Ultimate Movie Night:
Animated Films
for Kids and Families

———

Family Movie Night

Ultimate Movie Night: Animated Films for Kids and Families

Family Movie Night

Stephen White and
Eve White-Chapero

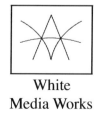

White
Media Works

Published by White Media Works
San Diego, California
www.whitemediaworks.com

ISBN 978-1-64145-135-2

<u>Dedication</u>

To Molly, Ada, Emi, Andre, Sarah, and Amanda,
connoisseurs of fine animation, all

Table of Contents

Table of Contents

Table of Contents

Table of Contents

Table of Contents

Table of Contents

Table of Contents

Table of Contents

Table of Contents

Appendices

Introduction

Ultimate Movie Night: Animated Films for Kids and Families was written to help families answer the dreaded Friday or Saturday night question: "What are we going to watch tonight?" Between cable and streaming and home media there are many choices, but our family often found it hard to settle on a movie that everyone could agree upon. We set out to create a guide to help people find the best animated films for a night of family viewing.

We've always found it interesting to know a little more about the movies we watch, so we have also included some basic information about each film, including when it was released, the writer and director, the voice actors, music highlights, and some facts about each title.

Many people don't pay that much attention to who wrote or directed animated films, but as with live-action films, this is one of the best ways we've found to locate other movies we're likely to enjoy. A list of some directors of note is included in an appendix at the end of the book.

You may find a number of surprises as you look at the voice actors. Some, like Billy Connolly, Ellen DeGeneres, or Patrick Warburton, have such distinctive voices they're easier to identify, but others are less well-known. Do you know which film starred Julia Roberts, Nicolas Cage, Meryl Streep, Paul Giamatti, Lily Tomlin and Ricardo Montalban? Or which film included Charlize Theron, Ralph Fiennes, Matthew McConaughey, and George Takei? Or which eight (eight!) animated Disney films Alan Tudyk appeared in? (Answers: *The Ant Bully, Kubo and the Two Strings,* and *Wreck It Ralph, Frozen, Big Hero 6, Zootopia, Moana, Ralph Breaks the Internet, Frozen II,* and *Raya and the Last Dragon*).

The Music Highlights section includes popular songs as well as the composers of each film's score. Getting to know the world of composers can be rewarding, from Disney mainstays Alan Menken (*The Little Mermaid, Beauty and the Beast, Aladdin, Tangled*), Henry Jackman (*Big Hero 6, Winnie the Pooh*), and Michael Giacchino (*The Incredibles, Coco, Zootopia*), to the creepy scores of Danny Elfman (*The Nightmare Before Christmas, Frankenweenie, Corpse Bride*), to the big name composers John Williams (*The Adventures of Tintin, Star Wars: The Clone Wars*), Alan Silvestri (*The Croods, Lilo & Stitch, The Polar Express*), James Horner (*Balto, The Land Before Time*), Hans Zimmer (*Madagascar, The Road to El Dorado, Kung Fu Panda*), and John Powell (*How to Train Your Dragon, Kung Fu Panda, The Lorax*).

The "Film Facts" section includes interesting trivia, information on "Easter eggs" (hidden references or images in films), and additional appearances such as shorts or sequels, as well as a heads up about mid-credits or post-credits scenes that many families miss.

Writing this book has been both enjoyable and educational, as we have had a chance to revisit many old favorites, and to watch many films we had never seen before. The new films were often surprising, as several titles we didn't think we would like turned out to be very good.

The process of selecting films for the book was a challenge, as there are thousands of animated films. We made our best effort to choose movies that are worthwhile, either for pure entertainment value, artistic excellence, or cultural literacy. Most of the titles included were originally theatrical films, but some home media releases and television films found their way into the book as well.

The majority of titles are in the one- to two-hour range, but we also included a handful of shorter choices that may be useful on occasion, such as the classic Chuck Jones shorts (*Rikki-Tiki-Tavi, The Cricket in Times Square, How the Grinch Stole Christmas!*), the Peanuts holiday specials (*A Charlie Brown Christmas, It's the Great Pumpkin, Charlie Brown*), and *My Little Pony: Equestria Girls* specials.

There are many worthy films we were not able to include. In the interest of making the selections family-friendly, we've limited ourselves to movies in the G to PG range. Films rated PG-13 will be covered in a future volume, as well as some wonderful PG films that we believe are a better fit for an older audience, such as *Watership Down* or Studio Ghibli's *Only Yesterday.*

While certain films are geared exclusively to a younger audience, many of the best films can entertain on multiple levels at once, and often go beyond mere entertainment, carrying important messages about life, personal development, and identity. One of the biggest challenges of a family movie night can be finding a movie that kids, teens, and adults can all enjoy watching together (a couple of lists are included at the back of the book to help with this). We've found that younger kids and older kids can watch the same movie in different ways.

While the younger kids are taking in the story, older kids may be more entertained by finding the deeper meaning of the film, identifying voice actors, catching hidden Easter eggs, or noticing continuity errors. Letting older kids read the entry for the movie in this book before watching the film (skipping the synopsis if they don't like spoilers!) may make the experience more interesting for them.

Families enjoy movies together for many reasons: to help children learn about the world, to let parents share movies they've loved, to laugh together, or to learn something new alongside each other.

There are also lots of ways to have a movie night. Whether you're just gathering everyone in the household to watch something together, inviting local family, or adding some friends to the mix, sharing a film is a great opportunity for a get-together.

Ingredients to consider for a great animated film movie night:

Popcorn (of course)
Pizza
Drinks
Family and friends
The movie, preferably chosen in advance
This book (to settle arguments about who voiced which role, etc.)

With over 350 films, there are about seven years worth of movies for a weekly movie night included in this book. We hope you have as much fun watching them as we did.

Roll film!

Stephen White and Eve White-Chapero
San Diego, 2021

Film Listings

Abominable (PG)

Theatrical release date: September 27, 2019
Country: USA, China
Production Company: DreamWorks Animation, Pearl Studio, China Film Co-Production
Length: 97 minutes
Directed by: Jill Culton, co-director Todd Wilderman
Written by: Jill Culton

Synopsis: Teenage violinist Yi befriends a yeti, nicknamed Everest, which has escaped from captivity in a facility owned by cruel businessman Mr. Burnish. Yi sets out to return Everest to his family, accompanied by chatty Peng and the image-conscious Jin, pursued by Burnish's team. As the quartet travels across China, Everest reveals special powers, growing blueberries, dandelions, and vegetation to help them escape Burnish and his chief scientist Dr. Zara. When a mountaintop confrontation finally occurs, a sudden change of heart leads to many unexpected consequences for everyone.

Cast: Chloe Bennet as Yi
Albert Tsai as Peng
Tenzing Norgay Trainor as Jin
Joseph Izzo as Everest
Sarah Paulson as Dr. Zara

Eddie Izzard as Burnish
Tsai Chin as Nai Nai
Michelle Wong as Yi's Mom
Rich Dietl as Goon Leader
James Hong as Yak Herder

Music Highlights: "Girl's Gotta" (Bissell/Stroup) performed by Danger Twins, "Dreams" (Beaudreau/Bissell) performed by Philip Beaudreau, "Fix You" (Martin/Berryman/Buckland/Champion) performed by Coldplay, "Beautiful Life" (Rexha/Fleur/Zammarelli/Black/Tempest) performed by Bebe Rexha. Music by Rupert Gregson-Williams.

Film Facts

• Chloe Bennet, voice of Yi, voiced Chase in *Tinker Bell and the Legend of the NeverBeast* (2014), and played Daisy Johnson (Quake) in the *Agents of S.H.I.E.L.D.: Slingshot* mini-series (2016).
• Tenzing Norgay Trainor, voice of Jin, is best known for playing Parker in the Disney Channel comedy *Liv and Maddie* (2013-2017). He is the grandson of Tenzing Norgay, who was the first Sherpa to reach the peak of Mount Everest alongside Sir Edmund Hillary.
• Albert Tsai, voice of Peng, played Fred in *Coop and Cami Ask the World* (2018).
• British comedian Eddie Izzard, voice of Burnish, also did voice acting in the animated films *The Wild* (2006), *Igor* (2008), *Cars 2* (2011), *Rock Dog* (2016), and *The Lego Batman Movie* (2017), as well as voicing swashbuckling rat Reepicheep in *The Chronicles of Narnia: Prince Caspian* (2008).
• The film stirred international controversy by including a map with the "Nine-Dash Line," that identified disputed areas of the South China Sea as belonging to China, which has been aggressively expanding its maritime claims.
• *Abominable* followed *Smallfoot* (2018) and *Missing Link* (2019), two other recent films about large, furry, mythical creatures.

Adventures in Zambezia (G)

Theatrical release date: December 28, 2012 (South Africa)
Country: South Africa   South African title: *Zambezia*
Production Company: Triggerfish Animation Studios
Length: 83 minutes
Directed by: Wayne Thornley
Screenplay by: Raffaella Delle Donne, Anthony Silverston, Wayne Thornley, Andrew Cook

Synopsis: Pursued by two hungry marabou storks, Gogo, an elderly saddle-billed stork, and Tini, a yellow weaver bird, are on a mission to take a basket of young birds to the island of Zambezia, the City of Birds. On the way they meet Kai, a young Peregrine falcon, who invites them to stay, but the marabou soon catch up to them and Kai's father, Tendai, asks them to move on. Kai follows them, and Tendai overhears the marabou conspiring with the huge lizard Budzo to attack Zambezia. The group finally reaches Zambezia, ruled by the eagle Sekhuru. Kai is impressed with the swift flying of the Hurricanes that patrol Zambezia, and asks to try out to be part of the team, getting a spot as a Hurricane trainee. When the marabou capture several weavers, Tini finds they have also captured Tendai. Sekhuru sends the Hurricanes in pursuit of the marabou, and Kai is asked to stay back, but goes on a night mission with a slick Nightjar, Ezee, and Zoe, Sekhuru's daughter. The trio find the marabou and learn of the alliance between the marabou and the lizard, but when they return, Kai is chastised for disobeying orders. Sekhuru finally tells Kai the truth about his father's tragic history in Zambezia, and why he has never wanted to return. When Kai frees his father, the two of them must rally the birds of Zambezia, before Budzo reaches the eggs on the island.

Cast: Jeremy Suarez as Kai
Abigail Breslin as Zoe
Leonard Nimoy as Sekhuru
Jeff Goldblum as Ajax
Samuel L. Jackson as Tendai
Jenifer Lewis as Gogo
Jim Cummings as Budzo/Marabous

Richard E. Grant as Cecil
Jamal Mixon as Ezee
David Shaughnessy as Morton
Noureen DeWulf as Pavi
Tania Gunadi as Tini
Deep Roy as Mushana
Phil LaMarr as Announcer Bird

Music Highlights: "Say Hello to Zambezia" (Bruce Retief) performed by Gang of Instrumentals, "Easy Easy" (Bruce Retief) performed by Gang of Instrumentals, "Get Up" (Bruce Retief) performed by Zolani Mohala, "Out of the Mist" (Bruce Retief) performed by Ludovic Mampuya, "Vukani" (Zwai Bala) performed by Zwai Bala, Mushana's and Spring Celebration Music (Didas Bonazebi/ Ludovic Mampuya). Music by Bruce Retief.

Film Facts

- The Zambezi River is the fourth-longest river in Africa.
- This was the first feature of Cape Town, South Africa's Triggerfish, makers of *Khumba* (2013).
- The film won the "Best Animation" award at the Africa Movie Academy Awards.

The Adventures of Ichabod & Mr. Toad (Approved)

Theatrical release date: October 5, 1949
Production Company: Walt Disney Productions
Length: 68 minutes
Directed by: Jack Kinney, Clyde Geronimi, James Algar
Written by: Erdman Penner, Winston Hibler, Joe Rinaldi, Ted Sears, Homer Brightman, Harry Reeves, based on *The Legend of Sleepy Hollow* by Washington Irving and *The Wind in the Willows* by Kenneth Grahame

---

Synopsis: A package film pairing two animated tales from classic literature. "The Story of Mr. Toad," drawn from Kenneth Grahame's *The Wind in the Willows,* follows the spendthrift J. Thaddeus Toad, Esq., as he trades the deed of Toad Hall to obtain a motorcar. "The Story of Ichabod Crane" is drawn from Washington Irving's "The Legend of Sleepy Hollow," depicting the fearful schoolteacher's encounter with the dreaded Headless Horseman.

Cast: Bing Crosby as Ichabod, Brom Bones, "Sleepy Hollow" narrator
Basil Rathbone as "Adventures of Mr. Toad" narrator, Policeman
Eric Blore as Mr. Toad
Pat O'Malley as Cyril Proudbottom
John Ployardt as the Prosecutor
Colin Campbell as Mole
Campbell Grant as Angus MacBadger
Claude Allister as Ratty

Music Highlights: "Ichabod" (Don Raye/Gene de Paul) performed by Bing Crosby, "Katrina" (Raye/de Paul) performed by Bing Crosby, "The Headless Horseman" (Raye/de Paul) performed by Bing Crosby, "Merrily on Our Way (to Nowhere in Particular)" (Churchill & Wolcott/Morey & Gilbert) performed by Eric Blore and Pat O'Malley, "Auld Lang Syne" (Traditional/Burns). Music by Oliver Wallace.

Film Facts

• This was 11th of the Walt Disney animated classics, and the sixth and final of the Disney "package" films of the 1940s, combining two shorter featurettes into a full length film.
• Mel Blanc, the Warner Bros./*Looney Toons* voice actor most famous as the voice of Bugs Bunny, provided an uncredited singing voice for the horse Cyril Proudbottom.
• Planning for *The Wind in the Willows*, which was originally intended to be a full-length feature, began in 1938 after the success of *Snow White and the Seven Dwarfs*. Animation work began in 1941, but the project was plagued by production interruptions due to financial struggles, an animators strike, and a number of layoffs at Walt Disney Productions.
• English writer A.A. Milne, author of the Winnie the Pooh stories, had previously adapted Toad's adventures as a play, *Toad of Toad Hall*, which debuted in 1929. In a curious coincidence, by 1966 it would be Milne's own stories being adapted, as Disney created the first Winnie the Pooh short, "Winnie the Pooh and the Honey Tree."
• Package films such as *Saludos Amigos, Fun and Fancy Free,* and *The Adventures of Ichabod and Mr. Toad* were prompted by Disney's limited resources due to the U.S. government tapping the studio to produce films to support the war effort.

The Adventures of Tintin (PG)

Theatrical release date: December 21, 2011
Production Company: Columbia Pictures, Paramount Pictures, Nickelodeon Movies, Amblin Entertainment
Length: 107 minutes
Directed by: Steven Spielberg
Screenplay by: Steven Moffat and Edgar Wright & Joe Cornish, based on *The Adventures of Tintin* by Hergé

Synopsis: After unsuspecting journalist Tintin buys a model of a ship called the Unicorn at a flea market, he is pursued by two men intent on acquiring the ship: an Interpol officer, and the ruthless collector Ivanovitch Sakharine. While chasing a cat in Tintin's apartment, his dog Snowy accidentally breaks the model, revealing a small scroll which Tintin unknowingly kicks under a cabinet. Tintin goes out to research the real Unicorn, finding the model has vanished when he returns. Snowy shows Tintin the scroll, but it is soon stolen by a pickpocket, just before Tintin and Snowy are themselves captured by Sakharine's henchmen. After being held prisoner on a ship with the ship's captain, Archibald Haddock, the trio make their escape, soon learning that there are three models of the Unicorn, each with a scroll which, when combined, show the location of the lost treasure of the actual Unicorn. The race is on to solve the mystery and find the treasure before Sakharine does.

Cast: Jamie Bell as Tintin
Andy Serkis as Captain Haddock/
     Sir Francis Haddock
Daniel Craig as Sakharine/Red Rackham
Nick Frost as Thomson
Simon Pegg as Thompson

Daniel Mays as Allan/Pirate Flunky #1
Gad Elmaleh as Ben Salaad
Toby Jones as Silk
Joe Starr as Barnaby
Enn Reitel as Nestor/Mr. Crabtree
Mackenzie Crook as Tom/Pirate Flunky #2

Music Highlights: Score by John Williams.

Film Facts

• *The Adventures of Tintin* (originally *Les Aventures de Tintin*) was a series of French/Belgian comic books and comic strips by Belgian cartoonist Georges Remi, who used the pen name Hergé, first appearing in 1929.
• The story for the film is drawn from the Tintin stories "The Crab with the Golden Claws," "The Secret of the Unicorn," and "Red Rackham's Treasure."
• This was director Steven Spielberg's first animated film. Spielberg was an admirer of Hergé, and included an artist who resembled Hergé in the flea market scene (at about the 4:07 mark). The artist asks Tintin, "Have I drawn you before?" Tintin replies, "Occasionally."
• A sequel was planned, to be titled *Tintin and the Temple of the Sun,* but fell through. Steven Spielberg and Peter Jackson have both expressed ongoing interest in developing a sequel.
• Nickelodeon had previously aired *The Adventures of Tintin* animated TV series (1991-1992).

Aladdin (G)

Theatrical release date: November 25, 1992
Production Company: Walt Disney Pictures, Walt Disney Feature Animation
Length: 90 minutes
Directed by: John Musker and Ron Clements
Written by: Ron Clements & John Musker, Ted Elliott & Terry Rossio

Synopsis: "Street rat" Aladdin, accompanied by his monkey, Abu, has a chance encounter with the lovely princess Jasmine, daughter of the benevolent Sultan of Agrabah. Caught up in the evil plans of the Sultan's Grand Vizier, Jafar, Aladdin is taken to the Cave of Wonders, where a magic carpet guides him to an enchanted lamp containing a manic blue genie. When Jafar's evil schemes threaten Jasmine and the Sultan, Aladdin is put to the test.

Cast: Scott Weinger as Aladdin
Robin Williams as Genie
Linda Larkin as Princess Jasmine
Jonathan Freeman as Jafar

Frank Welker as Abu the monkey/Cave of Wonders/Rajah
Gilbert Gottfried as Iago
Douglas Seale as The Sultan
Charlie Adler as Gazeem/Melon Merchant/Nut Merchant

Music Highlights: "A Whole New World" (Alan Menken/Tim Rice) performed by Lea Salonga and Brad Kane, "Friend Like Me" (Alan Menken/Howard Ashman) performed by Robin Williams, "Prince Ali" (Alan Menken/Howard Ashman) performed by Robin Williams. Music by Alan Menken.

Film Facts

• *Aladdin*, the 31st Disney animated classic, was one of the studio's biggest successes of the 1990s, earning positive reviews and grossing over $504 million worldwide. It was the highest-grossing film of 1992 and the highest-grossing animated film of all time (until *The Lion King* broke that record).
• The story was drawn from the Middle Eastern folk tale collection *One Thousand and One Nights*.
• *Aladdin* was a key part of the 1989-1999 "Disney Renaissance" that began with *The Little Mermaid* (1989), which was also directed by Musker and Clements.
• "A Whole New World" won the "Best Original Song" Academy Award at the 65th Academy Awards, and the "Song of the Year" Grammy at the 36th Annual Grammy Awards.
• Genie impersonations included Arnold Schwarzenegger (36:28), Ed Sullivan (36:43), Groucho Marx (36:57), Señor Wences (38:12), William F. Buckley (39:39/1:16:08), Peter Lorre (39:57), Robert De Niro (40:25), Pinocchio (44:45), Julius Caesar (45:37), Arsenio Hall (45:50), Walter Brennan (49:30), Ethel Merman (50:10), Rodney Dangerfield (54:10), and Jack Nicholson (54:14).
• "Arabian Nights" was edited on the soundtrack reissue, replacing a lyric referencing cutting off an ear with a description of geography and hot weather.
• There are brief cameos by Pinocchio (44:45), Sebastian from *The Little Mermaid* (45:35), and a toy of the Beast from *Beauty and the Beast* (46:58).
• In the 1993 book *Aladdin: The Making of an Animated Film*, Robin Williams is credited as "the actor signed to play the Genie." Williams was upset with the studio over the film's advertising.
• After their second huge success, Musker and Clements would go on to direct the Disney films *Hercules* (1997), *Treasure Planet* (2002), *The Princess and the Frog* (2009), and *Moana* (2016).

Aladdin: *The Return of Jafar* (G)

Home media release date: May 20, 1994
Production Company: Walt Disney Video Premiere, Walt Disney Television Animation,
Walt Disney Animation Australia, Walt Disney Animation Japan
Length: 69 minutes
Directed by: Toby Shelton, Tad Stones, Alan Zaslove
Written by: Kevin Campbell, Mirith J.S. Colao, Bill Motz, Steve Roberts, Dev Ross, Bob Roth, Jan
Strnad, Brian Swenlin, story by Duane Capizzi, Douglas Langdale, Mark McCorkle, Robert Schooley,
Tad Stones

Synopsis: Aladdin, despite his luxurious life with princess Jasmine and the Sultan in the palace of Agrabah, continues to crave adventure. He thwarts a robbery by the evil Abis Mal and his gang, only to run into the sarcastic parrot Iago, who has escaped from the enchanted lamp, where he has abandoned the Sultan's disloyal Grand Vizier Jafar. When Abis Mal seeks revenge, Iago accidentally saves Aladdin's life, gaining him admission to the palace. Unfortunately for Aladdin, Abis Mal comes across the lamp where Jafar is imprisoned, and the two conspire to get their revenge on Aladdin.

Cast: Scott Weinger as Aladdin
Linda Larkin as Jasmine
Dan Castellaneta as Genie
Jonathan Freeman as Jafar
Gilbert Gottfried as Iago
Jason Alexander as Abis Mal
Val Bettin as Sultan

Jeff Bennett as Thief
Brad Kane as Aladdin's singing voice
Liz Callaway as Princess Jasmine's singing voice
B.J. Ward as Street Mother
Jim Cummings as Razoul
Frank Welker as Abu the Monkey

Music Highlights: "Forget About Love" (Patty Silversher/Michael Silversher) performed by Liz Callaway, Brad Kane, and Gilbert Gottfried, "You're Only Second Rate" (Randy Peterson/Kevin Quinn) performed by Jonathan Freeman, "I'm Looking Out for Me" (Randy Peterson/Kevin Quinn) performed by Gilbert Gottfried. Music by Mark Watters.

Film Facts

• This film, released on VHS in May, 1994, introduced the *Aladdin* TV series, which began broadcasting in September, 1994.
• The film was originally titled *The Return of Jafar,* and later sensibly revised to *Aladdin: The Return of Jafar.*
• Dan Castellaneta (best known for voicing Homer Simpson on *The Simpsons*) took on the role of Genie in this film, taking over from Robin Williams.
• This release was generally seen as a disappointment after the success of the original film.
• The singing voice for Jasmine was provided by Liz Callaway, and Aladdin's by Brad Kane.
• Three songs from *The Return of Jafar* ("Forget About Love," "You're Only Second Rate," "I'm Looking Out for Me") appeared on the *Aladdin and the King of Thieves* soundtrack.

Aladdin and the King of Thieves (NR)

Home media release date: August 13, 1996
Production Company: Walt Disney Television Animation
Length: 80 minutes
Directed by: Tad Stones
Written by: Mark McCorkle and Robert Schooley

Synopsis: Aladdin learns that his father, Cassim, is the leader of the legendary Forty Thieves, who try to steal the oracle, an enchanted scepter which grants to whoever possesses it the answer to one question. Aladdin hopes that his father can attend his wedding to Princess Jasmine. He seeks out the thieves' lair and defeats Sa'luk to earn a place among the thieves, but his hopes are dashed when Cassim is caught trying to steal. Aladdin frees him, and follows him to the Vanishing Isle, home of the Hand of Midas, a magical item which can turn anything to gold. Soon Cassim must decide what the real treasure in his life is.

Cast: Val Bettin as Sultan of Agrabah
Jim Cummings as Razoul
Gilbert Gottfried as Iago the Parrot
Linda Larkin as Princess Jasmine
Jerry Orbach as Sa'luk

John Rhys-Davies as Cassim, the King of Thieves
Scott Wienger as Aladdin
Frank Welker as Abu the Monkey
Robin Williams as Genie

Music Highlights: "Party in Agrabah" (David Friedman) performed by Robin Williams, Brad Kane, Liz Callaway, Merwin Foard, and Gilbert Gottfried, "Out of Thin Air" (David Friedman) performed by Brad Kane and Liz Callaway, "Welcome to the Forty Thieves" (Randy Peterson/Kevin Quinn) performed by Scott Barnes, Don Bradford, Merwin Foard, David Friedman, Paul Kandel, Peter Samuel, Gordon Stanley, Guy Stroman. Music by Mark Watters, Carl Johnson.

Film Facts

• Aladdin's second feature-length sequel is based on "Ali Baba and the Forty Thieves," another tale in *One Thousand and One Nights*.
• Genie pop culture references: Tinker Bell (1:25), Rocky Balboa, *Rocky* (2:33), Woody Allen (4:22), Robin Leach (8:00), White Rabbit, *Alice in Wonderland* (9:00), Forrest Gump (15:53), Mrs. Doubtfire (35:00), the Marx Brothers (35:20), Elvis Presley (36:00), Bob Hope and Bing Crosby (36:40), ED-209, *RoboCop*/Cylon, *Battlestar Galactica* (43:15), Pocahontas (43:56), the Sorcerer's Apprentice (44:55), Einstein (45:36), Shaquille O'Neal (46:02), Vito Corleone, *The Godfather* (46:33), Pluto (49:21), Ozzie Nelson, *Ozzie & Harriet* (1:07:28), Richard Dawson, *Family Feud* (1:07:10), Mickey Mouse, "Steamboat Willie" (1:14:37), *Aliens* (1:21:20). Genie also dresses Jasmine as Cinderella (36:18) and Snow White (36:20), as well as holding up cards to make her look like Ariel, Minnie Mouse, and Jessica Rabbit (36:20).
• At the end of the film, Aladdin and Jasmine walk past Prince Uncouthma, a recurring character from the *Aladdin* animated series (1:15:30).
• The soundtrack CD included "Party in Agrabah," "Out of Thin Air," "Welcome to the Forty Thieves," "Father and Son," "Are You In or Out?" and "Arabian Nights Reprise."

Alice in Wonderland (G)

Theatrical release date: July 28, 1951
Production Company: Walt Disney Productions
Length: 75 minutes
Directed by: Clyde Geronimi, Hamilton Luske, Wilfred Jackson
Written by: Winston Hibler, Ted Sears, Bill Peet, Erdman Penner, Joe Rinaldi, Milt Banta, Bill Cottrell, Dick Kelsey, Joe Grant, Dick Huemer, Del Connell, Tom Oreb, John Walbridge, based on *Alice's Adventures in Wonderland* and *Through the Looking-Glass* by Lewis Carroll

Synopsis: After following the White Rabbit down a hole leading to Wonderland, Alice has some ups and downs as she encounters a series of fantastic creatures and places, including the Cheshire Cat, Tweedledee and Tweedledum, the Mad Hatter, and the Queen of Hearts.

Cast: Kathryn Beaumont as Alice
Ed Wynn as the Mad Hatter
Richard Haydn as the Caterpillar
Sterling Holloway as the Cheshire Cat
Jerry Colonna as the March Hare
Verna Felton as the Queen of Hearts
Pat O'Malley as Tweedledee/Tweedledum/Walrus
Bill Thompson as the White Rabbit and the Dodo

Music Highlights: "In a World of My Own" (Bob Hilliard/Sammy Fain) performed by Kathryn Beaumont, "I'm Late" (Bob Hilliard/Sammy Fain) performed by Bill Thompson, "All in the Golden Afternoon" (Bob Hilliard/Sammy Fain) performed by Kathryn Beaumont, "The Unbirthday Song" (Mack David/Al Hoffman/Jerry Livingston) performed by Ed Wynn and Jerry Colonna, "Very Good Advice" (Bob Hilliard/Sammy Fain) performed by Kathryn Beaumont. Music by Oliver Wallace.

Film Facts

• *Alice in Wonderland* is the 13th of the Disney animated classics. The original book by Lewis Carroll (pen name of Charles Dodgson) was *Alice's Adventures in Wonderland* (1865). Disney's film also drew from Carroll's sequel, *Through the Looking-Glass* (1871).
• Walt Disney first developed a film inspired by *Alice's Adventures in Wonderland* in 1933, with the Laugh-O-Gram Studio short "Alice's Wonderland," which mixed a live-action Alice (Virginia Davis) with an animated environment.
• When Laugh-O-Gram went bankrupt, Disney moved to Hollywood, and began a series of live-action/animated shorts called the "Alice Comedies." By 1933 Disney was considering a feature-length Alice film, but shelved the project when Paramount released a live-action *Alice in Wonderland* in December, 1933.
• A 1933 screen test was filmed with early film star Mary Pickford as a possible lead for a live-action film, and later Ginger Rogers was considered for the role, but ultimately an animated film was produced.
• In one of the earliest Disney cameos, José Carioca from *Saludos Amigos* (1943) and *The Three Caballeros* (1944) appears as a juror, at the bottom right of the jury box (1:07:18, 1:09:05).
• Over 30 songs were written for the film, the most of any Disney feature. Songwriters included lyricist Bob Hilliard and composer Sammy Fain ("In a World of My Own," "All in the Golden Afternoon," "I'm Late") and Tin Pan Alley songwriters Mack David, Al Hoffman and Jerry Livingston ("The Unbirthday Song").

Anastasia (G)

Theatrical release date: November 21, 1997
Production Company: 20th Century Fox, Fox Animation Studios, Fox Family Films
Length: 94 minutes
Directed by: Don Bluth, Gary Goldman
Written by: Susan Gauthier & Bruce Graham, Bob Tzudiker & Noni White

Synopsis: In 1916 the evil Rasputin places a curse on the family of Nicholas Romanov, the Czar of Imperial Russia, and revolutionary soldiers storm the palace. The young Anastasia and her grandmother, Marie, are helped by a servant boy to flee the palace, but are separated in the confusion. Ten years later, the whereabouts of the princess Anastasia are a mystery. Anya, a young woman suffering from amnesia, hopes to go to Paris to find her family, but cannot get an exit visa. Con-men Dimitri and Vladimir recruit Anya to pose as Anastasia, in the hopes of claiming a reward from her grandmother. Rasputin, aided by the bumbling white bat Bartok, does his best to derail their plans, but they arrive safely. Marie is skeptical due to the many imposters she has encountered, but Anastasia's ability to answer questions about her childhood finally convinces Marie — and herself — that she is the real Anastasia. She learns that Dimitri is the servant boy who helped her escape ten years ago, and together they must face Rasputin's continued efforts to destroy them.

Cast: Meg Ryan as Anastasia
John Cusack as Dimitri
Kelsey Grammer as Vladimir
Christopher Lloyd as Rasputin
Hank Azaria as Bartok

Bernadette Peters as Sophie
Kirsten Dunst as Young Anastasia
Angela Lansbury as The Dowager Empress Marie
Rick Jones as Czar Nicholas/Servant/Soldier
Andrea Martin as Phlegmenkoff/Old Woman

Music Highlights: Music by Stephen Flaherty/Lyrics by Lynn Ahrens: "A Rumor in St. Petersburg" performed by Jonathan Dokuchitz, Kelsey Grammer, and the Townspeople, "Journey to the Past" performed by Liz Callaway, "Once Upon a December" performed by Liz Callaway, "In the Dark of the Night" performed by Jim Cummings and Creatures, "Paris Holds the Key (To Your Heart)" performed by Bernadette Peters, Jonathan Dokuchitz, and Ensemble, "At the Beginning" performed by Richard Marx and Donna Lewis, "Journey to the Past" performed by Aaliyah, "Once Upon a December" performed by Deana Carter. Score by David Newman.

Film Facts

• Anastasia is based on the historical figure the Grand Duchess Anastasia Nikolaevna of Russia. Although the film supposes she survived, the actual Anastasia was killed with her family on July 17, 1918, by a group of Bolsheviks in Yekaterinburg.
• The music box in the film was an actual gift from Marie Feoderovna to Anastasia. The working title for the film was *The Music Box*.
• Liz Callaway (*Beauty and the Beast*, *The Return of Jafar*) provided the singing voice of Anastasia.
• The song "Paris Holds the Key" includes cameos of Josephine Baker, Maurice Chevalier, Isadora Duncan, Sigmund Freud, Charles Lindbergh, Claude Monet, Auguste Rodin, and Gertrude Stein.

Anina (TV-G)

Theatrical release date: April 19, 2013 (Uruguay)
Country: Uruguay   Language: Spanish
Production Company: Palermo Animación, Raindogs Cine, Antorcha Films
Length: 79 minutes
Directed by: Alfredo Soderguit
Screenplay by: Federico Ivanier, Alfredo Soderguit, Julián Goyoaga, Alejo Schettini, Germán Tejeira, based on the novel by Sergio López Suárez

Synopsis: The young girl Anina Yatay Salas is teased by her classmates because each of her names is a "capicúa," a palindrome. One day she bumps into a large girl, Yisel, who is called "the elephant," making her drop her sandwich, leading to a fight. Anina and Yisel see the principal, who gives them a unique punishment: each of them get an envelope closed with sealing wax, that they must not open for a full week. Even worse, they are not allowed to tell their classmates what their punishment was. Finally Anina tells her friend Florencia, who proposes that Anina open Yisel's envelope. They begin following Yisel, seeing her arrive at her home, where she is seen talking to Anina's crush, Jonathan. At school, Anina and Florencia try to look in Yisel's backpack during recess, but when it looks like they will be caught, Florencia lets herself be discovered to protect Anina. Their teacher chooses Anina and Yisel to oversee the class first aid kit, and when Yisel leaves the room, Anina looks in her backpack for her envelope, instead finding postcards from her father, who is in Australia. The week finally passes, when a classmate, Pablo, pretends to be a tightrope walker and falls after Anina cries out. Instead of blaming her, Yisel protects her from a mean teacher. Anina has a nightmare about the envelope, and when she wakes, the seal is broken and the envelope is empty. At the market, Anina learns that Yisel's mother is struggling while her father is away in Australia. When they meet with the principal, Anina confesses she opened her envelope, and is told that the principal just wanted her to think about what happened. She learns from the experience, starting a friendship with Yisel and feeling more confident.

Cast: Federica Lacaño as Anina
Guillermina Pardo as Florencia
Lucía Parrilla as Yisel
María Mendive as Madre de Anina (Mother)
César Troncoso as Padre de Anina (Father)

Cristina Morán as Directora (Principal)
Gimena Fajardo as Maestra Agueda (teacher)
Florencia Zabaleta as Maestra Aurora (teacher)
Roberto Suárez as Vecina Pocha (neighbor)
Petru Valenski as Vecina Tota (neighbor)

Music Highlights: "Alguien" (Pesoa) performed by Guillermo Pesoa, "Con Sangre la Letra Entra" (Ariosa/Otero), "Bolero Sideral" (Keoroglián/Otero/Antuña). Music by Gaston Otero, Bruno Boselli.

Film Facts

- The film was submitted for the "Best Foreign Language Film" Academy Award, but not selected.
- The bus ticket Anina gives Yisel (1:13:20) is special because the number is a palindrome (01610).
- Director Alfredo Soderguit illustrated the book *Anina Yatay Salas* (2003) by Sergio López Suárez.

The Ant Bully (PG)

Theatrical release date: July 28, 2006
Production Company: Legendary Pictures, Playtone, DNA Productions
Length: 88 minutes
Directed by: John A. Davis
Written by: John A. Davis, based on the book by John Nickle

Synopsis: After Lucas Nickle is bullied by larger kid, he turns to bullying the ants of a colony near his house. The wizard-alchemist ant Zoc develops a potion that shrinks Lucas to the size of an ant, and he is taken before the Ant Queen. Lucas is sentenced to live and work in the ant colony. The kind Hova volunteers to teach Lucas "the destroyer" the ways of ants. In trying to find his place in the colony, Lucas learns about foraging, accompanied by Hova, Zoc, the spirited scout ant Fugax, and the forceful Kreela, and survives an attack of wasps. As he learns the ways of the ants, Lucas tries to cancel a planned visit by the exterminator, but Zoc remains suspicious of him, and chases him from the colony. When Lucas is eaten by a frog, Zoc reconsiders, rescuing Lucas, leading the two of them to finally see eye to eye. Working together, Lucas, the ants, and the wasps join forces in a battle to cut the dreaded exterminator down to size. Returned to human size, Lucas remembers the value of working together, as he and the smaller kids in the neighborhood re-negotiate their relationship with the local bully.

Cast: Julia Roberts as Hova
Nicolas Cage as Zoc
Meryl Streep as Queen
Paul Giamatti as Stan Beals
Zach Tyler Eisen as Lucas Nickle
Regina King as Kreela

Bruce Campbell as Fugax
Lily Tomlin as Mommo
Cheri Oteri as Doreen Nickle
Larry Miller as Fred Nickle
Allison Mack as Tiffany Nickle
Ricardo Montalban as Head of Council

Music Highlights: Score by John Debney.

Film Facts

• The film was based on the 1999 children's book *The Ant Bully* by John Nickle.
• Some roles were re-cast during production, including Lily Tomlin replacing Shirley MacLaine as the voice of Mommo (Lucas's grandmother), and Bruce Campbell replacing Alan Cumming as the voice of Fugax.
• This was Ricardo Montalban's last role (as the Head of Council) before his death in 2009.
• The film was produced by Tom Hanks and Gary Goetzman's production company Playtone. Hanks proposed the film after reading the book with one of his children.
• A Masonic Square and Compass is seen on Lucas's grandmother's rocking chair (10:07).
• A video game was made for Windows, GameCube, Game Boy Advance, PlayStation 2, and Wii.
• The film's score was released, as well as the CD *The Ant Bully: Music Inspired by the Motion Picture*, featuring ant-themed music, naturally including Adam and the Ants.

April and the Extraordinary World (PG)

Theatrical release date: Nov 11, 2015 (France/Belgium), Mar 25 (US limited), Apr 8, 2016 (US wide)
Country: France, Canada, Belgium   French title: *Avril et le Monde Truqué*
Production Company: Je Suis Bien Content, StudioCanal, Kaibou Production, Need Productions
Length: 105 minutes
Directed by: Christian Desmares, Franck Ekinci
Screenplay by: Franck Ekinci & Benjamin Legrand, based on an original idea by Benjamin Legrand, original graphic creation Tardi

Synopsis: In an alternate reality, Napoleon III seeks a formula for invincible soldiers. During this research, two lizards achieve the power of speech, but escape. Years later, famous scientists begin mysteriously disappearing, limiting technological progress. In 1931 France, coal power has given way to burning wood. Needing more wood, the French eye an attack on North America, and force scientists to work on developing invincible soldiers. A serum is developed in secret by the elderly Prosper Franklin with his son Paul and Paul's wife Annette. They flee from a police raid, led by Gaspar Pizoni, with their daughter April and the talking cat Darwin, and April and Darwin escape with the serum. Ten years later, Pizoni has April tailed by the pickpocket Julius. Darwin, now an elderly cat on the verge of death, is revived by the Ultimate Serum. Just as Julius finds her hideout, April's father, still alive, contacts her from a secret airship containing all the missing scientists, helping her find her grandfather, Prosper. Prosper is soon captured, but April and Julius are able to rescue him, and they escape in a mysterious vehicle, which reveals who is really behind the disappearance of the scientists, and the fantastic goal of their Project is soon revealed.

Cast:

Role	English	French
Avril/April Franklin	Angela Galuppo	Marion Cotillard
Darwin	Tony Hale	Philippe Katerine
Prosper "Pops" Franklin	Tony Robinow	Jean Rochefort
Paul Franklin	Mark Camacho	Olivier Gourmet
Annette Franklin	Macha Grenon	Macha Grenon
Julius	Tod Fennell	Marc-André Grondin
Gaspar Pizoni	Paul Giamatti	Bouli Lanners
Chimène	Susan Sarandon	Anne Coesens
Rodrigue	J.K. Simmons	Benoît Brière

Music Highlights: "Chargez! Chargez!" (Perrine Capron/Claire Tillier/Franck Ekinci) performed by Claire Tillier, "Les Molécules de l'Amour" (Perrine Capron/Claire Tillier/Franck Ekinci) performed by Claire Tillier. Music by Valentin Hadjadj.

Film Facts

• Artist Jacques Tardi is a popular French writer and cartoonist, creator of Adèle Blanc-Sec.
• Tardi and Benjamin Legrand also collaborated on the graphic novel *Tueur de Cafards* (1984).
• The film won the "Best Animated Feature Film" César Award, a top honor in France.

The Aristocats (G)

Theatrical release date: December 24, 1970
Production Company: Walt Disney Productions
Length: 78 minutes
Directed by: Wolfgang Reitherman
Written by: Larry Clemmons, Vance Gerry, Ken Anderson, Frank Thomas, Eric Cleworth, Julius Svendsen, and Ralph Wright, based on a story by Tom McGowan and Tom Rowe

---

Synopsis: A scheming butler attempts to do away with a wealthy French matron's beloved cat Duchess and her three kittens, Berlioz, Marie, and Toulouse, because the cats are listed first in her will. When the felines find themselves far from home they are aided by the streetwise alley cat Thomas O'Malley and a variety of other animals in their efforts to return home and give the butler his just desserts.

Cast: Phil Harris as Thomas O'Malley
Eva Gabor as Duchess
Dean Clark as Berlioz
Liz English as Marie
Gary Dubin as Toulouse

Hermione Baddeley as Madame Adelaide Bonfamill
Roddy Maude-Roxby as Edgar the Butler
Sterling Holloway as Roquefort
Scatman Crothers as Scat Cat

Music Highlights: "The Aristocats" (Sherman/Sherman) performed by Maurice Chevalier, "She Never Felt Alone" (Sherman/Sherman) performed by Robie Lester, "Scales and Arpeggios" (Sherman/Sherman) performed by Liz English, Gary Dubin, Dean Clark, and Robie Lester, "Thomas O'Malley Cat" (Terry Gilkyson) performed by Phil Harris, "Ev'rybody Wants To Be A Cat" (Floyd Huddleston/Al Rinker) performed by cast. Music by George Bruns.

Film Facts

• O'Malley's full name is Abraham De Lacy Giuseppe Casey Thomas O'Malley (O'Malley the alley cat).
• *The Aristocats* was the last film to be personally approved by Walt Disney, before he died in 1966.
• The film was originally planned as a two-part live-action animal story for the TV series *Walt Disney's Wonderful World of Color*, but was eventually re-conceptualized as an animated film.
• Louis Armstrong was originally going to voice Scat Cat, but withdrew due to an illness.
• A 1943 Looney Tunes cartoon was titled "The Aristo-Cat."
• Several people worked on both *The Aristocats* and *The Jungle Book* (1967), including director Reitherman, Phil Harris as Thomas O'Malley (Baloo in *The Jungle Book*), and Sterling Holloway as Roquefort (Kaa in *The Jungle Book*), with music by the Sherman Brothers (including the theme, "The Aristocats" sung by Frenchman Maurice Chevalier, "Scales and Arpeggios," and "She Never Felt Alone"). Terry Gilkyson (composer of "The Bare Necessities" from *The Jungle Book*) contributed "Thomas O'Malley Cat."
• Production began on a sequel in 2005, but was canceled by the following year, when John Lasseter became chief creative officer of Disney and Pixar, and canceled all sequels.

Arthur and the Invisibles (PG)

Theatrical release date: November 29, 2006 (France, limited), January 12, 2007 (US)
Country: France French title: *Arthur et les Minimoys*
Production Company: Avalanche Productions, Metro Voices, Canal+
Length: 94 minutes
Directed by: Luc Besson
Written by: Luc Besson and Céline Garcia, based on the book by Luc Besson

---

Synopsis: Arthur, back in Connecticut after a year in his boarding school, stays with his grandmother, who tells Arthur about her adventures with his grandfather, Archibald, including his encounter with the tiny Minimoys. Arthur learns that his grandmother will be evicted if they can't find his grandfather's buried treasure of rubies. He soon finds secret messages left by his grandfather, allowing him to enter the world of the Minimoys. The Minimoy King tells Arthur that his grandfather's rubies are located in Necropolis, ruled by the wizard Maltazard, or "the evil M," located in the seven lands, from which no one ever returns. During an attack by Matazard's minions, the Seides, Arthur draws the Minimoy's sword of power, and goes on a quest with Princess Selenia into the seven lands. They face many perils, but persevere into the heart of Necropolis, in the hopes of saving their homes and families.

Cast: Freddie Highmore as Arthur
Mia Farrow as Daisy (grandmother)
Madonna as Princess Selenia
Jimmy Fallon as Betameche
David Bowie as Maltazard
Robert De Niro as King
Harvey Keitel as Miro
Snoop Dogg as Max

David Suchet as Narrator
Emilio Estevez as Ferryman
Rob Corddry as Seides
Nate Corddry as Seides
Erik Per Sullivan as Baby Bug/Mino
Chazz Palminteri as The Travel Agent
Anthony Anderson as Koolomassai
Jason Bateman as Darkos

Music Highlights: "Let's Dance" (Bowie) performed by David Bowie, "Theme from S-Express" (Gabriel/Moore) performed by S-Express, "You Never Can Tell" (Berry) performed by Chuck Berry, "Lonesome Town" (Knight) performed by Ricky Nelson, "Stayin' Alive" (Barry Gibb/Robin Gibb/ Maurice Gibb) performed by The Bee Gees, "Disco Science" (Deal/Ahmadzaï) performed by Mirwais Ahmadzaï, "Quest for Love" (Remanda/Kilcher) performed by Jewel, "It's a Beautiful Day" (Elijah Harris/Lee Harris/Da Octopusss) performed by Elijah Harris. Score by Eric Serra.

Film Facts

• The original French title of the film was *Arthur et les Minimoys*. The Weinstein Company edited the film in the U.S., to minimize the love story between Arthur and Selenia.
• The role of Princess Selenia was voiced by different pop singers in different countries: Paula Vesala (Finland), Mylène Farmer (France), Nena (Germany), Tamta (Greece), and Robyn (Sweden).
• The film was followed by the sequels *Arthur and the Revenge of Maltazard* (2009) and *Arthur 3: The War of the Two Worlds* (2010), and the animated TV series *Arthur and the Minimoys* (2017).

Arthur Christmas (PG)

Theatrical release date: November 23, 2011
Production Company: Aardman Animations, Columbia Pictures, Sony Pictures Animation
Length: 97 minutes
Directed by: Sarah Smith, co-directed by Barry Cook
Written by: Peter Baynham and Sarah Smith

> **Synopsis**: Santa Claus, specifically the 20th Santa Claus, runs a high tech Christmas operation, with a massive flying sled-craft and a team of stealthy elves to help deliver presents and fill stockings. Santa is assisted by his older son Steve, who ably coordinates the global operation, and his kindly but bumbling younger son Arthur, who works in Letters. A glitch leads to a Christmas gift going undelivered, and when Steve and Santa settle for the present being delivered late, Arthur, egged on by Santa's father, Grandsanta, takes the traditional sleigh (with stowaway elf Bryony Shelfley) to deliver the present. Many obstacles complicate their efforts, and Santa and Steve's willingness to allow a child to go without a gift on Christmas leads to a crisis of faith among the elves. Steve, Santa, and Mrs. Santa finally join the effort to deliver the gift, giving each of them a chance to reconsider their roles in the family.

Cast: James McAvoy as Arthur
Hugh Laurie as Steve
Bill Nighy as Grandsanta
Jim Broadbent as Santa
Imelda Staunton as Mrs. Santa
Ashley Jensen as Bryony

Marc Wootton as Peter
Laura Linney as North Pole Computer
Eva Longoria as Chief De Silva
Ramona Marquez as Gwen
Michael Palin as Ernie Clicker
Joan Cusack as Lead Elf

Music Highlights: "Make Someone Happy" (Betty Comden/Adolph Green/Jule Styne) performed by Bill Nighy. End credits: "Santa Claus Is Comin' To Town" (J. Fred Coots/Haven Gillespie) performed by Justin Bieber (with fragments of "ABC" and "I Want You Back"). Score by Harry Gregson-Williams.

Film Facts

• The film's working title was *Operation Rudolph*.
• The elf putting down railroad track in front of him (6:20) imitates a scene in the Wallace & Gromit short film *The Wrong Trousers* (27:29).
• One of the news stories about the sleigh features a Tom Hanks-like voice reporting on a "steam train flying around" (53:38), referencing *The Polar Express* (2004), starring Hanks.
• There is no Trelew, Mexico, but there is a Trelew, Argentina.
• A poster in Gwen's room (1:23:58) shows the Aardman Animation show *Chop Socky Chooks* (2007-2008), and Steve steps on a squeaky toy (1:24:54) of Aardman's *Shaun the Sheep* (2007-2020).
• Jim Broadbent also played Santa in the live-action family film *Get Santa* (2014).

Atlantis: The Lost Empire (G)

Theatrical release date: June 15, 2001
Production Company: Walt Disney Pictures, Walt Disney Feature Animation
Length: 95 minutes
Directed by: Gary Trousdale and Kirk Wise
Screenplay by: Tab Murphy, story by Kirk Wise & Gary Trousdale, Joss Whedon, Bryce Zabel & Jackie Zabel, Tab Murphy

---

Synopsis: The year is 1914, and Milo Thatch, a linguist who has spent years researching Atlantis, is chosen by wealthy eccentric Preston B. Whitmore, who offers an expedition to find the lost civilization, accompanied by a team of explorers: Commander Lyle Tiberius Rourke, Lt. Helga Katrina Sinclair, mechanic Audrey Rocio Ramirez, radio operator Wilhelmina Bertha Packard, demolitions expert Vinny Santorini, Dr. Joshua Strongbear Sweet, geologist Gaetan "Mole" Molière, Smithsonian representative Fenton Q. Harcourt, and chef Cookie Farnsworth. When they are successful, Milo learns that his language skills are needed to aid the Atlanteans in activating the source of their power.

Cast: Michael J. Fox as Milo Thatch
Corey Burton as Gaetan "The Mole" Moliere
Claudia Christian as Helga Katrina Sinclair
James Garner as Commander Lyle Tiberius Rourke
John Mahoney as Preston B. Whitmore
Phil Morris as Dr. Joshua Strongbear Sweet

Leonard Nimoy as King Kashekim Nedakh
Don Novello as Vincenzo "Vinny" Santorini
Jacqueline Obradors as Audrey Rocia Ramirez
Florence Stanley as Whlhelmina Bertha Packard
David Ogden Stiers as Fenton Q. Harcourt
Cree Summer as Princess "Kida" Kidagakash

Music Highlights: "Where the Dream Takes You" (Diane Warren/James Newton Howard) performed by Mya. Score by James Newton Howard.

Film Facts

• Leonard Nimoy, voice of King Kashekim Nedakh, is best known for playing Mr. Spock on the original *Star Trek* series (1966-1969). Other well-known actors include Don Novello (Father Guido Sarducci on *Saturday Night Live*), James Garner (*The Rockford Files, Maverick*), John Mahoney (*Frasier*), Claudia Christian (*Babylon 5*), Phil Morris (Jackie Chiles on *Seinfeld*), Jacqueline Obradors (*NYPD Blue*), and Cree Summer (*A Different World*).
• The line "Dive, dive, five degrees down bubble," as the submarine descends, comes from the classic Disneyland ride "Submarine Voyage."
• Directors Gary Trousdale and Kirk Wise had previously co-directed *Beauty and the Beast* (1991) and *The Hunchback of Notre Dame* (1996).
• Linguist Marc Okrand was hired to develop the Atlantean language, with the written version created by John Emerson.
• A pre-release edit of the film began with a "Viking Prologue" (included on the DVD and Blu-ray of the film), which introduced the Shepherd's journal shown in the film, but did not let the audience know about the population of Atlantis. The decision was made to create a new prologue that depicted the destruction of Atlantis.

Atlantis: Milo's Return (G)

Home media release date: May 13, 2003
Production Company: DisneyToon Studios, Walt Disney Television Animation, Toon City Animation
Length: 70 minutes
Directed by: Tad Stones, Toby Shelton, Victor A. Cook
Screenplay by: Thomas Hart, Henry Gilroy, Kevin Hopps, Tad Stones, Stephen Engelhart, Marty Isenberg

Synopsis: A series of three stories taking place after *Atlantis: The Lost Empire*. In part 1, as the Atlanteans rebuild their city, Milo's team is shipwrecked near a village terrorized by a giant Kraken. In part 2 (beginning at 29 minutes), the team is called to Arizona to investigate phantom "sand coyotes." In part 3 (beginning at 52 minutes), a stolen Atlantean spear leads the team to a castle in Iceland, built by an eccentric who casts himself as a modern day Odin of Norse mythology, seeking to initiate Ragnarok, the end of this world. The recovered spear finally brings Atlantis to the surface world.

Cast: James Taylor as Milo
Cree Summer as Kida
John Mahoney as Whitmore
Jacqueline Obradors as Audrey & Nurse
Don Novello as Vinny
Corey Burton as Mole

Phil Morris as Sweet
Florence Stanley as Packard
Frank Welker as Obby & Mantell
Steven Barr as Cookie
Clancy Brown as Volgud
Jan Gilpin as Inger

Music Highlights: Original music by Don Harper.

Film Facts

• Michael J. Fox was replaced by James Arnold Taylor as the voice of Milo Thatch, but several of the original actors reprised their roles, including Cree Summer (Princess Kida), John Mahoney (Preston B. Whitmore), Corey Burton (Gaetan "The Mole" Moliere), Don Novello (Vincenzo "Vinny" Santorini), Jacqueline Obradors (Audrey Rocia Ramirez), Phil Morris (Dr. Joshua Strongbear Sweet), and Florence Stanley (Wilhelmina Bertha Packard).
• The three segments from *Atlantis: Milo's Return* were created as part of a planned series called *Team Atlantis* which was never fully developed.
• An online interview with voice director Greg Weisman referenced connections between the *Gargoyles* universe and that of Atlantis, including a planned episode that would feature Puck/Demona from the *Gargoyles* series (1994-1997).
• Don L. Harper also wrote music for the Disney films *The Lion King 1 & 1/2* and *Tarzan & Jane*.
• In the Bonus Material section of the DVD there is alternate ending to the first segment of the story, featuring the Kraken, which is very brief, just lasting a few seconds, but which gives the story a very different ending.
• Additional appearances: *Atlantis: The Lost Empire* (2001), plus games *Atlantis: The Lost Empire* (2001), *Atlantis: The Lost Empire - Trial by Fire* (2001), *The Lost Empire - The Lost Games* (2001).

Balto (G)

Theatrical release date: December 22, 1995
Production Company: Amblimation, Amblin Entertainment, Universal Pictures
Length: 78 minutes
Directed by: Simon Wells
Screenplay by: Cliff Ruby, Elana Lesser, David Steven Cohen, Roger S.H. Schulman

Synopsis: A grandmother tells her granddaughter a tale of Nome, Alaska, in 1925. Top sled dog Steele is fast but arrogant, looking down on the stray Balto, who dreams of being a sled dog. When the little girl Rosy's hat blows away into the path of Steele's sled, Balto outruns Steele to save it, impressing Rosy's dog Jenna. Despite Jenna's admiration, Balto is ashamed he is a dog-wolf hybrid. Jenna learns that Rosy and other children are sick with diphtheria, and the terrible Alaskan weather makes it difficult to get an antitoxin to the town, so plans are made for a dogsled team to pick up the medicine from a rail station. Dogs compete for a spot on the team, and despite interference from Steele's henchdogs Nikki, Kaltag, and Star, Balto finishes first, only to be passed over due to being part wolf. When Steele's team gets lost, Balto resolves to find them, accompanied by the grouchy goose, Boris, and the playful polar bears, Muk and Luk. An encounter with a huge bear almost ends their mission, until Jenna unexpectedly arrives, and after the bear perishes by falling through the ice over a lake, she explains that they need to take the mountain trail. Seeking to go faster, Balto goes on alone, finally finding the team, but Steele's pride prevents him from accepting help, and he refuses to let Balto take the medicine. During a fight, Steele tumbles off a cliff, allowing Balto to lead the team, but the bitter Steele marks trees to confuse the way back. It's only by embracing his wild side that Balto can find the help he needs to lead the mission home.

Cast: Kevin Bacon as Balto
Bob Hoskins as Boris (goose)
Bridget Fonda as Jenna
Jim Cummings as Steele
Phil Collins as Muk and Luk
Jack Angel as Nikki
Danny Mann as Kaltag

Robbie Rist as Star
Juliette Brewer as Rosy
Sandra Searles Dickson as Sylvie and Dixie/
    Rosy's Mother
Miriam Margolyes as Grandma Rosy/
    Extra Voices
Lola Bates-Campbell as Granddaughter

Music Highlights: "Reach for the Light" (James Horner/Barry Mann/Cynthia Weil) performed by Steve Winwood. Music by James Horner.

Film Facts

• The film is based on a true story, in which the dog Togo led the dogsled team first, and Balto finished the journey. Togo's story is told in the live-action film *Togo* (2019).
• The bronze statue of Balto is in New York's Central Park, near the Tisch Children's Zoo.
• The real Balto was a Siberian Husky, not part wolf.
• The film generated two sequels, *Balto: Wolf Quest* (2002) and *Balto III: Wings of Change* (2004).

Bambi (G)

Theatrical release date: August 21, 1942
Production Company: Walt Disney Productions
Length: 70 minutes
Directed by: David D. Hand
Story direction by: Perce Pearce, story adaptation by Larry Morey, story development by George Stallings, Melvin Shaw, Carl Fallberg, Chuck Couch, Ralph Wright

---

Synopsis: A young fawn named Bambi is born and followed over a year. He faces frightening dangers, as his mother is killed by a hunter and his forest home is destroyed by a fire, but he also finds the friendship of Thumper the rabbit and Flower the skunk, as well as the guidance of Friend Owl, and his father, the Great Prince of the Forest. As spring approaches, Bambi discovers love, falling under the spell of the doe Faline, but soon finds he must fight the stag Ronno to win his place with her.

Cast: Bambi: Bobby Stewart (baby), Donnie Dunagan (young), Hardie Albright (adolescent), John Sutherland (adult)
Thumper: Peter Behn (young), Tim Davis (adolescent), Sam Edwards (adult)
Flower: Stan Alexander (young), Tim Davis (adolescent), Sterling Holloway (adult)
Faline: Cammie King Conlon (young), Ann Gillis (adult)
Thumper's Mother: Margaret Lee
The Great Prince of the Forest: Fred Shields
Bambi's Mother: Paula Winslow
Friend Owl: Will Wright

Music Highlights: "Love is a Song" (Frank Churchill/Larry Morey) performed by Donald Novis, "Looking for Romance (I Bring You a Song)" (Churchill/Morey), "Little April Shower" (Churchill/Morey), "Let's Sing a Gay Little Spring Song" (Churchill/Morey), "Twitterpated" (H. Bliss/R. Sour/H. Manners), "Thumper Song" (Bliss/Sour/Manners). Music by Frank Churchill, Edward Plumb.

Film Facts

- The fifth Disney animated classic, *Bambi* was based on the 1923 novel *Bambi, a Life in the Woods* (originally *Bambi: Eine Lebensgeschichte aus dem Walde*) by Austrian writer Felix Salten (Salten was born in Hungary, but raised in Austria).
- Thumper was called "Bobo" in an early script. He did not appear in Salten's book.
- The scene of Bambi's mother eating grass (41:00) turned up in the Donald Duck short "No Hunting" (1955) and in a number of Disney films: *The Sword in the Stone* (1963) at 7:07, *The Jungle Book* (1967) at 47:26, and *Beauty and the Beast* (1991) at 0:27. Bambi and his mother both appear in *The Rescuers* (1977) at 53:07.
- The animators studied the movements of deer, rabbits, and skunks, going to the Los Angeles Zoo, even setting up a small zoo at the studio which included a pair of deer named Bambi and Faline.
- The off-screen shooting of Bambi's mother was famously traumatic for director Steven Spielberg, and sparked Paul McCartney's interest in animal rights.
- The film was released in 1942, during World War II, to very mixed reviews, and fell slightly short of breaking even during its initial release. Critical and popular evaluations of the film improved over the years, as it was re-released in theaters several times.

Bambi II (G)

Home media release date: February 7, 2006 (theatrical release in Argentina on January 26, 2006)
Production Company: Walt Disney Pictures, DisneyToon Studios, DisneyToon Studios Australia, Toon City Animation (Philippines)
Length: 74 minutes
Directed by: Brian Pimental
Screenplay by: Alicia Kirk, story by Brian Pimental and Jeanne Rosenberg, inspired by the book *Bambi* by Felix Salten

---

Synopsis: Taking place after the loss of Bambi's mother, the young deer Bambi is raised by his father, The Great Prince of the Forest. Bambi and the Great Prince both face struggles, as Bambi wrestles with his fears and his father deals with his sudden and unexpected role raising Bambi.

Cast: Patrick Stewart as The Great Prince
Alexander Gould as Bambi
Keith Ferguson as Friend Owl
Brendon Baerg as Thumper
Nicky Jones as Flower
Andrea Bowen as Faline
Anthony Ghannam as Ronno

Music Highlights: "There is Life" (David Friedman) performed by Alison Krauss, "First Sign of Spring" (Michelle Lewis/Daniel Petty) performed by Michelle Lewis, "Through Your Eyes" (Richard Marx/Dean Pitchford) performed by Martina McBride. Music by Bruce Broughton.

Film Facts

• *Bambi II* was released theatrically in some countries (Australia, Austria, Brazil, the Dominican Republic, France, Italy, Mexico, and the UK), but only on DVD/VHS in the United States.
• Researchers spent weeks in Maine studying the forest, as they did for the original *Bambi* (1942).
• Patrick Stewart took over the role of The Great Prince of the Forest from Fred Shields. The lines "Your mother can't be with you anymore. Come…" are drawn from the original *Bambi*.
• Alexander Gould, who voiced Bambi, also voiced Nemo in *Finding Nemo* (2003).
• At one point British screen legend Christopher Lee was expected to provide the voice of a man in the forest, but the role was cut by the time the film was finalized.
• Working titles for the project included *Bambi and the Great Prince* and *Bambi and the Great Prince of the Forest,* before *Bambi II* was chosen.
• Though critical reviews were mixed, DVD and Blu-ray sales totaled $117.4 million, and the film won an Annie Award for "Best Home Entertainment Production."
•The video game *Bambi: The Fawn's Journey* was released shortly before the film.
• This film was the final VHS release from Walt Disney Home Entertainment. *Cars* was the last Pixar VHS release.

Barbie franchise

Barbie began as the famous doll by the Mattel toy company, introduced in 1959. A pair of specials in 1987 were followed by many home media films, as well as several shorts and a few TV series:

Barbie and the Rockers: Out of This World (1987) TV special (also on VHS)
Barbie and the Sensations: Rockin' Back to Earth (1987) TV special (also on VHS)

Film Title	Songs/Music
Barbie in The Nutcracker (2001)	Tchaikovsky's *Nutcracker* Ballet
Barbie as Rapunzel (2002)	"Constant As the Stars Above"
Barbie: Swan Lake (2003)	"Wings" performed by Leslie Mills
Barbie as The Princess and the Pauper (2004)	"Written in Your Heart"
Barbie Fairytopia (2005)	"A Rainbow in Your Eyes"
Barbie and the Magic of Pegasus (2005)	"Hope Has Wings"
Barbie Fairytopia: Mermadia (2006)	Music by Eric Colvin
The Barbie Diaries (2006)	"This Is Me"
Barbie in The 12 Dancing Princesses (2006)	"Shine"
Barbie Fairytopia: Magic of the Rainbow (2007)	"You Are the Most"
Barbie as The Island Princess (2007)	"Here on My Island"/"I Need to Know"
Barbie Mariposa (2008)	Music by Eric Colvin
Barbie & The Diamond Castle (2008)	"Connected"
Barbie in A Christmas Carol (2008)	"Jolly Old Saint Nicholas"
Barbie Presents Thumbelina (2009)	Music by Eric Colvin
Barbie and The Three Musketeers (2009)	"All for One"
Barbie in A Mermaid Tail (2010)	"Queen of the Waves"
Barbie: A Fashion Fairytale (2010)	"Life is a Fairytale"
Barbie: A Fairy Secret (2011)	"Can You Keep a Secret"
Barbie: Princess Charm School (2011)	"You Can Tell She's a Princess"
Barbie: A Perfect Christmas (2011)	"A Perfect Christmas"
Barbie in A Mermaid Tail 2 (2012)	"Do the Mermaid"
Barbie: The Princess & the Popstar (2012)	"Here I Am"
Barbie in The Pink Shoes (2013)	"Keep on Dancing"
Barbie Mariposa & the Fairy Princess (2013)	"Only a Breath Away"
Barbie & Her Sisters in A Pony Tale (2013)	"You're the One"
Barbie: The Pearl Princess (2014)	"Light Up the World"
Barbie and the Secret Door (2014)	"If I Had Magic"
Barbie in Princess Power (2015)	"Soaring"
Barbie in Rock 'N Royals (2015)	"What If I Shine"/"Finale Mash Up"
Barbie & Her Sisters in The Great Puppy Adventure (2015)	"The Greatest Day"
Barbie Spy Squad (2016)	"Strength in Numbers"
Barbie: Star Light Adventure (2016)	"Shooting Star"
Barbie and Her Sisters in A Puppy Chase (2016)	"Live in the Moment"
Barbie: Video Game Hero (2017)	"Change the Game"
Barbie: Dolphin Magic (2017)	"Treasure"
Barbie: Princess Adventure (2020)	"Life in Color"/"Try It On"

Barbie: Life in the Dreamhouse animated shorts (2012-2015)
Barbie Dreamtopia shorts (2016), *Barbie: Dreamtopia* TV film (2016), *Barbie Dreamtopia: Festival of Fun* TV film (2017), *Barbie Dreamtopia: The Series* (2017-2018)
Barbie: Dreamhouse Adventures animated TV series (2018-2021)

Barbie in The Nutcracker (TV-Y)

Limited theatrical release date: October 23, 2001 Home media release date: December 11, 2001
Production Company: Mainframe Entertainment, Mattel Entertainment
Length: 78 minutes
Directed by: Owen Hurley
Written by: Linda Engelsiepen, Hilary Hinkle, Rob Hudnut, based on the tale by E. T. A. Hoffmann, *The Nutcracker* ballet by Pyotr Ilyich Tchaikovsky

Synopsis: When Barbie's sister Kelly is struggling with ballet, Barbie tells her the tale of Clara, who receives the gift of a nutcracker from her aunt. On Christmas Eve Clara falls asleep, only to wake to find her nutcracker is alive, battling the Mouse King and his soldiers. The Mouse King shrinks Barbie, and together Clara and the Nutcracker fight off the mice. In order to grow Barbie back to her normal size, they set off to find the Sugarplum Princess, on an island across the sea of storms. Along the way they must evade the Mouse King's soldiers, with some help from Captain Candy and Major Mint. Barbie figures out that the Nutcracker used to be Prince Eric. When the Nutcracker, the Major, and the Captain are captured, friendly fairies fly Barbie to the Mouse King's castle, where she frees her friends, leading to a final battle between the Nutcracker and the Mouse King. The Nutcracker and Clara's shared bravery leads to the defeat of the Mouse King and a most unexpected appearance of the Sugarplum Princess.

Cast: Kelly Sheridan as Barbie/Clara
Kirby Morrow as The Nutcracker/Prince Eric
Tim Curry as The Mouse King
Peter Kelamis as Pimm the Bat
Christopher Gaze as Major Mint
Ian James Corlett as Captain Candy

Chantal Strand as Kelly
Kathleen Barr as Aunt Elizabeth Drosselmayer/ Owl
French Tickner as Grandfather Drosselmayer
Alex Doduk as Tommy
Britt McKillip as Peppermint Girl

Music Highlights: Music by Arnie Roth, based on Tchaikovsky's *Nutcracker* Ballet, performed by The London Symphony Orchestra.

Film Facts

• This is Barbie's theatrical/home media debut, following the TV specials *Barbie and the Rockers: Out of This World* (1987) and *Barbie and the Sensations: Rockin' Back to Earth* (1987), which were later released on VHS.
• The film had a week-long limited theatrical release beginning October 23, 2001.
• Kelly Sheridan, voice of Barbie, is a prolific voice actress, including roles in *My Little Pony: Friendship is Magic* (Cheerilee, Starlight Glimmer), *X-Men: Evolution* (Scarlet Witch), *Inuyasha* (Sango), *LoliRock* (Praxina), and *Ninjago* (Gayle Gossip).
• The film's computer animation was not as developed as it was for subsequent titles in the series.
• Prussian author E. T. A. Hoffmann wrote the 1816 story "The Nutcracker and the Mouse King," which Pyotr Ilyich Tchaikovsky adapted into the 1892 ballet *The Nutcracker*.

Barbie as Rapunzel (NR)

Home media release date: October 1, 2002
Production Company: Mainframe Entertainment, Mattel Entertainment
Length: 84 minutes
Directed by: Owen Hurley
Written by: Cliff Ruby & Elana Lesser

Synopsis: Rapunzel is a servant to the sorceress Gothel, who has raised her since she was an infant. Deep in the forest, behind a magic wall, Rapunzel spends her days cooking and cleaning for Gothel, kept company by the white rabbit Hobie, and purple dragon Penelope. One day she discovers a secret room and finds a hand mirror with an engraved message, given to her on her first birthday, although Gothel said she adopted Rapunzel a few days after she was born. She discovers a tunnel leading to a town outside the castle, where Rapunzel saves a little girl from falling into a deep hole, and meets Prince Stefan. Gothel is angry Rapunzel left the castle, destroying her paintings and imprisoning her in a tower. With the help of a magic paintbrush, Rapunzel paints a picture of the town she visited, which she walks through into the real town. Stefan takes Rapunzel to a silver smith, who says his brother made the magic paintbrush. The brother lives in Wilhelm's kingdom, but they cannot visit it due to a feud between King Frederick and King Wilhelm. Stefan invites her to the castle's masked ball. Rapunzel returns to her tower so Penelope's father, the dragon Hugo, will not be blamed for her escape, but Gothel discovers her invitation to the ball. She cruelly cuts off Rapunzel's hair, destroys her magic paintbrush, puts a magic barrier on the castle, and chains Hugo, going to the ball disguised as Rapunzel. Rapunzel's honest nature allows her to escape the tower, and when she arrives at the castle, she learns the real reason for the feud between the kingdoms, as well as the truth about her own past.

Cast: Kelly Sheridan as Barbie/Rapunzel
Anjelica Huston as Gothel
Cree Summer as Penelope (dragon)
Ian James Corlett as Hobie (rabbit)/Palace Guard
Mark Hildreth as Stefan
David Kaye as Hugo (dragon)/General
Peter Kelamis as Otto/Skinny Swordsman
Russell Roberts as King Frederick
Christopher Gaze as King Wilhelm
Terry Klassen as Fat Swordsman/Baker
Chantal Strand as Kelly/Katrina
Danny McKinnon as Tommy
Britt McKillip as Melody
Jocelyne Loewen as Lorena

Music Highlights: "Rapunzel Theme" (Arnie Roth) performed by Becky Taylor, "Wish Upon a Star" (Nicals Molinder/Joacim Persson/Pelle Ankarberg) performed by Samantha Mumba, "Constant As the Stars Above" (Rob Hudnut/Arnie Roth), performed by Jessica Brown. Music by Arnie Roth.

Film Facts

• The baker (16:22) and the guard (32:00) both also appear in *Barbie as The Princess and the Pauper,* the baker at 22:08 and the palace guard at 1:08:52.
• Antonín Dvořák's Symphony No. 9 (the "New World Symphony") is heard in the film.

Barbie as The Princess and the Pauper (NR)

Home media release date: September 28, 2004
Production Company: Mainframe Entertainment, Mattel Entertainment
Length: 85 minutes
Directed by: William Lau
Written by: Cliff Ruby & Elana Lesser

Synopsis: Princess Anneliese is born on the same day as Erika, a poor peasant girl. When Anneliese's kingdom runs out of money, the Queen plans to marry Anneliese off to the nearby King Dominick, who is looking for a wife, while Erika is working as an indentured servant to Madame Carp to work off her parents' debt. On a secret visit to the town, Anneliese meets Erika, and they are both surprised at their resemblance. After returning to the palace, Anneliese is kidnaped by the henchmen of the Queen's wicked advisor Preminger, but her loyal tutor Julian knows something is amiss. He persuades Erika to pose as Anneliese, while they learn what happened. Anneliese escapes and returns to the castle, but the guards are so convinced that Erika is Anneliese that they won't let her in the palace. She happens upon Madame Carp, who, taking her to be Erika, puts her to work. The king's "page" turns out to be King Dominick himself in disguise, but Preminger is determined to marry the Queen, trapping both Princess Anneliese and Julian in a mine. With courage and teamwork, Anneliese and Erika work to expose Preminger's scheme.

Cast: Kelly Sheridan as Princess Anneliese/Erika
Melissa Lyons as singing Princess Anneliese
Julie Stevens as singing Erika
Mark Hildreth as King Dominick
Mark Luna as singing King Dominick
Alessandro Juliani as Julian
Martin Short as Preminger

Kathleen Barr as Serafina/Bertie
Ian James Corlett as Wolfie/Guard #3
Ellen Kennedy as Queen Genevieve
Pam Hyatt as Madame Carp
Brian Drummond as Nick/Guard #1
Jan Rabson as Midas/Nack
Colin Murdock as Royal Scheduler

Music Highlights: "Free" (Megan Cavallari/Amy Powers) performed by Melissa Lyons and Julie Stevens, "How Can I Refuse?" (Cavallari/Powers/Rob Hudnut) performed by Martin Short, "I Am a Girl Like You" (Cavallari/Powers), performed by Melissa Lyons and Julie Stevens, "To Be a Princess" (Cavallari/ Powers/Hudnut) performed by Alessandro Juliani and Julie Stevens, "The Cat's Meow" (Cavallari/Powers/Hudnut) performed by Julie Stevens, "If You Love Me for Me" (Cavallari/Powers) performed by Mark Luna and Julie Stevens, "Written in Your Heart" (Cavallari/Powers/Hudnut) performed by Melissa Lyons and Julie Stevens. Score by Arnie Roth.

Film Facts

• The story is based on Mark Twain's 1881 novel *The Prince and the Pauper*. Other films based on the story include the Mickey Mouse featurette "The Prince and the Pauper" (1990), and *Curious George: Royal Monkey* (2019).
• Two characters from *Barbie as Rapunzel* (2002) appear: the baker (22:08) and the palace guard (1:08:52). The baker is seen in *Barbie as Rapunzel* at 16:22, the guard at 32:00.

Barbie in the 12 Dancing Princesses (TV-Y)

Home media release date: September 19, 2006
Production Company: Mainframe Entertainment, Mattel Entertainment
Length: 83 minutes
Directed by: Greg Richardson
Written by: Cliff Ruby & Elana Lesser

Synopsis: The princesses of King Randolph are invited to a royal ball by the kingdom of Bulovia, but do not conduct themselves with royal bearing. The king invites his cousin, the Duchess Rowena (and her monkey Brutus), to come prepare his daughters for royal life. Unbeknownst to the king, Rowena is harsh with the princesses, dressing them in ugly gray gowns, taking their belongings, and locking them in their room. After reading a tale of an enchanted land, Genevieve finds an opening to the magical world from their room. The princesses dance throughout the night, only to return to their unpleasant life during the day. Their father begins to fall ill, and it is discovered that Rowena has been poisoning him. The princesses try to return home, but are trapped when Rowena orders the entrance to the magical land destroyed. Working together with Derek, a loyal servant of the king, the princesses must find a way to return and save their father from Rowena, who has seized power as the queen.

Cast: Kelly Sheridan as Geneveive
Catherine O'Hara as Rowena
Nicole Oliver as Ashlyn/Twyla
Jennifer Copping as Blair
Lalainia Lindbjerg as Courtney
Kathleen Barr as Delia
Chiara Zanni as Edeline

Adrienne Carter as Fallon
Ashleigh Ball as Hadley/Ilsa
Britt McKillip as Janessa
Maddy Capozzi as Kathleen
Chantal Strand as Lacey
Shawn Macdonald as Derek
Christopher Gaze as King Randolph

Music Highlights: Themes by Felix Mendelssohn (Symphony No. 3/"Scottish," Symphony No. 4/ "Italian," A Midsummer Night's Dream), "Derek's Tune" (trad., arr. Roth), "Birthday Song" (trad., arr. Roth) performed by Melissa Lyons, "Sacerdotes Domini" (William Byrd, arr. Jeffrey Bernstein) performed by Occidental College Women's Glee Club. End credits: "Shine" (Roth/Powers/Hudnut) performed by Cassidy Ladden. Music by Arnie Roth.

Film Facts

• The story is based on the Brothers Grimm tale "The Twelve Dancing Princesses."
• The sisters of Genevieve are seen in *Barbie as The Island Princess* (2007) at the palace (46:13, 1:08:40), and Genevieve's dress is also shown (41:21).
• The emissary of Bulovia bears a strong resemblance to Preminger in *Barbie as The Princess and the Pauper* (2004).
• In a brief scene at the dinner table, Courtney is supposed to be holding a book (as she was a few seconds before), but nothing is in her hand (5:00).

Barbie as The Island Princess (TV-Y)

Home media release date: September 18, 2007
Production Company: Mattel Entertainment, Rainmaker Entertainment
Length: 86 minutes
Directed by: Greg Richardson
Written by: Cliff Ruby & Elana Lesser

Synopsis: When mystery girl Ro washes up on the beach of an island, she is raised by the red panda Sagi, the peacock Azul, and the elephant Tika, in a tropical paradise. When Prince Antonio's ship arrives at the island one day, Ro has a chance to try to get some answers about her past. Ro and her animal friends return with Antonio to the kingdom of Apollonia. Ro is amazed to see the people and kingdom, but soon Antonio is informed by the king that he is to marry Princess Luciana, daughter of Queen Ariana. Ariana reveals that she wants revenge on the king, after her family was punished many years ago for plotting to kill the king. Antonio protests that he does not want to marry Luciana, as he loves Ro, but his father insists. Wanting Ro out of the way, Luciana uses a sleeping herb to put the king's animals to sleep, blaming it on Ro. The king orders Ro sent back to her island, but she risks everything to return to save the animals, proving her worthiness in the process.

Cast: Kelly Sheridan as Ro/Rosella
Melissa Lyons as Rosella's singing voice
Alessandro Juliani as Prince Antonio
Christopher Gaze as Sagi
Steve Marvel as Azul/Minister
Susan Roman as Tika
Garry Chalk as Frazer/Calvin
Russell Roberts as King Peter

Patricia Drake as Queen Danielle/
    Mama Pig
Bets Malone as Tallulah
Britt McKillip as Rita
Carly McKillip as Gina
Chantal Strand as Sofia
Andrea Martin as Queen Ariana
Candice Nicole as Princess Luciana

Music Highlights: "Here On My Island" performed by Melissa Lyons, Steve Marvel, Christopher Gaze and Susan Roman, "Right Here In My Arms" performed by Melissa Lyons, "A Brand New Shore" performed by Alessandro Juliani, Susan Roman, Christopher Gaze, Steve Marvel and Kelly Sheridan, "I Need To Know" performed by Melissa Lyons and Alessandro Juliani, "Love Is For Peasants" performed by Andrea Martin and Candice Nicole, "At The Ball" performed by Bets Malone, Gaze, Lyons, Roman and Marvel, "The Rat Song" performed by Scott Page-Pagter and Ian James Corlett,"Always More" performed by Melissa Lyons, "When We Have Love" performed by cast, Water Music by Handel, "I Need To Know (Pop Version)" performed by Cassidy Ladden.
All songs: music by Megan Cavallari, lyrics by Amy Powers and Rob Hudnut. Score by Arnie Roth.

Film Facts

• The sisters of Genevieve, the heroine of *Barbie in The 12 Dancing Princesses* (2006), are seen at the palace (46:13, 1:08:40), and Genevieve's dress is also shown (41:21).
• Wolfie, the barking cat from *Barbie as The Princess and the Pauper* (2004) also appears (53:51).
• Matt, the mime rat, is listed in the credits as "voiced by himself."

Barbie and The Three Musketeers (TV-Y)

Home media release date: September 15, 2009
Production Company: Mattel Entertainment, Rainmaker Entertainment
Length: 81 minutes
Directed by: William Lau
Written by: Amy Wolfram

Synopsis: Corinne has had an agreement with her mother that when she turned 17, she could go to Paris to be a musketeer. She sets out with a letter of introduction from her father, d'Artagnan, to Monsieur Treville, who is in charge of guarding the royal family. She is turned away as too inexperienced, but when a dog chases her cat, Miette, Corinne runs into the palace, and is recruited by the demanding Madame de Bossé to prepare for an upcoming palace ball, alongside the fashion-conscious Viveca, the dancer Aramina, and the violinist Renée. After a suspicious incident in which a chandelier almost falls on Prince Louis, the seemingly feeble old housekeeper Hélène notices the girls' exceptional skills as they fend off debris from the chandelier. Hélène, who is much stronger than she appeared, takes them to a secret musketeer training room, agreeing to train them. When the rope securing the prince's hot air balloon is cut, Corinne manages to save him, after which the musketeers in training overhear the regent planning to do away with the prince at the costume ball. After their warning to Monsieur Treville is ignored, Corinne and her crew must save the day.

Cast: Kelly Sheridan as Barbie as Corinne
Tim Curry as Philippe
Kira Tozer as Viveca
Willow Johnson as Aramina
Dorla Bell as Renée
Nicole Oliver as Corinne's Mother/
    Fancy Dress Girl #1
Merrilyn Gann as Madame de Bossé
Kathleen Barr as Hélène/Fancy Dress Girl #2

Mark Hildreth as Prince Louis
Michael Dobson as Bertram/Musketeer Guard
Bernard Cuffling as Monsieur Treville
Brad Swaile as Serge/Handsome Man
Amelia Henderson as Miette (cat)
Tabitha St. Germain as Miette Walla
Brian Dobson as Brutus (dog)/Regent Guard #2
David Kaye as Alexander/Driver
Terry Klassen as Pig/Regent Guard #1/Henchman

Music Highlights: "Making My Way" (Leslie Mills/Chris Pelcer) performed by Leslie Mills, "All For One" (Amy Powers/Jeannie Lurie/Gabriel Mann/Rob Hudnut) performed by Keely Hawkes, "Unbelievable" (Ian Alec Harvey Dench/James Saul Atkin/Zachary Sebastian Rex/James Foley/Mark Simon Decloedt/Derran Gene Brownson, orig. by EMF). Score by Eric Colvin.

Film Facts

• Don't miss the "Bloopers" bonus feature on the DVD.
• The story is based on the 1844 novel *The Three Musketeers* by Alexandre Dumas. Corinne's initial mishaps with her three friends mirrors D'Artagnan's experience with the musketeers in the book.
• Several characters from the novel are shown or mentioned, including Monsieur Treville, Countess de Winter, and Constance. Renée and Aramina's names come from the musketeer Rene Aramis.

Batman: Mask of the Phantasm (PG)

Theatrical release date: December 25, 1993
Production Company: Warner Bros. Animation
Length: 76 minutes
Directed by: Eric Radomski, Bruce W. Timm
Screenplay by: Alan Burnett, Paul Dini, Martin Pasko, Michael Reaves, story by Alan Burnett

Synopsis: As Batman is in the process of catching a group of criminals, a mysterious figure with a scythe, the Phantasm, ends up killing crime boss Chuckie Sol. Once the police arrive, they see Batman and assume he was responsible. While Bruce Wayne is at a party, he is reminded of his old flame Andrea Beaumont and his first days fighting crime. When criminal associate Buzz Bronski visits Chuckie Sol's grave, the Phantasm crushes him with a tombstone, and again, Batman is blamed for the death. While still dressed as Batman, Bruce visits his parents' grave, and is seen by Andrea. He follows her and sees her on a date, leading to more memories of his early struggle to honor the promise he made to his late parents to fight crime, and his desire to have a normal life with Andrea. In the present, criminal boss Salvatore Valestra is told Batman is the one killing criminal leaders. Batman puts together that Valestra is next on the Phantasm's list, and goes to see him. While at his home, he sees a photo of Andrea's father with the three crime bosses. Another flashback reveals Bruce proposed to Andrea, after which a group of criminals was seen meeting with Andrea's father, and the next day Andrea's engagement ring was returned with a note saying she was "too young" to get married. In the present, at the dilapidated site of Gotham's World Fair celebration, Valestra asks the Joker for protection. Batman shows up in Andrea's home, asking her about the photo of the crime bosses with her father, but she refuses to talk. When the Phantasm comes to kill Salvatore, he's already dead, and the Joker catches him on film. Batman must end the Phantasm's killing spree, and come to terms with his past.

Cast: Kevin Conroy as Batman
Dana Delany as Andrea Beaumont
Hart Bochner as Arthur Reeves
Stacy Keach, Jr. as Phantasm/Carl Beaumont
Abe Vigoda as Salvatore Valestra
Dick Miller as Chuckie Sol

John P. Ryan as Buzz Bronski
Efrem Zimbalist Jr. as Alfred
Bob Hastings as Commissioner Gordon
Robert Costanzo as Detective Bullock
Mark Hamill as The Joker
Marilu Henner as additional voices

Music Highlights: "I Never Even Told You" (Siedah Garrett/Glen Ballard) performed by Tia Carrere, Music by Shirley Walker.

Film Facts

• The film was made by many of the cast and crew of *Batman: The Animated Series* (1992–1995).
• The story is based on the graphic novels *Batman: Year One* and *Batman: Year Two*.
• The World's Fair song is "There's a Great Big Beautiful Tomorrow" by the Sherman Brothers.

Batman & Mr. Freeze: SubZero (NR)

Home media release date: March 17, 1998
Production Company: Warner Bros. Animation
Length: 67 minutes
Directed by: Boyd Kirkland
Written by: Randy Rogel & Boyd Kirkland

Synopsis: Mr. Freeze is lying low in the Arctic, hunting for fish with his two polar bears, providing food for the Inuit boy Koonak, and keeping watch over his medically ill wife Nora, who is suspended in a solution until a cure can be found for her. When by chance a submarine destroys the tube holding Nora's body, the crew is soon frozen. Seeking a cure for his wife, Mr. Freeze returns to Gotham, consulting with Dr. Gregory Belson, who determines a cure may be possible, but can find no donors who are a match with Nora's blood type. Mr. Freeze bribes Belson to find a living donor, targeting Barbara Gordon (who sometimes goes by the name Batgirl). While Barbara and Dick Ward (also known as Robin), are on a date at a nightclub, Freeze attacks, kidnapping Barbara. From background sounds on a phone call, Batman and Robin determine where Barbara is being held, taking the Batwing to her location on an offshore oil drilling platform. Meanwhile, Mr. Freeze and Belson prepare to operate on Barbara, but when Koonak objects, Barbara is able to escape. Even when Batman and Robin arrive, Mr. Freeze and his polar bears are formidable foes, with their battle leading to the destruction of the platform. Mr. Freeze is believed to have died in an explosion, and soon after, Nora is able to receive medical help to save her life, news which is happily received by an interested party in the Arctic.

Cast: Kevin Conroy as Batman
Michael Ansara as Mr. Freeze
Loren Lester as Robin
Efrem Zimbalist Jr. as Alfred
George Dzundza as Dr. Gregory Belson
Robert Costanzo as Detective Bullock

Bob Hastings as Commissioner Gordon
Mary Kay Bergman as Barbara Gordon
Marilu Henner as Veronica Vreeland
Dean Jones as Dean Arbagast
Mari Devon as Summer Gleeson
Liane Schirmer as Renee Montoya

Music Highlights: "I Only Have Eyes for You" (Harry Warren/Al Dubin) performed by The Flamingos. Music by Michael McCuistion.

Film Facts

• Mr. Freeze first appeared in the comic *Batman* #121, February, 1959, originally called Mr. Zero. He appeared in two episodes of *Batman: The Animated Series* (1992-1995), "Heart of Ice" (season 1, episode 14) and "Deep Freeze" (season 2, episode 19).
• This was the second animated film produced by the *Batman: The Animated Series* cast and crew.
• This release received favorable comparisons to the live-action *Batman & Robin* (1997), released the previous year.

Batman: Mystery of the Batwoman (PG)

Home media release date: October 21, 2003
Production Company: Warner Bros. Animation
Length: 75 minutes
Directed by: Curt Geda, sequence directors Jennifer Graves, Tim Maltby
Written by: Michael Reaves, story by Alan Burnett

Synopsis: The mysterious Batwoman appears, attacking criminals trafficking plasma rifles for the Penguin. While investigating at the Penguin's factory, Batman and Robin find the Batwoman, just before the factory blows up from a charge she set, destroying additional illegal arms. While at a department store, Bruce Wayne meets Kathy Duquesne, daughter of the gangster Carlton Duquesne, who persuades Wayne to help her escape her father's bodyguards, and Wayne begins to suspect she is the Batwoman. After the Batwoman shows up to photograph documents at the Penguin's headquarters, the Penguin fires Carlton Duquesne as his head of security. Kathy Duquesne takes Wayne to the Penguin's Iceberg Lounge, where the Batwoman appears again, restraining the Penguin with a high-tech metal like the one the clumsy scientist Rocky demonstrated for Wayne Tech, and it appears that Rocky is actually Batwoman. As a battle breaks out, Batman obtains a piece of the metal, giving it to detective Sonia Alacana. Rocky visits a prison to see her boyfriend Kevin, who was framed by the Penguin, saying she's close to a breakthrough, just needing someone in Penguin's organization to talk. Desperate for assistance, the Penguin hires the fearsome Bane to protect him. Meanwhile, Batman learns that Rocky was seen at the same time as Batwoman, despite his hunch that she was the vigilante. The true identity of the Batwoman is tied to several injustices, and a showdown with Bane on the Penguin's ship takes place as Batman discovers the Batwoman's true target.

Cast: Kevin Conroy as Batman
Kimberly Brooks as Kathy Duquesne
Kelly Ripa as Rocky
Elisa Gabrielli as Sonia
Kyra Sedgwick as Batwoman
David Ogden Stiers as Penguin
Kevin Michael Richardson as Carlton Duquesne

John Vernon as Rupert Thorne
Hector Elizondo as Bane
Efrem Zimbalist Jr. as Alfred
Eli Marienthal as Robin
Tara Strong as Barbara Gordon
Bob Hastings as Commissioner Gordon
Robert Costanzo as Detective Bullock

Music Highlights: "Batman: The Animated Series" Theme (Shirley Walker), "Betcha Neva" (Dave James/Alan Ross/Natasha Bedingfield) performed by Cherie. Music by Lolita Ritmanis.

Film Facts

- The film is tied to *Batman: The Animated Series/The New Batman Adventures/Batman Beyond*.
- Kathy Duquesne's name is inspired by Kathy Kane, the secret identity of Batwoman in the comics.
- The DVD includes the animated short "Chase Me."

Beauty and the Beast (G)

Theatrical release date: November 22, 1991
Production Company: Walt Disney Pictures, Walt Disney Feature Animation
Length: 84 minutes/Special Edition 91 minutes
Directed by: Gary Trousdale and Kirk Wise
Screenplay by: Linda Woolverton

Synopsis: A poor inventor stumbles upon a magical castle where the prince has been transformed into a terrible Beast, and the servants into animated objects. The inventor is kept prisoner, but released with the agreement that he send a replacement, and his daughter Belle insists on going in his place. Belle endures life with the harsh Beast, who gradually begins to soften, and Bell unexpectedly begins to care for him. Belle is allowed to leave to tend to her ill father, and an angry mob led by the hunter Gaston, jealous of Belle's affection for the Beast, attacks the castle. The love between Belle and the Beast is transformative.

Cast: Paige O'Hara as Belle
Robby Benson as Beast
Richard White as Gaston
Jerry Orbach as Lumiere
David Ogden Stiers as Cogsworth

Angela Lansbury as Mrs. Potts
Bradley Michael Pierce as Chip
Rex Everhart as Maurice
Jesse Corti as LeFou
Hal Smith as Philippe

Music Highlights: "Belle" performed by Paige O'Hara & cast, "Be Our Guest" performed by Jerry Orbach & cast, "Gaston" performed by Richard White, Jesse Corti, and chorus, "Something There" performed by Paige O'Hara & Robby Benson, "Beauty and the Beast" performed by Angela Lansbury, "The Mob Song" performed by Richard White and chorus. End credits: "Beauty and the Beast" performed by Céline Dion and Peabo Bryson. All songs: music by Alan Menken, lyrics by Howard Ashman. Score by Alan Menken.

Film Facts

• *Beauty and the Beast* was the 30th Walt Disney animated classic and the third film of the Disney Renaissance, after *The Little Mermaid* (1989) and *The Rescuers Down Under* (†990).
• The "Beauty and the Beast" story is based on the French fairy tale "La Belle et la Bête" by Gabrielle-Suzanne de Villeneuve, in her 1740 collection of fairy tales *La Jeune Américaine, et les contes marins,* also influenced by Jeanne-Marie Leprince de Beaumont's adaptation of the tale and Jean Cocteau's classic 1946 film.
• Lyricist Howard Ashman and composer Alan Menken had provided the Oscar-winning music for *The Little Mermaid* (1989), and went on to compose music for *Aladdin* (1992).
• The 2002 Special Edition VHS/DVD added a new Menken/Ashman song, "Human Again."
• *Beauty and the Beast* won Academy Awards for "Best Song" ("Beauty and the Beast") and "Best Score," and was the first animated film ever to be nominated for "Best Picture."
• The Beast is named Prince Adam, though this is never indicated in the film.
• The film's success led to animated sequels, a 1994 Broadway musical, and a 2017 live-action film.
• The film is dedicated to lyricist Howard Ashman, who died of AIDS-related complications in 1991.

Beauty and the Beast: The Enchanted Christmas (G)

Home media release date: November 11, 1997
Production Company: Walt Disney Video Premiere, Walt Disney Television Animation, Walt Disney Animation Canada
Length: 72 minutes
Directed by: Andy Knight
Written by: Flip Kobler & Cindy Marcus and Bill Motz & Bob Roth

---

Synopsis: Taking place in-between events in the first film, Belle tries to bring Christmas to the castle, which the grief-stricken Beast had banned. The court composer Forte, transformed into a huge pipe organ, manipulates the Beast's ill-humor, aided by the naive piccolo Fife.

Cast: Paige O'Hara as Belle
Robby Benson as Beast
Jerry Orbach as Lumiere
David Ogden Stiers as Cogsworth
Bernadette Peters as Angelique
Tim Curry as Forte
Haley Joel Osment as Chip

Frank Welker as Phillippe/Sultan
Jeff Bennett as Axe/Poke
Jim Cummings as Various
Kath Soucie as Enchantress
Paul Reubens as Fife
Angela Lansbury as Mrs. Potts

Music Highlights: "Stories" (Rachel Portman/Don Black) performed by Paige O'Hara, "As Long as There's Christmas" (Portman/Black) performed by Bernadette Peters, "Don't Fall in Love" (Portman/Black) performed by Tim Curry, "A Cut Above the Rest" (Portman/Black) performed by Jerry Orbach, David Ogden Stiers, and Paige O'Hara. "As Long as There's Christmas" (Portman/Black) performed by Peabo Bryson and Roberta Flack. Music by Rachel Portman.

Film Facts

• Prior to this film, the series *Sing Me a Story with Belle* (1995-1999) offered live-action acting and puppets intercut with classic Disney animated shorts.
• The working title for the film was *Beauty and the Beast: A Christmas Belle*.
• The story's original villain was slated to be Avenant, Gaston's younger brother, seeking revenge on Belle and the Beast (Avenant was the name of a character in Jean Cocteau's classic 1946 live-action *Beauty and the Beast*).
• Lyricist Don Black has worked extensively in film, and is perhaps best known for writing the lyrics to the title song from the 1966 film *Born Free*.
• This was the first animated Disney film to feature music by a female composer, Rachel Portman. Portman also composed the score for the unrelated film *Belle* (2013).
• A soundtrack CD mixed original songs (including "As Long As There's Christmas" sung by Peabo Bryson and Roberta Flack) with instrumentals and Christmas carols sung by Paige O'Hara.
• Angelique appears in *Mickey's Once Upon a Christmas* (1999) as a Christmas ornament.
• The 2002 Special Edition VHS/DVD featured a video of "As Long As There's Christmas" by Swedish pop girl group Play.

Beauty and the Beast: *Belle's Magical World* (G)

Home media release date: February 17, 1998
Production Company: Walt Disney Television Animation, Walt Disney Video Premiere
Length: Original release 70 minutes/Special Edition 92 minutes
Directed by: Bob Kline
Writers: "The Perfect Word" written by Richard Cray, "Fifi's Folly" written by Alice Brown and Carter Crocker, "Mrs. Potts' Party" written by Nancy Greystone and Richard Cray, "Broken Wing" story by Chip Hand, written by Carter Crocker and Sheree Guitar.

Synopsis: A montage of short stories which, like *The Enchanted Christmas,* fall in between the opening and ending of the first *Beauty and the Beast* film. Stories include "The Perfect Word" (1:00), "Fifi's Folly" (24:19), and "Broken Wing" (1:08:25). The 2011 Special Edition DVD added a fourth story, "Mrs. Potts' Party" (45:32).

Cast: Robby Benson as The Beast
Paige O'Hara as Belle
David Ogden Stiers as Cogsworth
Jerry Orbach as Lumiere
Jeff Bennett as Crane
Jim Cummings as Webster
Gregory Grudt as Chip

Rob Paulsen as LePlume
Kimmy Robertson as Fifi the Featherduster
Anne Rogers as Mrs. Potts
Frank Welker as Sultan the Footstool
April Winchell as Chandeleria
Joanne Worley as Armoire the Wardrobe

Music Highlights: "Listen With Our Hearts" (Michael & Patty Silversher) from "The Perfect Word," performed by Belle (Paige O'Hara), "A Little Thought" (Michael & Patty Silversher) from "Mrs. Potts' Party" performed by Belle (Paige O'Hara). Music by Harvey R. Cohen.

Film Facts

• As would be the case with Disney's *Atlantis* a few years later, an animated *Beauty and the Beast* television series was considered for possible release, and some episodes were created as part of this process, but eventually the decision was made not to produce the series. The episodes that were created for the series were repurposed for this home media release, tied together by animations of a storybook page turning.
• Composers Michael and Patty Silversher also wrote songs for *Aladdin: The Return of Jafar* (1994), and *The Little Mermaid II: Return to the Sea* (2000).
• A book similar to Webster, the dictionary in the story "The Perfect Word," originally appeared as a large puppet on the live-action/animated short television series *Sing Me a Story with Belle* (1995-1997).
• The original 1998 title of the release on VHS was simply *Belle's Magical World,* but upon re-release it was re-titled *Beauty and the Beast: Belle's Magical World.* The 1998 VHS featured three stories, the 2003 Special Edition VHS/DVD included a fourth story, "Mrs. Potts' Party."
• The 2011 DVD features an episode of *Sing Me a Story with Belle.*

Bee Movie (PG)

Theatrical release date: November 2, 2007
Production Company: DreamWorks Animation, Columbus 81 Productions, Pacific Data Images
Length: 91 minutes
Directed by: Simon J. Smith, Steve Hickner
Written by: Jerry Seinfeld and Spike Feresten & Barry Marder & Andy Robin

Synopsis: Barry, a young bee who needs to choose his occupation, can't stand the idea of committing to just one job for the rest of his life. On a dare, he makes a flight with pollen gatherers, but gets separated and meets the human Vanessa. Barry and Vanessa hit it off (to the irritation of Ken, a man Vanessa was dating before Barry arrived), and when Barry is horrified to learn that humans steal honey from bees, she helps him sue the human race. Barry wins the lawsuit, and all the honey is returned to the bees. Despite their victory, bee society breaks down when the hive stops working to make honey, leaving it up to Barry to help the bees rediscover their team spirit.

Cast: Jerry Seinfeld as Barry B. Benson
Renée Zellweger as Vanessa Bloome
Matthew Broderick as Adam Flayman
Patrick Warburton as Ken
John Goodman as Layton T. Montgomery
Chris Rock as Mooseblood

Kathy Bates as Janet Benson
Barry Levinson as Martin Benson
Oprah Winfrey as Judge Bumbleton
Larry Miller as Buzzwell
Rip Torn as Lou Lo Duca
Michael Richards as Bud Ditchwater

Music Highlights: "Sugar Sugar" (Jeff Barry/Andy Kim) performed by The Archies, "Here Comes the Sun" (George Harrison) performed by Sheryl Crow. End credits: "Thinkin' Bee" (Marc Shaiman/Jerry Seinfeld) performed by Jerry Seinfeld and Matthew Broderick. Music by Rupert Gregson-Williams.

Film Facts

• A series of three humorous trailers were made, showing disastrous efforts to film *Bee Movie* as a live-action film.
• Celebrity cameos included Sting, Ray Liotta, Carl Kasell, and Larry King as "Bee Larry King."
• Several actors previously worked on the NBC sitcom *Seinfeld* (1989-1998): Jerry Seinfeld, Patrick Warburton (David Puddy), Michael Richards (Kramer), Larry Miller (the Doorman), and Mario Joyner (Lamar). The name of Barry's father, Martin Benson, also comes from the *Seinfeld* episode "The Pez Dispenser," and Jerry's girlfriend in the first season of *Seinfeld* was named Vanessa.
• The scene with Barry floating in the pool (29:35) is based on the film *The Graduate* (1967).
• The bear brought into the courtroom (48:58) strongly resembles Vincent from the DreamWorks Animation film *Over the Hedge* (2006).
• Caricatures of Disney's Winnie the Pooh and Piglet are shown as the honey is reclaimed (1:02:31).
• The line "Turn your key, sir" (1:03:24), and the dual key-turn are drawn from Matthew Broderick's film *WarGames* (1983).

Big Hero 6 (PG)

Theatrical release date: November 7, 2014
Production Company: Walt Disney Pictures, Walt Disney Animation Studios
Length: 102 minutes
Directed by: Don Hall and Chris Williams
Screenplay by: Jordan Roberts, Dan Gerson, Robert L. Baird

Synopsis: Hiro Hamada, a gifted but trouble-prone teenage robotics engineer, is brought by his older brother Tadashi to the university robotics lab where he works, meeting Go Go, Honey Lemon, Wasabi, and Fred, and the head of the robotics program, Robert Callaghan. To get into the university program Hiro creates "microbots," a swarm of tiny mentally-controlled robots that can be shaped into whatever is imagined. During a fire Tadashi runs into a building to try to save professor Callaghan, but an explosion leaves Hiro alone in the world. Hiro accidentally activates one of Tadashi's projects, Baymax, an inflatable medical robot, and the two are led by one of Hiro's microbots to a warehouse where they find microbots being produced on a mass scale, and where they escape a confrontation with a masked man. Before long they are joined by Tadashi's colleagues: Go Go, Honey Lemon, Wasabi, and Fred, forming a team to stop the villain who has stolen Hiro's technology.

Cast: Scott Adsit as Baymax
Ryan Potter as Hiro
Daniel Henney as Tadashi
T.J. Miller as Fred
Jamie Chung as Go Go

Damon Wayans Jr. as Wasabi
Genesis Rodriguez as Honey Lemon
James Cromwell as Robert Callaghan
Alan Tudyk as Alistair Krei
Maya Rudolph as Cass

Music Highlights: "Immortals" (Hurley/Trohman/Stump/Wentz) performed by Fall Out Boy, "Boca Dulce Boca" (Salgado/Santander) performed by José Luis Rodríguez, "Eye of the Tiger" (Peterik/Sullivan) performed by Survivor. Score by Henry Jackman.

Film Facts

• The 54th of the Disney animated classics, *Big Hero 6* was originally a comic book series published by Marvel, first appearing as *Sunfire & Big Hero 6 #1* (September, 1998). The first issue of a five-issue *Big Hero 6* mini-series in 2008 was the first appearance of Fred and Wasabi.
• At the 87th Academy Awards in 2015 *Big Hero 6* won the "Best Animated Feature" award.
• Disney acquired Marvel Entertainment in 2009. *Big Hero 6* was the first Disney animated feature film featuring Marvel characters.
• The *Big Hero 6* team is racially diverse: Hiro (Japanese), Fred (Caucasian), Go Go (Korean), Honey Lemon (Latina), Wasabi (African-American), and Baymax (robot).
• Several cameos are scattered throughout the film, including references or characters from *Lilo & Stitch* (2002), *Wreck-It Ralph* (2012), *Frozen* (2013), and *Zootopia* (2016).
• Additional appearances: the animated TV series *Big Hero 6: The Series* (2017-2020), promoted by a few sets of shorts: "Baymax and…" (6 shorts), "Big Chibi 6: The Series" (12 shorts), "Baymax Dreams" (3 shorts), and "Baymax and Mochi" (3 shorts).

The Black Cauldron (PG)

Theatrical release date: July 24, 1985
Production Company: Walt Disney Pictures, Walt Disney Feature Animation
Length: 80 minutes
Directed by: Ted Berman, Richard Rich
Story by: David Jonas, Al Wilson, Vance Gerry, Roy Morita, Ted Berman, Peter Young, Richard Rich, Art Stevens, Joe Hale, based on *The Chronicles of Prydain* series by Lloyd Alexander

---

Synopsis: Young Taran is dissatisfied with his work as assistant pig-keeper for the magician Dallben, until he learns that Henwen, the pig he has been caring for, has mystical powers. He also learns that the evil Horned King is seeking the powerful Black Cauldron, and plans to use Henwen's powers to get it. Dallben sends Taran away to hide Henwen, but the pig is captured by the Horned King's minions. Accompanied by the curious creature Gurgi, the Princess Eilonwy, the bard Fflewddur Fflam, and the tiny Fairfolk, Taran decides to destroy the Black Cauldron rather than let it fall into evil hands. The treacherous Horned King, however, will not be defeated so easily, requiring the ultimate sacrifice.

Cast: Grant Bardsley as Taran
Susan Sheridan as Eilonwy
Freddie Jones as Dallben
Nigel Hawthorne as Fflewddur
Arthur Malet as King Eidilleg
John Byner as Gurgi and as Doli
Lindsay Rich as Fairfolk

Brandon Call as Fairfolk
Gregory Levinson as Fairfolk
Eda Reiss Merin as Orddu
Adele Malis-Morey as Orwen
Billie Hayes as Orgoch
Phil Fondacaro as Creeper
John Hurt as The Horned King

Music: Score by Elmer Bernstein.

Film Facts

• The 25th of the Disney animated classics, *The Black Cauldron* was based on the first two books in *The Chronicles of Prydain,* a series of novels by American author Lloyd Alexander that draw upon Welsh mythology.
• This was the first Disney animated feature to receive a PG rating (*The Black Hole,* from 1979, was the first live-action Disney film to receive this rating).
• This was also the first animated Disney feature not to have any songs. Elmer Bernstein's score generally received positive reviews from critics.
• Director Tim Burton worked as a conceptual artist on this film, years before *The Nightmare Before Christmas* (1993), *Alice in Wonderland* (2010), *Alice Through the Looking Glass* (2016), and *Dumbo* (2019).
• This was the first Disney film to make use of computer-generated imagery (CGI), creating several special effects, such as bubbles, a floating orb, and the Black Cauldron.
• Elmer Bernstein's soundtrack score was released on CD by Varèse Sarabande in 1985, and was much sought after by collectors. It was reissued by Intrada in 2012.
• The author, Lloyd Alexander, saw little similarity between *The Black Cauldron* and his work.

Bolt (PG)

Theatrical release date: November 21, 2008
Production Company: Walt Disney Pictures, Walt Disney Animation Studios
Length: 96 minutes
Directed by: Chris Williams and Byron Howard
Screenplay by: Dan Fogelman and Chris Williams

Synopsis: Bolt, a Hollywood canine who believes he really possesses super powers, accidentally ends up across the country. Believing his co-star Penny is in great danger, Bolt sets out to save her, aided by the cynical stray cat Mittens and the true-believer hamster Rhino. Though Bolt learns his powers aren't real, it turns out there are true villains to contend with.

Cast: John Travolta as Bolt
Miley Cyrus as Penny
Susie Essman as Mittens
Mark Walton as Rhino
Malcolm McDowell as Dr. Calico
James Lipton as The Director
Greg Germann as The Agent

Diedrich Bader as Veteran Cat
Nick Swardson as Blake
J.P. Manoux as Tom
Dan Fogelman as Billy
Kari Wahlgren as Mindy
Chloë Moretz as Young Penny
Randy Savage as Thug

Music Highlights: "Barking at the Moon" (Jenny Lewis) performed by Jenny Lewis, "I Thought I Lost You" (Miley Cyrus/Jeffrey Steele) performed by Miley Cyrus and John Travolta, "Dog-Face Boy" (Burston/Campbell/Delaoglou/Kilmister) performed by Motörhead. Score by John Powell.

Film Facts

• The 48th Disney animated classic, the film's original title was *American Dog,* written by Chris Sanders (*Lilo & Stitch*), who was slated to direct the film as well. Differences over the direction of the film led to Sanders being replaced by directors Chris Williams and Byron Howard. Sanders went on to co-write and co-direct *How to Train Your Dragon* in 2010 and *The Croods* in 2013.
• Despite their extensive on-screen interactions, some of the lead actors never met in person — even John Travolta (Bolt) and Susie Essman (Mittens).
• Susie Essman, voice of Mittens, appeared as Susie Greene in *Curb Your Enthusiasm*.
• Mark Walton, voice of Rhino, had previously done voice acting in the Disney films *Chicken Little* (2005) and *Home on the Range* (2004). Walton is a Disney artist who did some temporary ("scratch") readings of lines for Rhino, but the producers liked his work so much they cast him in the role.
• James Lipton (The Director) is the host of the *Inside the Actors Studio* television series on Bravo.
• Bolt's look is based on the American White Shepherd breed.
• The film was paired in theaters with Pixar's *Cars Toons* short "Tokyo Mater."
• A game based on the film was released for PC, PS2, PS3, Wii, Xbox 360, and Nintendo DS.
• The DVD includes the bonus 4-minute short "Super Rhino" (2009) showing what a hamster with super powers might look like (as well as an inside joke for *Hanna Montana* fans).

The Book of Life (PG)

Theatrical release date: October 17, 2014
Production Company: Reel FX Creative Studios, 20th Century Fox, Chatrone
Length: 95 minutes
Directed by: Jorge R. Gutiérrez
Screenplay by: Jorge R. Gutiérrez & Doug Langdale

Synopsis: On a field trip to a museum on the Day of the Dead, the children are shown the Book of Life, containing all the stories of the world. They learn of the kind La Muerte, ruler of the Land of the Remembered afterlife, the trickster Xibalba, ruler of the Land of the Forgotten, and the Candle Maker, who keeps everything in balance. Xibalba proposes a wager to La Muerte: the best friends Manolo (who has lost his mother) and Joaquin (son of the late Captain Mondragon) are both interested in Maria. If Joaquin marries Maria, Xibalba will stop interfering in the human world, but if Manolo marries her, Xibalba will rule the Land of the Remembered. In disguise, La Muerte gives Manolo a blessing, and Xibalba gives Joaquin a medal that will not allow him to be hurt and will give him immeasurable courage. He is told to keep it hidden, as there is a bandit king, Chakal, who would stop at nothing to get it back. Maria is charmed by Manolo's kindness, so Xibalba cheats to get Manolo into the Land of the Remembered, not counting on the power of a pure heart.

Cast: Diego Luna as Manolo
Zoe Saldana as Maria
Channing Tatum as Joaquin
Ron Perlman as Xibalba
Christina Applegate as Mary Beth
Ice Cube as Candle Maker
Kate del Castillo as La Muerte

Hector Elizondo as Carlos Sanchez
Danny Trejo as Skeleton Luis
Carlos Alazraqui as General Posada/Dali/Chuy
Ana de la Reguera as Skeleton Carmen
Emil-Bastien Bouffard as Young Manolo
Elias Garza as Young Joaquin
Genesis Ochoa as Young Maria

Music Highlights: "I Will Wait" (Dwane/Lovett/Marshall/Mumford) performed by Joe Matthews and Diego Luna, "Creep" (Hammond/Hazlewood/C. Greenwood/J. Greenwood/O'Brien/Selway/Yorke) performed by Diego Luna, "I Love You Too Much" (Paul Williams/Gustavo Santaolalla) performed by Diego Luna, "Can't Help Falling in Love" (Creatore/Weiss/Peretti) performed by Diego Luna, "The Apology Song" (Williams/Santaolalla) performed by Diego Luna, "No Matter Where You Are" (Alvarado/Alvarado) performed by Diego Luna, Zoe Saldana and Plácido Domingo, "Live Life" (Campany/Grigg/Uecke/Uecke) performed by Jesse & Joy, "The Apology Song" (Paul Williams/Gustavo Santaolalla) performed by La Santa Cecilia. Music by Gustavo Santaolalla.

Film Facts

- Writer/director Jorge Gutiérrez has expressed interest in creating a trilogy of films.
- Characters in Gutiérrez's *El Tigre: The Adventures of Manny Rivera* (2007) make cameos (4:11).
- The film drew many comparison's with Pixar's *Coco* (2017), released three years later.
- The DVD included an animated short, *The Adventures of Chuy*.

The Boss Baby (PG)

Theatrical release date: March 31, 2017
Production Company: DreamWorks Animation
Length: 97 minutes
Directed by: Tom McGrath
Written by: Michael McCullers, based on the book by Marla Frazee

---

Synopsis: Imaginative seven year old Tim Templeton loves being the center of his parents' attention, but his world is turned upside down when he sees a baby arrive in a taxi, wearing a tiny business suit and carrying a briefcase. Inexplicably, Tim's parents are oblivious to the oddity of this, and when Tim learns that the baby can talk, sent on a mission from Baby Corp to stop puppies from cutting into the babies' share of love, his parents ignore his efforts to expose the Boss Baby for what he is. Though they begin as adversaries, Tim and the Boss Baby agree to work together, going with their parents to their work, Puppy Co. If they can accomplish the mission of discovering Puppy Co's top secret puppy project, Boss Baby can return to Baby Corp, which would be fine with Tim. Unfortunately, the puppy project is more diabolical than they suspected, requiring a team of babies to save the day.

Cast: Alec Baldwin as Boss Baby
Steve Buscemi as Francis Francis
Jimmy Kimmel as Dad
Lisa Kudrow as Mom
Tobey Maguire as Adult Tim/Narrator
Miles Bakshi as Tim
James McGrath as Wizzie/Elvis Impersonator

Conrad Vernon as Eugene
ViviAnn Yee as Staci
Eric Bell, Jr. as Triplets
David Soren as Jimbo
Edie Mirman as Big Boss Baby
James Ryan as Story Bear
Walt Dohrn as Photographer

Music Highlights: "Blackbird" (Lennon/McCartney), "Alla en El Rancho Grande" (Trad.) performed by Mariachi Real de San Diego, "Cheek to Cheek" (Berlin) performed by Fred Astaire, "Ladies Night" (Bell/Bell/Brown/Muhammad/Smith/Taylor/Thomas/Toon) performed by Kool & The Gang, "The Tra La La Song (One Banana Two Banana)" (Winkless/Ziegler/Barkan) performed by The Banana Splits, "Theme from S.W.A.T." (De Vorzon) performed by Rhythm Heritage, "C.C. Rider" (arr. Presley) performed by Elvis Presley, "(Every Time I Turn Around) Back In Love Again" (Hanks/Grey) performed by L.T.D., "Everybody Loves Babies" (Smith) performed by David P. Smith, "Viva Las Vegas" (Pomus/Shuman) performed by Elvis Presley. End credits: "What The World Needs Now Is Love" (Bacharach/David) performed by Missi Hale. Music by Hans Zimmer and Steve Mazzaro.

Film Facts

• Tim's shirt reads "01" (7:23), but after Boss Baby arrives it reads "02" (8:10).
• Wizzy the Wizard quotes Gandalf of *The Lord of the Rings*: "He shall not pass!" "Fly, you fools!"
• Director Tom McGrath (*Madagascar, Megamind*) makes a cameo as the TV Chef.
• Tim's daughter's hospital crib reads 3/31/17 (1:27:26), which was the theatrical release date of *The Boss Baby*.
• The film was nominated for the "Best Animated Feature" Academy Award.

The Boxcar Children (G)

Theatrical release date: April 8, 2014 (premiere at Toronto International Film Festival, Canada)
Production Company: Castaway Hammerhead Productions, Village Roadshow Pictures
Length: 86 minutes
Directed by: Mark A.Z. Dippe and Dan Chuba, co-directed by Kyungho Jo
Written by: Justin Merz and Zach Strauss, based on the book by Gertrude Chandler Warner

---

Synopsis: Four siblings, Henry, Jess, Violet, and Benny, are on their own after their parents have passed away. They fear their grandfather, who did not get along with their mother, and ask to stay the night at a bakery. The couple there plan to send Benny to an orphanage, so they flee. As the bakers look for them, the children run and hide in an abandoned boxcar. Despite their challenges, Henry helps Benny face his fears by appealing to his imagination, they find blueberries to eat, and they befriend a stray dog that they name "Watch." A nearby junkyard provides dishes and utensils, and the boxcar begins to feel more like a home. Henry begins working for a local man, Dr. Moore, mowing his lawn and working in his yard. When Dr. Moore needs more help with his cherry harvest, all four children go to his home to help. Dr. Moore sees a notice in the paper from the children's grandfather, and takes them to the Silver City Field Day community celebration, where Henry wins a race. Later, Violet becomes ill, and Henry brings Dr. Moore, who takes the children back to his house. The next day a man called "Mr. Henry" comes to visit the house, and the children get to know how kind the man is. They finally discover that Mr. Henry is actually their grandfather, James Henry Alden, and come to understand the truth about him.

Cast: Illeana Douglas as Mary
Mackenzie Foy as Violet
Zachary Gordon as Henry
Joey King as Jessie
Jadon Sand as Benny

Martin Sheen as Grandfather Alden
J.K. Simmons as Dr. Moore
D.B. Sweeney as Baker
Audrey Wasilewski as Baker's Wife

Music Highlights: Music by Kenneth Burgomaster.

Film Facts

• The film was based on *The Boxcar Children* series of books by Gertrude Chandler Warner, begun in 1924. Warner wrote 19 books, and other authors continued the series, totaling over 150 titles.
• The National Education Association named the book in the "Teachers' Top 100 Books for Children" 2007 poll, and the School Library Journal included the book in its "Top 100 Chapter Books" in 2012.
• The film debuted at TIFF Kids, an offshoot of the Toronto International Film Festival.
• The bakery at the beginning of the film, Chandler, is named after Gertrude Chandler Warner.
• Additional appearances: the animated sequel *The Boxcar Children: Surprise Island* (2018), with voice actors Martin Sheen, J.K. Simmons, and Jadon Sand reprising their roles.

The Boxtrolls (PG)

Theatrical release date: September 26, 2014
Production Company: Laika, Focus Features
Length: 96 minutes
Directed by: Anthony Stacchi, Graham Annable
Screenplay by: Irena Brignull & Adam Pava, based upon the book *Here Be Monsters!* by Alan Snow

Synopsis: The Boxtrolls, mysterious, box-wearing creatures who live below the English town of Cheesebridge, take a baby from the Trubshaw family, and the town exterminator, Archibald Snatcher, is hired to eliminate the trolls. At night there is a curfew, when the trolls roam the streets, looking for mechanical objects, and fleeing from the exterminator and his cruel thugs. In the underground troll world, caves strewn with machines they tinker with, the human baby, "Eggs," grows up among the trolls, raised by the kindly troll Fish. Over time their numbers diminish, as the exterminator hunts them down. Lord Portley-Rind, leader of the white-hatted aristocrats who run the town, is more focused on eating fancy cheeses than governing, but his spirited daughter Winifred sees Eggs with the trolls, just before Fish is captured. Eggs enters the strange human world to find Fish, and Winifred points him to the exterminators, led by Snatcher, who is obsessed with emulating the cheese eating aristocrats. Eggs finds that the exterminators have the captured trolls working as slave labor, along with the father of Eggs, whom Snatcher claimed was eaten by the trolls. When Winifred hears what's happened, she and Eggs escape into the troll tunnels, where they learn the truth of how Eggs ended up with the trolls, and how Snatcher is developing a terrible weapon. When the adults won't listen, they need to take action to expose the evil hiding in plain sight.

Cast: Ben Kingsley as Snatcher
Isaac Hempstead Wright as Eggs
Elle Fanning as Winnie Portley-Rind
Dee Bradley Baker as Fish/Wheels/Bucket
Steve Blum as Shoe/Sparky
Toni Collette as Lady Cynthia Portley-Rind
Jared Harris as Lord Portley-Rind
Nick Frost as Mr. Trout

Richard Ayoade as Mr. Pickles
Tracy Morgan as Mr. Gristle
Simon Pegg as Herbert Trubshaw
Pat Fraley as Fragile/Sweets
Fred Tatasciore as Clocks/Specs
Nika Futterman as Oil Can/Knickers
Maurice LaMarche as Sir Langsdale
James Urbaniak as Sir Broderick/Workmen

Music Highlights: "The Boxtrolls Song" (Eric Idle) performed by Mark Orton, Loch Lomond, & Sean Patrick Doyle, "Quattro Sabatino" (Marianelli) performed by Peter Harris, Alex Tsilogiannis, Thomas Kennedy, & Edmund Saddington, "Little Boxes" (Malvina Reynolds) performed by Loch Lomond, "Some Kids" (Donaldson/Young) performed by Loch Lomond. Music by Dario Marianelli.

Film Facts

• The film was nominated for the "Best Animated Feature" Academy Award and Golden Globe.
• A brief mid-credits scene appears (1:29:54).
• Alan Snow's 550-page novel *Here Be Monsters!* offers a much more complicated story and world.

Boy and the World (PG)

Theatrical release date: January 17, 2014
Country: Brazil   Portuguese title: *O Menino e o Mundo*
Production Company: Filme de Papel
Length: 80 minutes
Directed by: Alê Abreu
Written by: Alê Abreu

Synopsis: A boy is shown playing with animals and exploring the world around him. One day his father, who often entertained the boy by playing his flute, must leave, taking his suitcase and leaving by train. The boy has memories of times with his father, and finally packs a photo of his family in a suitcase of his own, going to the train tracks. A storm sends the boy to a new place, where he sees his suitcase and the picture of his family. He meets an old man who wears a shirt like his, and his dog, going with them and joining a large group of people picking cotton. Later a *carnaval* crowd passes by, dressed in colorful clothes, playing instruments, and singing. Back at the cotton picking operation, a boss comes by, and dismisses workers seen as unfit, including the old man. The boy travels with the man and his dog, walking with a cart and using the cart as a boat when a storm hits, ending up under a pink tree. The boy sees his father on a passing truck of workers, and follows after the truck. He finds a factory where the cotton is woven into fabric, and ends up on a bus of workers leaving the factory and going into the city. The boy follows the last worker on the bus, who wears an orange shirt and rainbow cap, to his home. The next day they go to an outdoor market, where the worker performs music as a one-man band, while the boy plays with a kaleidoscope, wandering onto a barge that takes fabric to be turned into clothes. He later returns to the worker, and they sneak into the abandoned fabric factory, where the owner of the factory replaces the workers with a machine. The boy sees his father's train, but once he reaches it, many men who look like his father get out. There is a battle between the army and the people, shown as a rainbow colored bird, which is destroyed by the army, followed by scenes of destruction of the Amazon rainforest and increasing industrialization. The boy races back to his home. Scenes of the boy planting the pink tree as a child are followed by the boy, wearing an orange shirt and rainbow cap, leaving home as a young man.

Cast: Vinicius Garcia as Menino
Felipe Zilse as Jovem/additional voices
Alê Abreu as Velho

Lu Horta as Mãe
Marco Aurélio Campos as Pai

Music Highlights: Music by Ruben Feffer, Gustavo Kurlat.

Film Facts

• The film was nominated for the "Best Animated Feature Film" Academy Award.
• The language in the film is Portuguese spoken backwards.

Brave (PG)

Theatrical release date: June 22, 2012
Production Company: Pixar Animation Studios, Walt Disney Pictures
Length: 93 minutes
Directed by: Mark Andrews, Brenda Chapman, co-directed by Steve Purcell
Screenplay by: Mark Andrews, Steve Purcell and Brenda Chapman & Irene Mecchi, story by Brenda Chapman

Synopsis: Fiercely independent Scottish princess Merida of Clan Dun Broch chafes at expectations of formality, preferring to scale mountains, use her longbow, and enjoy the freedoms extended to her three young brothers. When Queen Elinor expects her to marry the winner of the Highland Games, Merida seeks magical help to change her mother's mind. Unwittingly turning the Queen into a bear, Merida and her mother must work together to undo the damage done, and keep King Fergus from mistaking the Queen for Mor'du, a demon bear to which he lost his leg.

Cast: Kelly MacDonald as Merida
Billy Connolly as Fergus
Emma Thompson as Elinor
Julie Walters as The Witch
Robbie Coltrane as Lord Dingwall
Kevin McKidd as Lord MacGuffin
Craig Ferguson as Lord MacIntosh
Sally Kinghorn as Maudie
Eilidh Fraser as Maudie
Peigi Barker as Young Merida
Kevin McKidd as Young MacGuffin
Steven Cree as Young MacIntosh
Steve Purcell as The Crow
Callum O'Neill as Wee Dingwall
Patrick Doyle as Martin
John Ratzenberger as Gordon

Music Highlights: "Touch the Sky" (Mark Andrews/Alex Mandel) performed by Julie Fowlis, "Into the Open Air" (Alex Mandel) performed by Julie Fowlis, "Learn Me Right" (Mumford & Sons) performed by Birdy with Mumford & Sons, "Song of Mor'du" (Patrick Doyle/Steve Purcell) performed by Billy Connolly/cast, "Noble Maiden Fair" (Patrick Doyle) performed by Emma Thompson/Peigi Barker. Score by Patrick Doyle.

Film Facts

- *Brave* was the 13th Pixar feature, originally titled *The Bear and the Bow*.
- Merida was the first Pixar character to become a Disney princess, and the first princess not to have a love interest in the film (soon followed by *Moana*).
- The story was originally written by Brenda Chapman, who was to have been the film's sole director, but differences with John Lasseter led to her replacement by Mark Andrews.
- Ever-present Pixar institution John Ratzenberger voiced Gordon the guard.
- Easter eggs: A wood carving of Sully from *Monsters, Inc.* (32:40), the *Toy Story* Pizza Planet truck (32:43), A113 in Roman Numerals, ACXIII, above the door (33:10).
- The film won the "Best Animated Feature" Academy Award and Golden Globe.
- Additional appearances: "The Legend of Mor'du" short (2012). Merida appears in *Sofia the First* season 3, episode 5, "The Secret Library," is a character in season 5 of the live-action-series *Once Upon a Time* (aired 2015-2016), and makes a hilarious cameo in *Ralph Breaks the Internet* (2018).

The Brave Little Toaster (NR)

Theatrical release date: July 10, 1987
Production Company: Hyperion Pictures, Kushner-Locke, Wang Film Productions
Length: 90 minutes
Directed by: Jerry Rees
Screenplay by: Jerry Rees & Joe Ranft, screen story by Jerry Rees, Joe Ranft, Brian McEntee, based on the novella by Thomas M. Disch

Synopsis: In an abandoned cottage, one by one different appliances come to life. The Toaster, Radio, Lampy, the vacuum cleaner Kirby, and electric blanket Blanky work to clean the house, as they have every day since their Master left. Blanky thinks the Master is returning, and cries when he does not. The Air Conditioner claims the Master will never return, and after a man puts a "For Sale" sign in the front yard, the Toaster says they need to set out to find their Master. Their journey is not an easy one, with Blanky carried away in a windstorm and Lampy burned out by a lightning bolt. Through teamwork and perseverance, they make their way through the wilderness. They are rescued from sinking into the mud by a man with a second hand shop. They flee the shop, finding their Master's home, but he is away visiting the cottage they came from. The home appliances toss the new arrivals into a dumpster, and they are hauled away to the junkyard. Their former companion, the TV, shows the Master their location. He arrives just before the appliances are destroyed by the trash compactor, and when his own safety is at risk, the brave little Toaster makes the ultimate sacrifice.

Cast: Jon Lovitz as Radio
Tim Stack as Lampy/Zeke
Timothy E. Day as Blanky/Young Master
Thurl Ravenscroft as Kirby
Deanna Oliver as Toaster
Phil Hartman as Air Conditioner/
      Hanging Lamp
Joe Ranft as Elmo St. Peters
Judy Toll as Mish-Mash/Two-Face Sewing Machine
Wayne Kaatz as Rob
Colette Savage as Chris
Mindy Stern as Mother/Two-Face Sewing Machine
Jim Jackman as Plugsy
Jonathan Benair as Black and White TV

Music Highlights: "Tutti-Frutti" (Penniman/La Bostrie) performed by Little Richard, "City of Light" (Van Dyke Parks) performed by Deanna Oliver, Timothy Stack, Thurl Ravenscroft, Jerry Rees and Timothy E. Day, "Hidden Meadow" (Bob Walter/Rick Johnston), "My Mammy" (Donaldson/Young/ Lewis) performed by Al Jolson, "It's a B-Movie" (Parks) performed by Phil Hartman, Timothy Stack, Thurl Ravenscroft, Jerry Rees, Timothy E. Day and appliances, "Cutting Edge" (Parks) performed by cast, "Worthless" (Parks) performed by cast, "April Showers" (Silvers/DeSylva) performed by Jerry Rees. Music by David Newman.

Film Facts

- *The Brave Little Toaster* was published in *The Magazine of Fantasy and Science Fiction* in 1980.
- This was the first animated film ever shown at the Sundance Film Festival, screening in 1988.
- Sequels: *The Brave Little Toaster to the Rescue* (1997), *The Brave Little Toaster Goes to Mars* (1998).

Brother Bear (G)

Theatrical release date: November 1, 2003
Production Company: Walt Disney Pictures, Walt Disney Feature Animation
Length: 85 minutes
Directed by: Aaron Blaise & Robert Walker
Screenplay by: Tab Murphy and Lorne Cameron & David Hoselton and Steve Bencich &
Ron J. Friedman

> **Synopsis**: After killing a bear to avenge his oldest brother Sitka, Kenai, a member of an Inuit tribe, is transformed into a bear himself. As he pursues a way to undo this change, he is hunted by a second brother, Denahi, who believes the bear he is chasing killed Kenai. Along the way Kenai is schooled in the ways of bears by Koda, a recently orphaned cub, as well as benefitting from comic relief by two argumentative moose, Rutt and Tuke.

Cast: Joaquin Phoenix as Kenai
Jeremy Suarez as Koda
Jason Raize as Denahi
Rick Moranis as Rutt

Dave Thomas as Tuke
D. B. Sweeney as Sitka
Joan Copeland as Tanana
Michael Clarke Duncan as Tug

Music Highlights: "Great Spirits" (Phil Collins) performed by Tina Turner, "Transformation" (Collins) performed by The Bulgarian Women's Choir, "Welcome" (Collins) performed by The Blind Boys of Alabama and Phil Collins with Oren Waters, "On My Way" (Collins) performed by Phil Collins and Jeremy Suarez, "No Way Out (Theme from Brother Bear)" (Collins) performed by Phil Collins, "Look Through My Eyes" (Collins) performed by Phil Collins. Score by Mark Mancina and Phil Collins.

Film Facts

• The 44th Disney animated classic, the initial story idea for *Brother Bear* was to create a bear version of Shakespeare's *King Lear,* focused on an old bear and his three daughters (just as *The Lion King* drew from *Hamlet*).
• The filmmakers visited Kodiak Island, the Denali National Park, and the Kenai Fjords National Park in Alaska (places with names similar to Koda, Denahi, and Kenai), studying landscapes and learning about Native culture. They sought language assistance from Angayuqaq Oscar Kawagley, a professor at the University of Alaska, Fairbanks, who translated dialogue into Yup'ik.
• Phil Collins and Mark Mancina previously provided music for Disney's *Tarzan* (1999).
• Kenai says "I'm not a beaver, I'm a bea- No, I mean, I'm not a bear, I'm a man!" In *The Sword and the Stone* (1963), Wart says, "I'm not a boy — I mean, I'm not a squirrel, I'm a boy!"
• A highlight of the film was the bickering Canadian moose duo of Rutt and Tuke (Rick Moranis and Dave Thomas, co-stars of the 1983 Canadian comedy *Strange Brew*).
• The DVD includes the music video for "Look Through My Eyes" by Phil Collins.
• A video game based on the film was released for PC, GameBoy Advance, and mobile phones.
• Additional appearances: *Brother Bear 2* (2006). "On My Way" and "Welcome" on *Sing Along Songs: Brother Bear - On My Way* VHS/DVD (2003).

Brother Bear 2 (G)

Home media release date: August 29, 2006
Production Company: DisneyToon Studios, DisneyToon Studios Australia, Project Firefly, Toon City Animation
Length: 74 minutes
Directed by: Benjamin Gluck
Screenplay by: Rich Burns

Synopsis: Prior to being turned into a bear, Kenai and Nita formed an engagement bond when Kenai gave Nita an amulet. When Nita later seeks to marry, the spirits demand that she go with Kenai to Hokani Falls on the eve of the equinox to destroy the amulet, accompanied by the irrepressible cub Koda. Meanwhile, scene-stealing moose Rutt and Tuke are in search of moosettes. During their journey both Kenai and Nita rekindle tender feelings, sparking jealousy in Koda.

Cast: Patrick Dempsey as Kenai
Mandy Moore as Nita
Jeremy Suarez as Koda
Rick Moranis as Rutt
Dave Thomas as Tuke
Andrea Martin as Anda

Catherine O'Hara as Kata
Wanda Sykes as Innoko
Wendie Malick as Aunt Siqiniq
Kathy Najimy as Aunt Taqqiq
Michael Clarke Duncan as Tug
Jim Cummings as Bering & Chikoot

Music Highlights: "Welcome to This Day" (Melissa Etheridge) performed by Melissa Etheridge, "It Will Be Me" (Melissa Etheridge) performed by Melissa Etheridge, "Feels Like Home" (Matthew Gerrard/Robbie Nevil) performed by Melissa Etheridge and Josh Kelley. Score by Dave Metzger.

Film Facts

• "Nita" means "bear" in the Choctaw language.
• Kenai, originally voiced by Joaquin Phoenix in the first film, is played by Patrick Dempsey, who appeared in *Enchanted* (2007) as well as playing Dr. Derek Shepherd on *Grey's Anatomy*.
• Jason Marsden was originally slated to voice the role of Kenai, and is even heard in an early trailer for the film.
• Newcomer Mandy Moore voiced Kenai's childhood love Nita, four years before she would voice Rapunzel in *Tangled* (2010).
• The sequel was produced by DisneyToon Studios and Disney Animation Australia, along with Project Firefly, an animation company established by workers from the Disney Feature Animation Florida after the studio shut down in early 2004.
• The soundtrack for *Brother Bear 2* was issued as a digital download, but was not issued on CD or other media.
• The popularity of the moose duo, Rutt and Tuke, is reflected in the slogan emblazoned across the DVD cover, "The Moose Are On The Loose,"
• After this film Rick Moranis retired from TV and film acting until 2018.

The Bugs Bunny/Road-Runner Movie (G)

Theatrical release date: September 28, 1979
Production Company: Chuck Jones Enterprises, Warner Bros.
Length: 98 minutes
Directed by: Chuck Jones
Written by: Mike Maltese and Chuck Jones

Synopsis: Bugs Bunny, relaxing at home, reflects on his life, including the invention of chase films, and the many "fathers" he has had, focusing on Chuck Jones. Several of Bugs's adventures are presented, including "Hare-Way to the Stars," "Rabbit Seasoning"*, "Duck Dodgers in the 24½th Century," "Robin Hood Daffy"*, "Duck Amuck," "Bully for Bugs," "Ali Baba Bunny," "Rabbit Fire," "For Scent-imental Reasons"*, "Long-Haired Hare"*, "What's Opera, Doc?," "Operation: Rabbit." The Road-Runner cartoons include "Fast and Furry-ous"*, "Going! Going! Gosh!", "Zipping Along," "Stop! Look! And Hasten!", "Guided Muscle," "Gee Whiz-z-z-z-z-z", "There They Go-Go-Go!", "Zoom and Bored," "Whoa, Be-Gone!", "Hip Hip-Hurry!", "Hot-Rod and Reel!", "Wild About Hurry," "Hopalong Casualty," "Zip 'n' Snort," "To Beep or Not to Beep," "Beep Prepared."*
NOTE: shorts with an asterisk are edited.

Cast: Mel Blanc as Bugs Bunny/Daffy Duck/ Porky Pig/Marvin the Martian/ Wile E. Coyote/Pepe le Pew/ Dr. I.Q. High/Hassan

Arthur Q. Bryan as Elmer Fudd
Paul Julian as Road Runner
Nicolai Shutorev as Giovanni Jones
singing voice

Music Highlights: Music by Carl Stalling and Milt Franklyn.

Film Facts

• The original title of the film was *The Great American Chase*.
• The Looney Tunes/Merrie Melodies shorts were produced from 1939 to 1969, followed by *The Bugs Bunny/Road-Runner Movie* (1979), *The Looney, Looney, Looney Bugs Bunny Movie* (1981), *Bugs Bunny's 3rd Movie: 1001 Rabbit Tales* (1982), *Daffy Duck's Movie: Fantastic Island* (1983), and *Daffy Duck's Quackbusters* (1988). After Mel Blanc died in 1989, the archival compilation *The Looney Tunes Hall of Fame* (1991) was followed by *Space Jam* (1996), *Looney Tunes: Back in Action* (2003) and *Space Jam: A New Legacy* (2021).
• The film was issued on VHS and on DVD, appearing on the 2005 *Looney Tunes Movie Collection* DVD, along with *Bugs Bunny's 3rd Movie: 1001 Rabbit Tales*.
• Phil Monroe co-directed the "Bugs at Home" scenes.
• Bugs Bunny's carrot-juice waterfall house is based on the 1935 Frank Lloyd Wright house called Fallingwater in Laurel Highlands, in southwest Pennsylvania.
• There were competing claims of who "created" Bugs Bunny, including some comments by Bob Clampett overstating his role, prompting Chuck Jones to educate filmgoers about Bugs' many "fathers." Inadvertently left off the list was Bugs' first father, Ben "Bugs" Hardaway.

A Bug's Life (G)

Theatrical release date: November 25, 1998
Production Company: Pixar Animation Studios, Walt Disney Pictures
Length: 95 minutes
Directed by: John Lasseter, co-directed by Andrew Stanton
Screenplay by: Andrew Stanton, Donald McEnery & Bob Shaw

Synopsis: After the hapless ant Flik accidentally destroys the food supply prepared for the annual visit of a grasshopper gang that rules over the ants, he leaves in search of help to free the colony. Enlisting the circus troupe of P.T. Flea, Flik inspires the colony to rebel against the grasshoppers.

Cast: Dave Foley as Flik
Kevin Spacey as Hopper
Julia Louis-Dreyfus as Atta
Hayden Panettiere as Dot
Phyllis Diller as Queen
Richard Kind as Molt
David Hyde Pierce as Slim
Joe Ranft as Heimlich

Denis Leary as Francis
Jonathan Harris as Manny
Madeline Kahn as Gypsy Moth
Bonnie Hunt as Rosie
Michael McShane as Tuck/Roll
John Ratzenberger as P.T. Flea
Brad Garrett as Dim
Roddy McDowall as Mr. Soil

Music Highlights: "The Time of Your Life" (Randy Newman) performed by Randy Newman, "A Bug's Life Suite" (instrumental). Score by Randy Newman.

Film Facts

• *A Bug's Life* was the 2nd Pixar film, following *Toy Story* (1995).
• The initial story idea was discussed, along with ideas for *Toy Story 2, Monsters, Inc.* and *Finding Nemo,* at a lunch attended by Pixar's story team: John Lasseter, Andrew Stanton, Pete Docter, and Joe Ranft. The story was originally called *Bugs,* and is loosely based on Aesop's fable "The Ant and the Grasshopper."
• Walt Disney produced a 1934 short film "The Grasshopper and the Ants."
• Flik has cameo appearances in an outtake from *Toy Story 2,* during the end credits of *Cars,* and as a toy in *Toy Story 3.*
• The story line bears some resemblance to Akira Kurosawa's classic 1954 film *Seven Samurai.*
• Pixar and rival studio DreamWorks sparred over the similarities between *A Bug's Life* and *Antz.*
• Many of the voice actors had appeared in sitcoms, including Dave Foley (*NewsRadio*), Julia Louis-Dreyfus (*Seinfeld*), David Hyde Pierce (*Frasier*), Richard Kind (*Mad About You, Spin City*), and Brad Garrett (*Everybody Loves Raymond*).
• Several actors also appeared in other Disney/Pixar films: Dave Foley (*Monsters University*), Hayden Panettiere (*Dinosaur, Ice Princess*) Richard Kind (*Cars, Inside Out*), David Hyde Pierce (*Treasure Planet*).
• Additional appearances: *Sing Along Songs: Flik's Musical Adventure* VHS (1999)/DVD (2005), *It's Tough to Be a Bug!* 9-minute 3D film at Walt Disney World/California Adventure theme parks.

Cars (G)

Theatrical release date: June 9, 2006
Production Company: Pixar Animation Studios, Walt Disney Pictures
Length: 117 minutes
Directed by: John Lasseter, co-directed by Joe Ranft
Screenplay by: Dan Fogelman, John Lasseter, Joe Ranft, Kiel Marray & Phil Lorin, Jorgen Klubien, original story by John Lasseter, Joe Ranft, Jorgen Klubien

Synopsis: On his way to seek the Piston Cup, arrogant, hot-shot race car Lightning McQueen runs afoul of the local law enforcement in rural Radiator Springs. As he impatiently bides his time performing community service, he begins to question the superficial life he has led.

Cast: Owen Wilson as Lightning McQueen
Paul Newman as Doc Hudson
Bonnie Hunt as Sally Carrera
Larry the Cable Guy as Mater
Cheech Marin as Ramone
Tony Shalhoub as Luigi
Guido Quaroni as Guido
Jenifer Lewis as Flo
Paul Dooley as Sarge
Michael Wallis as Sheriff
George Carlin as Fillmore
Katherine Helmond as Lizzie

Music Highlights: "Real Gone" (John Shanks/Sheryl Crow) performed by Sheryl Crow, "Life is a Highway" (Tom Cochrane) performed by Rascal Flatts, "Our Town" (Randy Newman) performed by James Taylor. Score by Randy Newman.

Film Facts

• *Cars,* the 7th Pixar film, began as a screenplay titled *The Yellow Car* written by Jorgen Klubien, focused on an electric car, later developed by John Lasseter into *Route 66*, ultimately becoming *Cars* with story additions by Joe Ranft.
• Lightning McQueen is not named after actor Steve McQueen, but after the late Pixar animator Glenn McQueen.
• Birds from the 2000 Pixar short "For the Birds" make a cameo in the desert (17:44).
• The story of *Cars* closely parallels that of the 1991 Michael J. Fox comedy *Doc Hollywood*.
• The cast of the film included cameos by a number of race car drivers, including Mario Andretti, Dale Earnhardt Jr., Richard Petty, Michael Schumacher, and Darrell Waltrip, as well as announcer Bob Costas, and promoter Humpy Wheeler. The Rust-eze brothers were voiced by Tom and Ray Magliozzi, hosts of the National Public Radio show *Car Talk*.
• Pixar mainstay John Ratzenberger plays Mack, and end credit parodies Hamm Truck in *Toy Car Story* (*Toy Story*), the Abominable Snow Plow in *Monster Trucks, Inc.* (*Monsters, Inc.*), and P.T. Flea Car (P.T. Flea in *A Bug's Life*).
• Be sure to watch the end credits for a number of additional animated clips.
• *Cars: The Video Game* was made for Mac/PC/PS 2/Xbox/GameCube/Wii/Game Boy Advance/DS.
• Additional appearances: "Mater and the Ghost Light" short (2006), *Cars Toons* TV series (2008-2014), *Cars Toon: Mater's Tall Tales* DVD/Blu-ray (2010), *Cars 2* (2011), and *Cars 3* (2017).

Cars 2 (G)

Theatrical release date: June 24, 2011
Production Company: Pixar Animation Studios, Walt Disney Pictures
Length: 106 minutes
Directed by: John Lasseter, co-directed by Brad Lewis
Screenplay by: Ben Queen, original story by John Lasseter, Brad Lewis, Dan Fogelman

---

Synopsis: Lightning McQueen is drafted into an international race, during which Mater unknowingly engages with secret agents who seek to stop a villainous plot from being enacted. Down home hijinks and mayhem ensue.

Cast: Larry the Cable Guy as Mater
Owen Wilson as Lightning McQueen
Michael Caine as Finn McMissile
Emily Mortimer as Holley Shiftwell
Eddie Izzard as Sir Miles Axlerod
John Turturro as Francesco Bernoulli
Brent Musburger as Brent Mustangburger
Joe Mantegna as Grem
Thomas Kretschmann as Professor Z
Peter Jacobson as Acer

Bonnie Hunt as Sally
Darrell Waltrip as Darrell Cartrip
Franco Nero as Uncle Topolino
David Hobbs as David Hobbscap
Patrick Walker as Mel Dorado
Tony Shalhoub as Luigi
Jaff Garlin as Otis
Michel Michelis as Tomber
Jason Isaacs as Siddeley/Leland Turbo
Lloyd Sherr as Fillmore/Combat Ship

Music Highlights: "You Might Think" (Ric Ocasek) performed by Weezer (orig. by The Cars), "Polyrhythm" (Yasutaka Nakata) performed by Perfume, "Mon Coeur Fait Vroum (My Heart Goes Vroum)" (Michael Giacchino/Scott Langteau) performed by Bénabar, "Collision of Worlds" (Paisley/Williams) performed by Brad Paisley and Robbie Williams, "Nobody's Fool" (Brad Paisley) performed by Brad Paisley. Score by Michael Giacchino.

Film Facts

• *Cars 2* was Pixar's 12th film. It was the first film by the studio to receive substantial negative reviews, and the first not to be nominated for an Academy Award.
• Mater's license plate reads A113, an homage to the CalArts classroom where John Lasseter, Brad Bird, Pete Docter, and Andrew Stanton attended. The number appears in each Pixar film.
• Cameos: Gusteau's restaurant from *Ratatouille* (renamed "Gastow's," 50:06), a portrait of *Brave* characters in a London pub (1:25:38), The *Toy Story* Pizza Planet Truck (1:36:14/1:37:44).
• John Ratzenberger makes his usual Pixar film voice acting appearance as Mack.
• For international versions of the film, the filmmakers cast a variety of local race car drivers in the place of Jeff Gorvette, voiced by stock car racer Jeff Gordon, including Frosty (voiced by Mark Winterbottom) in Australia, Sebastian Schnell (Sebastian Vettel) in Germany, Flash (Jan Nilsson) in Sweden, Memo Rojas in Latin America, Vitaly Petrov in Russia, and Fernando Alonso in Spain.
• *Cars 2: The Video Game* was made for Mac/PC/PS 3/Xbox 360/Wii/Nintendo DS and 3DS.
• Additional appearances: *Cars* (2006), "Mater and the Ghost Light" (2006), *Cars Toons* TV series (2008-2014), *Cars Toon: Mater's Tall Tales* DVD/Blu-ray (2010), *Cars 3* (2017).

Cars 3 (G)

Theatrical release date: June 16, 2017
Production Company: Pixar Animation Studios, Walt Disney Pictures
Length: 102 minutes
Directed by: Brian Fee
Screenplay by: Kiel Murray, Bob Peterson, Mike Rich, original story by Brian Fee, Ben Queen, Eyal Podell & Jonathon E. Stewart

> **Synopsis**: Racer Lightning McQueen finds himself overtaken by a new generation of faster cars, ending up in a racetrack crash as he tries to keep up. After recovering physically he is persuaded to return to racing, training with the spirited coach Cruz Ramirez. When his preparation stalls, he seeks out Smokey, the guru who trained his late mentor, Doc. In contrast to McQueen's belief that Doc regretted the end of his racing days, Smokey reveals that Doc's training with McQueen was the highlight of his life. McQueen learns that there's more to his life, and more to Ramirez, than he originally thought.

Cast: Owen Wilson as Lightning McQueen
Cristela Alonzo as Cruz Ramirez
Chris Cooper as Smokey
Nathan Fillion as Sterling
Larry the Cable Guy as Mater
Armie Hammer as Jackson Storm
Ray Magliozzi as Dusty
Tony Shalhoub as Luigi
Bonnie Hunt as Sally
Lea DeLaria as Miss Fritter
Kerry Washington as Natalie Certain
Bob Costas as Bob Cutlass
Margo Martindale as Louise Nash
Darrell Waltrip as Darrell Cartrip
Isiah Whitlock Jr. as River Scott
Bob Peterson as Chick Hicks

Music Highlights: "Run That Race" (Auerbach) performed by Dan Auerbach, "Ride" (Ward/Bogart/Bassett) performed by ZZ Ward with Gary Clark Jr., "King's Highway" (Petty) performed by James Bay (orig. by Tom Petty & the Heartbreakers), "Glory Days" (Springsteen) performed by Andra Day (orig. by Bruce Springsteen), "Drive My Car" (Lennon/McCartney) performed by Jorge Blanco (orig. by The Beatles), "Freeway of Love" (Walden/Cohen) performed by Lea DeLaria (orig. by Aretha Franklin). Score by Randy Newman.

Film Facts

• *Cars 3* was the 18th Pixar film, returning the franchise to good standing with critics and filmgoers after the misfire of *Cars 2*.
• In considering story ideas, the creative team was intrigued with the idea of what comes next for athletes when a new generation begins to take over the field, with both Brian Fee and story supervisor Scott Morse drawing on their experience as parents in developing the story.
• Cruz Ramirez was voiced by Cristela Alonzo, a comedian known for the sitcom *Cristela* on ABC, which made her the first Latina to create, produce, write, and star in her own US television show.
• The film includes a post-credit Mater animation (1:01). The *Cars 3* Blu-ray/DVD include the short "Lou," and the Blu-ray/Digital HD version include the short "Miss Fritter's Racing Skoool."
• The *Cars 3: Driven to Win* video game was made for PS3/PS4/Xbox 360/Xbox One/Switch/Wii U.
• The Citroën 2CV is a tribute to Japanese director Hayao Miyazaki's film *The Castle of Cagliostro*.

Castle in the Sky (PG)

Theatrical release date: August 2, 1986
Country: Japan Japanese title: *Tenkû no Shiro Rapyuta*
Production Company: Studio Ghibli/Tokuma Shoten
Length: 125 minutes
Directed and written by: Hayao Miyazaki

Synopsis: An airship carrying the girl Sheeta, the captive of government agent Muska, is attacked by air pirates Captain Dola and her sons. In the commotion Sheeta falls from the airship, inexplicably floating gently down to a mining town, where she befriends the spirited boy Pazu. They are soon pursued by both Dola and her sons and troops led by Muska. After falling off a high bridge, thanks to a special crystal on Sheeta's necklace, Sheeta and Pazu float gently to the ground, ending up in the mines. Sheeta reveals she is an orphan, who lived at her family home until some men took her away. They find Pazu's uncle Pom in the mine, who shows them an area where the rocks glow with the mineral aetherium, and tells them that the legendary floating city of Lapuda is made crystals like the one Sheeta wears. Sheeta tells Pazu she inherited a traditional family name with the necklace: "Lucita Toel Ul Laputa," just before they are captured by Muska, who shows Sheeta a robot that had fallen from Laputa, and tells Sheeta she is heir to the throne of Laupta. Muska tells Sheeta to recite ancient words to activate her stone, also activating the lifeless robot of Laputa, which comes to Sheeta's rescue until Pazu can rescue her. When Muska obtains Sheeta's dropped crystal, it's a race to see who can reach Laputa first.

Cast:	English (1998)	English (1989)	Japanese
Sheeta	Anna Paquin/Debi Derryberry	Lara Cody	Keiko Yokozawa
Pazu	James Van Der Beek	Barbara Goodson	Mayumi Tanaka
Dola	Cloris Leachman	Rachel Vanowen	Kotoe Hatsui
Muska	Mark Hamill	Jeff Winkless	Minori Terada
Uncle Pom	Richard Dysart	Edward Mannix	Fujio Tokita
General	Jim Cummings	Mike Reynolds	Ichirō Nagai
Boss	John Hostetter	Clifton Wells	Hiroshi Ito
Charles	Michael McShane	Barry Stigler	Takuzō Kamiyama
Louie	Mandy Patinkin	Dave Mallow	Yoshito Yasuhara
Henri	Andy Dick	Eddie Frierson	Sukekiyo Kamiyama

Music Highlights: "Kimi Wo Nosete" (Miyazaki/Hisaishi) performed by Azumi Inoue, "Moshimo Sora Wo Tobetara" (L: Takashi Matsumoto/Kyôhei Tsutsumi) performed by Obata Yoko. Music by Joe Hisaishi.

Film Facts

• The flying island Laputa was included in Jonathan Swift's 1726 novel *Gulliver's Travels*.
• The design of Laputa was influenced by the castle at Paronella Park, Queensland, Australia.
• Laputa's fox squirrels also appeared in Miyazaki's *Nausicaä of the Valley of the Wind* (1984).

A Cat in Paris (PG)

Theatrical release date: Oct 15, 2010 (Premiere), Dec 15, 2010 (France), Jun 1, 2012 (limited US)
Country: France **French title**: *Une Vie de Chat* (lit. *A Cat's Life*)
Production Company: Folimage, Lunanime, Digit Anima, France 3 Cinéma, Emage Animation
Length: 70 minutes
Directed by: Alain Gagnol and Jean-Loup Felicioli
Written by: Alain Gagnol

Synopsis: A black cat lives in two worlds: during the day he goes by the name Dino and lives with the girl Zoé, the daughter of the Jeanne, chief of police, and Zoé's nanny, Claudine. At night the cat accompanies the jewel thief Nico, under the name Mr. Cat. After a jewelry theft, Nico puts a fish bracelet on the cat, who takes it to Zoé. It isn't long before Zoé's mother has the bracelet identified as stolen, after which Zoé follows the cat, which leads her to the notorious criminal Victor Costa and his gang, which is planning to steal an invaluable work of art, the Colossus of Nairobi. When things start to look bad for Zoé, help arrives from an unexpected source. Before the story is resolved it becomes clear that appearances can be deceiving, when it comes to both friends and foes.

Cast:

Role	English	French
Victor Costa	J.B. Blanc	Jean Benguigui
Nico	Steve Blum	Bruno Salomone
Jeanne (police chief/Zoé's mother)	Marcia Gay Harden	Dominique Blanc
Claudine	Anjelica Huston	Bernadette Lafont
Lucas	Matthew Modine	Bernard Bouillon
Zoé	Lauren Weintraub	Oriane Zani
Mister Baby/Zookeeper	Mike Pollock	Jacques Ramade
Mister Hulot	Philippe Hartmann	Jean-Pierre Yvars
Mister Frog	Gregory Cupoli	Patrick Ridremont
Mister Potato	Marc Thompson	Patrick Descamps

Music Highlights: "I Wished on the Moon" (Dorothy Parker/Ralph Rainger) performed by Billie Holiday, "Une Vie de Chat" / "A Cat in Paris" (Serge Besset) performed by Bulgarian Symphony Orchestra - SIF309. Music by Serge Besset.

Film Facts

• *A Cat in Paris* was nominated for the "Best Animated Feature" Academy Award in the United States, and the "Best Animated Film" César Award in France.
• The film premiered at the Saint-Quentin Ciné-Jeune Film Festival in France on October 15, 2010, and received a 2012 limited release in the US after appearances at a couple of film festivals.
• Co-directors Gagnol and Felicioli also collaborated on the shorts "L'egoïste" (1997), "Le Nez à la Fenêtre" (2000), "Le Couloir" (2005), "Mauvais Temps" (2006), "Un Plan d'Enfer" (2016), "The Cat's Regret" (2018), the short series *Les tragédies minuscules* (1999), and the film *Phantom Boy* (2015). Several of their short works were collected on the video *Pris de Court* (2008).

The Cat Returns (G)

Theatrical release date: July 19, 2002 (Japan), July 13, 2005 (US)
Production Company: Studio Ghibli, Hakuhodo, Mitsubishi, Nippon Television Network
Length: 75 minutes
Directed by: Hiroyuki Morita
Screenplay by: Reiko Yoshida, English screenplay by Cindy Davis Hewitt and Donald H. Hewitt, based on the 2002 manga "Baron: Neko no Danshaku" by Aoi Hiiragi

Synopsis: The kind but disorganized girl Haru happens upon a grey cat carrying a parcel in its mouth, which stops in the middle of a busy street. Haru darts out to save the cat, which, to her shock, speaks to her, saying she will be rewarded later. That night Haru sees a parade of cats outside her home, with the Cat King carried on a litter. He presents her with a list of gifts she will receive in repayment for saving the life of Prince Lune. Soon her yard is filled with cat tails, cats follow her to school, her locker is filled with mice, and an envoy of the King tells her she is to marry Prince Lune. Haru, not wanting to marry a cat, hears a voice that says she must follow a white cat to the Cat Bureau. At the Bureau she meets an animated statuette called the Baron, the statue bird Toto, and the grumpy cat Muta. The royal cats remain set on Haru marrying the prince, and carry her off to the Cat Kingdom, where she meets Yuki, a servant cat she helped years before. Haru is transformed into a cat, and begins to fall under the cats' spell, but she is reminded of her true identity by the Baron, and with help from Muta and Prince Lune, they work to escape the cat kingdom once and for all.

Cast:

Role	English	Japanese
Haru Yoshioka	Anne Hathaway	Chizuru Ikewaki
Baron Humbert von Gikkingen	Cary Elwes	Yoshihiko Hakamada
Muta/Renaldo Moon	Peter Boyle	Tetsu Watanabe
Toto	Elliott Gould	Yôsuke Saitô
The Cat King	Tim Curry	Tetsurō Tanba
Prince Lune	Andrew Bevis	Takayuki Yamada
Yuki	Judy Greer	Aki Maeda
Natori	René Auberjonois	Kenta Satoi
Natoru	Andy Richter	Mari Hamada
Naoko Yoshioka	Kristine Sutherland	Kumiko Okae
Hiromi	Kristen Bell	Hitomi Satō

Music Highlights: "Kaze Ni Naru" (Ayano Tsuji) performed by Ayano Tsuji. Music by Yuji Nomi.

Film Facts

• This is a sequel of sorts to Studio Ghibli's *Whisper of the Heart* (1995), also with the Baron.
• The film began when a Japanese theme park requested that Studio Ghibli make a 20-minute short featuring cats. The original project was canceled, but the story later developed into a feature film.
• Aoi Hiiragi's story "Baron: Neko no Danshaku" was published in the manga *Animage,* May, 2002.

Cats Don't Dance (G)

Theatrical release date: March 26, 1997
Production Company: Turner Feature Animation, Warner Bros. Animation
Length: 75 minutes
Directed by: Mark Dindal
Screenplay by: Roberts Gannaway and Cliff Ruby and Elana Lesser and Theresa Pettengill, story by Mark Dindal & Robert Lence & Brian McEntee & Rick Schneider & David Womersley & Kelvin Yasuda

Synopsis: Danny, an idealistic cat who aspires to be a singer and actor, travels from his home in Kokomo, Indiana, to the Hollywood of the 1930s, lucking into a minor role in a Mammoth Pictures musical with child star Darla Dimple. Danny is guided by overworked studio employee Sawyer, a beautiful white cat, but rather than delivering his simple line of "meow," begins hamming it up, to Darla's fury, which increases when Danny accidentally tangles her in a rope. Danny is put in his place, but is soon cheered up by Pudge the Penguin, and by meeting the kindly studio mascot Woolie Mammoth. Woolie explains that Sawyer was once a singer and dancer, but like many others, was worn down by Hollywood, where only humans are stars. Darla pretends to offer the animals a chance to audition for studio head L.B. Mammoth, but they are soon betrayed when Darla floods the soundstage. Danny has a plan for a comeback, turning Darla's premiere into their promised audition.

Cast: Scott Bakula as Danny
Jasmine Guy as Sawyer (singing: Natalie Cole)
Ashley Peldon as Darla Dimple (singing: Lindsay Ridgeway)
Kathy Najimy as Tillie Hippo
John Rhys-Davies as Woolie Mammoth
George Kennedy as L.B. Mammoth
Rene Auberjonois as Flanigan
Hal Holbrook as Cranston
Don Knotts as T.W.
Betty Lou Gerson as Frances
Matthew Herried as Pudge
Frank Welker as Farley Wink

Music Highlights: "Our Time Has Come" (Martin Page) performed by James Ingram and Carnie Wilson, "Danny's Arrival Song" (Randy Newman) performed by Scott Bakula, "Little Boat on the Sea" (Newman) performed by Lindsay Ridgeway/Scott Bakula, "Animal Jam Session" (Newman) performed by Scott Bakula, "Big and Loud" (Newman) performed by Lindsay Ridgeway, "Pack Up Your Troubles in Your Old Kit Bag" (Felix Powell/George Asaf) performed by Kathy Najimy, "Tell Me Lies" (Newman) performed by Natalie Cole, "Nothing's Gonna Stop Us Now" (Newman) performed by Natalie Cole, Scott Bakula, and Kathy Najimy. End credits: "I Do Believe" (Simon Climie/Will Downing) performed by Will Downing, "Tonight I'm Going Out with You" (Bill Elliott) performed by Bill Elliott & His Orchestra. Music by Steve Goldstein.

Film Facts

• Darla's huge butler Max was voiced by director Mark Dindal.
• Period films referenced: *Gone With the Wind* (1939), *The Wizard of Oz* (1939), *King Kong* (1933).
• End credits humor (1:14:15): "No animals were harmed during the making of this film. Although, some were erased and had to be redrawn."
• The film won the "Best Animated Feature" Annie Award.

Charlotte's Web (G)

Theatrical release date: March 1, 1973
Production Company: Hanna-Barbera Productions, Sagittarius Productions
Length: 94 minutes
Directed by: Charles Nichols and Iwao Takamoto
Story by: Earl Hamner Jr., based on the book *Charlotte's Web* by E.B. White

Synopsis: One spring morning, when a pig has had piglets, farmer John Arable is set to kill the runt of the litter, when his daughter, the kindhearted Fern, persuades him to hold off. Fern and the piglet, named Wilbur, become fast friends, and are seldom apart. Once Wilbur is grown her father sells Wilbur to Fern's uncle, Homer Zuckerman. While at Zuckerman's farm Wilbur learns he is to be slaughtered for meat. Despite his distress, Wilbur meets the spider Charlotte, who tries to come up with a plan to save Wilbur's life. She works through the night to spin a web spelling out "SOME PIG." Great crowds come to see the miraculous web and pig, and Wilbur is famous for while, but over time things go back to normal, and a hornet caught in Charlotte's web destroys the words. The Goose suggests "TERRIFIC" as a second web message, and again crowds gather and wane. After one more web-word, "RADIANT," Wilbur is off to the county fair, hoping to win a prize. Charlotte, Templeton the rat, and Wilbur go to the fair, where Charlotte spins one last word for Wilbur, "HUMBLE," before her life is over, and the lives of her 514 children are just beginning.

Cast: Debbie Reynolds as Charlotte
Paul Lynde as Templeton
Henry Gibson as Wilbur
Rex Allen as Narrator
Martha Scott as Mrs. Arable
Dave Madden as Ram
Danny Bonaduce as Avery Arable
Don Messick as Jeffrey/Lamb/Spectators/Uncle

Herb Vigran as Lurvy
Agnes Moorehead as The Goose
Pam Ferdin as Fern Arable
Joan Gerber as Edith Zuckerman/Mrs. Fussy
Robert Holt as Homer Zuckerman
John Stephenson as Mr. Arable/Parking Officer
William B. White as Henry Fussy

Music Highlights: "There Must Be Something More" performed by Pam Ferdin, "I Can Talk" performed by Henry Gibson, "Chin Up" performed by Debbie Reynolds, "Mother Earth and Father Time" performed by Debbie Reynolds, "We've Got Lots in Common" performed by Henry Gibson, Debbie Reynolds, Dave Madden, and chorus, "A Veritable Schmorgasboard" performed by Agnes Moorehead and Paul Lynde, "Deep in the Dark" performed by Debbie Reynolds, "Charlotte's Web" performed by chorus, "Zuckerman's Famous Pig" performed by Barbershop Quartet. All songs by Richard M. Sherman and Robert B. Sherman. Score by Irwin Kostal.

Film Facts

- Charlotte's full name is Charlotte A. Cavatica.
- Don Messick, voice of the young goose Jeffrey, is famous for voicing Scooby-Doo.
- Author E.B. White, who was reluctant for a film to be produced, reportedly disliked the film.
- Tony Randall recorded Templeton's lines, but was not the right fit. He was replaced by Paul Lynde.

Chicken Little (G)

Theatrical release date: November 4, 2005
Production Company: Walt Disney Pictures, Walt Disney Feature Animation
Length: 81 minutes
Directed by: Mark Dindal
Screenplay by: Steve Bencich & Ron J. Friedman, Ron Anderson, story by Mark Dindal, Mark Kennedy

---

Synopsis: Chicken Little develops a reputation as an alarmist after he is hit with an acorn and tries to warn the town of imminent danger, and even worse, is an embarrassment to his father. Little befriends fellow schoolyard misfits Abby Mallard, Fish Out of Water, and Runt of the Litter. When an octagon-shaped alien artifact lands in his window, Little and his friends stumble upon an alien ship, and are soon pursued by ominous alien robots and connecting with a small orange three-eyed alien. In the midst of an alien invasion, Little finally confronts his father and professes his affection for Abby, and they work together to correct the confusion that began the invasion in the first place.

Cast: Zach Braff as Chicken Little
Garry Marshall as Buck Cluck
Don Knotts as Mayor Turkey Lurkey
Patrick Stewart as Mr. Woolensworth
Amy Sedaris as Foxy Loxy
Steve Zahn as Runt of the Litter
Joan Cusack as Abby Mallard
Wallace Shawn as Principal Fetchit
Harry Shearer as Dog Announcer
Fred Willard as Melvin - Alien Dad
Catherine O'Hara as Tina - Alien Mom
Patrick Warburton as Alien Cop

Music Highlights: "One Little Slip" (Ed Robertson/Steven Page) performed by Barenaked Ladies, "Stir It Up" (Danny Sembello/Alta Sherral Willis) performed by Joss Stone and Patti LaBelle, "Shake a Tail Feather" (Otha Hayes/Verlie Rice/Andre Williams) performed by the Cheetah Girls (orig. by The Five Du-Tones). Score by John Debney.

Film Facts

• The 46th Disney animated classic, *Chicken Little* was the first fully computer animated feature film produced by Disney (not including Pixar films, which were just distributed by Disney at this time).
• A brief scene from *Raiders of the Lost Ark* is shown in a movie theater (at 2:06) as a giant round water tower rolls through Chicken Little's town.
• Actors considered for the title role included Matthew Broderick and Michael J. Fox.
• As Buck Cluck drives Chicken Little to school, note the Bull in a china shop (4:53).
• Veteran comedian Don Knotts (voice of Mayor Turkey Lurkey) starred in the live-action Disney films *The Apple Dumpling Gang* (1975), *No Deposit, No Return* (1976), *Gus* (1976), *Herbie Goes to Monte Carlo* (1977), and *The Apple Dumpling Gang Rides Again* (1979), in addition to playing Barney Fife on the *Andy Griffith Show*. This film was was Knotts' last work.
• A second movie was planned, to be called *Chicken Little 2: The Ugly Duckling Story,* but production was halted when John Lasseter was appointed Chief Creative Officer of Walt Disney Feature Animation in 2006 and canceled all sequels.

Chicken Run (G)

Theatrical release date: June 23, 2000
Production Company: Aardman Animations, DreamWorks Animation, Pathé
Length: 84 minutes
Directed by: Peter Lord & Nick Park
Screenplay by: Karey Kirkpatrick, based on an original story by Peter Lord & Nick Park

---

Synopsis: The chickens on Tweedy's Farm are harassed by the wicked Mr. and Mrs. Tweedy and their vicious dogs, where those who don't produce eggs are done away with. The determined chicken Ginger leads the flock in efforts to escape their imprisonment on the farm (digging under the fence, tunneling, dressing up as a human), but their efforts are always thwarted. When escaped circus rooster Rocky the Flying Rooster crash lands on the farm, he reluctantly agrees to teach the chickens to fly in exchange for hiding him from the circus. The chickens begin a training regimen, but their problems mount when the Tweedys plan to convert the farm to poultry production.

Cast: Julia Sawalha as Ginger
Mel Gibson as Rocky
Lynn Ferguson as Mac
Imelda Staunton as Bunty
Jane Horrocks as Babs

Tony Haygarth as Mr. Tweedy
Miranda Richardson as Mrs. Tweedy
Phil Daniels as Fetcher (the rat)
Timothy Spall as Nick (the rat)
Benjamin Whitrow as Fowler (the rooster)

Music Highlights: "Ave Maria" (Franz Schubert) performed by Gracie Fields, "Barwick Green" (Arthur Wood), "Over the Waves" ["Sobre las Olas"] (Juventino Rosas), "The Wanderer" (Ernest Maresca) performed by Dion, "Flip Flop and Fly" (Charles Calhoun/Lou Willie Turner) performed by Ellis Hall (orig. by Big Joe Turner). Music by John Powell and Harry Gregson-Williams.

Film Facts

• Co-director Nick Parks had two pet chickens named Ginger and Rocky when he was growing up.
• Mel Gibson is, in fact, American by birth, despite the common misconception that he is Australian due to his long residence in that country.
• Real chickens don't have teeth, but they were added to the chicken's beaks to make them more expressive. Real chickens also don't talk.
• Some scenes were an homage to other films. Ginger being pulled on a trolley through the tunnel (6:05) is inspired by *The Great Escape* (1963), Ginger grabbing her hat just as the pie machine door comes down (52:54) references *Raiders of the Lost Ark* (1981), the line "I've met a lot of hard boiled eggs in my time, but you're twenty minutes," is drawn from Billy Wilder's film *Ace in the Hole* (1951), Mac's glasses are modeled after those of Dustin Hoffman's character Louis Dega in *Papillon* (1973), and "A cling-on, Captain, the engines can't take it!" (1:14:15) is of course a reference to Scotty in *Star Trek* (1966-1969).
• Nick Park's Aardman Animations is best known for the popular Wallace and Gromit shorts and films.
• It was belatedly announced in 2018 that a sequel to the film was in development.

Cinderella (G)

Theatrical release date: March 4, 1950
Production Company: Walt Disney Productions
Length: 74 minutes
Directed by: Wilfred Jackson, Hamilton Luske, Clyde Geronimi
Story: William Peed, Erdman Penner, Ted Sears, Winston Hibler, Homer Brightman, Harry Reeves, Kenneth Anderson, Joe Rinaldi, from the original classic by Charles Perrault

Synopsis: After cruel mistreatment by her stepmother and stepsisters, Cinderella is told she can attend a royal ball for Prince Charming if she can get her chores done and find a gown to wear. With help from animals she has befriended, she is ready for the ball, but her jealous stepsisters destroy her gown. Cinderella's fairy godmother provides a gown and carriage. Cinderella charms the Prince at the ball, leaving behind a glass slipper as the only sign of her identity. The Prince seeks to marry the woman he met at the ball, and undertakes a search to see whose foot fits the glass slipper. Cinderella's stepmother locks her away to prevent the Prince from learning she is the one he seeks. The animals free Cinderella, but her stepmother causes the glass slipper to shatter. Fortunately Cinderella can prove her identity, as she has the other glass slipper.

Cast: Irene Woods as Cinderella
Eleanor Audley as Lady Tremaine
Verna Felton as Fairy Godmother
Rhoda Williams as Drizella

James MacDonald as Bruno/Gus/Jaques
Luis van Rooten as King/Grand Duke
Don Barclay as Doorman
William Phipps/Mike Douglas as Prince Charming

Music Highlights: "A Dream is a Wish Your Heart Makes" performed by Ilene Woods, "So This Is Love" performed by Ilene Woods and Mike Douglas, "Bibbidi-Bobbidi-Boo" performed by Verna Felton and chorus, "The Work Song" performed by chorus. All songs written by Mack David/Jerry Livingston/Al Hoffman. Music by Oliver Wallace, Paul J. Smith.

Film Facts

• The 12th Walt Disney animated classic, this film gave Disney a second iconic "princess," after Snow White. The castle from the film would also become iconic, both as part of the Walt Disney logo, and as one of the most famous locations at Disneyland.
• Disney's first Cinderella animation was a 1922 short while working at Laugh-O-Gram studios.
• Helene Stanley was a live-action model filmed to provide guidance for animation. The cat Lucifer was modeled after a cat owned by animator Ward Kimball.
• Verna Felton, who voiced the Fairy Godmother, would later voice the role of the fairy Flora in *Sleeping Beauty* (1959).
• The Walt Disney Music Company was formed to release the soundtrack for this film.
• Additional appearances: *Cinderella II* (2002), *Cinderella III* (2007), "The Favorite Gift" read-along with still photos on *Princess Stories Vol. 1: A Gift From the Heart* DVD (2004), and the live-action *Cinderella* (2015), directed by Kenneth Branagh, starring Lily James and Cate Blanchett.

Cinderella II: Dreams Come True (G)

Home media release date: February 26, 2002
Production Company: Walt Disney Video Premiere, Walt Disney Television Animation
Length: 73 minutes
Directed by: John Kafka
Writers: "Aim to Please" screenplay by Jill Blotevogel and Tom Rogers, "Tall Tail" screenplay by Jule Selbo and Tom Rogers, "An Uncommon Romance" screenplay by Tom Rogers

Synopsis: This film is a montage of three stories: • "Aim to Please": After their marriage, Prince Charming is called away, and Cinderella must plan a royal banquet at the castle. Cinderella rejects the rigid royal traditions and resolves to plan the banquet her way, inviting a mix of royalty and commoners. The King's initial consternation soon gives way to delight. • "Tall Tail": Jac's wish to be human is granted, but he soon finds he is more helpful as a mouse. • "An Uncommon Romance": Cinderella plays matchmaker between her sister Anastasia and a smitten baker.

Cast: Jennifer Hale as Cinderella
Rob Paulsen as Jaq/Grand Duke/Baker/
    Sir Hugh Bert/Flower Vendor
Corey Burton as Gus/Mert/Stable Hand
Andre Stojka as The King
Susanne Blakeslee as Stepmother

Russi Taylor as Fairy Godmother/Drizella/Mary
    Mouse/Beatrice/Countess Le Grande/Daphne
Tress MacNeille as Anastasia/Pretty Woman
Holland Taylor as Prudence
Christopher Daniel Barnes as The Prince
Frank Welker as Lucifer/Pom Pom/Bruno

Music Highlights: "Follow Your Heart" (Alan Zachary/Michael Weiner) performed by Brooke Allison, "The World Is Looking Up to You" (Randy Rogel) performed by Brooke Allison, "It's What's Inside That Counts" (Randy Rogel) performed by Brooke Allison, "Put It Together (Bibidi Bobidi Boo)" (Michael Bradford/Mack David/Al Hoffman/Jerry Livingston) performed by Brooke Allison. Score by Michael Tavera.

Film Facts

• The three stories were originally developed as episodes of a planned Cinderella television series, which ultimately was canceled, animated by Walt Disney Television Animation and Walt Disney Video Premiere (better known as Disney MovieToons, and later Disneytoon Studios).
• Jennifer Hale, who voiced Cinderella, is a prolific voice actress, including Jessie on *The Real Adventures of Jonny Quest* (1996-1997), Ms. Marvel on *The Avengers: Earth's Mightiest Heroes* (2010-2012), and Commander Shepard and May O'Connell on the *Mass Effect* video game series.
• The voice of Prince Charming was provided by Christopher Daniel Barnes, who voiced Prince Eric in *The Little Mermaid* (1989).
• Susanne Blakeslee, voice of Lady Tremaine in this film, also voiced Cruella De Vil in *101 Dalmatians II: Patch's London Adventure* (2000).
• The songs from the film were included on the *Princess Favorites* compilation CD (Walt Disney Records, 2002).

Cinderella III: A Twist in Time (G)

Home media release date: February 6, 2007
Production Company: DisneyToon Studios, Walt Disney Pictures, DisneyToon Studios Australia, Toon City Animation
Length: 70 minutes
Directed by: Frank Nissen
Screenplay by: Dan Berendsen, Margaret Heidenry, Colleen Ventimilia, and Eddie Guzelian

---

Synopsis: After obtaining the Fairy Godmother's wand, Cinderella's stepmother and stepsisters Anastasia and Drizella turn time back to the day after the Royal Ball. They use the wand so the glass slipper fits the foot of Anastasia, and to alter Prince Charming's memory so he believes she is the one he fell in love with. Cinderella's loyal mouse friends Jaq and Gus discover what is happening, and together they expose the truth - with the help of the unlikeliest of allies.

Cast: Jennifer Hale as Cinderella
Tami Tappan Damiano as Cinderella singing voice
C. D. Barnes as Prince Charming
Susanne Blakeslee as Lady Tremaine
Tress MacNeille as Anastasia
Lesli Margherita as Anastasia singing voice

Russi Taylor as Drizella/Fairy Godmother
Andre Stojka as The King
Holland Taylor as Prudence
Rob Paulsen as the Grand Duke/Jaq
Corey Burton as Gus
Frank Welker as Lucifer

Music Highlights: "Perfectly Perfect" (Alan Zachary/Michael Weiner), performed by Bridgit Mendler, Lesli Margherita, Russi Taylor, Rob Paulsen, and Corey Burton, "More Than a Dream" (Alan Zachary/Michael Weiner) performed by Tami Tappan Damiano, "Anastasia's Theme" (Alan Zachary/Michael Weiner) performed by Lesli Margherita, "At the Ball" (Alan Zachary/Michael Weiner) performed by Rob Paulson and Corey Burton, "I Still Believe" (Matthew Gerrard/Bridget Benenate) performed by Hayden Panettiere. Music by Joel McNeely.

Film Facts

• After complaints that *Cinderella II: Dreams Come True* (2002) was poorly produced, many critics and viewers were pleasantly surprised with the quality of *Cinderella III*.
• Though produced after *Cinderella II*, *Cinderella III* takes place immediately after the first film.
• Don't miss the final scene during the credits (1:08).
• The film was directed by experienced storyboard artist, story artist, director, and production designer Frank Nissen, who had worked on *Dinosaur* (2000), *Mickey • Donald • Goofy: The Three Musketeers* (2004), and *Pooh's Heffalump Movie* (2005).
• The majority of the voice cast from *Cinderella II* returned for this film, including Jennifer Hale as Cinderella, C. D. Barnes as Prince Charming, Susanne Blakeslee as Lady Tremaine, Tress MacNeille as Anastasia, and Russi Taylor as Drizella.
• Cinderella was slated to appear on the planned second volume of the *Disney Princess Enchanted Tales* home media series, but the series was canceled. A song from Cinderella's unreleased segment, "Happiness Was Made to Share," was included on the 2009 reissue of *Disney Princess Enchanted Tales: Follow Your Dreams* (2007).

Cloudy With a Chance of Meatballs (PG)

Theatrical release date: September 18, 2009
Production Company: Columbia Pictures, Sony Pictures Animation
Length: 90 minutes
Directed by: Phil Lord, Christopher Miller
Written by: Phil Lord & Christopher Miller, based upon the book *Cloudy With a Chance of Meatballs* written by Judi Barrett & illustrated by Ron Barrett

---

Synopsis: Flint Lockwood, a creative inventor whose concepts have often ended in disaster, sets his mind on creating a machine which can turn water into food. After a spectacular invention failure, which destroys the town's opening ceremony for the Sardine Land theme park, Flint's device causes hamburgers to rain out of the sky, documented by aspiring TV reporter Sam Sparks. After years of disappointing his father, Flint is delighted by the recognition his success brings him, but still doesn't win his father's approval. Even worse, the food creator begins to show signs of strain. Pressured by the mayor to create even bigger food for the ceremonial opening of the town, renamed Chewandswallow, Flint pushes the machine past the safety point, creating chaos with a spaghetti tornado. Flint's efforts to turn off the machine are thwarted by the major, who programs the machine to create a massive buffet that will afflict the whole world. Finally encouraged by his father, Flint creates a flying car in the hopes of reaching the machine and shutting it down.

Cast: Bill Hader as Flint Lockwood
Anna Faris as Sam Sparks
James Caan as Tim Lockwood
Andy Samberg as "Baby" Brent
Bruce Campbell as Mayor Shelbourne
Mr. T as Earl Devereaux

Bobb'e J. Thompson as Cal Devereaux
Benjamin Bratt as Manny
Neil Patrick Harris as Steve (the monkey)
Al Roker as Patrick Patrickson
Lauren Graham as Fran Lockwood
Will Forte as Joe Towne

Music Highlights: "Sunshine, Lollipops and Rainbows" (Howard Liebling/Marvin Hamlisch) performed by Lesley Gore, "Promises" (Trevor Rabin) performed by Trevor Rabin, "Sirius" (Alan Parsons/Eric Woolfson) performed by The Alan Parsons Project. End credits: "Raining Sunshine" (Matthew Gerrard/Jay Landers/Charlie Midnight) performed by Miranda Cosgrove. Score by Mark Mothersbaugh.

Film Facts

• The film was originally directed by Paul & Gaëtan Brizzi, who were replaced by Phil Lord & Christopher Miller, who were also removed from the project before finally returning to complete it.
• Lord and Miller previously worked together on the animated TV comedy *Clone High* (2002-2003).
• Earl Devereaux (voiced by Mr. T) breaks through a tortilla chip, forming a letter T (1:07:22).
• Miranda Cosgrove, singer of "Raining Sunshine," is well known for her role as Carly in the Nickelodeon comedy *iCarly*.

Coco (PG)

Theatrical release date: November 21, 2017
Production Company: Pixar Animation Studios, Walt Disney Pictures
Length: 105 minutes
Directed by: Lee Unkrich, Adrian Molina
Screenplay by: Adrian Molina and Matthew Aldrich, original story by Lee Unkrich, Jason Katz, Matthew Aldrich and Adrian Molina

> **Synopsis**: Young Miguel is determined to play music like his hero, film star Ernesto de la Cruz, and his family is just as determined to stop him, as his great great grandfather left the family to be a musician. As the Mexican holiday Día de los Muertos approaches, Miguel finds a partial photo of his great great grandfather, dressed the same as Ernesto de la Cruz. When Miguel goes to borrow de la Cruz's guitar from his tomb for a performance, he is transported to the afterlife, a city populated by skeletons. To return, he must get the blessing of a member of his family, setting him on a quest to find de la Cruz. In the process, Miguel and his family learn a lot about forgiveness, understanding, and love, across generations.

Cast: Anthony Gonzalez as Miguel
Gael García Bernal as Héctor
Benjamin Bratt as Ernesto de la Cruz
Alanna Ubach as Mamá Imelda
Renee Victor as Abuelita
Jaime Camil as Papá
Alfonso Arau as Papá Julio
Herbert Siguenza as Tío Oscar/Tío Felipe
Gabriel Iglesias as Clerk
Lombardo Boyar as Plaza Mariachi/Gustavo
Ana Ofelia Murguía as Mamá Coco
Natalia Cordova-Buckley as Frida Kahlo
Selene Luna as Tía Rosita
Edward James Olmos as Chicharrón
Sofía Espinosa as Mamá
Carla Medina as Departures Agent

Music Highlights: "Remember Me" (Kristen Anderson-Lopez/Robert Lopez) performed by Gael García Bernal/Gabriella Flores/Libertad García Fonzi, and by Anthony Gonzalez/Ana Ofelia Murguía, and by Benjamin Bratt, "Un Poco Loco" (Germaine Franco/Adrian Molina) performed by Anthony Gonzalez and Gael García Bernal, "Proud Corazon" (Franco/Molina) performed by Anthony Gonzalez. Score by Michael Giacchino.

Film Facts

• The 19th Pixar film, *Coco* won Academy Awards for "Best Animated Feature" and "Best Original Song" ("Remember Me"), the "Best Animated Feature Film" Golden Globe, and several Annie Awards, and became the highest grossing film of all time in Mexico.
• The voice cast featured a number of actors of Mexican ancestry, including Anthony Gonzalez (Miguel), Gael Garcia Bernal (Héctor), Alanna Ubach (Mamá Imelda), Ana Ofelia Murguía (Mamá Coco), and Edward James Olmos (Chicharrón).
• John Ratzenberger makes his customary Pixar film appearance as Juan Ortodoncia, a skeleton in the Land of the Dead who has bad teeth. He has a one-word part ("Gracias").
• Disney sought to trademark the phrase "Día de los Muertos," leading to an outcry from Mexican-Americans. Cartoonist Lalo Alcaraz was part of this protest. Disney quickly dropped the trademark bid, and ended up hiring Alcaraz as a consultant for the film.

Coraline (PG)

Theatrical release date: February 6, 2009
Production Company: Laika Entertainment, Focus Features, Pandemonium
Length: 100 minutes
Directed by: Henry Selick
Screenplay by: Henry Selick, based on the book by Neil Gaiman

Synopsis: Coraline Jones moves into the Pink Palace Apartments, housed in a spooky mansion. Her parents are working hard to finish a gardening catalog, leaving little time for Coraline. She meets the grandson of the landlady, Wybie, as well as a wild black cat. Wybie gives Coraline an odd doll from his grandmother's trunk that looks just like her, with buttons for eyes. In her apartment Coraline notices a small door in the living room, but its opening is bricked up. Late that night, Coraline sees a mouse go through the little door, following it into a parallel world, where she meets her Other Mother and Other Father, who have buttons for eyes, and who are not distracted by their work. While Coraline in intrigued with this new world, the black cat, able to speak on this side, warns her that the world is not as benevolent as it seems. Her Other Mother tells Coraline she can stay, if she is willing to have buttons sewn over her eyes. Coraline begins to realize that the other world is much more menacing than it seemed, and that getting out of it will not be easy. NOTE: Despite its PG rating, the disturbing content in this film make it appropriate for older viewers.

Cast: Dakota Fanning as Coraline Jones
Teri Hatcher as Mel Jones/Other Mother/Beldam
Jennifer Saunders as Miss April Spink/Other Spink
Dawn French as Miss Miriam Forcible/Other Forcible
Keith David as The Cat
John Hodgman as Charlie Jones/Other Father
Robert Bailey Jr. as Wyborne "Wybie" Lovat
Ian McShane as Mr. Sergei Alexander Bobinsky/
      Other Bobinsky

Aankha Neal as Sweet Ghost Girl
George Selick as Ghost Boy
Hannah Kaiser as Tall Ghost Girl
Harry Selick as Photo Friend
Marina Budovsky as Photo Friend
Emerson Hatcher as Magic Dragonfly
Jerome Ranft as Mover
Christopher Murrie as Toy
Jeremy Ryder as Toy

Music Highlights: "Sirens of the Sea" (Henry Selick) performed by Michele Mariana, "Other Father Song" (They Might Be Giants) performed by They Might Be Giants, "Nellie Jean" (Kent Melton) performed by Kent Melton, "Dreaming" (Bruno Coulais) performed by Bruno Coulais, The Children's Choir of Nice, and Teri Hatcher. Music by Bruno Coulais.

Film Facts

- Wybie was not in the original novel.
- The dollar bill given to the mover as a tip (3:15) shows director Henry Selick's face.
- The Other Father wears slippers (17:59) of *Monkeybone* (2001), directed by Henry Selick.
- A post-credits scene appears (1:39:36).
- "JERK WAD" (1:40:13) was the code to enter a contest for Nike "Coraline Dunks" shoes.

Corpse Bride (PG)

Theatrical release date: September 23, 2005
Production Company: Tim Burton Productions, Laika Entertainment, Patalex II Productions
Length: 77 minutes
Directed by: Tim Burton, Mike Johnson
Screenplay by: John August and Caroline Thompson and Pamela Pettler

Synopsis: The high class but cash-poor parents of Victoria Everglot lament the necessity of her arranged marriage to Victor Van Dort, the son of socially climbing fish merchants. At their first meeting, on the eve of their marriage, Victor charms Victoria with his piano playing, but his nerves make it difficult for him to memorize his wedding vows. He goes for a walk in the woods to practice his vows, placing the ring on what seems to be a tree branch. The branch turns out the be the skeletal hand of Emily, who accepts Victor's vows and takes him to the Land of the Dead. The creepy Lord Barkis tells Victor's family that he was seen on the arm of another woman, and Victor learns that Emily was robbed and murdered by her fiancé, and ever since has waited for someone to come ask for her hand in marriage. Emily agrees to go to the Land of the Living with Victor to meet his parents. Victor leaves Emily in the forest, going to see Victoria, but when Emily finds out about this she takes them back to the Land of the Dead, hurt and confused by Victor's coldness. Back in the land of the living, Lord Barkis seeks to marry Victoria. As Victor and Emily get to know each other, Victor agrees to marry Emily, but she does not want to ruin Victoria's chance for happiness. The truth comes out about Lord Barkis, who gets his just deserts, and Emily is finally at peace.

Cast: Johnny Depp as Victor Van Dort
Helena Bonham Carter as Corpse Bride (Emily)
Emily Watson as Victoria Everglot
Tracey Ullman as Nell Van Dort/Hildegarde
Paul Whitehouse as William Van Dort/
    Mayhew/Paul The Head Waiter
Joanna Lumley as Maudeline Everglot
Albert Finney as Finis Everglot

Richard E. Grant as Barkis Bittern
Christopher Lee as Pastor Galswells
Michael Gough as Elder Gutknecht
Jane Horrocks as Black Widow Spider/
    Mrs. Plum
Enn Reitel as Maggot/Town Crier
Deep Roy as General Bonesapart
Danny Elfman as Bonejangles

Music Highlights: "According to Plan" (Elfman/August) performed by Finney, Lumley, Ullman, and Whitehouse, "Remains of the Day" (Elfman/August) performed by Elfman, Horrocks, Paul Baker, Alison Jiear, and Gary Martin, "Tears to Shed" (Elfman/August) performed by Carter, Horrocks, and Reitel, Tannhauser: Pilgrim's Chorus (Richard Wagner) performed by Simon Preston, "The Wedding Song" (Elfman) performed by Elfman, Horrocks, Baker, Jiear, and Martin. Music by Danny Elfman.

Film Facts

- Tim Burton's films include *The Nightmare Before Christmas* (1993) and *Frankenweenie* (2012).
- The piano reads "Harryhausen" (8:58), for legendary stop-motion animator Ray Harryhausen.
- The film was nominated for the "Best Animated Feature" Academy Award.

The Cricket in Times Square (NR)

Broadcast date: April 24, 1973
Production Company: Chuck Jones Enterprises
Length: 24 minutes
Directed by: Chuck Jones
Written by: Chuck Jones, from the book by George Selden, illustrated by Garth Williams

Synopsis: Chester C. Cricket is just about to enjoy a family's picnic in Connecticut, when a sudden thunderstorm sends the family running for cover. Chester is swept up in the family's picnic basket, ending up lost in Times Square. He is given a place to stay by Mario, a kind boy working in a news stand, and befriended by Tucker the Mouse, and Tucker's improbable friend Harry the Cat. A passing music teacher gives Chester a golden cricket cage, telling an old Chinese legend about a truthful man whom the gods protected by turning him into a cricket, and since that day crickets have sung songs of truth. Tucker and Harry give Chester a two-month anniversary feast, putting on the radio. As Chester rubs his wings together to play along with music on the radio, everyone is astounded at how well he plays, including Chester himself. An accidental fire at the news stand makes Mario's mother suspicious of the cricket, but Chester's beautiful music softens her anger. Tucker dreams up a scheme for Chester to learn a wide repertoire so his music can save the news stand. Chester charms the crowds in Times Square, saving the newsstand, but when autumn comes, he tells his friends he must return to his home, as a cricket belongs in the country in the autumn.

Cast: Mel Blanc as Tucker the Mouse/Paul
Les Tremayne as Chester C. Cricket/
      Harry the Cat/Father/Music Teacher

June Foray as Mother
Kerry MacLane as Mario Bellini

Music Highlights: Music by Dean Elliot.

Film Facts

• Chuck Jones is best known as a director of Looney Tunes shorts, featuring Bugs Bunny, the Road Runner, and many more. Mel Blanc, voice of Tucker the Mouse, provided voices for most of the Looney Tunes characters.
• The 1960 children's book *The Cricket in Times Square* by George Selden, illustrated by Garth Williams, won the Newbery Honor in 1961.
• Chuck Jones Enterprises also produced several titles featuring Looney Tunes characters, the TV specials *The Cat in the Hat* (1971), *A Christmas Carol* (1971), *Rikki-Tikki-Tavi* (1975), *The White Seal* (1975), *Mowgli's Brothers* (1976), *Raggedy Ann and Andy in The Great Santa Claus Caper* (1978), *Raggedy Ann and Raggedy Andy in the Pumpkin Who Couldn't Smile* (1979), and *A Chipmunk Christmas* (1981), the films *The Phantom Tollbooth* (1970) and *The Bugs Bunny/Road-Runner Movie* (1979), and of course the TV film *Daffy Duck and Porky Pig Meet the Groovie Goolies* (1972).
• Additional appearances: *A Very Merry Cricket* (1973) and *Yankee Doodle Cricket* (1975).

The Croods (PG)

Theatrical release date: March 22, 2013
Production Company: DreamWorks Animation
Length: 98 minutes
Directed by: Chris Sanders & Kirk DeMicco
Screenplay by: Kirk DeMicco & Chris Sanders, story by John Cleese, Kirk DeMicco, Chris Sanders

---

Synopsis: In prehistoric times, Eep, a young cave woman, lives with her family, the Croods, fighting for survival in their brief forays out of their cave to find food. Eep is frustrated by the rules of hiding in the cave and avoiding anything new. One day a stranger named Guy arrives with the news that the world is ending, predicting earthquakes and collapse of the land. Their cave is crushed in one of these earthquakes, forcing the family out into the world. After several run-ins with dangerous animals, Guy saves the family, and together they journey to find safety. Tension emerges between Eep's father, Grug, who has kept the family safe by encouraging fear of anything new, and Guy, who values change and adaptation, a tension which is worsened by Eep and Guy's interest in each other. Grug must learn to face his own fears, to help his family do more than just survive, emerging from their cave to follow the light.

Cast: Nicolas Cage as Grug (father)
Emma Stone as Eep (daughter)
Ryan Reynolds as Guy
Catherine Keener as Ugga (mother)
Cloris Leachman as Gran
Clark Duke as Thunk (son)
Chris Sanders as Belt
Randy Thom as Sandy (baby)

Music Highlights: "Shine Your Way" (Alan Silvestri/Glen Ballard/Kirk DeMicco/Chris Sanders) performed by Owl City and Yuna. Score by Alan Silvestri.

Film Facts

• Chris Sanders contributed to several Disney films, including *Beauty and the Beast* (1991), *Aladdin* (1992), *The Lion King* (1994), and *Mulan* (1998), before co-directing *Lilo & Stitch* (2002) and *How to Train your Dragon* (2010).
• Kirk DeMicco co-wrote the screenplay of the animated films *Quest for Camelot* (1998) and *Space Chimps* (2008).
• *The Croods* was first conceived as a stop-motion animation film by Aardman Animations, to be titled *Crood Awakening*. John Cleese (Monty Python) and Kirk DeMicco were separately developing a film based on Roald Dahl's book *The Twits* (1980). The two projects were combined, initially focused on two cavemen, one embracing change and one resistant to it. After the poor performance of the film *Flushed Away* (2006), DreamWorks and Aardman Animations ended their relationship, Cleese dropped out, and the story developed a focus on the Croods as a family.
• The colorful sabertooth tiger that pursues Grug throughout the film was called a "Macawnivore," created by artist Leighton Hickman.
• Composer Alan Silvestri previously worked with Chris Sanders on *Lilo & Stitch* (2002).

The Croods: A New Age (PG)

Theatrical release date: November 25, 2020
Production Company: DreamWorks Animation
Length: 95 minutes
Directed by: Joel Crawford
Screenplay by: Kevin Hageman & Dan Hageman and Paul Fisher & Bob Logan,
story by Kirk DeMicco, Chris Sanders

Synopsis: Guy has become a part of the Croods family pack, but it isn't long before he and Eep are dreaming of having a place of their own. Grug discovers a huge walled off garden, and after the family gorges, they are trapped in a net. They are freed by Phil and Hope Betterman, friends of Guy's family, who live in a beautiful home with their daughter Dawn. Phil and Hope, put off by the Croods' primitive ways, hope to keep Guy as a companion for Dawn, and to move the Croods along. Eep shows Dawn the joys of life outside the walls, as Mr. Betterman works to get Grug on board with leaving Guy behind. Guy enjoys the safety of the walls, and accidentally insults Eep as a "cave girl," leading to their breakup. Annoyed by Phil's manipulation, Grug and Ugga eat all the Betterman's bananas, not knowing that the bananas are the only thing that keeps a troop of punch monkeys at bay. Guy, Grug, and Phil are captured by the monkeys, and learn that the monkeys used to have bananas to give to a huge monster, but when their water was diverted by Phil, they needed a new source of bananas. The women follow to save the men, inspired by Gran's motivational Thunder Sisters history. As the monkeys prepare to sacrifice Grug, Guy, and Phil, the Thunder Sisters stage a spectacular rescue, and the two families reconsider their ideal living situation.

Cast: Nicolas Cage as Grug
Emma Stone as Eep
Ryan Reynolds as Guy
Catherine Keener as Ugga
Cloris Leachman as Gran
Clark Duke as Thunk

Leslie Mann as Hope Betterman
Peter Dinklage as Phil Betterman
Kelly Marie Tran as Dawn Betterman
Kailey Crawford as Sandy
Christopher Sanders as Belt
James Ryan as Sash

Music Highlights: "I Think I Love You" (Romeo) performed by The Partridge Family, "True" (Kemp) performed by Spandau Ballet, "Feel the Thunder" (A. Haim/D. Haim/E. Haim/Ariel Rechtshaid) performed by HAIM, "I Think I Love You" (Romeo) performed by Tenacious D, "We Are Here Together" (Mark Mothersbaugh) performed by Jack Black & HAIM. Score by Mark Mothersbaugh.

Film Facts

• Kirk DeMicco and Chris Sanders, directors of *The Croods* (2013), were originally to direct the sequel, but the film was canceled in 2016 before being revived, with Joel Crawford directing.
• The Blu-ray includes the Croods shorts "Family Movie Night: Little Red Bronana Bread" and "Dear Diary: World's First Pranks" as well as the non-Croods short "To: Gerard."
• The film was nominated for the "Best Animated Feature Film" Golden Globe.

Curious George (G)

Theatrical release date: February 10, 2006
Production Company: Imagine Entertainment, Universal Pictures, FatCat Animation Studio
Length: 87 minutes
Directed by: Matthew O'Callaghan
Screenplay by: Ken Kaufman, story by Ken Kaufman and Mike Werb

Synopsis: When Mr. Bloomsberry's museum falls on hard times, accident-prone museum lecturer Ted volunteers to help by finding the famous, rare, incredible Lost Shrine of Zagawa. After acquiring some bright yellow adventuring attire, Ted travels to Africa and encounters a curious monkey, as well as a disappointingly tiny statue of Zagawa. Mr. Bloomsberry mistakenly believes the statue is huge, and promotes the discovery to an eager public. When Ted returns, he discovers the curious monkey has stowed away, and his exploration begins causing havoc in Ted's apartment building. Ted soon finds himself evicted from his building, humiliated at the museum, and sleeping in the park with the monkey, which he soon names George. Ted's friend Clovis creates a magnification device that can be used to magnify the tiny Zagawa statue, but Bloomsberry's jealous son Junior causes George to break the device, and Bloomsberry decides to close the museum. George is captured by animal control, and sent on a ship back to Africa. After talking with his friend Maggie, Ted has a change of heart and races to the ship, finding not just George, but also learning that the tiny Zagawa statue is a map to the real treasure of Zagawa.

Cast: Frank Welker as George
Will Ferrell as Ted - Man with the Yellow Hat
Eugene Levy as Clovis
Dick Van Dyke as Mr. Bloomsberry
Drew Barrymore as Maggie
David Cross as Junior

Billy West as Manager
Jeff Bennett as Salesman
Michael Chinyamurindi as Edu
Michael Sorich as Seen It Cab Driver
Ed O'Ross as Ivan
Joan Plowright as Ms. Plushbottom

Music Highlights: "Upside Down" (Johnson) performed by Jack Johnson, "Talk of the Town" (Johnson) performed by Jack Johnson, "People Watching" (Johnson) performed by Jack Johnson. Score by Heitor Pereira.

Film Facts

• The ship Ted travels on, the H.A. Rey (11:37), is named for the co-writer of the Curious George children's books, with his wife, Margret Rey. The character of Maggie was named after Margret.
• The blue pajamas that fall on George's head look like Blue from Nick Jr.'s *Blues Clues* (20:42).
• In the French children's book that first featured George, *Cecily G. and the Nine Monkeys* (1939), George was originally named Fifi.
• At one point the film was considered as a live-action/animation hybrid.
• Additional appearances: the PBS Kids children's television show *Curious George* (2006-2020), *Curious George 2: Follow That Monkey!* (2009), *Curious George 3: Back to the Jungle* (2015), *Curious George: Royal Monkey* (2019), and *Curious George: Go West, Go Wild* (2020).

Curious George 2: Follow That Monkey! (G)

Home media release date: March 2, 2010 (July 10, 2009 in Denmark)
Production Company: Imagine Entertainment, Universal Animation Studios, Toon City Animation
Length: 80 minutes
Directed by: Norton Virgien
Screenplay by: Chuck Tately, story by Chuck Tately and Darrell Rooney

---

Synopsis: While Ted (the Man With the Yellow Hat) is preoccupied with a presentation to the museum's Board of Directors, George can't wait to go to Piccadilly's circus to see a baby elephant. Maggie convinces Ted to take George, where he ends up backstage with the elephant, Kayla. The two of them disappear, as the elephant is unhappy in the circus. George learns that Kayla misses her family in California, so they set off by train to take her back, with Ted unintentionally joining them at the last minute. Ted falls off the train, and while trying to place a reassuring call to the circus, ends up sounding like he has kidnapped Kayla. "Danno" Wolfe, a bumbling circus security officer, begins pursuing them, but Kayla accidentally disconnects the back three train cars. As the authorities begin to catch up with them, Ted must decide if he's willing to risk everything to help Kayla.

Cast: Frank Welker as George/Cow
Amy Hill as Flower Pot Lady/Irate Woman
Ed O'Ross as Ivan the Doorman
Jeff Bennett as Ted
Fred Tatasciore as Mr. Bloomsberry

Nickie Bryar as Maggie/Teen Boy
Jamie Kennedy as "Danno" Wolfe
Catherine Taber as Tina
Tim Curry as Piccadilly
Jeff McNeal as Kayla/Hog/Tonga/Layla

Music Highlights: "Life Less Ordinary" (Carbon Leaf) performed by Carbon Leaf, "The Friendship Song" (Carbon Leaf) performed by Carbon Leaf, "California Sun" (Henry Glover/Morris Levy) performed by Brian Wilson (orig. by Joe Jones), "On a Roll" (Carbon Leaf) performed by Carbon Leaf, "Heart of the Day" (Carbon Leaf) performed by Carbon Leaf, "Let Your Troubles Roll" (Carbon Leaf) performed by Carbon Leaf. End credits: "Walking in the Sun" (Carbon Leaf) performed by Carbon Leaf. Score by Heitor Pereira.

Film Facts

• The film was originally to be titled *Curious George 2: Monkey on the Run*.
• A few new actors joined the cast: Jeff Bennett replaced Will Ferrell as Ted, Nickie Bryar replaced Drew Barrymore as Maggie, and Fred Tatasciore replaced Dick Van Dyke as Mr. Bloomsberry.
• Famous comedian Jerry Lewis voiced the role of the Stationmaster.
• The automated phone tree Ted listens to includes the language of Klingon, from *Star Trek* (22:00). The number is erroneously given as *cha'* (two), when of course it should have been *wej* (three).
• The image of George sleeping under the elephant Kayla's ear (28:30) is inspired by a picture in Margret Rey and H. A. Rey's children's book *Curious George Takes a Job* (1947).
• Jackie Greene recorded the song "Follow That Monkey," which is included on the soundtrack but is not in the film.

Curious George 3: Back to the Jungle (G)

Home media release date: June 23, 2015
Production Company: Imagine Entertainment, Universal 1440 Entertainment
Length: 81 minutes
Directed by: Phil Weinstein
Written by: Chuck Tately

Synopsis: George and Ted, the Man with the Yellow Hat, are approached by Hal Houston of the Global Space Agency (GSA) and his assistant Andrew, asking George to help with a problem in Central Africa. Heavy rains have been causing flooding, and the GSA has set up Project Stop Flooding, a series of dams to keep the water under control. They need George to bring back a malfunctioning Regional Dam Synchronizer, or RDS, from a satellite in space. Ted reluctantly allows George to begin training for the mission. George successfully gets the RDS, but when he begins playing with water in the space capsule, a malfunction causes the capsule to crash land. George is able to eject in central Africa, and Ted goes searching. Once George is found, he's happy to take off his space suit, and he and the man try to find their way back to civilization. On the way, the man is caught in a net by the gorilla Seymour and Dr. Naja Kulinda, who runs an animal preserve. Ted is mistaken for a poacher, but the confusion is eventually cleared up. They are almost rescued by Hal Houston, but George's space suit is sighted far away, and Houston leaves. Dr. Kulinda shows George and Ted around the preserve, and they find the tower where the RDS is supposed to go. A serious storm approaches, so George and Ted make the perilous journey to the space capsule to get the RDS and install it before the storm causes terrible flooding.

Cast: Frank Welker as Curious George
Jeff Bennett as Ted
Gwendoline Yeo as Popcorn Vender/
    Automated Voice
John Goodman as Hal Houston
Phil LaMarr as Plane Mechanic/Dam Operator
Alex Polinsky as Tech Andrew
Angela Bassett as Dr. Kulinda
Dee Bradley Baker as Additional voices
Steve Josefson as Additional voices

Music Highlights: "Up for Anything" (Nolan) performed by Mark Lennon/Nick Nolan, "Superman" (Nolan) performed by Ralph Saenz & Nick Nolan, "Welcome to Paradise" (Nolan) performed by Plain White T's, "Beautiful Wild" (Nolan) performed by Kipp Lennon & Nick Nolan, "Together Forever" (Nolan) performed by Kipp Lennon & Nick Nolan. Music by Heitor Pereira.

Film Facts

• The dialogue has references other films about space missions, including "the right stuff" (14:28) from *The Right Stuff* (1983) and "Houston, we have a problem" (21:02) from *Apollo 13* (1995).
• Compared to the other films in the series, this entry received less favorable reviews.
• The film was followed by *Curious George: Royal Monkey* (2019), and *Curious George: Go West, Go Wild* (2020).

Curious George: Royal Monkey (G)

Home media release date: September 10, 2019
Production Company: Universal 1440 Entertainment, Imagine Entertainment, Universal Animation
Length: 86 minutes
Directed by: Doug Murphy
Screenplay by: Dan Wicksman & Nuria Wicksman and Cliff Ruby & Elana Lesser and Joe Stillman, story by Dan Wicksman & Nuria Wicksman

Synopsis: After working hard on a project, Ted, the Man With the Yellow Hat, agrees to take George to the Castleland theme park. Their trip is delayed by an unexpected visit from the royal family of Simiana to the museum, including the royal monkey Philippe. A mixup leads George to switch places with Philippe, thinking the royal family is taking him to Castleland, while Philippe ends up reluctantly going home with Ted. Ted resolves to teach George better manners, and is amazed at his improvement in neatness, while George is dazzled by the royal residence. Although they are puzzled by his odd behavior, George begins to charm the royal family, and cheers up Princess Isabel, who is sad about her coronation, which she fears will lead to a life of boring meetings as an official member of the royal court. The King is displeased with Isabel's behavior, and Ted worries that he's been too hard on George, who isn't acting like himself. Ted sees a news report showing mishaps caused by George, and realizes the monkeys got switched. Still yearning for some fun before her coronation, Isabel and George join a traditional horse derby, before they return home to find Ted and Philippe. They learn that the King is so serious because he was hurt when people laughed at him for playing the tuba on his own coronation day. They all arrive in time to get Isabel to her coronation, and to give her father another chance at happiness.

Cast: Frank Welker as George/Philippe
Jeff Bennett as Ted/Butler/Announcer
Daniela Bobadilla as Princess Isabel
Philip Anthony-Rodriguez as King Gustavo
Eliza Schneider as Ana/Fruit Cart Lady
Ed O'Ross as Ivan the Doorman/Firefighter
Adrienne C. Moore as Doris
Mick Wingert as Mayor/Nature Show Narrator/ Worker

Music Highlights: "A Perfect World" (Michele Brourman/Amanda McBroom) performed by Rob Trow, "Ride, Ride, Ride" (Brourman/McBroom) performed by Rob Trow, "Now You Know" (Brourman/McBroom) performed by Rob Trow, "Nothing Seems Right Anymore" (Brourman/ McBroom) performed by Rob Trow. End credits: "Diamond in the Sun" (Andy Grammer) performed by Andy Grammer. Music by Germaine Franco.

Film Facts

• The story is based on Mark Twain's oft-imitated 1881 novel *The Prince and the Pauper*.
• George's scene of grabbing at a plane while holding onto a tower (14:06) recalls King Kong's climb of the Empire State Building.
• Amanda McBroom and Michele Brourman also wrote music for *The Land Before Time* films.

Despicable Me (PG)

Theatrical release date: July 9, 2010
Production Company: Universal Pictures, Illumination Entertainment
Length: 95 minutes
Directed by: Chris Renaud, Pierre Coffin
Screenplay by: Cinco Paul & Ken Daurio, based on a story by Sergio Pablos

Synopsis: Cruel criminal mastermind Gru is at the top of his field, supported by his colleague Dr. Nefario and a horde of yellow, goggle and overall-wearing minions, until he learns that he has been upstaged by the orange warmup suit-wearing braggart Vector, who steals one of the pyramids in Egypt. Gru hatches a plan to steal a shrink ray from Vector's fortress so he can steal the moon, but after he fails to break in, he is shocked to see that Vector allows three orphans in to buy cookies they are selling. Gru adopts the orphans, Margo, Edith, and Agnes, with the plan of using them to infiltrate Vector's headquarters. Gru is able to steal the shrink ray, while he acts as a father to the girls — albeit an awkward one. Dr. Nefario, concerned that Gru is distracted by the girls, calls the orphanage to have them returned. Gru succeeds in shrinking the moon, but realizes how important the girls have become to him, rushing back to see their ballet, only to find that they have been kidnapped by Vector. Vector soon learns just how much Gru has come to care for his children.

Cast: Steve Carell as Gru
Jason Segel as Vector
Russell Brand as Dr. Nefario
Julie Andrews as Gru's Mom
Will Arnett as Mr. Perkins
Kristen Wiig as Miss Hattie
Miranda Cosgrove as Margo
Dana Gaier as Edith
Elsie Fisher as Agnes
Pierre Coffin as minons: Tim, Bob, Mark, Phil, Stuart
Chris Renaud as Dave the Minion
Jemaine Clement as Jerry the Minion
Mindy Kaling as Tourist Mom

Music Highlights: "Despicable Me" (Williams) performed by Pharrell Williams, "Fun, Fun, Fun" (Williams) performed by Pharrell Williams, "Prettiest Girls" (Williams) performed by Pharrell Williams, "You Should Be Dancing" (Barry Gibb/Robin Gibb/Maurice Gibb) performed by The Bee Gees. Music by Heitor Pereira.

Film Facts

- The original title of the film was *Evil Me*.
- Margo's t-shirt shows the Lorax (12:32), from Illumination Entertainment's film *The Lorax* (2012).
- The Bank of Evil sign reads, "Formerly Lehman Brothers" (15:00).
- The storybook *Sleepy Kittens* (1:02:26) was produced as an actual children's board book.
- Gru shares his name with the nefarious Russian intelligence operation GRU.
- Gru's ticket to the girls' "Swan Lake" performance is 072069 (seen at 1:13:18). The date of first lunar landing was July 20, 1969.
- Additional appearances: *Despicable Me 2* (2013), *Minions* (2015), *Despicable Me 3* (2017), and *Minions: The Rise of Gru* (2021).

Despicable Me 2 (PG)

Theatrical release date: July 3, 2013
Production Company: Universal Pictures, Illumination Entertainment
Length: 98 minutes
Directed by: Pierre Coffin, Chris Renaud
Written by: Cinco Paul & Ken Daurio

Synopsis: Gru is taken by secret agent Lucy Wilde to an intelligence briefing by Silas Ramsbottom at the Anti-Villain League, showing him that a lab stolen from the arctic circle contained a serum, PX-41, which can produce terrible mutations. Gru's partner, Dr. Nefario, departs to resume a life of crime, while Gru is drafted to go undercover with Lucy at the Paradise Shopping Mall, as bakery employees, seeking to find the stolen PX-41 serum. Gru suspects that Mexican restaurant owner Eduardo Pérez may actually be the infamous villain El Macho. Even worse, Pérez's son, Antonio, takes a liking to Gru's daughter, Margo. Ramsbottom tells Gru that it was wig store owner Floyd Eagle-san who stole the PX-41 serum, and Lucy tells him she's moving to Australia, leaving Gru heartbroken. Gru learns that Dr. Nefario is working with El Macho, using the PX-41 serum to turn minions into purple monsters. Lucy realizes her love for Gru, but is captured by El Macho. Dr. Nefafrio returns to Gru's side with an antidote for the minions, but El Macho will not be so easy to beat, especially when he takes the PX-41 serum himself, becoming a huge purple monster.

Cast: Steve Carell as Gru
Kristen Wiig as Lucy
Benjamin Bratt as Eduardo Pérez/El Macho
Miranda Cosgrove as Margo
Russell Brand as Dr. Nefario
Ken Jeong as Floyd Eagle-san
Steve Coogan as Silas Ramsbottom
Elsie Fisher as Agnes
Dana Gaier as Edith
Moises Arias as Antonio Pérez
Nasim Pedrad as Jillian
Kristen Schaal as Shannon
Pierre Coffin as Kevin/Bob/Stuart
Chris Renaud as Minions/Italian Waiter

Music Highlights: "Another Irish Drinking Song" (DiCostanzo/Sabourin) performed by Pierre Coffin, "Just a Cloud Away" (Williams) performed by Pharrell Williams, "I Swear" (Baker/Myers) performed by Pierre Coffin, "Y.M.C.A." (Belolo/Morali/Willis) performed by Village People/Pierre Coffin, "Scream" (Williams) performed by Cee-Lo Green, "Happy" (Williams) performed by Pharrell Williams, "Despicable Me" (Williams) performed by Pharrell Williams. Music by Heitor Pereira.

Film Facts

- The minions emulate the famous "Lunch Atop a Skyscraper" photograph (19:05).
- The same boy whose balloon Gru popped in *Despicable Me* has a stuffed bear pop (28:00).
- Margo's shirt (41:33) shows Wangan-Kun of the Japanese TV series *Bayside Shakedown* (1997).
- The song the minions sing as "Underwear" (1:27:05) is actually "I Swear" by All-4-One.
- The film and Pharrell Williams' "Happy" received Academy Award nominations.
- Several mid-credits scenes appear (beginning at 1:30:45).

Despicable Me 3 (PG)

Theatrical release date: June 30, 2017
Production Company: Illumination, Universal Pictures
Length: 89 minutes
Directed by: Pierre Coffin, Kyle Balda, co-directed by Eric Guillon
Written by: Cinco Paul & Ken Daurio

Synopsis: Former child actor Balthazar Bratt, star of the *Evil Bratt* TV show in the 80s, has taken up a life of crime after adolescence ruined the cuteness that made him a star. Former super villain Gru and his wife Lucy Wilde are sent by the Anti-Villain League (AVL) to stop Bratt from stealing the Dumont diamond. Although Gru is able to prevent the theft, Bratt escapes, and new AVL director Valerie Da Vinci fires Gru and Wilde. The couple return home to their daughters, Margo, Edith, and Agnes, and Gru's horde of short yellow minions, but most of the minions depart when Gru declines to return to a life of villainy. Unexpected news comes from Gru's twin brother, Dru, and the family travels to Freedonia to meet him. Dru reveals to Gru that their father was the supervillain the Bald Terror, and asks that Gru teach him to become a villain. Gru resists, but when Bratt succeeds in stealing the Dumont diamond, Gru and Dru work together to get it back, only to find they have different goals in mind. Once Bratt stoops to kidnapping the children, differences are put aside.

Cast: Steve Carell as Gru/Dru
Kristen Wiig as Lucy
Trey Parker as Balthazar Bratt
Miranda Cosgrove as Margo
Dana Gaier as Edith

Nev Scharrel as Agnes
Pierre Coffin as Minions/Museum Director
Steve Coogan as Fritz/Silas Ramsbottom
Julie Andrews as Gru's Mom
Jenny Slate as Valerie Da Vinci

Music Highlights: "Take My Breath Away" (Moroder/Whitlock) performed by Berlin, "María" (Edit) (Porter/Escolar/Blake) performed by Ricky Martin, "Despicable Me" (Williams) performed by Pharrell Williams, "There's Something Special" (Williams) performed by Pharrell Williams, "Fun, Fun, Fun" (Williams) performed by Pharrell Williams, "I Am the Very Model of a Modern Major-General" (Gilbert/Sullivan), "Physical" (Kipner/Shaddick) performed by Olivia Newton-John, "99 Luftballons" (Karges/Petersen) performed by Nena, "Into The Groove" (Madonna/Bray) performed by Madonna, "Hug Me" (Williams/Parker) by Pharrell Williams/Trey Parker, "Bad" (Jackson) performed by Michael Jackson, "Sussudio" (Collins) performed by Phil Collins, "Fight Night" (Arnold/Ball/Cephus/Marshall) performed by Migos, "Take on Me" (Furuholmen/Harket/Waaktaar) performed by A-Ha, "Chuck Berry" (Williams) by Pharrell Williams, "Freedom" (Williams/Brown/Criss/Gist) by Pharrell Williams, "Doowit" (Williams) by Pharrell Williams, "Money For Nothing" (Knopfler/Sting) performed by Dire Straits, "Yellow Light" (Williams) by Pharrell Williams. Score by Heitor Pereira.

Film Facts

- The Grinch on Margo's shirt (23:35), and a *Sing* poster (39:34) are a nod to two Illumination films.
- "Freedonia" comes from the classic Marx Brothers film *Duck Soup* (1933).
- Additional appearances: followed by *Minions: The Rise of Gru* (2021).

Dinosaur (PG)

Theatrical release date: May 19, 2000
Production Company: Walt Disney Pictures, Walt Disney Feature Animation, The Secret Lab
Length: 82 minutes
Directed by: Ralph Zondag, Eric Leighton
Screenplay by: John Harrison and Robert Nelson Jacobs, based on an original screenplay by Walon Green, story by Thom Enriquez, John Harrison, Robert Nelson Jacobs, Ralph Zondag

Synopsis: After an iguanodon egg ends up on an island among a pack of lemurs, they raise the baby, Aladar, as one of their own. Meteors begin to decimate their island, and a grown Aladar takes his family to the mainland, where they join a herd of dinosaurs led by the arrogant iguanodon Kron, headed for a dinosaur nesting ground. Aladar objects to Kron's brutal leadership, eventually leading to a confrontation with the survival of the group hanging in the balance.

Cast: D.B. Sweeney as Aladar (iguanodon)
Alfre Woodward as Pilo (lemur)
Ossie Davis as Yar (lemur)
Max Casella as Zini (lemur)
Hayden Panettiere as Suri (lemur)

Samuel E. Wright as Kron (iguanodon)
Julianna Margulies as Neera (iguanodon)
Joan Plowright as Baylene (brachiosaurus)
Della Reese as Eema (styracosaurus)

Music Highlights: Score by James Newton Howard.

Film Facts

• The 39th of the Disney animated classics, *Dinosaur* features an unusual mix of live-action backgrounds and computer generated dinosaurs and other creatures.
• Hayden Panettiere had appeared as Dot in *A Bug's Life* (1998), and Samuel E. Wright famously voiced Sebastian in *The Little Mermaid* (1989).
• Kate Bush wrote a song for the film, but it was ultimately not used, either because Bush refused to change the lyrics or because test audiences did not respond well to it, depending on who you believe. The song was reportedly redeveloped as "Lyra" from *The Golden Compass*.
• *Dinosaur* was first proposed in 1988 as a stop-motion animation project by directors Paul Verhoeven and Phil Tippett. The film ended up featuring photographic/live-action backgrounds with computer generated dinosaurs.
• Despite its depiction in the film, a carnotaurus is actually smaller than an iguanodon.
• An opening scene of a meteor headed toward Earth was scrapped when a similar scene opened the film *Armageddon* (1998).
• A video game was made for Windows, PlayStation, PS2, Dreamcast, and Game Boy Color.
• Disney had created surprisingly few dinosaur films prior to this release, including the Stravinsky "Rite of Spring" dinosaur sequence in *Fantasia* (1940), and the edited 1985 Touchstone film *Dinosaur...Secret of the Lost Legend* broadcast on *The Magical World of Disney* in 1989. Several years later Pixar would release *The Good Dinosaur* (2015).

Disney Princess Enchanted Tales: Follow Your Dreams (G)

Home media release date: September 4, 2007
Production Company: DisneyToon Studios, Toon City Animation
Length: 56 minutes
Directed by: David Block
Written by: Denise Gruska (Aurora: "Keys to the Kingdom"), Shirley Pierce (Jasmine: "More Than a Peacock Princess"), Tom Rogers (Princess intros and narration)

Synopsis: A pair of stories feature Aurora from *Sleeping Beauty,* and Princess Jasmine from *Aladdin*, focused on the theme of perseverance. In "Keys to the Kingdom," Princess Aurora is in charge while the rest of the royal family is away for a conference, declining the assistance of the good fairies, Flora, Fauna, and Merryweather. When her responsibilities begin to feel overwhelming, Aurora resorts to using Merryweather's magic wand with unexpected results, leading her to conclude that she is better able to solve problems using her own skills. In "More Than a Peacock Princess," Princess Jasmine, bored with her royal activities and duties, takes on the role of Royal Assistant Educator at the Royal Academy of Young Scholars. Her unruly pupils leave Jasmine feeling discouraged, but her kind servant Aneesa urges her to practice perseverance. She soon has an opportunity to persevere, as she helps stable boy Hakeem to find Sahara, the Sultan's runaway horse.

Cast: Erin Torpey as Princess Aurora
Corey Burton as King Stefan
Barbara Dirikson as Queen Leah
Roger Craig Smith as Prince Phillip
Jeff Bennett as King Hubert
Barbara Dirikson as Flora
Russi Taylor as Fauna

Tress MacNeille as Merryweather
Linda Larkin as Princess Jasmine
Jeff Bennett as The Sultan
Frank Welker as Abu
Gilbert Gottfried as Iago
Frank Welker as Rajah
Zack Shada as Hakeem

Music Highlights: "Keys to the Kingdom" (Amy Powers/Russ DeSalvo) performed by Cassidy Ladden as Aurora, "Peacock Princess" (Amy Powers/Russ DeSalvo) performed by Lea Salonga as Jasmine and Gilbert Gottfried as Iago, "I've Got My Eyes On You" (Amy Powers/Russ DeSalvo) performed by Lea Salonga as Jasmine. Score by Jeff Danna.

Film Facts

• This was the first animated story featuring Aurora since she first appeared in *Sleeping Beauty* in 1959. She had previously appeared as a background character in the *House of Mouse* (2001-2003).
• The DVD includes a bonus feature music video of Belle singing "You'll Never Lose This Love."
• This DVD was originally to be called *A Kingdom of Kindness*, with an alternate story featuring Aurora, paired with a story featuring Belle from *Beauty and the Beast*. A preview of the unreleased version can be found on the first *Brother Bear 2* DVD.
• The original DVD includes a preview for a planned second DVD, *Honesty*, to feature Cinderella and Mulan. *Follow Your Dreams* was reissued in 2009 with a bonus disc featuring "Happiness Was Made to Share" by Cinderella and "Working for a Dream" by Mulan from the unreleased volume.

Doug's 1st Movie (G)

Theatrical release date: March 26, 1999
Production Company: Walt Disney Pictures, Jumbo Pictures, Walt Disney Television Animation
Length: 77 minutes
Directed by: Maurice Joyce
Written by: Ken Scarborough

Synopsis: Doug Funnie and his best friend Skeeter are searching for a legendary lake monster, and local bully Roger and his friends make a fake monster to trick them. Skeeter sees through their disguise, but they are all startled when a real muddy creature emerges from the lake. Back at school, the Valentine's Day dance is approaching, and Doug invites his crush, Patti Mayonnaise, to organize the dance with him. Unfortunately, Guy Graham, an upperclassman who also likes Patti, horns in on the dance committee. Doug and Skeeter are overjoyed when Skeeter's camera has captured a photo of the lake monster, and when the monster shows up at Skeeter's house, it turns out it's a gentle creature that they name Herman Melville. They tell Mr. Dink and his wife, Mayor Tippi Dink, about the monster, which seems to have been created by pollution in the lake caused by businessman Mr. Bluff. They are concerned that Bluff will kill the story if they tell the newspaper, so they plan a press conference, but when Guy tells Mr. Bluff about the monster, he tries to cover it up. Doug has second thoughts, and cancels the press conference to protect Herman, which makes Patti think Doug was lying. As Mr. Bluff schemes to cover up the whole matter, aided by Guy, Roger makes a robot, Robocrusher, which cares for him a little too much. Doug and Skeeter work hard to do what's right, despite the risks required.

Cast: Thomas McHugh as Doug Funnie/Lincoln
Fred Newman as Skeeter/Mr. Dink/Porkchop/Ned
Chris Phillips as Roger Klotz/Boomer/Larry/
　　Mr. Chiminy
Constance Shulman as Patti Mayonnaise
Frank Welker as Herman Melville
Doug Preis as Mr. Funnie/Mr. Bluff/Willie/
　　Chalky/Bluff Agent #1

Guy Hadley as Guy Graham
Alice Playten as Beebe Bluff/Elmo
Eddie Korbich as Al Sleech/Moo Sleech/
　　Robocrusher
David O'Brien as Stentorian (Quailman)
　　Announcer
Doris Belack as Mayor Tippi Dink
Becca Lish as Judy Funnie/Mrs. Funnie/Connie

Music Highlights: "Disney's Doug: Original Theme" (Sawyer), "Deep Deep Water" (Sawyer/Osborn/Garvey) performed by Dan Sawyer, "Deep Deep Water" (Sawyer/Osborn/Garvey) performed by SHeDAISY, "Mona Mo" (Sawyer/Newman) performed by Dan Sawyer & Fred Newman. End credits: "Someone Like Me" (Squier/Lodin) performed by Michael Africk. Music by Mark Watters.

Film Facts

• The film was planned as a home media release, but after Nickelodeon's *The Rugrats Movie* (1998) was successful in theaters, it was decided to release it theatrically.
• Additional appearances: *Doug* (Nickelodeon 1991-1994) and *Doug* (Disney 1996-1999) TV series.

DuckTales the Movie: Treasure of the Lost Lamp (G)

Theatrical release date: August 3, 1990
Production Company: Walt Disney Television Animation, Disneytoon Studios, Walt Disney Pictures, Walt Disney Animation France
Length: 74 minutes
Directed by: Bob Hathcock
Screenplay by: Alan Burnett

Synopsis: Scrooge McDuck and his adventurous nephews, Huey, Dewey, and Louie, have high hopes when a chest believed to contain the legendary treasure of Collie Baba and the 40 Thieves is found at a desert dig site. When they arrive, accompanied by Webby Vanderquack and pilot Launchpad McQuack, they are disappointed to find there is no treasure, but when a map is found, the explorers set off on a new treasure hunt. They are aided by the thief Dijon, unaware that he is working for Merlock, an evil wizard who wants a magic lamp hidden in Collie Baba's treasure. When the treasure is finally located inside a pyramid, Webby Vanderquack picks up the lamp, having no idea what it is. Merlock and Dijon steal the treasure, not knowing that Webby has the one item they truly want. The children soon learn the lamp contains a Genie, and each get three wishes, but it isn't long before Merlock and Dijon are back, for a struggle to see who can retain control of the lamp.

Cast: Alan Young as Scrooge
Terence McGovern as Launchpad McQuack
Russi Taylor as Huey/Dewey/Louie/Webby
Richard Libertini as Dijon
Christopher Lloyd as Merlock

June Foray as Mrs. Featherby
Chuck McCann as Duckworth
Joan Gerber as Mrs. Beakley
Rip Taylor as Genie

Music Highlights: "Ducktales Theme" (Mark Mueller) performed by Jeffrey Pescetto. Score by David Newman.

Film Facts

• This was the first animated theatrical film released by Walt Disney that was produced by Disney Television Animation, rather than the Walt Disney Feature Animation department.
• The Indiana Jones films were inspired by Carl Barks' *Uncle Scrooge* comics, including the temple weight trigger and rolling boulder (see "The Seven Cities of Cibola" from *Uncle Scrooge* #7, 1954).
• A figure that looks like Indiana Jones is seen at the Explorer's Club (43:57).
• Posters for *The DuckTales Movie* and *Raiders of the Lost Ark* were both designed by Drew Struzan.
• The buried pyramid is from the Carl Barks' "Pyramid Scheme" (*Uncle Scrooge* #25, 1959).
• When Collie Baba's treasure is found, Scrooge is briefly seen wearing his customary blue frock coat, instead of his explorer outfit (12:14).
• The Donald Duck short "Dude Duck" (1951) was shown with the film in theaters.
• Additional appearances: *DuckTales* animated television series (1987-1990), *DuckTales* animated television series reboot (2017-2019).

Dumbo (G)

Theatrical release date: October 31, 1941 (premiere Oct 23, 1941 at Broadway Theater, New York)
Production Company: Walt Disney Productions
Length: 64 minutes
Supervising Director: Ben Sharpsteen, Sequence directors Norman Ferguson, Wilfred Jackson,
Bill Roberts, Jack Kinney, Sam Armstrong
Screen story by: Joe Grant, Dick Huemer, based on the book by Helen Pearl and Harold Pearl

---

Synopsis: After being teased and tormented by humans and elephants alike for his unusually large ears, circus elephant Dumbo is befriended by Timothy Q. Mouse, who helps him learn to fly, helping Dumbo to attain his freedom.

Cast: Edward Brophy as Timothy Q. Mouse
Verna Felton as Mrs. Jumbo
Sterling Holloway as Mr. Stork
Cliff Edwards as Jim Crow

Herman Bing as The Ringmaster
Billy Bletcher as a Clown
Margaret Wright as Casey Jr.

Music Highlights: "Look Out for Mr. Stork," "Casey Jr.," "Roustabouts," "Baby Mine," "Pink Elephants on Parade," "When I See An Elephant Fly." All songs music by Oliver Wallace/ Frank Churchill, lyrics by Ned Washington.

Film Facts

• Dumbo had a smaller budget than any Disney film, yet did better than *Pinocchio* (1940) and *Fantasia* (1940) at the box office.
• In the original book, Dumbo's friend was a bird named Red Robin rather than Timothy Q. Mouse.
• Elephants were brought to the Disney studio so the animators could study their movements.
• The film is among the shortest of Disney's features, clocking in at only 64 minutes. RKO urged Disney to lengthen the film, shorten it, or release it as a B film, but he refused. RKO finally relented.
• The Disney animators went on strike for five weeks during the process of creating the film, and at the time of its creation, Walt Disney Productions was in financial jeopardy, as complications from World War II led both *Pinocchio* (1940) and *Fantasia* (1940) to fare poorly at the box office. *Dumbo* broke this streak, and helped return the studio to a more stable footing.
• Verna Felton voiced the Fairy Godmother in *Cinderella* (1950), the Queen of Hearts in *Alice in Wonderland* (1951), Aunt Sarah in *Lady and the Tramp* (1955), Flora in *Sleeping Beauty* (1959), and the elephant Winifred in *The Jungle Book* (1967). Sterling Holloway voiced Flower in *Bambi* (1942), the Cheshire Cat in *Alice in Wonderland* (1951), Kaa in *The Jungle Book* (1967), Roquefort in *The Aristocats* (1970), and Winnie the Pooh in *The Many Adventures of Winnie the Pooh* (1977). Cliff Edwards voiced Jiminy Cricket in *Pinocchio* (1940) and in *Fun and Fancy Free* (1947).
• Additional appearances: *Dumbo's Circus* puppet television show (1985-1986), the *Dumbo* live-action theatrical film (2019).
• A sequel, *Dumbo II,* was planned and in development to the point that it was announced on the *Dumbo* "60th Anniversary Edition" DVD (2001). Director Robert C. Ramirez (*The Brave Little Toaster to the Rescue*) was to helm the project, but the release was canceled in 2006 when John Lasseter was appointed Chief Creative Officer of Walt Disney Animation Studios.

Early Man (PG)

Theatrical release date: February 16, 2018
Production Company: Aardman Animations, Summit Entertainment, BFI, StudioCanal
Length: 89 minutes
Directed by: Nick Park
Screenplay by: Mark Burton and James Higginson, story by Mark Burton and Nick Park

Synopsis: In the Neo-Pleistocene age, a small, round meteor lands, beginning the game of football (soccer). Many years later, the caveman Dug, with his wild boar dog Hognob, live in a Stone Age tribe, alongside Chief Bobnar, Treebor, Magma, Barry, Mr. Rock, Asbo, Thongo, Gravelle, Grubup, and the unintelligible Eemak. After a successful rabbit hunt, the caveman tribe is driven out of their valley by a party of Bronze-Age warriors with armored mammoths and advanced weapons. Dug and Hognob are accidentally brought into their village, and Dug ends up as the goalie in a football game. Dug challenges the governor, Lord Nooth, to a football match: if the cavemen win, they keep their valley, but if they lose, they spend the rest of their lives in a mine. When the one ball the cavemen had gets crushed, Dug sneaks into the village to get another, meeting the expert football player Goona, who joins the caveman team, since she has never been allowed to play in the village. Nooth gets nervous when he realizes the cavemen have been playing football for hundreds of years, and schemes to sabotage the cavemen by showing Dug cave paintings of his tribe always losing football games. For all their skill, the Bronzers are not truly a team, giving Dug and Goona a chance — a small chance — at victory.

Cast: Eddie Redmayne as Dug
Tom Hiddleston as Lord Nooth
Maisie Williams as Goona
Timothy Spall as Chief Bobnar
Miriam Margolyes as Queen Oofeefa
Rob Brydon as the Message Bird/Brian/
    Bryan
Kayvan Novak as Dino/Jurgend

Richard Ayoade as Treebor
Selina Griffiths as Magma
Johnny Vegas as Asbo
Mark Williams as Barry
Gina Yashere as Gravelle
Richard Webber as Grubup
Simon Greenall as Eemak/Thongo
Nick Park as Hognob

Music Highlights: "Tiger Feet" (Chinn/Chapman) performed by New Hope Club (orig. by Mud), "Hope" (Brad Simpson) performed by The Vamps, "I Predict a Riot" (Rix/Baines/White/Hodgson/ Wilson) performed by The Kaiser Chiefs. End credits: "Good Day" (Jamie N. Commons/Benjamin Epand) performed by New Hope Club. Music by Harry Gregson-Williams and Tom Howe.

Film Facts

• Football references: "Oofeefa" sounds like the football association FIFA, Jurgend is based on the German footballer Jürgen Klinsmann, Brian and Bryan are inspired by British announcers Brian Moore and Alan Hansen, and "Early Man United" refers to the Manchester United football team.
• Aardman Animations' Wallace and Gromit make a cameo appearance in a crowd scene (58:11), and a penguin from the Wallace & Gromit short "The Wrong Trousers" also appears (1:00:40).

Eleanor's Secret (NR)

Theatrical release date: December16, 2009 (France/Belgium/Switzerland)
Country: France, Italy   French title: *Kérity, la Maison des Contes* (lit. "Kérity, the House of Tales")
Production Company: Prana Studios, Tremendous Entertainment
Length: 80 minutes
Directed by: Dominique Monféry
Screenplay by: Anik Le Ray & Alexandre Révérend, story by Anik Le Ray

Synopsis: The family of seven year old Nat has inherited his Aunt Eleanor's home after she passed away at the age of 99. The house has a secret room, that Eleanor told Nat he would be able to see one day. The family comes to stay for the summer, and though Nat's sister Angelica teases him about not being able to read yet, the two of them enjoy the nearby beach. When they return, their parents tell them that Eleanor wrote them a letter. She leaves Angelica a porcelain doll, and leaves Nat the key to the secret room. Nat nervously opens the door, and to his disappointment, he finds the room holds a huge library. When repairs on the house become expensive, his parents propose they sell the books, asking Nat to pick one out that he would like to keep. Nat goes to the library, and when a book falls of the shelf, is suddenly buffeted about by words and pages. Small characters from the books come to life, explaining all the books are first editions, and that Nat is the "great reader, successor to Eleanor." Nat is delighted to meet the characters he knows and loves. They ask him to read the magic spell printed on the wall: "Just because it's a story, doesn't mean it's not real," saying he only has once chance to say it, and needs to read it by noon. The Wicked Fairy, who doubts Nat is the real replacement, shrinks Nat down. Pickall, the junk man, is called by Nat's parents to take all the books from the house, and Nat, accompanied by Alice and the White Rabbit from Wonderland and an ogre, sets out on a quest to save them all.

Cast:

Role	English	French
Nathaniel	Arthur Dubois	Pascal Berger
Angelica	Stéphane Flamand	Stéphane Flamand
Mom	Sharon Mann	Julie Gayet
Dad	David Gasman	Denis Podalydès
Eleanor	Jodi Forrest	Jeanne Moreau
Alice	Hester Wilcox	Prunelle Rulens
Ogre	David Gasman	Chilly Gonzalez
Carabosse	Christine Flowers	Liliane Rovère

Music Highlights: Music by Christophe Héral.

Film Facts

• The film premiered October 22, 2009 at the Rome Film Festival.
• Monféry directed the 2003 Disney short "Destino" & *Franklin & the Turtle Lake Treasure* (2006).
• The film won the "Best Feature Award" at the Providence Children's Film Festival in 2011.

84

The Emperor's New Groove (G)

Theatrical release date: December 15, 2000
Production Company: Walt Disney Pictures, Walt Disney Feature Animation
Length: 78 minutes
Directed by: Mark Dindal
Screenplay by: David Reynolds, story by Chris Williams, Mark Dindal

Synopsis: Arrogant Incan emperor Kuzco reveals his plans to demolish a nearby village to make way for a vacation spot, and shortly thereafter callously fires his evil advisor Yzma. Yzma's attempt to kill Kuzco is inadvertently thwarted by her incompetent henchman Kronk, but in the process Kuzco is turned into a llama. Seeking help from Pacha, a resident of the village he planed to destroy, Kuzco finally begins to learn humanity once he is no longer human.

Cast: David Spade as Emperor Kuzco
John Goodman as Pacha
Eartha Kitt as Yzma
Patrick Warburton as Kronk
Wendie Malick as Chicha
Kellyann Kelso as Chaca
Eli Russell Linnetz as Tipo
Bob Bergen as Bucky/Fly stuck in web

Music Highlights: "Perfect World" (Sting/Dave Hartley) performed by Tom Jones, "My Funny Friend and Me" (Sting/Dave Hartley) performed by Sting, "Snuff Out the Light (Yzma's Song)" (Sting/David Hartley) performed by Eartha Kitt, "Walk the Llama Llama" (Sting/David Hartley) performed by Rascal Flatts, "One Day She'll Love Me" (Sting/David Hartley) performed by Sting and Shawn Colvin. Score by John Debney.

Film Facts

• Disney's 40th animated classic, *The Emperor's New Groove* was originally titled *Kingdom of the Sun*. In the original story proposed by Roger Allers and Matthew Jacobs, the greedy emperor gains his freedom by trading places with an identical peasant (à la *The Prince and the Pauper*), until the witch Yzma calls upon Supay, the god of death, to destroy the sun, which will allow her to stay beautiful forever. Yzma transforms the emperor into a llama and obtains the pauper's silence by threatening to expose his identity. Along the way the pauper falls in love with the emperor's fiancé, while the emperor falls in love with Mata the llama-herd. Sting, former frontman of The Police, wrote a series of songs for the film. Storyboard artist Chris Williams and director Mark Dindal re-developed the story, hiring comedy writer David Reynolds to write the screenplay.
• Eartha Kitt, voice of Yzma, is best known as Catwoman from the 1960s *Batman* TV series.
• The capital of the ancient Inca empire was named Cuzco, phonetically the same as Kuzco.
• Trudie Styler (Sting's wife) made a documentary, *The Sweatbox* (2002), chronicling the torturous development of the film.
• Patrick Warburton's character Kronk was chosen as the lead of the sequel.
• Additional appearances: *Kronk's New Groove* (2005), *The Emperor's New School* animated TV series (2006-2008).

The Emperor's New Groove: *Kronk's New Groove* (G)

Home media release date: December 13, 2005
Production Company: DisneyToon Studios, Toon City Animation
Length: 72 minutes
Directed by: Elliot M. Bour & Saul Andrew Blinkoff
Screenplay by: Tom Rogers, story by Tony Leondis & Michael LaBash and Tom Rogers

---

Synopsis: Kronk is working as a successful fry cook, but Yzma plays on his desire to win his father's approval to get him to help her sell snake oil to the local population. He works to redeem himself as camp counselor for the Junior Chipmunk troop, and loses his heart to another counselor, Ms. Birdwell, but they have a falling out. Kronk finally faces his father, though his panic to impress him leads him to pretend Pacha's family is his own, and soon the deception collapses around him. It is only when he finally confesses and realizes the importance of his friends that he finally earns the approval of his father and reconciles with Ms. Birdwell.

Cast: Patrick Warburton as Kronk
Tracey Ullman as Ms. Birdwell
Eartha Kitt as Yzma
David Spade as Kuzco
John Goodman as Pacha
Wendie Malick as Chicha
John Mahoney as Papi

John Fiedler as Rudy
Jeff Bennett as Old Man/Gollum-Rudy
Bob Bergen as Bucky
Patti Deutsch as Waitress
Jessie Flower as Chaca
Anthony Ghannam as Huayna
Eli Russell Linnetz as Tipo

Music Highlights: "Be True to Your Groove" (Peter Lurye) performed by Sandy Barber and Peter Lurye, "Feel Like a Million" (Jeanine Tesori) performed by Eartha Kitt, "Let's Groove" (Maurice White/Wayne Vaughn) performed by Earth, Wind & Fire, "Camp Chippamunka" (Randy Petersen/ Kevin Quinn) performed by Nicholas Harper, Eli Russell Linnetz, Zoe Merrill, Madison Moore, Aaron Page, and Bobbi Page. Score by Mark Watters.

Film Facts

• Patrick Warburton has acted/voiced a range of characters, including the Tick, David Puddy on *Seinfeld,* and Flynn in the *Skylanders* video game series, also appearing in *Buzz Lightyear of Star Command* animated TV series (2000-2001), *Home on the Range* (2004), and *Chicken Little* (2005).
• Yzma, in semi-cat form, is voiced by Eartha Kitt, recalling her role as Catwoman in the 1966-1968 *Batman* television series.
• Kronk's full name is revealed as Kronker Pepikrankenitz.
• The classic Disneyland ride "It's a Small World" is referenced in the film (14:11).
• One of the characters imitates Gollum from *The Hobbit/Lord of the Rings,* greedily saying, "My precious." (22:25).
• Additional appearances: Follows *The Emperor's New Groove* (2000), followed by *The Emperor's New School* Disney Channel animated TV series (2006-2008).

Epic (PG)

Theatrical release date: May 24, 2013
Production Company: 20th Century Fox Animation, Blue Sky Studios
Length: 102 minutes
Directed by: Chris Wedge
Screenplay by: James V. Hart & William Joyce and Dan Shere and Tom J. Astle & Matt Ember, story by William Joyce & James V. Hart and Chris Wedge

Synopsis: When M.K. goes to visit her father, Professor Radcliffe Bomba, she's concerned about his belief that there's a race of tiny people that are an important part of the ecosystem. The Leafmen of Moonhaven, soldiers of the kind Queen Tara, fight against the decay of the Boggans, led by the cruel Mandrake and his son Dagda. Mandrake plots to destroy Queen Tara before she can choose an heir, which will continue the life of the forest. As the Queen is choosing a Royal Pod to be her heir, the Boggans attack. The leader of the Leafmen, Ronin, tries to protect the Queen, but she is shot by an arrow, plummeting to the ground, where she's found by M.K. The Queen passes her essence on to the Pod, giving it to M.K., who shrinks to the Queen's size. The Queen tells M.K. to take the Pod to wise glowworm Nim Galuu, just before her spirit departs into the sky. M.K. and Ronin, joined by Nod, a Leafman dropout, reach Nim Galuu, and learn that the Pod must bloom in the moonlight. While Nod is distracted by M.K., Mandrake steals the Pod, planning for it to bloom in darkness, so he can use it to destroy the forest. The Pod is retrieved, but Mandrake will not let it go so easily, requiring Nod to join the Leafmen, and M.K. to get some big reinforcements.

Cast: Amanda Seyfried as Mary Katherine "M.K." Bomba
Josh Hutcherson as Nod
Colin Farrell as Ronin
Christoph Waltz as Mandrake
Aziz Ansari as Mub (slug)
Chris O'Dowd as Grub (snail)
Pitbull as Bufo (toad)
Jason Sudeikis as Professor Radcliffe Bomba
Steven Tyler as Nim Galuu (glowworm)
Beyoncé Knowles as Queen Tara
Blake Anderson as Dagda
Judah Friedlander as Larry
Thomas F. Wilson as Finn

Music Highlights: "Same Changes" (Talan/Tannen) performed by The Weepies with Brad Gordon, "In the Sweet Bye and Bye" (Bennett/Webster/Batiste) performed by Magnificent Seventh's Brass Band, "Gonna Be Alright" (Stinson/Saadiq) performed by Steven Tyler, "Hell" (Maxwell) performed by Squirrel Nut Zippers. End credits: "Rise Up" (Hollis/Woodard/Sia/Beyoncé) performed by Beyoncé. Music by Danny Elfman.

Film Facts

• The film's original title was *Leaf Men*, based on the 1996 book *The Leaf Men and the Brave Good Bugs* by William Joyce, author of *A Day With Wilbur Robinson*, and *Guardians of Childhood* series. The films *Meet the Robinsons* (2007) and *Rise of the Guardians* (2012) were based on these books.
• Steven Tyler, voice of Nim Galuu, is best known as the lead singer of rock band Aerosmith.

Ernest & Celestine (PG)

Theatrical release date: May 23, 2012 (Cannes), December 12, 2012 (France)
Country: Belgium, France, Luxembourg   **French title**: *Ernest et Célestine*
Production Company: La Parti Productions, Les Armateurs, Melusine Productions
Length: 80 minutes
Directed by: Stéphane Aubier, Vincent Patar, Benjamin Renner
Written by: Daniel Pennac, based on the books by Gabrielle Vincent

---

Synopsis: Celestine lives in an orphanage with other mice, cared for by the Gray One, who warns them about the dangers of bears. Ernest the bear, coming out of hibernation, is famished, and heads into the bear city to perform as a one-bear band, hoping to get tips from passersby, but his instruments are confiscated by the police. Celestine and two other mice sneak into the city, tasked with gathering bears' teeth and bringing them back for mouse dentists to use, as mice depend upon their teeth. Celestine, far behind in her tooth quota, gets trapped in a trash can, and Ernest finds her sleeping there. After Ernest almost eats her, Celestine convinces him to feast in a nearby candy store instead. Ernest is caught by the police, and Celestine frees him. In return, Ernest agrees to steal a big bag of teeth from the bear dentist for her, making her a hero among the mice. Ernest ends up napping in the mouse orphanage, panicking the mice. Celestine helps him escape, and they flee to Ernest's house. Ernest tries to throw Celestine out, but with nowhere to go, she claims his cellar. The pair overcome their mistrust of each other, and Ernest learns Celestine wants to be an artist, while Celestine learns that Ernest wanted to be a musician. When they are finally captured by the police, their kindness and loyalty shine through.

Cast:

Role	English	French
Ernest	Forest Whitaker	Lambert Wilson
Celestine	Mackenzie Foy	Pauline Brunner
The Grey One	Lauren Bacall	Anne-Marie Loop
The Rat Judge	Paul Giamatti	Pierre Baton
The Dentist	William H. Macy	Dominique Collignon
Lucienne	Megan Mullally	Brigitte Virtudes
Georges	Nick Offerman	Patrice Melennec
The Bear Judge	Jeffrey Wright	Féodor Atkine
Chief Police of Bears	David Boat	Vincent Grass

Music Highlights: Music by Vincent Courtois, lyrics by Thomas Fersen (English).

Film Facts

• Many cultures have a legend of a mouse tooth fairy.
• The film was nominated for the "Best Animated Feature" Academy Award, and won the "Best Animated Film" César Award in France.
• A poster for Aubier and Patar's *A Town Called Panic* (2009) is seen in the child bear's room.

Fantasia (G)

Theatrical release date: November 13, 1940
Production Company: Walt Disney Productions
Length: 1940 version 124 minutes (1942 general release 81 minutes, 1946 version 115 minutes)
Supervising Director: Ben Sharpsteen, see below for segment directors
Written by: Joe Grant, Dick Huemer

Synopsis: A series of short animations inspired by pieces of classical music.

Cast: Leopold Stokowski as himself - the Conductor
Deems Taylor as himself
Walt Disney as Mickey Mouse

James McDonald as percussionist
Julietta Novis as Ave Maria soloist
Paul J. Smith as violinist

Music (performed by the Philadelphia Orchestra, conducted by Leopold Stokowski):
• Johann Sebastian Bach - *Toccata and Fugue in D Minor*: orchestra, clouds, abstracts (dir. Samuel Armstrong). • Piotr Ilyich Tchaikovsky - *Nutcracker Suite*: fairies, flowers, mushrooms, fish (dir. Samuel Armstrong). • Paul Dukas - *The Sorcerer's Apprentice*: Mickey Mouse (dir. James Algar). • Igor Stravinsky - *Rite of Spring*: dinosaurs (dir. Bill Roberts/Paul Satterfield). • Intermission/Meet the Soundtrack, • Ludwig van Beethoven - *Symphony No. 6 in F Major* (Pastoral): centaurs/fauns/Bacchus/Zeus (dir. Ford Beebe Jr./Hamilton Luske). • Amilcare Ponchielli - *Dance of the Hours*: ostriches/hippos/elephants/alligators (dir. Norm Ferguson/T. Hee). • Modest Mussorgsky - *Night on Bald Mountain*: devil/spirits / Franz Schubert - *Ave Maria*: procession of light (dir. Wilfred Jackson).

Film Facts

• The third of the Disney animated classics, *Fantasia* was one of Disney's grandest creations, but it didn't begin as a feature film. The original plan was for "The Sorcerer's Apprentice" sequence to be a *Silly Symphonies* short, part of a series of musical shorts Disney released from the late 1920s to the late 1930s. Disney wanted to create a special film to boost the popularity of Mickey Mouse, and after a chance meeting with conductor Leopold Stokowski, it was agreed that Stokowski would conduct a studio orchestra for the short. As production costs grew, the strategy of combining the short with other shorts set to classical music appeared wise, as there was no way the short could recoup the production costs on its own. The working title for the new film was *The Concert Feature*.
• *Fantasia* premiered as a limited release in thirteen U.S. cities, on November 13, 1940. Ticket prices were higher than usual, and theatergoers had to book their seats in advance. Ushers were hired to direct people to their seats, and each viewer was provided with a program.
• "The Sorcerer's Apprentice" was based on Goethe's 1797 poem "Der Zauberlehrling." The name of the Sorcerer is Yen Sid — note what it spells backwards.
• Walt Disney provided the voice of Mickey Mouse until 1946, including *Fantasia*.
• When additional scenes with Deems Taylor were added in 2000, the audio was so damaged that his voice was overdubbed by versatile voice actor Corey Burton in the entire film.
• The film won two special Academy Awards, one given to Leopold Stokowski and his associates for "the creation of a new form of visualized music," and one given to Walt Disney and his associates for "outstanding contribution to the advancement of the use of sound in motion pictures."
• Additional appearances: *Fantasia 2000* (1999).

Fantasia 2000 (G)

Theatrical release date: December 31, 1999
Production Company: Walt Disney Pictures, Walt Disney Feature Animation
Length: 74 minutes
Host sequence director: Don Hahn. See below for segment directors.
Host sequences written by: Don Hahn, Irene Mecchi, David Reynolds.

Synopsis: As with the original *Fantasia,* a series of short animations inspired by pieces of classical music.

Cast: Hosts: Steve Martin, Itzhak Perlman, Quincy Jones, Bette Midler, James Earl Jones, Penn & Teller, James Levine, Angela Lansbury

Music (performed by the Chicago Symphony Orchestra, directed by James Levine):
• Ludvig van Beethoven, *Symphony No. 5*: Abstract butterflies (Dir. Pixote Hunt)
• Ottorino Respighi, *Pines of Rome*: Whales in flight (Dir. Hendel Butoy)
• George Gershwin, *Rhapsody in Blue*: Scenes in a city (Dir. Eric Goldberg)
• Dmitri Shostakovich, *Piano Concerto No. 2, Allegro, Opus 102*: The Steadfast Tin Solder (Dir. Hendel Butoy)
• Camille Saint-Saëns, *Carnival of the Animals,* Finale: Flamingo with a yo-yo (Dir. Eric Goldberg)
• Paul Dukas, *The Sorcerer's Apprentice*: Mickey Mouse (Dir. James Algar)
• Sir Edward Elgar, *Pomp and Circumstance* - Marches 1, 2, 3, and 4: Donald and Daisy Duck on Noah's Ark (Dir. Francis Glebas)
• Igor Stravinsky, *Firebird Suite* - 1919 Version: Forest nymph (Dir. Gaëtan Brizzi, Paul Brizzi)

Film Facts

• *Fantasia 2000* is the 38th of the Disney animated classics.
• The film was clearly modeled after the first film, with Beethoven's 6th Symphony replaced by his 5th, Igor Stravinsky's *Rite of Spring* replaced by his *Firebird Suite,* and Shostakovich's *Piano Concerto No. 2* standing in for Bach's *Toccata and Fugue* as the keyboard piece. "The Sorcerer's Apprentice" was the only segment repeated from the first *Fantasia* film.
• The DVD includes the shorts "Melody" (1953) and "Toot, Whistle, Plunk and Boom" (1953).
• A tiny Mickey and Minnie can be seen on the roof of the ark after the rain (56:27).
• Disney's plan for the original *Fantasia* (1940) was to continue to develop new shorts based on classical pieces, keeping *Fantasia* in theaters but replacing some of the initial seven shorts with the new entries on an ongoing basis. This plan never materialized due to prohibitive costs.
• Over the years a number of sequel ideas were considered. Wolfgang Reitherman and Mel Shaw, two of Disney's original animators, began to develop a film to be called *Musicana*, that would feature shorts with music from around the world and stories drawn from folk tales, but it was never put into production. Jeffrey Katzenberg reportedly approached André Previn about work on a *Fantasia* sequel to feature music by the Beatles, but Previn declined.
• Additional appearances: Sequel to *Fantasia* (1940). A second sequel, *Fantasia 2006,* began development in 2002, for which the musical shorts "One by One," "Lorenzo," and "The Little Matchgirl" were created, but the film was canceled in 2004.

Fantastic Mr. Fox (PG)

Theatrical release date: November 25, 2009
Production Company: American Empirical Pictures, Indian Paintbrush, Regency Enterprises
Length: 87 minutes
Directed by: Wes Anderson
Screenplay by: Wes Anderson and Noah Baumbach, based on the novel by Roald Dahl

Synopsis: After a close scrape while Mrs. Fox is pregnant, Mr. Fox agrees to give up his days of theft, becoming a newspaper columnist. Wanting to leave the family foxhole for a tree, Mr. Fox moves across from the nasty farmers Boggis, Bunce, and Bean. Mr. and Mrs. Fox and their peculiar, cape-wearing son Ash are soon visited by Ash's accomplished cousin Kristofferson. Unable to resist temptation, Mr. Fox plans to rob all three farmers, joined by Kylie the opossum, and later by Kristofferson. The farmers conspire to kill Mr. Fox, shooting off his tail, and when he escapes into the tree, begin trying to dig the foxes out. The foxes tunnel down into the earth, but the farmers use digging machines and explosives. Underground, the foxes run into Badger and other animals, upset about the digging Mr. Fox has stirred up. Turning disadvantage to their favor, Mr. Fox leads a raid to clean out all three farms, ending in a giant feast. Ash, tired of being underestimated, convinces Kristofferson to try to retrieve Mr. Fox's tail, but Kristofferson is captured. Recognizing his neglect has led Ash to feel insecure, Mr. Fox apologizes, and decides to turn himself in to the farmers. When Bean's henchman Rat tries to take Ash, Mr. Fox defeats him, and changes his mind about surrender, orchestrating a rescue operation to save Kristofferson.

Cast: George Clooney as Mr. Fox
Meryl Streep as Mrs. Fox
Jason Schwartzman as Ash
Bill Murray as Badger
Wally Wolodarsky as Kylie
Eric Anderson as Kristofferson
Michael Gambon as Franklin Bean
Willem Dafoe as Rat

Owen Wilson as Coach Skip
Jarvis Cocker as Petey
Wes Anderson as Weasel
Karen Duffy as Linda Otter
Robin Hurlstone as Walter Boggis
Hugo Guinness as Nathan Bunce
Helen McCrory as Mrs. Bean

Music Highlights: "Heroes and Villains" (Wilson/Parks) performed by The Beach Boys, "Street Fighting Man" (Jagger/Richard) performed by The Rolling Stones, "Petey's Song" (Cocker/Anderson/Baumbach) performed by Jarvis Cocker, "I Get Around" (Wilson/Love) performed by The Beach Boys, "Boggis, Bunce, and Bean" (L: Dahl/M: Desplat) performed by The London Oratory School Schola, "Let Her Dance" (Fuller) performed by Bobby Fuller Four. Music by Alexandre Desplat.

Film Facts

- Mr. Fox's study (14:50) is closely modeled after Roald Dahl's "Writing Hut," where he worked.
- The "Bandit Hats" ad in the newspaper (11:56) is surrounded by quotes drawn from Dahl's book.
- The film was nominated for the "Best Animated Feature" Academy Award and Golden Globe.

Ferdinand (PG)

Theatrical release date: December 15, 2017
Production Company: Blue Sky Studios, 20th Century Fox Animation
Length: 108 minutes
Directed by: Carlos Saldanha
Screenplay by: Robert L. Baird and Tim Federle and Brad Copeland, screen story by Ron Burch & David Kidd and Don Rhymer, based upon the book *The Story of Ferdinand* by Munro Leaf, and illustrations by Robert Lawson

Synopsis: Ferdinand, a young bull who loves flowers more than fighting, sees his father taken off to a bullfight, from which he does not return. Distraught, Ferdinand flees the ranch where he's lived with other bulls, ending up on a flower grower's farm, cared for by the kindly Nina, alongside the dog Paco. One year he is told he is too big to go to the annual Flower Festival, but makes his way over anyway. A bee sting causes him to rampage through the festival, and he is taken back to the ranch where he grew up. He meets his childhood companions as well as the chatty goat Lupe, who tries to train him to take on the visiting bullfighter El Primero. Ferdinand begins to sneak out, but learns that no bull ever wins a bull fight, and returns to persuade all the bulls to leave. The aggressive Valiente attacks Ferdinand, who breaks Valiente's horn while defending himself. Finally escaping the ranch, the bulls are pursued by the ranchers. Ferdinand approaches the ranchers to save his friends, and ends up in the ring with El Primero. Ferdinand has a chance to kill El Primero, but lets him live. El Primero returns with a sword, but the crowd calls for mercy.

Cast: John Cena as Ferdinand
Kate McKinnon as Lupe
Anthony Anderson as Bones
Bobby Cannavale as Valiente/Valiente's father
Peyton Manning as Guapo
Gina Rodriguez as Una (hedgehog)

Miguel Ángel Silvestre as El Primero
David Tennant as Angus
Lily Day as Nina
Juanes as Juan
Jerrod Carmichael as Paco
Tim Nordquist as Maquina

Music Highlights: "Home (Film Version)" (Jonas/Tranter/Monson) performed by Nick Jonas, "Watch Me" (Jonas/Evigan/Douglas/Tucker/Bianco) performed by Nick Jonas, "I Know You Want Me (Calle Ocho)" (Seraphine/Bosco/Gonella/Perez/Wolinski/Fasano/Bello) performed by Pitbull, "Freedom" (Jagger/Richards, additional material by Perez/Pearl) performed by Pitbull, "España Cañi" (Narro/Tallada), "Home" (Jonas/Tranter/Monson) performed by Nick Jonas, "Lay Your Head on Me" (Izquierdo/Johnson/Aristizabal/Lomax/Johnson) performed by Juanes. Music by John Powell.

Film Facts

• The 1936 children's book *The Story of Ferdinand* was written by Munro Leaf and Robert Lawson.
• Walt Disney produced a 1938 short, "Ferdinand the Bull," also based on the book.
• The film was nominated for the "Best Animated Feature" Academy Award and Golden Globe.
• A brief mid-credits scene appears (1:40:04).

FernGully: The Last Rainforest (G)

Theatrical release date: April 10, 1992
Production Company: FAI Films, Kroyer Films, Youngheart Productions
Length: 76 minutes
Directed by: Bill Kroyer
Screenplay by: Jim Cox, based on the stories of "FernGully" by Diana Young

> **Synopsis**: In the rainforest FernGully, years after the powerful fairy Magi had trapped the destructive spirit Hexxus in a tree, the young fairy Crysta meets Batty Koda, a bat who says he was trapped by humans, which the fairies thought had gone extinct. Crysta flies to Mount Warning in the hopes of finding a human, where she finds the lumberjack Zak, marking trees to be cut. While trying to spray an insect with paint, he accidentally marks the tree imprisoning Hexxus for destruction. When a tree nearly falls on him, Crysta shrinks Zak to fairy size. Hexxus is freed when his tree is destroyed, and sends the lumberjacks toward FernGully to destroy it. The fairies face the twin challenges of the destructive machinery of the humans and the evil of Hexxus, requiring great sacrifice to protect the forest.

Cast: Tim Curry as Hexxus
Samantha Mathis as Crysta
Christian Slater as Pips
Jonathan Ward as Zak
Robin Williams as Batty Koda
Grace Zabriskie as Magi Lune

Geoffrey Blake as Ralph
Robert Pastorelli as Tony
Cheech Marin as Stump
Tommy Chong as Root
Tone-Loc as Goanna
Townsend Coleman as Knotty

Music Highlights: "Life Is a Magic Thing" (Thomas Dolby) performed by Johnny Clegg, "A Dream Worth Keeping" (Webb/Silvestri) performed by Sheena Easton, "Batty Rap" (Dolby/Young/Young) performed by Robin Williams, "Lithuanian Lullaby" (trad.) performed by Veronika Povilioniene "If I'm Goanna Eat Somebody (It Might As Well Be You)" (Jimmy Buffett/Mike Utley) performed by Tone Loc, "Spis, Li Milke Le" (Gueorgui Mintchev) performed by Le Mystere des Voix Bulgares, "Toxic Love" (Dolby) performed by Tim Curry, "Bamnqobile" (Joseph Shabalala) performed by Ladysmith Black Mambazo, "Raining Like Magic" (Raffi) performed by Raffi, "Tri Jetrve" (trad.) performed by Zbor i orkestar KUD, "Land of a Thousand Dances" (Chris Kenner) performed by Guy, "Some Other World" (Bruce Roberts/Elton John) performed by Elton John. Music by Alan Silvestri.

Film Facts

- Diana Young's book *FernGully* was published in 1992.
- The film was screened at the United Nations General Assembly on April 22, 1992, for Earth Day.
- Mount Warning is a real location, in New South Wales, Australia.
- The soundtrack of the film is quite eclectic, including a mix of pop and world music.
- This was Robin Williams's first animated film, just before his appearance as Genie in *Aladdin* (1992). Disney was reportedly not pleased with his involvement, and sought to get him to withdraw.
- Elton John's "Some Other World" came two years before his work on *The Lion King* (1994).
- Additional appearances: *FernGully 2: The Magical Rescue* home media release (1998).

Finding Nemo (G)

Theatrical release date: May 30, 2003
Production Company: Pixar Animation Studios, Walt Disney Pictures
Length: 100 minutes
Directed by: Andrew Stanton, co-directed by Lee Unkrich
Screenplay by: Andrew Stanton, Bob Peterson, David Reynolds, original story by Andrew Stanton

---

Synopsis: After losing his wife and recently laid eggs to a predator, clownfish father Marlin is overprotective of his one surviving son, Nemo, and is horrified when Nemo is scooped up by a scuba-diving dentist. Marlin must face his own fears in his quest to find his son, aided by the memory-impaired but helpful fish Dory. Meanwhile, Nemo seeks to escape the dentist's fish tank before he is given as a gift to the dentist's treacherous niece.

Cast: Albert Brooks as Marlin
Ellen DeGeneres as Dory
Alexander Gould as Nemo
Willem Dafoe as Gill
Brad Garrett as Bloat
Allison Janey as Peach
Austin Pendelton as Gurgle

Stephen Root as Bubbles
Vicki Lewis as Deb/Flo
Joe Ranft as Jacques
Geoffrey Rush as Nigel
Andrew Stanton as Crush
Elizabeth Perkins as Coral
Bob Peterson as Mr. Ray

Music Highlights: "Beyond the Sea" (Charles Trenet/Jack Lawrence) performed by Robbie Williams. Score by Thomas Newman.

Film Facts

• *Finding Nemo,* the 5th Pixar film, was the brainchild of Andrew Stanton, one of the core creative team at Pixar. The story drew from Stanton's childhood visits to the dentist, where he was fascinated with the aquarium, imagining that the fish wanted to return to the ocean, as well as his experiences as a parent, including the impulse to be overprotective.
• Ellen Degeneres was cast as the scattered Dory, after Stanton saw Degeneres "change the subject five times before finishing one sentence" in an episode of *Ellen.*
• William H. Macy was originally chosen to play Marlin, and recorded all of his dialogue, but ultimately the directors hired Albert Brooks for the part.
• Thomas Newman, composer of the *Finding Nemo* score, is a cousin of Randy Newman.
• The film was re-released in 3D on September 14, 2012.
• An Easter Egg is included on the second disc of the DVD: From the Bonus Features menu select the return icon, and select the green fish.
• Pixar in-jokes: The dentist's camera number is A-113 (14:52), the Pizza Planet truck is seen outside the dentist's office (1:00:52).
• The film won the "Best Animated Film" Academy Award, among many other awards, and was included in the American Film Institute's list of the top 10 American animated films.
• A *Finding Nemo* video game was released for PC, GameCube, PS2, Xbox, Game Boy Advance.
• Additional appearances: Followed by *Finding Dory* (2016).

Finding Dory (PG)

Theatrical release date: June 17, 2016 (premiere June 8, 2016, El Capitan Theatre, Los Angeles)
Production Company: Pixar Animation Studios, Walt Disney Pictures
Length: 97 minutes
Directed by: Andrew Stanton, co-directed by Angus MacLane
Screenplay by: Andrew Stanton, Victoria Strouse, original story by Andrew Stanton

---

Synopsis: Dory, a blue surgeonfish with a serious case of short-term memory loss, grows up with supportive parents, but ends up wandering off on an adventure that takes her far from home (chronicled in *Finding Nemo*). A fragmentary recollection of her past sets her on a journey to find her home and parents, accompanied by clownfish Marlin and Nemo. After being captured by the Marine Life Institute, Dory works with the grouchy octopus Hank to escape, while Marlin and Nemo try to help from the outside. Dory's quest ends in a spectacular — and unforgettable — conclusion.

Cast: Ellen DeGeneres as Dory
Albert Brooks as Marlin
Ed O'Neill as Hank
Kaitlin Olson as Destiny
Hayden Rolence as Nemo
Ty Burrell as Bailey
Diane Keaton as Jenny
Eugene Levy as Charlie

Sloane Murray as Young Dory
Idris Elba as Fluke
Dominic West as Rudder
Bob Peterson as Mr. Ray
Kate McKinnon as Wife Fish
Bill Hader as Husband Fish (Stan)
Sigourney Weaver as Sigourney Weaver
Alexander Gould as Passenger Carl

Music Highlights: "Unforgettable" (Gordon) performed by Sia (orig. by Nat King Cole). Score by Thomas Newman.

Film Facts

• *Finding Dory,* the 17th Pixar film, gives us the backstory on Dory's life, which is helpful, as Dory is not able to provide it herself.
• Dory is a "regal blue tang," a type of surgeonfish.
• Alexander Gould, the original voice of Nemo, was replaced by Hayden Rolence, as Gould's voice had changed since 2003.
• After the credits there is an update on the still-plastic bagged "Tank Gang" from Finding Nemo.
• Easter Eggs: A picture of Darla from *Finding Nemo* is in the background at the Marine Life Institute (22:02). The transport truck includes the CalArts classroom number "A113" (1:19:48). Riley from *Inside Out* is among the kids visiting the MLI (30:40). A seawater supply pipe (1:01:00) is labeled "TL59," short for Tomorrowland 1959, the location and year that the "Submarine Voyage" ride appeared at Disneyland.
• Ratzenberger role: A crab named Bill at the Marine Institute.
• The DVD/Blu-ray include the short "Piper" (2016) which accompanied *Finding Dory* in the theater, with a new short "Marine Life Interviews" (2016), included on the Blu-ray.
• Additional appearances: *Finding Nemo* (2003), "Marine Life Interviews" short (2016).

Flushed Away (PG)

Theatrical release date: November 3, 2006
Production Company: Aardman Animations, DreamWorks Animation
Length: 85 minutes
Directed by: David Bowers, Sam Fell
Screenplay by: Dick Clement & Ian La Frenais and Chris Lloyd & Joe Keenan and Will Davies, story by Sam Fell and Peter Lord and Dick Clement & Ian La Frenais

Synopsis: When his family leaves on vacation, Roddy the rat enjoys having the run of his fine Kensington home, but is soon joined by the uncouth sewer rat Sid. When Roddy tries to flush the unwelcome guest, Sid turns the tables, and Roddy ends up in the sewer, finding Ratropolis, a city of rats. Seeking to return home, he asks for help from savvy boat owner Rita, just before henchmen of the criminal boss the Toad burst in to retrieve a ruby. Roddy and Rita are almost iced, but escape with the ruby. Recognizing the ruby as glass, Roddy breaks it, but offers to get Rita real gems if she helps him get home. They set out on Rita's boat, and are pursued by agents of the Toad, who reveals he was the favored pet of Prince Charles, until he was displaced by a pet rat and flushed away. Toad sends Le Frog to retrieve the "master cable" Rita is wearing as a belt. Le Frog briefly takes the cable, but Rita and Roddy escape, though Rita's beloved boat is lost in the process. They finally arrive at Roddy's home, and Rita gets her gems. After Rita leaves, Roddy realizes that Ratropolis is at risk of being flushed away, and Toad reveals his plan to replace the rat city with a toad city.

Cast: Hugh Jackman as Roddy
Kate Winslet as Rita
Ian McKellen as The Toad
Jean Reno as Le Frog
Bill Nighy as Whitey
Andy Serkis as Spike
Shane Richie as Sid

Kathy Burke as Rita's Mum
David Suchet as Rita's Dad
Miriam Margolyes as Rita's Grandma
Rachel Rawlinson as Tabitha
Susan Duerden as Mother
Miles Richardson as Father
John Motson as Football Commentator

Music Highlights: "Dancing with Myself" (Idol/James) performed by Billy Idol, "Are You Gonna Be My Girl?" (Cester/Munce) performed by Jet, "She's a Lady" (Anka), "Don't Worry, Be Happy" (Bobby McFerrin), "Ice Cold Rita" (Keenan/Baxter), "Bohemian Like You" (Taylor) performed by Dandy Warhols, "Mr. Lonely" (Vinton/Allan), "Proud Mary" (Fogerty) performed by Tina Turner. End credits: "What's New Pussycat?" (Bacharach/David) performed by Tom Jones, "Wonderful Night" (Cook/Daumont) performed by Fatboy Slim. Music by Harry Gregson-Williams.

Film Facts

• The Aardman Animations film *Chicken Run* appears as a DVD on a shelf (2:49).
• Roddy holds up the costume of the X-Men's Wolverine (1:58), a role played by Hugh Jackman in the *X-Men* film series.
• A mid-credits scene appears (1:16:19).
• Credits joke: "No slugs were a-salted during the making of this film." (1:24:12).

The Fox and the Hound (G)

Theatrical release date: July 10, 1981
Production Company: Walt Disney Productions
Length: 83 minutes
Directed by: Art Stevens, Ted Berman, Richard Rich
Story by: Larry Clemmons, Ted Berman, David Michener, Peter Young, Burny Mattinson, Steve Hulett, Earl Kress, Vance Gerry.

Synopsis: An unlikely friendship forms between a young fox kit, Tod, and a bloodhound puppy, Copper, before they know they are supposed to be adversaries. In time Copper is taught to be a hunting dog and the pair's friendship is tested by the expectations of their roles.

Cast: Mickey Rooney as Tod
Kurt Russell as Copper
Pearl Bailey as Big Mama
Jack Albertson as Amos Slade
Sandy Duncan as Vixey
Jeanette Nolan as Widow Tweed
Pat Buttram as Chief

John Fiedler as Porcupine
John McIntire as Badger
Dick Bakalyan as Dinky
Paul Winchell as Boomer
Keith Mitchell as Young Tod
Corey Feldman as Young Copper

Music Highlights: "Best of Friends" (Johnston/Fidel) performed by Pearl Bailey, "Lack of Education" (Stafford) performed by Pearl Bailey, "A Huntin' Man" (Stafford) performed by Jack Albertson, "Goodbye May Seem Forever" (Rich/Patch) performed by Jeanette Nolan, "Appreciate the Lady" (Stafford) performed by Pearl Bailey. Music by Buddy Baker.

Film Facts

• The 24th Disney animated classic, *The Fox and the Hound* was based on the rare 1967 novel by Daniel P. Mannix, written for adults. The idea for a film based based on the novel was proposed by Wolfgang Reitherman, the veteran Disney animator and director who had been involved in almost every key Disney film from *Snow White and the Seven Dwarfs* (1937) on.
• Reitherman was appointed director of the film, paired with co-director Art Stevens, who had been working at Disney since *Fantasia* (1940), and had recently co-directed *The Rescuers* (1977). The up and coming filmmakers involved with this film included Brad Bird (*The Incredibles*), Chris Buck (*Tarzan, Frozen*), Tim Burton (*The Nightmare Before Christmas*), Ron Clements & John Musker (*The Little Mermaid*), John Lasseter (*Toy Story*), and Henry Selick (*James & the Giant Peach*).
• Kurt Russell appeared in several Disney films, but this was his only voice acting role.
• This was the last Disney film with significant input from the members of the "Nine Old Men," Disney's old guard animators, including Frank Thomas, Ollie Johnston, and Woolie Reitherman.
• Tensions between the older and younger animators led to Don Bluth leaving Disney with a number of other animators to form Don Bluth Productions, delaying production of the film.
• A "songs and story" record was issued instead of a full soundtrack. "Best of Friends" is found on *Disney's Greatest 3* CD, *Classic Disney* Vol. 2 CD, and the *Music of Disney: Legacy in Song* box.
• Additional appearances: Followed by *The Fox and the Hound 2* (2006) home media release.

The Fox and the Hound 2 (G)

Home media release date: December 12, 2006
Production Company: DisneyToon Studios, Toon City Animation, Hot Donut Productions
Walt Disney Pictures
Length: 69 minutes
Directed by: Jim Kammerud
Written by: Rich Burns and Roger S. H. Schulman.

Synopsis: The friendship between Tod the fox and Copper the hound is strained as Copper seeks stardom with canine musicians the Singin' Strays, under the leadership of the arrogant Cash, hoping to perform at the Grand Ole Opry. Cash's singing partner Dixie and Tod are both neglected, as is a cricket, until the fox and the hound are reminded of where their loyalties truly lie.

Cast: Reba McEntire as Dixie
Patrick Swayze as Cash
Jonah Bobo as Tod
Harrison Fahn as Copper

Jeff Foxworthy as Lyle
Vicki Lawrence as Granny Rose
Stephen Root as Talent Scout
Jim Cummings as Waylon/Floyd

Music Highlights: "Friends for Life" (Marcus Hummon) performed by One Flew South, "We're in Harmony" (Will Robinson) performed by The Singin' Strays: Reba McEntire, Patrick Swayze, Vicki Lawrence, Jim Cummings, Harrison Fahn, "Hound Dude" (Will Robinson) performed by Josh Gracin, Patrick Swayze, "Good Doggie, No Bone!" (Marcus Hummon) performed by Reba McEntire, "Blue Beyond" (Gordon Kennedy/Blair Masters) performed by Trisha Yearwood, "We Go Together" (Marcus Hummon) performed by Little Big Town with the Singin' Strays, "You Know I Will" (Gordon Kennedy) performed by Lucas Grabeel, "We're in Harmony" (Will Robinson) performed by Chip Davis. Score by Joel McNeely.

Film Facts

• Disney celebrated the twenty-fifth anniversary of *The Fox and the Hound* with the release of this home media film.
• The producers of the film went to Nashville to ask country songwriters to write original songs for different scenes in the film.
• Reba McEntire voiced Artemis on two episodes of *Hercules: The Animated Series* (1998-1999): "Hercules and the Falling Star" and "Hercules and the Caledonian Boar."
• Bonuses on the original DVD included "The Making of the Music" featurette, and the 1939 short "Goofy and Wilbur." The 2011 and 2017 two-movie Blu-ray editions included "Unlikely Friends," a collection of stories of surprising animal friendships.
• This was one of the last home media sequels Disney produced (along with *Bambi II* and *Brother Bear 2*) before John Lasseter's decision to cancel all new Disney sequels.
• Some home media releases pair the film with *The Fox and the Hound* (1981), and one 2014 release added *Oliver & Company* (1988).
• Additional appearances: *The Fox and the Hound* (1981).

Frankenweenie (PG)

Theatrical release date: October 5, 2012
Production Company: Walt Disney Pictures, Tim Burton Productions
Length: 87 minutes
Directed by: Tim Burton
Screenplay by: John August, based on a screenplay by Lenny Ripps, story by Tim Burton

---

Synopsis: The young Victor Frankenstein loves making home monster movies and playing with his dog, Sparky. When he wants to participate in his school's science fair, his father insists he also play baseball. During the game, Victor hits the ball, but Sparky breaks his leash and chases the ball, and is tragically killed by a car. When his science teacher, Mr. Rzykruski, shows how electricity can activate the muscles of a dead frog, Victor immediately plans to bring Sparky back. Using his knowledge of science, Victor harnesses the power of lightning and reanimates Sparky. Victor's classmate Edgar finds out about Sparky, and forces Victor to reanimate a fish for him, which he plans to use to win the science fair, but the fish, which is almost invisible, soon vanishes altogether. Victor's parents finally discover Sparky, who runs away, wandering into the Dutch Day fair, and eventually curling up on his grave. Edgar lets it slip that Victor reanimated Sparky, and his classmates break into Victor's lab, planning a experiments of their own, with monstrous results. Victor and Sparky work to save Victor's peers from their own creations, and despite the mayor's hostility, Sparky demonstrates his heroic nature.

Cast: Catherine O'Hara as Mrs. Frankenstein/
    Weird Girl/Gym Teacher
Martin Short as Mr. Frankenstein/
    Mr. Burgemeister/Nassor
Martin Landau as Mr. Rzykruski
Charlie Tahan as Victor Frankenstein

Atticus Shaffer as Edgar "E" Gore
Winona Ryder as Elsa Van Helsing
Robert Capron as Bob
James Hiroyuki Liao as Toshiaki
Conchata Ferrell as Bob's Mom
Tom Kenny as New Holland Towns Folk

Music Highlights: "Six Powerful Cues (a)" (Wilfred William Burns), "Death of the Alien 1" (Harry Bluestone/Emil Cadkin), "Savage Episode" (Len Stevens), "Green Peppers" (Sol Lake) performed by Herb Alpert & The Tijuana Brass, "Elsa's Song" (John August/Danny Elfman) performed by Winona Ryder, "Folkloric" (Alfred Kluten), "Carousel" (Craig Austin) performed by Craig Austin, "Strange Love" (Karen Orzolek) performed by Karen O. Music by Danny Elfman.

Film Facts

• *Frankenweenie* was originally a 1984 short by Tim Burton, included on the Blu-ray of the film.
• The doghouse-shaped tombstone of Zero from Tim Burton's *The Nightmare Before Christmas* (1993) is included in the pet cemetery (20:01). Sparky's tombstone also appears in Disneyland's annual "Haunted Mansion Holiday" makeover of the Haunted Mansion attraction.
• The Blu-ray includes the short "Captain Sparky vs. the Flying Saucers."
• The film was nominated for the "Best Animated Feature" Academy Award and Golden Globe.

Free Birds (PG)

Theatrical release date: November 1, 2013
Production Company: Reel FX Creative Studios
Length: 91 minutes
Directed by: Jimmy Hayward
Screenplay by: Scott Mosier and Jimmy Hayward, story by David I. Stern & John J. Strauss

Synopsis: Reggie has grown up on a turkey farm, the only resident aware that they are being fattened up for the Thanksgiving kill. He is chosen by the President of the United States as a ceremonially pardoned turkey, and after briefly enjoying a luxurious life in the White House, Reggie is kidnapped by the large, intense turkey Jake, part of the Turkey Freedom Front, who has been told by the "Great Turkey" about a time machine, which they can use to stop Thanksgiving. They end up in a secret U.S. military base where an experimental time machine is being tested, and flee from security into the machine, just as it activates. The machine, identifying itself as S.T.E.V.E., offers to take them anywhere — or any *when* — and Reggie impulsively chooses the first Thanksgiving. They meet the native alpha turkey Ranger, his charming sister Jenny, and their father, Chief Broadbeak. While going out in the woods to disarm traps, Reggie falls for Jenny, and when hunting dogs chase them, they seek refuge in S.T.E.V.E., where Reggie begins to hope that Jenny might join him in the future. Once they get back, Reggie joins Jake on a mission to destroy the Pilgrims' weapons, to try to prevent Thanksgiving. They are successful in their mission, but discovered by the angry Pilgrims, and must make hard choices in order to secure their future.

Cast: Owen Wilson as Reggie
Woody Harrelson as Jake
Amy Poehler as Jenny
George Takei as S.T.E.V.E.
Colm Meaney as Myles Standish
Keith David as Chief Broadbeak
Dan Fogler as Governor Bradford
Jimmy Hayward as Ranger/Leatherbeak/
President /Hazmats
Kaitlyn Maher as President's Daughter
Carlos Alazraqui as Amos
Jeff Biancalana as General Sagan/Hazmats
Danny Carey as Danny
Carlos Ponce as Narrator/Alejandro

Music Highlights: "Up Around the Bend" (John C. Fogerty) performed by Social Distortion (orig. by Creedence Clearwater Revival), "Back in Time" (Marshall Manning) performed by MattyBRaps. Music by Dominic Lewis.

Film Facts

• The line "Those are some angry birds" (1:17:35) references the *Angry Birds* game/franchise.
• The working title of the film was simply *Turkeys*.
• S.T.E.V.E. was voiced by George Takei (Sulu in the *Star Trek* franchise). Takei's catchphrase, "Oh, my!" is included (1:23:46), as it is in the 2016 film *Kubo and the Two Strings* (11:04).
• Governor William Bradford, Myles Standish, and Chief Massasoit are actual historical figures.
• A mid-credits scene appears (1:25:28).

From Up on Poppy Hill (PG)

Theatrical release date: July 16, 2011 (Japan), March 15, 2013 (limited US release)
Country: Japan   **Japanese title**: *Kokuriko-zaka Kara*
Production Company: Studio Ghibli, NTN, Dentsu, Hakuhodo DYMP, Walt Disney Japan, Toho
Length: 91 minutes
Directed by: Gorō Miyazaki
Screenplay by: Hayao Miyazaki and Keiko Niwa

Synopsis: In Japan in the 1960s, Umi Matsuzaki lives in her grandmother's boarding house in the port city of Yokohama, cooking and caring for her sisters and the borders. Her father was killed in the Korean War, and her mother is studying in America. Every morning Umi raises naval flags in her front yard. At her high school, Shun Kazama, editor of the student newspaper, publishes a poem about Umi's flags, and later participates in a risky jump from a roof into a pool. When Umi's sister Sora wants to get Shun's autograph, Umi reluctantly accompanies her to the Latin Quarter, a run-down building that houses the school's many clubs. Umi begins helping with the paper, and later helps work to save the Latin Quarter from being demolished, getting closer with Shun. One day Umi shows Shun a photo of her father and two other sailors. It turns out Shun has the same photo, and questions arise about whether Umi and Shun might have the same father. As Umi learns more about her past, she also needs to face hard truths about her future.

Cast:

Role	English	Japanese
Umi Matsuzaki	Sarah Bolger	Masami Nagasawa
Shun Kazama	Anton Yelchin	Junichi Okada
Hana Matsuzaki	Edie Mirman	Keiko Takeshita
Ryoko Matsuzaki	Jamie Lee Curtis	Jun Fubuki
Miki Hokuto	Gillian Anderson	Yuriko Ishida
Akio Kazama	Chris Noth	Nao Ōmori
Yoshio Onodera	Bruce Dern	Takashi Naito
Shirō Mizunuma	Charlie Saxton	Shunsuke Kazama
Chief Director Tokumaru	Beau Bridges	Teruyuki Kagawa
Sora Matsuzaki	Isabelle Fuhrman	Haruka Shiraishi
Riku Matsuzaki	Alex Wolff/Raymond Ochoa	Tsubasa Kobayashi
Saori Makimura	Christina Hendricks	Eiko Kanazawa

Music Highlights: "Sayonara no Natsu ~Kokuriko-zaka kara~" ("Summer of Farewells - From Up on Poppy Hill") (Yukiko Marimura/Kôichi Sakata) performed by Aoi Teshima, "Ue wo Muite Arukô" (Rokusuke Ei/Hachidai Nakamura) performed by Kyû Sakamoto. Music by Satoshi Takebe.

Film Facts

• The film is based on Chizuru Takahashi and Tetsuro Sayama's graphic novel *Kokurikozaka Kara*.
• The ship at the end of the film has an oval sign reading "Ghibli" (1:24:50), after the studio.
• In the Japanese version, director Gorō Miyazaki voices the school's world history teacher.

Frozen (PG)

Theatrical release date: November 27, 2013
Production Company: Walt Disney Pictures, Walt Disney Animation Studios
Length: 102 minutes
Directed by: Chris Buck and Jennifer Lee
Screenplay by: Jennifer Lee, Story inspired by "The Snow Queen" by Hans Christian Anderson, story by Chris Buck, Jennifer Lee, Shane Morris

Synopsis: Princess Elsa is cursed with an uncontrolled power to create ice and snow, and bears guilt from accidentally injuring her sister, Anna as a child. When the sisters are orphaned, Elsa is crowned Queen, and after Anna impetuously gets engaged on Anna's coronation day, Elsa's power is revealed to the shocked kingdom, leading her to flee to find refuge in an ice castle. Seeking to persuade her sister to return, Anna commandeers the help of ice cutter Kristoff and his reindeer, Sven, but Elsa inadvertently strikes Anna's heart with ice, making her gravely ill. Sven's adoptive family, the trolls, explain that only an act of true love can save her, but Anna's situation looks dire when she learns her love is not so true.

Cast: Kristen Bell as Anna
Idina Menzel as Elsa
Jonathan Groff as Kristoff
Josh Gad as Olaf
Santino Fontana as Hans
Alan Tudyk as Duke
Ciaran Hinds as Pabbie/Grandpa

Chris Williams as Oaken
Stephen J. Anderson as Kai
Maia Wilson as Bulda
Edie McClurg as Gerda
Robert Pine as Bishop
Maurice LaMarche as King

Music Highlights: "Do You Want to Build a Snowman?" performed by Kristen Bell/Agatha Lee Morin/Katie Lopez, "For the First Time in Forever" performed by Kristin Bell/Idina Menzel, "Love is an Open Door" performed by Kristen Bell/Santino Fontana, "Let it Go" performed by Idina Menzel, "Fixer Upper" performed by Maia Wilson/cast. All songs by Kristen Anderson-Lopez and Robert Lopez. Score by Christophe Beck.

Film Facts

• The 53rd Disney animated classic, *Frozen* is inspired by Hans Christian Andersen's story "The Snow Queen." Four key character names combine to approximate Andersen's full name: Hans Kristoff Anna-Sven.
• The song "Spring Pageant" was omitted from the film, but included on the 2-disc soundtrack.
• Elsa was going to be the villain, kidnapping Anna from her wedding and freezing her heart.
• The frightening snow monster created by Elsa is named Marshmallow.
• Elsa's castle changes color depending her emotional state.
• When Elsa is crowned, the bishop says, in Old Norse (similar to Icelandic): "Sem hón heldr inum helgum eignum ok krýnd í þessum helga stað ek té fram fyrir yðr…" translating to: "As she holds the holy properties, and is crowned in this holy place, I present to you...Queen Elsa of Arendelle."
• Additional appearances: Followed by "Frozen Fever" short (2015), "Olaf's Frozen Adventure" featurette (2017), *Frozen II* (2019).

Frozen II (PG)

Theatrical release date: November 22, 2019
Production Company: Walt Disney Animation Studios, Walt Disney Pictures
Length: 103 minutes
Directed by: Chris Buck, Jennifer Lee
Screenplay by: Jennifer Lee, story by Jennifer Lee, Chris Buck, Marc E. Smith, Kristen Anderson-Lopez, Robert Lopez. Story inspired by "The Snow Queen" by Hans Christian Andersen

> **Synopsis**: In their youth, Anna and Elsa's father told them a story of a forest protected by spirits of air, fire, water, and earth. Their grandfather, King Runeard, built a dam as a symbol of peace between Arendelle and the forest tribe of Northuldra. A celebration in the forest unexpectedly turned into a battle. Their mother told them of a river, Ahtohallan, that held answers to the past. In the present, as Kristoff tries to get up the courage to propose to Anna, Elsa begins hearing a mysterious call, and wakes the sprits of the forest, leading to strong winds and an earthquake in Arendelle. The trolls tell Elsa that she must go to the Enchanted Forest to find the truth and right a wrong of the past. Entering the forest, they find the native people, as well as soldiers from Arendelle, who have been frozen in time. As Elsa makes contact with the angry elemental spirits, she learns the truth about what happened in the forest many years ago, and needs to trust her loved ones to help her set it right.

Cast: Kristen Bell as Anna
Idina Menzel as Elsa
Josh Gad as Olaf
Jonathan Groff as Kristoff
Sterling K. Brown as Mattias
Evan Rachel Wood as Iduna

Alfred Molina as Agnarr
Martha Plimpton as Yelena
Jason Ritter as Ryder
Rachel Matthews as Honeymaren
Jeremy Sisto as King Runeard
Ciarán Hinds as Pabbie

Music Highlights: "All Is Found" performed by E. Wood, "Some Things Never Change" performed by cast, "Into the Unknown" performed by I. Menzel/Aurora Aksnes, "When I Am Older" performed by J. Gad, "Reindeer(s) Are Better Than People (Cont.)" performed by J. Groff, "Lost in the Woods" performed by J. Groff, "Show Yourself" performed by cast, "The Next Right Thing" performed by K. Bell. End credits: "Into the Unknown" performed by Panic! at the Disco, "All Is Found" performed by Kacey Musgraves, "Lost in the Woods" performed by Weezer. All songs by Kristen Anderson-Lopez & Robert Lopez. "Vuelie" (Fjellheim/Beck) performed by Cantus and cast. Score by Christophe Beck.

Film Facts

- *Frozen II* was Disney Animation Studio's 58th animated classic.
- The haunting song that calls Elsa to the forest is a kind of "kulning," a Scandinavian herding call.
- The Northuldra tribe is based on the Sámi people of Scandinavia.
- Olaf's invisible "Samantha" (29:09) is a reference to the BBC radio comedy panel game show *I'm Sorry I Haven't a Clue,* which featured an invisible "Samantha" as well as a "Sven."
- A post-credits scene (1:42:00) features Olaf, Marshmallow, and some friends.

Fun and Fancy Free (Approved)

Theatrical release date: September 27, 1947
Production Company: Walt Disney Productions
Length: 70 minutes
Production Supervisor: Ben Sharpsteen. Directed by: Jack Kinney, Bill Roberts, Hamilton Luske
Story by: Homer Brightman, Harry Reeves, Ted Sears, Lance Nolley, Eldon Dedini, Tom Oreb, "Bongo" from an original story by Sinclair Lewis

Synopsis: A package film featuring two stories: "Bongo" depicts a circus bear who escapes to the wild, and must learn the ways of nature as well as the customs of bears if he is to win the heart of Lulubelle. "Mickey and the Beanstalk" puts Mickey, Goofy, and Donald Duck in the "Jack and the Beanstalk" fairy tale, trying to outwit Willie the Giant and retrieve the stolen Golden Harp.

Cast: Edgar Bergan as himself, Charlie McCarthy, and Mortimer Snerd
Dinah Shore as narrator of "Bongo"
Luana Patten as herself
Anita Gordon as the Singing Harp
Cliff Edwards as Jiminy Cricket
Billy Gilbert as Willie the Giant
Clarence Nash as Donald Duck
Pinto Colvig as Goofy
Walt Disney as Mickey Mouse
Music by The Kings Men, The Dinning Sisters, The Starlighters

Music Highlights: "Lazy Countryside" (Worth) performed by Dinah Shore, "Too Good to Be True" (Kaye/Daniel) performed by Dinah Shore, "I'm a Happy Go Lucky Fellow" (Washington/Daniel) performed by Dinah Shore, "My Favorite Dream" (William Walsh/Ray Noble) performed by Anita Gordon, "Say It with a Slap" (Kaye/Daniel) performed by Dinah Shore, "Fun and Fancy Free" (Benjamin/Weiss) performed by Cliff Edwards, "My What a Happy Day" (Walsh/Noble) performed by Anita Gordon, "Fee Fi Fo Fum" (Smith/Quenzer) performed by Billy Gilbert. Music director Charles Wolcott. Score by Paul Smith, Oliver Wallace, and Eliot Daniel.

Film Facts

• The 9th Disney animated classic, and the fourth of the Disney "package" films, *Fun and Fancy Free* paired two shorter films due to limited resources caused by World War II.
• "Mickey and the Beanstalk" was originally intended to be a full-length feature called *The Legend of Happy Valley,* an adaptation of "Jack and the Beanstalk." Mickey had previously tangled with giants in the short "Giantland" (1933), and in "The Brave Little Tailor" (1938).
• "Bongo" was inspired by the children's story *Little Bear Bongo,* by author Sinclair Lewis.
• This was Walt Disney's last film performance as Mickey Mouse, succeeded by Jimmy MacDonald.
• "I'm a Happy Go Lucky Fellow" was originally written for *Pinocchio* (1940).
• Prolific actor Billy Gilbert (Willie the Giant) had previously voiced Sneezy in *Snow White and the Seven Dwarfs* (1937).
• Dinah Shore's "Lazy Countryside" was released as a 78 RPM single in 1947 (Columbia 37884), and is included on her *Cocktail Hour* collection (Columbia River, 2000) and the compilation *Essential Hollywood & Broadway Musicals* CD 2.

The Girl Who Leapt Through Time (TV-PG)

Theatrical release date: July 15, 2006 (Japan)
Country: Japan   **Japanese title**: *Toki o Kakeru Shôjo*
Production Company: Madhouse
Length: 98 minutes
Directed by: Mamoru Hosoda
Screenplay by: Satoko Okudera, based on the novel by Yasutaka Tsutsui

Synopsis: High school student Makoto Konno enjoys hanging out with her friend Yuri and playing baseball with her male friends Chiaki and Kousuke, but struggles with grades and always being late. While she is returning notebooks to a science lab, she sees an odd round object on the floor, leading her to collapse and have a mysterious vision of passing through a landscape with horses and people, then rushes through a technological landscape. On the way home her bicycle brakes fail, and she flies into the path of an oncoming train. The next thing she knows she is lying on the ground a few minutes before the train passed. Her aunt, Auntie Witch, tells her she experienced a "time leap." Makoto experiments with intentional time leaps for selfish reasons, but Auntie Witch raises the question of whether her good fortune may lead to someone else's suffering. When Chiaki asks Makoto if she'd like to start dating, she time leaps to avoid the issue, and when her classmate Takase is taunted and bullied, in a rage he throws a fire extinguisher which hits her friend Yuri. Makoto is horrified when an even worse tragedy occurs, and she cannot stop it because she has used up her time leaps. Chiaki unexpectedly offers help, at great personal cost, and explains more about Makoto's time leaps. Chiaki's sacrifice makes it possible for Makoto to help him in return.

Cast:

Role	English	Japanese
Makoto Konno	Emily Hirst	Riisa Naka
Chiaki Mamiya	Andrew Francis	Takuya Ishida
Kousuke Tsuda	Alex Zahara	Mitsutaka Itakura
Yuri Hayakawa	Kristie Marsden	Ayami Kakiuchi
Kaho Fujitani	Natalie Walters	Mitsuki Tanimura
Miyuki Konno	Shannon Chan-Kent	Yuki Sekido
Kazuko Yoshiyama	Saffron Henderson	Sachie Hara
Moriko Uesugi	Tabitha St. Germain	Shiori Yohari
Sekimi Nowake	Marÿke Hendrikse	Sonoka Matsuoka

Music Highlights: "Ganetto" (Hanako Oku) performed by Hanako Oku, "Kawaranai Mono" (Hanako Oku) performed by Hanako Oku. Music by Kiyoshi Yoshida.

Film Facts

• This film was the first to win the "Animation of the Year" Japan Academy Prize.
• The story is based on Yasutaka Tsutsui's 1967 novel *Toki o kakeru shôjo*, with several changes.
• Initially given a small release, demand for the film grew through word of mouth.

The Good Dinosaur (PG)

Theatrical release date: November 25, 2015
Production Company: Pixar Animation Studios, Walt Disney Pictures
Length: 93 minutes
Directed by: Peter Sohn
Screenplay by: Meg LeFauve, original concept and development by Bob Peterson, story by Peter Sohn, Erik Benson, Meg LeFauve, Kelsey Mann, Bob Peterson

---

Synopsis: In an alternate universe, an asteroid that struck the Earth and wiped out the dinosaurs never did, and dinosaur culture and technology evolves over time. A family of farming dinosaurs is plagued by a pest that keeps stealing their food, a wild young human. After the death of his father in a flood, young dinosaur Arlo and the pest are swept away by a river, leaving them far from home. Though wary of each other at first, Arlo and the pest, soon named "Spot," begin to work together, finding they share more than they thought.

Cast: Jeffrey Wright as Poppa
Frances McDormand as Momma
Maleah Padilla as Young Libby
Ryan Teeple as Young Buck
Jack McGraw as Young Arlo
Marcus Scribner as Buck
Raymond Ochoa as Arlo

Jack Bright as Spot
Peter Sohn as Pet Collector
Steve Zahn as Thunderclap
Mandy Freund as Downpour
Steven Clay Hunter as Coldfront
A.J. Buckley as Nash
Anna Paquin as Ramsey

Soundtrack Highlights: Score by Mychael Danna and Jeff Danna.

Film Facts

• *The Good Dinosaur*, the 16th Pixar film, was conceived in 2009 by Bob Peterson, co-writer of *Finding Nemo* (2003), co-director of *Up* (2009), and co-writer of *Cars 3* (2017), in collaboration with Peter Sohn, who had worked as a story artist, animator, and voice actor on many Pixar films.
• This was the first Pixar film to be scored by two composers, brothers Mychael Danna and Jeff Danna.
• Research for the film included trips to Wyoming, Oregon, and Montana to see open spaces and diverse landscapes, as well as studying the movements of elephants as an analogue for animating the dinosaurs.
• John Ratzenberger makes his customary Pixar appearance as the velociraptor Earl.
• Easter Eggs: A tiny asteroid in the first scene momentarily becomes the Pizza Planet truck from *Toy Story* (1:02), "A113" appears in the bird pen sticks (7:13), the octopus Hank from Pixar's upcoming *Finding Dory* is at the bottom left of the water Arlo falls into (39:32), and the yellow ball with a star from the "Luxo Jr." short appears (40:58).
• The short "Sanjay's Super Team" was shown with the film in theaters, and is included on the DVD/Blu-ray.
• *The Good Dinosaur: Dino Crossing* video game was released for mobile phones.
• Additional appearances: "Hide and Seek" promotional short on the Blu-ray (2016).

A Goofy Movie (G)

Theatrical release date: April 7, 1995
Production Company: Disney MovieToons, Walt Disney Television Animation, Walt Disney Animation Australia, Walt Disney Animation France, Walt Disney Animation Canada
Length: 78 minutes
Directed by: Kevin Lima
Screenplay by: Jymn Magon, Chris Matheson, Brian Pimental, story by Jymn Magon

Synopsis: It's not easy raising a teen, and Goofy's son Max is a handful. It's also not easy being a teen, and Max is frequently embarrassed by his father's antics. After Max gets in trouble at school, Goofy resolves to take him on a cross-country road trip to fish at Lake Destiny, Idaho, recreating a trip he made with his own father. Before they depart, Max is desperate to impress his crush, Roxanne, and impulsively boasts that he will be onstage at a concert by pop idol Powerline. The travails of the trip test the father-son bond of both Goofy and Max, but also help them understand each other better. They're on track to a better relationship, as long as they can survive the perils of the road.

Cast: Bill Farmer as Goofy
Jason Marsden as Max Goof
Jim Cummings as Pete
Kellie Martin as Roxanne
Rob Paulsen as P.J. Pete
Wallace Shawn as Principal Mazur
Jenna von Oÿ as Stacey
Frank Welker as Bigfoot
Kevin Lima as Lester
Jo Anne Worley as Miss Maples

Music Highlights: "I 2 I" (Patrick DeRemer/Roy Freeland) performed by Tevin Campbell featuring Rosie Gaines, "After Today" (Tom Snow/Jack Feldman) performed by Aaron Lohr and chorus, "Stand Out" (Patrick DeRemer/Roy Freeland) performed by Tevin Campbell, "On the Open Road" (Tom Snow/Jack Feldman) performed by Bill Farmer, Aaron Lohr, and chorus, "Lester's Possum Park" (Kevin Quinn/Randy Peterson) performed by Kevin Quinn and chorus, "Nobody Else But You" performed by Bill Farmer and Aaron Lohr (Tom Snow/Jack Feldman). Score by Carter Burwell, additional music/orchestration by Don Davis.

Film Facts

• This was the third Disney MovieToons film, after *DuckTales the Movie: Treasure of the Lost Lamp* (1990) and *The Return of Jafar* (1994). It followed the animated TV series *Goof Troop* (1992), and was originally conceived as a TV special, but along the way was upgraded to a theatrical release.
• Director Kevin Lima made a cameo as Lester, of Lester's Possum Park.
• Kevin Quinn, singer/co-writer of "Lester's Possum Park," went on to play Xander in the *Jessie* spin-off *Bunk'd* (2015-2019).
• At the end of the song "Stand Out," the edge of a decoration that looks like Ariel from *The Little Mermaid* (1989) is seen (10:38). During the song "On the Open Road," Mickey Mouse and Donald Duck are seen trying to hitch a ride (29:05).
• Additional appearances: *Sport Goofy in Soccermania* TV special (1987), *Goof Troop* TV series (1992), *An Extremely Goofy Movie* (2000), *Mickey • Donald • Goofy: The Three Musketeers* (2004).

Goofy: *An Extremely Goofy Movie* (G)

Home media release date: February 29, 2000
Production Company: Walt Disney Video Premiere, Walt Disney Television Animation, Walt Disney Animation Australia
Length: 78 minutes
Directed by: Douglas McCarthy
Screenplay by: Scott Gorden

Synopsis: It's a difficult transition for Goofy when his son, Max, goes to college, and he is fired after his distracted state leads to a catastrophe on the job at the toy assembly factory. He is advised to get a college degree so he can find a new job. When Max gets to campus, he admires skilled skateboarder Bradley Uppercrust III, head of Gamma Mu Mu fraternity. Uppercrust, impressed with Max's skateboarding, invites him to complete with Gamma Mu Mu in the college X Games competition, but Max declines when his best friends P.J. and Bobby are excluded. A rivalry forms between Max and Uppercrust, and to make things even worse, Goofy enrolls at the same college, promising more embarrassing antics. Max introduces Goofy to the college librarian, Sylvia Marpole, in the hopes that she will keep him occupied. By blind luck Goofy seems to be able to skateboard, and is invited by Uppercrust to join his team, setting the stage for a competition like no other.

Cast: Bill Farmer as Goofy
Jason Marsden as Max Goof
Jeff Bennett as Bradley Uppercrust, III/
    Unemployment Lady/Chuck the Sportscaster
Jim Cummings as Pete
Brad Garrett as Tank
Vicki Lewis as Beret Girl in Cafe

Bebe Neuwirth as Sylvia Marpole
Rob Paulsen as P.J. Pete
Pauly Shore as Bobby Zimmeruski
Paddi Edwards as Receptionist at Office
Kath Soucie as Co-Ed/Cafe Cashier
Jenna von Oÿ as Co-Ed
Cree Summer-Francks as Co-Ed/Girl at Club

Music Highlights: "Future's So Bright I Gotta Wear Shades" (MacDonald) performed by Pat Benatar & Neil Giraldo (orig. by Timbuk 3), "Right Back Where We Started From" (Edward/Tubbs) performed by Cleopatra (orig. by Maxine Nightingale), "Knock On Wood" (Floyd/Cropper) performed by Carmen Carter (orig. by Eddie Floyd), "Don't Give Up" (Bartek) performed by Carl Graves, Carmen Carter, John Avila & Terrence A. Carson, "You Make Me Feel Like Dancing" (Sayer/Poncia) performed by Carmen Carter & Donnie McClurkin (orig. Leo Sayer). Music by Steve Bartek.

Film Facts

• The use of the X Games was a bit of cross-promotion, as Disney acquired ESPN in 1996.
• The names of Donald Duck's nephews, Huey, Dewey and Louie, are briefly mentioned (9:37).
• One of the crowd watching Max skate is wearing Goofy's customary green hat, orange shirt, vest, and blue pants (31:42).
• Vocalist Carmen Carter sang on the soundtracks of *The Lion King II* (1998), *Cinderella 2: Dreams Come True* (2002), *The Lion King 1 1/2* (2004), and *Brother Bear 2* (2006).
• Additional appearances: *Sport Goofy in Soccermania* TV special (1987), *Goof Troop* animated TV series (1992), *A Goofy Movie* (1995), *Mickey • Donald • Goofy: The Three Musketeers* (2004).

The Great Mouse Detective (G)

Theatrical release date: July 2, 1986
Production Company: Walt Disney Pictures, Walt Disney Feature Animation
Length: 74 minutes
Directed by: John Musker, Dave Michener, Ron Clements, Burny Mattinson
Story adapted by: Pete Young, Vance Gerry, Steve Hulett, Ron Clements, John Musker, Bruce M. Morris, Matthew O'Callaghan, Burny Mattinson, David Michener, Melvin Shaw, based on the *Basil of Baker Street* book series by Eve Titus and Paul Galdone

---

Synopsis: When the toymaker Flaversham is abducted, leaving his daughter Olivia as the only witness, Basil of Baker Street, the great mouse detective, is called into service. Basil is soon led into a confrontation with his nemesis, the evil Professor Ratigan, whose treacherous plans must be stopped.

Cast: Vincent Price as Professor Ratigan
Barrie Ingham as Basil
Val Bettin as Dawson
Susanne Pollatschek as Olivia

Candy Candido as Fidget
Diana Chesney as Mrs. Judson
Eve Brenner as The Mouse Queen
Alan Young as Flaversham

Music Highlights: "The World's Greatest Criminal Mind" (Henry Mancini/Larry Grossman/Ellen Fitzhugh) performed by Vincent Price, "Goodbye, So Soon" (Henry Mancini/Larry Grossman/Ellen Fitzhugh) performed by Vincent Price, "Let Me Be Good to You" (Melissa Manchester) performed by Melissa Manchester. Music by Henry Mancini.

Film Facts

• The 26th Disney animated classic, *The Great Mouse Detective* is based on the book series *Basil of Baker Street* by Eve Titus, illustrated by Paul Galdone. The film was directed by John Musker, Dave Michener, Ron Clements, and Burny Mattinson, who had worked together on *The Fox and the Hound* (1981). Musker and Clements would later direct *The Little Mermaid* (1989), *Aladdin* (1992), *Hercules* (1997), *Treasure Planet* (2002), *The Princess and the Frog* (2009), and *Moana* (2016).
• The studio's success with *The Rescuers* (1977) led Disney to consider a similar zoological crime fighting story, and Titus' writings were raised as a possibility. The story was not pursued right away due to its similarity to *The Rescuers,* but this was reconsidered by 1980 as the difficult work on *The Black Cauldron* (1985) ground on.
• Vincent Price was famous for his many classic horror films, and ranked *The Great Mouse Detective* as one of his favorite roles.
• The management at Disney sought to include a song that might achieve radio success, initially considering pop artists which would sound quite out of place in London before the turn of the century. They settled on Melissa Manchester, who wrote and sang "Let Me Be Good to You."
• Basil Rathbone, famous for his live-action portrayals of Sherlock Holmes, appears in a brief cameo (22:48).
• Additional appearances: "The World's Greatest Criminal Mind" on *Sing-Along Songs Vol. 10: Beauty and the Beast: Be Our Guest* 1991/1994 VHS.

The Grinch (PG)

Theatrical release date: November 9, 2018
Production Company: Universal Pictures, Universal Animation Studios, Illumination Entertainment
Length: 85 minutes
Directed by: Yarrow Cheney, Scott Mosier
Screenplay by: Michael LeSieur & Tommy Swerdlow, based on the book *How The Grinch Stole Christmas!* by Dr. Seuss

---

Synopsis: The mean-spirited Grinch, with his beleaguered dog Max, lives high above the happy town of Whoville, where overworked Donna Who, mother of Cindy-Lou Who and her twin brothers, tries to balance work and family. As Christmas approaches, the Grinch, an orphan embittered by being left out of holiday celebrations, schemes to steal Christmas, believing that if he takes their gifts and decorations, the Whos will be deprived of the joy he never shared. As the Grinch schemes to steal the joy of Whoville, Cindy-Lou Who schemes to capture Santa Claus, in the hopes of helping her mother. When Cindy-Lou traps the Grinch, her simple kindness gnaws at him, making him uneasy as he steals the Who gifts and decorations. On Christmas morning, just as he is about to topple the stolen gifts, he hears the Whos singing, helping him realize that Christmas isn't about material possessions, but about what's inside.

Cast: Benedict Cumberbatch as The Grinch
Cameron Seely as Cindy-Lou Who
Rashida Jones as Donna Who
Pharrell Williams as Narrator
Tristan O'Hare as Groopert

Kenan Thompson as Mr. Bricklebaum
Sam Lavagnino as Ozzy
Ramone Hamilton as Axl
Angela Lansbury as Mayor McGerkle
Scarlett Estevez as Izzy

Music Highlights: Score by Danny Elfman.

Film Facts

• The lonely Grinch plays the Eric Carmen hit "All By Myself" on the organ (20:05).
• The bat that Cindy Lou and Groopert use to rise to their treehouse says "Theodor" (33:32), in honor of Dr. Theodor Seuss Geisel, better known as Dr. Seuss. Similarly, the sewing machine the Grinch uses to make his Santa suit is called "Theodor" (53:50).
• In *Despicable Me 3* (2017), the Grinch appears on a t-shirt worn by Margo, Gru's oldest daughter (23:35). *The Grinch* also references *Despicable Me,* with the Grinch wearing Gru's scarf (41:02), a snowman representing the minion Carl (9:03), and Edith's unicorn from *Despicable Me 3* (53:03). A stuffed animal resembling Snowball from *The Secret Life of Pets* (2016) also appears in Cindy-Lou's room (55:48).
• The Grinch wears distinctive red and white stripes on his scarf (25:05) and his tie (1:14:50), inspired by Dr. Seuss's classic *The Cat in the Hat.*
• The Grinch says that he's been putting up with the Whos and Christmas for 53 years. Dr. Seuss was 53 years old when he wrote *How the Grinch Stole Christmas!*

Happy Feet (PG)

Theatrical release date: November 17, 2006
Production Company: Warner Bros., Village Roadshow Pictures, Kennedy Miller Productions
Length: 108 minutes
Directed by: George Miller
Written by: George Miller, John Collee, Judy Morris, Warren Coleman

---

Synopsis: Mumble, the just-hatched penguin chick of Norma Jean and Memphis, has an odd tap dance in his walk, and when he is asked to identify his heartsong so he can find a mate, it comes out as tap dance. As he grows, Mumble faces dangers from predators including a skua seabird and a leopard seal, as well as scorn from his peers for not having a heartsong. Mumble befriends a group of Adelie penguins, but ends up blamed by the penguin elder Noah for a famine that has hit the area. His father asks him to renounce his friends and his odd dancing ways, but Mumble explains that he can't. He is exiled, and he and his friends set out to discover the true cause of the famine. They seek the self-professed guru Lovelace, and are joined by Mumble's love, Gloria. Ultimately, Mumble sets out alone, pursuing a massive ship that is capturing the penguins' fish. He meets the "aliens" responsible for the famine, and charms them with his dance, bringing global awareness of the penguins' plight.

Cast: Elijah Wood as Mumble
Robin Williams as Ramón/Lovelace
Brittany Murphy as Gloria
Hugh Jackman as Memphis
Nicole Kidman as Norma Jean
Hugo Weaving as Noah the Elder
Anthony LaPaglia as Boss Skua
E. G. Daily as baby Mumble

Magda Szubanski as Miss Viola
Miriam Margolyes as Mrs. Astrakhan
Fat Joe as Seymour
Steve Irwin as Trev
Carlos Alazraqui as Nestor
Lombardo Boyar as Raul
Jeffrey Garcia as Rinaldo
Johnny Sanchez as Lombardo

Music Highlights: "Kiss" (Prince), "Heartbreak Hotel" (Axton/Durden/Presley), "In My Room" (Wilson/Usher) performed by E.G. Daily & Sydney Children's Choir, "Do It Again" (Wilson/Love) performed by The Beach Boys, "Somebody to Love" (Mercury) performed by Brittany Murphy, "Candela" (Cariello/De Jesus) performed by Da Madd Dominikans, "My Way" (François/Revaux/Anka) performed by Robin Williams, "Boogie Wonderland" (Lind/Willis) performed by cast, "Leader of the Pack" (Barry/Greenwich/Morton) performed by Dan Navarro, "The End" (Lennon/McCartney) performed by k.d. lang, "I Wish" (Stevie Wonder) performed by Patti LaBelle, Yolanda Adams and Fantasia Barrino, "Hit Me Up" (KNS/Farrell) performed by Gia Farrell, "The Joker" (Miller/Curtis/Ertegun) performed by Jason Mraz. Music by John Powell.

Film Facts

- The film won the "Best Animated Feature" Academy Award and got a Golden Globe nomination.
- A DVD bonus scene, "Mumble Meets a Blue Whale," features the late conservationist Steve Irwin.
- The sequel *Happy Feet Two* followed in 2011.

Hercules (G)

Theatrical release date: June 27, 1997
Production Company: Walt Disney Pictures, Walt Disney Feature Animation
Length: 93 minutes
Directed by: John Musker and Ron Clements
Screenplay by: Ron Clements & John Musker, Donald McEnery & Bob Shaw and Irene Mecchi

Synopsis: Hercules, son of Zeus, is prophesied to stop Hades' rise to power. He is stolen by Hades' minions, but not having the heart to dispose of him as planned, the minions leave him on Earth in demi-god form. As a young man Hercules finally learns his identity, and trains with Philocetes (Phil) to prove he is a true hero and regain his godhood. Along the way Hercules falls for Megara (Meg), a mortal whose soul belongs to Hades. Meg's fatal injury leads Hercules to visit the underworld, risking everything to bring Meg back.

Cast: Tate Donovan as Hercules
Joshua Keaton as Young Hercules
Roger Bart as Young Hercules singing
Danny DeVito as Phil
James Woods as Hades

Susan Egan as Meg
Bobcat Goldthwait as Pain
Matt Frewer as Panic
Rip Torn as Zeus
Samatha Eggar as Hera

Music Highlights: "The Gospel Truth" performed by Lillias White, Cheryl Freeman, LaChanze, Roz Ryan, and Vaneese Thomas (The Muses), "Go the Distance" performed by Roger Bart, "One Last Hope" performed by Danny DeVito, "Zero to Hero" performed by Lillias White, Tawatha Agee, Cheryl Freeman, LaChanze, Roz Ryan, and Vaneese Thomas, "I Won't Say (I'm in Love)" performed by Susan Egan, "A Star is Born" performed by The Muses. All songs: music by Alan Menken, lyrics by David Zippel. Score by Alan Menken.

Film Facts

• The 35th Disney animated classic (and the 8th Disney Renaissance film), *Hercules* was directed by Ron Clements and John Musker, the duo behind *The Little Mermaid* (1989) and *Aladdin* (1992).
• Susan Egan, the actress who voiced Meg, has recorded a series of albums, also appearing in *Lady and the Tramp II* (2001), and providing the voice of Meg in *Hercules: The Animated Series* (1998-1999), *Hercules: Hero to Zero* (1999), and the *Kingdom Hearts II* video game.
• Belinda Carlisle of The Go-Go's recorded "I Won't Say (I'm in Love)" for a 1997 CD single.
• In developing the film's visual style, English cartoonist Gerald Scarfe was hired as a production designer, as Clements and Musker admired his work. His fluid artwork was a challenge for the animators, but gave the film a very distinctive look.
• Composer Alan Menken had worked with Clements and Musker on both *The Little Mermaid* (1989) and *Aladdin* (1992), this time collaborating with lyricist David Zippel. At John Musker's request, a gospel style was incorporated into the songs, in stark contrast to Menken's plan to provide a more classic Greek sound.
• A *Hercules* video game was released for PlayStation and Game Boy.
• Additional appearances: *Hercules: Zero to Hero* 1998 VHS, *Hercules: The Animated Series* (1998-1999).

Hercules: Zero to Hero (NR)

Home media release date: August 17, 1999
Production Company: Walt Disney Television Animation, Walt Disney Video Premiere, Walt Disney Animation Australia, Toon City Animation (Philippines), Walt Disney Animation Japan
Length: 70 minutes
Directed by: Bob Kline
Written by: Madellaine Paxson ("Hercules and the Yearbook"), Mark McCorkle/Robert Schooley ("Hercules and the First Day of School"), Greg Weisman ("Hercules and the Grim Avenger"), Gary Sperling ("Hercules and the Visit from Zeus")

Synopsis: Picking up after the events of the *Hercules* film, after Hades' defeat, Hercules has married Meg and looks back on his years at Prometheus Academy, a school attended by both mortals and immortals. The film's stories are drawn from four episodes of *Hercules: The Animated Series* (1998-1999) which were edited together. The episode "Hercules and the Yearbook," which featured Hercules looking back at different memories, was used as a framing device tying the different episodes together.

Cast: Tate Donovan as Hercules
Susan Egan as Meg
Robert Costanzo as Phil
Frank Welker as Pegasus
French Stewart as Icarus
Sandra Bernhard as Cassandra
Corey Burton as Zeus
James Woods as Hades

Bobcat Goldthwait as Pain
Matt Frewer as Panic
Paul Shaffer as Hermes
Eric Stoltz as Theseus
Richard Simmons as Physedipus
Eric Idle as Parenthesis
Diedrich Bader as Adonis
Jodi Benson as Helen of Troy

Music Highlights: "Zero to Hero" Main Title Theme (music by Alan Menken, lyrics by David Zippel) performed by Lillias White, Tawatha Agee, Cheryl Freeman, LaChanze, Roz Ryan, and Vaneese Thomas. Music by Adam Berry.

Film Facts

• Megara, or "Meg" as she is often known, appears in the episode "Hercules and the Yearbook," which begins the film. Original film actress Susan Egan returns to voice the part.
• This title is one of the few home media releases associated with a major Disney film that is only available on VHS. It has never been issued on DVD.
• The combination of different episodes through the use of a framing device was also used in the home media releases *Belle's Magical World* (1998), *Tarzan and Jane* (2002), and *Atlantis: Milo's Return* (2003).
• Composer Adam Berry also wrote music for the *Buzz Lightyear of Star Command* TV series, the *Kim Possible* TV series, and the *Big Hero 6* animated TV series.
• This release was the final title in the *Hercules* franchise, apart from cameo appearances on *House of Mouse* (2001-2003).
• Additional appearances: *Hercules* (1997), and *Hercules: The Animated Series* (1998-1999).

Home (PG)

Theatrical release date: March 27, 2015
Production Company: DreamWorks Animation
Length: 94 minutes
Directed by: Tim Johnson
Screenplay by: Tom J. Astle & Matt Ember, based upon the novel *The True Meaning of Smekday* by Adam Rex

Synopsis: Fleeing from the fearsome Gorg, Captain Smek leads the alien race the Boov to hide on Earth, relocating the humans to Happy Humanstown. The quirky, clumsy Boov named Oh moves into a vacated apartment building, and when trying to invite his neighbors to a housewarming party, hits the wrong button on his phone and invites the entire galaxy — including the Gorg. While fleeing the enraged Boov, Oh runs into the girl Tip Tucci and her cat Pig, who were separated from Tip's mother Lucy, and have been hiding among the Boov. Oh and Tip make a truce, striking out for Paris, so Tip can find out where her mother is, driving Tip's car, which Oh has outfitted with convenience store machines. After evading the Boov, they learn that Oh's phone password is needed to cancel his message before the Gorg receive it. Oh cancels it just in time, and they learn that Tip's mother is in Australia. The Boov briefly catch up with Tip and Oh, but they escape, finally making it to Australia. After an argument with Tip, Oh returns to the Boov and saves them from the Gorg, so the Boov make him their leader. After helping Tip find her mother, Oh finally discovers why the Gorg are chasing the Boov — if he can just get them to talk before they destroy the planet.

Cast: Jim Parsons as Oh
Rihanna as Gratuity "Tip" Tucci
Steve Martin as Captain Smek
Jennifer Lopez as Lucy Tucci
Matt Jones as Kyle
Brian Stepanek as Gorg Commander/
  Father/Boov
April M. Lawrence as Boov Announcer

Music Highlights: "Run To Me" (Yip/Romulus/Reeves/McCullough/Coffee) performed by Clarence Coffee Jr, "Dancing in the Dark" (Hermansen/Eriksen/Dean/McDonald/Fenty) performed by Rihanna, "Towards the Sun" (Carvalho/Baker/Fenty) performed by Rihanna, "As Real as You and Me" (Jerkins/Williams/Fenty) performed by Rihanna. "Only Girl (In the World)" (Hermansen/Eriksen/Johnson/WIlhelm) performed by Rihanna, "Cannonball" (Hermansen/Eriksen/Ellestad/Hanna/Haynie) performed by Kiesza, "Drop That" (Plant/Fenty) performed by Rihanna. End credits: "Red Balloon" (Hermansen/Eriksen/Aitchison/Høiberg) performed by Charli XCX, "Feel the Light" (Hermansen/Eriksen/Ellestad/Haynie) performed by Jennifer Lopez. Music by Lorne Balfe and Stargate.

Film Facts

- The film premiered at the Boulder International Film Festival on March 7, 2015.
- Steve Martin previously appeared in the DreamWorks film *The Prince of Egypt* (1998).
- Additional appearances: the prequel short "Almost Home," shown with *Mr. Peabody and Sherman* (2014) and *Rio 2* (2014), and animated TV series *Home: Adventures with Tip & Oh* (2016–2018).

Home on the Range (PG)

Theatrical release date: April 2, 2004
Production Company: Walt Disney Pictures, Walt Disney Feature Animation
Length: 76 minutes
Directed by: Will Finn and John Sanford
Written by: Will Finn and John Sanford, story by Will Finn, John Sanford, Michael LaBash, Sam Levine, Mark Kennedy, Robert Lence

Synopsis: After Maggie the Cow's herd was stolen by Alameda Slim and the Willie Brothers Gang, she ends up on the Patch of Heaven farm, where she meets fellow cows Grace and Mrs. Calloway. With the farm at risk of foreclosure, the cows pursue Alameda Slim to collect the reward money, aided by the peg-leg rabbit Lucky Jack, in competition with Rico the bounty hunter and Buck the horse.

Cast: Roseanne Barr as Maggie (cow)
Judi Dench as Mrs. Caloway (cow)
Jennifer Tilly as Grace (cow)
Steve Buscemi as Wesley
G.W. Bailey as Rusty (dog)
Cuba Gooding, Jr. as Buck (horse)
Randy Quaid as Slim

Lance Legault as Junior (buffalo)
Charles Dennis as Rico (bounty hunter)
Sam J. Levine as The Willie Brothers
Joe Flaherty as Jeb, the Goat
Richard Riehle as Sheriff
Carol Cook as Pearl (farmer)

Music Highlights: "(You Ain't) Home on the Range" and "Home on the Range (Echo Mine Reprise)" performed by Tim Blevins, Gregory Jbara, William H. Parry, Wilbur Pauley and Peter Samuel, "Little Patch of Heaven" performed by k.d. lang, "Yodle-Adle-Eedie-Idle-Oo" performed by Randy Quaid, Randy Erwin, and Kerry Christenson, "Will the Sun Ever Shine Again" performed by Bonnie Raitt, "Wherever the Trail May Lead" performed by Tim McGraw, "Anytime You Need a Friend" performed by The Beu Sisters. All songs music by Alan Menken, lyrics by Glenn Slater. Score by Alan Menken.

Film Facts

• The 45th of the Disney animated classics, *Home on the Range* was directed by Will Finn and John Sanford. The film began as a treatment titled *Sweating Bullets* written by Mike Gabriel, co-director of *The Rescuers Down Under* (1990) and director of *Pocahontas* (1995), originally focusing on a timid human cowboy who has to contend with the dreaded Slim, a ghostly cattle rustler. Directors Finn and Sanford added elements of the Pied Piper of Hamelin story and a deaf girl, and the protagonist later became a dude, then a boy, then a little bull, and finally the trio of cows.
• The role of Wesley was written for actor Steve Buscemi.
• Patrick Warburton voiced the minor role of Patrick the horse.
• Alan Menken provided the music for the film, working with lyricist Glenn Slater on a series of Western-themed songs.
• A *Home on the Range* video game was released for Game Boy Advance.
• The *Sing Along Songs: Home on the Range: Little Patch of Heaven* 2004 VHS/DVD, included "Little Patch of Heaven," "Yodel-Adle-Eedle-Idle-Oo," and "Anytime You Need a Friend."

Hoodwinked! (PG)

Theatrical release date: January 13, 2006
Production Company: Kanbar Entertainment, Kanbar Animation, Blue Yonder Films
Length: 80 minutes
Directed by: Cory Edwards, co-directed by Todd Edwards, Tony Leech
Screenplay by: Cory Edwards & Todd Edwards and Tony Leech, story by Todd Edwards & Cory Edwards

Synopsis: The Wolf, dressed as Granny Puckett, accosts Red, also known as Little Red Riding Hood. As Red faces the Wolf, a tied-up Granny emerges from the closet, just before the Woodsman bursts in. The police arrive on the scene, and detective Nicky Flippers tries to get to the bottom of things. Each of the suspects tells their tale. Red describes how someone was after Granny's recipes, and she overcome several obstacles to get the recipe book to Granny's house. Next, the Wolf, actually a reporter, tells the story of his investigation of the Goody Bandit. The Woodsman is next, explaining he is an actor named Kirk trying to get a role in a Paul's Bunion Cream commercial, and was instructed by a casting director to work on his inner woodsman. When it's Granny's turn, she explains she secretly lives a very active lifestyle (enjoying extreme skiing), but ended up tied in the closet. As the threads of the four stories are woven together, the real Goody Bandit is revealed.

Cast: Anne Hathaway as Red
Glenn Close as Granny
Jim Belushi as The Woodsman
Patrick Warburton as The Wolf
Anthony Anderson as Detective Bill Stork
David Ogden Stiers as Nicky Flippers

Xzibit as Chief Grizzly
Chazz Palminteri as Woolworth
Andy Dick as Boingo
Cory Edwards as Twitchy
Benjy Gaither as Japeth the Goat
Ken Marino as Raccoon Jerry

Music Highlights: "Great Big World" (T. Edwards) performed by Anne Hathaway, "Little Boat" (Rogers) performed by Daniel Rogers, "Be Prepared" (T. Edwards) performed by Benjy Gaither, "Runaway" (Greene) performed by Joshua J. Greene, "Schnitzel Song" (T. Edwards) performed by Fleming McWilliams feat. Jim Belushi, "The Real G" (C. Edwards/Painter) performed by Cory Edwards, "Tree Critter" (T. Edwards) performed by Todd Edwards, "Blow Your House Down" (Ely Buendia) performed by Pupil, "Eva Deanna" (T. Edwards) performed by Todd Edwards, "Glow" (T. Edwards) performed by Todd Edwards, "Red is Blue" (T. Edwards) performed by Ben Folds, "Top of the Woods" (T. Edwards) performed by Andy Dick, End credits: "Critters Have Feelings" (T. Edwards) performed by Todd Edwards, "Bounce" (C. Edwards/John Mark Painter), performed by Todd Collins. Music by John Mark Painter.

Film Facts

- *Hoodwinked!* was an independent film, funded by Maurice Kanbar, with a low $8 million budget.
- The Wolf is based on Chevy Chase's character Fletch, also a reporter seeking to solve a mystery.
- Additional appearances: *Hoodwinked Too* (2011), which received unfavorable reviews.

Horton Hears a Who! (PG)

Theatrical release date: March 14, 2008
Production Company: Blue Sky Studios, Dr. Seuss Enterprises, 20th Century Fox Animation
Length: 86 minutes
Directed by: Jimmy Hayward, Steve Martino
Screenplay by: Cinco Paul & Ken Daurio, based upon the book by Dr. Seuss

---

Synopsis: The tiny Whos, in their town of Whoville, live on a dust speck, which is carried through the air one day in the Jungle of Nool. The Whos are heard by the kind elephant Horton, who wishes to help them, but the snooty Kangaroo discourages Horton from speaking of such silly matters. Horton begins talking with the Mayor of Whovile, who has his own difficulties in getting the residents of Whoville to believe him when he describes a giant elephant in the sky. Even worse, the Kangaroo persuades the evil vulture Vlad to steal the pink flower upon which the dust speck rests, dropping it in a field of millions of identical pink flowers. Horton patiently sifts through the masses of flowers, finally finding the dust speck flower, only to be tied and caged by a mob generated by the Kangaroo. Every Who must pull together to try to make enough noise to be heard by the skeptical mob, before their dust speck is dropped in boiling beezlenut oil.

Cast: Jim Carrey as Horton
Steve Carell as Mayor
Carol Burnett as Kangaroo
Will Arnett as Vlad
Seth Rogen as Morton
Dan Fogler as Councilman/
      Yummo Wickersham
Isla Fisher as Dr. Mary Lou Larue

Jonah Hill as Tommy
Amy Poehler as Sally O'Malley
Jaime Pressly as Mrs. Quilligan
Charles Osgood as Narrator
Josh Flitter as Rudy
Niecy Nash as Miss Yelp
Jesse McCartney as JoJo
Shelby Adamowsky as Hedy/Hooly

Music Highlights: "Quickie" (Thomas Foyer) performed by Thomas Foyer, "Swingville Sashay" (Muff & Rezz) performed by Muff & Rezz, "Agua Melao" (Candido) performed by Gilberto Candido, "The Blue Danube" (instrumental) (Johann Strauss II), "Can't Fight This Feeling" (Kevin Cronin) performed by cast (orig. by REO Speedwagon). Music by John Powell.

Film Facts

• The children's book *Horton Hears a Who!* was published in 1954.
• References to other Dr. Seuss stories are sprinkled throughout the film, including green eggs and ham from, well, *Green Eggs and Ham* (12:38), the hat from *500 Hats of Bartholomew Cubbins* (16:25), the *Cat in the Hat* cat and fish (18:21), "Thidwick" from *Thidwick the Big-Hearted Moose* (30:16), and the observatory in the shape of the Cat in the Hat's hat (41:41).
• A portrait that the Mayor shows JoJo (14:32) is based on Theodor Geisel (aka Dr. Seuss).
• "Burt from Accounting" is holding a "Who Sky" mug that is based on the Blue Sky logo (1:03:30).
• *Horton Hears a Who!* was previously adapted into a half-hour 1970 TV special.

Hotel Transylvania (PG)

Theatrical release date: September 28, 2012
Production Company: Columbia Pictures, Sony Pictures Animation, Happy Madison Productions
Length: 91 minutes
Directed by: Genndy Tartakovsky
Written by: Peter Baynham and Robert Smigel, story by Todd Durham and Dan Hageman & Kevin Hageman

---

Synopsis: Protective single dad Dracula has created a castle far from humans, determined to keep his pledge to his late wife to protect their daughter Mavis. The castle becomes the popular monster tourist destination Hotel Transylvania. All is well until Mavis's 118th birthday, when her father promised she could see the outside world. To protect her, Dracula creates a fake town stocked with zombies posing as hostile humans to scare Mavis back to the safety of the castle. Just when he thinks they are safe, clueless hiker Jonathan wanders into the castle, assuming all the monsters are people in costumes. A panicked Dracula disguises him as a Frankenstein monster to avoid attracting attention, but Johnny catches Mavis's eye anyway. A human-vampire romance begins to develop, but Dracula convinces Johnny that it is safer for Mavis if he leaves. Johnny pretends to hate monsters and storms off, leaving Mavis's heartbroken. Seeing her despair, Dracula has a change of heart, and gathers his crew to try to bring Johnny back.

Cast: Adam Sandler as Dracula
Andy Samberg as Jonathan
Selena Gomez as Mavis
Kevin James as Frankenstein
Fran Drescher as Eunice
Steve Buscemi as Wayne

Molly Shannon as Wanda
David Spade as Griffin
CeeLo Green as Murray
Jon Lovitz as Quasimodo
Brian George as Suit of Armor
Luenell as Shrunken Heads

Music Highlights: "The Zing" (Sandler/Smigel/White) performed by Andy Samberg, CeeLo Green, Selena Gomez, Adam Sandler and Kevin James. "Problem (The Monster Remix)" (Dr. Luke/Walter/Gomez/Adams) performed by Becky G featuring Will.i.am. Score by Mark Mothersbaugh.

Film Facts

• A short related to the film, "Goodnight Mr. Foot," was shown before *Hotel Transylvania* in theaters, and is included on the DVD/Blu-ray.
• Dracula lives in Transylvania, which is now part of Romania, and the license plate on his hearse, reading UNDEAD, is accurately shown as a Romanian plate (5:10).
• Mavis has a painting of Selena Gomez, who voices Mavis, in her room (10:41).
• In "You're My Zing," Jonathan references Nala and Simba from Disney's *The Lion King* (1994) (1:21:04).
• The film began production in 2006, going through six directors by the time it was completed.

Hotel Transylvania 2 (PG)

Theatrical release date: September 25, 2015
Production Company: Columbia Pictures, Sony Pictures Animation
Length: 89 minutes
Directed by: Genndy Tartakovsky
Written by: Robert Smigel & Adam Sandler, based on characters created by Todd Durham

Synopsis: Dracula's daughter Mavis and her human love Jonathan are married, and soon have a son, Dennis. Anxious for Dennis to get his fangs, Dracula takes Dennis out with Frankenstein, Wayne the wolf-man, Murray the mummy, Griffin the Invisible Man (and, somewhat reluctantly, Blobby), to let each monster inspire Dennis to find his "inner monster" by watching them in action. Meanwhile, Jonathan and Mavis visit the human world, where Mavis is enchanted with the wonders of the 24-hour mini-mart and the skate park, but is unsure whether life among humans is right for them after time with Jonathan's family. Dracula's plans go awry, but Dennis ends up having a great time. Things get complicated when Mavis invites Dracula's very old school father, Vlad, to Dennis's birthday party. Vlad is shocked and judgmental when he learns that Dennis is half-human, but soon realizes that it's not the monster in the fight, it's the fight in the monster.

Cast: Adam Sandler as Dracula
Andy Samberg as Jonathan
Selena Gomez as Mavis
Kevin James as Frankenstein
Steve Buscemi as Wayne
David Spade as Griffin
Keegan-Michael Key as Murray
Asher Blinkoff as Dennis

Fran Drescher as Eunice
Molly Shannon as Wanda
Megan Mullally as Grandma Linda
Nick Offerman as Grandpa Mike
Dana Carvey as Dana
Rob Riggle as Bela
Mel Brooks as Vlad
Jonny Solomon as Blobby

Music Highlights: "I'm in Love With a Monster (Remix)" (Samuels/Reece/Mancuso/Etienne/Coulter) performed by Fifth Harmony, "Monster Mash" (Leonard Capizzi/Bobby Pickett) performed by Bobby "Boris" Pickett, "Worth It" (Collins/Eriksen/Hermansen/Kaplan/Renea) performed by Fifth Harmony, "Johnny's Girl" (Baxter/Sandler/Smigel), "Daddy's Girl" (Sandler/Smigel), "Suffer, Suffer, Scream In Pain" (Taylor/Sandler/Smigel, based on "Twinkle, Twinkle, Little Star," M: trad., L: Jane Taylor), "Friends Forever" (Baxter/Sandler/Smigel), "Nutsy Koo Koo" (Worster/Sandler/Smigel), "Phantom" (Baxter/Sandler/Smigel). Music by Mark Mothersbaugh.

Film Facts

• Jonathan's vampire costume is based on Gary Oldman's look in *Bram Stoker's Dracula* (1992).
• The video Mavis angrily shows Dracula features a photo of Dr. Frankenstein from *Young Frankenstein* (1974) and the Joker from the *Batman* TV series (1966-1968).
• A man tells Dracula "Love your chocolate cereal!" (36:29) referring to Count Chocula cereal.
• A game based on the film was made for mobile phones.

Hotel Transylvania 3 (PG)

Theatrical release date: July 13, 2018
Production Company: Columbia Pictures, Sony Pictures Animation, MRC
Length: 97 minutes
Directed by: Genndy Tartakovsky
Written by: Genndy Tartakovsky and Michael McCullers

Synopsis: To get away from the stress of Hotel Transylvania, the young vampire Mavis, her husband Johnny, her son Dennis, and her father Dracula, book passage on the cruise ship Legacy, joined by several of their friends. Dracula, who has been in mourning for his late wife Martha, is surprised to find himself attracted to the captain of the Legacy, Ericka. Unbeknownst to Dracula, Ericka is the great-granddaughter of his old foe Abraham Van Helsing. Van Helsing, now more machine than man, is hiding on the ship, with a plan to destroy the monsters upon their arrival in Atlantis. Unable to wait, Ericka attempts to kill Dracula, and Frankenstein and Murray overhear her lamenting that she has been unable to "get" him, thinking she's interested in him romantically. Dracula asks her on a date, during which Ericka begins to fall for Drac, to her surprise. Ericka is torn between her family's hostility and her feelings for Dracula, and finally breaks things off with him, retrieving an Instrument of Destruction for Van Helsing. When the monsters have a huge dance party at Atlantis, Van Helsing uses ancient music to summon a giant Kraken to destroy the monsters, but Johnny fights back with positive, inspirational music.

Cast: Adam Sandler as Dracula
Andy Samberg as Johnny
Selena Gomez as Mavis
Kevin James as Frankenstein
Fran Drescher as Eunice
Steve Buscemi as Wayne
Molly Shannon as Wanda
David Spade as Griffin

Keegan-Michael Key as Murray
Jim Gaffigan as Van Helsing
Kathryn Hahn as Ericka
Asher Blinkoff as Dennis
Chris Parnell as Stan/Fish Man
Joe Jonas as The Kraken
Chrissy Teigen as Crystal
Mel Brooks as Vlad

Music Highlights: "I'm in Love With a Monster" (Samuels/Reece/Mancuso/Etienne/Coulter) performed by Fifth Harmony, "I See Love" (Robin/Allan/Schoorl/McIldowie) performed by Jonas Blue/Joe Jonas, "Float" (Nam/Grigg/Powell) performed by Eric Nam, "It's Party Time" (Foster/Bublé) performed by Joe Jonas, "Seavolution" (Verwest), "Wave Rider" (Verwest), and "Tear It Down" (Verwest) performed by Tiësto, "Good Vibrations" (Wilson/Love) performed by The Beach Boys, "Don't Worry Be Happy" (McFerrin) performed by Bobby McFerrin, "Macarena" (Romero/Ruiz) performed by Los del Río. Music by Mark Mothersbaugh.

Film Facts

• The DVD/Blu-ray include the shorts "Puppy!" and "Goodnight Mr. Foot."
• The film's story was based in part on writer/director Tartakovsky's terrible vacation experiences.
• The plane wing gremlin (15:12) recalls *The Twilight Zone* episode "Nightmare at 20,000 Feet."

How the Grinch Stole Christmas! (NR)

Theatrical release date: December 18, 1966
Production Company: Cat in the Hat Productions, MGM Animation/Visual Arts
Length: 26 minutes
Directed by: Chuck Jones, co-director Ben Washam
Written by: Dr. Seuss, additional story Irv Spector and Bob Ogle

---

Synopsis: The Grinch, a nasty, reclusive grouch, has spent 53 years at the top of Mount Crumpit, putting up with the insufferable joy, noise, and singing of the Whos down in Whoville every Christmas season. He develops the awful plan to dress up as Santa Claus and steal the Whos holiday decorations and gifts, leaving them to cry on Christmas morning. Dressing his dog Max as a reindeer, the Grinch strikes out with his sleigh, stealing stockings, presents, lights, and Christmas trees. When he is caught red-handed by the 2 year old Cindy Lou Who, the Grinch lies to the child, telling her he is fixing a light on the tree. On Christmas morning, the Grinch listens eagerly for the sobbing of the Whos, but is shocked to hear singing instead. He realizes that Christmas is not about ribbons, tags, packages, boxes or bags, leading to a literal change of heart. Unfortunately, just as the Grinch sees the light, the sleigh with the Whos Christmas things begins to slide off the mountain. The Grinch must draw upon the strength that his new understanding provides.

Cast: Boris Karloff as Narrator/The Grinch   Dal McKennon as Max
June Foray as Cindy Lou Who

Music Highlights: "Welcome Christmas/Trim Up the Tree" (lyrics Dr. Seuss/music Albert Hague) performed by cast, "You're a Mean One, Mr. Grinch" (lyrics Dr. Seuss/music Albert Hague) performed by Thurl Ravenscroft. Songs by Albert Hague, additional music by and orchestra conducted by Eugene Poddany.

Film Facts

• The special was based on Dr. Seuss's 1957 children's book *How the Grinch Stole Christmas!*
• Director Chuck Jones, best known for directing many classic Looney Tunes episodes, worked with Dr. Seuss on the 1940s *Private Snafu* shorts produced for the military.
• Thurl Ravenscroft, uncredited singer of "You're a Mean One, Mr. Grinch," voiced Tony the Tiger in Frosted Flakes cereal TV commercials, and a Wickersham Brother in the *Horton Hears a Who!* TV special (1970), as well as appearing in Disney's *The Aristocats* (1970) and *One Hundred and One Dalmatians* (1961).
• A soundtrack LP was issued in 1966 on the MGM label Leo the Lion Records.
• Additional appearances: the animated prequel *Halloween is Grinch Night* (1977), the animated special *The Grinch Grinches the Cat in the Hat* (1982), the live-action *How the Grinch Stole Christmas* (2000), and the animated film *The Grinch* (2018).
• The specials *How the Grinch Stole Christmas!* (1966), *Halloween is Grinch Night* (1977), and *The Grinch Grinches the Cat in the Hat* (1982) are included on the 2012 DVD box set *Dr. Seuss: Holidays on the Loose*.

How to Train Your Dragon (PG)

Theatrical release date: March 26, 2010
Production Company: DreamWorks Animation
Length: 98 minutes
Directed by: Chris Sanders and Dean DeBlois
Screenplay by: Will Davies and Dean DeBlois & Chris Sanders, based on the book by Cressida Cowell

Synopsis: Hiccup has grown up in a Viking village, but has never fit in. As the village deals with a persistent dragon problem, Hiccup's thoughtful methods are a poor fit with the rough and tumble ways of the Vikings, to the constant disappointment of his father, Stoick, the chief of the village. When Hiccup manages to trap a Night Fury, a dragon which has never been defeated, he doesn't have the heart to kill it, freeing it instead. The Night Fury's tail was damaged, preventing it from flying away, and despite his fear, Hiccup gradually befriends the dragon, naming it Toothless and inventing a replacement tail fin so it can fly. Along with the other young vikings, Astrid, Snotlout, Fishlegs, Tuffnut and Ruffnut, Hiccup is required to train in fighting dragons, but spends his free time learning all about Toothless, and using this knowledge to tame dragons rather than attacking them, figuring out that everything the Vikings thought they knew about dragons is wrong. Hiccup, who is expected to become a dragonslayer, vows to put things right between humans and dragons once and for all, but to do so he must find a way to heal the mistrust on both sides.

Cast: Jay Baruchel as Hiccup
Gerard Butler as Stoick
Craig Ferguson as Gobber
America Ferrera as Astrid
Jonah Hill as Snotlout
Christopher Mintz-Plasse as Fishlegs
T.J. Miller as Tuffnut

Kristen Wiig as Ruffnut
Robin Atkin Downes as Ack
Philip McGrade as Starkard
Kieron Elliott as Hoark the Haggard
Ashley Jensen as Phlegma the Fierce
David Tennant as Spitelout

Music Highlights: "Sticks and Stones" (Jónsi) performed by Jónsi. Music by John Powell.

Film Facts

• DeBlois & Sanders co-directed *Lilo & Stitch* (2002). Sanders also co-directed *The Croods* (2013).
• Cressida Cowell wrote a series of 12 novels on dragons, beginning with *How to Train Your Dragon* (2003), *How to Be a Pirate* (2004), and *How to Speak Dragonese* (2005).
• Additional appearances: *How to Train Your Dragon 2* (2014) and *How to Train Your Dragon: The Hidden World* (2019), shorts "Legend of the BoneKnapper Dragon" (2010, 17 min.), "Book of Dragons" (2011, 17 min.), "Dragons: Gift of the Night Fury" (2011, 22 min.), "Dragons: Dawn of the Dragon Racers" (2014, 26. min.), "How to Train Your Dragon: Homecoming" (2019, 22 min.), and TV series *Dragons: Riders of Berk* (2012-2013), *Dragons: Defenders of Berk* (2013-2014), *Dragons: Race to the Edge* (2015-2018), and *Dragons: Rescue Riders* (2019-2020).

How to Train Your Dragon 2 (PG)

Theatrical release date: June 13, 2014
Production Company: DreamWorks Animation, distributed by 20th Century Fox
Length: 102 minutes
Directed by: Dean DeBlois
Written by: Dean DeBlois, based on the *How to Train Your Dragon* book series by Cressida Cowell

Synopsis: Humans and dragons now live in harmony. Rather than participating in dragon races, Hiccup and his Night Fury dragon Toothless are off making a map of dragons in the lands around the island of Berk. In the process, he and Astrid run across a huge mass of ice with the frozen wreckage of ships. As they approach, Astrid's dragon is captured by a net, and they meet Eret and the dragon trappers of Drago Bludvist, who is building a dragon army. Stoick, chief of Berk and Hiccup's father, knows Drago as a merciless madman, explaining that Drago killed the other Viking chieftains when they would not follow him. Hiccup remains determined to try to get Drago to see that peace is possible. When Hiccup is captured by a mysterious figure named Valka, he begins to learn more about both his past and his future. While Hiccup is gone, Astrid, Snotlout, Fishlegs, Tuffnut and Ruffnut attempt a rescue, believing that Hiccup has been captured by Drago Bludvist. Unfortunately, once Drago learns of Berk and its dragons, he sets his sights on conquering the island. It turns out that Drago has a massive Bewilderbeast, and Hiccup learns at a great price that some people can't be reasoned with.

Cast: Jay Baruchel as Hiccup
Cate Blanchett as Valka
Gerard Butler as Stoick
Craig Ferguson as Gobber
America Ferrera as Astrid
Jonah Hill as Snotlout
Christopher Mintz-Plasse as Fishlegs
T.J. Miller as Tuffnut
Kristen Wiig as Ruffnut
Djimon Hounsou as Drago
Kit Harington as Eret
Kieron Elliott as Hoark the Haggard
Philip McGrade as Starkard
Andrew Ableson as Ug
Gideon Emery as Teeny
Randy Thom as Toothless

Music Highlights: "Where No One Goes" (Jon Thor Birgisson/John Powell) performed by Jónsi and John Powell, "For the Dancing and the Dreaming" (Shane MacGowan/Birgisson/Powell) performed by Gerard Butler, Craig Ferguson and Mary Jane Wells, "Into a Fantasy" (Alexander Rybak) performed by Alexander Rybak. Music by John Powell.

Film Facts

• Dean DeBlois wrote the role of Valka with Cate Blanchett in mind.
• The animated series *Dragons: Race to the Edge* (2015-2018) takes place before this film.
• The film was nominated for the "Best Animated Feature" Academy Award, and won the "Best Animated Feature Film" Golden Globe and Annie awards.
• Dean DeBlois agreed to make this film if he could also make a third, creating a full trilogy.

How to Train Your Dragon: The Hidden World (PG)

Theatrical release date: February 22, 2019
Production Company: DreamWorks Animation, Dentsu, Fuji Television
Length: 104 minutes
Directed by: Dean DeBlois
Written by: Dean DeBlois, based on the *How to Train Your Dragon* book series by Cressida Cowell

Synopsis: Hiccup, chief of the Vikings of Berk, has assembled a team of dragon riders, freeing dragons captured by trappers and bringing them back to Berk. The dragon killer Grimmel the Grisly works with the trappers to defeat the Vikings of Berk, while Hiccup has his own plan, to find the Hidden World, a legendary land all dragons are said to come from, and relocate everyone there. Hiccup's dragon, Toothless, comes across a white female Light Fury, and soon after finds a dragon trap in the woods. Grimmel appears in Hiccup's house, telling him he will destroy Berk if Hiccup does not give him Toothless. Hiccup proposes to the people of Berk that they find the Hidden World. They travel to the west, and stop at an area they call New Berk. The Light Fury finds Toothless there, and he follows her, beginning a courtship, but is unable to follow far due to his injured tail. Hiccup makes him a new tail fin, and Toothless sets off to find her. Meanwhile Valka, Hiccup's mother, rides out to make sure they weren't followed, and is attacked by Grimmel's forces, returning to tell Hiccup they are being tracked. Hiccup and the dragon riders go on a stealth mission to try to stop Grimmel, but are quickly caught. They escape, but Hiccup's confidence is shaken when Toothless has not returned after leaving with the Light Fury. Astrid takes Hiccup to look for Toothless, and they finally find the Hidden World. When the dragons there threaten Hiccup, Toothless saves him, but Grimmel arrives to capture Toothless, and take all of Berk's dragons with him. It falls to Astrid to remind Hiccup of the leader he can be: the kind willing to sacrifice everything for those he loves, and inspiring the same loyalty in others.

Cast: Jay Baruchel as Hiccup
America Ferrera as Astrid
F. Murray Abraham as Grimmel
Cate Blanchett as Valka
Gerard Butler as Stoick
Craig Ferguson as Gobber
Jonah Hill as Snotlout

Christopher Mintz-Plasse as Fishlegs
Kristen Wiig as Ruffnut
Kit Harington as Eret
Justin Rupple as Tuffnut
Robin Atkin Downes as Ack
Kieron Elliott as Hoark
Julia Emelin as Griselda the Grevious

Music Highlights: "Together from Afar" (Jónsi) performed by Jónsi. Music by John Powell.

Film Facts

- *The Hidden World* was the third installment of a planned trilogy.
- The home media releases included the DreamWorks shorts "Bilby" and "Bird Karma."
- The film was nominated for the "Best Animated Feature" Academy Award and Golden Globe.

Howl's Moving Castle (PG)

Theatrical release date: Sep 5, 2004 (Venice Film Festival), Nov 20, 2004 (Japan), Jun 17, 2005 (US)
Country: Japan Japanese title: *Hauru No Ugoku Shiro*
Production Company: Studio Ghibli, Dentsu, Mitsubishi
Length: 119 minutes
Directed by: Hayao Miyazaki
Written by: Hayao Miyazaki, from the novel by Diana Wynne Jones

Synopsis: The young milliner Sophie meets a curious man who says he is being followed, asking her to come with him. It isn't long before they're pursued by a horde of slithering black creatures, and the man levitates them both to safety. Sophie is later visited at her hat shop by the Witch of the Waste, who turns her into an old woman. She makes her way to the Waste, where witches and wizards dwell. Howl's "moving castle," walking on chicken legs, finally comes by, allowing Sophie inside where she meets the trapped fire spirit Calcifer, the young apprentice Markl, and finally Howl. She gives the castle a thorough cleaning, while Howl tries to cope with two kingdoms determined to go to war with each other. When he is summoned to see the king, Howl asks Sophie to go in his place. The king's sorceress, Madame Suliman, attempts to use Sophie to catch Howl, but he is able to rescue her, after Suliman shows them a vision of Howl as a large bird-like creature. Howl and Calcifer use their magic to move the castle, but the war continues to threaten everyone's safety. Sophie must try to solve the mysteries surrounding Howl, before it's too late.

Cast: Role	English	Japanese
Sophie Hatter	Jean Simmons/Emily Mortimer (young)	Chieko Baisho
Howl	Christian Bale	Takuya Kimura
Witch of the Waste	Lauren Bacall	Akihiro Miwa
Calcifer	Billy Crystal	Tatsuya Gashuin
Markl	Josh Hutcherson	Ryūnosuke Kamiki
Suliman	Blythe Danner	Haruko Kato
Lettie	Jena Malone	Yayoi Kazuki
Honey	Mari Devon	Mayuno Yasokawa
Prince Justin/Turnip Head	Crispin Freeman	Yō Ōizumi
King of Ingary	Mark Silverman	Akio Ōtsuka

Music Highlights: "Sekai no Yakusoku" (Yumi Kimura) performed by Chieko Baisho. Score by Joe Hisaishi.

Film Facts

• The film was critically hailed, receiving a "Best Animated Feature" Academy Award nomination.
• Science fiction/fantasy writer Diana Wynne Jones wrote three books in the "Howl Series," *Howl's Moving Castle* (1986), *Castle in the Air* (1990), and *House of Many Ways* (2008).
• As is often the case, the book provides a much fuller understanding of the story.

The Hunchback of Notre Dame (G)

Theatrical release date: June 21, 1996
Production Company: Walt Disney Pictures, Walt Disney Feature Animation
Length: 91 minutes
Directed by: Gary Trousdale and Kirk Wise
Screenplay by: Tab Murphy, Irene Mecchi, Bob Tzudiker & Noni White, and Jonathan Roberts, animation story by Tab Murphy, from the Victor Hugo novel *Notre Dame de Paris*

Synopsis: Taken from his gypsy parents as a baby, Quasimodo was raised in Notre Dame cathedral as a bell ringer, with only three stone gargoyles as his companions. Schooled by the harsh judge Frollo, Quasimodo longs to live in the larger world. After inadvertently being crowned the King at the Festival of Fools, Quasimodo is enchanted with the lovely gypsy Esmeralda, and understanding what it is to be an outsider, seeks to help her find freedom, and in the process finds his own.

Cast: Tom Hulce as Quaimodo
Demi Moore as Esmeralda
Tony Jay as Frollo
Kevin Kline as Phoebus
Paul Kandel as Clopin
Jason Alexander as Hugo
Charles Kimbrough as Victor
Mary Wickes as Laverne

David Ogden Stiers as Archdeacon
Mary Kay Bergman as Quasimodo's Mother
Corey Burton as Brutish Guard
Jim Cummings as Guards and Gypsies
Bill Fagerbakke as Oafish Guard
Heidi Mollenhauer as Esmeralda (singing voice)
Frank Welker as Baby Bird

Music Highlights: "The Bells of Notre Dame" performed by Paul Kandel, David Ogden Stiers, Tony Jay/chorus, "Out There" performed by Tom Hulce and Tony Jay, "Topsy Turvy" performed by Paul Kandel and crowd, "The Court of Miracles" performed by Paul Kandel/chorus, "Someday" performed by All-4-One. All songs music by Alan Menken, lyrics by Stephen Schwartz. Score by Alan Menken.

Film Facts

• The 34th Disney animated classic, and seventh of the Disney Renaissance, *The Hunchback of Notre Dame* was directed by Kirk Wise and Gary Trousdale, a duo known for directing *Beauty and the Beast* (1991), and who would later collaborate on *Atlantis: The Lost Empire* (2001). The story was based on Victor Hugo's 1831 novel *The Hunchback of Notre-Dame*.
• Some much needed comic relief was provided by a trio of stone gargoyles, voiced by Charles Kimbrough as Victor, Jason Alexander as Hugo (Victor-Hugo — get it?), and Mary Wickes as LaVerne (as in the Andrews Sisters: Maxine, Patty, and LaVerne).
• Music was a key element of the film, provided by composer Alan Menken, a Disney mainstay, and lyricist/composer Stephen Schwartz (*Godspell*, 1971, *Pippin*, 1972, *Wicked*, 2003).
• During the song "Out There" there are cameos from a few Disney characters, including Belle of *Beauty and the Beast,* reading a book as she walks, the flying carpet from *Aladdin,* and Pumbaa from *The Lion King* (15:05).
• Additional appearances: *The Hunchback of Notre Dame II* (2002).

The Hunchback of Notre Dame II (G)

Home media release date: March 19, 2002
Production Company: Walt Disney Pictures, Walt Disney Video Premiere, Walt Disney Television Animation, Walt Disney Animation Japan
Length: 68 minutes
Directed by: Bradley Raymond
Screenplay by: Jule Selbo and Flip Kobler & Cindy Marcus

Synopsis: Quasimodo is smitten with a circus performer, Madellaine, on the *Jour d'Amour* ("day of love"), but soon learns she is part of a criminal gang when Madellaine leads Quasimodo away from the bell tower during the theft of the jewel-encrusted *La Fidele* bell. Unbeknownst to Quasimodo, Madellaine's deception was to prevent an attack by the cruel circus master Sarousch. When Sarousch attempts to flee the city by holding hostage Phoebus and Esmeralda's son, Zephyr, Madellaine has an opportunity to redeem herself in Quasimodo's eyes.

Cast: Jason Alexander as Hugo
Jennifer Love Hewitt as Madellaine
Tom Hulce as Quasimodo
Paul Kandel as Clopin
Charles Kimbrough as Victor
Kevin Kline as Phoebus
Michael McKean as Sarousch
Demi Moore as Esmeralda
Haley Joel Osment as Zephyr
Jane Withers as Laverne

Music Highlights: "I'm Gonna Love You (Madellaine's Love Song)" (Jennifer Love Hewitt/Chris Canute) performed by Jennifer Love Hewitt, "Le Jour d'Amour" (Randy Petersen/Kevin Quinn) performed by Jason Alexander, Tom Hulce, Paul Kandel, Charles Kimbrough, and Jane Withers, "An Ordinary Miracle" (Walter Edgar Kennon) performed by Tom Hulce, "I'd Stick With You" (Kennon) performed by Tom Hulce and Haley Joel Osment, "Fa La La La Fallen in Love" (Kennon) performed by Jason Alexander, Charles Kimbrough, and Mary Jay Clough. Music by Carl Johnson.

Film Facts

• When Jennifer Love Hewitt learned that her character did not have a song in the film, she co-wrote one and submitted it to the producers, who used it during the end credits.
• DVD bonus features include "Behind the Scenes with Jennifer Love Hewitt" and Hugo (Jason Alexander) performing the peculiar jazz poem, "It's Not Easy Being a Gargoyle."
• Director Bradley Raymond previously directed *Pocahontas II: Journey to a New World* (1998), and a segment of *Mickey's Once Upon a Christmas* (1999), going on to direct *The Lion King 1½* (2004), and three Tinker Bell films.
• Jane Withers replaced Mary Wickes as the gargoyle LaVerne. Wickes passed away during the filming of the first movie, with Withers stepping in to complete her lines.
• No soundtrack was released from the film. "I'm Gonna Love You (Madellaine's Love Song)" appears on *Disney's Superstar Hits* CD (2002).
• Additional appearances: Follows *The Hunchback of Notre Dame* (1996). Quasimodo and Esmeralda appeared in some episodes of *House of Mouse* (2001-2003).

Ice Age (PG)

Theatrical release date: March 15, 2002
Production Company: Blue Sky Studios, 20th Century Fox Animation
Length: 81 minutes
Directed by: Chris Wedge, co-directed by Carlos Saldanha
Screenplay by: Michael Berg, Michael J. Wilson and Peter Ackerman, story by Michael J. Wilson

Synopsis: Feeling the coming ice age, a great migration of dinosaurs and other prehistoric animals are heading south. The socially awkward Sid the Sloth runs afoul of two rhino-like brontotheres, and is rescued by the lonely mammoth Manny, tagging along with him. Nearby, the sabertooth tiger Diego is asked to capture a baby during a raid on a human camp, but the baby's mother escapes with him, depositing the baby with Sid and Manny before vanishing into the river. Diego appears, and pretends to want to return the child to the humans. Diego agrees to guide Manny and Sid to the baby's home, secretly leading them to his pack so they can devour Manny. A sighting of the humans causes Diego to lead the group into an ice cave shortcut, where Manny sees cave paintings that recall his lost mate and child, killed by hunters, explaining both his sadness and why he needs to return the human child. After Manny saves his life, Diego reconsiders his treachery, and the trio becomes an unlikely herd.

Cast: Ray Romano as Manfred
John Leguizamo as Sid
Denis Leary as Diego
Goran Visnjic as Soto
Jack Black as Zeke
Cedric "the Entertainer" as Rhino (Carl)

Stephen Root as Rhino (Frank)/Start
Diedrich Bader as Saber-Toothed Tiger (Oscar)
Alan Tudyk as Saber-Toothed Tiger/Dodo
Lorri Bagley as Female Sloth (Jennifer)
Jane Krakowski as Female Sloth (Rachel)
Peter Ackerman as Dodo/Freaky Mammal

Music Highlights: "Sound Off (Duckworth Chant)" (Willie Duckworth/Bernard Lentz), "Send Me on My Way" (Liz Berlin/John Buynak/Jim Dispirito/Jim Donovan/Michael Glabicki/Patrick Norman/Jenn Wertz) performed by Rusted Root, "The Comedians" (Dmitri Kabalewsky). Music by David Newman.

Film Facts

• Scrat, voiced by director Chris Wedge, resembles an extinct animal called a cronopio.
• The group passes Stonehenge, and Manny remarks, "It'll never last." (40:31).
• The cave paintings are inspired by the cave paintings of the Lascaux Cave in France (48:15).
• The film was nominated for the "Best Animated Feature" Academy Award.
• Additional appearances: *Ice Age: The Meltdown* (2006), *Ice Age: Dawn of the Dinosaurs* (2009), *Ice Age: A Mammoth Christmas* special (2011), *Ice Age: Continental Drift* (2012), *Ice Age: The Great Egg-Scapade* (2016), *Ice Age: Collision Course* (2016).
• *Ice Age* shorts: "Gone Nutty" (2002), "No Time for Nuts" (2006), "Scrat's Continental Crack-up" (2010), "Scrat's Continental Crack-up: Part 2" (2011), "Cosmic Scrat-tastrophe" (2015), "Scrat: Spaced Out" (2016).

Ice Age: The Meltdown (PG)

Theatrical release date: March 31, 2006
Production Company: Blue Sky Studios, 20th Century Fox Animation
Length: 91 minutes
Directed by: Carlos Saldanha
Screenplay by: Peter Gaulke & Gerry Swallow and Jim Hecht, story by Peter Gaulke, Gerry Swallow

Synopsis: Sid has opened a camp for kids, getting help from his adoptive herd-mates, the mammoth Manny and the saber toothed tiger Diego. While there, Fast Tony the armadillo predicts flooding that will lead to the end of the world, and they soon see evidence that the ice is indeed melting. The animals begin a migration to avoid the coming flood, as two carnivorous prehistoric sea monsters are released from an ancient block of ice. Manny, who feared he was the last mammoth, is delighted to find Ellie, a female mammoth who was raised in an opossum family and thinks she is just a very large opossum. Ellie and her two opossum "brothers," Crash and Eddie, join the herd. Manny finally convinces Ellie she's a mammoth, but quickly offends her by making it sound like they should be a couple simply to continue the mammoth species. After apologies are made, and Sid is kidnapped by a tribe of mini-sloths who try to sacrifice him in a fire pit, they finally reach higher ground, where a huge boat awaits. Unfortunately, hot geysers block their path, and Ellie is trapped by the rising water. The herd pulls together to survive the flood, only to encounter a mammoth surprise, leaving Manny and Ellie with a choice to make about their future.

Cast: Ray Romano as Manny
John Leguizamo as Sid
Denis Leary as Diego
Seann William Scott as Crash
Josh Peck as Eddie

Queen Latifah as Ellie
Will Arnett as Lone Gunslinger Vulture
Jay Leno as Fast Tony
Chris Wedge as Scrat
Alan Tudyk as Cholly

Music Highlights: "Food Glorious Food" (Lionel Bart). Music by John Powell.

Film Facts

• The songs Sid sings include "One" (Harry Nilsson), popularized by Three Dog Night, Buffalo Springfield's "For What It's Worth" (Stills), and the traditional "If You're Happy and You Know It."
• The vulture song "Food Glorious Food" is from the 1960 stage musical/1968 musical film *Oliver!*
• Though not stated in the film, the sea monsters are named Cretaceous (a Metriorhynchus) and Maelstrom (a Globidens).
• The DVD and Blu-ray include the short "No Time for Nuts," as well as the brief extra "Outtake Prank."
• Scenes from the film were used in commercials for the candy Airheads.
• The next film in the series is *Ice Age: Dawn of the Dinosaurs* (2009).
• Carlos Saldanha also directed Blue Sky Studios's *Rio* (2011) and *Ferdinand* (2017).

Ice Age: Dawn of the Dinosaurs (PG)

Theatrical release date: July 1, 2009
Production Company: Blue Sky Studios, 20th Century Fox Animation
Length: 94 minutes
Directed by: Carlos Saldanha, co-directed by Michael Thurmeier
Screenplay by: Michael Berg & Peter Ackerman and Mike Reiss and Yoni Brenner, story by Jason Carter Eaton

Synopsis: While the prehistoric rodent Scrat falls for a flying squirrel, the mammoth Manny is on edge as his mate Ellie is pregnant. Sabertooth tiger Diego does not feel cut out for a domestic life, and departs, telling Sid the sloth that the friends' time as a herd is over. Sid, wanting to find a new herd himself, comes across three huge eggs, and the dinosaurs which hatch from them imprint upon Sid as their "mother." The baby dinosaurs lead a pack of kids of many species to a playground Manny built for when his baby is born. The dinosaurs cause chaos on the playground, leading to its destruction, just before their actual mother, a T. Rex, appears. She retrieves the three baby T. Rex's, and Sid along with them, taking them to an underground world of dinosaurs. They are soon joined by Diego, Manny, Ellie, Crash and Eddie, and the herd meets the weasel Buck, who agrees to take them through the treacherous terrain, hoping to avoid the terrifying creature he calls "Rudy." They make their way past the Jungle of Misery, the Chasm of Death, and the Plates of Woe, finally reaching Lava Falls, where dinosaur newborns are cared for. Complications arise when Ellie goes into labor just as Sid needs to be rescued. Manny and Diego fight predators closing in on Ellie, while Buck takes Crash and Eddie to save Sid. All goes well, until the dreaded Rudy appears.

Cast: Ray Romano as Manny
John Leguizamo as Sid
Denis Leary as Diego
Simon Pegg as Buck
Queen Latifah as Ellie
Seann William Scott as Crash
Josh Peck as Eddie
Chris Wedge as Scrat

Bill Hader as Gazelle
Kristen Wiig as Pudgy Beaver Mom
Karen Disher as Scratte
Joey King as Beaver Girl
Jane Lynch as Diatryma Mom
Frank Welker as Momma/Rudy
Eunice Cho as Madison
Carlos Saldanha as Dinosaur Babies/Flightless Bird

Music Highlights: "You'll Never Find Another Love Like Mine" (Gamble/Huff) performed by Lou Rawls, "Walk the Dinosaur" (Fagenson/Jacobs/Weiss) performed by Queen Latifah, "Alone Again (Naturally)" (O'Sullivan) performed by Chad Fischer. Music by John Powell.

Film Facts

- The film was condensed into the 14-minute *Ice Age: Dawn of the Dinosaurs: The 4-D Experience*.
- The Blu-ray combo pack includes two Scrat shorts, "Gone Nutty" and "No Time for Nuts."
- The original title of the film was *Ice Age: A New Beginning,*
- Gilbert O'Sullivan's "Alone Again (Naturally)" gets new lyrics for Scrat's acorn (1:14:48).

Ice Age: Continental Drift (PG)

Theatrical release date: July 13, 2012
Production Company: Blue Sky Studios, 20th Century Fox Animation
Length: 88 minutes
Directed by: Steve Martino, Michael Thurmeier
Screenplay by: Michael Berg and Jason Fuchs, story by Michael Berg and Lori Forte

Synopsis: Teen mammoth Peaches is growing, wanting to be more independent and spend time with her friend Louis, a molehog, which her father Manny is uneasy about. The sloth Sid briefly reunites with his family as they pass through, dropping Sid's grandmother off for Sid to take care of. When Peaches sneaks off to see the other teens, Manny humiliates her in front of the other young mammoths, leading Peaches to say she wishes Manny wasn't her father. The ground begins breaking apart, and Manny, Diego, and Sid are set adrift on an ice floe, soon finding Sid's Granny in a tree on the floe. In the middle of the ocean, their floe is captured by the aggressive ape Captain Gutt. When Gutt refuses to allow Manny to return to his family. the herd fights back, and Gutt's huge iceberg splits apart, with Manny, Diego, Sid, and Granny ending up with the tiger-like Smilodon Shira. They arrive at an island, where Gutt has landed as well. After joining forces with the rodent-like hyrax, and with help from Shira, the herd commandeers Gutt's ship, but is soon pursued by an enraged Gutt. Peaches begins to change to please her crush, Ethan, who persuades her to turn her back on Louis, but she soon regrets her choice. Manny leads the group across the ocean, passing perils such as sirens, only to find that when he finally locates Ellie and Peaches, they're being held prisoner by Gutt. Led by the tiny molehog Louis, the herd pulls together to fight Gutt and his henchmen, with some help from Shira and Granny's pet whale "Precious."

Cast: Ray Romano as Manny
John Leguizamo as Sid
Denis Leary as Diego
Queen Latifah as Ellie
Seann William Scott as Crash
Josh Peck as Eddie
Peter Dinklage as Captain Gutt

Wanda Sykes as Granny (sloth)
Jennifer Lopez as Shira (Smilodon)
Josh Gad as Louis (molehog)
Keke Palmer as Peaches (woolly mammoth)
Nick Frost as Flynn (elephant seal)
Aziz Ansari as Squint (rabbit)
Drake as Ethan (mammoth)

Music Highlights: "Master of the Seas" (Adam Schlesinger) performed by cast. End Credits: "We Are (Family) (Theme from Ice Age: Continental Drift)" (Ester Dean) performed by cast, "Chasing the Sun" (Gleave/Smith) performed by The Wanted. Music by John Powell.

Film Facts

- The blue face paint on the hyrax is a reference to *Braveheart* (1995).
- Two shorts were made: "Scrat's Continental Crack-Up" & "Scrat's Continental Crack-Up: Part 2."
- Activision released a game based on the film, *Ice Age: Continental Drift – Arctic Games* (2012).

Ice Age: Collision Course (PG)

Theatrical release date: July 22, 2016
Production Company: Blue Sky Studios, 20th Century Fox Animation
Length: 95 minutes
Directed by: Michael Thurmeier, co-director Galen Tan Chu
Screenplay by: Michael Wilson and Michael Berg and Yoni Brenner, story by Aubrey Solomon

Synopsis: Relationship changes are in the air for the herd, as Peaches, the daughter of mammoths Manny and Ellie, is going to marry the clumsy Julian, sabertooths Diego and Shira are considering having a cub, and Sid's girlfriend leaves him. After a mini-asteroid shower hits the earth, the weasel Buck explains that he's discovered a stone pillar that describes how previous giant asteroid impacts had led to extinctions, and a new round of extinction is coming. The herd travels to the site of the asteroid impacts to try to stop the coming catastrophe, and despite the interference of the pesky dromaeosaurs Gavin, Gertie, and Roger, they learn that the asteroids that have already fallen are magnetic, and could change the course of the coming giant asteroid if they were sent into space. Unfortunately, creatures in Geotopia, a community in one of the asteroids from long ago led by Shangri Llama, need the mini-asteroids to attain immortality. Sid falls for Brooke, one of the Geotopians, and ends up destroying their immortality when he tries to give one of their crystals to Brooke. The Geotopians are finally convinced to help the herd, using a volcano to launch the crystals into space. Disaster averted, the herd returns for Peaches' wedding.

Cast: Ray Romano as Manny
John Leguizamo as Sid
Denis Leary as Diego
Queen Latifah as Ellie
Simon Pegg as Buck
Seann William Scott as Crash
Josh Peck as Eddie
Keke Palmer as Peaches

Adam DeVine as Julian
Neil deGrasse Tyson as Neil deBuck Weasel
Jesse Tyler Ferguson as Shangri Llama
Jessie J as Brooke
Jennifer Lopez as Shira
Wanda Sykes as Granny
Nick Offerman as Gavin
Stephanie Beatriz as Gertie

Music Highlights: "Mi Padrino El Diablo" (Lozolla/Ortega) performed by La Trakalosa De Monterrey, "Crazy in Love" (Beyoncé/Record/Carter/Harrison) performed by Sarai Howard, "Fireball" (Frederic/Perez/Juber/Ryan/Peyton/Spargur/Schuller) performed by Ali Dee, "Dream Weaver" (Wright) performed by Gary Wright, "Let's Get It On" (Gaye/Townsend) performed by Don Peake, "My Superstar" (Geringas/Leonti) performed by Jessie J/Tha Vill, "Dream Weaver" (Wright) performed by Trent Harmon. Music by John Debney.

Film Facts

• Related shorts: "Cosmic Scrat-tastrophe" (shown with *The Peanuts Movie*), "Scrat: Spaced Out."
• "Bring Scrat Home" on a promotional poster referenced "Bring Him Home" from *The Martian*.
• After this release, the spin-off film *Ice Age: Adventures of Buck Wild* was announced.

The Illusionist (PG)

Theatrical release date: Feb 16, 2010 (Berlin International Film Festival), Jun 16, 2010 (France/UK)
Country: France/UK   French title: *L'illusionniste*
Production Company: Pathé, Django Films, Ciné B, France 3 Cinéma, Canal+, CinéCinéma
Length: 80 minutes
Directed by: Sylvain Chomet
Screenplay by: Jacques Tati, adapted by Sylvain Chomet

Synopsis: In 1959 Paris, a lackluster stage magician and his temperamental rabbit are dismissed from their theater engagement, traveling to London, and then on to Scotland. During a brief residency at a pub, the magician's kindness to the young cleaning woman Alice leads her to follow him to Edinburgh, where he performs at the Royal Music Hall, and they take a room at the Little Joe Hotel, where several other artists stay. When items catch Alice's eye, the illusionist buys them for her, but must take odd jobs to afford their expenses, while Alice kindly shares food with their down-on-their-luck neighbors at the hotel. The illusionist is hired to draw crowds to Jenner's department store, and while visiting him there, Alice bumps into a young man she'd noticed from the neighborhood, and they begin to fall in love. The illusionist sees them together, and departs the city after setting his rabbit free.

Cast: Jean-Claude Donda as The Illusionist/
French Cinema Manager
Eilidh Rankin as Alice
Duncan MacNeil: Additional Voices

Raymond Mearns: Additional Voices
James T. Muir: Additional Voices
Tom Urie: Additional Voices
Paul Bandey: Additional Voices

Music Highlights: "My Girl Blue" (Malcolm Ross) performed by The Britoons, "Love of Another Man" (Malcolm Ross) performed by The Britoons, "Molly Jean" (Malcolm Ross) performed by The Britoons, "Chanson Illusionist" (Sylvain Chomet) performed by Didier Gustin, Jil Aigrot, and Frédéric Lebon. End credits: "Les Follies" (John Leach/George Fenton). Score by Sylvain Chomet.

Film Facts

• The original story was a semi-autobiographical script written by the French mime and comic actor Jacques Tati. The live-action film that the illusionist walks in on (1:07:40) is Tati's *Mon Oncle* (1958). Just before he enters the theater he resembles Tati's character Monsieur Hulot.
• Some parallels have been noted between Alice and Alice in Wonderland, including her name, blue and white dress, and white rabbit companion.
• The fish and chips restaurant menu draws its Lobster Thermidor description from the classic 1970 *Monty Python's Flying Circus* sketch "Spam."
• There is a brief post-credits scene (1:19:31).
• The fictional band "The Britoons" featured Malcolm Ross, Iain Stoddart, and Leo Condie. Ross was a member of the influential Scottish post-punk band Josef K and Edwyn Collins' Orange Juice.
• The film was nominated for the "Best Animated Feature" Academy Award and Golden Globe.
• Chomet also directed the short "The Old Lady and the Pigeons" and the animated film *The Triplets of Belleville* (2003).

The Incredibles (PG)

Theatrical release date: November 5, 2004
Production Company: Pixar Animation Studios, Walt Disney Pictures
Length: 115 minutes
Directed by: Brad Bird
Written by: Brad Bird

Synopsis: After some well-publicized mishaps, the government outlawed superhero activity, consigning the former heroes to mundane occupations. Two of these heroes, Mr. Incredible and Elastigirl, do their best to adapt to civilian life as Bob and Helen Parr, but Mr. Incredible chafes at this bland existence, and begins to perform furtive super-good deeds. Mr. Incredible jumps at the chance to help a mysterious benefactor defeat an out of control robot. All is not as it seems, and Elastigirl is soon on the trail of the missing Mr. Incredible, accompanied by their children, Violet and Dash, who have powers of their own.

Cast: Craig T. Nelson as Bob Parr/Mr. Incredible
Holly Hunter as Helen Parr/Elastigirl
Sarah Vowell as Violet Parr
Spencer Fox as Dashiell Parr (Dash)
Eli Fucile/Maeve Andrews as Jack-Jack
Samuel L. Jackson as Lucius Best/Frozone

Jason Lee as Buddy Pine/Syndrome
Wallace Shawn as Gilbert Huph
Brad Bird as Edna Mode (E)
Bret Parker as Kari
John Ratzenberger as Underminer

Music Highlights: Score by Michael Giacchino.

Film Facts

• *The Incredibles,* the 6th Pixar film, quickly became a fan favorite, and a top film of 2004. It was written and directed by Brad Bird, who had previously directed and co-written *The Iron Giant* (1999). The process of creating *The Iron Giant* was demanding, leaving Bird pondering the balance between career and family life, a tension that became a core theme in *The Incredibles*.
• Bird's film *The Iron Giant* led to John Lasseter's invitation to pitch *The Incredibles* to Pixar.
• There are some parallels between *The Incredibles* and Alan Moore's adult graphic novel *Watchmen*. Coincidence or conspiracy?
• John Ratzenberger's role in the film is the Underminer: "Behold, the Underminer! I'm always beneath you, but nothing is beneath me!"
• *The Incredibles* is the only Pixar film not to feature the Pizza Planet truck.
• The film won the "Best Animated Feature" Academy Award.
• Pixar Easter egg: The number A-113 appears three times: Mirage mentions room A-113, Mr. Incredible is held in on Level "A1" in cell "13," and the control room shows Level A1, section 13.
• The streets shown on Mr. Incredible's GPS are near the Pixar Animation Studios building in Emeryville, California.
• A video game was made for Mac, PC, GameCube, PS2, Xbox, and Game Boy Advance.
• Additional appearances: "Jack Jack Attack" short (2004), *Incredibles 2* (2018), "Auntie Edna" short (2018).

Incredibles 2 (PG)

Theatrical release date: June 15, 2018
Production Company: Pixar Animation Studios, Walt Disney Pictures
Length: 118 minutes
Directed by: Brad Bird
Written by: Brad Bird

Synopsis: Following a destructive battle with supervillain the Underminer, the Superhero Relocation Program is shuttered, leaving the Parr family with no support. To make matters worse, Violet's secret identity is discovered by classmate Tony Rydinger. Businessman Winston Deavor believes that sending heroes on secret missions can win back the trust of the public, and Elastigirl reluctantly agrees to help, leaving Bob to care for the kids at home. Elastigirl's defeat of the evil Screenslaver seems like the win they were looking for, but as is often the case with supervillains, all is not as it seems…

Cast: Craig T. Nelson as Bob Parr/Mr. Incredible
Holly Hunter as Helen Parr/Elastigirl
Sarah Vowell as Violet Parr
Huck Milner as Dashiell Parr (Dash)
Catherine Keener as Evelyn Deavor
Eli Fucile as Jack-Jack
Bob Odenkirk as Winston Deavor
Samuel L. Jackson as Lucius Best/Frozone
Michael Bird as Tony Rydinger
Sophia Bush as Voyd
Brad Bird as Edna Mode (E)
Phil LaMarr as Krushauer/Helectrix
Isabella Rossellini as Ambassador
Adam Gates as Chad Brentley

Music Highlights: Score by Michael Giacchino. The soundtrack also includes a cappella versions of "Here Comes Elastigirl - Elastigirl's Theme," "Chill or Be Chilled - Frozone's Theme," "Pow! Pow! Pow! - Mr. Incredible's Theme" and "The Glory Days" performed by DCappella.

Film Facts

• *Incredibles 2,* the 20th Pixar film, was once again written and directed by Brad Bird.
• John Ratzenberger's customary Pixar role was the Underminer. *Incredibles 2* picks up where the Underminer cliffhanger from the first film left off.
• The Parr's residence at the beginning of the film, the Safari Court, is based on the Safari Inn, a motel in Burbank, California, near the Walt Disney Company.
• Screenslaver's flashing lights posed a risk to those prone to seizures, leading some theaters to post warnings prior to the film.
• The newscaster's attire and background (56:15) resemble those in the 1987 Holly Hunter film *Broadcast News*.
• The film was accompanied by the Pixar short "Bao" (2018).
• Brad Bird's sons did voice acting for the film: Tony Rydinger was voiced by Michael Bird, and Jack-Jack's monster vocalizations were created by Nick Bird. Edna Mode was once again voiced by Brad Bird himself.
• Additional appearances: Follows *The Incredibles* (2004), and "Jack Jack Attack" short (2004), followed by "Auntie Edna" short (2018), included on Blu-ray.

Inside Out (PG)

Theatrical release date: June 19, 2015
Production Company: Pixar Animation Studios, Walt Disney Pictures
Length: 95 minutes
Directed by: Pete Docter, co-directed by Ronnie Del Carmen
Screenplay by: Pete Docter, Meg Lefauve, Josh Cooley, original story by Pete Docter, Ronnie Del Carmen

Synopsis: Riley faces a crisis at the age of 11 when, after growing up in Minnesota, she moves with her parents to San Francisco. Parallel to the outer world that Riley is aware of, in her mind five core emotions (Joy, Sadness, Fear, Anger, and Disgust) work through a console to manage Riley's responses to the world, while a few Core Memories power her personality. After many years of Joy dominating Riley's emotional world, a struggle in the Headquarters ends up casting out Joy and Sadness, who struggle to return while the other emotions to scramble to respond to Riley's new life.

Cast: Amy Poehler as Joy
Phyllis Smith as Sadness
Richard Kind as Bing Bong
Bill Hader as Fear
Lewis Black as Anger
Mindy Kaling as Disgust
Kaitlyn Dias as Riley

Diane Lane as Mom
Kyle MacLachlan as Dad
Paula Poundstone as Forgetter Paula
Bobby Moynihan as Forgetter Bobby
Paula Pell as Dream Director & Mom's Anger
Dave Goelz as Subconscious Guard Frank
Frank Oz as Subconscious Guard Dave

Music Highlights: Score by Michael Giacchino.

Film Facts

• The 15th Pixar film, *Inside Out* was widely hailed as groundbreaking in its symbolic representation of how humans experience emotion.
• The story underwent many changes, and at one point the struggles to make the film were so serious that director Pete Docter feared he might be dismissed from Pixar. In the end the film won the "Best Animated Feature" Academy Award, Annie Award, and Golden Globe.
• The film draws upon the research of Dr. Paul Ekman, whose work included focus on six core emotions in humans (anger, disgust, fear, joy, sadness, and surprise) and Dr. Dacher Keltner at UC Berkeley.
• There is an extra scene during the end credits (1:26:19).
• The short "Lava" preceded *Inside Out* in its theatrical release and is on the Blu-ray/DVD.
• Easter eggs: Colette from *Ratatouille* is on a magazine (6:06), the birds from the "For the Birds" short are on the phone line (7:36), and the memory orbs include scenes from the film *Up* (various). Riley's classmate wears a shirt with the same skull logo as Andy's neighbor Sid in *Toy Story* (22:14), and the park is the same as in *Toy Story* (4:41). Pixar easter egg mainstays the Pizza Planet truck (37:45), the Luxo ball (38:53), and A113 (1:13:54) also appear.
• Additional appearances: The short "Riley's First Date?" (2015), included on the Blu-ray.

The Iron Giant (PG)

Theatrical release date: August 6, 1999
Production Company: Warner Bros. Feature Animation
Length: 86 minutes
Directed by: Brad Bird
Screenplay by: Tim McCanlies, screen story by Brad Bird, based on *The Iron Man* by Ted Hughes

Synopsis: In 1957, off the coast of Maine, a giant robot hurtles into the ocean from space. The next day, young Hogarth hears talk of the event, and goes out into the woods searching for it. He finds the huge robot eating iron at a power plant, where it accidentally electrocutes itself. When it later recovers, Hogarth runs away, and is picked up by his skeptical mother. Government agent Kent Mansley arrives to investigate the power plant destruction, and his car is soon eaten by the unseen robot. Hogarth befriends the robot in the woods, beginning to teach it words. When the robot begins to eat railroad tracks, Hogarth gets him to put the rails back, but the robot is hit by the train and damaged. Hogarth brings the robot home, where it reassembles itself. It is almost seen at the house by Agent Mansley, so Hogarth takes the robot to the scrap yard run by junk artist Dean McCoppin. Agent Mansley continues his interrogation, but Hogarth finally shakes him, finding the robot doing "arts and crafts" at Dean's direction at the scrap yard. When the army is finally called in, Dean makes the "metal man" look like one of his junk art creations. Even after the robot shows it is friendly, the army attacks, but when a nuclear missile sent to destroy the robot threatens to destroy the town of Rockwell, the Iron Giant clearly shows its benevolent nature.

Cast: Jennifer Aniston as Annie Hughes
Harry Connick Jr. as Dean McCoppin
Vin Diesel as The Iron Giant
James Gammon as Foreman Marv Loach/
    Floyd Turbeaux

Cloris Leachman as Mrs. Tensedge
Christopher McDonald as Kent Mansley
John Mahoney as General Rogard
Eli Marienthal as Hogarth Hughes
M. Emmet Walsh as Earl Stutz

Music Highlights: "Honeycomb" (Merrill) performed by Jimmie Rodgers, "I Got a Rocket in My Pocket" (Logsdon/McAlpin) performed by Jimmy Lloyd, "Comin' Home Baby" (Dorough/Tucker) performed by Mel Tormé, "Blue Rumba" (Black) performed by Pepe Dominguin, "Genius After Hours" (Charles) performed by Ray Charles, "Capitolizing" (Gonzales) performed by Babs Gonzales, "Cha-Hua-Hua" (Ross/Lubin) performed by Eddie Platt, "Blues Walk" (Donaldson) performed by Lou Donaldson, "Let's Do the Cha Cha" (Boyd/Nance) performed by The Magnificents, "Searchin'" (Leiber/Stoller) performed by The Coasters. Music by Michael Kamen.

Film Facts

- Feature directorial debut of Brad Bird, who went on to direct *The Incredibles* and *Ratatouille*.
- Hogarth has posters from 1950s science fiction films, such as *Forbidden Planet* (58:24).
- The film won the "Best Animated Feature Film" Annie Award.
- Limited marketing led to a poor box office showing, but the film has developed a cult following.

Jack and the Cuckoo-Clock Heart (PG)

Theatrical release date: February 5, 2014 (France), September 24, 2014 (US limited release)
Country: France   French title: *Jack et la Mécanique du Coeur*
Production Company: Duran, EuropaCorp, France 3 Cinéma, uFilm, Walking the Dog
Length: 93 minutes
Directed by: Stéphane Berla, Mathias Malzieu
Screenplay by: Mathias Malzieu, based on his novel *The Boy with the Cuckoo-Clock Heart*

Synopsis: When Jack's mother is in a snowstorm in Edinburgh just before giving birth, the midwife Madeleine saves Jack by replacing his icy heart with a cuckoo-clock. Left in Madeleine's care, he must live by three rules: never touch the hands of the heart, keep his temper under control, and never fall in love, or his cuckoo-clock heart will stop forever. Madeleine finally takes Jack out to see the world, where he's smitten with the blind-without-her-glasses Miss Acacia. He convinces Madeleine to allow him to go to school, where he is bullied by Joe, finally having a confrontation in which he fears he's killed Joe. Jack flees, meeting filmmaker Georges Méliès, and they set out for Andalusia to find Miss Acacia. They find her at the Extraordinarium circus, where Jack takes a job at the Ghost Train ride to be near her, but she tells Jack she loves someone else. Jack finally learns that he is the one from her past that she's in love with, and gives her the key to his clock heart. Their happiness is shattered when Joe returns, accusing Jack of attacking him. Miss Acacia rejects Jack, and he returns to Edinburgh. When she follows to give him the key, Jack refuses to use it.

Cast:

Role	French	English
Jack	Mathias Malzieu	Orlando Seale
Miss Acacia	Olivia Ruiz	Samantha Barks
Madeleine	Marie Vincent/Emily Loizeau	Barbara Scaff
Méliès	Jean Rochefort	Stéphane Cornicard
Joe	Grand Corps Malade	Harry Sadeghi

Music Highlights: "The Coldest Ever Day on Earth" (Malzieu) by Dionysos/Seale/Scaff, "Miss Sprite" (Malzieu) by Dionysos/Dormer/Seale/Barks, "Joe's Theme" (Grand Corps Malade) by Dionysos/Sadeghi, "The Cuckoo Clock's Panic" (Malzieu) by Dionysos/Seale/Samuels, "A Man with No Tricks" (Malzieu) by Dionysos/Seale/Cornicard, "Malagueña" (Galarza/Burgos/Burgos) by Olivia Ruiz, "La Chica Chocolate" (Malzieu) by Ruiz, "King of the Ghost Train" (Malzieu/Dionysos/Daviaud) by Dionysos/Seale, "My Lady Key" (Malzieu) by Dionysos/Seale/Barks, "Quijote" (Blanc/Canac/Maktav) by Ruiz, "Joe's Return" (Grand Corps Malade) by Dionysos/Sadeghi, "Death Song" (Malzieu/Dionysos/Daviaud) by Dionysos/Seale, "Whatever the Weather" (Malzieu/Dionysos/Daviaud) by Dionysos/Seale, "Hamac of Clouds" (Malzieu/Dionysos/Daviaud) by Seale, "Jack et la Mécanique du Coeur" (Malzieu/Dionysos/Daviaud) by Dionysos/Seale.

Film Facts

• The film is inspired by *La Mécanique du Cœur* (2007), an album by the French rock band Dionysos, which was itself based on a book by Mathias Malzieu, the band's frontman.

James and the Giant Peach (PG)

Theatrical release date: April 12, 1996
Production Company: Walt Disney Pictures, Allied Filmmakers, Skellington Productions
Walt Disney Productions
Length: 79 minutes
Directed by: Henry Selick
Screenplay by: Karey Kirkpatrick, Jonathan Roberts & Steve Bloom, based on the book by
Roald Dahl

Synopsis: James Trotter, an orphan whose parents were tragically eaten by a rhinoceros, is placed with his cruel Aunt Spiker and Aunt Sponge. James kindly rescues as spider from his aunts, and soon receives a magic bag of crocodile tongues from an old man. When one of the tongues is dropped near a peach tree, a huge peach grows, which Spiker and Sponge turn into a tourist attraction. James enters a hole in the peach to find a collection of large insects and worms: Mr. Centipede, Mr. Earthworm, the Glowworm, Mr. Grasshopper, Mrs. Ladybug, and Miss Spider. They launch the peach into the ocean and embark on a journey to New York.

Cast: Simon Callow as Grasshopper
Richard Dreyfuss as Centipede
Jane Leeves as Ladybug
Joanna Lumley as Aunt Spiker
Miriam Margolyes as Glowworm

Pete Postlethwaite as Old Man
Susan Sarandon as Spider
Paul Terry as James
David Thewlis as Earthworm
Miriam Margolyes as Glowworm

Music Highlights: "My Name is James" (Newman) performed by Paul Terry with Drew Harrah, "Sail Away" (Coward) performed by Noël Coward, "That's the Life" (Newman) performed by Richard Dreyfuss, Susan Sarandon, Jane Leeves, Simon Callow, and Miriam Margolyes, "Heroes Return" (Steck) instrumental, "Family" (Newman) performed by Callow, Dreyfuss, Leeves, Sarandon, Thewlis, Margolyes, and Terry, "Eating the Peach" (Newman/Dahl) performed by Richard Dreyfuss, Susan Sarandon, Simon Callow, Jane Leeves, Paul Terry, and David Thewlis, "Good News" (Newman) performed by Randy Newman. Music by Randy Newman.

Film Facts

- The first 20 minutes of the film are live-action, followed by stop-motion animation inside the peach, and a mix of live-action and animation when the group reaches New York City.
- Singer-songwriter Randy Newman's best-known soundtrack work is for Pixar films, beginning with *Toy Story* (1995).
- Director Henry Selick's previous Disney film was *The Nightmare Before Christmas* (1993), also using stop-motion animation. He later directed *Coraline* (2009).
- The Pirate Captain's head is the head of Jack Skellington from *The Nightmare Before Christmas*.
- Grasshopper plays James part of Bach's Partita for Violin Solo No. 3 in E Major.
- Andy Partridge of the English band XTC was to write the film's music, but withdrew.
- Disney later released Roald Dahl's *The BGF* (2016).

The Jungle Book (G)

Theatrical release date: October 18, 1967
Production Company: Walt Disney Productions
Length: 78 minutes
Directed by: Wolfgang Reitherman
Story: Larry Clemmons, Ralph Wright, Ken Anderson, Vance Gerry, inspired by the Rudyard Kipling "Mowgli" stories

---

Synopsis: A human child, Mowgli, is raised by a pack of wolves, aided by Baloo the bear and Bagheera the panther, but hunted by the fierce tiger Shere Khan. After some misadventures with Kaa the snake and King Louie's wild jungle monkeys, Mowgli is drawn to the human world, and must decide whether he wishes to move beyond simply having the "bare necessities."

Cast: Phil Harris as "Baloo" the Bear
Sebastian Cabot as "Bagheera" the Panther
Louis Prima as "King Louie" of the Apes
George Sanders as "Shere Khan" the Tiger
Sterling Holloway as "Kaa" the Snake

J. Pat O'Malley as "Col. Hathi" the Elephant
Bruce Reitherman as "Mowgli" the Man Cub
Verna Felton/Clint Howard as Elephants
Darleen Carr as The Girl

Music Highlights: "The Bare Necessities" (Terry Gilkyson) performed by Phil Harris, "I Wan'na Be Like You" (Sherman/Sherman) performed by Louis Prima and Phil Harris, "Colonel Hathi's March (The Elephant Song)" (Sherman/Sherman) performed by J. Pat O'Malley and chorus, "Trust in Me" (Sherman/Sherman) performed by Sterling Holloway. Music by George Bruns.

Film Facts

• *The Jungle Book*, the 19th of the Disney animated classics, was the last film Walt Disney personally produced, as he died during the title's production.
• Walt Disney was much more involved in developing *The Jungle Book* than he had been with *The Sword in the Stone* (1963), offering extensive input in story meetings and urging the writers to deviate from the original stories by Kipling as needed.
• The three sons of director Wolfgang Reitherman, one of Disney's "nine old men," had roles in Disney films: Bruce as Mowgli in *The Jungle Book* and Christopher Robin in "Winnie the Pooh and the Honey Tree," and Richard and Robert as Wart in *The Sword in the Stone*.
• The soundtrack of the film is considered one of Disney's classics, with music composed by the Sherman Brothers, including King Louie/Louis Prima's "I Wan'na Be Like You," and Kaa/Sterling Holloway's hypnotic "Trust in Me," as well as Terry Gilkyson's iconic "The Bare Necessities" sung by Baloo/Phil Harris.
• "Trust in Me" was originally written for *Mary Poppins* as "The Land of Sand" with other lyrics.
• In the Hindi language, *baloo* means bear, *bagheera* means panther, *hathi* means elephant, and *shere khan* means tiger king.
• The Beatles were approached to voice the vultures (who were modeled on the band), but declined.
• Additional appearances: *The Jungle Book 2* (2003), characters in the animated TV series *TaleSpin* (1990-1991) and *Jungle Cubs* (1996-1998), and the live-action version of *The Jungle Book* (2016).

The Jungle Book 2 (G)

Theatrical release date: February 14, 2003
Production Company: Walt Disney Pictures, DisneyToon Studios, Walt Disney Animation Australia, Walt Disney Animation France, Tandem Films, Toon City Animation, Spaff Animation
Length: 72 minutes
Directed by: Steve Trenbirth
Screenplay by: Karl Geurs, additional written material by Carter Crocker, Evan Spiliotopoulos, David Reynolds, Roger S.H. Schulman, Tom Rogers

> **Synopsis**: Picking up after the events in *The Jungle Book,* Mowgli is living in the man-village with Shanti, the mysterious girl from the end of the first film, and the little boy Ranjan. Tired of his life among humans, Mowgli returns to the jungle with Baloo, soon followed by Shanti and Ranjan, who plan to rescue him, believing he is in danger. The dreaded tiger Shere Khan does end up threatening Mowgli and Shanti, leaving Mowgli with an appreciation for his life in the village as well as the jungle.

Cast: John Goodman as Baloo
Haley Joel Osment as Mowgli
Mae Whitman as Shanti
Connor Funk as Ranjan
Bob Joles as Bagheera

Tony Jay as Shere Khan
John Rhys-Davies as Ranjan's Father
Jim Cummings as Kaa/Colonel Hathi/
M.C. Monkey
Phil Collins as Lucky

Music Highlights: "I Wan'na Be Like You (The Monkey Song)" (Richard M. Sherman/Robert B. Sherman) performed by Smash Mouth, "Jungle Rhythm" (Lorraine Feather/Paul Grabowsky) performed by Haley Joel Osment, Mae Whitman, and Connor Funk, "W-I-L-D" (Lorraine Feather/Paul Grabowsky) performed by John Goodman, "Colonel Hathi's March" (Richard M. Sherman/Robert B. Sherman) performed by Bob Joyce, Rick Logan, Guy Maeda, and Jerry Whitman, "The Bare Necessities" (Terry Gilkyson) performed by John Goodman and Haley Joel Osment, "Right Where I Belong" (Lorraine Feather/Joel McNeely) performed by Windy Wagner. Original score by Joel McNeely.

Film Facts

- When Shanti goes to get water (5:28) she briefly hums "My Own Home," the song that first drew Mowgli to the village in *The Jungle Book* (1967).
- Pumbaa, the warthog from *The Lion King,* appears during the song "W-I-L-D" (44:17).
- This release was originally planned as a direct-to-video release, but the decision was later made to release it theatrically.
- King Louie was not included in the film because Disney could not agree on terms with the widow of Louis Prima.
- Prior to this film, Bob Hilgenberg and Rob Muir wrote a sequel screenplay that was not developed.
- Additional appearances: Sequel to *The Jungle Book* (1967), characters in *TaleSpin* animated TV series (1990-1991) and *Jungle Cubs* animated TV series (1996-1998), and the live-action version of *The Jungle Book* (2016).

Kahlil Gibran's The Prophet (PG)

Theatrical release date: Sep 6, 2014 (Toronto International Film Festival), Aug 7, 2015 (US)
Country: United States, Canada, Lebanon, France, Qatar
Production Company: Ventanarosa, Doha Film Institute, Financière Pinault, Participant Media
Length: 85 minutes
Directed by: Roger Allers, segments: "On Freedom": Michal Socha, "On Children": Nina Paley, "On Marriage": Joann Sfar, "On Work": Joan Gratz, "On Eating & Drinking": Bill Plympton, "On Love": Tomm Moore, "On Good & Evil": Mohammed Saeed Harib, "On Death": Gaëtan Brizzi/Paul Brizzi
Screenplay by: Roger Allers, inspired by the book *The Prophet* by Kahlil Gibran

---

Synopsis: On the island of Orphalese, young Almitra has not spoken since her father died two years earlier, and has a propensity for causing trouble for the vendors at the local market, aided by a crafty seagull. One day, instead of going to school, Almitra follows her mother Kamila to her work, as a housekeeper for Mustafa, a writer and artist on house arrest. Mustafa is kind with Almitra, and he soon gets word that he is free, on the condition that he immediately returns to his home country. The grouchy Sergeant and clumsy young soldier Halim escort Mustafa toward his ship, followed by Almitra, with stops at a wedding and a café, where Mustafa dispenses wisdom along the way. Halim seeks Mustafa's advice, confessing he loves Kamila, but is afraid to tell her. Instead of taking Mustafa to his ship, the Sergeant begins to take him into a building, leading to unrest and a struggle between the people and the soldiers, which Mustafa calms. He is taken to a military officer, who asks Mustafa to sign a paper disavowing his writings, or face death. Mustafa will not sign the paper, and is given a night in prison to think the matter over. Halim, Kamila, and Almitra seek to free Mustafa, but he says he must face what awaits him. He asks Almitra to gather his writings and share them with the people. As the people gather outside his prison, Mustafa tells them not to mourn, as he will be reborn.

Cast: Liam Neeson as Mustafa
Salma Hayek-Pinault as Kamila
John Krasinski as Halim
Frank Langella as Pasha
Alfred Molina as Sergeant
Quvenzhané Wallis as Almitra

Assaf Cohen as Baker/Date Seller/Groom
John Kassir as Baker/Man in Turban/
    Donkey Driver/English Tourist/Fisherman
Nick Jameson as Grocer/Male Guest/
    Grandpa/Male Villager
Fred Tatasciore as Orange Seller/Bride's Father/Drummer

Music Highlights: "Attaboy" (Duncan/Meyer/Thile) performed by Yo-Yo Ma, Stuart Ian Duncan, Edgar A. Meyer, Chris Thile, "On Children" (Gibran/Rice) performed by Damien Rice, "On Love" (Gibran/Hannigan) performed by Glen Hansard and Lisa Hannigan. Music by Gabriel Yared.

Film Facts

- Lebanese-American Kahlil Gibran's book *The Prophet* was originally published in 1923.
- Salma Hayek-Pinault, the film's producer and the voice of Kamila, is of Lebanese descent.
- The film premiered at the Toronto International Film Festival on September 6, 2014.

Kiki's Delivery Service (G)

Theatrical release date: July 29, 1989
Country: Japan   Japanese title: *Majo no Takkyūbin*
Production Company: Studio Ghibli
Length: 103 minutes
Directed by: Hayao Miyazaki
Screenplay by: Hayao Miyazaki, based on the 1985 novel by Eiko Kadono, illustrated by Akiko Hayashi

Synopsis: When a witch reaches age 13, the tradition is that she must leave home for a year. When the perfect clear night comes, the good-natured young witch Kiki leaves with her cat Jiji, finding a busy town without without a witch. She befriends Osono, a kind bakery owner, who offers her a place to stay in her attic, and Kiki agrees to work at the bakery for room and board. During a delivery, a stuffed cat is lost, so Jiji stands in for the toy while Kiki tries to find it. Kiki finally finds the toy at an artist's house in the woods. The artist fixes a rip in the toy, and Jiji is freed. Kiki continues to make deliveries, helping customers with their troubles, but doing so makes her late for a party she was invited to by the boy Tombo. After flying in the rain she becomes ill, and when she's better, Osono arranges for Kiki to deliver a package to Tombo. They share a bike ride, but when Tombo's friends arrive, one of whom has been unkind to Kiki, she leaves, finding that her magic begins to fade. The artist who helped her visits, and they discuss the importance of "trusting your spirit." When Tombo is carried away by a runaway zeppelin, Kiki has to find the inner strength to save him.

Cast:

Role	English (1997)	English (1990)	Japanese
Kiki	Kirsten Dunst	Lisa Michelson	Minami Takayama
Jiji	Phil Hartman	Kerrigan Mahan	Rei Sakuma
Osono	Tress MacNeille	Alexandra Kenworthy	Keiko Toda
Ursula	Janeane Garofalo	Edie Mirman	Minami Takayama
Tombo	Matthew Lawrence	Eddie Frierson	Kappei Yamaguchi
Fukuo	Brad Garrett	Greg Snegoff	Kōichi Yamadera
Kokiri	Kath Soucie	Barbara Goodson	Mieko Nobusawa
Okino	Jeff Bennett	John Dantona	Kōichi Miura
Madame	Debbie Reynolds	Melanie MacQueen	Haruko Kato
Barsa	Edie McClurg	Edie Mirman	Hiroko Seki

Music Highlights: "Soaring" (Forest) performed by Sydney Forest, "Rouge no Dengon" (Yumi Arai) performed by Yumi Matsutoya, "I'm Gonna Fly" (Forest) performed by Sydney Forest, "Yasashisa ni Tsutsumareta Nara" (Yumi Arai) performed by Yumi Matsutoya. Music by Joe Hisaishi.

Film Facts

• The bus that nearly hits Kiki says "Studio Ghibli" on the side (16:05).
• A live-action re-make of *Kiki's Delivery Service* was released in 2014.
• Sunao Katabuchi (*In This Corner of the World*) was originally going to direct the film, but after extensive work on the story, Hayao Miyazaki assumed the role, with Katabuchi as assistant director.

Kirikou and the Sorceress (NR)

Theatrical release date: December 9, 1998 (France)
Country: France/Belgium/Luxembourg   French title: *Kirikou et la Sorcière*
Production Company: France 3 Cinéma, Les Armateurs, Monipoly Prod., Odec Kid, Rija Studio
Length: 71 minutes
Written and Directed by: Michel Ocelot

Synopsis: The boy Kirikou is born in a West African village, able to talk and walk at birth. He is told that a drought has been caused by the wicked sorceress, Karaba, who has killed Kirikou's father and uncles, except for the youngest uncle. Kirikou joins his uncle to fight Karaba, hiding under his hat and warning his uncle of Karaba's attacks. Karaba thinks the hat is magical, and agrees to spare Kirikou's village if she is given the hat. Kirikou runs off to make a fake hat for one of Karaba's robots to take back to her. Karaba next demands all of the gold in the village, and burns down the hut of a woman who kept a gold necklace. The sorceress sends her boat to capture the children of the village, but Kirikou cuts holes to sink it. Karaba tries again with an enchanted tree, but again Kirikou saves them. Hoping to fix the drought, Kirikou climbs into the Forbidden Spring, finding a monster inside that is drinking all the water. He slays the monster, restoring water to the village. When Kirikou asks why Karaba is so evil, his mother tells him only his grandfather, the Wise Man of the Mountain, can answer his question. Kirikou's mother shows him a tunnel, and after he gets lost, he follows some animals out. When he finally reaches his grandfather, he learns that Karaba did not cause the drought, and does not eat her foes as people say. He also learns that Karaba is suffering from a poison thorn in her spine, which also gives her magic power. Kirikou resolves to remove the thorn, leading to a transformation in both Karaba and his village. NOTE: As is the custom in areas of Africa, the women are topless, and children are naked.

Cast:	Role	French	English
	Kirikou	Doudou Gueye Thiaw/William Nadylam-Yotnda/Sebastien Hebrant	Theodore Sibusiso Sibeko
	Karaba	Awa Sene Sarr	Antoinette Kellermann
	Uncle	Tshilombo Lubambu	Fezile Mpela
	The Mother	Maimouna N'Diaye	Kombisile Sangweni
	The Old Man	Robert Liensol	Mabutho Kid Sithole

Music Highlights: "Kirikou" (Youssou N'Dour) performed by Bouba Mendy.

Film Facts

• Director Michel Ocelot often uses silhouettes, and a few scenes in this film make use of these.
• Michel Ocelot also directed *Azur & Asmar* (2006) and *Tales of the Night* (2011).
• Additional appearances: the animated films *Kirikou et les Bêtes Sauvages* (2005), *Kirikou et les Hommes et les Femmes* (2012), plus the stage musical, *Kirikou et Karaba* (2007).

Klaus (PG)

Theatrical release date: November 15, 2019
Production Company: Netflix Animation, Sergio Pablos Animation Studios, Atresmedia Cine
Length: 96 minutes
Directed by: Sergio Pablos, co-directed by Carlos Martínez López
Screenplay by: Sergio Pablos, Jim Mahoney, Zach Lewis, original story by Sergio Pablos

---

Synopsis: After Jesper Johansson, the lazy, entitled son of the Royal Postmaster General, intentionally flounders through the Royal Postal Academy, his father assigns him to establish postal service in the frozen wasteland of Smeerensberg. He soon finds himself in the middle of a vicious feud between the Krum clan and the Ellingboe clan. He bumps into the town's bitter teacher, Alva, who has been forced into selling fish as the feuding clans will not send their children to mingle with the enemy at school. After Jesper fails to get anyone in town to send a letter, a child accidentally drops a drawing. Desperate for some kind of mail, Jesper puts the drawing into an envelope, before fleeing from the boy's frightening father. He soon goes to see the woodsman outside of town, dropping the drawing, which shows the boy, sadly standing at his window. Klaus, the large woodsman with a white beard, gives Jesper a toy to deliver to the boy, but due to the traps around the house, they deliver the toy through the chimney. The next morning, three more children have letters for Jesper to deliver to Mr. Klaus. The Krum and Ellingboe children begin playing with the toys together, to the horror of their parents. As more children begin writing letters and getting toys, rumors begin to develop about the mysterious Klaus, who is said to come down the chimney, put toys in stockings, and leave coal for naughty children. The town begins to transform as the children play together, good deeds are done, and the school resumes, so children can learn to write letters. Though he is tested by the leaders of the clans who want to maintain their feud, he is guided by Klaus's belief that "A true act of goodwill always sparks another."

Cast: Jason Schwartzman as Jesper
J.K. Simmons as Klaus
Rashida Jones as Alva
Will Sasso as Mr. Ellingboe
Neda Margrethe Labba as Márgu
Sergio Pablos as Pumpkin/Olaf

Norm MacDonald as Mogens
Joan Cusack as Mrs. Krum
Evan Agos as Ellingboe Boy
Sky Alexis as Ellingboe Girl 2
Jaeden Bettencourt as Krum Boy/Jesper's Son
Teddy Blum as Small Ellingboe Boy

Music Highlights: "Invisible" (Justin Tranter, Jussifer and Caroline Pennell) performed by Zara Larsson. Music by Alfonso G. Aguilar.

Film Facts

• The film is the directorial debut of Sergio Pablos, who worked at Disney, and developed the story for Illumination Entertainment's *Despicable Me* (2010) and Warner Animation's *Smallfoot* (2018).
• *Klaus* was nominated for the "Best Animated Feature" Academy Award and Annie Award, winning the Annie Award.

Kubo and the Two Strings (PG)

Theatrical release date: August 19, 2016
Production Company: Focus Features, Laika Entertainment
Length: 101 minutes
Directed by: Travis Knight
Screenplay by: Marc Haimes and Chris Butler, story by Shannon Tindle and Marc Haimes

---

Synopsis: In feudal Japan, the baby Kubo's grandfather steals his eye, and his mother flees with Kubo in a boat on a storm-tossed sea, hitting her head when the boat capsizes. Years later the young Kubo cares for his often catatonic mother, supporting them with performances in the local market using origami figures that he magically animates when he plays his shamisen. He tells the story of the samurai Hanzo, Kubo's father, who seeks a magical sword, breastplate, and helmet, and who is attacked by the evil Moon King. His mother warns Kubo never to be out at night, but when he hears that he might be able to talk with spirits in the graveyard after dark, he goes to try to reach the spirit of his father. While there he encounters his frightening, levitating twin aunts, who seek to take his other eye to his grandfather. Kubo tries to flee, and is rescued by his mother, who strikes a chord on his shamisen to momentarily stop his aunts. She tells Kubo that he must "find the armor," and animates an insect on his robe, which flies him away. Kubo wakes to find himself in the snowy Far Lands with the no-nonsense Monkey, who tells him his mother used the last of her magic to animate her so she could protect Kubo. She tells Kubo his aunts will pursue him relentlessly, and they must find the armor before they are captured. On the way they encounter an insect-like samurai cursed to wander the lands with no memory, who believes that Kubo's father Hanzo was his master. He joins their party, pledging to protect Kubo. Many challenges await them, as they discover the true importance of family and identity.

Cast: Art Parkinson as Kubo
Charlize Theron as Mother
Brenda Vaccaro as Kameyo
Cary-Hiroyuki Tagawa as Hashi
Meyrick Murphy as Mari
George Takei as Hosato

Rooney Mara as The Sisters
Ralph Fiennes as Moon King
Matthew McConaughey as Beetle
Minae Noji as Minae
Alpha Takahashi as Aiko
Laura Miro as Miho

Music Highlights: "While My Guitar Gently Weeps" (George Harrison) performed by Regina Spektor (orig. by The Beatles). Music by Dario Marianelli.

Film Facts

- Travis Knight was an animator on *Coraline* (2009), *ParaNorman* (2012) and *The Boxtrolls* (2014).
- "Hosato" is George Takei's middle name. Takei's catchphrase, "Oh, my!" is included (11:04), as it is in the 2013 film *Free Birds* (1:23:46).
- The fire-breathing chicken is an actual Japanese folklore *yōkai*, called Basan, Basabasa, or Inuhōō.
- Monkey has a scar under her eye, just as Kubo's mother does.

Kung Fu Panda (PG)

Theatrical release date: June 6, 2008
Production Company: DreamWorks Animation, Paramount Pictures
Length: 92 minutes
Directed by: Mark Osborne, John Stevenson
Screenplay by: Jonathan Aibel & Glenn Berger, story by Ethan Reiff & Cyrus Voris

Synopsis: The clumsy panda Po dreams of being a kung fu legend, while working in the noodle restaurant of his adoptive father, the goose Mr. Ping. Meanwhile at the Jade Palace, Master Shifu's training of the Furious Five, Tigress, Monkey, Crane, Viper, and Mantis, is interrupted when Shifu's master, the turtle Oogway, has had a vision that the vicious snow leopard Tai Lung will escape from prison. They agree to use the Dragon Scroll, which will make a chosen one into the Dragon Warrior. In what seems like a random accident, Po lands in front of Master Oogway, and is named the Dragon Warrior, to Shifu's horror. Shifu and the Furious Five reluctantly begin training Po, with disastrous results. They get word that Tai Lung has indeed escaped, and even worse, Master Oogway departs from the mortal realm, just after imploring Master Shifu to complete Po's training. Po progresses rapidly, and is finally deemed ready for the Dragon Scroll. When the mysterious scroll contains less of a revelation than expected, Po returns home in disappointment, until unexpected wisdom from his father sends him back to face Tai Lung, finally believing in himself.

Cast: Jack Black as Po
Dustin Hoffman as Shifu
Angelina Jolie as Tigress
Ian McShane as Tai Lung
Jackie Chan as Monkey
Seth Rogen as Mantis
Lucy Liu as Viper

David Cross as Crane
Randall Duk Kim as Oogway
James Hong as Mr. Ping
Dan Fogler as Zeng
Michael Clarke Duncan as Commander Vachir
Wayne Knight as Gang Boss

Music Highlights: "Kung Fu Fighting" (Douglas) performed by Cee-Lo Green and Jack Black (orig. by Carl Douglas). Music by Hans Zimmer and John Powell.

Film Facts

• The filmmakers studied Chinese culture for years in developing the film, basing the martial arts of the Furious Five on actual styles, studying Asian music, and making use of chi/qi energy points.
• A post credits scene (1:31:19) features Po and Shifu.
• The film was nominated for the "Best Animated Feature" Academy Award and Golden Globe.
• Additional appearances: "Kung Fu Panda: Secrets of the Furious Five" short (2008, 25 min.), "Kung Fu Panda Holiday" short (2010, 21 min.), *Kung Fu Panda 2* (2011), "Kung Fu Panda: Secrets of the Masters" short (2011, 23 min.), *Kung Fu Panda: Legends of Awesomeness* series (2011-2016), *Kung Fu Panda 3* (2016), *Kung Fu Panda: The Paws of Destiny* series (2018-2019).

Kung Fu Panda 2 (PG)

Theatrical release date: May 26, 2011
Production Company: DreamWorks Animation
Length: 90 minutes
Directed by: Jennifer Yuh Nelson
Written by: Jonathan Aibel & Glenn Berger

Synopsis: Fireworks were invented by the Peacocks of Gongmen City, but where others saw beauty, the young Shen saw power in using them as gunpowder. A prophecy stated that a warrior of black and white would defeat him, so Shen began doing away with all the pandas, and was banished from the city. Years later, as Master Shifu explains to the panda Po that he must learn inner peace, word comes that Shen's henchmen are raiding the musician village, stealing metal. During the battle, Po has a flash of memory, recalling himself as a baby with his mother. He returns home talk to his father, the goose Mr. Ping, who finally tells him he was adopted, after he was found in an alley. When Lord Shen uses a terrible weapon to kill Master Thundering Rhino, Po sets out to stop him, aided by the Furious Five: Tigress, Monkey, Mantis, Viper, and Crane. Lord Shen returns to Gongmen City, and during a confrontation with Shen, Po learns that Shen was there when Po was separated from his parents. Shen escapes, but Po follows, seeking answers about his past. During their battle Shen tells Po his parents didn't love him, then shoots him with a cannon, the blast carrying his body far away. Po is found by Shen's Soothsayer, who helps him recall that his parents sacrificed themselves protecting him from Shen's attack. With renewed determination, Po sets out to confront Shen and fulfill the prophecy, finding inner peace in the heat of battle.

Cast: Jack Black as Po
Angelina Jolie as Tigress
Dustin Hoffman as Shifu
Gary Oldman as Shen
Jackie Chan as Monkey
Seth Rogen as Mantis
Lucy Liu as Viper

David Cross as Crane
James Hong as Mr. Ping
Michelle Yeoh as Soothsayer
Danny McBride as Wolf Boss
Dennis Haysbert as Master Ox
Jean-Claude Van Damme as Master Croc
Victor Garber as Master Rhino

Music Highlights: "Joy" (Liu Mingyuan) performed by China Broadcasting Chinese Orchestra, "Tricked Pickpocket" (Éric Serra) performed by Éric Serra. Music by Hans Zimmer and John Powell.

Film Facts

• Michelle Yeoh, voice of the Soothsayer, starred in *Crouching Tiger, Hidden Dragon* (2000). The instrumental piece "Tricked Pickpocket" is from the 2003 film *Bulletproof Monk*, starring Chow Yun-fat, another star of *Crouching Tiger, Hidden Dragon*.
• The peacock Shen uses the Choy Li Fut/Cai Li Fo martial arts style, using his tail as a metal fan.
• The film was nominated for the "Best Animated Feature" Academy Award.
• Subtitles considered for the film included "Pandamoneum" and "The Kaboom of Doom."

Kung Fu Panda 3 (PG)

Theatrical release date: January 29, 2016
Production Company: DreamWorks Animation, Pearl Studio (as Oriental DreamWorks)
Length: 95 minutes
Directed by: Jennifer Yuh Nelson, Alessandro Carloni
Written by: Jonathan Aibel & Glenn Berger

Synopsis: In the spirit realm, the wicked bull Kai confronts the kind master Oogway, stealing his chi as part of his plan to return to the mortal realm. Back at the Jade Palace, master Shifu announces he is retiring, putting the panda Po, the clumsy Dragon Master, in charge of training the Furious Five. Kai sends a team of jade warriors to capture Oogway's students. Po's long-lost father Li Shan shows up, but their reunion is cut short when Kai's warriors attack the Jade Palace. A scroll reveals how Kai was Oogway's best friend, but when a group of pandas healed an injured Oogway, Kai was corrupted, and banished by Oogway to the spirit realm. Po agrees to go with Li to learn about chi among the pandas, accompanied by his stowaway father Ping. Kai defeats a band of opponents, turning Crane and Mantis into possessed jade warriors, and marches on the Jade Palace, destroying it along with Oogway's statue. Tigress escapes to warn Po, whose father finally confesses he doesn't know the secret of chi. The panda village volunteers to help Po, and he realizes they all have natural strengths which will help them fight. When Po must take the fight to the spirit realm, Li Shan finally realizes how to provide him the chi he needs to win.

Cast: Jack Black as Po
Bryan Cranston as Li
Dustin Hoffman as Shifu
Angelina Jolie as Tigress
J.K. Simmons as Kai
Jackie Chan as Monkey
Seth Rogen as Mantis
Lucy Liu as Viper

David Cross as Crane
Kate Hudson as Mei Mei
James Hong as Mr. Ping
Randall Duk Kim as Oogway
Steele Gagnon as Bao
Liam Knight as Lei Lei
Wayne Knight as Big Fun/Hom-Lee
Barbara Dirickson as Grandma Panda

Music Highlights: "I'm So Sorry" (Reynolds/Sermon/McKee/Platzman) performed by Imagine Dragons, "Kung Fu Fighting (Celebration Time)" (Carl Douglas) performed by Shanghai Roxi Musical Studio Choirs and Metro Voices, London. End Credits: "Try" (Vincent Fang/Celeste Syn/Patrick Brasca) performed by Patrick Brasca feat. Jay Chou, "Kung Fu Fighting" (Douglas) performed by The Vamps (orig. by Carl Douglas). Music by Hans Zimmer.

Film Facts

• The DVD/Blu-ray include the shorts "Everybody Loves a Panda Party" and "Panda Paws."
• Pandas rolling instead of walking is based on actual panda behavior.
• The film was followed by *Kung Fu Panda: The Paws of Destiny* animated TV series (2018-2019).
• More sequels have been discussed, with some plans calling for six films in all.

Lady and the Tramp (G)

Theatrical release date: June 22, 1955
Production Company: Walt Disney Productions
Length: 76 minutes
Directed by: Hamilton Luske, Clyde Geronimi, Wilfred Jackson
Story: Erdman Penner, Joe Rinaldi, Ralph Wright, Don Dagradi, from the story by Ward Greene

Synopsis: Pampered house-dog Lady has her world turned upside-down when the arrival of a new baby leads her to flee from the housesitting Aunt Sarah and her wicked Siamese cats. Rescued by the scruffy-but-noble Tramp, Lady learns about the perils and pleasures of life on the street. Lady is eventually caught by the dogcatcher, and Aunt Sarah chains her in the backyard. When a rat threatens the new baby, Lady's frantic barks bring Tramp to save the day, but Aunt Sarah mistakenly thinks Tramp was causing trouble, sending him to the pound. Lady's friends Trusty and Jock chase the dogcatcher's wagon, freeing Tramp, but Trusty is seriously injured in the process. Trusty heals in the end, and when they return to Lady's home, it is the Tramp's turn to learn a new way of life.

Cast: Peggy Lee as Darling/Si/Am/Peg
Barbara Luddy as Lady
Larry Roberts as Tramp
Bill Thompson as Jock
Bill Baucom as Trusty
Stan Freberg as Beaver

Verna Felton as Aunt Sarah
Alan Reed as Boris
George Givot as Tony
Dallas McKennon as Toughy
Lee Millar as Jim Dear

Music Highlights: "He's a Tramp" (Sonny Burke/Peggy Lee) performed by Peggy Lee, "La La Lu" (Sonny Burke/Peggy Lee) performed by Peggy Lee, "The Siamese Cat Song" (Sonny Burke/Peggy Lee) performed by Peggy Lee, "Bella Notte (This is the Night)" (Sonny Burke/Peggy Lee) performed by George Givot. Musical score by Oliver Wallace.

Film Facts

• The 15th Disney animated classic, *Lady and the Tramp* was a combination of two stories. In 1937, story artist Joe Grant proposed the project *Lady,* based on events in Grant's household, when his dog was dethroned by his new baby. The story didn't have enough "bite," so Disney suggested adding elements of Ward Greene's 1945 *Cosmopolitan* story, "Happy Dan, The Cynical Dog." A group of Disney's top writers, Erdman Penner, Joe Rinaldi, and Ralph Wright, were joined by Don DaGradi in fashioning the story into a film; meanwhile, Greene published a 1953 novel, *Lady and the Tramp: The Story of Two Dogs,* drawing from his story and from Grant's.
• The name "Tramp" thankfully beat out other possibilities, which included Bozo, Homer, and Rags. The cats Si and Am were originally called "Nip" and "Tuck."
• In the editing process, the famous "spaghetti kiss" scene was almost cut, as Disney found it silly.
• Scamp, a minor character who was unnamed in the film, had comic strip from 1955 to 1988.
• Additional appearances: *Lady and the Tramp II: Scamp's Adventure* (2001), and the live-action version of *Lady and the Tramp* (2019).

Lady and the Tramp II: Scamp's Adventure (G)

Home media release date: February 27, 2001
Production Company: Walt Disney Video Premiere, Walt Disney Television Animation, Walt Disney Animation Australia
Length: 69 minutes
Directed by: Darrell Rooney, co-directed by Jeannine Roussel
Screenplay by: Bill Motz & Bob Roth

> **Synopsis:** Lady and the Tramp's son Scamp escapes to pursue life with the junkyard dogs, led by Buster, a former associate of the Tramp's. He meets Angel, a good-hearted stray who envies the home that Scamp has abandoned. Scamp sees home differently after life on the street.

Cast: Scott Wolf as Scamp
    Roger Bart as Scamp (singing)
Alyssa Milano as Angel
    Susan Egan as Angel (singing)
Chazz Palminteri as Buster
Jeff Bennett as Tramp/Jock/Trusty
Jodi Benson as Lady
Bill Fagerbakke as Mooch (sheepdog)
Mickey Rooney as Sparky (Irish Wolfhound)
Bronson Pinchot as Francois (Boston Terrier)
Cathy Moriarty as Ruby (Afghan Hound)
Mary Kay Bergman as Si
Debi Derryberry as Annette
Barbara Goodson as Darling
Nick Jameson as Jim Dear
Tress MacNeille as Aunt Sarah/Am
Andrew McDonough as Junior
Rob Paulsen as Otis (Chinese Crested)
Kath Soucie as Collette/Danielle
Frank Welker as Reggie (Bullmastiff)

Music Highlights: "(Prologue) Welcome Home" (Manchester/Gimbel) performed by Jodi Benson, Jeff Bennett, Jim Cummings, Debi Derryberry, Michael Gough, Kath Soucie, "World Without Fences" (Melissa Manchester/Normal Gimbel) performed by Roger Bart, "Junkyard Society Rag" (Manchester/Gimbel) performed by Jess Harnell, Bill Fagerbakke, Melissa Manchester, Cathy Moriarty, Mickey Rooney, Broson Pinchot, "I Didn't Know I Could Feel This Way" (Manchester/Gimbel) performed by Roger Bart and Susan Egan, "Always There" (Manchester/Gimbel) performed by Roger Bart, Jeff Bennett, Jodi Benson, Susan Egan, "Bella Note (This is the Night)" (Peggy Lee/Sonny Burke) performed by Joy Enriquez and Carlos Ponce. Music score by Danny Troob.

Film Facts

• *Lady and the Tramp II: Scamp's Adventure* takes place shortly after the end of the first film.
• Roger Bart and Susan Egan provided the singing voices for Scamp and Angel; they previously provided voices for Hercules and Meg in the film *Hercules* (1997).
• Adult contemporary singer Melissa Manchester, who wrote and sang "Let Me Be Good to You" for *The Great Mouse Detective* (1986), wrote a handful of songs for the soundtrack, including "Welcome Home."
• The core creative team had worked together on *The Lion King II* (1998), including co-directors Darrell Rooney and Jeannine Roussel, and writers Bill Motz and Bob Roth. Motz & Roth were a writing duo who had contributed to several Disney animated TV series.
• Additional appearances: Sequel to *Lady and the Tramp* (1955).

The Land Before Time franchise

The Land Before Time (1988). Littlefoot, Cera, Ducky, Petrie, and Spike must make their way to the Great Valley.

The Land Before Time II: The Great Valley Adventure (1994). Cera leads her friends into the Mysterious Beyond, where they meet the egg-stealing dinosaurs Ozzie and Strut.

The Land Before Time III: The Time of the Great Giving (1995). When a meteorite cuts off their water supply, Littlefoot and his friends set out to find a new source of water.

The Land Before Time IV: Journey Through the Mists (1996). Strange creatures are said to live in the Land of Mists, where Littlefoot must journey to get medicine for his grandfather.

The Land Before Time V: The Mysterious Island (1997). Swarming Leaf Gobblers eat the food in the Great Valley, and the young dinosaurs end up on the Mysterious Island, where sharptooths dwell.

The Land Before Time VI: The Secret of Saurus Rock (1998). When the twin baby threehorns Dinah and Dana run away, Littlefoot, Cera, Ducky, Petrie, and Spike set out to bring them back.

The Land Before Time VII: The Stone of Cold Fire (2001). Littlefoot sees a "stone of cold fire" fall from the sky, and goes looking for it in the Mysterious Beyond with his companions.

The Land Before Time VIII: The Big Freeze (2001). Snow comes to the Great Valley for the first time, and Mr. Thicknose helps the dinosaurs find Spike and Ducky in the Mysterious Beyond.

The Land Before Time IX: Journey to the Big Water (2002). Heavy rains end up stranding the colorful dolphin-like Mo, and he needs the help of the young dinosaurs to get back to the Big Water.

The Land Before Time X: The Great Longneck Migration (2003). Littlefoot, his grandparents, and all the other Longnecks have a dream that draws them to a huge gathering, to save the sun.

The Land Before Time XI: Invasion of the Tinysauruses (2005). When all the delicious treesweets in the Great Valley disappear, everyone suspects Littlefoot, but they soon learn of a colony of tiny longnecks.

The Land Before Time XII: The Great Day of the Flyers (2006). Petrie is worried about the approaching Great Day of the Flyers, but gets some good advice from the fuzzy dinosaur Guido.

The Land Before Time XIII: The Wisdom of Friends (2007). The dinosaurs help Loofah and Doofah, who have lost their way while traveling to the Berry Valley.

The Land Before Time XIV: Journey of the Brave (2016). When his father, Bron, has been stranded after a volcano erupted, Littlefoot goes to find him, with the help of a Pteranodon named Etta.

The Land Before Time animated TV series (2007–2008)

152

The Land Before Time (G)

Theatrical release date: November 18, 1988
Production Company: Amblin Entertainment, Sullivan Bluth Ltd.
Length: 69 minutes
Directed by: Don Bluth
Screenplay by: Stu Krieger, story by Judy Freudberg & Tony Geiss

Synopsis: In the dangerous land of dinosaurs, leafeaters head west in search of food in the Great Valley. On the way, the baby longneck dinosaur Littlefoot hatches, traveling with his mother and grandparents. Littlefoot begins to play with the young triceratops Cera, but their parents tell them to stay with their own kind. When Littlefoot and Cera follow a frog, a Tyrannosaurus Rex attacks, and Littlefoot's mother is terribly injured while protecting the young dinosaurs. An earthquake separates Littlefoot from his grandparents and Cera from her parents, and soon after, Littlefoot's mother dies. The kind Rooter encourages Littlefoot to keep going. Littlefoot tries to persuade Cera to come with him to the Great Valley, but she refuses, preferring to look for her family. Littlefoot is soon joined by the bigmouth Ducky and the flyer Petrie. Cera catches up with them later, after a run-in with the temporarily stunned Tyrannosaurus Rex. Ducky finds a sleepy, just-hatched spiketail, which she names Spike, who joins their band. Working together, the hungry young dinosaurs are able to eat the leaves of a tree. Their journey is complicated by Cera's stubbornness, lava, tarpits, and the threat of sharptooths, but by helping each other they finally find the Great Valley, where Cera reunites with her father and Littlefoot finds his grandparents.

Cast: Judith Barsi as Ducky
Burke Byrnes as Daddy Topps
Gabriel Damon as Littlefoot
Bill Erwin as Grandfather
Pat Hingle as Narrator/Rooter
Candy Hutson as Cera
Will Ryan as Petrie
Helen Shaver as Littlefoot's Mother

Music Highlights: "If We Hold On Together" (James Horner/Will Jennings) performed by Diana Ross. Music by James Horner.

Film Facts

• Littlefoot is an Apatosaurus ("longneck"), Cera is a Triceratops ("threehorn"), Ducky is a Saurolophus ("bigmouth"), Petrie is a Pteranodon ("flyer"), and Spike is a Stegosaurus ("spiketail").
• Petrie wraps Littlefoot's leaf around him (32:49), resembling the crow Jeremy from *The Secret of NIMH* (1982), when he is "undercover."
• Executive Producers Steven Spielberg and George Lucas advised many edits to cut or tone down overly scary scenes, leading to a relatively short running time. The cuts led to re-sequencing certain scenes, so the one-eyed Tyrannosaurus Rex (14:27) later mysteriously has both eyes (31:52).
• Pizza Hut offered a series of hand puppets to promote the film.
• Additional appearances: See *The Land Before Time* franchise page.

The Last Unicorn (G)

Theatrical release date: November 19, 1982
Production Company: Rankin/Bass Productions, Topcraft, ITC Films
Length: 93 minutes
Directed by: Arthur Rankin, Jr. and Jules Bass
Screenplay by: Peter S. Beagle, based on his novel *The Last Unicorn*

Synopsis: A unicorn overhears two hunters saying that she is the last unicorn. Unable to believe she is the last, she asks a passing butterfly if it has seen any others. The butterfly tells her the Red Bull of King Haggard had pushed all the unicorns to the ends of the earth. The unicorn leaves her forest, searching for others of her kind. The caravan of the witch Mommy Fortuna finds the unicorn sleeping, and she is captured. She meets the witch's magician, Schmendrick, who agrees to free her, then the unicorn frees the harpy Celaeno before she and Schmendrick depart. Schmendrick is captured by Captain Cully and his band, but escapes, accompanied by Molly Grue, another member of Cully's company. The unicorn finally approaches the castle of King Haggard, and when the ferocious Red Bull threatens her, Schmendrick transforms the unicorn into the woman Amalthea. They meet the unhappy King Haggard, and his son, Prince Lir, who seeks to win Lady Amalthea's favor. As the unicorn remains in Lady Amalthea's guise, she becomes confused and anxious. The wise palace cat explains that the unicorn must face the Red Bull, by finding the tunnel to the Red Bull's lair, "when the wine drinks itself, when the skull speaks, when the clock strikes the right time." King Haggard reveals that unicorns were the only thing that made him happy, and he used the Red Bull to drive them into the sea, where he could possess them. In a confrontation with the Red Bull, Prince Lir seeks to defend the unicorn, and is struck down. The unicorn's resolve to protect him finally helps her to turn the tide on the Red Bull.

Cast: Alan Arkin as Schmendrick
Jeff Bridges as Prince Lir
Mia Farrow as Unicorn/Amalthea
Tammy Grimes as Molly Grue
Robert Klein as The Butterfly
Angela Lansbury as Mommy Fortuna

Christopher Lee as King Haggard
Keenan Wynn as Captain Cully/Harpy
Paul Frees as Mabruk/The Tree/The Cat
Rene Auberjonois as The Skull
Theodore Gottlieb as Ruhk
Don Messick as The Cat

Music Highlights: "The Last Unicorn" (Jimmy Webb) performed by America, "Man's Road" (Jimmy Webb) performed by America, "Now That I'm a Woman" (Jimmy Webb) performed by Mia Farrow, "In the Sea" (Jimmy Webb) performed by America, "That's All I've Got to Say" (Jimmy Webb) performed by Jeff Bridges and Katie Irving. Music by Jimmy Webb.

Film Facts

- Peter S. Beagle's novel *The Last Unicorn* was published in 1968.
- The animation was completed at the Tokyo studio Topcraft, which later became Studio Ghibli.
- The song "The Last Unicorn" was covered by Kenny Loggins, Groove Coverage, and Dan Avidan.

Leap! (PG)

Theatrical release date: October 19, 2016 (Mon Premier Festival, France), August 25, 2017 (USA)
Country: Canada, France   **French title**: *Ballerina*
Production Company: L'Atelier Animation, Quad Productions, Main Journey, Caramel Film
Length: 89 minutes
Directed by: Éric Summer and Éric Warin
Screenplay by: Carol Noble, Laurent Zeitoun, Éric Summer, based on a story by Éric Summer, Laurent Zeitoun, based on an idea by Éric Summer

---

Synopsis: Félicie and Victor are children in an orphanage in France. Félicie dreams of dancing ballet, and one day she and Victor flee to Paris. The pair are separated, and Félicie talks her way into assisting Odette, the cleaner at the home of the wealthy and cruel Régine Le Haut. Régine's daughter, Camille Le Haut, who is as cruel as her mother, is waiting to be admitted to the Paris Opera Ballet school. She insults Félicie and breaks her music box, the only possession she brought with her to the orphanage. Angry at her mistreatment, Félicie impersonates Camille, taking her place at the ballet school, but does not impress her teacher, Mérante. Meanwhile, Victor, who dreams of being an inventor, begins working for Gustave Eiffel, who is building the Eiffel Tower. Odette agrees to train Félicie in dance. Mérante dismisses one dancer from the class each day, and Félicie works hard not to get cut. Odette repeatedly asks her. "Why do you dance?" Félicie's deception is discovered, but Mérante, impressed with her hard work, insists that she be able to participate in a crucial audition for the Nutcracker. Félicie does not do well in her audition, but finally realizes why she dances.

Cast: Elle Fanning as Félicie
Nat Wolff as Victor
Carly Rae Jepsen as Odette
Maddie Ziegler as Camille
Terence Scammel as Mérante
Tamir Kapelian as Rudolph

Kate McKinnon as Regine
Joe Sheridan as Director of Opera
Elena Dunkelman as Dora
Soshana Sperling as Nora
Jamie Watson as Greasy Guard
Bronwen Mantel as Mother Superior

Music Highlights: "You Know It's About You" (Braide/Wrabel) performed by Magical Thinker featuring Stephen Wrabel, "Rainbow" (Kreviazuk/Kotara.McInnis) performed by Liz Huett, "Be Somebody" (Kreviazuk/NZA/Salter/Pompetzki/Remmler) performed by Chantal Kreviazuk, "Unstoppable" (Matías Mora/Mia Minichiello) performed by Camila Mora, "Blood, Sweat and Tears" (Braide/Getz/Quiñones) performed by Magical Thinker feat. Dezi Paige, "Suitcase" (Furler/Braide) performed by Sia, "Confident" (Ilya/Kotecha/Martin/Lovato) performed by Demi Lovato, "Cut to the Feeling" (Jepsen/Wilcox/Nolan) performed by Carly Rae Jepsen, "Runaways" (Jepsen/Parish/Hollander) performed by Carly Rae Jepsen. Music by Klaus Badelt.

Film Facts

• Aurélie Dupont and Jérémie Bélingard of the Paris Opera Ballet choreographed the film's dance.
• Dane DeHaan voiced Victor and Julie Khaner voiced Regine in the French version.
• Mel Brooks voiced Luteau in the US version.

Legend of the Guardians: The Owls of Ga'Hoole (PG)

Theatrical release date: September 24, 2010
Production Company: Village Roadshow Pictures, Animal Logic, Cruel and Unusual Films, GOG
Length: 97 minutes
Directed by: Zack Snyder
Screenplay by: John Orloff and Emil Stern, based on the *Guardians of Ga'hoole* novels by Kathryn Lasky

Synopsis: Young owl siblings Soren, a dreamer, and Kludd, a realist, are raised with their sister Eglantine by their parents, Noctus and Marella, and their nursemaid, the snake Mrs. P. A Tasmanian devil attacks Soren and Kludd when they accidentally tumble out of their tree. Unable to fly yet, they are snatched away by the cruel owls Jutt and Jatt, and taken to St. Aegolius, led by the "Pure Ones," Metal Beak and his wife, General Nyra. They are told this is their new home. Soren defends the small elf owl Gylfie, and they are assigned to be "pickers," gathering metal flecks for the Pure Ones' weapon. Kludd declines to join them, becoming a soldier. Jutt and Jatt brainwash the new owls by "moonblinking" them, but Gylfie and Soren resist. One of the enforcers, Grimble, perceives that they have escaped being moon blinked, and offers to teach them to fly, telling them to find the sea of Hoolemere and warn the guardians of Ga'hool. They are discovered by Nyra and Kludd, and when Nyra attacks Grimble, Kludd decides to help her rather than returning home. Soren and Gylfie flee, and are soon joined by the timid Digger, the poet-warrior Twilight, and Mrs. P, caught by Twilight. A wise echidna guides the band to find the Guardians at the Tree of Ga'Hoole. The leaders, Boron and Barran, ask the skeptical Allomere and two soldiers to investigate St. Aegolius, but they are ambushed. Allomere is able to return, confirming the threat of the Pure Ones, and the Guardians prepare to do battle to stop their evil plan.

Cast: Jim Sturgess as Soren
Emily Barclay as Gylfie
Ryan Kwanten as Kludd
Helen Mirren as Nyra
Geoffrey Rush as Ezylryb/The Lyze of Kiel
Hugo Weaving as Noctus and Grimble
Abbie Cornish as Otulissa

Anthony LaPaglia as Twilight
Miriam Margolyes as Mrs. Plithiver
Sam Neill as Allomere
Richard Roxburgh as Boron
David Wenham as Digger
Joel Edgerton as Metal Beak
Adrienne DeFaria as Eglantine

Music Highlights: "To the Sky" (Adam Young) performed by Owl City, "Coming Home" (Lisa Gerrard/Harry Gregson-Williams) performed by Lisa Gerrard, "The Host of the Seraphim" (Lisa Gerrard/Brendan Perry) performed by Dead Can Dance. Music by David Hirschfelder.

Film Facts

- The film is based on the first 3 books of Kathryn Lasky's 16-book *Guardians of Ga'Hoole* series.
- The character of Allomere did not appear in the books.
- Director Zack Snyder went on to direct many of the DC Comics/DC Extended Universe films.

The LEGO Movie (PG)

Theatrical release date: February 7, 2014
Production Company: Warner Animation Group, Village Roadshow Pictures, LEGO Group
Length: 100 minutes
Directed by: Christopher Miller, Phil Lord
Screenplay by: Phil Lord & Christopher Miller, story by Dan Hageman & Kevin Hageman and Phil Lord & Christopher Miller

Synopsis: The seemingly very ordinary Emmet Brickowski is believed to be the Special one who will fulfill an ancient (8.5 years old) prophecy to recover the Piece of Resistance which can stop the Kragle, a weapon stolen by President Business, which can freeze the world. When Emmet is captured by Bad Cop and almost melted down, he is rescued by the fierce Wyldstyle, and taken to the wise Vitruvius. Emmet learns that Wyldstyle and Vitruvius are both Master Builders, who need no instructions to create. Though Emmet's cluelessness casts doubt on his abilities, his visions of "the Man Upstairs" provide hope that he may truly be the Special one.

Cast: Chris Pratt as Emmet Brickowski
Elizabeth Banks as Wyldstyle/Lucy
Will Ferrell as Lord Business/
      President Business/The Man Upstairs
Morgan Freeman as Vitruvius
Alison Brie as Unikitty
Nick Offerman as Metal Beard
Liam Neeson as Bad Cop/Good Cop/Pa Cop
Jadon Sand as Finn

Will Arnett as Batman/Bruce Wayne
Channing Tatum as Superman
Cobie Smulders as Wonder Woman
Jonah Hill as Green Lantern
Anthony Daniels as C-3PO
Billy Dee Williams as Lando
Keith Ferguson as Han Solo
Todd Hansen as Gandalf
Amanda Farinos as Mom

Music Highlights: "Everything is Awesome (The Awesome!! Version)" (Patterson/Bartholomew/Harriton/Schaffer/Samberg/Taccone) performed by Jo-Li feat. The Lonely Island, "Everything is Awesome (Awesome Remixxx!!!)" performed by Tegan & Sara feat. The Lonely Island, "War Cry" (Hegna/Werner) performed by Federale, "Everything is Awesome (Saloon Version)" (Patterson) performed by Peter Zachos, "Get Ready for This (Yar Mix)" (Wilde/DeCoster/Slijngaard/Harris) performed by 2 Unlimited, "How Ya Gonna Keep 'Em Down On The Farm" (Young/Lewis/Donaldson) performed by Judy Garland, "Untitled Self Portrait" (Mothersbaugh/Arnett/Lord/Miller) performed by Will Arnett, "Everything is Awesome (Unplugged)" (Patterson) performed by Shawn Patterson and Sammy Allen. Music by Mark Mothersbaugh.

Film Facts

- The LEGO Company designates the employees who design their sets as "Master Builders."
- Vitruvius was an ancient Roman architect, who wrote *De Architectura*.
- A tube marked "Magic Portal" refers to a 1989 brickfilm (stop motion LEGO film) of this name.
- Wyldstyle shows several LEGO "realms" to Emmet (19:50), including Pirate's Cove, Knight's Club, Viking's Landing, Clown Town, LEGO Friends, Speed Racer, BIONICLE, and Fabuland.

The LEGO Batman Movie (PG)

Theatrical release date: February 10, 2017
Production Company: Warner Animation Group, DC Ent., RatPac Ent., Lego System A/S
Length: 104 minutes
Directed by: Chris McKay
Screenplay by: Seth Grahame-Smith and Chris McKenna & Erik Sommers and Jared Stern & John Whittington, story by Seth Grahame-Smith

Synopsis: The Joker steals a plane filled with explosives, explaining that he has a plan to take over Gotham City with a horde of Batman's enemies. Batman saves the day, but is troubled when the city's new Commissioner, Barbara Gordon, says the city should no longer rely on Batman. Joker and the villains are poised to attack, but unexpectedly turn themselves in. Uneasy over the Joker's plan, Batman acquires the Phantom Zone Projector from Superman, accompanied by the recently-adopted Dick Grayson, soon code-named Robin. They break into Arkham Asylum and use the projector on the Joker. While in the Phantom Zone, the Joker recruits a host of ferocious villains, including Sauron, Voldemort, Medusa, and Daleks, all freed by Harley Quinn. Facing an unimaginable threat, Batman must also conront what he fears most: forming relationships and trusting others.

Cast: Will Arnett as Batman/Bruce Wayne
Michael Cera as Robin/Dick Grayson
Rosario Dawson as Batgirl/Barbara Gordon
Ralph Fiennes as Alfred Pennyworth
Siri as 'Puter
Zach Galifianakis as Joker
Jenny Slate as Harley Quinn

Jason Mantzoukas as Scarecrow
Conan O'Brien as The Riddler
Doug Benson as Bane
Billy Dee Williams as Two-Face
Zoë Kravitz as Catwoman
Kate Micucci as Clayface
Riki Lindhome as Poison Ivy

Music Highlights: "Who's the (Bat)Man" (Hefti/Wakili/Deskins/Pointer/Fisher/Rabinowitz/Lamot) performed by Patrick Stump, "Forever" (Tranter/Crean/Pyne/Whittle) performed by DNCE, "Man in the Mirror" (Ballard/Garrett) performed by Richard Cheese & Lounge Against The Machine, "(I Just) Died in Your Arms" (Eede) performed by Cutting Crew, "Invincible" (Rimes/Arian) performed by Kirsten Arian, "One" (Nilsson) performed by Harry Nilsson. End credits: "Friends Are Family" (Sernel/Love/Benjamin/Lewis/Miller) performed by Oh, Hush! feat. Will Arnett, "I Found You" (Balfe/Genn) performed by Fraser Murray. Music by Lorne Balfe.

Film Facts

• The Batman films referred to (19:16) include *Batman: The Movie* (1966), *Batman* (1989), *Batman Returns* (1992), *Batman Forever* (1995), *Batman & Robin* (1997), *Batman Begins* (2005), *The Dark Knight* (2008), *The Dark Knight Rises* (2012), and *Batman v Superman: Dawn of Justice* (2016).
• Ellie Kemper (of *Unbreakable Kimmy Schmidt*) voices Phyllis, the Phantom Zone gatekeeper.
• Polka-Dot Man, Mime, Eraser-Man, Kite-Man, and Condiment King (4:34) are indeed Batman villains. The Bat shark repellent (38:28) is also mentioned in *Batman: The Movie* (1966).
• The director intentionally contrasted the grimmest Batman with the most optimistic Robin.

The LEGO Movie 2: The Second Part (PG)

Theatrical release date: February 8, 2019
Production Company: Warner Animation Group, Rideback, Vertigo Ent., Animal Logic
Length: 107 minutes
Directed by: Mike Mitchell
Screenplay by: Phil Lord & Christopher Miller, story by Phil Lord & Christopher Miller and Matthew Fogel

Synopsis: Duplo aliens invade Bricksburg, which eventually becomes Apocalypseburg. The seemingly invincible General Mayhem invites five guests to a wedding, but when Wyldstyle refuses, the General captures her, Unikitty, Batman, MetalBeard, and the spaceman Benny, taking them in a spaceship to meet the alien Queen Watevera Wa'Nabi. The queen plans to marry Batman, which they fear will bring about the catastrophic Armamageddon. Emmett follows the captives through the Stairgate, meting Rex Dangervest, a super-confident adventurer with a dinosaur-crewed spaceship, who works with Emmet to stop the wedding. The five Lego prisoners are given the spa treatment, and all except Wyldstyle begin to support the wedding. When General Mayhem is at risk of falling to her doom, Wyldstyle reluctantly saves her, and learns the shocking truth about the wedding, and Armamageddon.

Cast: Chris Pratt as Emmet Brickowski/Rex Dangervest
Elizabeth Banks as Wyldstyle/Lucy
Will Arnett as Batman
Tiffany Haddish as Queen Watevra Wa'Nabi
Stephanie Beatriz as General Mayhem/Sweet Mayhem
Alison Brie as Unikitty/Ultrakatty
Nick Offerman as MetalBeard
Charlie Day as Benny
Maya Rudolph as Mom
Will Ferrell as President Business/Dad

Jadon Sand as Finn
Brooklynn Prince as Bianca
Channing Tatum as Superman
Jonah Hill as Green Lantern
Richard Ayoade as Ice Cream Cone
Noel Fielding as Balthazar
Jason Momoa as Aquaman
Cobie Smulders as Wonder Woman
Ralph Fiennes as Alfred Pennyworth
Todd Hansen as Gandalf/Swamp Creature

Music Highlights: "Everything Is Awesome (Tween Dream Remix)" (Patterson) performed by Garfunkel & Oates w/Eban Schletter, "5:15" (Miller/Guetta) performed by Stephanie Beatriz, "Welcome to the Systar System" (Lajoie) performed by Yossi/Esther Guetta/Fiora Cutler, "Not Evil" (Lajoie) performed by Tiffany Haddish, "Catchy Song" (Lajoie/High) performed by Dillon Francis feat. T-Pain & Lay Lay, "Gotham City Guys" (Lajoie) performed by Tiffany Haddish/Will Arnett, "Super Cool" (Hansen + Samberg/Schaffef/Taccone) performed by Beck feat. Robyn & Lonely Island, "Come Together Now" (Johnson/Schifino) performed by Matt & Kim, "Hello Me and You (Superorganism)" performed by Superorganism. Music by Mark Mothersbaugh.

Film Facts

- Director Mike Mitchell voices a few roles, including Sherry Scratchen-Post and the octopus Eight.
- Basketball stars Sheryl Swoopes and Gary Payton make brief cameo appearances.
- The film was promoted with the short series "Saving Bricksburg" and "Emmet's Holiday Party."

Lilo & Stitch (PG)

Theatrical release date: June 21, 2002
Production Company: Walt Disney Pictures, Walt Disney Feature Animation
Length: 85 minutes
Written and Directed by: Chris Sanders & Dean DeBlois

Synopsis: Mad scientist Jumba's experiment 626, a shape-shifting alien with a penchant for troublemaking, crash lands in Hawaii. After taking the form of a dog, the alien is adopted and named Stitch by Lilo Pelekai, a precocious misfit with an Elvis fixation being raised by her sister Nani. Jumba and high-strung scientist Pleakley are assigned to bring him back, though their efforts are thwarted by Stitch, efforts which are monitored by ex-CIA agent Cobra Bubbles, curiously now working as a child welfare officer. Stitch begins to question his purpose and his place in the universe, finding that his *ohana* (family) may be on Earth.

Cast: Daveigh Chase as Lilo
Christopher Michael Sanders as Stitch
Tia Carrere as Nani
David Ogden Stiers as Jumba
Kevin McDonald as Pleakley
Ving Rhames as Cobra Bubbles
Zoe Caldwell as Grand Councilwoman
Jason Scott Lee as David
Kevin Michael Richardson as Captain Gantu
Susan Hegarty as Rescue Lady

Music Highlights: "Hawaiian Roller Coaster Ride" (Silvestri/Ho'omalu) and "He Mele No Lilo" (Silvestri/Ho'omalu) performed by Mark Keali'i Ho'omalu/Hamehameha Schools Children's Chorus, "Stuck On You" (Schroeder/McFarland) performed by Elvis Presley, "Heartbreak Hotel" (Axton/Durden) performed by Elvis Presley, "Burning Love" (Linde) performed by Wynonna. Score by Alan Silvestri.

Film Facts

• The 42nd Disney animated classic, *Lilo & Stitch* was unlike anything the studio had done before, with aliens in Hawaii, a social worker who looks more like one of the "men in black," and beneath the chaos, a meditation on the children's story "The Ugly Duckling" and what it means to be part of a family. The film was co-written and co-directed by Chris Sanders and Dean DeBlois, who had worked together on *Mulan* (1998).
• Stitch was originally developed by Chris Sanders in the 1980s for a children's book. The story was originally set in Kansas, but relocated to Hawaii, changing its character significantly.
• The title of the song "He Mele No Lilo" means "A Song for Lilo."
• A DVD bonus features spoofs of coming attractions trailers featuring Stitch disrupting classic scenes from *Beauty and the Beast*, *The Little Mermaid*, *The Lion King*, and *Aladdin*.
• Future antagonist Dr. Hamsterviel is among the inmates when Jumba is imprisoned (8:37).
• The directors appeared in a cameo, running by after Stitch is acting up at the beach (45:06). Chris Sanders is wearing sunglasses, and Dean DeBlois has a beard and a cap with a smiley face.
• Filmmakers traveled to Kauai for research, studying aspects of Hawaiian culture such as the hula.
• Additional appearances: Followed by *Stitch! The Movie* home media (2003), *Lilo & Stitch: The Series* (2003-2006), *Lilo & Stitch 2: Stitch Has a Glitch* (2005), *Leroy & Stitch* home media (2006), *Stitch!/Suticchi!* Japanese TV series (2008-2011), *Stitch & Ai* Chinese animated TV series (2017).

Lilo and Stitch: *Stitch! The Movie* (G)

Home media release date: August 26, 2003
Production Company: Walt Disney Television Animation
Length: 64 minutes
Directed by: Tony Craig, Bobs Gannaway
Written by: Jess Winfield, Bobs Gannaway

Synopsis: After the events of the first film, alien Stitch is living with Lilo and her sister Nani, joined by mad scientist Jumba and Pleakley. Jumba had named Stitch "experiment 626," and secretly kept the other 625 experiments with him. The evil but diminutive Dr. Hamsterviel hires Captain Gantu to steal the experiments, and in the process, two experiments are freed: "Sparky," who thrives on electricity, and "Reuben," who has a gift for making sandwiches.

Cast: Daveigh Chase as Lilo
Chris Sanders as Stitch
Tia Carrere as Nani
David Ogden Stiers as Jumba
Kevin McDonald as Pleakley

Ving Rhames as Cobra Bubbles
Dee Bradley Baker as David Kawena
Kevin Michael Richardson as Captain Gantu
Jeff Bennett as Dr. Hamsterviel
Rob Paulsen as Reuben

Music Highlights: "Aloha, E Komo Mai" (Danny Jacob/Ali B. Olmo) performed by Jump 5. Original music by Michael Tavera.

Film Facts

• After the success of *Lilo & Stitch* (2002), Walt Disney Television Animation planed to develop an animated TV series based on the film. *Stitch! The Movie* was developed as a "backdoor pilot" to introduce the series, directed by Tony Craig and Bobs Gannaway, and written by Jess Winfield and Bobs Gannaway.
• Craig and Gannaway were well-known at Disney, having directed numerous episodes of the animated TV series *The Lion King's Timon & Pumbaa* (1995-1999), *101 Dalmatians: The Series* (1997-1998), *House of Mouse* (2001-2003), and *The Emperor's New School* (2006-2008). Co-writer Winfield had also worked on different TV series, writing for *101 Dalmatians: The Series* (1997-1998), *Buzz Lightyear of Star Command* (2000-2001), and *The Legend of Tarzan* (2001-2003).
• The end of the film set the stage for the animated TV series to come, poising Lilo and Stitch to track down the other 623 of Jumba's 626 experiments, and with each possessing very different appearances and powers, ample variety was assured.
• In terms of continuity, the events in this film and the animated TV series take place after those in *Lilo & Stitch 2: Stitch Has a Glitch* (2005), despite its later release date.
• Jumba and Pleakley have a final scene after the closing credits (60:00).
• Pleakley's name is Wendy Pleakley. He is male, but wears female clothes at times.
• The original title of the film was *Lilo & Stitch: A New Ohana*.
• A DVD game called *Lilo & Stitch's Island of Adventures* was released in 2003.

Lilo & Stitch 2: Stitch Has a Glitch (PG)

Home media release date: August 20, 2005
Production Company: Walt Disney Pictures, DisneyToon Studios, DisneyToon Studios Australia
Length: 68 minutes
Directed by: Tony Leondis and Michael LaBash
Screenplay by: Tony Leondis & Michael LaBash and Alexa Junge and Eddie Guzelian

Synopsis: After living happily with Lilo's family, steadily building his "goodness level," Stitch begins having difficulties, interfering with Lilo's hopes to win the same hula competition her mother won years before. As Lilo worries about Stitch's strange behavior and the upcoming hula competition, Pleakley serves as a relationship counselor for Nani and David, with disastrous results. It emerges that Stitch is malfunctioning, and will self-destruct without assistance from Jumba. Lilo recognizes that Stitch needs help, and hopes that it's not too late to give it.

Cast: Chris Sanders as Stitch
Dakota Fanning as Lilo
Tia Carrere as Nani
David Ogden Stiers as Jumba

Kevin McDonald as Pleakley
Kunewa Mook as Kumu
Jason Scott Lee as David

Music Highlights: "Always" (Alexa Junge/Jeanine Tesori) performed by Mark Keali'i Ho'omalu, Dennis and David Kamakahi, Hayley Westenra, Johnson Enos, "I Need Your Love Tonight" (Reichner/Wayne) performed by Elvis Presley, "Rubberneckin'" (Warren/Jones) performed by Elvis Presley, "A Little Less Conversation" (Strange/Davis) performed by Elvis Presley, "Hawaiian Roller Coaster Ride" (Silvestri/Ho'omalu) performed by Jump 5, "He Makana Ke Aloha (A Gift of Love)" (Kunewa Mook). Original score composed by Joel McNeely.

Film Facts

• In the story chronology, the events in this film follow *Lilo & Stitch* (2002), but come before *Stitch! The Movie* (2003).
• The DVD includes "The Origin of Stitch" bonus short, which is best viewed after the film, as it connects the events from *Lilo & Stitch 2: Stitch Has a Glitch* to those in *Stitch! The Movie* (2003).
• Daveigh Chase was occupied voicing Lilo in the *Lilo & Stitch: The Series*, making it difficult for her to take on this role as well. Chase's friend, Dakota Fanning, agreed to fill in as Lilo for this film.
• At one point in the film Lilo tells Stitch about the legend of Hi'iakaikapoliopele, recounted in the 2012 book *The Epic Tale of Hiiakaikapolipele* by Ho'oulumahiehie and Puakea Nogelmeier, translated by M. Puakea Nogelmeier.
• Kunewa Mook, as Kumu, the mellow hula instructor, also appeared in *Lilo & Stitch* (2002), *Stitch! The Movie* (2003), and *Lilo & Stitch: The Series* (2003-2006).
• Additional appearances: Follows *Lilo & Stitch* (2002), *Stitch! The Movie* (2003), and *Lilo & Stitch: The Series* (2003-2006), followed by *Leroy & Stitch* (2006), *Stitch!/Suticchi!* Japanese anime TV series (2008-2011), *Stitch & Ai* Chinese animated TV series (2017).

Lilo & Stitch: *Leroy & Stitch* (G)

Home media release date: June 23, 2006
Production Company: Walt Disney Pictures, Walt Disney Television Animation
Length: 73 minutes
Directed by: Tony Craig, Bobs Gannaway
Written by: Bobs Gannaway, Jess Winfield

Synopsis: Picking up after each of Jumba's experiments has found its niche, Jumba, Pleakley and Stitch go their separate ways, but after Captain Gantu springs Dr. Hamsterviel from prison, they force Jumba to create an evil red version of Stitch, which is copied hundreds of times to form an army. Jumba's experiments join forces to hold off the army, until Lilo and Stitch discover an unexpected secret weapon, where Elvis meets "aloha."

Cast: Daveigh Chase as Lilo
Chris Sanders as Stitch/Leroy
David Ogden Stiers as Jumba
Kevin McDonald as Pleakley
Tia Carrere as Nani
Kevin Michael Richardson as Gantu
Rob Paulsen as Reuben
Jeff Bennett as Dr. Hamsterviel
Zoe Caldwell as Grand Councilwoman

Bobcat Goldthwait as Nosy
Jillian Henry as Elena
Lili Ishida as Yuki
Tress MacNeille as Bonnie/Poxy/Gigi/
    Topper/Felix/Melty/Amnesio/
    Cannonball
Rocky McMurray as Clyde
Liliana Mumy as Mertle Edmonds
Ving Rhames as Cobra Bubbles

Music Highlights: "Aloha 'Oe" (Lili'uokalani) performed by Elvis Presley, "I'm So Lonesome I Could Cry" (Hank Williams) performed by Elvis Presley, "Jailhouse Rock" (Jerry Leiber/Mike Stoller) performed by Elvis Presley, "Don't Be Cruel" (Otis Blackwell) performed by Everlife, "Aloha 'Oe" (Lili'uokalani) performed by Daveigh Chase as Lilo, Chris Sanders as Stitch, and Rob Paulsen as Reuben. Score by J.A.C. Redford.

Film Facts

• While *Stitch! The Movie* (2003) served as a backdoor pilot for the animated television series *Lilo & Stitch: The Series* (2003-2006), *Leroy & Stitch* served as the series finale.
• The end credits include a list of all 626 of Jumba's experiments.
• After this film Chris Sanders and Dean DeBlois left Disney to develop *How to Train Your Dragon* (2010) at DreamWorks Animation. Sanders also co-directed *The Croods* (2013).
• Hamsterviel gives the coordinates of the black hole as 12211979 (at 34:30). The release date of the live-action Disney film *The Black Hole* was 12/21/1979.
• Timon and Pumbaa from *The Lion King* can be seen in the stadium crowd (on the right at 58:43).
• The *Lilo & Stitch Hawaiian Album* CD included a handful of Elvis Presley songs and the Lilo, Stitch, and Reuben version of "Aloha 'Oe" from the film, as well as some tracks from the original *Lilo & Stitch* (2002) film, and *Stitch! The Movie* (2003).
• It seemed for a time that *Leroy and Stitch* was the end of the line for the Lilo & Stitch franchise, until new animated television series were developed in Japan (*Stitch*) and China (*Stitch & Ai*), and a live-action film was announced.

The Lion King (G)

Theatrical release date: June 24, 1994
Production Company: Walt Disney Pictures, Walt Disney Feature Animation
Length: 88 minutes/Special Edition 89 minutes
Directed by: Roger Allers and Rob Minkoff
Screenplay by: Irene Mecchi and Jonathan Roberts and Linda Woolverton

Synopsis: Young Simba's father, the lion king Mufasa, is killed due to the actions of Simba's evil uncle, Scar. Scar makes Simba think the "accident" was his fault, leaving Scar as ruler when Simba flees. Despite the guilt that haunts him, Simba tries to live a carefree life with the meerkat Timon and warthog Pumbaa, until he is called back by his childhood playmate Nala, to try to save the drought-plagued Pride Lands from Scar and his hyaena lackeys.

Cast: Jonathan Taylor Thomas as young Simba
Matthew Broderick as adult Simba
James Earl Jones as Mufasa
Jeremy Irons as Scar
Moira Kelly as adult Nala
Niketa Calame as young Nala
Ernie Sabella as Pumbaa

Nathan Lane as Timon
Robert Guillaume as Rafiki
Rowan Atkinson as Zazu
Madge Sinclair as Sarabi
Whoopi Goldberg as Shenzi
Cheech Marin as Banzai
Jim Cummings as Ed

Music Highlights: "Circle of Life" performed by Carmen Twillie/"Nants' Ingonyama" performed by Lebo M, "I Just Can't Wait to Be King" performed by Jason Weaver, Laura Williams, and Rowan Atkinson, "Hakuna Matata" performed by Nathan Lane, Ernie Sabella, Jason Weaver, and Joseph Williams, "Be Prepared" performed by Jeremy Irons, "Can You Feel the Love Tonight" performed by Nathan Lane, Ernie Sabella, Sally Dworsky, Joseph Williams, and Kristie Edwards. All songs by Tim Rice and Elton John. Score by Hans Zimmer.

Film Facts

- The 32nd Disney animated classic, and the 5th film of the Disney Renaissance, *The Lion King* was the highest-grossing film of 1994. The idea for a film set in Africa came from Roy E. Disney, Jeffrey Katzenberg, and Peter Schneider, further developed by Charlie Fink. The first film treatment was written by sci-fi author Thomas Disch, titled *King of the Kalahari,* which screenwriter Linda Woolverton (*Beauty and the Beast*), began expanding into drafts of a script, titled *King of the Beasts* and later *King of the Jungle.*
- George Scribner (*Oliver & Company,* 1988), was initially chosen to direct, and Roger Allers was later added as a co-director. Elton John was asked to provide music for the film, with lyrics provided by frequent Andrew Lloyd Webber collaborator Tim Rice. Scribner objected to making the film a musical and withdrew, with animator and writer Rob Minkoff joining as the new co-director.
- An unused Timon/Pumbaa song "Warthog Rhapsody" is on *Rhythm of the Pride Lands* CD 1995
- Additional appearances: *The Lion King II: Simba's Pride* (1998), *The Lion King 1 1/2* (2004), *Timon & Pumbaa* animated TV series (1995-1999), *The Lion Guard* animated TV series (2015-2019), and *The Lion King* (2019) computer animated re-make.

The Lion King II: Simba's Pride (G)

Home media release date: October 27, 1998
Production Company: Walt Disney Video Premiere, Walt Disney Television Animation. Walt Disney Animation Australia
Length: 81 minutes
Directed by: Darrell Rooney
Screenplay by: Flip Kobler & Cindy Marcus, additional written material by Jenny Wingfield, Linda Voorhees, Gregory Poirier, Bill Motz & Bob Roth, Mark McCorkle & Robert Schooley, Jonathan Cuba

---

Synopsis: Simba and Nala's daughter, Kiara, ends up falling in love with Kovu, son of Zira, a former follower of Scar and leader of the outcast lions in the Pridelands. Simba's determination to keep them apart, and to keep the exiled lions away from Pride Rock, are challenged by Kiara.

Cast: Matthew Broderick as Simba
Neve Campbell as Kiara
Andy Dick as Nuka
Robert Guillaume as Rafiki
James Earl Jones as Mufasa

Moira Kelly as Nala
Nathan Lane as Timon
Jason Marsden as Kovu
Suzanne Pleshette as Zira
Ernie Sabella as Pumbaa

Music Highlights: "He Lives In You" (Mark Mancina/Jay Rifkin/Lebo M) performed by Lebo M, "We Are One" (Tom Snow/Marty Panzer/Jack Feldman) performed by Cam Clarke, Charity Sanoy, and Ladysmith Black Mambazo, "My Lullaby" (Joss Whedon/Scott Warrender) performed by Suzanne Pleshette, Crysta Macalush, and Andy Dick, "Love Will Find a Way" (Tom Snow/Jack Feldman) performed by Liz Callaway and Gene Miller. Music by Nick Glennie-Smith.

Film Facts

• Enthusiasm for *The Lion King* was so high at Disney that a sequel was in the works before the first film was released. Director Darrell Rooney (who would later direct *Lady and the Tramp II: Scamp's Adventure* and *Mulan II*) was hired for the project, with a screenplay largely written by husband and wife team Flip Kobler and Cindy Marcus (*Beauty and the Beast: The Enchanted Christmas, Pocahontas II, The Hunchback of Notre Dame II*), with additional input from a number of writers.
• Suzanne Pleshette voices Zira, the mother of Kovu, voiced by Jason Marsden. Pleshette and Marsden later provided the voices for Yubaba and Haku in the English dub of Hayao Miyazaki's *Spirited Away* (2001).
• In an argument over who was to watch Kiara, Timon calls Pumbaa a "fat fat fatty." This line comes from the Broadway musical *The Producers,* which starred…Matthew Broderick (voice of Simba) and Nathan Lane (voice of Timon).
• Voice actors providing singing voices included Cam Clarke (Simba), Liz Callaway (adult Kiara), Charity Sanoy (young Kiara), Crysta Macalush (young Vitani), and Gene Miller (adult Kovu).
• A CD titled *Return to Pride Rock: Songs Inspired by Disney's The Lion King II: Simba's Pride* (1999) featured songs from the soundtrack, but an official soundtrack, *The Lion King II: Simba's Pride,* wasn't issued until 2004.

The Lion King 1 & 1/2 (G)
The Lion King 3: Hakuna Matata

Home media release date: February 10, 2004
Production Company: Walt Disney Pictures, DisneyToon Studios, DisneyToon Studios Australia, Sparx Animation Studios, Spaff Animation
Length: 77 minutes
Directed by: Bradley Raymond
Screenplay by: Tom Rogers

Synopsis: The events of the first Lion King film are told from the perspective of Timon the meerkat and Pumbaa the warthog, giving the film a decidedly more whimsical tone. Timon, unsatisfied with life among his meerkat community, tries to make sense of the wise Rafiki's admonition to "look beyond what you see," setting off on a journey to find where he belongs, encountering Pumbaa and Simba along the way.

Cast: Nathan Lane as Timon
Ernie Sabella as Pumbaa
Julie Kavner as Mom
Jerry Stiller as Uncle Max
Matthew Broderick as Simba
Robert Guillaume as Rafiki
Moira Kelly as Nala

Whoopi Goldberg as Shenzi
Cheech Marin as Banzai
Jim Cummings as Ed
Edward Hibbert as Zazu
Jason Rudofsky as Flinchy
Matt Weinberg as Young Simba

Music Highlights: "Digga Tunnah" (Martin Erskine/Seth J. Friedman) performed by Lebo M and Johnny Clegg, "That's All I Need" (Tim Rice/Elton John) performed by Nathan Lane, "Hakuna Matata" (Tim Rice/Elton John) performed by Nathan Lane and Ernie Sabella, "The Lion Sleeps Tonight" (Luigi Creatore/Hugo Peretti/George David Weiss) performed by Lebo M (orig. Solomon Linda), "Nants' Ingonyama" (Lebo M) performed by Lebo M. Music by Don L. Harper.

Film Facts

• An announcement in *Variety* indicated that *The Lion King 1 & 1/2* would be released in 2001, but that date proved to be somewhat ambitious, as the film did not arrive in stores until February, 2004.
• Elton John and Tim Rice's "That's All I Need" was originally written for the first film as "Warthog Rhapsody," available on CDs *Rhythm of the Pride Lands* (1995)/*The Best of the Lion King* (2011).
• A different account of how Timon and Pumbaa met each other is given in the *Timon & Pumbaa* animated TV series episode "Once Upon a Timon" (season 2, episode 19).
• Disney characters making cameos at the end of the film include Mickey Mouse; Snow White and the Seven Dwarfs; Beast, Mrs. Potts, Chip, and Belle (*Beauty and the Beast*); Genie, Aladdin, Jasmine, and Magic Carpet (*Aladdin*); Lady and the Tramp; Hyacinth Hippo (*Fantasia*); Goofy; Stitch (*Lilo & Stitch*); Mad Hatter (*Alice in Wonderland*); Rabbit (*Winnie the Pooh*); Donald Duck; Peter Pan, Tinker Bell, and the Lost Boys (*Peter Pan*); Pocahontas; Mowgli and Baloo (*The Jungle Book*); Quasimodo, Hugo, Victor, and Laverne (*The Hunchback of Notre Dame*); Terk (*Tarzan*); Dumbo; Flora, Fauna, and Merryweather (*Sleeping Beauty*); and Br'er Bear (*Song of the South*).

The Little Mermaid (G)

Theatrical release date: November 17, 1989
Production Company: Walt Disney Pictures, Walt Disney Feature Animation
Length: 83 minutes
Directed by: John Musker and Ron Clements
Written by: John Musker and Ron Clements, based on the fairy tale by Hans Christian Andersen

---

Synopsis: The mermaid Ariel, daughter of King Triton, enjoys exploring with her friend Flounder, and trying the patience of the crab Sebastian, Triton's court composer. Despite being a princess, Ariel tires of her life underwater, longing to be part of the human world that fascinates her. After saving the human Prince Eric from drowning, Ariel agrees to give her voice to the sea witch Ursula in exchange for human legs, so she can see the surface world. If she is kissed by Prince Eric within three days, she will remain human, but if not, she will become Ursula's slave. Ariel and Eric are drawn to each other, but before their kiss, Ursula interferes, casting a spell over Eric. Ariel, Sebastian, and the seagull Scuttle must work to counter Ursula's cunning and deception.

Cast: Jodi Benson as Ariel
Christopher Daniel Barnes as Eric
René Auberjonois as Louis
Pat Carroll as Ursula
Paddi Edwards as Flotsam & Jetsam
Buddy Hackett as Scuttle

Jason Marin as Flounder
Kenneth Mars as Triton
Edie McClurg as Carlotta
Will Ryan as Seahorse
Ben Wright as Grimsby
Samuel E. Wright as Sebastian

Music Highlights: "Part of Your World" (Howard Ashman/Alan Menken) performed by Ariel/Jodi Benson), "Kiss the Girl" (Ashman/Menken) performed by Sebastian/Samuel E. Wright, "Under the Sea" (Ashman/Menken) performed by Sebastian/Samuel E. Wright. Original score by Alan Menken.

Film Facts

• The 28th of the Disney animated classics, and the film that sparked the Disney Renaissance, *The Little Mermaid* marked a new kind of Disney film, charming both audiences and critics alike.
• Back in the 1930s Walt Disney had considered making a film based on Hans Christian Anderson's fairy tales, including "The Little Mermaid" and "The Snow Queen" (later adapted into *Frozen*).
• "Part of Your World" was almost cut from the film shortly before its release.
• As King Triton arrives for the opening concert, tiny images of Mickey Mouse, Donald Duck, Goofy, and Kermit the Frog are visible scattered in the audience (3:42-3:44).
• Ben Wright (Grimsby) had previously voiced Roger in *101 Dalmatians*.
• Lyricist Howard Ashman joined the project in 1987, making the key suggestion that Sebastian have a Jamaican accent rather than an English one. Ashman brought on board composer Alan Menken, his former collaborator on the off-Broadway musical *Little Shop of Horrors* (1982).
• The film won Academy Awards for Best Original Score and Best Original Song ("Under the Sea").
• Additional appearances: *The Little Mermaid* animated TV series (1992-1994), *The Little Mermaid II: Return to the Sea* (2000), *The Little Mermaid: Ariel's Beginning* (2008).

The Little Mermaid II: Return to the Sea (G)

Home media release date: September 19, 2000
Production Company: Walt Disney Video Premiere, Walt Disney Television Animation, Walt Disney Animation Canada
Length: 75 minutes
Directed by: Jim Kammerud, co-directed by Brian Smith
Screenplay by: Elizabeth Anderson and Temple Mathews

Synopsis: Celebration of the birth of Ariel and Eric's daughter, Melody, is cut short when the deceased sea witch Ursula's sister Morgana tries to kidnap the child. To protect her daughter, Ariel is forced to keep Melody away from the sea, under the watchful eye of the crab Sebastian. Melody begins sneaking into the sea, and after finding a locket with her name on it, is tricked into visiting Morgana and stealing Triton's trident for her. With help from intrepid penguin/walrus team Tip and Dash, Melody tries to defeat Morgana and bridge the gap between land and sea.

Cast: Jodi Benson as Ariel
Samuel E. Wright as Sebastian
Tara Charendoff as Melody
Pat Carroll as Morgana
Buddy Hackett as Scuttle
Kenneth Mars as King Triton

Max Casella as Tip
Stephen Furst as Dash
Rob Paulsen as Prince Eric
Clancy Brown as Undertow
Cam Clarke as Flounder
Rene Auberjonois as Chef Louis

Music Highlights: "Down to the Sea" (Silversher/Silversher) performed by Jodi Benson, Rob Paulsen, Clancy Brown, Key E. Kuter, & Samuel E. Wright, "For a Moment" (Silversher/Silversher) performed by Jodi Benson & Tara Charendoff, "Tip & Dash" (Silversher/Silversher) performed by Max Casella, Stephen Furst, & Tara Charendoff, "Here on the Land and Sea" (Silversher/Silversher) performed by Jodi Benson, Tara Charendoff, & Samuel E. Wright. End credits: "Part of Your World" (Ashman/Menken) performed by Chely Wright. Music by Danny Troob.

Film Facts

• After the first home media release in 2000, the appearance of Ariel's sisters Adela and Aquata during the opening song "Down to the Sea" was changed for the 2008 reissue (3:25).
• Ariel and Eric's daughter, Melody, was voiced by Tara Charendoff, a prolific voice actress later known as Tara Strong, who also voiced Twilight Sparkle on *My Little Pony: Friendship is Magic.*
• The 2008 DVD reissue included the deleted song "Gonna Get My Wish" as a bonus feature.
• The soundtrack CD includes four songs from the film, supplemented by Sebastian singing a variety of cover songs.
• Michael Silversher and Patty Silversher (Aladdin: *The Return of Jafar,* Beauty and the Beast: *Belle's Magical World*) provided the songs for the film, including the lively opening title "Down to the Sea," and the finale, "Here on the Land and Sea." Disney fixture Danny Troob (*Beauty and the Beast, Aladdin, The Lion King, Pocahontas, Hercules*) provided the film's score.
• Additional appearances: Follows *The Little Mermaid* (1989), *The Little Mermaid* animated TV series (1992-1994), followed by the prequel *The Little Mermaid: Ariel's Beginning* (2008).

168

The Little Mermaid: Ariel's Beginning (G)

Home media release date: August 26, 2008
Production Company: DisneyToon Studios
Length: 77 minutes
Directed by: Peggy Holmes
Screenplay by: Robert Reece and Evan Spiliotopoulos, story by Jule Selbo and Jenny Wingfield

Synopsis: Taking place before the first Little Mermaid film, King Triton's heart is broken when his wife is lost in an accident with a pirate ship, and he forbids music in the kingdom. Ariel's curiosity is piqued by a chance musical encounter with the little fish Flounder, and she discovers an underground (undersea) music club. After Ariel persuades her sisters (Adella, Andrina, Alana, Aquata, Arista, and Attina) to join her at the club, evil governess Marina Del Rey betrays them to King Triton. Aided by the crab Sebastian, Ariel risks everything to help her father remember the music he has renounced.

Cast: Jodi Benson as Ariel
Samuel E. Wright as Sebastian
Jim Cummings as King Triton
Sally Field as governess Marina Del Rey
Jeff Bennett as Benjamin
Parker Goris as Flounder
Lorelei Hill Butters as Queen Athena

Ariel's sisters
Tara Strong as Adella and Andrina
Jennifer Hale as Alana
Grey DeLisle as Aquata and Arista
Kari Wahlgren as Attina

Music Highlights: "Jump in the Line" (Bell/Samuel/de Leon/Oller) performed by Samuel E. Wright et al., "Just One Mistake" (Jeanine Tesori) performed by Sally Field, "Athena's Song" (Jeanine Tesori) performed by Andrea Robinson, "I Remember" (Jeanine Tesori) performed by Jodi Benson. Score by James Dooley.

Film Facts

• *The Little Mermaid: Ariel's Beginning* was originally titled *The Little Mermaid III* (as seen in a teaser on *The Little Mermaid* Platinum Edition DVD, issued in 2006.
• Peggy Holmes, who had previously worked as an actress, dancer, and choreographer, made her feature directorial debut with this film. She had previously directed the segment "Belles on Ice" from *Mickey's Twice Upon a Christmas*, and would go on to direct the Disney Fairies films *Secret of the Wings* (2012) and *The Pirate Fairy* (2014).
• "Jump in the Line" was popularized in the West by Harry Belafonte in 1961, credited as written by Raymond Bell (a pseudonym for Belafonte). It was originally written by Lord Kitchener, stage-name of Aldwyn Roberts, a song with which he won the 1946 Trinidad Carnival Road March. It was recorded in 1952 by Woody Herman and his Third Herd.
• After this release Ariel made a cameo appearance in *Ralph Breaks the Internet* (2018).
• Additional appearances: Prequel to *The Little Mermaid* (1989), *The Little Mermaid* animated TV series (1992-1994), and *The Little Mermaid II: Return to the Sea* (2000).

The Little Prince (PG)

Theatrical release date: Jul 29, 2015 (France), Aug 5, 2016 (USA), May 22, 2015 (Cannes premiere)
Country: France/Italy   **French title**: *Le Petit Prince*
Production Company: Method Animation, ON Animation, Orange Studio, LPPTV, M6, Lucky Red
Length: 108 minutes
Directed by: Mark Osborne
Screenplay by: Irena Brignull, Bob Persichetti, based on *Le Petit Prince* by Antoine de Saint-Exupéry

Synopsis: When a Little Girl has over-prepared her answers for an admission interview at Werth Academy, her mother buys a house in the district so she can still attend. The Mother reveals a detailed life plan for the Girl, before going off to work, but the plan gets altered when an airplane propeller bursts through both the fence and the wall of the house. The eccentric Aviator next door apologizes and gives the Girl a huge jar of pennies with a handful of toys inside, including a small figure of The Little Prince from the classic children's book. The Aviator sends her a letter describing his adventure in the Sahara desert, where he met the Little Prince, going on to tell the girl about the Prince's tiny planet, and his journeys to different planets, where he met the Fox. The Aviator gives the Girl a stuffed fox, but when the story has an upsetting turn, the girl stops visiting, and is shocked when the Aviator is suddenly taken to the hospital. The Girl and the Fox strike out in her neighbor's plane, to find help for the Aviator from the Little Prince himself. As it happens, the Prince is not himself, and after the Girl helps him remember who he is, they escape and he helps her to understand the Aviator's story, and how "It is only with the heart that one can see rightly." The Girl returns to the Aviator to apologize for her absence.

Cast: Jeff Bridges as The Aviator
Mackenzie Foy as The Little Girl
Rachel McAdams as The Mother
Riley Osborne as The Little Prince
Marion Cotillard as The Rose
Bud Cort as The King

Ricky Gervais as The Conceited Man
Albert Brooks as The Businessman
James Franco as The Fox
Benicio Del Toro as The Snake
Paul Rudd as Mr. Prince
Paul Giamatti as The Academy Teacher

Music Highlights: "Turn Around" (Zimmer/Camille) vocals by Camille, "Equation" (Zimmer/Camille/Ducol) vocals by Camille, "Le Tour de France en Diligence" (Zimmer/Camille/Stornetta) vocals by Camille, "Hop Hop" (Trenet) performed by Charles Trenet, "Quand J'étais Petit je Vous Aimais" (Trenet) performed by Charles Trenet, "Don't Let It Bother You" (Gordon/Revel) performed by Fats Waller, "Boum" (Trenet) performed by Charles Trenet, "En Quittant une Ville" (Trenet) performed by Charles Trenet. Music by Hans Zimmer & Richard Harvey featuring Camille.

Film Facts

• The film debuted in the US on Netflix on August 5, 2016.
• A mid-credits scene appears (1:38:49).
• Director Mark Osborne pitched the story close to 400 times in the process of making the film.

Long Way North (PG)

Theatrical release date: June 16, 2015 (France premiere), September 30, 2016 (US)
Country: France/Denmark   French title: *Tout en Haut du Monde*
Production Company: Sacrebleu Productions, Maybe Movies, France 3 Cinéma. 2 Minutes, Nørlum
Length: 81 minutes
Directed by: Rémi Chayé
Screenplay by: Claire Paoletti and Patricia Valeix, adapted by Fabrice de Costil

Synopsis: Sacha, a 15 year old Russian girl, is preparing for her debutante ball. Her grandfather, the explorer Oloukine, never returned from a voyage to the North Pole. The Prince Tomsky objects to a new library wing being named for Oloukine, due to the failure of the trip. Sacha learns that her grandfather's ship, the Davaï, took a different course than they thought, so the Tsar's agents looked in the wrong place when they tried to find it. At the ball she tries to get the Prince to review the matter, but he takes offense, jeopardizing her father's chance to be appointed ambassador to Rome. Her father is angry and disappointed in Sacha, who is convinced that they could find his ship and regain their family's honor. Sacha sets out to find a ship to the frozen north. She trades her earrings for passage, and after a long voyage into icy waters, they finally find a lifeboat from the Davaï. When a huge block of ice sinks their ship and seriously injures the captain, the party's only hope for survival is to find the Davaï — if it even exists. As rations are short, and a blizzard sets in, the crew blames Sacha for their misfortune. Sacha strikes out alone and learns the truth of her grandfather's fate.

Cast:

Role	English	French
Sasha	Chloé Dunn	Christa Théret
Oloukine	Geoffrey Greenhill	Féodor Atkine
Katch	Tom Perkins	Thomas Sagols
Larson	Antony Hickling	Rémi Caillebot
Nadya	Claire Harrison-Bullett	Audrey Sablé
Tomsky	Tom Morton	Fabien Briche
Father	Martin Lewis	Rémi Bichet
Mother	Bibi Jacob	Julienne Degenne
Maloney	Leslie Clack	Bruno Magnes
Lund	Peter Hudson	Loïc Houdré
Mowson	Tom Morton	Cyrille Monge
Frenchy	Martin Lewis	Stéphane Pouplard

Music Highlights: Music by Jonathan Morali.

Film Facts

• Rémi Chayé worked on *The Secret of Kells* (2009), *Eleanor's Secret* (2009), and *The Painting* (2011).
• Actress Christa Théret (Sacha) was recognized for her acting in the live-action film *Renoir* (2012).
• The film won the "Audience Award" at the Annecy International Animation Film Festival.
• A very brief post-credits scene appears (1:21:20).

The Lorax (PG)

Theatrical release date: March 2, 2012
Production Company: Universal Pictures, Illumination Entertainment, Dr. Seuss Enterprises
Length: 96 minutes
Directed by: Chris Renaud, Kyle Balda
Screenplay by: Cinco Paul & Ken Daurio, based on the book by Dr. Seuss

Synopsis: Eager to impress Audrey, the girl of his dreams, the teenager Ted travels to see the mysterious Once-ler in search of a real tree, which don't exist in Thneedville, a town which requires air to be provided by the scheming Mr. O'Hare, proprietor of O'Hare Air. Outside of town, high in a tower, the Once-ler tells Ted his sad tale of how he is to blame for the loss of Thneedville's trees. In his youth, the Once-ler struck out to create the multi-purpose garment the "Thneed," finding an idyllic valley where he could chop down Trufula trees for raw materials. The cutting of the trees summoned the Lorax, the guardian of the forest. The Once-ler scoffed at the warnings of the Lorax, engaging in a battle over the forest, bringing in his obnoxious family to mass-produce Thneeds. Their greed led to the destruction of the natural beauty of the valley, and also led to Thneedville's need to import air. The Once-ler gives Ted the last Trufula seed, and Audrey, Ted, and Ted's grandmother must find a way to show the citizens of Thneedville that trees really do matter, before O'Hare takes the seed.

Cast: Danny DeVito as The Lorax
Ed Helms as The Once-ler
Zac Efron as Ted
Taylor Swift as Audrey

Betty White as Grammy Norma
Rob Riggle as Mr. O'Hare
Jenny Slate as Ted's Mom
Nasim Pedrad as Once-ler's Mom

Music Highlights: "Thneedville" (John Powell/Cinco Paul), "O'Hare Air Jingle" (Chad Fischer) performed by Chad Fischer, "Everybody Needs a Thneed" (John Powell/Cinco Paul) performed by The 88 and Ed Helms, "How Bad Can I Be" (John Powell/Cinco Paul/Kool Kojak) performed by Ed Helms, "Let It Grow" (John Powell/Cinco Paul) performed by cast, "These Trees" (John Powell/Cinco Paul) performed by Ed Helms. End credits: "Let It Grow (Celebrate the World)" (Christopher Stewart/Ester Dean/Cinco Paul/John Powell/Aaron Pearce) performed by Ester Dean. Music by John Powell.

Film Facts

• Ted and Audrey are named after Dr. Theodor Seuss Geisel, better known as Dr. Seuss, and his wife, Audrey Geisel.
• The film made its theatrical premiere on March 2, 2012, on what would have been Dr. Seuss's 108th birthday.
• Two Easter eggs refer to *Despicable Me* (2010), Illumination Entertainment's previous hit film: a toy minion is seen in Ted's drawer (9:04), and Ted's sneakers say "Gru's Shoes" with a picture of a minion (14:28). Similarly, in *Despicable Me* Margo wears a t-shirt with the face of the Lorax (12:32). The money used in the film seems to show the mayor of Whoville (45:41).
• A previous 24-minute version of *The Lorax* was produced in 1972, broadcast on television.

The Loud House Movie (TV-Y7)

Streaming release date: August 20, 2021
Production Company: Nikelodeon Films/Nickelodeon Animation Studios
Length: 83 minutes
Directed by: Dave Needham
Screenplay by: Kevin Sullivan, Chris Viscardi

Synopsis: Lincoln Loud helps his sisters with their many weekend activities, but at a celebration dinner for their accomplishments, Lincoln is locked out of the restaurant and forgotten. He confides in his best friend Clyde that he wishes he could be in good at something, like everyone else seems to be. When Clyde tells Lincoln he followed in the footsteps of his ancestors, Lincoln learns his family came from Scotland. The family travels to Loch Loud, a town founded by their ancestors, meeting Angus, the grounds keeper at Loud Castle, the Loud family's ancestral home. The castle caretaker Morag is displeased when the family returns. Lincoln learns that — of course — there were many sisters who used to live in the castle, but is overjoyed to hear that there was also an esteemed Duke. Angus shows the girls a just-hatched dragon which comes back to the castle. Getting in the spirit, Lincoln dresses up in royal fashion, and is told he can only become a duke by helping the people of the town. Lincoln wins over the town and is crowned Duke, but Morag lets slip that her family drove away the Loud's predecessors. When she tries to make history repeat, the ghost of Lucille Loud, an ancestor from 400 years ago, helps solve the mystery.

Cast: Asher Bishop as Lincoln/The Duke
David Tennant as Angus
Michelle Gomez as Morag
Jill Talley as Mom/1600's Mom
Brian Stepanek as Dad/1600's Dad
Catherine Taber as Lori
Liliana Mumy as Leni/1600's Leni
Nika Futterman as Luna
Cristina Pucelli as Luan
Jessica DiCicco as Lynn/Lucy
Grey Griffin as Lola/Lana/Lily/Scoots
Lara Jill Miller as Lisa/1600's Lisa
Katy Townsend as Lucille/Mrs. Scroggins/
Old Aggie

Music Highlights: "Life is Better Loud" (Rockwell/Lewis) performed by Doug Rockwell & Michelle Lewis, "Ordinary Me" (Oh, Hush!/DeWolfe) performed by Asher Bishop, "Now or Never" (Oh, Hush!/DeWolfe) performed by Oh, Hush! x graywolfe, "This Town Was Named for You" (Rosenblatt/Kozak/Swirsky) performed by David Tennant, cast and Distant Cousins, "I Wanna Be the Duke" (Oh, Hush!/Richert/DeWolfe) performed by Asher Bishop & David Tennant, "Loud Castle Theme Song" (Rockwell/Lewis) performed by Doug Rockwell, "The Duchess I Will Be" (Fink/Piker/Gleed/Yaeger) performed by Michelle Gomez, "My Way Back Home" (Lennertz/White) performed by Tide Lines, "Let's Get Lost" (Rosenblatt/Kozak/Swirsky) performed by Distant Cousins. Music by Philip White.

Film Facts

• David Tennant (Angus) is a well known Scottish actor, who played Dr. Who from 2005-2010.
• Additional Appearances: *The Loud House* animated TV series (2016-2021), spinoff animated TV series *The Casagrandes* (2019).

Luca (PG)

Theatrical/streaming release date: June 18, 2021 (premiere June 13, 2021 at Aquarium of Genoa)
Production Company: Pixar Animation Studios, Walt Disney Pictures
Length: 95 minutes
Directed by: Enrico Casarosa
Screenplay by: Jesse Andrews, Mike Jones, story Enrico Casarosa, Jesse Andrews, Simon Stephenson

Synopsis: The young sea monster Luca is curious about the "land monsters" in the human world. His protective mother wants to keep him far from the surface, but one day he learns that his grandmother went to the surface in the guise of a human. As he is looking for human artifacts on the sea floor, he runs into an older boy doing the same. The boy, Alberto, takes him to the surface, where they both transform into human form. Alberto and his father have lived in a small Italian village, and Luca is intrigued with this new world, and with Alberto's adventurous spirit. When he is away too long, Luca's parents find his human artifacts, and plan to send him to the deep sea with his uncle. Before he has to leave, Luca and Alberto plan to visit "Vespa island" (Portorosso), hoping to ask "Signor Vespa" for a scooter. In town, they run into the swaggering Ercole, who says he bought his new scooter with his winnings from the Portorosso Cup race. They are rescued by the ambitious girl Giulia, who plans to beat Ercole in the race this year, and the boys ask to be on Giulia's team. They help Giulia's father, Massimo, catch fish to earn money to enter the race. Fearing for his safety, Luca's parents reluctantly follow him into the human world. Giulia, Luca, and Alberto begin training for the race, but when Luca begins to share Giulia's love of learning, Alberto gets jealous, and during a struggle, is revealed as a sea monster. Giulia learns Luca is a sea monster too, and Luca learns Alberto was also keeping a secret. In the end, the underdogs pull together to overcome the challenges of the race, as well as the prejudices of the town.

Cast: Jacob Tremblay as Luca Paguro
Jack Dylan Grazer as Alberto Scorfano
Emma Berman as Giulia Marcovaldo
Saverio Raimondo as Ercole Visconti
Maya Rudolph as Daniela Paguro

Marco Barricelli as Massimo Marcovaldo
Jim Gaffigan as Lorenzo Paguro
Peter Sohn as Ciccio
Lorenzo Crisci as Guido
Marina Massironi as Signora Marsigliese

Music Highlights: "Un Bacio A Mezzanotto" (Giovannini/Garinei/Kramer) performed by Quartetto Cetra, "Il Gatto a La Volpe" (Bennato) performed by Edoardo Bennato, "Andavo A Cento All'Ora" (Migliacci/Buttici/Cantini) performed by Gianni Morandi, "Tintarella di Luna" (De Filippi/Migliacci) performed by Mina, "Fatti Mandare Dalla Mamma A Prendere Il Latte" (Bacalov/Migliacci) performed by Gianni Morandi, "Viva la Pappa col Pomodoro" (Rota/Wertmüller) performed by Rita Pavone. End credits: "Citta Vuota" (Pomus/Shuman) performed by Mina. Music by Dan Romer.

Film Facts

• Portorosso was shown in an ad on a travel agency window in Pixar's previous film, *Soul* (57:39).
• A post-credits scene appears (1:33:45).
• Easter eggs: Hank (*Finding Dory*), Donald Duck, Pixar Luxo ball, Pizza Planet truck.

Madagascar (PG)

Theatrical release date: May 27, 2005
Production Company: DreamWorks Animation, PDI/DreamWorks
Length: 86 minutes
Directed by: Eric Darnell, Tom McGrath
Written by: Mark Burton & Billy Frolick and Eric Darnell & Tom McGrath

Synopsis: After living in captivity at the Central Park Zoo, the zebra Marty reaches his 10th birthday, and wishes to return to living free in the wild. His friend Alex, a lion who is popular at the zoo, tries to help Marty see the benefits of living in the zoo, but Marty is still itching to leave. When he learns of a breakout by the zoo's crafty penguins, led by the determined Skipper, Marty follows them. He is soon pursued by Alex, the hippopotamus Gloria, and the giraffe Melman, all hoping to bring Marty back home. The four friends and penguins are captured at Grand Central Station, but when there is a public outcry over keeping them in captivity, they are put on a ship heading to a wildlife preserve in Kenya. The ever-scheming penguins hijack the ship, setting course for Antarctica, in the process knocking Alex, Marty, Gloria, and Melman's crates overboard. They end up on the island of Madagascar, and though they enjoy the idyllic aspects of island life, they also face many perils, including the carnivorous cat-like fossas, hunger, and the singing, narcissistic lemur King Julien XIII. When Alex's hunger gets the better of him, he's exiled to the land of the fossas. The return of the penguins provides the promise of a return home, if they can just find a way to contain Alex's newly awakened predatory instincts.

Cast: Ben Stiller as Alex
Chris Rock as Marty
David Schwimmer as Melman
Jada Pinkett Smith as Gloria
Sacha Baron Cohen as Julien
Cedric the Entertainer as Maurice
Andy Richter as Mort
Tom McGrath as Skipper/Fossa/
    Panicky Man on Subway

Christopher Knights as Private
Chris Miller as Kowalski
Conrad Vernon as Mason
Eric Darnell as Zoo Announcer/Lemur #1/
    Fossa/Subway Car Announcer
David Cowgill as Police Horse
Steve Apostolina as Police Officer
Elisa Gabrielli as Old Lady
Devika Parikh as News Reporter

Music Highlights: "I Like To Move It, Move It" (Erick Morillo/Mark Quashie) performed by Reel 2 Real featuring Mad Stuntman. Music by Hans Zimmer.

Film Facts

• The film developed a similar idea to Disney's *The Wild* (2006), which began production first.
• Post-credits, Gloria appears in a parody of Disney's Tinker Bell (1:25:40).
• Additional appearances: *Madagascar: Escape 2 Africa* (2008), *Madagascar 3: Europe's Most Wanted* (2012), "The Madagascar Penguins in a Christmas Caper" short (2005), "Merry Madagascar" short (2009), "Madly Madagascar" short (2013), *The Penguins of Madagascar* TV series (2008-2015), *All Hail King Julien* TV series (2014-2017), *Madagascar: A Little Wild* TV series (2020).

Madagascar: Escape 2 Africa (PG)

Theatrical release date: November 7, 2008
Production Company: DreamWorks Animation, Pacific Data Images
Length: 89 minutes
Directed by: Eric Darnell, Tom McGrath
Written by: Etan Cohen and Eric Darnell & Tom McGrath

Synopsis: After showing the backstory of how Alex the lion ended up in the Central Park Zoo, we pick up the story of Alex, Marty the zebra, Melman the giraffe, and Gloria the hippopotamus, as they prepare to fly back from Madagascar, joined by the lemurs King Julien, Maurice, and Mort, and the chimpanzees Mason and Phil, in an old plane flown by the penguins from the zoo. The plane makes an emergency landing in Africa when it runs out of fuel, where Alex is reunited with his parents. As the penguins repair the plane, Marty finds a herd of zebras and fits right in, Gloria catches the eye of Moto Moto the hippo, and Melman becomes a witch doctor for a tower of giraffes. Things get complicated when the scheming Makunga works to dethrone Alex's father as the alpha lion of the pride, Marty begins to experience an identity crisis, Melman is caught up in hypochondria, and Gloria's flirtation with Moto Moto causes tension between her and Melman. There may yet be hope for the quarreling quartet, if they can just find a way to pull together.

Cast: Ben Stiller as Alex
Chris Rock as Marty/Additional Zebras
David Schwimmer as Melman
Jada Pinkett Smith as Gloria
Sacha Baron Cohen as Julien
Cedric the Entertainer as Maurice
Andy Richter as Mort
Bernie Mac as Zuba

Alec Baldwin as Makunga
Sherri Shepherd as Mom
will.i.am as Moto Moto
Elisa Gabrielli as Nana
Tom McGrath as Skipper
Chris Miller as Kowalski
Christopher Knights as Private
Conrad Vernon as Mason

Music Highlights: "The Traveling Song" (Zimmer/will.i.am) performed by will.i.am, "Big and Chunky" (Zimmer/will.i.am) performed by will.i.am, "Best Friends" (Zimmer/will.i.am) performed by will.i.am, "She Loves Me" (Zimmer/will.i.am) performed by will.i.am, "I Like To Move It" (Erick Morillo/Mark Quashie) performed by will.i.am. Music and songs by Hans Zimmer and will.i.am.

Film Facts

• The film was originally to be subtitled *The Crate Escape,* a play on the title of the classic Steve McQueen film *The Great Escape* (1963).
• The similarity of the lion power struggle's to Disney's *The Lion King* recalled other instances of DreamWorks films emulating Disney, given the similarities of *Antz* (1998) to *A Bug's Life* (1998), and the first *Madagascar* (2005) to *The Wild* (2006).
• The tag line on the film poster was "Still together. Still lost."
• The DVD and Blu-ray included two episodes of *The Penguins of Madagascar* series.

Madagascar 3: Europe's Most Wanted (PG)

Theatrical release date: June 8, 2012
Production Company: DreamWorks Animation, PDI/DreamWorks
Length: 93 minutes
Directed by: Eric Darnell, Conrad Vernon, Tom McGrath
Screenplay by: Eric Darnell and Noah Baumbach

Synopsis: Still trying to return to the Central Park Zoo, Alex the lion, Marty the zebra, Melman the giraffe, and Gloria the hippopotamus, joined by their lemur friends King Julien, Maurice, and Mort, head to Monte Carlo to retrieve their overdue penguin companions. Escaping the disturbed Animal Control officer Captain Chantel DuBois, who has her sights set on Alex as a trophy, the team is waylaid again when their plane crashes. After catching a ride on a circus train, they pose as circus animals, meeting the sea lion Stefano, the jaguar Gia, the tiger Vitaly, and the bear Sonya. The zoo animals join the circus animals for a catastrophic performance in Rome, and it comes to light that Vitaly, the star performer of the act, suffered a traumatic incident with fire during a performance, and has not been the same since. Alex persuades the troop to develop a fresh approach, which makes all the difference. After finally making it back to the zoo, Alex, Marty, Melman, and Gloria begin to reconsider where their home really is.

Cast: Ben Stiller as Alex
Chris Rock as Marty
David Schwimmer as Melman
Jada Pinkett Smith as Gloria
Sacha Baron Cohen as Julien
Cedric the Entertainer as Maurice
Andy Richter as Mort
Tom McGrath as Skipper
Frances McDormand as Captain Chantal Dubois

Jessica Chastain as Gia
Bryan Cranston as Vitaly
Martin Short as Stefano
Chris Miller as Kowalski
Christopher Knights as Private
Conrad Vernon as Mason
Vinnie Jones as Freddie the Dog
Steve Jones as Jonesy the Dog
Nick Fletcher as Frankie the Dog

Music Highlights: "Afro Circus/I Like to Move It" (Erick Morillo/Mark Quashie) performed by Chris Rock and Sacha Baron Cohen. Music by Hans Zimmer.

Film Facts

• The film followed a few seasons of the TV series *The Penguins of Madagascar* (2008-2015), and was followed by the spin-off film *Penguins of Madagascar,* released November 26, 2014.
• All three directors had voice acting parts, Tom McGrath as Skipper, Conrad Vernon as Mason, and Eric Darnell as the Comandante/Zoo Official.
• The song Captain Chantel DuBois sings is "Non, Je Ne Regrette Rien," written in 1956, and popularized by Édith Piaf in 1960, dedicated by Piaf to the French Foreign Legion.
• Chantel DuBois's prison escape is modeled after *The Shawshank Redemption* (1994).

Make Mine Music (Approved)

Theatrical release date: August 15, 1946
Production Company: Walt Disney Productions
Length: 75 minutes (edited U.S. home media version 67 minutes)
Directed by: Jack Kinney, Clyde Geronimi, Hamilton Luske, Bob Cormack, Josh Meador.
Production Supervisor: Joe Grant. Story: Homer Brightman, Dick Huemer, Dick Kinney, John Walbridge, Tom Oreb, Dick Shaw, Eric Gurney, Sylvia Holland, T. Hee, Ed Penner, Dick Kelsey, Jim Bodrero, Roy Williams, Cap Palmer, Jesse Marsh, Erwin Graham

---

Synopsis: A series of animated shorts set to classical music and popular music from the 1940s, including performances by singers Andy Russell, Jerry Colonna, Dinah Shore, The Andrews Sisters, and Nelson Eddy, and big band music by Benny Goodman and his Orchestra. It was followed by the similar *Melody Time* (1948).

Cast/Segments: • "Make Mine Music" (Ken Darby/Eliot Daniel) opening by chorus

• "A Rustic Ballad: The Martins and the Coys" (Al Cameron/Ted Weems) by The King's Men (deleted from U.S. home media)

• "A Tone Poem: Blue Bayou" (Bobby Worth/Ray Gilbert) sung by the Ken Darby Chorus

• "A Jazz Interlude: All the Cats Join In" (Eddie Sauter/Alec Wilder/Ray Gilbert) featuring Benny Goodman and his Orchestra

• "A Ballad in Blue: Without You" (Osvaldo Farrés/Ralph Maria Siegel/Ray Gilbert) by Andy Russell

• "A Musical Recitation: Casey at the Bat" (poem by Ernest Lawrence Thayer, music by Ray Gilbert/ Ken Darby/Eliot Daniel) by Jerry Colonna, also includes includes "A Hot Time in the Old Town" (Theo A. Metz)

• "Ballade Ballet: Two Silhouettes" (Charles Wolcott/Ray Gilbert) by Tania Riabouchinska and David Lichine - The Dance, Dinah Shore - The Song

• "A Fairy Tale with Music: Peter and the Wolf" (Serge Prokofieff) told by Sterling Holloway

• "After You've Gone" (Turner Leighton/Henry Creamer) by The Goodman Quartet

• "A Love Story: Johnnie Fedora and Alice Bluebonnet" (Allie Wrubel) sung by The Andrews Sisters

• "Opera Pathetique: The Whale Who Wanted to Sing at the Met" by Nelson Eddy, including "Shortnin' Bread" (James Whitcomb Riley), "Largo al Factotum" (Gioachino Rossini/Cesare Sterbini) from *The Barber of Seville*, "Chi me Freno in Tal Momento?" (Gaetano Donizetti/ Salvatore Cammarano) from *Lucia de Lammermoor*, "Pseudo I Pagliacci Passage" (Nelson Eddy), "Tristan und Isolde" excerpt (Richard Wagner), "Mefistofele" (Arrigo Bolto), "Mag der Himmel Euch Verbegen" (Friedrich von Flotow/Friedrich Wilhelm Riese) from *Martha*.

Film Facts

• The 8th Disney animated classic, and the third of six Disney "package" films in the 1940s, *Make Mine Music* offered an eclectic mix of animated vignettes set to music.
• "Without You" was originally called "Tres Palabras" by Osvaldo Farrés.

Mary and the Witch's Flower (PG)

Theatrical release date: July 8, 2017
Country: Japan   **Japanese title**: *Meari to Majo no Hana*
Production Company: Studio Ponoc
Length: 103 minutes
Directed by: Hiromasa Yonebayashi, English-language director Giles New
Screenplay by: Riko Sakaguchi and Hiromasa Yonebayashi, English-language screenplay adaptation by David Freedman & Lynda Freedman, based on the novel *The Little Broomstick* by Mary Stewart

Synopsis: Mary is staying with her great-aunt Charlotte before her school term begins. Bored and lonely, she runs into a neighbor boy, Peter, and later follows Peter's cats, Tib and Gib, into the woods, to a patch of glowing blue flowers. The gardener tells her they're "Fly-by-Night," said to valued by witches for their magic. Later, in the forest, the flowers dissolve into a mist that covers Tib and Gib. The following day Mary goes into the forest, finding a broom. Tib tosses a glowing blue substance on Mary's hands, and an image of a flower appears on each palm, also bringing the broom to life, which whisks her and Tib off to Endor College for witches, where headmistress Madam Mumblechook shows her around, and introduces her to Doctor Dee. Madam Mumblechook learns that Mary has discovered the "Fly-by-Night" flowers, and sends her back home. Once there she finds that Peter has gone missing, and a vision from Mumblechook tells her that Peter has been kidnapped, and will only be returned if Mary brings the Fly-by-Night flowers to Endor. Mary uses a crushed Fly-by-Night to fly the flowers back, but is trapped herself, imprisoned with Peter and the "failures" of Doctor Dee's transformation experiments. Still able to use magic, Mary undoes the transformations of the animals, but Peter is caught as they are escaping. The broom takes Mary to a magical cottage, where she learns more about Endor and her own history, which may help her as she returns to Endor, determined to save Peter.

Cast:

Role	English	Japanese
Mary Smith	Ruby Barnhill	Hana Sugisaki
Madam Mumblechook	Kate Winslet	Yûki Amami
Doctor Dee	Jim Broadbent	Fumiyo Kohinata
Flanagan	Ewen Bremner	Jirô Satô
Great-Aunt Charlotte	Lynda Baron	Shinobu Ôtake
Peter	Louis Ashbourne Serkis	Ryûnosuke Kamiki
Miss Banks	Morwenna Banks	Eri Watanabe
The Red-Haired Witch	Teresa Gallagher	Hikari Mitsushima

Music Highlights: "Rain" (Nakajin/Fukase/Saori) performed by Sekai no Owari. Music by Takatsugu Muramatsu.

Film Facts

• This is Studio Ponoc's debut, written/directed by Studio Ghibli alumnus Hiromasa Yonebayashi.
• The "witch of Endor" is referred to in the Bible, in 1 Samuel 28.

Maya the Bee Movie (G)

Theatrical release date: September 4, 2014 (South Korra), March 5, 2015 (USA)
Production Company: Studio 100 Film, Buzz Studios, Fish Blowing Bubbles, Flying Bark Prod.
Length: 89 minutes
Directed by: Alexs Stadermann
Written by: Fin Edquist, Marcus Sauermann, story by Alexs Stadermann

Synopsis: The spirited young bee Maya is born into a busy beehive, showing an unusual ability to dream and have fun that most bees lack. She soon runs into the Queen, but the nasty Royal Advisor Buzzlina angrily sends her back to school. Maya ends up outside, and while excitedly exploring, meets the kind grasshopper Flip, who shows her the meadow before returning her to the hive. When a group of hornets arrive, Buzzlina urges the Queen to force them to leave. Maya finally ends up at school, where she meets her teacher, Miss Cassandra, and makes a new friend, Willi. Buzzlina steals the Queen's royal jelly, planning to blame the theft on the hornets, and when Maya sees her with the jelly, Buzzlina banishes Maya from the hive. Willi soon follows, and they meet the young hornet Sting, nicknamed Buzzywump, who has been told terrible stories about bees, but soon changes his mind when they save him from a spider. Sting guides them to Jitterbug Hollow to see Flip. A pair of clumsy ants destroy the wasp camp, and the wasps believe the bees were to blame, while Buzzlina seizes power in the hive, making it look like the wasps killed the Queen. Maya, Willi, and Sting have to work together to prevent a war between the bees and wasps.

Cast: Coco Jack Gillies as Maya
Kodi Smit-McPhee as Willi
Joel Franco as Sting (hornet)
Richard Roxburgh as Flip (grasshopper)
Justine Clarke as Miss Cassandra
Jacki Weaver as Buzzlina Von Beena
Andy McPhee as Hank (hornet)

Miriam Margolyes as The Queen
David Collins as Arnie (ant)
Shane Dundas as Barney (ant)
Jimmy James Eaton as Paul (ant)
Heather Mitchell as The Nurse
Noah Taylor as Crawley
Cameron Ralph as Momo (moth)

Music Highlights: "Bee Yourself" (Engelhardt/Mountzouris/Gates-Foale) performed by Roxburgh, Loau, Jurevicius, and Meneses, "Let Your Feelers Down" (Gates-Foale/Stephen/Lenon/Bedelis) performed by Ute Engelhardt, Kevin Jones, Ricky Rock, Franky, and Stravroula Mountzouris. End credits: "Here Comes Maya the Bee" (Eede/Verthulst/Bourlon) performed by Myra Maud, "Maya Dance" (Verhulst/Bourlon/Eede) performed by Myra Maud. Music by Ute Engelhardt.

Film Facts

• Maya is from Waldemar Bonsels' German children's book *The Adventures of Maya the Bee* (1912).
• Additional appearances: *Maya the Honey Bee* Japanese anime TV series (1975–1980), *Maya the Bee* animated TV series (2012-2017), *Maya the Bee: The Honey Games* film (2018), and *Maya the Bee: The Golden Orb* film (2021).

Meet the Robinsons (G)

Theatrical release date: March 30, 2007
Production Company: Walt Disney Pictures, Walt Disney Animation Studios
Length: 95 minutes
Directed by: Stephen Anderson
Written by: Jon Bernstein, Michelle Spitz, Don Hall, Nathan Greno, Aurian Redson, Joe Mateo, and Stephen Anderson, based on the book *A Day With Wilbur Robinson* by William Joyce

> **Synopsis**: Lewis, a 12-year-old inventor and long-term orphanage resident, is brought by Wilbur Robinson to the future in order to thwart the schemes of the "bowler hat guy," who, along with the robot hat "Doris," has stolen a time machine from the home of the colorful Robinson family.

Cast: Angela Bassett as Mildred
Daniel Hansen/Jordan Fry as Lewis
Matthew Josten as Michael "Goob" Yagoobian
John H.H. Ford as Mr. Harrington
Dara McGarry as Mrs. Harrington/Receptionist
Tom Kenny as Mr. Willerstein
Laurie Metcalf as Lucille Krunklehorn
Don Hall as Coach
Paul Butcher as Stanley
Tracey Miller-Zarneke as Lizzy
Wesley Singerman as Wilbur
Jessie Flower as Young Franny
Stephen John Anderson as Bowler Hat Guy/Bud
Ethan Sandler as Doris/CEO/Spike/Dmitri
Harland Williams as Carl
Nathan Greno as Lefty
Kellie M. Hoover as Aunt Billie
Don Hall as Gaston
Adam West as Uncle Art
Stephen Anderson as Tallulah

Music Highlights: "Another Believer" (Wainwright/de Vries) performed by Rufus Wainwright, "The Future Has Arrived" (Elfman) performed by The All-American Rejects, "Where is Your Heart At?" (Wainwright) performed by Jamie Cullum, "Give Me the Simple Life" (Ruby/Bloom) performed by Jamie Cullum, "Little Wonders" (Thomas) performed by Rob Thomas, "The Motion Waltz (Emotional Commotion)" (Wainwright) performed by Rufus Wainwright. Score by Danny Elfman.

Film Facts

• The 47th of the Disney animated classics, *Meet the Robinsons* was based on the book *A Day With Wilbur Robinson* by William Joyce. Initially considered as a possible live-action film, it was eventually deemed more appropriate for animation.
• An early script caught the attention of Renaissance man Stephen Anderson (animator, storyboard artist, writer, voice actor, director), who sought the opportunity to direct the film, having been adopted himself.
• Director Stephen Anderson also worked on Disney's *Tarzan* (1999), *The Emperor's New Groove* (2000), *Bolt* (2008), and *Winnie the Pooh* (2011).
• The phrase "Keep moving forward" is drawn from a quote by Walt Disney.
• A photo of Walt Disney appears on the wall of the orphanage (3:21).
• A sequel was planned, to be called *Meet the Robinsons 2: First Date*, with animation to be provided by DisneyToon Studios, but upon his 2006 appointment as CCO of Disney and Pixar, John Lasseter canceled all sequels that were planned or in production.

Megamind (PG)

Theatrical release date: November 5, 2010
Production Company: DreamWorks Animation, Pacific Data Images
Length: 95 minutes
Directed by: Tom McGrath
Written by: Alan Schoolcraft & Brent Simons

Synopsis: An alien sent to Earth at the same time as the hero Metro Man, Megamind landed in a jail, where he was raised, while Metro Man had all the breaks. Turning to a life of crime, aided only by the fish-like Minion, Megamind is constantly thwarted by Metroman, until one day, after an attack by Megamind, Metro Man's costume lands at Megamind's feet, filled only with a skeleton. After his initial delight, Megamind finds that he is bored and lonely without his nemesis. Seeking to restore balance in his life, he creates a hero, using Metro Man's DNA to turn reporter Roxanne Ritchi's hapless cameraman Hal Stewart into the hero "Tighten." Disguised as Bernard, curator of the Metro Man Museum, Megamind begins to date Roxanne, and starts to question whether he wants to be a villain. When his disguise glitches, Roxanne rejects him, and he angrily sets up a battle with Tighten. To Megamind's surprise, Tighten has been using his powers for evil, as being a hero was too much work. In an effort to figure out how to beat Tighten, Roxanne and Megamind visit Metro Man's old secret sanctum, where they make a shocking discovery. As Tighten continues to wreak havoc on the city, Megamind takes on an entirely new role.

Cast: Will Ferrell as Megamind
Brad Pitt as Metro Man
Tina Fey as Roxanne Ritchi
Jonah Hill as Tighten/Hal Stewart
David Cross as Minion
Ben Stiller as Bernard

Justin Theroux as Megamind's Father
Jessica Schulte as Megamind's Mother
Tom McGrath as Lord Scott/Prison Guard
Emily Nordwind as Lady Scott
J.K. Simmons as Warden
Brian Hopkins as Prisoner

Music Highlights: "Bad to the Bone" (Thorogood) performed by George Thorogood & The Destroyers, "A Little Less Conversation (Junkie XL Remix)" (Davis/Strange) performed by Elvis Presley, "Highway to Hell" (Scott/Young/Young) performed by AC/DC, "Alone Again Naturally" (O'Sullivan) performed by Gilbert O'Sullivan, "Mr. Blue Sky" (Jeff Lynne) performed by ELO, "Back in Black" (Johnson/Young/Young) performed by AC/DC, "Welcome to the Jungle" (Rose/Adler/Stradlin/Hudson/McKagan) performed by Guns N' Roses, "Bad" (Jackson) performed by Michael Jackson. Music by Hans Zimmer and Lorne Balfe.

Film Facts

• The film was originally titled *Master Mind*, then *Oobermind*, before finally becoming *Megamind*.
• A mid-credits scene appears (1:28:19) featuring Minion.
• Additional Appearances: "Megamind: The Button of Doom" short (2010), as well as a handful of comics: *The Reign of Megamind* (2010) by WildStorm, and 5 issues by Ape Comics (2010-2011).

Melody Time (Approved)

Theatrical release date: May 27, 1948
Production Company: Walt Disney Productions
Length: 72 minutes
Production Supervisor: Ben Sharpsteen, directed by Clyde Geronimi, Wilfred Jackson, Hamilton Luske, Jack Kinney
Story: Winston Hibler, Erdman Penner, Harry Reeves, Homer Brightman, Ken Anderson, Ted Sears, Joe Rinaldi, Bill Cottrell, Art Scott, Jesse Marsh, Bob Moore, John Walbrdige. "Little Toot" by Hardie Gramatky

---

Synopsis: A series of animated shorts set to music from the 1940s, similar to *Make Mine Music* (1946). Featured performers include Frances Langford, pianist Jack Fina, the Andrews Sisters, bandleader Fred Waring and His Pennsylvanians, Mickey Mouse Club Mouseketeer Dennis Day, Roy Rogers, Trigger, Bob Nolan and the Sons of the Pioneers.

Cast/Segments: • "Melody Time" theme (Benny Benjamin/George Weiss) sung by Buddy Clark, as Master of Ceremonies
• "Once Upon a Wintertime" (Bobby Worth/Ray Gilbert) sung by Frances Langford: Ice-skating sweethearts
• "Bumble Boogie" (Nikolai Rimsky-Korsakov, arr. Jack Fina) by Freddy Martin & His Orchestra, featuring Jack Fina on Piano: Bumblebee tries to escape "an instrumental nightmare"
• "The Legend of Johnny Appleseed"/"The Lord is Good to Me"/"Get on the Wagon Rolling West"/ "There's a Lot of Work Out There to Do"/"Apple Feast" (Gannon/Kent) by Dennis Day
• "Little Toot" (Allie Wrubel) sung by The Andrews Sisters: The little tugboat who couldn't behave gets a chance to accomplish a big deed
• "Trees" (poem by Joyce Kilmer, music by Oscar Rasbach) by Fred Waring and His Pennsylvanians: Trees through the seasons
• "Blame it on the Samba" (Nazareth/Gilbert) by Ethel Smith & The Dinning Sisters: Donald Duck, José Carioca, and the Aracuan bird introduced in *The Three Caballeros* (1944)
• "Blue Shadows on the Trail" (Daniel/Lange) by Roy Rogers, Bob Nolan and the Sons of the Pioneers/"Sweet Sue" (Daniel/Lange) by Roy Rogers, Sons of the Pioneers, "Pecos Bill" (Daniel/Lange) by Roy Rogers and Trigger, Bob Nolan and the Sons of the Pioneers, Children: Bobby Driscoll, Luana Patten

---

Film Facts

• The 10th of the Disney animated classics, and the fifth of the Disney "package" films of the 1940s, *Melody Time* presented another set of musical animated shorts, after *Make Mine Music* (1946).
• Working titles for the film included *Sing About Something* and *All in Fun*.
• "Bumble Boogie" adapts Rimsky-Korsakov's "Flight of the Bumble Bee." "Little Toot" is based on a 1939 story by Hardie Gramatky. "Trees" was based on the 1913 poem "Trees" by Joyce Kilmer. "Blame it on the Samba" adapts Ernesto Nazareth's 1914 polka "Apanhei-te, Cavaquinho."
• The song "The Lord is Good to Me" is included on *The Music of Disney: Legacy in Song* box.
• Segments of both *Melody Time* and its predecessor, *Make Mine Music*, were combined in 1955 to create *Music Land*, a film provided to RKO Radio Pictures, to satisfy Disney's contract.

Mickey • Donald • Goofy: The Three Musketeers (G)

Home media release date: August 17, 2004
Production Company: Walt Disney Pictures, DisneyToon Studios, DisneyToon Studios Australia, Toon City Animation
Length: 68 minutes
Directed by: Donovan Cook
Written by: Evan Spiliotopoulos, David M. Evans

Synopsis: The Three Musketeers come to the rescue when paupers Mickey Mouse, Donald Duck, Goofy, and Pluto are robbed by bandits. Mickey receives a musketeer hat, and is inspired to believe that he and his fellow janitors Donald and Goofy could become musketeers themselves, despite the scorn of Pete, the captain of the musketeers. The princess of France, Minnie Mouse, dreams of finding true love, but soon has more to worry about when a safe nearly falls on top of her. Unbeknownst to Minnie, Pete is scheming with the Beagle Boys to take over the throne, and decides to allow Mickey, Donald, and Goofy to be her bodyguards, considering them inept. To stop Pete and the Beagle Boys, the trio of musketeers must face their own shortcomings.

Cast: Wayne Allwine as Mickey Mouse
Tony Anselmo as Donald Duck
Bill Farmer as Goofy/Pluto
Russi Taylor as Minnie
Tress MacNeille as Daisy

Jim Cummings as Pete
April Winchell as Clarabelle
Jeff Bennett as The Beagle Boys
Maurice LaMarche as The Beagle Boys
Rob Paulsen as The Troubadour

Music Highlights: "All For One and One For All" (music Offenbach's *Orpheus in the Underworld*/lyrics by Chris Otsuki) performed by Rob Paulsen, "Love So Lovely" (music Tchaikovsky's *Nutcracker* and *Romeo and Juliet*/lyrics by Chris Otsuki) performed by Rob Paulsen, "Sweet Wings of Love" (music Strauss' *The Blue Danube*/lyrics by Chris Otsuki) performed by Rob Paulsen, "Petey's King of France" (music Grieg's *Peer Gynt*/lyrics by Chris Otsuki), performed by Peg Leg Pete/Jim Cummings, "Chains of Love" (music Bizet's *Carmen*/lyrics by Chris Otsuki) performed by Bill Farmer and April Winchell, "This is the End" (music Beethoven's *Symphony No. 5*/lyrics by Chris Otsuki), "L'Opera" (music Arthur Sullivan/lyrics by W.S. Gilbert, from *The Pirates of Penzance* and *Princess Ida*) performed by Jess Harnell. Score by Bruce Broughton.

Film Facts

- The classic novel *The Three Musketeers* (1844) by Alexandre Dumas inspired the film.
- In shorts from the 1930s Pete was known as "Peg Leg Pete." In this film he appears with a peg leg for the first time since these shorts.
- The songs in the opera are from Gilbert and Sullivan's *The Pirates of Penzance* and *Princess Ida*.
- In the game *Kingdom Hearts 3D: Dream Drop Distance,* the setting from this film is included as the world "Country of the Musketeers."
- Mickey, Donald, & Goofy appeared in "Mickey and the Beanstalk" in *Fun and Fancy Free* (1947).

Mickey's Once Upon a Christmas (NR/TV-G)

Home media release date: November 9, 1999
Production Company: Walt Disney Video Premiere, Walt Disney Television Animation
Length: 66 minutes
Directors/Writers: "Donald Duck: Stuck on Christmas" Directed by: Bradley Raymond. Screenplay by: Charlie Cohen, story inspired by "Christmas Every Day" by William Dean Howells. "A Very Goofy Christmas" Directed by: Jun Falkenstein, Bill Speers. Screenplay by Scott Gorden & Tom Nance, Carter Crocker. "Mickey & Minnie's Gift of the Magi" Directed by: Toby Shelton, Associate Director Bill Speers, Unit Director Keith Ingham. Screenplay by: Richard Cray, Temple Mathews

Synopsis: A series of three Christmas vignettes. In "Donald Duck: Stuck On Christmas," Donald's nephews wish for it to be Christmas every day. To their initial delight, their wish is granted, but they soon find that a daily Christmas is not a magical experience, and that there's more to the holiday than just getting gifts. In "A Very Goofy Christmas," when Goofy's son Max questions Santa's existence, Goofy tries to help by dressing up as Santa, but his plan backfires. It's Max's turn to try to help Goofy before the real Santa arrives and helps Max learn about his father's love for him. In "Mickey and Minnie's Gift of the Magi," Mickey plans to get Minnie a gold chain for her watch, trading his beloved harmonica to afford it. Minnie, meanwhile, has traded in her watch to get Mickey a case for his harmonica, leaving both of them without their material treasures, but rich in love.

Cast: Wayne Allwine as Mickey Mouse
Russi Taylor as Minnie Mouse/
      Huey/Dewey/Louie
Tony Anselmo as Donald Duck
Diane Michelle as Daisy Duck
Tress MacNeille as Chip/Daisy/
      Aunt Gurtie
Alan Young as Uncle Scrooge McDuck

Bill Farmer as Goofy/Pluto
Corey Burton as Dale
Shaun Fleming as Young Max Goof
Jim Cummings as Pete/Postman/Santa/
      Police/Fire Chief
Jeff Bennett as Mortimer
Gregg Berger as Mr. Anderson
Kelsey Grammer as Narrator

Music Highlights: "Deck the Halls" (Trad./lyrics Thomas Oliphant) performed by cast: Wayne Allwine, Tony Anselmo, Bill Farmer, Tress MacNeille, Russi Taylor, "We Wish You a Merry Christmas" (Trad.) performed by cast, "Jingle Bells" (James Pierpont) performed by cast, "Deck the Halls" (Trad./lyrics Thomas Oliphant) performed by SHeDAISY. Music by J. Eric Schmidt.

Film Facts

• "Donald Duck: Stuck On Christmas" was inspired by the 1892 short story "Christmas Every Day" by William Dean Howells, which was made into a 1996 TV film.
• "Mickey and Minnie's Gift of the Magi" was based on the 1905 short story "The Gift of the Magi" by O. Henry.
• SHeDAISY released a *Deck the Halls* CD single (Lyric Street Records, 1999).
• Additional appearances: Preceded by *Mickey's Christmas Carol* featurette (1983), followed by *Mickey's Twice Upon a Christmas* (2004).

Mickey's Twice Upon a Christmas (G)

Home media release date: November 9, 2004
Production Company: DisneyToon Studios, Blur Studio, Sparx Animation France
Length: 68 minutes
Directed by: Matthew O'Callaghan. "Belles on Ice" Story/Story director: Peggy Holmes. Screenplay: Bill Motz & Bob Roth and Peggy Holmes. "Christmas: Impossible" Story director: Matthew O'Callaghan. Story: Chad Fiveash & James Patrick Stoteraux. Screenplay: Chad Fiveash & James Patrick Stoteraux and Matthew O'Callaghan. "Christmas Maximus" Story director: Theresa Pettengill. Story: Theresa Pettengill. Screenplay: Bill Motz & Bob Roth and Shirley Pierce. "Donald's Gift" Story director: Carole Holliday. Story: Carole Holliday. Screenplay: Jim Peronto and Carole Holliday. "Mickey's Dog-Gone Christmas" Story director: Matthew O'Callaghan. Story: Colin Goldman and Matthew O'Callaghan. Screenplay: Michael Shipley & Jim Bernstein and Shirley Pierce.

Synopsis: Like its predecessor, *Mickey's Twice Upon a Christmas* presents a series of holiday vignettes. In "Belles on Ice," Minnie Mouse and Daisy Duck show their competitive side in an ice skating competition that ends up bringing in the hippos and alligators from *Fantasia* (1940), until they realize they've gone too far. In "Christmas: Impossible," Huey, Dewey, and Louie have regrets about their bad behavior on Christmas Eve, requiring a trip to the North Pole to try to get off Santa's "naughty" list. In "Christmas Maximus," Goofy's son Max brings his girlfriend Mona to meet Goofy, who wastes no time in embarrassing Max by bringing out baby pictures and wiping cocoa off his face. Max finally realizes Goofy does what he does out of love, and fortunately Mona understands. In "Donald's Gift," Donald is annoyed by the holiday hustle and bustle, seeking only peace, quiet, and hot chocolate. His annoyance is frustrating to Daisy and his nephews, but ultimately he is able to find his holiday spirit in song and helping others. In "Mickey's Dog-Gone Christmas," Mickey is harsh after Pluto accidentally knocks down the Christmas tree. Pluto runs away, ending up at the North Pole, becoming an honorary reindeer. It isn't long before both Mickey and Pluto want to reconcile, joining the gang for Christmas carols.

Cast: Wayne Allwine as Mickey Mouse
Tony Anselmo as Donald Duck
Bill Farmer as Goofy/Pluto
Russi Taylor as Minnie Mouse/
      Huey/Dewey/Louie
Tress MacNeille as Daisy Duck
Alan Young as Uncle Scrooge McDuck

Jason Marsden as Max Goof
Kellie Martin as Mona
Chuck McCann as Santa Claus
Jeff Bennett as Donner/Elves
Jim Cummings as Blitzen
Clive Revill as Narrator
Edie McClurg as Santa's Workshop Announcer

Music Highlights: "Make Me Look Good" (Jim Wise) performed by Tom Leonard. "Share This Day" (Danny Jacob/Matt Bissonette) performed by Josh Kelley. Score by Stephen James Taylor.

Film Facts

• At the beginning of the film the narrator begins to read *The Night Before Christmas,* an 1823 poem by Clement Clarke Moore, before beginning the proper story.
• Kellie Martin, voice of Mona, also voiced Max's crush, Roxanne, in *A Goofy Movie* (1995).

Minions (PG)

Theatrical release date: July 10, 2015
Production Company: Illumination Entertainment, Universal Pictures
Length: 91 minutes
Directed by: Pierre Coffin, Kyle Balda
Written by: Brian Lynch

Synopsis: Minions evolved long ago to serve the most despicable master they could, though keeping a master was not always easy. After settling in a snowy land, Kevin, leader of the Minions, goes with Stuart and Bob to find a new master. In 1960s England, they learn of the Villain-Con debut of Scarlet Overkill, whom the Minions come to serve, with her husband Herb. Kevin, Stuart and Bob are tasked with stealing the Queen's crown, which is a catastrophe, but in the process Bob pulls Excalibur from the stone, becoming the King of England. When Scarlet is enraged that they have not provided the crown to her, Bob changes the law to allow her to be Queen. Scarlet promptly betrays the Minions, sending them to the dungeon. They escape, but Scarlet soon has Bob and Stuart again. Kevin accidentally uses Scarlet's ultimate weapon machine, growing to a massive size, and his selfless willingness to protect his buddies saves the day, and leads the Minions to their next master: Gru.

Cast: Sandra Bullock as Scarlet Overkill
Jon Hamm as Herb Overkill
Michael Keaton as Walter Nelson
Allison Janney as Madge Nelson
Steve Coogan as Professor Flux/Tower Guard
Jennifer Saunders as The Queen
Geoffrey Rush as Narrator
Steve Carell as Young Gru
Pierre Coffin as The Minions
Katy Mixon as Tina
Michael Beattie as VNC Announcer/Walter Jr.
Hiroyuki Sanada as Sumo Villain

Music Highlights: "Happy Together" (Bonner/Gordon) performed by The Turtles, "19th Nervous Breakdown" (Jagger/Richards) performed by The Rolling Stones, "I'm a Man" (Winwood/Miller) performed by The Spencer Davis Group, "Break On Through (To the Other Side)" (Densmore/Krieger/Manzarek/Morrison) performed by The Doors, "Make 'Em Laugh" (Freed/Brown) vocal by Pierre Coffin, "Hair" (MacDermot/Rado/Ragni) performed by Pierre Coffin/Alex Dowding, "You Really Got Me" (Davies) performed by The Kinks, "The Letter" (Thompson) performed by The Box Tops, "My Generation" (Townshend) performed by The Who, "Theme From The Monkees" (Hart/Boyce) vocal by Pierre Coffin. End credits: "Got To Get You Into My Life" (Lennon/McCartney) performed by The Beatles, "Mellow Yellow" (Leitch) performed by Donovan, "Revolution" (Lennon/McCartney) performed by Coffin, Roberts, Poirel, Balda and Parodi. Score by Heitor Pereira.

Film Facts

• Kevin, Stuart, and Bob resemble Margo, Agnes, and Edith from the *Despicable Me* series.
• One scene re-enacts The Beatles' *Abbey Road* album cover, set to "Love Me Do" (59:45).
• Several mid-credits scenes appear (1:21:22), as well as an end-credits scene (1:28:19).
• Additional appearances: *Despicable Me* series, *Minions: 3 Mini-Movie Collection* (2016, with "Competition," "Cro-Minion," "Binky Nelson Unpacified"), *Minions Holiday Special* (2020).

Mirai (PG)

Theatrical release date: July 20, 2018
Country: Japan   Japanese title: *Mirai no Mirai*
Production Company: Studio Chizu, CTV, Dentsu, East Japan Marketing & Communications
Length: 98 minutes
Directed by: Mamoru Hosoda
Written by: Mamoru Hosoda

Synopsis: The parents of the young boy Kun bring home a new baby, Mirai, gradually leading Kun to feel jealous. In Kun's backyard he runs into a human version of Yukko, the family dog. Soon after, while his mother is away on a trip and his father is distracted with work, Kun is shocked to find an older version of Mirai. They work together to put away a set of Girls Day ceremonial dolls (which legend says must be put away to avoid a delay in her marriage), without being caught by Kun's father. After looking at photo albums with his mother, Kun visits his mother as a young girl, joining her in making a terrible mess. After struggling with learning to ride a bike, he sees his great-grandfather, riding a horse and motorcycle with him. After fussing over his clothes before going out, he thinks his parents have left without him, and sees himself alone in a train station. He is rescued by Mirai, who shows him the tree that indexes the moments of their family's history.

Cast:

Role	English	Japanese
Father	John Cho	Gen Hoshino
Mother	Rebecca Hall	Kumiko Aso
Great-grandfather (young)	Daniel Dae Kim	Masaharu Fukuyama
Kun	Jaden Waldman	Moka Kamishiraishi
Mirai	Victoria Grace	Haru Kuroki
Yukko	Crispin Freeman	Mitsuo Yoshihara
Grandmother	Eileen T'Kaye	Yoshiko Miyazaki
Mirai Ota (baby)	Kari Wahlgren	Kaede Hondo
Kun Ota (high schooler)	Evan Smith	Tasuku Hatanaka
Grandmother (young)	Valerie Arem	Yoshiko Miyazaki
Great-grandmother (young)	Stephanie Sheh	Asami Sanada
Mother (girl)	Madigan Kacmar	Sakura Saiga
Grandfather	Victor Brandt	Koji Yakusho

Music Highlights: "Mirai no Têma"/"Mirai's Theme" (Tatsurô Yamashita) and "Uta no Kisha"/"Song Train" (Tatsurô Yamashita) performed by Tatsurô Yamashita. Music by Masakatsu Takagi.

Film Facts

• The bookcase has books on architecture, including Bauhaus, Frank Lloyd Wright, and Zaha Hadid.
• The film was nominated for the "Best Animated Feature" Academy Award and Golden Globe.
• Writer/director Mamoru Hosoda's daughter is named Mirai, and many of the interactions of the characters in the story are based on his observations of his children.

Missing Link (PG)

Theatrical release date: April 12, 2019
Production Company: Laika Entertainment, Annapurna Pictures
Length: 93 minutes
Directed by: Chris Butler
Screenplay by: Chris Butler

Synopsis: Sir Lionel Frost is a "seeker of mythical beasts," hoping to provide proof of something extraordinary to the snobby gents at the Optimates Club in England. After an unsuccessful effort to get a photo of a prehistoric lake monster, Lionel is inspired by a letter from the New World reporting the existence of the "missing link" between humans and apes. He makes a deal with the insufferable Lord Piggot-Dunceby that if he can provide proof, he will be admitted into the Optimates Club. Despite his skepticism, Piggot-Dunceby hires a hit man to do away with Lionel. Traveling to Washington state, Lionel tracks down the legendary creature, which, to his surprise, can speak. Mr. Link reveals that he is the one who wrote to Lionel, as he is terribly lonely, hoping that Lionel could help him find the yeti in Himalayas. The pair thwart an attack by Piggot-Dunceby's hit man Willard Stenk, proceeding to visit Adelina Fortnight, the widow of Lionel's old partner, to get a map to the Himalayas. After Lionel attempts to steal the map, Adelina insists on joining their expedition. Unfortunately, Stenk remains on their tail, and even when they reach their destination, the yeti are unexpectedly...cold. A confrontation with Piggot-Dunceby gives Lionel a choice of whether to stay focused on seeking validation, or forging his own path.

Cast: Hugh Jackman as Sir Lionel Frost
David Walliams as Mr. Lemuel Lint
Stephen Fry as Lord Piggot-Dunceby
Matt Lucas as Mr. Collick
Zach Galifianakis as Mr. Link
Timothy Olyphant as Willard Stenk
Zoe Saldana as Adelina Fortnight
Amrita Acharia as Ama Lhamu

Ching Valdes-Aran as Gamu
Emma Thompson as The Elder
Humphrey Ker as Doorman/General Pugh
Adam Godley as Lord Bilge
Neil Dickson as Doctor Roylott
Ian Ruskin as Lord Scrivener
Matthew Wolf as Lord Ramsbottom
Darren Richardson as Alfie

Music Highlights: "Ol Joe Clark" (Traditional) performed by The Grascals. End credits: "Do-Dilly-Do (A Friend Like You)" (Walter Martin) performed by Walter Martin. Music by Carter Burwell.

Film Facts

• A statuette of Monkey from the Laika Entertainment film *Kubo and the Two Strings* (2016) is seen in Sir Lionel's drawer (7:18).
• Other Laika films include *Coraline* (2009), *ParaNorman* (2012) and *The Boxtrolls* (2014).
• The film was nominated for the "Best Animated Feature" Academy Award, and won the "Best Animated Feature Film" Golden Globe.

Mr. Peabody and Sherman (PG)

Theatrical release date: March 7, 2014
Production Company: DreamWorks Animation, Pacific Data Images, Bullwinkle Studios
Length: 92 minutes
Directed by: Rob Minkoff
Screenplay by: Craig Wright, additional screenplay material by Michael McCullers, based on "Peabody's Improbable History" from the *Rocky & Bullwinkle* TV series produced by Jay Ward

Synopsis: The genius talking dog Mr. Peabody, with his boy, Sherman, use the time travel invention the WABAC ("wayback") Machine to visit Paris at the time of the French Revolution, followed by an even bigger adventure: Sherman's first day of school. When Sherman is bullied by a mean girl, Penny, he bites her, prompting an investigation of Mr. Peabody. Seeking to settle the matter, Mr. Peabody invites Penny's family over for a visit. Penny accuses Sherman of lying when he says he'd spoken with George Washington, so Sherman shows her the WABAC, leaving her in ancient Egypt. With some difficulty they are able to rescue Penny, but run out of power and get stranded in the Renaissance, where Penny hijacks Leonardo da Vinci's flying machine, taking Sherman with her. Finally on their way back home, a detour to the Trojan War waylays them, as Sherman is angry that Mr. Peabody did not tell him his parenting was being investigated. Chaos is unleashed by a rip in the space-time continuum, but in the midst of the confusion, Sherman realizes who he really is.

Cast: Ty Burrell as Mr. Peabody
Max Charles as Sherman
Lauri Fraser as Marie Antoinette/Egyptian Woman
Guillaume Aretos as Robespierre
Patrice A. Musick as Teacher
Ariel Winter as Penny Peterson
Karan Brar as Mason
Josh Rush as Carl
Stephen Tobolowsky as Principal Purdy

Allison Janney as Ms. Grunion
Dennis Haysbert as Judge
Stephen Colbert as Paul Peterson
Leslie Mann as Patty Peterson
Zach Callison as King Tut
Stanley Tucci as Leonardo da Vinci
Patrick Warburton as Agamemnon
Mel Brooks as Albert Einstein
Rob Minkoff as Creepy Boy

Music Highlights: "Beautiful Boy (Darling Boy)" (Lennon) performed by John Lennon, "Way Back When" (Adam M. Roth/Fredrik Eriksson/Sebastian Fritze) performed by Grizfolk, "Kid" (Andre) performed by Peter Andre. Music by Danny Elfman.

Film Facts

• During Penny's visit, the music includes "Rhapsody in Blue" (George Gershwin), "Purple Haze" (Jimi Hendrix), "Tezka Radost" (Ondrej Smeykal), and "Aquarela do Brasil" (Ary Barroso).
• The janitor sweeping up at the end (1:22:31) is from the original *Rocky and Bullwinkle* show.
• Cameos include Bullwinkle J. Moose (1:04) and Dudley Do-Right's horse (17:38).
• Additional appearances: Based on the "Peabody's Improbable History" segments of the animated series *The Adventures of Rocky and Bullwinkle and Friends* (1959-1964), followed by the animated TV series *The Mr. Peabody & Sherman Show* (2015-2017).

The Mitchells vs. the Machines (PG)

Theatrical release date: April 23, 2021 Streaming date: April 30, 2021
Production Company: Columbia, Sony Pictures Animation, Lord Miller Prod., One Cool Films
Length: 113 minutes
Directed by: Mike Rianda, co-directed by Jeff Rowe
Written by: Mike Rianda and Jeff Rowe, story consultant Alex Hirsch

---

Synopsis: Katie Mitchell has always felt like a misfit, coping by making films. On the verge of leaving home for film school, Katie has a falling out with her father, who she's had a hard time getting along with. He tries to make it up to her by canceling her flight to California, and taking her on a family road trip. PAL technology mogul Mark unveils the PAL MAX robots, which promptly begin trying to take over the world. As humans are rounded up, the Mitchells have to work together to survive the apocalypse, while Mark tries to persuade PAL not to launch the imprisoned human race into space. At the Mall of the Globe, Katie gets two malfunctioning robots to upload a kill code to stop the revolution, but PAL sends an army of appliances to stop them. When the router is destroyed the upload fails, so the family heads to Silicon Valley to challenge the robot world with their ample human foibles.

Cast: Abbi Jacobson as Katie/Dog Cop
Danny McBride as Rick
Maya Rudolph as Linda
Mike Rianda as Aaron/Furbies/
      Talking Dog/Wifi Enthusiast
Eric André as Mark
Olivia Colman as PAL
Fred Armisen as Deborahbot 5000

Beck Bennett as Eric/PAL MAX Robots
Chrissy Teigen as Hailey Posey
John Legend as Jim Posey
Charlyne Yi as Abby Posey
Blake Griffin as PAL MAX Prime
Conan O'Brien as Glaxxon 5000
Doug the Pug as Monchi
Alex Hirsch as Dirk

Music Highlights: "Lamb and the Lion" (Breeck/Byron/Byron/Gray) performed by The Mae Shi, "Death to Los Campesinos!" and "Broken Heartbeats Sound Like Breakbeats" (Briggs et al.) performed by Los Campesinos!, "I Want More" (Utter/Vail/Connelly) performed by Bangs, "Nyan Cat" (Nakanishi) performed by daniwell, "Live Your Life" (Harris/Riddick/Smith) performed by T.I./ Rihanna, "California" (Boucher) performed by Grimes, "(Nothing But) Flowers" (Byrne/Frantz/ Harrison/N'Jock/Weymouth) performed by Talking Heads, "On the Verge" (Hanna/Fateman/Samson) performed by Le Tigre, "Battle without Honor or Humanity" (Hotei) performed by Tomoyasu Hotei, "Walk the Dinosaur" (Weiss/Jacobs/Fagenson) performed by Was Not Was, "Dreamy Wonder" (Rider) performed by Tempura Kidz, "Ironside" (Jones) performed by Quincy Jones, "Hoppípolla" and "Inní Mér Syngur Vitleysingur" (Dyrason/Sveinsson/Birgisson/Holm) performed by Sigur Rós. End credits: "On My Way" (Lahey/Payten/Strum) performed by Alex Lahey. Music by Mark Mothersbaugh.

Film Facts

- Mike Rianda and Jeff Rowe were writers for Disney's animated series *Gravity Falls* (2012-2016).
- Katie became the first openly LGBTQ central character of a mainstream animated film.
- The Mitchells are based on writer/director Mike Rianda's family.

Moana (PG)

Theatrical release date: November 23, 2016
Production Company: Walt Disney Pictures, Walt Disney Animation Studios
Length: 107 minutes
Directed by: John Musker & Ron Clements, co-directed by Chris Williams & Don Hall
Screenplay by: Jared Bush, story by Ron Clements & John Musker, Chris Williams & Don Hall, Pamela Ribon, Aaron Kandell & Jordan Kandell

---

Synopsis: As a gift to humanity, the demigod Maui stole the heart of goddess Te Fiti, but unintentionally caused the Earth to begin to die. Moana, the daughter of the chief of a Polynesian island, is in line to lead after her father, but is chosen by the ocean to get Maui to return the heart to Te Fiti. Among Moana's challenges: leaving her island when her people gave up seafaring generations ago, persuading the arrogant Maui to help, escaping the clutches of a giant collector crab, withstanding the wrath of the fiery Te Kā, and above all, finding the courage to remember who she truly is.

Cast: Auli'i Cravalho as Moana
Dwayne Johnson as Maui
Rachel House as Gramma Tala
Temuera Morrison as Chief Tui
Jemaine Clement as Tamatoa
Nicole Scherzinger as Sina

Alan Tudyk as Heihei, Villager #3
Oscar Kightley as Fisherman
Troy Polamalu as Villager #1
Puanani Cravalho as Villager #2
Louise Bush as Toddler Moana
Chris Jackson as Chief Tui (singing)

Music Highlights: "Where You Are" (Lin-Manuel Miranda/Opetaia Foa'i/Mark Mancina) performed by Christopher Jackson, Rachel House, Nicole Scherzinger, Auli'i Cravalho, Louise Bush, "How Far I'll Go" (Miranda) performed by Auli'i Cravalho, "We Know the Way" (Foa'i/Miranda) performed by Opetaia Foa'i, Lin-Manuel Miranda, Pasifika Voices, "You're Welcome" (Miranda) performed by Dwayne Johnson, "Shiny" (Miranda/Mancina) performed by Jemaine Clement. Score by Mark Mancina.

Film Facts

• The 56th of the Disney animated classics, the story of *Moana* was initially conceived by top directors John Musker and Ron Clements (*The Great Mouse Detective, The Little Mermaid, Aladdin, Hercules, Treasure Planet, The Princess and the Frog*), drawn from Polynesian mythology.
• The film was titled *Vaiana* in several European countries, and *Oceania* in Italy.
• The DVD/Blu-ray include the short "Inner Workings," the Blu-ray also includes "Gone Fishing."
• The song lyrics in the film are in English, Samoan, and the Polynesian language Tokelauan.
• Easter Eggs: the magic carpet from *Aladdin* appears in earth tones (17:19), the face of Baymax from *Big Hero 6* appears among the Kakamora pirates (47:57), Genie's lamp is among the treasure on Tamatoa's back (1:02:25), Maui briefly transforms into Sven, the reindeer from *Frozen* (1:02:46).
• Mini Maui became the first traditionally-animated character included in a computer-animated Disney film.
• Additional appearances: The short "Gone Fishing" (2017) from the *Moana* Blu-ray.

Monster House (PG)

Theatrical release date: July 21, 2006
Production Company: Columbia Pictures, Relativity Media, ImageMovers, Amblin Entertainment
Length: 91 minutes
Directed by: Gil Kenan
Screenplay by: Dan Harmon & Rob Schrab and Pamela Pettler, story by Dan Harmon & Rob Schrab

Synopsis: Teenager D.J. is concerned about his neighbor across the street, the cranky old man Nebbercracker, who shouts at kids who walk on his lawn and steals tricycles from small children. When D.J. and his friend Chowder are playing basketball, the ball rolls onto the old man's lawn. When D.J. tries to get it back, the old man seizes him, but then suddenly falls to the ground, and his body is wheeled away. That night D.J. gets a phone call, and when he calls the number back he can hear the phone ring at the house across the street. After Chowder begins teasing D.J. by mocking the house, the house comes alive, trying to eat Chowder. On Halloween morning, the boys panic as Jenny, a savvy girl from Westbrook Prep, approaches the house, which eats a wagon she's pulling. Fearing a catastrophe on Halloween as trick-or-treaters approach the evil house, the kids call the police, but the house plays dead. They turn to a video game expert, Skull, who tells them the house is possessed by Nebbercracker, and they must strike the heart of the house: the furnace. When the kids learn that they had things all wrong, and with some very unexpected help, they work to end the curse of the house. NOTE: Despite its PG rating, the disturbing content in this film make it appropriate for older viewers.

Cast: Mitchel Musso as D.J.
Sam Lerner as Chowder
Spencer Locke as Jenny
Steve Buscemi as Nebbercracker
Catherine O'Hara as Mom
Fred Willard as Dad
Maggie Gyllenhaal as Zee
Jason Lee as Bones

Kevin James as Officer Landers
Nick Cannon as Officer Lister
Jon Heder as Reginald "Skull" Skulinski
Kathleen Turner as Constance
Woody Schultz as Paramedic #1
Ian McConnel as Paramedic #2
Ryan Newman as Little Girl
Kevin the Dog as Himself

Music Highlights: "Merciful Hammer" (Sardy) performed by Ralph Saenz, D. Sardy, John Shmersal, and Bobby Jarzombek, "Thou Art Dead" (Kenan) performed by Gil Kenan, "A Little More Love" (John Farrar) performed by Olivia Newton-John. End credits: "Halloween" (Siouxsie Sioux/Steven Severin/Budgie/John McGeoch) performed by Siouxsie & the Banshees. Music by Douglas Pipes.

Film Facts

- The film was executive produced by Robert Zemeckis and Steven Spielberg.
- The heavy metal tape that Zee plays is by "Skull + Bones" (13:42), two characters in the film.
- Several mid-credits scenes appear (1:23:26).

A Monster in Paris (PG)

Theatrical release date: October 12, 2011
Country: France French title: *Un Monstre à Paris*
Production Company: EuropaCorp, Bibo Films, France 3 Cinéma
Length: 90 minutes
Directed by: Bibo Bergeron
Screenplay by: Stéphane Kazandjian & Bibo Bergeron, based on an original story by Bibo Bergeron

Synopsis: In the early 1900s in Paris, timid film projectionist Emile Petit dreams of asking out Maud, a woman he works with. Emile gets a ride with his colorful friend Raoul to pick up a part for a projector, as Raoul delivers fertilizer to the local botanical gardens. While there, the impetuous Raoul begins playing with chemicals in a lab, causing a sunflower to grow to a towering height, and an accident causes more chemicals to mix, resulting in a huge cloud of mist. Emile sees a creature in the shadows which leaps straight up, out of the building. Police Commissioner Victor Maynott, who is running for mayor, agrees to let his officer Pâté investigate sightings of the creature around the city. A fragment of film leads the police to Emile and Raoul, and they believe the creature is a flea that has grown to huge proportions. The flea, dressed in human clothes, comes to the alley of the theater of cabaret singer Lucille. Though initially fearful, Lucille hears the creature sing, and recognizes its kindness. She takes the creature in, disguising it as a person and making it part of her act, calling it "Francœur." When Maynott seeks to destroy the "monster," Lucille, Emile and Raoul try to save Francœur, revealing the true nature of all involved.

Cast:

Role	English	French
Raoul	Adam Goldberg	Gad Elmaleh
Emile	Jay Harrington	Sébastien Desjours
Victor Maynott	Danny Huston	François Cluzet
Inspector Pâté	Bob Balaban	Philippe Peythieu
Francœur	Sean Lennon	Matthieu Chedid
Lucille	Vanessa Paradis	Vanessa Paradis
Maud	Madeline Zima	Ludivine Sagnier
Madame Carlotta	Catherine O'Hara	Julie Ferrier
Albert	Matthew Géczy	Bruno Salomone

Music Highlights: "La Seine & I" (-M-) performed by Vanessa Paradis & Sean Lennon (US)/ Matthieu Chedid (France), "A Monster in Paris" (-M-) performed by Sean Lennon, "Love is in My Soul" (-M-/Krestek/Moan/DP) performed by Sean Lennon, "Just a Little Kiss" (-M-/Cyril Atef). Original music by -M- & Patrice Renson.

Film Facts

• The French voice actor for Francœur, musician Matthieu Chedid, performs under the name -M-.
• Two final brief scenes play during the credits, one at 1:23:35, and one at 1:29:38.
• French singer/actress Vanessa Paradis (Lucille) appears in both the French and English versions.

Monsters, Inc. (G)

Theatrical release date: November 2, 2001
Production Company: Pixar Animation Studios, Walt Disney Pictures
Length: 92 minutes
Directed by: Pete Docter, co-directed by Lee Unkrich, David Silverman
Screenplay by: Andrew Stanton, Daniel Gerson, original story by Pete Docter, Jill Culton, Jeff Pidgeon, Ralph Eggleston

Synopsis: Employees of Monsters, Inc. scare children to capture their screams, which produce electricity in the monster world, while avoiding touching children, which are said to be highly toxic to monsters. Top scarer Sullivan and his colleague Mike stumble across an evil plot to extract screams from children with a monstrous machine, and scramble to deal with the little girl "Boo" who escapes into their world. Their efforts lead to a new era at Monsters, Inc.

Cast: John Goodman as James P. Sullivan
Billy Crystal as Mike Wazowski
Mary Gibbs as Boo
Steve Buscemi as Randall
James Coburn as Waternoose
Jennifer Tilly as Celia
Bob Peterson as Roz

John Ratzenberger as Yeti
Frank Oz as Fungus
Daniel Gerson as Needleman & Smitty
Steve Susskind as Floor Manager
Bonnie Hunt as Flint
Jeff Pidgeon as Bile
Sam Black as George

Music Highlights: "If I Didn't Have You" (Randy Newman) performed by Billy Crystal and John Goodman. Music by Randy Newman.

Film Facts

• *Monsters, Inc.*, the 4th Pixar film, was the directorial debut of Pete Docter. The initial idea for the film was conceived at a legendary lunch during which Pixar's story team (John Lasseter, Andrew Stanton, Pete Docter, and Joe Ranft) proposed film ideas, including *A Bug's Life, Toy Story 2,* and *Finding Nemo*. Docter had imagined there were monsters in his closet in his childhood, and a movie about monsters met with approval from the team.
• Boo's actual name is Mary, as written on a picture she draws.
• The restaurant "Harryhausen's" is an homage to master stop-motion animator Ray Harryhausen.
• The real "Mike Wazowski" (technically Isadore "Mike" Oznowicz) is the father of Frank Oz, director/actor most famous for creating, voicing, and puppeting with the Muppets (Miss Piggy, Fozzie, Bert, Grover, Cookie Monster).
• Cameos: a Jessie doll from *Toy Story 2* and Nemo from *Finding Nemo* (1:18:40) in Boo's room.
• John Ratzenberger's standard Pixar film role is the Yeti.
• A video game was produced for Game Boy Advance, Game Boy Color, and PlayStation 2.
• Additional appearances: "Mike's New Car" short (2002) on *Monsters, Inc.* DVD, *Monsters University* (2013), "Party Central" short (2013) on *Pixar Short Films Collection, Volume 3* DVD/ Blu-ray, *Monsters at Work* animated TV series (2021).

Monsters University (G)

Theatrical release date: June 21, 2013
Production Company: Pixar Animation Studios, Walt Disney Pictures
Length: 104 minutes
Directed by: Dan Scanlon
Screenplay by: Daniel Gerson & Robert L. Baird, Dan Scanlon, story by Dan Scanlon, Daniel Gerson & Robert L. Baird

Synopsis: Taking place before *Monsters, Inc.*, Mike Wazowski and Jimmy "Sully" Sullivan, freshmen in the Scare Program at Monsters University, begin their college career as rivals. After they are both kicked out of their program, Mike makes a deal with Dean Hardscrabble that if he can win the annual Scare Games he will be readmitted into the program — but if he loses he will leave Monsters University. His fraternity, the socially awkward Oozma Kappa, is short one member, requiring Mike and Sully to reluctantly work together. Over the course of the games they learn respect for each other, but for the final test Sully doubts Mike's ability and tampers with equipment in order to win. After they are expelled they begin working at Monsters, Inc. energy company, working their way up from the mailroom.

Cast: John Goodman as Jimmy Sullivan
Billy Crystal as Mike Wazokski
Steve Buscemi as Randall
Helen Mirren as Dean Hardscrabble
Peter Sohn as Squishy
Joel Murray as Don
Sean P. Hays as Terri

Dave Foley as Terry
Charlie Day as Art
Alfred Molina as Professor Knight
Tyler Labine as Greek Council VP
Nathan Fillion as Johnny
Aubrey Plaza as Greek Council President
Bobby Moynihan as Chet

Music Highlights: "Monsters University" (Newman) performed by chorus, "Roar" (Axwell/Sebastian Ingrosso) performed by Axwell & Sebastian Ingrosso of Swedish House Mafia, "Island" (Mastodon) performed by Mastodon. Score by Randy Newman.

Film Facts

• The 14th Pixar film, *Monsters University* was a prequel, giving the backstory of how top scarer Sully met Mike Wazowski.
• John Ratzenberger reprises his role from *Monsters, Inc.* as the Yeti.
• A draft sequel to *Monsters, Inc.*, titled *Monsters, Inc. 2: Lost in Scaradise,* was partially developed by Disney's short-lived Circle 7 Animation division, but never released. The story centered on Mike and Sully attempting to visit Boo to give her a birthday present, only to find that she had moved.
• A Monsters University campus website was created, at monstersuniversity.com/edu covering topics such as MU sports, the MU Concert Choir, MU ID cards, and "A Message From the Dean."
• The online video game "Scare School Scamper" was based on the film.
• Additional appearances: *Monsters, Inc.* (2001), "Mike's New Car" short (2002) on *Monsters, Inc.* DVD/Blu-ray, "Party Central" short (2013) on *Pixar Short Films Collection, Volume 3* DVD/ Blu-ray, *Monsters at Work* animated TV series (2021).

Monsters vs. Aliens (PG)

Theatrical release date: March 27, 2009
Production Company: DreamWorks Animation
Length: 94 minutes
Directed by: Conrad Vernon, Rob Letterman
Screenplay by: Maya Forbes & Wallace Wolodarsky and Rob Letterman and Jonathan Aibel & Glenn Berger, story by Rob Letterman & Conrad Vernon

Synopsis: Susan Murphy's wedding to news weatherman Derek Dietl is interrupted by a meteorite, which strikes Susan, causing her to grow to a huge size and turning her hair white. She is captured and transported to a secret military facility for monsters, taking the name "Ginormica" and meeting fellow residents Dr. Cockroach Ph.D., the blue blob B.O.B., the massive Insectosaurus, and the Missing Link, an ape-fish. When a hostile alien probe begins wreaking havoc on Earth, the monsters are given a chance to earn their freedom if they can stop the chaos. In the process, Susan's time as a monster teaches her more about herself than she ever understood when she was just a human.

Cast: Reese Witherspoon as Susan Murphy/Ginormica
Seth Rogen as B.O.B.
Hugh Laurie as Dr. Cockroach Ph.D.
Will Arnett as The Missing Link
Kiefer Sutherland as General W.R. Monger
Rainn Wilson as Gallaxhar
Stephen Colbert as President Hathaway

Paul Rudd as Derek Dietl
Julie White as Wendy Murphy
Jeffrey Tambor as Carl Murphy
Amy Poehler as Computer
Ed Helms as News Reporter
Renée Zellweger as Katie
John Krasinski as Cuthbert

Music Highlights: "When You See Those Flying Saucers" (Coben/Grean) performed by The Buchanan Brothers, "Here Comes the Bride" (Traditional), "Planet Claire" (Mancini/Pierson/Schneider/Strickland/C. Wilson/R. Wilson) performed by Les Deux Love Orchestra, also by The B-52's, "Axel F." (Faltermeyer) performed by Harold Faltermeyer, "Reminiscing" (Goble) performed by Little River Band, "Roses Are Red" (Dif/Rasted/Norreen/Nystrøm/Hartmann/Langhoff) performed by Aqua, "Tell Him" (Berns) performed by The Exciters, "Who's Crying Now" (Cain/Perry) performed by Journey, "Close Encounters of the Third Kind" (Williams), "E.T.: The Extra-Terrestrial" (Williams), "Wooly Bully" (Samudio) performed by Sam the Sham and The Pharaohs, "Let's Get It Started" (Adams/Fratantuno/Gomez/Graves/Pajon Jr./ Pineda), "Purple People Eater" (Wooley) performed by Sheb Wooley. Music by Henry Jackman.

Film Facts

• The monsters are based on classic monster films: Ginormica on *Attack of the 50 Foot Woman* (1958), B.O.B. on *The Blob* (1958), The Missing Link on *Creature from the Black Lagoon* (1954), and Dr. Cockroach Ph.D. on *The Fly* (1958).
• There is a mid-credits scene (1:26:33).
• Additional appearances: "B.O.B.'s Big Break in Monster 3D" short (2009), "The Night of the Living Carrots" short (2012).

Mulan (G)

Theatrical release date: June 19, 1998
Production Company: Walt Disney Pictures, Walt Disney Feature Animation
Length: 88 minutes
Directed by: Barry Cook and Tony Bancroft
Screenplay by: Rita Hsiao, Christopher Sanders, Philip LaZebnik, Raymond Singer & Eugenia Bostwick-Singer, based on a story by Robert D. San Souci

---

Synopsis: After the Huns invade China, the Emperor decrees that each household must provide a male warrior. Seeking to spare her aged father, Mulan masquerades as a man, and is able to stop the Hun army when the other soldiers cannot, though her secret is discovered in the process. When Khan, the leader of the Huns, seeks to kill the Emperor, Mulan must again defy convention in the service of her country.

Cast: Ming-Na Wen as Mulan
B.D. Wong as Shang
Eddie Murphy as Mushu
Harvey Fierstein as Yao
Gedde Watanabe as Ling
Jerry S. Tondo as Chien-Po

Frank Welker as Khan
Pat Morita as The Emperor
Miguel Ferrer as Shan-Yu
George Takei as First Ancestor
June Foray as Grandmother Fa
James Hong as Chi-Fu

Music Highlights: "Honor to Us All" performed by Beth Fowler, Marnie Nixon, and Lea Salonga, "Reflection" performed by Lea Salonga, "I'll Make a Man Out of You" performed by Donny Osmond, "A Girl Worth Fighting For" performed by Harvey Fierstein, James Hong, Lea Salonga, Jerry Tondo, and Matthew Wilder. All songs by Matthew Wilder and David Zippel. Score by Jerry Goldsmith.

Film Facts

• The 36th of the Disney animated classics, *Mulan* was based on the Chinese legend of Hua Mulan. It was spearheaded by Walt Disney Feature Animation Florida, when Disney gave the studio the opportunity to produce a feature film.
• Disney management were interested in an Asian story, working with children's book author Robert D. San Souci, who wrote a book inspired by the ancient Chinese poem "The Song of Mu Lan" (sometimes called "The Ballad of Mulan") which served as the basis for the screenplay. Certain changes were made, including changing the protagonists name from Hua Mulan to Fa Mulan.
• Marni Nixon, who provided the singing voice for Grandmother Fa, had a number of uncredited singing parts, including Maria in *West Side Story* (1961), Eliza Doolittle in *My Fair Lady* (1964), and Disney's *Alice in Wonderland* (1951).
• The poem the film is based upon dates back to circa 6th century China.
• Additional appearances: Followed by *Mulan II* home media (2005), *Mulan* live-action (2020).
• The live-action *Mulan* (2020) was marred by controversy, as the actress portraying Mulan made comments supportive of Hong Kong police involved in a brutal crackdown on democracy protesters, as well as concern that some filming took place in the Xinjiang region, site of serious human rights abuses of China's Uyghur Muslims.

Mulan II (G)

Home media release date: February 1, 2005 (November 3, 2004 in Italy/Norway)
Production Company: Walt Disney Pictures, DisneyToon Studios
Length: 79 minutes
Directed by: Darrell Rooney and Lynne Southerland
Screenplay by: Michael Lucker & Chris Parker and Roger S.H. Schulman

Synopsis: The Emperor's three daughters, Mei, Ting Ting, and Su, are engaged to marry three princes in Qui Gong they have never met, to form an alliance with the Middle Kingdom. Mulan and Shang, aided by Yao, Ling, and Chein-Po, are enlisted to escort the princesses by as they travel to meet the princes they are to marry. The princesses begin to waver as they consider the concept of a duty to their heart, and the journey is further complicated by Mushu's effort to break up Mulan and Shang, so he can maintain his pedestal (and life of comfort) among the spirits of the ancestors.

Cast: Ming-Na as Mulan
B.D. Wong as Shang
Mark Moseley as Mushu
Lucy Liu as Mei
Harvey Fierstein as Yao
Sandra Oh as Ting Ting

Gedde Watanabe as Ling
Lauren Tom as Su
Jerry Tondo as Chein-Po
Pat Morita as The Emperor
George Takei as First Ancestor
Frank Welker as Cri-Kee

Music Highlights: "Lesson Number One" (Jeanine Tesori/Alexa Junge) performed by Lea Salonga, "Like Other Girls" (Jeanine Tesori/Alexa Junge) performed by Beth Blankenship, Mandy Gonzalez, and Judy Kuhn, "A Girl Worth Fighting For (Redux)" (Mattew Wilder/David Zippel/Alexa Junge) performed by Harvey Fierstein, Jerry Tondo, Gedde Watanabe, Randy Crenshaw, "(I Wanna Be) Like Other Girls" (Tesori/Junge) performed by Atomic Kitten, "Here Beside Me" (McNeely/Light) performed by Hayley Westenra. Music by Joel McNeely.

Film Facts

• Mark Moseley replaced Eddie Murphy as the voice of Mushu. Moseley also followed Murphy as the voice of Donkey in the *Shrek 2* video game by Knowwonder.
• Lea Salonga, the singing voice of Mulan, also provided Jasmine's singing voice in *Aladdin*, as well as voicing Mrs. Kusakabe from the English translation of Hayao Miyazaki's *My Neighbor Totoro*.
• The singing voices of the princesses were provided by Judy Kuhn (Ting-Ting), Beth Blankenship (Mei), and Mandy Gonzalez (Su).
• World champion ice skater (and Disney fan) Michelle Kwan had a one-line cameo as a village shopkeeper skating over to offer Chien-Po ginger (48:55).
• Additional appearances: *Mulan* (1998), *Mulan* live-action (2020). Mulan also appeared in the live-action series *Once Upon a Time*, and in the series finale *Sophia the First: Forever Royal* (2018).
• The film has been referred to by the alternate title *Mulan 2: The Final War.*
• A third Mulan film was planned, but was canceled along with all other sequels when John Lasseter became the Chief Creative Officer of Walt Disney Animation Studios.

Mune: Guardian of the Moon (PG)

Theatrical release date: October 14, 2015 (premiere Dec 6, 2014, Forum des Images, Paris, France)
Country: France   French title: *Mune, le Gardien de la Lune*
Production Company: Onyx Films, Kinology, ON Animation Studios
Length: 85 minutes
Directed by: Alexandre Heboyan & Benoît Philippon
Screenplay by: Benoît Philippon, adaptation & dialogue Benoît Philippon & Jérôme Fansten, story by Benoît Philippon

---

Synopsis: It is time for new Guardians to be chosen for the Sun and Moon. The arrogant Sohone is chosen to replace Xolal as the Guardian of the Sun for the People of the Day, and unexpectedly, the timid Mune is chosen instead of heir apparent Leeyoon to replace Yule as Guardian of the Moon. Deep inside the planet, the evil Necross schemes to steal back the sun, releasing two "evil corruptor" snakes to further his cause. They begin influencing Leeyoon, who convinces Sohone to try to get rid of Mune. While Sohone is distracted, devils Mox and Spleen steal the sun, and the bitter Necross plans to let the sun grow cold and die. Sohone supports Leeyoon in claiming to be the Guardian of the Moon, and while Mune initially flees, he returns, supported by Glim, a clever girl made of wax, helping Sohone find the sun in the Underworld, before Mune sets out to recover the wandering Temple of the Moon. Both guardians learn that they must rely on each other to prevail.

Cast:	English 2017	English 2014	French
Mune	Joshua J. Ballard	Joshua J. Ballard	Michaël Grégorio
Glim	Nicole Provost	Nicole Provost	Izïa Higelin
Sohone	Rob Lowe	Trevor Devall	Omar Sy
Leeyoon	Christian Slater	Michael Dobson	Féodor Atkine
Necross	Davey Grant	Davey Grant	Eric Herson-Macarel
Mox	Patton Oswalt	Sam Vincent	Michel Mella
Spleen	Ed Helms	Brian Drummond	Fabrice Josso
Phospho	Jeff Dunham	Davey Grant	Patrick Poivey
Xolal	Michael Dobson	Michael Dobson	Jean Claude Donda
Yule	Paul Dobson	Paul Dobson	Benoît Allemane

Music Highlights: "Happy" (Pierre Forestier/Guillaume Jaulin/Thomas Le Vexier/Derek Martin/ Sylvain Richard) performed by C 2 C feat. Derek Martin. Music by Bruno Coulais.

Film Facts

• The film was originally conceived as a short by writer Benoît Philippon, but the story would not fit within the confines of a short.
• The premiere took place in Paris at the Forum des Images theater on December 6, 2014, and in the U.S. at the New York International Children's Film Festival on March 14, 2015.

Music Land (Approved)

Theatrical release date: October 5, 1955
Production Company: Walt Disney Productions
Length: 75 minutes
Directors: Clyde Geronimi, Hamilton Luske, Wilfred Jackson, Robert Cormack, Jack Kinney, Josh Meador. Writers: Various

---

Synopsis: A varied collection of musical shorts, drawing segments from the previously released films *Make Mine Music* (1946) and *Melody Time* (1948), including performances by the Andrews Sisters, Benny Goodman (with both his Orchestra and his Quartet), Jerry Colonna, Fred Waring and His Pennsylvanians, Freddy Martin & His Orchestra, featuring Jack Fina on piano, Frances Langford, Ethel Smith & The Dinning Sisters, and Roy Rogers, Trigger, Bob Nolan and the Sons of the Pioneers.

• "Johnny Fedora and Alice Blue Bonnet" (Allie Wrubel) sung by The Andrews Sisters (from *Make Mine Music*)
• "Two for the Record": "All the Cats Join In" (Eddie Sauter/Alec Wilder/Ray Gilbert) featuring Benny Goodman and his Orchestra (from *Make Mine Music*)/"After You've Gone" (Turner Leighton/Henry Creamer) by The Goodman Quartet (from *Make Mine Music*)
• "Casey at the Bat" (poem by Ernest Lawrence Thayer, music by Ray Gilbert/Ken Darby/Eliot Daniel) by Jerry Colonna, also includes includes "A Hot Time in the Old Town" (Theo A. Metz) (from *Make Mine Music*)
• "Contrast in Rhythm": "Trees" (poem by Joyce Kilmer, music by Oscar Rasbach) by Fred Waring and His Pennsylvanians (from *Melody Time*)/"Bumble Boogie" (Nikolai Rimsky-Korsakov, arr. Jack Fina) by Freddy Martin & His Orchestra, featuring Jack Fina on piano (from *Melody Time*)
• "Once Upon a Wintertime" (Bobby Worth/Ray Gilbert) by Frances Langford (from *Melody Time*)
• "Blame It on the Samba" (Ernesto Nazareth/Ray Gilbert) by Ethel Smith & The Dinning Sisters (from *Melody Time*)
• "Blue Shadows on the Trail" (Eliot Daniel/Johnny Lange) by Roy Rogers, Bob Nolan and the Sons of the Pioneers (from *Melody Time*)/"Pecos Bill" (Eliot Daniel/Johnny Lange) by Roy Rogers and Trigger, Bob Nolan and the Sons of the Pioneers, Children: Bobby Driscoll, Luana Patten (from *Melody Time*)

Film Facts

• A 1935 Silly Symphonies short also had the name "Music Land."
• RKO Radio Pictures distributed Disney films since *Snow White and the Seven Dwarfs* (1937), but the company had experienced some turmoil from the erratic decisions of aviation tycoon Howard Hughes. Disney formed his own distribution company, Buena Vista Distribution, and fulfilled his contract with RKO by assembling a new "package film," drawing shorts from the films *Make Mine Music* (1946) and *Melody Time* (1948), and releasing the new anthology theatrically as *Music Land*.
• Two Benny Goodman numbers from *Make Mine Music*, "All the Cats Join In" and "After You've Gone," were released theatrically in April, 1954, as "Two for the Record," while "Trees" and "Bumble Boogie," both from *Melody Time*, were released as the 1955 short "Contrast in Rhythm."

My Beautiful Girl, Mari (TV-G)

Theatrical release date: January 18, 2002 (South Korea)
Country: South Korea   Korean title: *Mariiyagi* (lit. *The Story of Mari*)
Production Company: Daewoo Entertainment, Kuk Dong, Siz Entertainment
Length: 86 minutes
Directed by: Seong-gang Lee
Written by: Su-jeong Kang, Mi-ae Seo, Seong-gang Lee

Synopsis: Nam-woo, a young man who works in an office, reflects on his childhood in a small fishing village, a time of many worries, but also many wonders. His father has passed away, his grouchy grandmother is ill, his best friend, Jun-ho, is reluctantly moving to attend school in Seoul, leaving Nam-woo struggling with many feelings of loss. During a visit to a local store, Nam-woo finds a marble that seems to have the image of a girl floating inside it, but before he can look at it clearly, drops it in a case of many marbles. Later, when the stray cat Yo cannot be found, Nam-woo heads to an abandoned lighthouse to look for him. While there, Nam-woo find Yo, but also a peculiar floating fish that leads him to the top of the lighthouse. After a flash of light, Nam-woo and Yo find themselves falling, rescued by a flying girl all in white, and getting a ride on the fish, which has grown to a huge size. After a long journey he sees the girl again, resting on the nose of a huge furry creature, before waking to find himself in the field near the lighthouse. In ordinary life, Nam-woo watches as Jun-ho pines for Soog-y, and she becomes angry when a drawing of the two of them kissing appears at the school. When Nam-woo goes back to the lighthouse, he returns to the fantasy world, and finally gets to talk to Mari, the floating girl. During a terrible storm Nam-woo and Jun-ho go back to the broken lighthouse, hoping that Mari's light will save the fishing boat of Jun-ho's father. Jun-ho departs, promising to stay in touch. As an adult, Nam-woo's memory of Mari has faded, but when Jun-ho gives him the marble that held her image, Nam-woo thinks of her, and begins returning to the fantasy world.

Cast:

Role	English	Korean
Nam-woo	Alejandro Fallick	Deok-hwan Ryu
Adult Nam-woo	Jay Hickman	Byung-hun Lee
Jun-ho	Clint Bickham	In-gyu Sung
Adult Jun-ho	Chris Patton	Hyung-jin Gong
Nam-woo's Mom	Christine Auten	Jong-ok Bae
Nam-woo's Grandma	Shelley Calene-Black	Moon-hee Na
Jun-ho's Father	John Swasey	Hang-sun Jang
Soog-y	Kira Vincent-Davis	Na-ri Lee

Music Highlights: Music by Byung-woo Lee.

Film Facts

• The film was the Grand Prix Winner at the Annecy International Animated Film Festival in France.
• The English dub was directed and produced by Carl Macek (*Robotech*).

My Little Pony: Equestria Girls (TV-Y)

Home media release date: August 6, 2013 (premiere June 15, 2013 at Los Angeles Film Festival)
Production Company: DHX Media, Hasbro Studios, Studio B
Length: 72 minutes
Directed by: Jayson Thiessen
Written by: Meghan McCarthy

Synopsis: Twilight Sparkle's coronation is disrupted when Princess Celestia's former student, Sunset Shimmer, steals Twilight's crown, planning to misuse its power in another world. Twilight follows her through a portal, ending up in human form in a human world, accompanied by her dragon Spike, who becomes a dog. The stolen crown has been given to the human Principal Celestia, and Twilight is determined to get it back by being crowned Fall Formal princess. She soon meets counterparts to Fluttershy, Pinkie Pie, Rainbow Dash, Applejack, and Rarity, as well as the gallant Flash Sentry, and learns that Sunset Shimmer has used lies and intimidation to turn her friends against each other. It's up to Twilight to set things right, while contending with Sunset Shimmer's efforts to sabotage her.

Cast: Tara Strong as Twilight Sparkle
Ashleigh Ball as Applejack/Rainbow Dash
Andrea Libman as Pinkie Pie/Fluttershy
Tabitha St. Germain as Rarity/Princess Luna/
    Vice Principal Luna/Cup Cake
Cathy Weseluck as Spike
Rebecca Shoichet as Sunset Shimmer

Lee Tockar as Snips
Richard Ian Cox as Snails
Nicole Oliver as Princess Celestia/
    Principal Celestia/Cheerilee
Vincent Tong as Flash Sentry
Britt McKillip as Princess Cadance
Peter New as Big Macintosh/Drummer

Music Highlights: "My Little Pony Theme Song" (Daniel Ingram/Lauren Faust), "This Strange World" (Daniel Ingram) performed by Rebecca Shoichet, "Equestria Girls" (Daniel Ingram/Meghan McCarthy) performed by Shannon Chan-Kent, Ashleigh Ball, Kazumi Evans, Andrea Libman, and Rebecca Shoichet, "Time to Come Together" (Daniel Ingram/Meghan McCarthy) performed by Rebecca Shoichet, Shannon Chan-Kent, Kazumi Evans, Ashleigh Ball, and Andrea Libman, "This is Our Big Night" (Daniel Ingram/Meghan McCarthy) performed by Rebecca Shoichet, Shannon Chan-Kent, Kazumi Evans, Ashleigh Ball, and Andrea Libman, "A Friend for Life" (Daniel Ingram) performed by Jerrica Santos. Score by William Kevin Anderson.

Film Facts

- Many characters from the *My Little Pony* TV series made appearances, including the Great and Powerful Trixie, the Cutie Mark Crusaders, Cheerilee, DJ Pon-3, Photo Finish, Lyra Heartstrings, Octavia Melody, Sweetie Drops, and Derpy Hooves.
- Singing voices were provided by Rebecca Shoichet (Twilight Sparkle), Shannon Chan-Kent (Pinkie Pie), and Kazumi Evans (Rarity).
- A series of 12 *Equestria Girls Minis* shorts was released online from 2015 to 2018.
- The film was well-received, sparking a series of sequels.

My Little Pony: Equestria Girls: Rainbow Rocks (TV-Y)

Limited theatrical release date: September 27, 2014 Broadcast date: October 17, 2014
Home media release date: October 28, 2014
Production Company: DHX Media, Hasbro Studios
Length: 74 minutes
Directed by: Jayson Thiessen, co-director Ishi Rudell
Written by: Meghan McCarthy

Synopsis: Three mysterious siren singers appear at Canterlot High, bewitching the school into holding a battle of the bands, including their own trio, The Dazzlings. Twilight Sparkle and her friends are immune to the spell, and suspect foul play. Sunset Shimmer, former student of Princess Celestia, is able to get a message to Equestria, and Twilight Sparkle returns to help. They believe that the music of their band, The Rainbooms, which gives the band pony ears and tails when they play, will provide the magic they need to defeat the sirens. Twilight worries that she might not be able to come up with an effective counterspell, while Sunset Shimmer is painfully aware that she is not fully trusted after her past misdeeds. The evil magic of the sirens turns the students of Canterlot High against each other, and even the Rainbooms experience tensions in the band, ending up trapped under the stage. With the help of a friend, the Rainbooms are freed and finally begin listening to each other, finding that their own friendship and forgiveness is the magic that they were missing.

Cast: Tara Strong as Twilight Sparkle
Ashleigh Ball as Applejack/Rainbow Dash
Andrea Libman as Pinkie Pie/Fluttershy
Tabitha St. Germain as Rarity/
     Vice Principal Luna/Photo Finish
Cathy Weseluck as Spike
Rebecca Shoichet as Sunset Shimmer

Kazumi Evans as Adagio Dazzle/Octavia Melody
Maryke Hendrikse as Sonata Dusk
Diana Kaarina as Aria Blaze
Vincent Tong as Flash Sentry/Drummer
Kathleen Barr as Trixie Lulamoon
Nicole Oliver as Principal Celestia
Ingrid Nilson as Maud

Music Highlights: "Rainbow Rocks" (Daniel Ingram), "Better Than Ever" (Daniel Ingram/Meghan McCarthy), "Battle" (Ingram/McCarthy), "Bad Counter Spell" (Ingram/McCarthy), "Shake Your Tail" (Daniel Ingram/Amy Keating Rogers), "Under Our Spell" (Ingram/McCarthy), "Tricks Up My Sleeve" (Ingram/McCarthy), "Awesome As I Wanna Be" (Ingram/McCarthy), "Welcome to the Show" (Ingram/McCarthy), "Rainbooms Battle" (Ingram). End credits: "Shine Like Rainbows" (Ingram). Music by William Kevin Anderson.

Film Facts

• The DVD/Blu-ray include several "prequel shorts."
• A short but important final scene follows the credits (1:12:45).
• Singing voices were provided by Rebecca Shoichet (Twilight Sparkle), Kazumi Evans (Rarity), Shannon Chan-Kent (Pinkie Pie), Madeline Merlo (Sonata Dusk), and Shylo Sharity (Aria Blaze).
• A one-track remix CD single, "Equestria Girls" (feat. Danielkon) was released.

My Little Pony: Equestria Girls: Friendship Games (TV-Y)

Limited theatrical release date: September 17, 2015 Home media release date: October 13, 2015
Production Company: Hasbro Studios, DHX Media, Studio B
Length: 72 minutes
Directed by: Ishi Rudell, consulting director Jayson Thiessen
Written by: Josh Haber

Synopsis: In the upcoming Friendship Games, the Wondercolts of Canterlot High are facing off against the spoiled students of Crystal Prep, who have been on a winning streak. Back at Crystal Prep, social misfit Twilight Sparkle has been studying energy readings that are coming from Canterlot High. The competitive Crystal Prep principal Abacus Cinch, concerned that Canterlot High might finally win the Friendship Games, makes it clear that Twilight's admission into the Everton Independent Study Program depends on her helping Crystal Prep win the competition. On a visit to Canterlot High, Twilight learns that the energy she's been studying is the magic coming from Rainbow Dash, Pinkie Pie, Rarity, Applejack, and Fluttershy, who, mistaking her for the pony world Twilight, all seem to know her. Twilight's spectrometer pendant seems to capture the students' magic, and begins opening dimensional rips. Principal Cinch believes the magic can help her students win, urging Twilight to release the magic. When she does, the magic transforms her, temporarily driving her power-mad. The students' remaining magic transforms Sunset Shimmer as well, and it's up to Sunset to help Twilight avoid making the same mistakes she made.

Cast: Tara Strong as Twilight Sparkle
Rebecca Shoichet as Sunset Shimmer
Ashleigh Ball as Rainbow Dash/Applejack
Andrea Libman as Pinkie Pie/Fluttershy/Sweetie Drops
Tabitha St. Germain as Rarity/Vice Principal Luna
Cathy Weseluck as Spike
Iris Quinn as Principal Abacus Cinch

Nicole Oliver as Principal Celestia
Britt McKillip as Dean Cadance
Vincent Tong as Flash Sentry/Bus Driver
Andrew Francis as Shining Armor
Sienna Bohn as Sugarcoat
Sharon Alexander as Sour Sweet
Kelly Sheridan as Indigo Zap

Music Highlights: "Friendship Games" (Daniel Ingram), "CHS Rally Song" (Josh Haber/Daniel Ingram), "What More Is Out There?" (Josh Haber/Daniel Ingram), "ACADECA" (Daniel Ingram), "Unleash the Magic" (Josh Haber/Daniel Ingram). End credits: "Right There in Front of Me" (Daniel Ingram). Score by William Anderson.

Film Facts

• The "time travel loop" Twilight mentions (1:09:21) is shown in the *My Little Pony: Friendship is Magic* episode "The Cutie Re-Mark" (season 5, episode 25).
• Though not named in the film, Twilight's transformed state is called "Midnight Sparkle."
• Five promo shorts, included on the Blu-ray, were shown in August, 2015: "The Science of Magic," "Pinkie Spy," "All's Fair in Love & Friendship Games," "Photo Finished," and "A Banner Day."
• Kelly Sheridan (voice of Indigo Zap) is known for voicing Barbie in many home media films.

My Little Pony: Equestria Girls: Legend of Everfree (TV-Y7)

Broadcast release date: October 1, 2016 Home media release date: November 1, 2016
Production Company: DHX Media, Hasbro Studios
Length: 73 minutes
Directed by: Ishi Rudell
Written by: Kristine Songco, Joanna Lewis

Synopsis: The students of Canterlot High are looking forward to a vacation at Camp Everfree, but soon notice tension between the counselors Gloriosa Daisy and Timber Spruce. Twilight Sparkle begins to experience nightmares about Midnight Sparkle, the power-mad creature she turned into in *My Little Pony: Equestria Girls: Friendship Games,* and even worse, she fears she is experiencing uncontrolled magic when her belongings begin floating in her tent. As strange things begin happening at the camp, Twilight fears she is to blame. Around the campfire, Timber Spruce tells a tale of the ancient forest spirit Gaea Everfree that allowed his grandparents to build their camp, but that she would return one day to take back the land. The students suspect that Timber Spruce wants to get rid of the camp, but as the mystery deepens, they learn things are not always as they appear, and the source of the magic is more of a problem than they thought.

Cast: Tara Strong as Twilight Sparkle
Rebecca Shoichet as Sunset Shimmer
Ashleigh Ball as Rainbow Dash/Applejack/Lyra
Andrea Libman as Pinkie Pie/Fluttershy/Bonbon
Tabitha St. Germain as Rarity/Vice Principal
     Luna/Muffins
Cathy Weseluck as Spike
Enid-Raye Adams as Gloriosa Daisy

Brian Doe as Timber Spruce
Nicole Oliver as Principal Celestia
Vincent Tong as Flash Sentry/Sandalwood
Brian Drummond as Filthy Rich
Michael Dobson as Bulk Biceps
Kathleen Barr as Trixie Lulamoon
Richard Cox as Snails
Lee Tockar as Snips

Music Highlights: "The Legend of Everfree" (Kristine Songco/Joanna Lewis/Daniel Ingram), "The Midnight in Me" (Songco/Lewis/Ingram), "Embrace the Magic" (Songco/Lewis/Ingram), "We Will Stand For Everfree" (Songco/Lewis/Ingram), "Legend You Were Meant to Be" (Songco/Lewis/Ingram), "Hope Shines Eternal" (Ingram). Score by William Kevin Anderson.

Film Facts

• Apart from the human versions of the "mane six" (Twilight Sparkle, Rainbow Dash, Applejack, Pinkie Pie, Fluttershy, and Rarity) and Sunset Shimmer, *My Little Pony* characters Trixie, Sweetie Drops (AKA Bonbon), Derpy Hooves, Lyra Heartstrings, Bulk Biceps, and Snips and Snails appear.
• The premiere of the film took place on Discovery Kids in Brazil on September 24, 2016, a week before it debuted on Netflix in the U.S.
• Don't miss the brief final post-credits scene (1:12:38).
• A 6-song digital *Legend of Everfree* EP was released.
• Singing voices were provided by Shannon Chan-Kent (Pinkie Pie), Kazumi Evans (Rarity), Kelly Metzger (Gloriosa Daisy), and Rebecca Shoichet (Twilight Sparkle/Sunset Shimmer).

My Little Pony: The Movie (PG)

Theatrical release date: October 6, 2017
Production Company: Allspark Pictures/DHX/Lionsgate
Length: 109 minutes
Directed by: Jayson Thiessen
Screenplay by: Meghan McCarthy, Rita Hsiao, Michael Vogel, story by Meghan McCarthy, Joe Ballarini

Synopsis: Twilight Sparkle is stressing over organizing the Equestria Festival of Friendship, but the event is interrupted by the arrival of the evil Storm King's minions Tempest Shadow and Grubber, planning to steal the Princesses' power. When they begin turning ponies to stone, the Mane Six escape to search for the Queen of the Hippos. Crossing the desert, they find a run down town, and accept an offer of help from the cat Capper, as Twilight realizes they're looking for the Queen of the Hippogriffs. Capper's effort to sell the ponies is interrupted by Tempest's arrival. They are able to stow away on an airship, but are caught by former pirates, led by Captain Celaeno, working for the Storm King. Another interruption by Tempest allows them to escape, and they finally reach the undersea kingdom of the hippogriffs. When the Queen declines to help, Twilight tests the limits of friendship in her desperation to save Equestria, and is reminded of how important true friendship is.

Cast: Tara Strong as Twilight Sparkle
Ashleigh Ball as Rainbow Dash/Applejack
Tabitha St. Germain as Rarity/Princess Luna
Andrea Libman as Pinkie Pie/Fluttershy
Cathy Weseluck as Spike
Nicole Oliver as Princess Celestia
Britt McKillip as Princess Cadance

Emily Blunt as Tempest Shadow/Fizzlepop
Michael Peña as Grubber
Liev Schreiber as the Storm King
Taye Diggs as Capper
Zoe Saldana as Captain Celaeno
Kristin Chenoweth as Princess Skystar
Uzo Aduba as Queen Novo

Music Highlights: "We Got the Beat" (Caffey) performed by Rachel Platten (orig. The Go-Go's), "We Got This" (Ingram/Vogel) by cast, "I'm the Friend You Need" (Ingram/Vogel) performed by Taye Diggs/cast, "Time to Be Awesome" (Ingram/Vogel) by cast, "One Small Thing" (Ingram/Vogel) performed by cast, "Open Up Your Eyes" (Ingram/McCarthy/Vogel) performed by Emily Blunt, "Rainbow" (Furler/Shatkin/Notorleva) performed by Sia, "Off to See the World" (Forchhammer/Brown/Ristorp/Forrest/Pilegaard/Labrel) performed by Lukas Graham. Score by Daniel Ingram.

Film Facts

• The film takes place after season seven of *My Little Pony: Friendship is Magic*.
• Fan-favorite frenemy Discord appears in balloon animal form (5:44).
• Pinkie Pie's "Easy Bake Confetti Cannon" (11:54) is named after Hasbro's Easy Bake Oven, and Pinkie, Spike and Applejack collectively say "Hungry…Hungry…Hippos" (19:04), a Hasbro game.
• Pop singer Sia plays Songbird Serenade, whose image is based on Sia's.
• An earlier film was also titled *My Little Pony: The Movie* (1986), prior to the *My Little Pony: Friendship Is Magic* reboot.

My Little Pony: Equestria Girls: Tales of Canterlot High/Magical Movie Night DVD (TV-Y7)

Broadcast dates: "Dance Magic" June 24, 2017, "Movie Magic" July 1, 2017, "Mirror Magic" July 8, 2017 Home media release date: August 8, 2017
Production Company: DHX, Hasbro Studios
Length: 22 minutes each
Directors/writers: "Dance Magic" directed by Ishi Rudell/written by G.M. Borrow, "Movie Magic" directed by Ishi Rudell/written by Noelle Benvenuti, "Mirror Magic" directed by Ishi Rudell/written by Rachel Vine, Dave Polsky

---

Synopsis: In "Dance Magic," the Equestria Girls are raising funds for Camp Everfree, and Rarity enters their group in a music video contest. After Rarity mentions her plans to their rivals from Crystal Prep, she's horrified to learn they've stolen her ideas. As each group struggles to win, Rarity realizes cooperation is the solution. In "Movie Magic," the girls visit the set of the new Daring Do film, only to find that the props needed to complete the film have disappeared, with disgruntled actress Chestnut Magnifico their prime suspect. As they investigate, they learn there is more to the story. In "Mirror Magic," the new Daring Do film is about to premiere, and Juniper Montage holds a grudge against the girls. She finds a mirror that shows glamorous images of her, and begins granting her wishes. Sunset Shimmer runs out of journal pages, and returns to Ponyville to get a new one, meeting Starlight Glimmer. Juniper traps the girls inside the mirror, and their energy transforms Juniper into a powerful villain. It's up to Starlight Glimmer to help Juniper see what really matters.

Cast: Tara Strong as Twilight Sparkle
Rebecca Shoichet as Sunset Shimmer
Ashleigh Ball as Rainbow Dash/Applejack
Andrea Libman as Pinkie Pie/Fluttershy
Tabitha St. Germain as Rarity
Cathy Weseluck as Spike
Sharon Alexander as Sour Sweet
Sienna Bohn as Sugarcoat

Shannon Chan-Kent as Lemon Zest
Britt Irvin as Sunny Flare
Kelly Sheridan as Starlight Glimmer
Andy Toth as Canter Zoom/Boss
Ali Liebert as Juniper Montage
Kira Tozer as Chestnut Magnifico
Charles Zuckerman as Stalwart Stallion/
    Director

Music Highlights: "Dance Magic" (Daniel Ingram). Score by William Kevin Anderson.

Film Facts

• The three stories were streamed on Netflix as *My Little Pony: Equestria Girls: Tales of Canterlot High,* and released as the *My Little Pony: Equestria Girls: Magical Movie Night* DVD.
• Singing voices were provided by Kazumi Evans (Rarity) and Rebecca Shoichet (Twilight Sparkle).
• The song "Dance Magic" appears on the *My Little Pony: Equestria Girls: Friendship Games* CD.
• The Equestria Girls franchise continued the following year with the one hour TV special *My Little Pony: Equestria Girls: Forgotten Friendship*, broadcast on Discovery Family on February 17, 2018.

My Little Pony: Equestria Girls: Forgotten Friendship (TV-Y7)

Broadcast date: February 17, 2018
Production Company: DHX Media/Hasbro Studios
Length: 50 minutes (original)/44 minutes (edited)
Directed by: Ishi Rudell, co-director Katrina Hadley
Written by: Nick Confalone

Synopsis: Sunset Shimmer is working with the Equestria Girls on the yearbook at Equestria High, with the help of the easily forgotten student Wallflower Blush. The Great and Powerful Trixie is irritated that she is not to be named "Greatest and Powerfullest" in the yearbook (because it is not a category in the yearbook). During a gathering of the friends at the beach, Sunset Shimmer is shocked to find that the Equestria Girls have completely forgotten her transition from a bully to a friend, and soon learns that everyone at Equestria High has forgotten her redemption. Sunset travels to Ponyville, and learns of an ancient magical artifact called the Memory Stone that can erase memories. She reluctantly partners with Trixie to track down the Memory Stone, learning from Twilight that the Memory Stone is buried under three tall stones - the same three stones that Wallflower Blush has in the school garden. With the power of her geode, Sunset reads Wallflower's memory of using the stone to erase everyone's recollection of her. When Sunset confronts her, Wallflower tries to use the Memory Stone to try to erase the memories of all the Equestria Girls, even of each other. Sunset steps in front of the others to protect them, and they see it as a true act of friendship, joining together to help Wallflower remember what she really wants.

Cast: Ashleigh Ball as Applejack/Rainbow Dash/
    Nurse Redheart
Andrea Libman as Pinkie Pie/Fluttershy
Rebecca Shoichet as Sunset Shimmer
Tabitha St. Germain as Rarity/Princess Luna/
    Vice Principal Luna
Tara Strong as Twilight Sparkle/Princess Twilight Sparkle

Nicole Oliver as Princess Celestia
Cathy Weseluck as Spike
Kathleen Barr as Trixie Lulamoon
Shannon Chan-Kent as Wallflower Blush
James Kirk as Micro Chips
Ingrid Nilson as Maud Pie

Music Highlights: "Equestria Girls Forever" (Daniel Ingram) ft. Angelic, "We've Come So Far" (Nick Confalone/Daniel Ingram/Trevor Hoffmann), "Invisible" (Nick Confalone/John Jennings Boyd/ Lisette Bustamante). Music by William Kevin Anderson.

Film Facts

• The special was based on the book *A Friendship to Remember* (2017) by Perdita Finn.
• It premiered on Discovery Family on February 17, 2018 at 50 minutes, also later appearing in an edited 44 minute version.
• Singing voices were provided by Shannon Chan-Kent (Pinkie Pie), Kazumi Evans (Rarity), and Rebecca Shoichet (Twilight Sparkle).

My Little Pony: Best Gift Ever (TV-Y)

Broadcast date: October 27, 2018
Production Company: Allspark Animation, DHX, Hasbro Studios
Length: 44 minutes
Supervising director: Jim Miller, Directed by: Denny Lu, Mike Myhre
Written by: Michael Vogel

Synopsis: As Twilight Sparkle panics over buying gifts for all her friends for the winter Hearth's Warming Eve celebration, Apple Jack proposes they use a Hearth's Warming Helper buddy system, drawing names so they each just buy a gift for one pony. Pinkie Pie heads to Yakyakistan to get advice on Twilight's gift, Rarity plans to get a designer hat for Applejack, Fluttershy gives no hints to Rainbow Dash as to what she might like, and Spike trades Rainbow Dash's name to Fluttershy for Rarity's name. Applejack shops for Spike, as hucksters Flim & Flam trick Fluttershy into buying an awful Holly Hearthwarming doll. Rarity's hat accidentally gets sent to the wrong farm, but the young pony farmer who gets it is so enchanted Rarity doesn't have the heart to take it back. Discord takes Rainbow Dash on a mission to catch a cute winterchilla for Fluttershy, which soon turns into a monstrous winterzilla. Spike decides to make a sparkly umbrella for for Rarity, with disastrous results, and Twilight's recipe of Chancellor Puddinghead's magical pudding gets out of control. Though no one's gift turned out as planned, all agree that the best gift can never be bought.

Cast: Tara Strong as Twilight Sparkle
Andrea Libman as Pinkie Pie/Fluttershy
Ashleigh Ball as Applejack/Rainbow Dash
Cathy Weseluck as Spike
Tabitha St. Germain as Rarity/Muffins/Flurry Heart
John de Lancie as Discord
Sam Vincent as Flim
Garry Chalk as Prince Rutherford/Oak Nut
Meaghan Hommy as Alice
Scott McNeil as Flam
Ingrid Nilson as Limestone Pie/
     Maud Pie/Marble Pie/Butternut
Sean Thomas as Pistachio
Andrew Francis as Shining Armor
Britt McKillip as Princess Cadance
Alison Wandzura as Bori
Asia Mattu as Aurora

Music Highlights: "One More Day" (Michael Vogel/Daniel Ingram), "The True Gift of Gifting" (Michael Vogel/Daniel Ingram). Music by William Anderson.

Film Facts

• Three companion shorts were posted on the Hasbro YouTube channel on December 11, 2018: "Triple Pony Dare Ya" (3:25), "The Great Escape Room" (3:25), and "Mystery Voice" (3:25).
• Follows "School Raze" (season 8), and followed by "The Beginning of the End" (season 9).
• Singing voices were provided by Rebecca Shoichet (Twilight Sparkle), Kazumi Evans (Rarity), and Shannon Chan-Kent (Pinkie Pie).
• The Young Six (Sandbar, Smolder, Gallus, Ocellus, Yona, Silverstream) appear at the beginning.
• References include the *Home Alone 2* pigeon lady (2:08), *A Charlie Brown Christmas* (2:12), *Elf* (2:14), *Beauty and the Beast* (11:02), and Snake Eyes/Storm Shadows from *G.I. Joe* (27:57).

My Little Pony: Equestria Girls: Rollercoaster of Friendship (TV-Y7)

Broadcast date: July 6, 2018
Production Company: Hasbro Studios, DHX Media Vancouver
Length: 44 minutes/50 minutes
Directed by: Ishi Rudell, co-director Katrina Hadley
Written by: Nick Confalone

Synopsis: The new theme park Equestria Land is about to open. Both Applejack and Rarity apply for jobs at the park, but only Rarity is hired, based on her social media following. The park's shallow and demanding public relations manager, Vignette Valencia, is obsessed with appearances, and makes a wish that attracts a magical app to her phone, that takes photos of objects — or people — replacing them with a version she likes better. Vignette invites the Equestria Girls' band, the Rainbooms, to perform at the park's end of day parade, but as the day progresses, she begins to be dissatisfied with the Equestria Girls, taking photos of them one by one, leaving the original version of them in a nondescript white room. Applejack sees Vignette capture Rainbow Dash, but the rest of the Equestria Girls don't believe her, leading her to angrily leave. When Rarity is out of the room, Vignette captures Pinkie, Fluttershy, and Twilight as well, replacing the captured friends with versions she has modified to her liking. Vignette arrogantly admits what she is doing, leading to a confrontation with Rarity, who is not willing to betray her friends for appearances. She escapes and works with Applejack to free the others, and they all confront Vignette together.

Cast: Ashleigh Ball as Applejack/Rainbow Dash
Andrea Libman as Pinkie Pie/Fluttershy
Rebecca Shoichet as Sunset Shimmer/Designer
Tabitha St. Germain as Rarity/Granny Smith
Tara Strong as Twilight Sparkle

Tegan Moss as Vignette Valencia
James Kirk as Micro Chips
Sam Vincent as Flim
Scott McNeil as Flam
Richard Newman as Mr. Cranky Doodle

Music Highlights: "Equestria Girls Forever" theme (Daniel Ingram) ft. Angelic, "Photo Booth" (John Jennings Boyd/Lisette Bustamante/Nick Confalone) performed by Kazumi Evans, Ashleigh Ball, Rebecca Shoichet, and Andrea Libman. Score by William Kevin Anderson.

Film Facts

• An edited 44-minute version of the special debuted on Discovery Family on July 6, 2018. The full 50-minute version was posted in 5 episodes on Hasbro's YouTube channel: "All Bite & No Park" (Aug 31, 2018), "Frenemy Request" (Sep 7, 2018), "Applejack Investigates" (Sep 14, 2018), "Captured Images" (Sep 21, 2018), and "No Filter" (Sep 28, 2018). The 44 minute version was added to Netflix on October 1, 2018.
• The specials *Forgotten Friendship* and *Rollercoaster of Friendship* were on the 2018 UK DVD *Equestria Girls: The Specials*.
• Singing voices provided by Kazumi Evans as Rarity, and Rebecca Shoichet as Twilight Sparkle.

My Little Pony: Equestria Girls: Spring Breakdown (TV-Y7)

Broadcast date: March 30, 2019
Production Company: DHX Media Vancouver, Hasbro Studios, Allspark Animation
Length: 44 minutes
Directed by: Ishi Rudell, co-director Katrina Hadley
Written by: Nick Confalone

Synopsis: As the Equestria Girls enjoy a spring break cruise, Rainbow Dash begins anticipating "bad magic," and ends up getting Pinkie Pie banned from the buffet, scaring Fluttershy's animals, and worsening Applejack's seasickness. During an onboard musical performance by the Rainbooms, the power on the ship shuts down, leaving Rainbow convinced that bad Equestrian magic is at work. While Twilight is fixing the ship, Pinkie is on the verge of getting a bite of an elusive bundt cake, and Rarity is enchanted with ship worker Ragamuffin, when Rainbow pulls them all away to see a strange image in the sea, but nothing is there. Rainbow strikes out on her own to investigate, followed by Twilight and Sunset Shimmer. They find Rainbow stuck in quicksand, which Sunset recognizes as a portal to Equestria, and the three of them become ponies. They seek out Twilight Sparkle, and learn that the symbol Rainbow saw is that of the Storm King, seen in *My Little Pony: The Movie* (2017). Back on the cruise ship, a worsening storm is threatening everyone's safety. The Equestria Girls reunite and activate their powers to set things right, getting everyone to lifeboats and safe on an island, just before the ship goes down. The passengers seek assistance getting back home by a little detour through Equestria.

Cast: Ashleigh Ball as Rainbow Dash/Applejack/
    Parrot
Andrea Libman as Pinkie Pie/Fluttershy
Rebecca Shoichet as Sunset Shimmer
Tabitha St. Germain as Rarity

Tara Strong as Twilight Sparkle
Cathy Weseluck as Spike
Kathleen Barr as Trixie Lulamoon/
    Puffed Pastry
Jason Michas as Ragamuffin

Music Highlights: "Equestria Girls Forever" theme (Daniel Ingram) ft. Angelic, "All Good" (Jessica Vaughn/Jess Furman/Ethan Roberts) performed by Ashleigh Ball, Rebecca Shoichet, Andrea Libman, and Kazumi Evans. Score by William Kevin Anderson. Additional music by Matthew Sorensen.

Film Facts

• A 44-minute version of the special aired on Discovery Family on March 30, 2019. The full version (47:18) was posted in 6 episodes on Hasbro's YouTube channel: "Bon Voyage" (Apr 12, 2019), "Sea Legs" (Apr 19, 2019), "Tropical Depression" (Apr 26, 2019), "Friend Overboard" (May 3, 2019), "Hoofin' It" (May 10, 2019), and "That Sinking Feeling" (May 17, 2019).
• Twilight's "melting ponies" painting resembles Salvador Dali's iconic *The Persistence of Memory*.
• This special was included on *My Little Pony: Equestria Girls - Spring, Sunsets, Holidays* DVD.
• Singing voices provided by Kazumi Evans as Rarity and Rebecca Shoichet as Twilight Sparkle.

My Little Pony: Equestria Girls: Sunset's Backstage Pass (TV-Y7)

Broadcast date: July 27, 2019
Production Company: DHX Media Vancouver, Hasbro Studios, Allspark Animation
Length: 44 minutes
Directed by: Ishi Rudell, Katrina Hadley
Written by: Whitney Ralls

Synopsis: Sunset Shimmer and Pinkie Pie are thrilled to attend the Starswirled Music Festival, where they hope to see their favorite pop duo PostCrush, with Kiwi Lollipop (K-Lo) and Supernova Zap (Su-Z). Pinkie's enthusiasm causes problems which leads them to get kicked out of the festival, to Sunset's bitter disappointment. The following morning Sunset finds that she's reliving the previous day. Twilight explains that it may be a time loop, and Sunset thinks it may be Equestrian magic giving her another chance to see Postcrush. Though warned against it, Pinkie still gets them thrown out. When the day starts again, Sunset ditches Pinkie Pie and finally sees Postcrush, but feels guilty that Pinkie missed it. The next morning, the day starts again, and Pinkie suggests contacting Twilight Sparkle in Ponyville, who suspects the time loop is being caused by someone using a magical device called the Time Twirler. They discover that the villainous magical trio the Dazzlings (seen in *My Little Pony: Equestria Girls: Rainbow Rocks,* 2014), and suspect that they are behind the time loop, but soon learn the truth — about the importance of friendship over perfection — is more complicated.

Cast: Rebecca Shoichet as Sunset Shimmer
Andrea Libman as Pinkie Pie/Fluttershy/Bon Bon
Ashleigh Ball as Rainbow Dash/Applejack/
    Lyra
Tabitha St. Germain as Rarity/Announcer
Tara Strong as Twilight Sparkle
Lili Beaudoin as K-Lo (Kiwi Lollipop)
Mariee Devereux as Su-Z (Supernova Zap)
Kazumi Evans as Adagio Dazzle
Diana Kaarina as Aria Blaze
Maryke Hendrikse as Sonata Dusk
Michael Dobson as Security Guard
Kathleen Barr as Puffed Pastry
Lee Tockar as Snips/Festival Artist/Intern

Music Highlights: "Equestria Girls Forever" theme (Daniel Ingram) ft. Angelic, "True Original" (Jessica Vaughn/Jess Furman/her0ism) performed by Marie Hui, Arielle Tuliao, Rebecca Shoichet, Shannon Chan-Kent, "Find the Magic" (Jessica Vaughn/Jess Furman/Jarl Aanestad). Music by William Kevin Anderson, additional music by Matthew Sorensen.

Film Facts

• A 44-minute version of the special aired on Discovery Family on July 27, 2019. The full version (46:17) was posted in 6 episodes on Hasbro's YouTube channel: Part 1 (Sep 17, 2019), Part 2 (Sep 22, 2019), Part 3 (Sep 24, 2019), Part 4 (Sep 29, 2019), Part 5 (Oct 6, 2019), Part 6 (Oct 13, 2019).
• A youth novelization, *My Little Pony: Equestria Girls: Make Your Own Magic: Starswirl Do-Over* (2019) was published.
• This special was included on *My Little Pony: Equestria Girls - Spring, Sunsets, Holidays* DVD.

My Little Pony: Equestria Girls: Holidays Unwrapped (TV-Y7)

Broadcast date: November 2, 2019
Production Company: Allspark Animation, DHX Media Vancouver
Length: 46 minutes / 44 minutes
Directed by: Ishi Rudell, Katrina Hadley
Written by: Anna Christopher

Synopsis: • "Blizzard or Bust": After studying all night for a big test, the Equestria Girls still don't feel ready. A few snowflakes give them the idea to create a "snow day" to give them a reprieve, but their scheme is discovered. • "Saving Pinkie's Pie": Every year Pinkie bakes a soufflé for Rarity, but every year it deflates before she can deliver it. Pinkie and Sunset Shimmer plan the perfect route to quickly deliver the soufflé to Rarity's house, but are waylaid by an epic snowball fight. • "The Cider Louse Fools": Applejack invites Twilight to her family's annual cider-making party, which is often sabotaged by the Flim Flam brothers. Twilight develops a plan to thwart their interference. • "Winter Break-In": When the girls can't find the key for Sunset's storage locker to get toys for the holiday Toys for Kids Festival, an elaborate break-in is planned. • "Dashing Through The Mall": Rainbow Dash has forgotten to get a gift for Fluttershy, and has five minutes at the mall to find the right choice, getting suggestions from Fluttershy's brother, Zephyr. • "O' Come All Ye Squashful": Applejack proposes a new holiday tradition of annual group photos with a theme, and her friends reluctantly dress up as vegetables for the "cornucopia" Applejack suggests, only to find that they misread her intent.

Cast: Ashleigh Ball as Rainbow Dash/Applejack
Andrea Libman as Pinkie Pie/Fluttershy
Rebecca Shoichet as Sunset Shimmer
Tara Strong as Twilight Sparkle
Tabitha St. Germain as Rarity/Granny Smith/
      Photo Finish/Vice Principal Luna
Richard Newman as Mr. Cranky Doodle
Nicole Oliver as Principal Celestia

Vincent Tong as Flash Sentry
Richard Ian Cox as Snails/Lee Tockar as Snips
Kathleen Barr as Trixie Lulamoon
Michael Dobson as Bulk Biceps
Sam Vincent as Flim
Scott McNeil as Flam
Michelle Creber as Apple Bloom
Ryan Beil as Zephyr Breeze

Music Highlights: "Equestria Girls Forever" theme (Daniel Ingram) ft. Angelic. Score by William Kevin Anderson, additional music & orchestrations by Matthew Sorensen.

Film Facts

• A 44-minute version of the special aired on Discovery Family on November 2, 2019. The full version (46:00) was posted in 6 episodes on the My Little Pony YouTube channel: "Blizzard or Bust" (Nov 16, 2019), "Saving Pinkie's Pie" (Nov 22, 2019), "The Cider Louse Fools" (Nov 29, 2019), "Winter Break-In" (Dec 6, 2019), "Dashing Through The Mall" (Dec 13, 2019), "O' Come All Ye Squashful" (Dec 20, 2019).
• This special was included on *My Little Pony: Equestria Girls - Spring, Sunsets, Holidays* DVD.

My Neighbor Totoro (G)

Theatrical release date: April 16, 1988 (Japan), July 13, 1990 (US)
Production Company: Studio Ghibli, Tokuma Japan Communications, Nibariki
Length: 86 minutes
Directed by: Hayao Miyazaki
Written by: Hayao Miyazaki

Synopsis: When Satsuki moves to the countryside with her sister Mei and father Tatsuo, she hopes that the run-down house they move into will be haunted. She is less sure when she runs into a horde of fuzzy round black creatures that quickly vanish. Their kindly neighbor Nanny explains the creatures are soot sprites, and the girls meet Nanny's timid grandson Kanta. The family visits Satsuki and Mei's mother Yasuko in the hospital, after which Mei follows a pair of rabbit-like creatures into a tunnel in a tree, which she tumbles down to find a huge, sleepy gray creature she names Totoro. Mei's father is unsurprised, describing Totoro as the King of the Forest. Satsuki and Mei begin running into Totoro at odd times, striking up a friendship, as the strange and wonderful creature shows them his magic, but they struggle with tragedy as well, as their mother has a health setback, and Mei gets lost after an argument. Totoro turns out to be a powerful ally in times of need.

Cast:	Role	English (2005)	English (1989/1993)	Japanese
	Satsuki Kusakabe	Dakota Fanning	Lisa Michelson	Noriko Hidaka
	Mei Kusakabe	Elle Fanning	Cheryl Chase	Chika Sakamoto
	Tatsuo Kusakabe	Tim Daly	Greg Snegoff	Shigesato Itoi
	Yasuko Kusakabe	Lea Salonga	Alexandra Kenworthy	Sumi Shimamoto
	Totoro	Frank Welker		Hitoshi Takagi
	Kanta Ōgaki	Paul Butcher	Kenneth Hartman	Toshiyuki Amagasa
	Nanny	Pat Carroll	Natalie Core	Tanie Kitabayashi
	Catbus	Frank Welker	Carl Macek	Naoki Tatsuta
	Michiko	Ashley Rose Orr	Brianne Siddall	Chie Kojiro

Music Highlights: "Sampo"/"Hey Let's Go" (L: Reiko Nakagawa/M: Joe Hisaishi). "Tonari no Totoro"/"My Neighbor Totoro" (L: Hayao Miyazaki/M: Joe Hisaishi), English songs sung by Sonya Isaacs. Music by Joe Hisaishi.

Film Facts

• The film has certain similarities to the Alice in Wonderland stories, including tumbling down a tunnel to magical place and the Cheshire cat bus, but Miyazaki has denied these were intentional.
• In the 2005 English dub, Satsuki and Mei are voiced by real life siblings Dakota and Elle Fanning.
• Director Hayao Miyazaki's mother was hospitalized with tuberculosis when he was growing up.
• The name Totoro comes from Mei mispronouncing "tororu," the Japanese word for troll.
• While it was not initially successful, *Totoro* is now regarded as one of Studio Ghibli's best films.
• Totoro makes cameo appearances in Disney's 2010 film *Toy Story 3* (35:45, end credits).

Nausicaä of the Valley of the Wind (PG)

Theatrical release date: March 11, 1984 (Japan), June 13, 1985 (US, as *Warriors of the Wind*)
Country: Japan Japanese title: *Kaze no Tani no Naushika*
Production Company: Topcraft
Length: 117 minutes
Written and Directed by: Hayao Miyazaki, based on the manga by Hayao Miyazaki

Synopsis: A toxic jungle spreads across the land, 1,000 years after industrialized civilization collapsed, threatening humanity's survival. In the wasteland, Nausicaä, daughter of King Jihl, scavenges for useful materials such as the shells of the giant ohmu insects. Lord Yupa visits Nausicaä's small kingdom, the Valley of the Wind, giving Nausicaä a fox-squirrel, Teto, and telling the people that things are grim, with other kingdoms swallowed by the toxic waste or at war. When a Tolmekian airship crashes nearby, Nausicaä rescues Lastelle of Pejite, who was transported with a giant insect that threatens the safety of the Valley. The Tolmekian ship also carries what is feared to be one of the giant warriors that incinerated the Earth 1,000 years before. Soldiers from Tolmekia, led by Kushana, arrive and imprison the people of the Valley. Kushana has a plan to burn the toxic jungle. The wise Obaba protests, and when the Tolmekians kill King Jihl, Nausicaä must calm her people. Nausicaä reveals that she's learned that the soil is toxic, not the plants, but is soon taken prisoner by Kushana. The Tolmekian airships are attacked by a Pejite plane, crashing. Under the toxic jungle, Nausicaä finds Asbel, the twin brother of Princess Lastelle, and they discover that the trees have purified the deadly toxins. As the kingdoms struggle, Nausicaä tries to reveal the truth.

Cast:

Role	English	Japanese
Nausicaä	Alison Lohman	Sumi Shimamoto
Lord Yupa	Patrick Stewart	Goro Naya
Kushana	Uma Thurman	Yoshiko Sakakibara
Kurotowa	Chris Sarandon	Iemasa Kayumi
Asbel	Shia LaBeouf	Yōji Matsuda
Mito	Edward James Olmos	Ichirō Nagai
Pejite Mayor	Mark Hamill	Makoto Terada
Gikkuri	Jeff Bennett	Jōji Yanami
Obaba	Tress MacNeille	Hisako Kyōda
Lastelle's Mother	Jodi Benson	Akiko Tsuboi
Lastelle	Emily Bauer	Miina Tominaga

Music Highlights: "Kaze no Tani no Naushika" (Takashi Matsumoto/Haruomi Hosono) vocals by Narumi Yasuda, "Saranbande" (G.F. Händel). Music by Joe Hisaishi.

Film Facts

- Key personnel from the Topcraft studio went on to form Studio Ghibli with Hayao Miyazaki.
- Nausicaä is inspired by a character of the same name in Homer's classic epic poem *The Odyssey*.
- A substantially edited version of the film was released in the US in 1985 as *Warriors of the Wind*.

Next Gen (TV-PG)

Streaming date: September 7, 2018
Country: US/China/Canada
Production Company: Netflix, Baozou Manhua, Tangent Animation, Alibaba Pictures
Length: 106 minutes
Directed by: Kevin Adams & Joe Ksander
Story and screenplay by: The Baozou Family, Kevin Adams & Joe Ksander, based on the comic series "7723" by Wang Nima

Synopsis: After her parents separate, young Mai becomes angry and rebellious, finding herself annoyed by the increasingly technological world that surrounds her. Mai accidentally ends up in a robot lab, activating Project 7723, an advanced robot developed by Dr. Rice, the kindly partner of tech guru Justin Pin. The robot imprints upon Mai, and follows her after she leaves her backpack at the lab. Mai meets her mother at Justin Pin's unveiling of the new model of household Q-Bot robots, the Gen 6, which he hopes to place in every home. Apart from her frustration with the culture's excessive reliance on technology, Mai has to contend with the neighborhood soccer field bully, Greenwood. When the 7723 robot tracks her home to return her backpack, Mai is initially annoyed, but realizes the robot might help her solve all her problems. Mai is delighted to have some help, but it soon comes to light that the robot has to keep deleting memories to make room for new ones. Things heat up for everyone when they learn that Pin's Gen 6 robots are not as friendly as they seem, and Pin himself is not what he seems. 7723 makes the difficult choice to shut down its weapons systems to make room for more memories, which seem like the most precious thing of all, until it realizes that Mai's safety is even more precious.

Cast: John Krasinski as 7723/Project 77
Charlyne Yi as Mai
Jason Sudeikis as Justin Pin/Ares
Michael Peña as Momo
David Cross as Dr. Tanner Rice/Q-Bots

Constance Wu as Molly (mother)
Kiana Ledé as Greenwood
Anna Akana as Ani
Issac Ryan Brown as Ric
Reba Buhr as Diagnostic Computer

Music Highlights: "Rebel Girl" (Kathleen Hanna/Kathryn Wilcox/Tobi Vail/Billy Karren) performed by Bikini Kill, "Clay" (Grace VanderWaal/Autumn Rowe) performed by Grace VanderWaal, "GonnaWanna" (Julie Edwards/Lindsey Troy) performed by Deap Vally, "Clearly" (Grace VanderWaal/Neil Ormandy/Johnny Nash/Ido Zmishlany/Chloe Angelides/Michael Bywaters) performed by Grace VanderWaal (orig. by Johnny Nash). Music by Samuel Jones and Alexis Marsh.

Film Facts

• The film is based on the online Chinese comic *7723* by Wang Nima.
• The intensity of the violence and some themes in the film make it a better choice for older kids.
• A Chinese-American-Canadian production, the film raised the troubling use of technology by the Chinese government, such as facial recognition software to track its citizens.

The Nightmare Before Christmas (PG)

Theatrical release date: October 29, 1993
Production Company: Touchstone Pictures, Skellington Productions, reissue by Walt Disney Pictures
Length: 76 minutes
Directed by: Henry Selick
Screenplay by: Caroline Thompson, based on a story and characters by Tim Burton, adaptation by Michael McDowell

---

Synopsis: As the denizens of Halloween Town prepare to celebrate Halloween, Jack Skellington, the Pumpkin King, laments how weary he has become of the routine. While walking in the woods Jack happens upon a circle of seven trees which are portals to different holiday lands, and a visit to Christmas Town leaves Jack in wonderment. Upon his return, he tries to share his discovery of Christmas, with limited success. He finally decides that Halloween Town will emulate Christmas traditions, and that Santa will be held captive while Jack brings gifts to the people of the world, despite the misgivings of Jack's love, the ragdoll Sally. Jack soon learns that spooky gifts do not bring Christmas joy, and after saving Santa from the treacherous Oogie Boogie, it's Santa's turn to save Jack.

Cast: Chris Sarandon as Jack Skellington
Danny Elfman as Jack Skellington (singing voice)
Catherine O'Hara as Sally/Shock
William Hickey as Evil Scientist
Glenn Shadix as Mayor
Paul Reubens as Lock
Ken Page as Oogie Boogie
Ed Ivory as Santa
Susan McBride as Big Witch/WWD
Debi Durst as Corpse Kid/Corpse Mom/ Small Witch
Gregory Proops as Harlequin Demon/Devil/ Sax Player
Kerry Katz as Man Under Stairs/Vampire/ Corpse Dad
Randy Crenshaw as Mr. Hyde/Behemoth/ Vampire Corpse Dad
Sherwood Ball as Mummy/Vampire

Music Highlights: "This Is Halloween" performed by cast, "What's This?" performed by Danny Elfman, "Jack's Lament" performed by Danny Elfman, "Jack's Obsession" performed by cast, "Kidnap the Sandy Claws" performed by Paul Reubens, Catherine O'Hara, and Danny Elfman, "Making Christmas" performed by cast, "Oogie Boogie's Song" performed by Ken Page and Ed Ivory, "Poor Jack" performed by Danny Elfman, "Sally's Song" performed by Catherine O'Hara, "Town Meeting Song" performed by cast. All songs by Danny Elfman/Music by Danny Elfman.

Film Facts

• Burton's first Disney work was the unreleased short "Vincent" (1982), which was later included on *The Nightmare Before Christmas* Special Edition (2000)/Collector's Edition DVD (2008).
• The film's music was a key component to its success. Danny Elfman, frontman for the L.A. band Oingo Boingo, provided the score, as he did for many of Burton's films
• The phrase "tender lumplings" is based on the Oingo Boingo song "Tender Lumplings."
• This was the first animated Disney feature to use stop-motion instead of traditional animation.
• Additional appearances: *The Nightmare Before Christmas: Oogie's Revenge* PS2/Xbox game (2004).

Nocturna (TV-PG)

Theatrical release date: October 11, 2007 (Spain)
Country: Spain, France Language: Spanish
Production Company: Filmax Entertainment, Animakids Productions, Filmax Animation
Length: 80 minutes
Directed by: Adrià García, Víctor Maldonado
Screenplay by: Adrià García, Víctor Maldonado, Teresa Vilardell

---

Synopsis: Tim, a boy living in an orphanage, is afraid of the dark, counting on the light from the stars to get him through the long nights. The other children are annoyed by Tim's fear, especially when he won't retrieve a ball that rolls into the basement because it's dark, getting revenge by preventing Tim from opening the window to see the stars. Even more troubling, stars inexplicably begin disappearing. Tim goes to the roof of the orphanage, only to see his favorite star disappear. Tim soon meets a huge figure called the Cat Shepherd, along with his cat Tobermory. The magical Cat Shepherd is in charge of helping children sleep in peace, and Tim persuades the Shepherd to take him to the Night World to see Moka, the guardian of the night, hoping to get him to return the stars. When Moka doesn't help, the Cat Shepherd takes Tim to the Lighthouse of the Stars, and soon they are in the world of Nocturna, where the night is created. This world is threatened by a mysterious force, the Darkness, and Tim soon learns he had a part in creating the threat, and must face his fears if it is to be vanquished.

Cast: Imanol Arias as Pastor de Gatos
Carlos Sobera as Sr. Moka
Natalia Rodríguez as Estrella Polar
Lloyd F. Booth Shankley as Tim
Robert Paterson as Cat Shepherd
Patrick Pellegrin as Mister Pi
Patrick Noerie as Les Lumignons
Joe Lewis as Whisperer
Hervé Caradec as L'Informateur

Roger Carel as Moka
Philippe Peythieu as Murray,
    le lumignon courageux
Evelyne Grandjean as Ébouriffeuse #
Cathy Cerda as Ébouriffeuse #2
Florence Dumortier as Ébouriffeuse #3
Jean-Luc Reichmann as Chat-man,
    le Berger des chats

Music Highlights: Music by Nicolas Errèra.

Film Facts

• Adrià García and Víctor Maldonado were art directors for the Goya-winning film *El Cid: The Legend* (2003). García directed *My Family and the Wolf/Ma Famille et le Loup* (2019), and Maldonado was a character designer for *Trollhunters: Tales of Arcadia* TV series (2016).
• *Nocturna* won Spain's Goya Award for "Best Animated Film" (Mejor Película Animada), beating *Azur and Asmar, Betizu eta Urrezko Zintzarria,* and *En Busca de la Piedra Mágica.*
• The film was praised for its imaginative story, but also noted for having a slow pace.

The Nut Job (PG)

Theatrical release date: January 17, 2014
Production Company: RedRover Co. Ltd., ToonBox Entertainment, Gulfstream Pictures
Length: 85 minutes
Directed by: Peter Lepeniotis
Written by: Peter Lepeniotis, Lorne Cameron, story by Peter Lepeniotis, Daniel Woo

Synopsis: The park animals are anxious when their leader, Raccoon, announces that the park's food bank has run low for the winter, but have new hope when a nut cart is spotted nearby. The cart is run by robbers who are staking out a bank across the street. Raccoon sends the squirrels Andie and the egotistical Grayson to investigate, only to find that Surly Squirrel and the rat Buddy are already moving in on the cart. Surly's recklessness ends up destroying not just the nut cart, but all of the animals' remaining food, and Surly is banished from the park. Exiled into the city, Surly finds a nut shop, which is a front for the robbers, but is prevented from getting the nuts by the robbers' pug. Andie, also out looking for food, comes across the nut shop. She picks up a defective dog whistle which was tossed out by the robbers, making a deal to give the whistle to Surly in exchange for splitting the nuts in the shop. Surly uses the threat of the whistle to tame the dog, and plans are made to make a tunnel to get the nuts out. When complications arise there are signs that Raccoon is not the benevolent leader he seemed to be.

Cast: Will Arnett as Surly
Brendan Fraser as Grayson
Liam Neeson as Raccoon
Katherine Heigl as Andie
Stephen Lang as King
Maya Rudolph as Precious
Jeff Dunham as Mole

Gabriel Iglesias as Jimmy
Sarah Gadon as Lana
James Rankin as Fingers
Scott Yaphe as Lucky
Joe Pingue as Johnny
Annick Obonsawin as Jamie

Music Highlights: "N.E.V.E.R." (Alana da Fonseca/Ali Theodore) performed by Alana D, "Fish Out of Water" (Mansa Wakili/Colton Fisher/Jason Rabinowitz) performed by Leo Soul, "Great Intentions" (Jason French Muniz/Jason Rabinowitz/Colton Fisher/James Katalbas) performed by Damato, "Oh Well" (Zack Arnett, Jason Rabinowitz/Colton Fisher/James Katalbas) performed by Skully Boyz, "Push Play" (Colton Fisher/Jason Rabinowitz/Sixx Johnson) performed by Sixx Johnson, "Heist Man Trophy" (Eric Goldman) performed by The L.A. Outfit. End credits: "Gangnam Style" (Park Jai Sang/Yoo Gun Hyung) performed by Psy. Score by Paul Intson.

Film Facts

• For unclear reasons, the end credits featured an animated version of the South Korean singer Psy, performing his hit "Gangnam Style." A brief mid-credits scene follows (1:22:45).
• Additional appearances: The film is based on the short "Surly Squirrel" (2005, 11 min.), followed by *The Nut Job 2: Nutty by Nature* (2017).

Oliver & Company (G)

Theatrical release date: November 18, 1988
Production Company: Walt Disney Pictures, Walt Disney Feature Animation
Length: 74 minutes
Directed by: George Scribner
Screenplay by: Jim Cox, Timothy J. Disney, James Mangold

> **Synopsis**: A rewrite of Charles Dickens's *Oliver Twist,* Oliver is a stray kitten who follows streetwise mutt Dodger to the home of Fagin, a small-time criminal with a pack of dogs. Oliver is taken in by Jenny, the daughter of a wealthy family, and after Fagin gives up an attempt to hold Oliver for ransom, Jenny herself is kidnapped by Sykes, a powerful criminal who controls Fagin. Fagin is forced to reconsider his life and whether he is willing to take on Sykes to save Jenny.

Cast: Joey Lawrence as Oliver
Billy Joel as Dodger
Cheech Marin as Tito
Richard Mulligan as Einstein
Roscoe Lee Browne as Francis
Sheryl Lee Ralph as Rita
Dom DeLuise as Fagin
Taurean Blacque as Roscoe
Carl Weintraub as Desoto
Robert Loggia as Sykes
Natalie Gregory as Jenny
William Glover as Winston
Bette Midler as Georgette
Frank Welker as Carlo

Music Highlights: "Once Upon a Time in New York City" (Ashman/Mann) performed by Huey Lewis, "Why Should I Worry?" (Hartman/Midnight) performed by Billy Joel, "Streets of Gold" (Pitchford/Snow) performed by Ruth Pointer, "Perfect Isn't Easy" (Manilow/Feldman/Sussman) performed by Bette Midler, "Good Company" (Minkoff/Rocha) performed by Myhanh Tran. Score by J.A.C. Redford.

Film Facts

• The 27th of the Disney animated classics, *Oliver & Company* was the first film that began production under the tenure of CEO Michael Eisner and Chairman Jeffrey Katzenberg, both coming to Disney from Paramount Pictures. Story artist Pete Young successfully pitched a canine version of Charles Dickens' classic novel *Oliver Twist* (1837-1839).
• Several cameos are featured: Roger from *101 Dalmatians* (4:29), Peg, Jock, and Trusty from *Lady and the Tramp* (11:50), Pongo from *101 Dalmatians* (11:54), a photo of Ratigan from *The Great Mouse Detective* (34:25), and Mickey Mouse on a watch (53:56).
• The film is loosely based on Charles Dickens' classic novel *Oliver Twist,* with Oliver, Dodger, and Fagin keeping the same names as the characters in Dickens' book.
• Billy Joel's spirited "Why Should I Worry?" received a Golden Globe nomination for "Best Original Song."
• A video game was made in 1989 by Coktel Vision for PC computers.
• Additional appearances: Characters made cameo appearances on the *House of Mouse* animated TV series (2001-2003), including Dodger leading the song "Everybody Wants to Be a Dog."

One Hundred and One Dalmatians (G)

Theatrical release date: January 25, 1961
Production Company: Walt Disney Productions
Length: 79 minutes
Directed by: Wolfgang Reitherman, Hamilton S. Luske, Clyde Geronimi
Story by: Bill Peet, based on the book *The Hundred and One Dalmatians* by Dodie Smith

---

Synopsis: After introducing their owners, Roger and Anita, prolific Dalmatians Pongo and Perdita ("Perdy") inexplicably have a litter of 99 puppies. Anita's former school-mate, the unbalanced Cruella de Vil, conspires with two henchmen, Jasper and Horace, to capture the puppies in order to make a fur coat out of their pelts. Through courage, wits, and perseverance, the canine family works to make its way home while evading Cruella and her men, aided by the sheepdog Colonel, the horse Captain, and the tabby cat Sgt. Tibs.

Cast: Rod Taylor as Pongo
J. Pat O'Malley as Colonel/Jasper
Betty Lou Gerson as Cruella de Vil
Martha Wentworth as Nanny
Ben Wright as Roger

Cate Bauer as Perdita
Dave Frankham as Sgt. Tibs
Fred Worlock as Horace
Lisa Davis as Anita

Music Highlights: "Cruella de Vil" (Mel Leven) performed by Bill Lee as Roger and Lisa Davis as Anita, "Dalmatian Plantation" (Mel Leven) performed by Bill Lee as Roger, "Playful Melody" (Bruns/Dunham), "Kanine Krunchies Kommercial" (Mel Leven). Music by George Bruns.

Film Facts

• The 17th of the Disney animated classics, *One Hundred and One Dalmatians* was based on the children's novel *The Hundred and One Dalmatians* by Dodie Smith, and became one of Disney's most iconic films of the 1960s. Bill Peet was chosen by Walt Disney to develop the book into a film, which marked the first Disney film to be written by an individual rather than a team.

• Three of Disney's most renowned directors, Wolfgang Reitherman, Hamilton S. Luske, and Clyde Geronimi, collaborated on the film, with music provided by songwriter Mel Leven, including the classic "Cruella de Vil," as well as "Dalmatian Plantation."

• Dodie Smith, author of the children's novel *The Hundred and One Dalmatians,* owned many Dalmatians, including one named Pongo.

• It has been reported that Smith had the idea for her book when a friend saw all the Dalmatians next to each other, and remarked, "Those dogs would make a lovely fur coat."

• First released under the title *One Hundred and One Dalmatians,* the film was later called *101 Dalmatians*.

• Additional appearances: Followed by *101 Dalmatians: The Series* (1997-1998), *101 Dalmatians Christmas* (1999), *101 Dalmatians II: Patch's London Adventure* (2003), *Sing Along Songs: 101 Dalmatians: Pongo & Perdidta* (1996 VHS/2006 DVD), *101 Dalmatian Street* animated TV series (2018-2019), plus live-action *101 Dalmatians* (1996), *102 Dalmatians* (2000), and *Cruella* (2021).

101 Dalmatians Christmas (NR)

Home media release date: November 2, 1999
Production Company: Walt Disney Television Animation, Jumbo Pictures
Length: 44 minutes
Directed by: Peter Ferk ("Coup de Vil"), Victor Cook ("A Christmas Cruella")
Written by: Ken Koonce, Michael Merton

Synopsis: A home media special that combines two episodes from *101 Dalmatians: The Series*. In "Coup de Vil" (season 2, episode 41) Cruella's mother calls a De Vil family meeting at Cruella's home, Villa de Vil, telling her children that whoever is able to get the Dearly's land will inherit her fortune, forcing the puppies to defend their home. "A Christmas Cruella" (season 1, episode 11) is inspired by Charles Dickens' *A Christmas Carol,* as Cruella fires Anita on Christmas Eve. When Cruella is knocked out by a falling Christmas tree, visions of Cadpig, Rolly and Spot (as the ghosts of Christmas past, present, and future) help Cruella see the error of her ways.

Cast: Kath Soucie as Anita Dearly/Rolly/Cadpig
Tara Charendoff as Spot/Two-Tone/Vendela
Jeff Bennett as Roger Dearly/Lt. Pug/Sgt. Tibbs/
    Swamp Rat/P.H. DeVil
April Winchell as Cruella de Vil
Frank Welker as Scorch (ferret)/Steven the Alligator

Charlotte Rae as Nanny
David L. Lander as Horace Badun
Michael McKean as Jasper Badun
Rob Paulsen as Cecil B. DeVil
Cree Summer as Princess (cow)
Debi Mae West as Lucky

Music Highlights: Main Title Theme written, arranged, and produced by Randy Peterson, Kevin Quinn, and Tim Heintz. Music by Mark Watters, Dan Sawyer.

Film Facts

• Other Disney Christmas specials include *Mickey's Christmas Carol* (1983), *Winnie the Pooh & Christmas Too!* (1991), *Beauty and the Beast: The Enchanted Christmas* (1997), *Mickey's Once Upon a Christmas* (1999), *Mickey's Twice Upon a Christmas* (2004), *Disney Princess: A Christmas of Enchantment* (2005), Winnie the Pooh: *Super Sleuth Christmas Movie* DVD (2007), and *A Christmas Carol* (2009).
• Victor Cook, director of "A Christmas Cruella," also worked on the animated TV series *Buzz Lightyear of Star Command* (2000-2001), *The Legend of Tarzan* (2001-2003), and *Lilo & Stitch: The Series* (2003-2006). Peter Ferk, director of "Coup de Vil," directed several other episodes of *101 Dalmatians: The Series,* as well as *Sabrina, The Animated Series* (1999-2000) and *Pigs Next Door* (2000).
• The *101 Dalmatians Christmas* special is one of of the few Disney releases never to be re-issued on DVD or on Blu-ray.
• Additional appearances: Preceded by *One Hundred and One Dalmatians* (1961), *101 Dalmatians: The Series* (1997-1998), followed by *101 Dalmatians II: Patch's London Adventure* (2003), *101 Dalmatian Street* (2018-2019), plus the live-action *101 Dalmatians* (1996), *102 Dalmatians* (2000), and *Cruella* (2021).

101 Dalmatians II: Patch's London Adventure (G)

Home media release date: January 21, 2003
Production Company: Walt Disney Video Premiere, Walt Disney Television Animation,
Walt Disney Animation Japan
Length: 70 minutes
Directed by: Jim Kammerud and Brian Smith
Screenplay by: Jim Kammerud and Brian Smith, story by Garrett K. Schiff and Dan Root,
Brian Smith & Jim Kammerud

Synopsis: Patch, one of Pongo and Perdita's puppies, is accidentally left behind when the family moves, and makes use of the opportunity to meet his television hero, Thunderbolt, just as Thunderbolt faces replacement by the younger dog Li'l Lightning. Meanwhile, Cruella de Vil hires the German artist, Lars, to paint Dalmatian spots for her in an attempt to quell her Dalmatian fixation, but before long she relapses and is out for fur. When she captures the Dalmatian family, Patch and Thunderbolt, aided by Li'l Lightning, come to the rescue, but they soon come to realize that real life is not always like television.

Cast: Barry Bostwick as Thunderbolt
Jason Alexander as Lightning
Martin Short as Lars
Bobby Lockwood as Patch
Susanne Blakeslee as Cruella
Samuel West as Pongo
Muarice LaMarche as Horace

Jeff Bennett as Jasper
Jodi Benson as Anita
Tim Bentinck as Roger
Kath Soucie as Perdita
Mary Macleod as Nanny
Michael Lerner as Producer

Music Highlights: "Try Again" (Richard Gibbs/Dean Pichford) performed by Will Young, "I See Spots" (Randy Rogel) performed by Tim Bentinck, "One of a Kind" (Noko/Trevor Gray/Howard Gray/Richard Gibbs/Mel Levin) performed by Apollo 440. Score by Richard Gibbs.

Film Facts

• Thunderbolt, the canine television star at the center of the sequel, was briefly shown on TV in the original *One Hundred and One Dalmatians* (1961). In the sequel he is voiced by Barry Bostwick, borrowing from his role as the slick, superficial mayor in the *Spin City* sitcom.
• Several of the voice actors appeared in other Disney films, including Jodi Benson (Ariel in *The Little Mermaid*), Jason Alexander (Abis Mal in *Aladdin: The Return of Jafar*), Kath Soucie (Kanga in *Pooh's Heffalump Movie*), and Kathryn Beaumont (*Alice in Wonderland, Peter Pan*).
• The DVD bonus features includes a whimsical behind the scenes "dogumentary."
• Barry Bostwick played Mayor Randal Winston in the sitcom *Spin City,* exhibiting the same cheerful self-importance and dubious judgment as Thunderbolt. He later played another mayor, in Pixar's *Incredibles 2* (2018).
• Additional appearances: Follows *One Hundred and One Dalmatians* (1961), *101 Dalmatians: The Series* animated TV series (1997-1998), and *101 Dalmatians Christmas* (1999), followed by *101 Dalmatian Street* animated TV series (2018-2019).

Onward (PG)

Theatrical release date: March 6, 2020 (premiere Feb 21, 2020 at Berlin International Film Festival)
Production Company: Pixar Animation Studios, Walt Disney Pictures
Length: 102 minutes
Directed by: Dan Scanlon
Screenplay by: Dan Scanlon, Jason Headley, Keith Bunin, original story by Dan Scanlon, Keith Bunin, Jason Headley

Synopsis: Long ago, magic filled the world, but over time, the magic began to fade as the world turned to modern conveniences like electricity. In the present, elf bothers Ian and Barley Lightfoot live with their mother, Laurel, after they lost their father, Wilden, years ago. The shy Ian is turning 16, and dreams of getting his driver's license, being more social, and being like his dad, while Barley is outgoing and obsessed with fantasy and his van, Guinevere. Laurel gives Ian and Barley a gift that Wilden left for them: a visitation spell and a magic staff that are supposed to bring Wilden back for a day. The spell is interrupted, leaving only Wilden's bottom half. They set off on a quest to find a Phoenix gem to help them finish the spell. A visit to the Manticore's Tavern points them to Raven's Point, and they are soon followed by Laurel and the Manticore. After facing many perils, Ian fears all was for naught, but finally realizes that even though he did not have his father as he grew up, he always had someone there looking out for him.

Cast: Tom Holland as Ian Lightfoot
Chris Pratt as Barley Lightfoot
Julia Louis-Dreyfus as Laurel Lightfoot
Octavia Spencer as The Manticore
Mel Rodriguez as Colt Bronco
Kyle Bornheimer as Wilden Lightfoot
Lena Waithe as Officer Spector
Ali Wong as Officer Gore
Grey Griffin as Dewdrop (Pixie Dusters Leader)
Tracey Ullman as Grecklin (Pawn Shop Owner)
Wilmer Valderrama as Gaxton (College Friend)
George Psarras as Officer Avel

Music Highlights: "Carried Me with You" (Brandi Carlile/Phil Hanseroth/Tim Hanseroth) performed by Brandi Carlile, "Let's Get It On" (Marvin Gaye/Ed Townshend) performed by Marvin Gaye. Music by Mychael Danna, Jeff Danna.

Film Facts

• The short "Playdate with Destiny" with Maggie Simpson of *The Simpsons* played with the film.
• Pixar Easter eggs: a Dorothea Williams LP from Pixar's next film, *Soul* (5:57), the woods from *Brave* on Ian's calendar (13:14), the Pizza Planet truck (24:13), the Luxo ball on a shield (27:56), Remy from *Ratatouille* wearing a chef's hat (28:39), Triple Dent Gum from *Inside Out* (42:35), *The Sword in the Stone* (55:13), and A113 given as a police code (1:31:23).
• Burger Shire: "Now serving 2nd breakfast" referenced *The Lord of the Rings* (7:08).
• John Ratzenberger made his customary Pixar film appearance as Construction Worker Fenwick toward the end of the film (1:18:16).
• The beholder and the gelatinous cube are monsters from Dungeons & Dragons.
• Additional appearances: "Magic Gems" 3-minute short (2020).

Open Season (PG)

Theatrical release date: September 29, 2006
Production Company: Sony Pictures Animation, Columbia Pictures
Length: 86 minutes
Directed by: Jill Culton, Roger Allers, co-directed by Anthony Stacchi
Screenplay by: Steve Bencich & Ron J. Friedman and Nat Mauldin, screen story by Jill Culton and Anthony Stacchi, from an original story by Steve Moore and John Carls

Synopsis: The grizzly bear Boog is the main attraction in the town of Timberline's nature show. When the hunter Shaw shows up with the deer Elliot tied to his truck, Boog frees him. Elliot returns the favor by introducing Boog to candy, and it isn't long before the two of them are running wild in a convenience store, where Boog is captured. Back at his nature show, Boog is interrupted by Elliot, who is fleeing from Shaw. Boog, unhappy to see Elliot again, becomes aggressive, prompting panic in the show's audience. Boog's owner, Beth, shoots Boog and Elliot with a tranquilizer and they are sent to the Timberline National Forest, just before open season hunting begins. Anxious to return to the town, Boog and Elliot reluctantly work together, trying to get along with the wildlife and turning the tables on the hunters. Boog and Elliot both finally learn the importance of teamwork.

Cast: Martin Lawrence as Boog
Ashton Kutcher as Elliot
Gary Sinise as Shaw
Debra Messing as Beth
Billy Connolly as McSquizzy
Georgia Engel as Bobbie
Jon Favreau as Reilly

Jane Krakowski as Giselle
Gordon Tootoosis as Gordy
Patrick Warburton as Ian
Cody Cameron as Mr. Weenie
Nika Futterman as Rosie
Danny Mann as Serge
Jack McGee as Hunter

Music Highlights: "Wild Wild Life" (David Byrne) performed by Talking Heads, "I Wanna Lose Control" (Dana Gumbiner) performed by Deathray, "Walkin' After Midnight" (Alan Block/Don Hecht), "I Belong" (Paul Westerberg) performed by Pete Yorn, "The Teddy Bears' Picnic" (John W. Bratton/Jimmy Kennedy), "Good Day" (Paul Westerberg) performed by Paul Westerberg, "Wild As I Wanna Be" (Paul Westerberg) performed by Deathray. Score by Paul Westerberg and Ramin Djawadi.

Film Facts

• This release was the first Sony Pictures Animation film, followed by *Surf's Up* (2007).
• A mid-credits scene appears near the beginning of the credits (1:18:52).
• The initial story for the film came from *In the Bleachers* comic strip cartoonist Steve Moore.
• The Sacramento band Deathray included former Cake members Greg Brown and Victor Damiani.
• Additional appearances: "Boog and Elliot's Midnight Bun Run" short (2007), *Open Season 2* (2009), *Open Season 3* (2011), *Open Season: Scared Silly* (2016). All three feature-length sequels were issued direct-to-video.

Over the Hedge (PG)

Theatrical release date: May 19, 2006
Production Company: DreamWorks Animation
Length: 83 minutes
Directed by: Tim Johnson, Karey Kirkpatrick
Screenplay by: Len Blum and Lorne Cameron & David Hoselton and Karey Kirkpatrick

---

Synopsis: The hungry raccoon RJ tries to steal a huge haul of food from the sleeping bear Vincent, accidentally waking Vincent and destroying his food. RJ persuades Vincent to let him replace the food, and soon after, overhears a group of forest animals planning to forage for food, including the fatherly turtle Verne, the skunk Stella, the squirrel Hammy, father and daughter opossums Ozzie and Heather, and the porcupines Penny and Lou, with their kids Bucky, Spike and Quillo. They all happen upon a huge hedge wall, and when Verne checks it out, he has a series of misfortunes in suburbia. RJ persuades the animals to venture past the hedge to gather food, secretly planning to pass it on to Vincent. When the food theft begins to get out of hand, local businesswoman Gladys Sharp calls in an exterminator. The animals are grateful to RJ for his help, but Verne tries to return the food so the exterminator will be called off. The group chooses to follow RJ over Verne, but RJ finally realizes how real the threat of the exterminator is. They agree to make one last raid on Gladys's home, but all except RJ are captured, leaving the raccoon to decide what his priorities really are.

Cast: Bruce Willis as RJ
Garry Shandling as Verne
Steve Carell as Hammy
Wanda Sykes as Stella
William Shatner as Ozzie
Nick Nolte as Vincent
Thomas Haden Church as Dwayne
Allison Janney as Gladys

Eugene Levy as Lou
Catherine O'Hara as Penny
Avril Lavigne as Heather
Omid Djalili as Tiger
Sami Kirkpatrick as Bucky
Shane Baumel as Spike
Madison Davenport as Quillo
Zoe Randol as Mackenzie

Music Highlights: "Family of Me" (Ben Folds) performed by Ben Folds, "Heist" (Ben Folds) performed by Ben Folds, "Still" (Ben Folds) performed by Ben Folds, "Rockin' the Suburbs (Over the Hedge Version)" (Ben Folds) performed by Ben Folds, "Lost in the Supermarket" (Joe Strummer/Mick Jones/Paul Simonon/Topper Headon) performed by Ben Folds (orig. by The Clash). Music by Rupert Gregson-Williams.

Film Facts

• The film is based on the syndicated comic strip *Over the Hedge,* written by Michael Fry and illustrated by T. Lewis.
• A short post-credits scene appears (1:22:38).
• The traps are mapped out with Monopoly tokens: the car, the iron, etc. (51:40).
• The short film "Hammy's Boomerang Adventure" is included on the DVD/Blu-ray.

Over the Moon (PG)

Theatrical/Streaming release date: Oct 23, 2020 (premiere Oct 17, 2020 at Montclair Film Festival)
Country: US/China
Production Company: Glen Keane Productions, Janet Yang Productions, Netflix, Pearl Studio
Length: 95 minutes
Directed by: Glen Keane, co-director John Kahrs
Written by: Audrey Wells, additional screenplay material by Jennifer Yee McDevitt & Alice Wu

Synopsis: Fei Fei's mother tells her the legend of Chang'e, a moon goddess who took an immortality potion, which lifted her to the moon, separating her from her love, the archer Houyi. Fei Fei's mother passes away, and after a time her father begins seeing Mrs. Zhong, who has an 8 year old son, Chin, who annoys Fei Fei to no end. Fei Fei continues to believe in Chang'e, and hoping to prove she is real, she builds a rocket to travel to the moon, finding that Chin has stowed away. When they arrive they find the goddess Chang'e, who welcomes them, and says they may present their "gift." Fei Fei does not know what she means, but goes in search of the gift on the surface of the moon, accompanied by three biker chicks. They happen upon the wreckage of Fei Fei's ship, where they meet the "nervous talker" pangolin Gobi, who was exiled by Chang'e 1,000 years ago. The chicks steal a doll that might be the gift Chang'e wants, but Fei Fei determines a fragment of an amulet is the real gift, presenting it to Chang'e. Chang'e combines the halves, bringing Houyi back, but he tells her he cannot stay, and she has to move on, before fading away. The moon falls into darkness, as Chang'e mourns her loss. Fei Fei, who also knows grief, goes to help Chang'e, but the memory of the loss of her mother paralyzes her. Chang'e tells her she must move on, and they return to Earth, with Fei Fei understanding that she can now be open to connection.

Cast: Cathy Ang as Fei Fei
Phillipa Soo as Chang'e
Robert G. Chiu as Chin
Ken Jeong as Gobi
John Cho as Father

Ruthie Ann Miles as Mother
Margaret Cho as Auntie Ling and Gretch
Kimiko Glenn as Auntie Mei and Luly
Artt Butler as Uncle and Bill
Sandra Oh as Mrs. Zhong

Music Highlights: "On the Moon Above" performed by Ruthie Ann Miles, John Cho and Cathy Ang, "Mooncakes" performed by Miles, Cho and Ang, "Rocket to the Moon" performed by Ang, "Ultraluminary" performed by Phillipa Soo, "Hey Boy" performed by Phillipa Soo and Robert G. Chiu, "Wonderful" performed by Ken Jeong, "Yours Forever" performed by Phillipa Soo and Conrad Ricamora, "Love Someone New" performed by Soo and Ang, "On the Moon Above (The Tai Ching Dance Song)" (He Muyang) performed by Phoenix Legend. All songs by Christopher Curtis/Marjorie Duffield/Helen Park unless otherwise indicated. Score by Steven Price.

Film Facts

• Screenwriter Audrey Wells passed away during the film's production. She also wrote *A Dog's Purpose* (2017), *Under the Tuscan Sun* (2003) and *George of the Jungle* (1997).
• Chang'e appears in a number of Chinese legends.

The Painting (TV-PG)

Theatrical release date: November 23, 2011 (France), May 10, 2013 (US)
Country: France   French title: *Le Tableau*
Production Company: Blue Spirit Animation, Be-Films
Length: 80 minutes
Directed by: Jean-François Laguionie
Screenplay by: Anik Leray, English adaptation by Stephanie Sheh

---

Synopsis: In a beautiful painting of a castle, the "Alldunns" look down on the "halfies" (partially completed figures) and "sketchies" (early sketches of figures). A young Alldunn, Ramo, has a relationship with the halfie Claire, to the disapproval of his peers. The Alldunns have a meeting in which their leader, The Great Chandelier, proposes that The Painter will not return, and that the Alldunns should rule, but Ramo objects. During the meeting, the sketchie Gum is found, beaten, and thrown off a castle balcony. Ramo, Lola and the sketchie Quill flee the Alldunns in a boat, which takes them through a forest, and down a waterfall. Lola proposes they seek out The Painter, and when they reach the edge of the painting, Lola escapes the confines of the painting, ending up in a battle scene painting. Lola flees the scene with a young soldier, Magenta. They all end up in the artist's studio, talking with paintings of the half-nude woman Florence, the rhyming Harlequin, and a bitter Self-Portrait of the artist. Florence shows Lola the streets of Venice in the background of her painting, where she and Ramo join the festive Carnival of Venice, while Quill and Magenta find several artworks destroyed by The Painter. The Great Chandelier has Claire trapped in an effort to lure Ramo back. When Ramo finds a tube of paint, they get the Self-Portrait to aid them by painting. When the group returns to the Alldunn painting, they bring paint back for the sketchies and halfies, permanently altering the balance of power in their world.

Cast: Kamali Minter as Lola
Michael Sinterniklaas as Ramo
Eden Riegel as Claire
Marc Thompson as The Great Chandelier
Vinnie Penna as Quill
Colin DePaula as Gum
Spike Spencer as Magenta

Christopher Kromer as Graymorgen
Mary Elizabeth McGlynn as Florence
Steve Blum as Self-Portrait
Colleen O'Shaughnessey as Harlequin
J.B. Blanc as The Painter/Venice Painter
Sam Riegel as Silhouette
Dave B. Mitchell as Pierrot/Grim Reaper

Music Highlights: Music by Pascal Le Pennec.

Film Facts

• The art in the film is inspired by the work of artists Pierre Bonnard, Marc Chagall, André Derain, Henri Matisse, Amedeo Modigliani, and Pablo Picasso.
• Jean-François Laguionie also directed the animated films *Gwen: The Book of Sand* (1985), *Black Mor's Island* (2004), *Louise by the Shore* (2016), and *The Prince's Voyage* (2019).

ParaNorman (PG)

Theatrical release date: August 17, 2012
Production Company: Laika Entertainment, Focus Features
Length: 92 minutes
Directed by: Sam Fell and Chris Butler
Written by: Chris Butler

Synopsis: Norman's parents are concerned that he talks to his grandmother, who fell ill and died. As it turns out, Norman sees many dead people and animals, for which he is bullied at school. His school play re-enacts the hanging of a witch by the settlers of Blithe Hollow in 1712, and her curse on seven accusers to rise as the living dead. Norman is befriended by Neil, another boy who is bullied, and they are approached by Norman's eccentric uncle, Mr. Prenderghast, who warns Norman that he has to use his gift to stop the witch's curse. During a play performance he has a vision that "the dead are coming." Norman's uncle passes away, and passes on the job of holding back the witch's curse to Norman, telling him to find a book at his house and use it to stop the witch in the graveyard. He is followed by the bully Alvin, who takes the book from him before he can read from it, and the settlers begin to rise from their graves. Norman finally tries reading from the book, but it doesn't work, forcing him to flee. Norman's sister Courtney goes to Neil's house looking for Norman, and Neil explains he went to the graveyard. Courtney rides with Neil and his older brother Mitch to the graveyard, finding Norman and Alvin facing a zombie. As the other zombies close in, the five of them drive away. A call to Norman's classmate Salma sends them to City Hall to find out where Norman needs to read from the book, while the scrappy townspeople of Blithe Hollow take on the zombies. Norman finally scales a tower to read from the book, and gets a vision of what really happened back in 1712, and he resolves to finally set things right.

Cast: Kodi Smit-McPhee as Norman Babcock
Tucker Albrizzi as Neil
Anna Kendrick as Courtney Babcock
Casey Affleck as Mitch
Christopher Mintz-Plasse as Alvin
Leslie Mann as Sandra Babcock
Jeff Garlin as Perry Babcock

Elaine Stritch as Grandma
Bernard Hill as The Judge
Jodelle Ferland as Aggie
Tempestt Bledsoe as Sheriff Hooper
Alex Borstein as Mrs. Henscher
John Goodman as Mr. Prenderghast
Hannah Noyes as Salma

Music Highlights: "Na Na Na" (Winslow/Chick) performed by Dennis Winslow/Ronn L. Chick, "Minuetto (Boccherini)" (Arturo Chaney) performed by Arturo Chaney. End credits: "Little Ghost" (Jack White) performed by The White Stripes. Music by Jon Brion.

Film Facts

• *ParaNorman* was nominated for the "Best Animated Feature" Academy Award.
• A post-credits scene appears (1:31:57), showing construction of Norman's stop motion figure.
• Mitch became the first openly gay character in a mainstream animated film.

Peanuts/Charlie Brown Franchise

A Charlie Brown Christmas (1965)
Charlie Brown's All Stars! (1966)
It's the Great Pumpkin, Charlie Brown (1966)
You're in Love, Charlie Brown (1967)
He's Your Dog, Charlie Brown (1968)
It Was a Short Summer, Charlie Brown (1969)
Play It Again, Charlie Brown (1971)
You're Not Elected, Charlie Brown (1972)
There's No Time for Love, Charlie Brown (1973)
A Charlie Brown Thanksgiving (1973)
It's a Mystery, Charlie Brown (1974)
It's the Easter Beagle, Charlie Brown (1974)
Be My Valentine, Charlie Brown (1975)
You're a Good Sport, Charlie Brown (1975)
It's Arbor Day, Charlie Brown (1976)
It's Your First Kiss, Charlie Brown (1977)
What a Nightmare, Charlie Brown! (1978)
You're the Greatest, Charlie Brown (1979)
She's a Good Skate, Charlie Brown (1980)
Life Is a Circus, Charlie Brown (1980)
It's Magic, Charlie Brown (1981)
Someday You'll Find Her, Charlie Brown (1981)
A Charlie Brown Celebration (1982)
Is This Goodbye, Charlie Brown? (1983)
It's an Adventure, Charlie Brown (1983)
What Have We Learned, Charlie Brown? (1983)
It's Flashbeagle, Charlie Brown (1984)
Snoopy's Getting Married, Charlie Brown (1985)
You're a Good Man, Charlie Brown (1985)
Happy New Year, Charlie Brown! (1986)
Snoopy! The Musical (1988)
It's the Girl in the Red Truck, Charlie Brown (1988)
Why, Charlie Brown, Why? (1990)
Snoopy's Reunion (1991)
It's Spring Training, Charlie Brown (1992)
It's Christmastime Again, Charlie Brown (1992)
You're in the Super Bowl, Charlie Brown (1994)
It Was My Best Birthday Ever, Charlie Brown (1997)
It's the Pied Piper, Charlie Brown (2000)
A Charlie Brown Valentine (2002)
Charlie Brown's Christmas Tales (2002)
Lucy Must Be Traded, Charlie Brown (2003)
I Want a Dog for Christmas, Charlie Brown (2003)
He's a Bully, Charlie Brown (2006)
Happiness Is a Warm Blanket, Charlie Brown (2011)

Peanuts: *A Charlie Brown Christmas* (NR)

Broadcast date: December 9, 1965
Production Company: United Feature Syndicate, Lee Mendelson Film Prod., Bill Melendez Prod.
Length: 25 minutes
Directed by: Bill Melendez
Written by: Charles M. Schulz

Synopsis: Feeling depressed about the Christmas season, Charlie Brown accepts Lucy's offer to direct the upcoming Christmas play. He goes to buy a Christmas tree for the play, and chooses a small tree with sparse pine needles, to the scorn of the rest of the Peanuts gang. When Charlie Brown asks what Christmas is all about, Linus recites from the Bible. leading Charlie Brown to smile, no longer worrying what others think. He walks out with the little tree, but gets discouraged when a single ornament bends the tree over. The other kids, also inspired by Linus's words, borrow Snoopy's decorations, and fix the little tree up.

Cast: Peter Robbins as Charlie Brown
Bill Melendez as Snoopy
Christopher Shea as Linus Van Pelt
Tracy Stratford as Lucy Van Pelt
Cathy Steinberg as Sally Brown

Chris Doran as Schroeder/Shermy
Ann Altieri as Frieda
Sally Dryer as Violet
Karen Mendelson as Patty
Geoffrey Ornstein as Pig-Pen

Music Highlights: "Christmas Time Is Here" (Vince Guaraldi/Lee Mendelson) performed by The Vince Guaraldi Trio/St. Paul's Episcopal Church choir, San Rafael, CA, "Skating" (Guaraldi) performed by The Vince Guaraldi Trio, "Surfin' Snoopy" (Guaraldi) performed by The Vince Guaraldi Trio, "Christmas Is Coming" (Guaraldi) performed by The Vince Guaraldi Trio, "Charlie Brown Theme" (Guaraldi) performed by The Vince Guaraldi Trio, "Linus and Lucy" (Guaraldi) performed by The Vince Guaraldi Sextet, "Happiness Theme" (Guaraldi) performed by The Vince Guaraldi Trio, "O Tannenbaum" (Trad., lyrics Ernst Anschütz) performed by The Vince Guaraldi Trio, "Fur Elise" (Beethoven), "Jingle Bells" (Pierpont), "Greensleeves" (Trad.) performed by The Vince Guaraldi Trio. "Hark the Herald Angels Sing" (Charles Wesley/Felix Mendelssohn) performed by St. Paul's Episcopal Church choir.

Film Facts

• The producers chose to hire child actors, which, along with the jazz soundtrack and the absence of a laugh track, led to fears the special would be a flop. It was a surprise hit with critics and viewers.
• The special was sponsored by Coca-Cola, produced on a very tight six-month schedule.
• Given its tight production schedule, the special was completed just 10 days before its broadcast. Executives at CBS were reportedly not pleased with the final product, but had no alternative.
• The special won an Emmy for "Outstanding Children's Program" in 1966.
• The quote from the Bible (King James Version) is drawn from Luke 2:8-14.
• The phobias Lucy mentions are real terms: hypengyophobia, ailurophobia, climacaphobia, thalassophobia, gephyrophobia, and pantophobia.

Peanuts: *It's the Great Pumpkin, Charlie Brown* (NR)

Broadcast date: October 27, 1966
Production Company: United Feature Syndicate, Lee Mendelson Film Prod., Bill Melendez Prod.
Length: 25 minutes
Directed by: Bill Melendez
Written by: Charles M. Schulz

Synopsis: It's Halloween, and everyone is getting ready for "tricks or treats." Linus tells the Peanuts gang that the Great Pumpkin rises up out of the pumpkin patch that he thinks is the most sincere, and flies through the air with a bag of toys for all the children. Linus faces a lot of skepticism, but Charlie Brown's sister Sally believes, agreeing to go to the pumpkin patch with him. Charlie Brown is invited to his first party, a Halloween gathering at Violet's. First they go trick or treating, but Charlie Brown has a couple of problems. Apart from having a little trouble with the scissors when cutting out eye holes for his ghost costume, he somehow always receives a rock while the other kids get candy. Snoopy, meanwhile, is dressed as the World War I flying ace, making his way across the French countryside while behind enemy lines. Both Charlie Brown and Linus have their disappointments, but both of them remain determined to persevere.

Cast: Peter Robbins as Charlie Brown
Chris Shea as Linus
Sally Dryer as Lucy
Cathy Steinberg as Sally
Ann Altieri as Frieda/Violet
Lisa DeFaria as Patty
Bill Melendez as Snoopy
Glenn Mendelson as Schroeder/Shermy
Gail DeFaria as Pigpen

Music Highlights: "Linus and Lucy" (Guaraldi) performed by The Vince Guaraldi Sextet. Original score composed & performed by Vince Guaraldi, arranged & conducted by John Scott Trotter.

Film Facts

• The special was first broadcast on CBS on October 27, 1966, the second Peanuts special produced. It was very well received by the public and critics alike, and was nominated for an Emmy Award.
• Children across the country sent candy to Charlie Brown when he did not get any in the special.
• Linus writes that the Great Pumpkin is not known as well as Santa, but tells him that "perhaps being number two, you'll try harder." This is a paraphrase of an Avis rental car ad campaign, which suggested they tried harder because they were number two, after industry leader Hertz.
• The songs Schroeder plays at the Halloween party are "It's a Long Way to Tipperary," "There's a Long, Long Trail," "Pack Up Your Troubles in Your Old Kit-Bag," and "Roses of Picardy."
• Lucy appears on the front of the TV guide she is reading (6:48).
• This special inspired Ray Bradbury to write the story *The Halloween Tree* (1972).
• *Music from the Soundtrack It's the Great Pumpkin, Charlie Brown* was released on CD by Craft Recordings/Concord Music Group in 2018.
• Cathy Steinberg (Sally) was 6 years old during production, and had to hurry to complete her lines before one of her teeth feel out, which happened just as she finished recording.

Peanuts: *A Charlie Brown Thanksgiving* (TV-G)

Broadcast date: November 20, 1973
Production Company: Lee Mendelson Film Prod., Bill Melendez Prod., United Feature Syndicate
Length: 25 minutes
Directed by: Bill Melendez and Phil Roman
Written by: Charles M. Schulz

Synopsis: When Peppermint Patty's father is out of town, she invites herself over to Charlie Brown's house for Thanksgiving dinner, bringing along Marcie and Franklin. Charlie Brown doesn't know what to do, as he is going to his grandmother's for Thanksgiving and won't even be home for dinner. Linus proposes they have an early Thanksgiving dinner at Charlie Brown's, and with the help of Snoopy and Woodstock, they prepare a feast of popcorn, toast, jelly beans and pretzel sticks. Linus shares a little Thanksgiving history and a prayer, but Peppermint Patty is outraged that the meal offered is not a traditional Thanksgiving dinner. Feeling badly about her outburst, Patty asks Marcie to apologize to Charlie Brown for her. When the first meal runs over time, Charlie Brown's grandmother invites everyone over to her home for another Thanksgiving dinner.

Cast: Todd Barbee as Charlie Brown
Robin Kohn as Lucy
Stephen Shea as Linus
Hilary Momberger as Sally

Christopher DeFaria as Peppermint Patty
Jimmy Ahrens as Marcie
Robin Reed as Franklin

Music Highlights: "Charlie Brown Blues" (Guaraldi), "Thanksgiving Theme" (Guaraldi), "Peppermint Patty" (Guaraldi), "Little Birdie" (Guaraldi) performed by Vince Guaraldi, "Is It James or Charlie?" (Guaraldi), "Linus and Lucy" (Guaraldi), "Over the River and Through the Woods" (Lydia Maria Child) performed by Christopher DeFaria and cast.

Film Facts

• Lucy's only appearance in the special is to hold the football for Charlie Brown.
• Marcie calls Peppermint Patty "Priscilla" as if that is her real first name. In the January 15, 1972 *Peanuts* comic strip, Patty says her name is Patricia Reichardt.
• Director Bill Melendez "voiced" Snoopy and Woodstock.
• "Little Birdie," with vocals by Vince Guaraldi, is Guaraldi's only non-instrumental in the special.
• Christopher DeFaria, who voiced Peppermint Patty, is related to Lisa DeFaria and Gail DeFaria, who also acted in the franchise.
• The 40th anniversary DVD included "The Mayflower Voyagers," the first episode of the eight-part animated TV miniseries *This Is America, Charlie Brown* (1988-1989).
• The troubling depiction of Woodstock eating another bird was raised as a concern by producer Lee Mendelson, but he was outvoted by Charles M. Schulz and Bill Melendez.
• Some music from the special is included on the 1998 CD *Charlie Brown's Holiday Hits*.

234

Peanuts: *It's the Easter Beagle, Charlie Brown!* (NR)

Broadcast date: April 9, 1974
Production Company: Lee Mendelson Film Prod., Bill Melendez Prod., United Feature Syndicate
Length: 25 minutes
Directed by: Phil Roman
Written by: Charles M. Schulz

Synopsis: It's Easter time for the Peanuts gang. Lucy is getting ready to go shopping for Easter candy, but Linus tells Sally that on Easter Sunday the Easter Beagle passes colored eggs to all the good little kids. The gang goes to the shopping center, where Sally wants to get some new shoes, while Snoopy has fun trying on hats, looking at kaleidoscope eggs, and buying a birdhouse for Woodstock, who's been having a hard time with the rains. Sally is skeptical of Linus's tale of the Easter Beagle, after her bad experience with the Great Pumpkin on Halloween. Peppermint Patty tries to teach Marcy how to color Easter eggs, but Marcy fries the eggs, then puts them in a waffle iron. Snoopy checks on Woodstock's birdhouse, shocked to find it fully decorated inside, and accidentally destroys it, so they go to buy a new one. Peppermint Patty carefully instructs Marcy to boil a new batch of eggs, but Marcy cracks the eggs open and throws away the shells, making egg soup. Lucy looks forward to finding all the Easter eggs on the hunt, because she is the one who's hiding them, but a mysterious white hand (or paw) takes the eggs after she hides them. Charlie Brown is sad about being alone, Sally is bitter when the Easter Beagle doesn't arrive, and Peppermint Patty and Marcie are frustrated over their egg-coloring challenges. Things brighten when Snoopy, as the Easter Beagle, distributes the colored eggs, making everyone happy except Lucy, who's indignant to receive her own Easter egg from the beagle.

Cast: Todd Barbee as Charlie Brown/Schroeder
Melanie Kohn as Lucy
Stephen Shea as Linus
Linda Ercoli as Peppermint Patty
Lynn Mortensen as Sally
James Ahrens as Marcie

Music Highlights: "Easter Theme" (Vince Guaraldi) performed by Vince Guaraldi, Piano Sonata No. 3 in C Major I. Allegro con Brio (Ludwig van Beethoven), "Snoopy and Woodstock" (Guaraldi) performed by Vince Guaraldi, Minuet In G Major (Johann Sebastian Bach), Symphony No. 7 in A Major: II. Allegretto (Ludwig van Beethoven), Symphony No. 7 in A Major: I. Poco sostenuto – Vivace (Ludwig van Beethoven).

Film Facts

• Charles Schultz was a critic of the commercialization of Christmas. At the shopping mall there are signs that read "Only 246 shopping days until Xmas," "Buy Early" and "Buy Now" (5:46).
• The special was first broadcast on CBS in 1974, and repeated on the network annually until 2000.
• Lucy was voiced by Melanie Kohn. Previously Melanie's sister Robin also voiced Lucy.
• The film received an Emmy nomination for "Outstanding Children's Special."

The Peanuts Movie (G)

Theatrical release date: November 6, 2015
Production Company: Blue Sky Studios, 20th Century Fox Animation
Length: 88 minutes
Directed by: Steve Martino
Written by: Craig Schulz, Bryan Schulz, Cornelius Uliano

Synopsis: When the Little Red-Haired Girl moves into the neighborhood, Charlie Brown is immediately smitten with her, but is so nervous around her he can't speak. The talent show offers him a chance to show off his magic act, but he gives up his slot to help Sally finish her act. Hoping to impress his crush at the school dance, Charlie Brown learns some moves from Snoopy, but an incident with the sprinkler system leads to disaster. Meanwhile, Snoopy finds a typewriter and envisions himself as the World War I Fly Ace, flying with the Allied pilot Fifi, who is threatened by the Red Baron. Charlie Brown is matched up with with the Little Red-Haired Girl to write a book report, and is shocked to learn that he got a perfect score on an important school test, giving him sudden popularity and respect. When the Little Red-Haired Girl has to go out of town, he plans to impress her by writing a book report on Tolstoy's *War and Peace*. At an assembly to celebrate his perfect test score, Charlie Brown learns that Peppermint Patty actually got the perfect score, declining the award, and afterwards his book report is destroyed. Despite his misery, the Little Red-Haired Girl chooses to be Charlie Brown's pen pal, admiring his many good qualities.

Cast: Noah Schnapp as Charlie Brown
Hadley Belle Miller as Lucy
Mariel Sheets as Sally
Alex Garfin as Linus
Francesca Angelucci Capaldi as the Little
    Red-Haired Girl
Venus Omega Schultheis as Peppermint Patty
Rebecca Bloom as Marcie
Marelik "Mar Mar" Walker as Franklin

Noah Johnston as Schroeder
Madisyn Shipman as Violet
Anastasia Bredikhina as Patty
A.J. Tecce as Pigpen
Micah Revelli as Little Kid
William "Alex" Wunsch as Shermy
Kristin Chenoweth as Fifi
Bill Melendez as Snoopy/Woodstock

Music Highlights: "Skating" (Guaraldi) performed by the Vince Guaraldi Trio, "Linus and Lucy" (Guaraldi) performed by the Vince Guaraldi Trio, "Better When I'm Dancin'" (Trainor/Dixon) performed by Meghan Trainor, "Good to Be Alive" (M. Trainor/R. Trainor) performed by Meghan Trainor, "That's What I Like" (Sermstyle, et al.) performed by Flo Rida feat. Fitz, "Christmas Time Is Here" (Guaraldi/Mendelson) performed by the Vince Guaraldi Trio. Music by Christophe Beck.

Film Facts

- Troy "Trombone Shorty" Andrews "voiced" Miss Othmar and the Little Red-Haired Girl's mother.
- The film was nominated for the "Best Animated Feature Film" Golden Globe.
- Two mid-credits scenes are included (1:18:00, 1:19:32), and a short post-credits scene (1:27:46).

Penguins of Madagascar (PG)

Theatrical release date: November 26, 2014
Production Company: DreamWorks Animation, Pacific Data Images
Length: 92 minutes
Directed by: Eric Darnell, Simon J. Smith
Screenplay by: Michael Colton & John Aboud and Brandon Sawyer, story by Alan Schoolcraft & Brent Simons and Michael Colton & John Aboud

---

Synopsis: Years ago, in Antarctica, nonconformist penguins Skipper, Kowalski, and Rico find a lost penguin egg, which hatches, and Private becomes part of their family. Years later, the team infiltrates Fort Knox to get Private a bag of the discontinued Cheezy Dibbles snack. They are captured by the criminal octopus Dr. Brine, also known as Dave, but escape and meet the elite interspecies crime fighting team North Wind. When they get a threatening message from Dave, North Wind's leader has the penguins sedated and sent to Madagascar. The penguins break out, and end up in Shanghai. Things get personal when Dave kidnaps Private, leading the penguins to pursue him in North Wind's plane, but the craft is soon destroyed. The penguins and North Wind put their differences aside to fight Dave's minions.

Cast: Tom McGrath as Skipper
Chris Miller as Kowalski
Christopher Knights as Private
Conrad Vernon as Rico
John Malkovich as Dave
Benedict Cumberbatch as Agent Classified
Ken Jeong as Short Fuse
Annet Mahendru as Eva
Peter Stormare as Corporal
Andy Richter as Mort
Danny Jacobs as King Julien
Sean Charmatz as Cricket
Werner Herzog as Documentary Filmmaker
Stephen Kearin as Pilot/Aquarium Employee
Kelly Cooney as Mermaid Penguin
Chris Sanders as Antarctic Penguin

Music Highlights: "Afro Circus/I Like To Move It" (Rock/Morillo/Quashie) performed by Chris Rock and Danny Jacobs, "Fideo Del Oeste" (Rodriguez) performed by Chingon, "Nobody" (Park/Rhee) performed by Wonder Girls, "I Can Dream About You" (Hartman) performed by Dan Hartman, "Celebrate" (Pérez/Cedar/Franks/Isaac/Maddahi/Puth/Fekaris/Zesses) performed by Pitbull. Music by Lorne Balfe.

Film Facts

• Several names of actors are worked into the dialogue through wordplay, including Kevin Bacon, Drew Barrymore, Halle Berry, Nicolas Cage, Anthony Michael Hall, Helen Hunt, William Hurt, Hugh Jackman, Parker Posey, Charlize Theron, Elijah Wood. and Robin Wright.
• A mid-credits scene appears (1:21:19).
• Penguins of Madagascar home media include the DVDs *The Penguins' Whacked-Out Adventure* (2005), *Party with the Penguins* (2009), *All-Nighter Before Xmas* (2010), *Happy King Julien Day* (2010), *New to the Zoo* (2010), *I Was a Penguin Zombie* (2010), *Operation: Get Ducky* (2010), *Operation: Antarctica* (2011), and *Operation: Blowhole* (2012).

Peter Pan (G)

Theatrical release date: February 5, 1953
Production Company: Walt Disney Productions
Length: 77 minutes
Directed by: Hamilton Luske, Clyde Geronimi, Wilfred Jackson
Story: Ted Sears, Erdman Penner, Bill Peet, Winston Hibler, Joe Rinaldi, Milt Banta, Ralph Wright, Bill Cottrell, an adaptation of the play *Peter Pan* by Sir James M. Barrie

---

Synopsis: English children Wendy, John, and Michael Darling leave the care of Nana, their maternal St. Bernard nursemaid, to follow the eternally youthful sprite Peter Pan and the petulant pixie Tinker Bell to the island of Never Land, where they have adventures with mermaids, Indians, and the Lost Boys (Cubby, Slightly, Nibs, Tootles, and the Twins), while battling the wicked Captain Hook, Mr. Smee, and the pirates.

Cast: Bobby Driscoll as Peter Pan
Kathryn Beaumont as Wendy
Hans Conried as Captain Hook/Mr. Darling
Bill Thompson as Mr. Smee
Heather Angel as Mrs. Darling

Paul Collins as John
Tommy Luske as Michael
Candy Candido as Indian Chief
Tom Conway as Narrator

Music Highlights: "Second Star to the Right" (Cahn/Fain) performed by chorus, "You Can Fly, You Can Fly, You Can Fly!" (Cahn/Fain) performed by Bobby Driscoll, Kathryn Beaumont, Paul Collins, Tommy Luske, "A Pirate's Life" (Penner/Wallace) performed by chorus, "Following the Leader" (Hibler/Sears/Wallace) performed by Bobby Driscoll, Paul Collins, Tommy Luske, "What Made the Red Man Red?" (Cahn/Fain) performed by Candy Candido, "Your Mother and Mine" (Cahn/Fain) performed by Kathryn Beaumont, "The Elegant Captain Hook" (Cahn/Fain) performed by Hans Conried and Bill Thompson. Score by Oliver Wallace.

Film Facts

• The 14th of the Disney animated classics, *Peter Pan* was a substantial success for Disney. The film was based on the 1904 play and 1911 novel *Peter Pan, or The Boy Who Wouldn't Grow Up* by James M. Barrie.
• Actress Margaret Kerry was the live-action model for Tinker Bell.
• The film's opening narration, "All this has happened before, and it will happen again," is a recurring motif in the series *Battlestar Galactica* (2004-2009).
• The depiction of Native Americans (called both "Indians" and "Redskins" in the film) has drawn criticism of racial insensitivity. When a sequel was developed many years later, the Native Americans were absent from the story.
• Composer Sammy Fain had originally written the melody of "Second Star to the Right" for the unused *Alice in Wonderland* (1951) song "Beyond the Laughing Sky."
• Kathryn Beaumont, who voiced Wendy, also voiced Alice in *Alice in Wonderland* (1951).
• Additional appearances: Followed by *Peter Pan: Return to Never Land* (2002). See also *Jake and the Never Land Pirates* TV series (2011-2016) and the Tinker Bell/Disney Fairies series.

238

Peter Pan: *Return to Never Land* (G)

Theatrical release date: February 15, 2002
Production Company: Walt Disney Pictures, Disney MovieToons, Walt Disney Animation Australia, Walt Disney Animation Canada, Walt Disney Animation Japan, Cornerstone Animation
Length: 72 minutes
Directed by: Robin Budd, co-director Donovan Cook
Screenplay by: Temple Mathews

Synopsis: Wendy from the first *Peter Pan* film has grown up and has two children, 12-year-old Jane and 4-year-old Danny. With their father gone to serve in the war, Jane is skeptical of the tales their mother tells about Never Land — until Captain Hook mistakes her for Wendy and abducts her to hold as a hostage against Peter Pan. Jane must face her own anger and skepticism to decide whether she can believe in Peter, Tinker Bell, and herself.

Cast: Harriet Owen as Jane & Young Wendy
Blayne Weaver as Peter Pan
Corey Burton as Captain Hook
Jeff Bennett as Smee & Pirates
Kath Soucie as Wendy
Andrew McDonough as Danny
Roger Rees as Edward
Spencer Breslin as Cubby
Bradley Pierce as Nibs
Quinn Beswick as Slightly
Aaron Spann as Twins

Music Highlights: "I'll Try" (Jonatha Brooke) performed by Jonatha Brooke, "Second Star to the Right" (Sammy Cahn/Sammy Fain) performed by Jonatha Brooke, "Do You Believe in Magic" (John Sebastian) performed by BBMak. Score by Joel McNeely.

Film Facts

• Coming 49 years after the original *Peter Pan* (1953), *Return to Never Land* continued the legend of Never Land. Voice actor Blayne Weaver had begun voicing Peter Pan in *Mickey's Magical Christmas: Snowed in at the House of Mouse* (2001), and was chosen to continue the role.
• The Lost Boys were unnamed in the original film, but several are called by the same names as in Barrie's play, including Nibs (rabbit suit), Slightly (fox suit), Tootles (skunk suit), and the Twins (raccoon suits). "Cubby" (bear suit) was originally "Curly."
• With the working title of *Peter and Jane* or *Peter Pan II: Peter and Jane,* the film was originally intended to be a theatrical release, then changed to a home media release, and finally returned to a theatrical release.
• The "Pixie Powered Edition" DVD issued in 2007 offered 5 Disney Fairies shorts as bonuses.
• After complaints of racial insensitivity, the Native Americans from the first film are simply absent in *Return to Never Land,* missing an opportunity for a more thoughtful portrayal.
• The song "Second Star to the Right" is heard when Peter reunites with Wendy.
• Blayne Weaver continued to voice Peter Pan, including the *House of Mouse* animated TV series, the short "Mickey's PhilharMagic" (2003), and *The Lion King 1 1/2* (2004).
• Additional Appearances: *Peter Pan* (1953). See also *Jake and the Never Land Pirates* TV series (2011-2016) and the Tinker Bell/Disney Fairies series.

The Phantom Tollbooth (G)

Theatrical release date: November 7, 1970
Production Company: MGM Animation/Visual Arts
Length: 90 minutes
Directed by: Chuck Jones and Abe Levitow, live-action sequences directed by David Monahan
Screenplay by: Chuck Jones and Sam Rosen, based on the book by Norton Juster

---

Synopsis: Young Milo is bored, but when a huge tollbooth appears in his bedroom, a small car takes him to the Land Beyond. He visits the Land of Expectations and meets the Whetherman, but on the way to Dictionopolis he enters the Doldrums, full of sluggish creatures where nobody thinks and there's nothing to do. Milo begins to fall asleep there, but is woken by Tock the watchdog, who saves him from the Doldrums by getting him to think. Tock explains that the land used to be the Kingdom of Wisdom, but was divided into two states, Dictionopolis, kingdom of words, and Digitopois, kingdom of mathematics. Passing through the land Milo meets Kakofonous A. Dischord and the Awful DYNN, the Humbug, and the Spelling Bee, then learns from from Faintly Macabre the Not-So-Wicked Which that the Princess of Sweet Rhyme and the Princess of Pure Reason were banished to the Castle in the Air, after they declared words and numbers had equal value. King Azaz of Dictionopolis supports Milo's quest to free Rhyme and Reason, as does the MathemaGician. Overcoming the Senses Taker, the Terrible Trivium, the Demon of Insincerity, and the Gelatinous Giant, Milo faces the Demons of Ignorance, and finally meets the Princesses.

Cast: Butch Patrick as Milo
Mel Blanc as Officer Short Shrift/
    Dodecahedron/Demon of Insincerity
Daws Butler as Whether Man/Senses Taker/
    Terrible Trivium/Gelatinous Giant
Candy Candido as Awful DYNN
Hans Conried as King Azaz/
    The MathemaGician

June Foray as Ralph/Faintly Macabre/
    Princess of Pure Reason
Patti Gilbert as Princess of Sweet Rhyme
Shep Menken as Spelling Bee/Chroma the Great
Cliff Norton as Kakofonous A. Dischord/
    Tollbooth Speaker
Larry Thor as Tock the Watchdog
Les Tremayne as Humbug

Music Highlights: "Milo's Song" (Pockriss/Gimbel) performed by cast, "Don't Say There's Nothing to Do in the Doldrums" (Pockriss/Vance) performed by Mel Blanc, Butch Patrick, and Thurl Ravenscroft, "Time Is a Gift" (Pockriss/Gimbel) performed by Butch Patrick and Larry Thor, "Noise, Noise, Beautiful Noise" (Pockriss/Vance) performed by Cliff Norton and Candy Candido, "Word Market" (Pockriss/Gimbel) performed by Hans Conried, "Numbers Are the Only Thing That Count" (Pockriss/Gimbel) performed by Hans Conried, "Rhyme and Reason Reign" (Pockriss/ Gimbel) performed by cast. Music by Dean Elliott.

Film Facts

- Butch Patrick (Milo) is best known for playing Eddie on the TV sitcom *The Munsters* (1964-1966).
- Director Chuck Jones makes a cameo as a cable car passenger (3:47).
- Hans Conried and Candy Candido were both voice actors in Disney's *Peter Pan* (1953).

Phineas and Ferb the Movie: Across the 2nd Dimension (TV-G)

Broadcast date: August 5, 2011
Production Company: Disney Television Animation
Length: 78 minutes
Directed by: Robert F. Hughes and Dan Povenmire
Written by: Jon Colton Barry, Dan Povenmire, Jeff "Swampy" Marsh

Synopsis: After accidentally destroying his equipment, Phineas and Ferb help evil scientist Dr. Heinz Doofenshmirtz fix his Other-Dimension-inator, which opens a dimensional portal, while their secret agent pet platypus Perry stands helplessly by, as he cannot compromise his cover. Phineas, Ferb and Perry follow Doofenshmirtz through the portal, to a world where Doofenshmirtz 2D rules the tri-state area, Perry has become an evil platyborg, and a startlingly capable Candace leads a resistance movement. Phineas and Ferb finally discover Perry is a secret agent, and once they get over their shock, they all work together to escape the evil dimension. When they finally manage to get home, Doofenshmirtz 2D sends an army of evil robots through the portal, to take over the tri-state area in our world.

Cast: Vincent Martella as Phineas Flynn
Ashley Tisdale as Candace Flyn
Thomas Brodie-Sangster as Ferb Fletcher
Caroline Rhea as Linda Flynn-Fletcher
Richard O'Brien as Lawrence Fletcher
Dan Povenmire as Dr. Heinz Doofenshmirtz
Swampy Marsh as Major Francis Monogram

Alyson Stoner as Isabella Garcia-Shapiro
Maulik Pancholy as Baljeet Rai
Bobby Gaylor as Buford Van Stomm
Mitchel Musso as Jeremy Johnson
Tyler Mann as Carl
Dee Bradley Baker as Perry the Platypus
Kelly Hu as Stacy Hirano

Music Highlights: "Everything's Better with Perry" (Povenmire/Marsh/Martin Olson/Aliki Theofilopoulos/Antoine Guilbaud) performed by Robbie Wyckoff, "Brand New Best Friend" (Barry/Povenmire/Olson) performed by Dan Povenmire, "Summer (Where Do We Begin?)" (Povenmire/Marsh/Olson/Barry/Hughes) performed by Vincent Martella and Danny Jacob, "I Walk Away" (Barry) performed by Olivia Olson, "Brand New Reality" (Povenmire/Marsh/Olson/Barry/Bernstein) performed by Robbie Wyckoff and Danny Jacob, "Takin' Care of Things" (Povenmire/Marsh/Jacob) performed by Dan Povenmire/Danny Jacob, "Robot Riot" performed by Jaret Reddick/Dan Povenmire. "Kick It Up a Notch" (Saul Hudson/Povenmire/Marsh/Jacob) performed by Vincent Martella, Dan Povenmire, Slash, Aaron Daniel Jacob, Danny Jacob. Music by Danny Jacob.

Film Facts

• Doofenshmirtz and Doofenshmirtz 2D appear as Beatles John Lennon and Paul McCartney, the Blues Brothers, Simon and Garfunkel, Sherlock Holmes and Dr. Watson, Laverne and Shirley, Ralph Kramden and Edward Norton, Bob Hope and Bing Crosby, Lucy and Ethel, Laurel and Hardy, Fred Astaire and Ginger Rogers, the Lone Ranger and Tonto, and Lewis and Clark (16:00).
• "I'm Jeremy Johnson, I'm here to rescue you" (58:58) paraphrases *Star Wars: A New Hope* (1977), as Luke Skywalker frees Princess Leia from her cell on the Death Star.
• A scene featuring Olivia Olson as Doofenshmirtz's daughter, Vanessa, was cut from the film, but her name was left in the credits.

Phineas and Ferb the Movie:
Candace Against the Universe (TV-G)

Broadcast date: August 28, 2020
Production Company: Disney Television Animation
Length: 86 minutes
Directed by: Bob Bowen
Written by: Dan Povenmire, Jeff "Swampy" Marsh, Jon Colton Barry, Jim Bernstein, Joshua Pruett, and Kate Kondell & Jeffrey M. Howard and Bob Bowen

---

Synopsis: Candace, constantly thwarted in her efforts to expose the schemes of Phineas and Ferb, feels like the universe is against her. When Candace and Vanessa are transported to an alien ship, Phineas, Ferb, Isabella, Baljeet, and Buford team with Dr. Doofenshmirtz to rescue them, unknowingly bringing along a stowaway Perry the Platypus, sent to save Candace as well. After they dock with a huge alien ship, Candace sends Vanessa down to the surface of an alien planet, but accidentally jettisons all the other escape pods. Candace is taken to the alien leader, Super Super Big Doctor, who tells her she is the chosen one, as her body contains the rare element Remarkalonium, which will save their world. Candace and SSBD bond, sharing a girls day out. When her would-be rescuers reach Candace, SSBD secretly sends them to prison. Perry stops the prison truck, and fearful but friendly aliens show them the city of Cowardalia, explaining that SSBD enslaved their people with a spore-generating plant, which Candace was chosen to revive. Candace unintentionally sends SSBD on the path to conquer Earth, pitting Candace, Phineas and Ferb against the universe.

Cast: Vincent Martella as Phineas
Ashley Tisdale as Candace
David Errigo Jr. as Ferb
Dan Povenmire as Dr. Doofenshmirtz
Alyson Stoner as Isabella
Maulik Pancholy as Baljeet

Bobby Gaylor as Buford
Dee Bradley Baker as Perry/Mama
Olivia Olson as Vanessa
Ali Wong as Super Super Big Doctor
Wayne Brady as Stapler-Fist
Al Yankovic as Shirt Cannon Guy

Music Highlights: "Such a Beautiful Day" (Povenmire/Kirkpatrick), "Candace Against the Universe Theme" (Jacob), "Unsung Hero" (Povenmire/Marsh), "Meet Our Leader" (Povenmire/Olson/Micucci), "You Are the Chosen One" (Povenmire/Olson/Micucci), "Girls Day Out" (Povenmire/Kiriakou), "Adulting" (Povenmire/Olson/Culross), "This Is Our Battle Song" (Povenmire/Olson/Hughes/Pruett), "Us Against the Universe" (Povenmire/Marsh). End credits: "Silhouettes" (Povenmire/Jacob), "We're Back" (Povenmire/Marsh). Music by Danny Jacob.

Film Facts

- Dan Povenmire and Jeff "Swampy" Marsh make a live-action cameo (58:17).
- Baseball stadium cameos (1:01:51) include Ducky Momo, Giant Floating Baby Head, & Lotsmo.
- A mid-credits scene appears with the parents of Phineas, Ferb, and Candace (1:21:45).

Pinocchio (G)

Theatrical release date: February 7, 1940
Production Company: Walt Disney Productions
Length: 88 minutes
Supervising Directors: Ben Shaprsteen, Hamilton Luske, sequence directors Bill Roberts, Norman Ferguson, Jack Kinney, Wilfred Jackson, T. Hee
Story Adaptation: Ted Sears, Otto Englander, Webb Smith, Willian Cottrell, Joseph Sabo, Erdman Penner, Aurelius Battaglia, from the story by Collodi

---

Synopsis: Kind Geppetto carves the wooden marionette Pinocchio, and wishes on a star that his creation will become a real boy. Pinocchio is given life by the Blue Fairy, and told if he is guided by his "conscience," Jiminy Cricket, he can become a real boy, by being brave, truthful, and unselfish. The naive puppet is tempted away from school by the deceitful fox Honest John and Gideon the cat, and taken to perform in Stromboli's puppet show, soon regretting his choice. Pinocchio is again tempted by John and Gideon, going to the unruly Pleasure Island, before learning the island carries a curse. Pinocchio finally returns home, only to find that Geppetto was swallowed by a whale while trying to find Pinocchio. In trying to help another, Pinocchio's sacrifice helps him become who he wishes to be.

Cast: Dickie Jones as Pinocchio/Alexander
Cliff Edwards as Jiminy Cricket
Christian Rub as Geppetto
Evelyn Venable as The Blue Fairy

Walter Catlett as J. Worthington Foulfellow
Charles Judels as Stromboli
Mel Blanc as Gideon/Donkeys/Marionettes
Frankie Darro as Lampwick

Music Highlights: "When You Wish Upon a Star" performed by Cliff Edwards/chorus, "Little Wooden Head" performed by Christian Rub, "Give a Little Whistle" performed by Cliff Edwards and Dickie Jones, "Hi-Diddle-Dee-Dee" performed by Walter Catlett and Dickie Jones, "I've Got No Strings" performed by Dickie Jones. All songs by Ned Washington and Leigh Harline.

Film Facts

• The 2nd of the Disney animated classics, *Pinocchio* was based on *The Adventures of Pinocchio* by Italian writer Carlo Collodi (pen name of Carlo Lorenzini), first published as a magazine serial in 1881-1882, and printed as a children's novel in 1883.
• The character of Pinocchio was somewhat cruel in the original story.
• Mel Blanc recorded dialogue for Gideon, but it was later decided that the character would be mute.
• The Blue Fairy was voiced by Evelyn Venable, an actress who served as the model for the Columbia Pictures logo.
• The music won two Academy Awards, "Best Music, Original Score," and "Best Music, Original Song" for "When You Wish Upon a Star." The song "When You Wish Upon a Star" became a theme for Disney as a whole.
• During "When You Wish Upon a Star" the books *Peter Pan* and *Alice in Wonderland* are seen.
• Additional appearances: Jiminy Cricket appeared in *Fun and Fancy Free* (1947). "Geppetto" was an episode of *The Wonderful World of Disney* anthology series, broadcast on May 7, 2000.

The Pirates! Band of Misfits (PG)

Theatrical release date: March 28, 2012 (UK), April 27, 2012 (US)
Country: UK   UK title: *The Pirates! In an Adventure with Scientists!*
Production Company: Aardman Animations, Sony Pictures Animation
Length: 88 minutes
Directed by: Peter Lord, Jeff Newitt
Screenplay by: Gideon Defoe, based on Gideon Defoe's novels *The Pirates! in an Adventure with Scientists* and *The Pirates! in an Adventure with Whaling*

Synopsis: The Pirate Captain yearns to win the Pirate of the Year award, but is repeatedly shown up by flashy pirates like Black Bellamy. When his ship happens upon scientist Charles Darwin, the Captain learns that his "parrot" Polly is actually a dodo, which could win them a scientific prize and turn his luck around. Darwin and his house-chimp try to steal Polly, but are thwarted. The "Scientist Captain" wins an audience with Queen Victoria. Despite her hatred of pirates, she pardons the Captain, but soon after traps him and offers him a vast treasure in exchange for his dodo, treasure which helps him win the Pirate of the Year Award. Unfortunately, his pardon disqualifies him as a pirate. It's only after losing his award, his dignity, and his crew, that the Captain realizes what is really important to him.

Cast: Hugh Grant as The Pirate Captain
Martin Freeman as The Pirate with a Scarf
Imelda Staunton as Queen Victoria
David Tennant as Charles Darwin
Jeremy Piven as Black Bellamy
Salma Hayek as Cutlass Liz
Lenny Henry as Peg-Leg Hastings

Brian Blessed as The Pirate King
Anton Yelchin as The Albino Pirate (US)
Brendan Gleeson as The Pirate with Gout
Ashley Jensen as The Surprisingly
   Curvaceous Pirate
Al Roker as The Pirate Who Likes Sunsets
   and Kittens (US)

Music Highlights: "Fiesta" (Finer/MacGowan/Koetscher/Lindt) performed by The Pogues, "Swords of a Thousand Men" (Tudorpole) performed by Tenpole Tudor, "Train to Skaville" (Dillon) performed by The Ethiopians, "London Calling" (Jones/Strummer/Simonon/Headon) performed by The Clash, "I'm Not Crying" (McKenzie/Clement) performed by Flight of the Conchords, "Ranking Full Stop" (Steele/Wakeling/Morton/Charlery/Cox) performed by The Beat. End credits: "You Can Get It If You Really Want" (Cliff) performed by Desmond Dekker (orig. by Jimmy Cliff), "Alright" (Goffey/Coombes/Quinn) performed by Supergrass. Music by Theodore Shapiro.

Film Facts

• The Pirate with Gout's hat has a badge from the famous British children's show *Blue Peter* (6:02).
• A Blood Island sign mentions "Weston-Super-Mare" (7:44), a town near Aardman Animations.
• Charles Darwin offers 10 pounds for Polly (24:25). Darwin's image is on the UK's 10 pound note.
• Wallace (of Wallace & Gromit) makes a gold cameo, at the bottom right of the screen (54:25).
• A scene in London (1:04:28) mimics a scene from the 1968 musical *Oliver!* (30:49).
• Several short animations run during the credits (1:19:39).
• Additional appearances: "So You Want to Be a Pirate!" short (2012).

Planes (PG)

Theatrical release date: August 9, 2013
Production Company: Walt Disney Pictures, Disneytoon Studios
Length: 92 minutes
Directed by: Klay Hall
Screenplay by: Jeffrey M. Howard, original story by John Lasseter, Klay Hall, Jeffrey M. Howard

Synopsis: In the town of Propwash Junction, cropdusting plane Dusty Crophopper dreams of becoming a racing star. After entering the Wings Across the Globe race qualifiers, he just makes the cut when one of the other planes is disqualified. Realizing Dusty is in way over his head, veteran war plane Skipper reluctantly agrees to train him, including helping him work on his fear of heights. As the race progresses from country to country, Dusty must contend with the dirty tricks of conniving racing plane Ripslinger, a disappointing revelation about his mentor, and his own fear of heights. Fortunately he has the support of friends and determination to do more than what he was built for.

Cast: Dane Cook as Dusty Crophopper
Stacy Keach as Skipper
Brad Garrett as Chug
Teri Hatcher as Dottie
Julia Louis-Dreyfus as Rochelle
Priyanka Chopra as Ishani
John Cleese as Bulldog
Cedric the Entertainer as Leadbottom
Carlos Alazraqui as El Chupacabra
Roger Craig Smith as Ripslinger
Anthony Edwards as Echo
Val Kilmer as Bravo
Sinbad as Roper
Gabriel Iglesias as Ned/Zed
Brent Musburger as Brent Mustangburger
Colin Cowherd as Colin Cowling
Danny Mann as Sparky
Oliver Kalkofe as Franz/Fliegenhozen
John Ratzenberger as Harland

Music Highlights: "Nothing Can Stop Me Now" (Mark Holman) performed by Mark Holman, "You Don't Stop - NYC" (Ali "Dee" Theodore) performed by Chris Classic and Alana D, "Fly" (John Fields/Jon Stevens) performed by Jon Stevens and The Dead Daisies. Score by Mark Mancina.

Film Facts

• Echo and Bravo, the F/A-18F Super Hornets, are based on planes in the film *Top Gun* (1986). They are voiced by Anthony Edwards and Val Kilmer, both of whom appeared in *Top Gun*.
• The Bavarian castle resembles Neuschwanstein, a castle which inspired the Sleeping Beauty castle at Disneyland in Anaheim and Disneyland Park in Paris.
• Though this wasn't a Pixar film, John Ratzenberger had a guest appearance, as the jet tug Harland.
• The *Cars Toons* episode "Air Mater," a bonus on the *Cars 2* DVD/Blu-ray, released November 1, 2011, featured scenes in Propwash Junction, as well as appearances by Skipper and Sparky. At the end of the short Mater says, "They oughta make a whole movie about planes."
• Additional appearances: Takes place in the same universe as *Cars* (2006). Followed by *Planes: Fire & Rescue* theatrical film (2014).

Planes: Fire & Rescue (PG)

Theatrical release date: July 18, 2014 (premiere July 15, 2014 at El Capitan Theatre, Los Angeles)
Production Company: Walt Disney Pictures, Disneytoon Studios
Length: 84 minutes
Directed by: Bobs Gannaway
Story and screenplay by: Bobs Gannaway, Jeffrey M. Howard

Synopsis: Former cropdusting plane Dusty Crophopper has achieved his dream of becoming a racer since the Wings Around the Globe race, but the wear and tear of fast flying has taken its toll on his gearbox. Dusty's mechanic Dottie warns Dusty to avoid the strain of racing, but he can't resist testing his limits, accidentally causing a fire when he almost crash lands. In the resulting blaze, the airport's firefighting capacity is deemed inadequate, and Dusty volunteers to become a firefighter to keep the airport open. While training at Piston Peak National Park under the guidance of helicopter Blade Ranger, Dusty is fitted with pontoons to land in water, but his failing gearbox poses an ongoing challenge, and he learns that Blade has his own painful history as well. Both are put to the test when Piston Peak's superintendent, Cad Spinner, shows himself to be self-serving, putting others at risk.

Cast: Dane Cook as Dusty Crophopper
Ed Harris as Blade Ranger
Julie Bowen as Lil' Dipper
Curtis Armstrong as Maru
John Michael Higgins as Cad
Hal Holbrook as Mayday
Wes Studi as Windlifter
Brad Garrett as Chug
Teri Hatcher as Dottie
Stacy Keach as Skipper
Cedric the Entertainer as Leadbottom
Danny Mann as Sparky
Barry Corbin as Ol' Jammer
Regina King as Dynamite
Anne Meara as Winnie
Jerry Stiller as Harvey
Fred Willard as Secretary of the Interior
Dale Dye as Cabbie
Matt Jones as Drip
Bryan Callen as Avalanche

Music Highlights: "Runway Romance" (Bobs Gannaway/Danny Jacob) performed by Brad Paisley, "Still I Fly" (Windy Wagner/Michael "Smidi" Smith/Spencer Lee) performed by Spencer Lee, "All In" (Brad Paisley) performed by Brad Paisley. Score by Mark Mancina.

Film Facts

• The RV couple Harvey and Winnie celebrate their 50th wedding anniversary in the film. They were voiced by real life spouses Jerry Stiller and Anne Meara, who celebrated their 60th wedding anniversary in 2014, the year of the film's release.
• Blade Ranger's television show, *CHoPs,* is a loving parody of the 1980s action drama series *CHiPs,* starring Erik Estrada. Estrada voiced Nick "Loop'n" Lopez, Ranger's former partner.
• In some countries the film was titled *Planes 2: Fire & Rescue* or just *Planes 2.*
• *Cars* cameos: Lightning McQueen in the *New Torque Times* newspaper (2:17), "Rust-eze Medicated Bumper Ointment" (2:42), DinoCo oil cans (8:44), Sarge and Mayday in a photo (16:22).
• An end credits interlude shows the fate of Cad Spinner (1:16:10).

Planet 51 (PG)

Theatrical release date: November 20, 2009
Country: Spain, United Kingdom, United States
Production Company: Ilion Animation Studios, HandMade Films, TriStar Pictures
Length: 91 minutes
Directed by: Jorge Blanco, co-directed by Javier Abad, Marcos Martínez
Screenplay by: Joe Stillman, original idea by Javier Abad, Jorge Blanco, Marcos Martínez, Ignacio Pérez Dolset

Synopsis: In the alien society of Glipforg, resembling a futuristic 1950s, aliens are fearful of the frightening "humaniacs" in their horror films. Junior assistant curator of the planetarium Lem is best friends with conspiracy theorist Skiff, and on the verge of asking out Neera, the beautiful alien next door, when they are interrupted by guitar-toting social protester Glar. The domestic tranquility is broken when a spaceman, Captain Charles T. Baker, arrives from the sky. Baker is as startled to see the aliens as they are to see him, and flees, but when he is trapped in the planetarium, begins to befriend Lem. Baker explains that his ship is set to depart in 74 hours, and Lem reluctantly begins to help him. Unfortunately, the alien military has set up fences around Baker's ship. Neera says the astronaut is peaceful, but in a moment of panic when Baker is almost discovered, Lem claims the astronaut wants to use mind control on the population, to Neera's disappointment. Baker is finally captured by the alien military, which plans to remove his brain at a secret base. Lem risks his own safety by going to rescue Baker, aided by Neera, Skiff, and Baker's dog-like Rover unit. They are able to get Baker to his ship, but are intercepted by General Grawl. Lem tells the General he doesn't have to fear the unknown, but the General is not persuaded. When part of the base collapses on the General, Baker's courage demonstrates his honorable nature.

Cast: Dwayne Johnson as Captain Charles T. Baker
Jessica Biel as Neera
Justin Long as Lem
Gary Oldman as General Grawl
Seann William Scott as Skiff
John Cleese as Professor Kipple
Freddie Benedict as Eckle
Alan Marriott as Glar
Mathew Horne as Soldier Vesklin
James Corden as Soldier Vernkot

Music Highlights: "Lollipop" (Dixson/Ross) performed by Sophie Green (orig. by Ronald & Ruby), "Long Tall Sally" (Blackwell/ Johnson/Penniman) performed by John Sloman (orig. by Little Richard), "Greased Lightnin'" (Jacobs/Tracy) performed by Lance Ellington (orig. from *Grease*), "Stick It to the Man" (Cawte) performed by Tom Cawte and The Electric Hearts, "Tried to Save the World" (Cawte) performed by Tom Cawte and The Electric Hearts. Music by James Brett.

Film Facts

• The film's original title was *Planet One*, but it was changed when another company used the name.
• References are made to *Alien* (47:20), *Star Wars* (48:50) and *Terminator* (49:10).
• LEM stands for Lunar Excursion Module, part of NASA's Apollo program.
• A brief mid-credits scene appears (1:26:07).

Pocahontas (G)

Theatrical release date: June 23, 1995
Production Company: Walt Disney Pictures, Walt Disney Feature Animation
Length: 81 minutes
Directed by: Mike Gabriel and Eric Goldberg
Written by: Carl Binder, Susannah Grant, Philip LaZebnik, story by Glen Keane, Joe Grant, Ralph Zondag, Burny Mattinson, Ed Gombert, Kaan Kalyon, Francis Glebas, Robert Gibbs, Bruce Morris, Todd Kurosawa, Duncan Marjoribanks, Chris Buck

Synopsis: When an English ship arrives in the New World seeking to establish a settlement and find gold, Captain John Smith happens upon Pocahontas, daughter of Chief Powhatan. Pocahontas is reluctant to marry the serious warrior Kocoum her father has in mind for her, seeking to find her own path in life. As tensions rise between the English and the Native tribe, Pocahontas and John Smith seek to make peace between their peoples.

Cast: Irene Bedard as Pocahontas
      Judy Kuhn as Pocahontas singing
Mel Gibson as John Smith
David Ogden Stiers as Ratcliffe/Wiggins
John Kassir as Meeko
Frank Welker as Flit
Danny Mann as Percy

Linda Hunt as Grandmother Willow
Russell Means as Powhatan
Christian Bale as Thomas
Billy Connolly as Ben
Joe Baker as Lon
Michelle St. John as Nakoma
James Apaumut Fall as Kocoum

Music Highlights: "Just Around the Riverbend" performed by Judy Kuhn, "Colors of the Wind" performed by Judy Kuhn, "The Virginia Company" performed by chorus, "Listen With Your Heart" performed by Linda Hunt and Bobbi Page, "Mine, Mine, Mine" performed by David Ogden Stiers, Mel Gibson and chorus, "Savages" performed by David Ogden Stiers, Jim Cummings, and chorus. All songs by Alan Menken and Stephen Schwartz. Score by Danny Troob.

Film Facts

• The 33rd of the Disney animated classics, and the 6th film of the Disney Renaissance, *Pocahontas* sought to create a love story inspired by historical figures. Mike Gabriel and Eric Goldberg were assigned to direct the film after Gabriel, who had recently co-directed *The Rescuers Down Under* (1990), proposed the film at Disney CEO Michael Eisner and Chairman Jeffrey Katzenberg's "Gong Show" pitch competition.
• Irene Bedard had appeared in the live-action Disney film *Squanto: A Warrior's Tale* (1994).
• Music for the film was provided by composer Alan Menken (in his fourth animated Disney film, after *The Little Mermaid, Beauty and the Beast,* and *Aladdin*), working with lyricist/composer Stephen Schwartz (*Godspell, Pippin, Wicked*).
• Stephen Schwartz and Alan Menken collaborated again on *The Hunchback of Notre Dame* (1996).
• Actor John Candy was originally slated to voice a comedic turkey, "Redfeather," but the character was eliminated from the film when Candy died in 1994.
• Additional appearances: Followed by *Pocahontas II: Journey to a New World* (1998).

Pocahontas II: Journey to a New World (G)

Home media release date: August 4, 1998
Production Company: Walt Disney Video Premiere, Walt Disney Television Animation, Walt Disney Animation Australia, Walt Disney Animation Canada, Walt Disney Animation Japan
Length: 72 minutes
Directed by: Bradley Raymond & Tom Ellery
Screenplay by: Allen Estrin and Cindy Marcus & Flip Kobler

Synopsis: Lying about their voyage to America, Governor Ratcliffe persuades King James I of England to have John Smith arrested, but Smith falls out of sight and is presumed dead. King James sends diplomat John Rolfe to America to investigate Ratcliffe's claim that the Native Americans are hostile. Pocahontas is appointed chief Powhatan's representative to return with Rolfe in an effort to avoid war, accompanied by the stern Uttamatomakkin and stowaways Flit and Meeko. Ratcliffe manipulates Pocahontas, who is arrested, but is freed with the aid of an old friend. Pocahontas has to choose not only between two men, but also between hiding to preserve her safety or taking the risk of standing up to help her people.

Cast: Irene Bedard as Pocahontas
    Judy Kuhn as Pocahontas (singing voice)
Jim Cummings as King James
Russell Means as Powhatan
Donal Gibson as John Smith

David Ogden Stiers at Ratcliffe
Finola Hughes as Queen Anne
Jean Stapleton as Mrs. Jenkins
Linda Hunt as Grandmother Willow
Billy Zane as John Rolfe

Music Highlights: "Where Do I Go From Here?" (Marty Manzer/Larry Grossman) performed by Judy Kuhn, "What a Day in London" (Manzer/Grossman) performed by Judy Kuhn and chorus, "Wait 'Til He Sees You" (Manzer/Grossman) performed by Jean Stapleton and Billy Zane, "Things Are Not What They Appear" (Manzer/Grossman) performed by David Ogden Stiers, Craig Copeland, Roger Freeland, Phil Proctor, "Between Two Worlds" (Stacy Widelitz/Blaise Tosti) performed by Judy Kuhn and Billy Zane. Score by Lennie Niehaus.

Film Facts

• John Rolfe's servant, Mrs. Jenkins, serves tea in a teapot that strongly resembles Mrs. Potts, the teapot from *Beauty and the Beast* (32:42).
• Donal Gibson is the younger brother of Mel Gibson, who voiced John Smith in the first film.
• One of a crowd of women around John Smith is dressed somewhat like Snow White (1:03:58).
• As with the original film, some of the criticism of the sequel centered on historical inaccuracies. Pocahontas and John Rolfe had married in Jamestown in April, 1614, and brought their young son with them to England, in contrast to the film's portrayal of Pocahontas as feeling torn between Rolfe and Smith to the end. Pocahontas and her bodyguard Uttamatomakkin were not imprisoned at the Tower of London. The film showed William Shakespeare in a brief scene, getting an idea for the play *Hamlet,* no less, when Shakespeare actually wrote *Hamlet* in 1603, and died in June, 1616, six weeks before Pocahontas arrived in England. Ratcliffe had also died prior to the events in the film.
• Additional appearances: Follows *Pocahontas* (1995).

Pokémon franchise

The Pokémon franchise began with a pair of video games for the Game Boy system, *Pokémon: Red* and *Pokémon: Green,* released in Japan in 1996 (later released internationally as *Pokémon: Red Version* and *Pokémon: Blue Version*), leading to a popular trading card game and an animated TV series that has endured for many years. Pokémon has become the most financially successful media franchise in the world. Several films have been produced related to the animated TV show.

Pokémon animated TV series

Season 1: Indigo League Apr 1, 1997-Jan 21, 1999 (82 episodes)
Season 2: Adventures in the Orange Islands Jan 28, 1999-Oct 7, 1999 (36 episodes)
Season 3: The Johto Journeys Oct 14, 1999-Jul 27, 2000 (41 episodes)
Season 4: Johto League Champions Aug 3, 2000-Aug 2, 2001 (52 episodes)
Season 5: Master Quest Aug 9, 2001-Nov 14, 2002 (65 episodes)
Season 6: Advanced Nov 21, 2002-Aug 28, 2003 (40 episodes)
Season 7: Advanced Challenge Sep 4, 2003-Sep 2, 2004 (52 episodes)
Season 8: Advanced Battle Sep 9, 2004-Sep 29, 2005 (54 episodes)
Season 9: Battle Frontier Oct 6, 2005-Sep 14, 2006 (47 episodes)
Season 10: Diamond and Pearl Sep 28, 2006-Oct 25, 2007 (52 episodes)
Season 11: Diamond and Pearl: Battle Dimension Nov 8, 2007-Dec 4, 2008 (52 episodes)
Season 12: Diamond and Pearl: Galactic Battles Dec 4, 2008-Dec 24, 2009 (53 episodes)
Season 13: Diamond and Pearl: Sinnoh League Victors Jan 7, 2010-Sep 9, 2010 (34 episodes)
Season 14: Black & White Sep 23, 2010-Sep 15, 2011 (50 episodes)
Season 15: Black & White: Rival Destinies Sep 22, 2011-Oct 4, 2012 (49 episodes)
Season 16-A: Black & White: Adventures in Unova Oct 11, 2012-Apr 18, 2013 (25 episodes)
Season 16-B: Black & White: Adventures in Unova and Beyond Apr 25, 2013-Sep 26, 2013 (20 ep.)
Season 17: XY Oct 17, 2013-Oct 30, 2014 (48 episodes)
Season 18: XY: Kalos Quest Nov 13, 2014-Oct 22, 2015 (45 episodes)
Season 19: XYZ Oct 29, 2015-Oct 27, 2016 (47 episodes)
Season 20: Sun & Moon Nov 17, 2016-Sep 21, 2017 (43 episodes)
Season 21: Sun & Moon: Ultra Adventures Oct 5, 2017-Oct 14, 2018 (49 episodes)
Season 22: Sun & Moon: Ultra Legends Oct 21, 2018-Nov 3, 2019 (54 episodes)
Season 23: Journeys Nov 17, 2019-Dec 4, 2020 (48 episodes)
Season 24: Master Journeys Dec 11, 2020-2021 (16 episodes)

Pokémon animated films

Pokémon The First Movie: Mewtwo Strikes Back (1998)

Pokémon The Movie 2000: The Power of One (1999)

Pokémon The Movie 3: Spell of the Unown (2000)

Pokémon 4Ever (2001)

Pokémon Heroes The Movie: Latios and Latias (2002)

Pokémon Jirachi: Wish Maker (2003)

Pokémon The Movie: Destiny Deoxys (2004)

Pokémon: Lucario and the Mystery of Mew (2005)

Pokémon Ranger and the Temple of the Sea (2006)

Pokémon: The Rise of Darkrai (2007)

Pokémon: Giratina and the Sky Warrior (2008)

Pokémon: Arceus and the Jewel of Life (2009)

Pokémon: Zoroark: Master of Illusions (2010)

Pokémon the Movie: White: Victini and Zekrom (2011)

Pokémon the Movie: Black: Victini and Reshiram (2011)

Pokémon the Movie: Kyurem vs. the Sword of Justice (2012)

Pokémon the Movie: Genesect and the Legend Awakened (2013)

Pokémon the Movie: Diancie and the Cocoon of Destruction (2014)

Pokémon the Movie: Hoopa and the Clash of Ages (2015)

Pokémon the Movie: Volcanion and the Mechanical Marvel (2016)

Pokémon the Movie: I Choose You! (2017)

Pokémon the Movie: The Power of Us (2018)

Pokémon: Mewtwo Strikes Back: Evolution (2019)

Pokémon: Secrets of the Jungle (2020)

Live-Action/Animation Film

Pokémon: Detective Pikachu (2019)

Pokémon The First Movie: Mewtwo Strikes Back (G)

Theatrical release date: July 18, 1998 (Japan), November 10, 1999 (US)
Country: Japan   Japanese title: *Gekijōban Poketto Monsutā: Myūtsū no Gyakushū*
Production Company: Oriental Light and Magic (OLM), Nintendo, Warner Bros.
Length: 75 minutes (96 minutes with "Picachu's Winter Vacation")
Directed by: Kunihiko Yuyama
Screenplay by: Takeshi Shudo

Synopsis: Scientists have cloned and enhanced the Pokémon Mew, dubbed Mewtwo, giving it powerful psychic abilities. When Mewtwo's creator tries to control him, Mewtwo rebels, escaping with a plan to conquer the world. Elsewhere, Ash, Brock and Misty receive an invitation to a special Pokémon trainers gathering at a palace. When they arrive at New Island, Mewtwo reveals he has been cloning Pokémon and making them more powerful. As Ash and the other Pokémon trainers marshal their Pokémon to oppose Mewtwo, the Pokémon battle their doubles. Seeing the Pokémon's loyalty, Mewtwo realizes that it's what you do with the gift of life that determines who you are. Ash, Misty and Brock are released from the island, but Team Rocket is not so lucky.

Cast:

Role	English	Japanese
Ash Ketchum/Satoshi	Veronica Taylor	Rika Matsumoto
Pikachu	Ikue Ōtani	Ikue Ōtani
Misty/Kasumi	Rachael Lillis	Mayumi Iizuka
Brock/Takeshi	Eric Stuart	Yūji Ueda
Narrator	Rodger Parsons	Unshō Ishizuka
Togepi	Satomi Kōrogi	Satomi Kōrogi
Jessie/Musashi	Rachael Lillis	Megumi Hayashibara
James/Kojirō	Eric Stuart	Shinichiro Miki
Meowth/Nyāsu	Maddie Blaustein	Inuko Inuyama

Music Highlights: "Pokemon Theme" (Siegler/Loeffler) ft. Billy Crawford, "Vacation" (Fitzpatrick/ Deutsch) performed by Vitamin C, "Catch Me If You Can" (Trullinger/Steckler) performed by Angela, "Brother My Brother" (Loeffler/Schuckett/Emosia) performed by Blessid Union of Souls. End Credits: "We're a Miracle" (Chapman/Zippel/Aguilera) performed by Christina Aguilera, "Free Up Your Mind" (Lawrence/Chisolm/Bunton) performed by Baby Spice, "If Only Tears Could Bring You Back" (Pulice/Desalvo) performed by Midnight Sons, "Don't Say You Love Me" (Raven/Larsen/ Zizzo/Bralower) performed by M2M. Music by Shinji Miyazaki, Hirokazu Tanaka.

Film Facts

- The Complete Version adds the "Origin of Mewtwo" prologue and "Picachu's Winter Vacation."
- Burger King offered six 23 karat gold Pokémon cards, each in a plastic Poké Ball.
- The English adaptation of the film made Mewtwo more of a villain than in the original film.
- Ash, Misty, and Brock are known as Satoshi, Kasumi, and Takeshi in Japan.
- Mewtwo returned in the film *Pokémon: Mewtwo Strikes Back: Evolution* (2019).

252

The Polar Express (G)

Theatrical release date: November 10, 2004
Production Company: Castle Rock Ent., Shangri-La Ent., Playtone, ImageMovers, Golden Mean
Length: 100 minutes
Directed by: Robert Zemeckis
Screenplay by: Robert Zemeckis & William Broyles Jr., based on the book by Chris Van Allsburg

Synopsis: On Christmas Eve, a boy is astounded to find a train, the Polar Express, pull to a stop in front of his house. The conductor asks if he's coming to the North Pole. Though the boy is unsure, he gets on the train, finding a kind, brave girl and a "know-it-all" among the passengers, and uses the emergency stop to help a lonely boy, Billy, get on the train. When the girl forgets her ticket, the boy tries to get it to her, but it sips out of his grasp. The conductor takes the girl away, and the boy fears she will be thrown off the train. He finds her ticket and follows, making his way along the top of the train, where he meets a mysterious hobo. He finally catches up to the girl, finding her in the engine car. After a hair-raising episode over a frozen lake, they finally arrive at the North Pole, and learn that one of the children on the train will receive the first gift of Christmas. When Billy stays back on the train, believing that Christmas never works out for him, the boy and girl persuade him to go with them, but before they can disembark, the train car rolls away, sending them behind the scenes into Santa's workshop, ending up in a gigantic bag of gifts. They are rescued in time to see Santa Claus, but the boy realizes he cannot hear the bells on Santa's sleigh. When a bell falls off the sleigh, he wills himself to believe, and can finally hear the bell. The children from the train are addressed by Santa, and the boy receives the first gift of Christmas, asking for the bell from the sleigh. As they depart, the children's tickets are punched with words: "depend" for Billy, "lead" for the girl," and "believe" for the boy.

Cast: Tom Hanks as Hero Boy/Father/Conductor/ Hobo/Scrooge/Santa Claus/Narrator
Leslie Zemeckis as Mother
Eddie Deezen as Know-It-All

Nona Gaye as Hero Girl
Jimmy Bennett as Billy - Lonely Boy
Brendan King as Pastry Chef
Andy Pellick as Pastry Chef

Music Highlights: "The Polar Express" (Ballard/Silvestri), "Hot Chocolate" (Ballard/Silvestri) performed by Tom Hanks, "When Christmas Comes to Town" (Ballard/Silvestri) performed by Matt Hall/Meagan Moore, "Spirit of the Season" (Ballard/Silvestri), "Santa Claus is Comin' to Town" (Coots/Gillespie) performed by cast/Frank Sinatra, "Rockin' on Top of the World" (Ballard/Silvestri) performed by Steven Tyler. End credits: "Believe" (Ballard/Silvestri) performed by Josh Groban. Music by Alan Silvestri.

Film Facts

- The buildings at the center of the city are based on the Pullman Car Company factory in Chicago.
- An initial condition for granting the rights for the film was that it not be animated.
- *The Polar Express* author Chris Van Alsburg also wrote the books *Jumanji* and *Zathura*.

Ponyo (G)

Theatrical release date: July 19, 2008 (Japan), August 14, 2009 (US)
Country: Japan   Japanese title: *Gake No Ue No Ponyo* (lit. "Ponyo on the Cliff")
Production Company: Studio Ghibli
Length: 101 minutes
Directed by: Hayao Miyazaki
Screenplay by: Hayao Miyazaki

Synopsis: Brunhilde, the small red-haired daughter of Fujimoto, a powerful wizard who lives underwater, goes for a ride on a jellyfish and ends up stuck in a jar. A young boy, Sōsuke, finds her and frees her from the jar, carrying her off before Fujimoto's watery minions can recover her. Sōsuke names her Ponyo and takes her to his school, next door to his mother's work at a senior center. To Sōsuke's surprise, Ponyo begins to speak, telling Sōsuke she loves him, just before Fujimoto captures her back. Fujimoto explains he was once human, but left to serve the Earth. Ponyo tells him she wants to be human and loves Sōsuke, willing herself to have legs, but Fujimoto wishes for her to remain innocent forever, using his powers to shrink her down. Her sisters free her, and she uses Fujimoto's magic to turn herself human. The magic she unleashes throws the universe out of balance, causing a tsunami. Fujimoto confesses to Ponyo's mother, Gran Mamare, what has happened, and she explains that Ponyo became a human because of her love for Sōsuke. Ponyo chooses to live as a human, and Gran Mamare restores balance to the universe.

Cast:

Role	English	Japanese
Ponyo	Noah Cyrus	Yuria Nara
Sōsuke	Frankie Jonas	Hiroki Doi
Lisa (Sōsuke's mother)	Tina Fey	Tomoko Yamaguchi
Kōichi (Sōsuke's father)	Matt Damon	Kazushige Nagashima
Gran Mamare	Cate Blanchett	Yūki Amami
Fujimoto	Liam Neeson	George Tokoro
Ponyo's sisters	Akiko Yano	Akiko Yano
Toki	Lily Tomlin	Kazuko Yoshiyuki
Yoshie	Betty White	Tomoko Naraoka

Music Highlights: "Gake no ue no Ponyo" (Kondô/Miyazaki/Hisaishi) performed by Takaaki Fujioka, Naoya Fujimaki & Nozomi Ohashi, "Ponyo on the Cliff by the Sea" (Kondô/Miyazaki/Hisaishi) performed by Noah Cyrus & Frankie Jonas, "Umi No Okâsan" (Miyazaki/Hisaishi) performed by Masako Hayashi. Music by Joe Hisaishi.

Film Facts

• Ponyo is inspired by Brunhilde from Richard Wagner's opera cycle *Der Ring des Nibelungen*.
• Sōsuke is inspired by Natsume Sōseki's novel *The Gate* (*Mon*), with a character of the same name.
• The film won the "Animation of the Year" Japan Academy Film Prize.

Porco Rosso (PG)

Theatrical release date: July 18, 1992 (Japan), December 16, 1994 (US)
Country: Japan   **Japanese title**: *Kurenai no Buta*
Production Company: Studio Ghibli
Length: 94 minutes
Directed by: Hayao Miyazaki
Written by: Hayao Miyazaki

Synopsis: In 1929 Europe, the humanoid pig bounty hunter Porco Rosso is called in to defend a ship carrying a group of school girls from the Mamma Aiuto Gang air pirates. After thwarting the pirates, Rosso meets the American pilot Donald Curtis at the Hotel Adriano, run by the singer Madame Gina. It is revealed that Rosso used to be human, and is under a curse. A group of air pirates, the Pirate Federation, continues to attack ships, and threatens Rosso. Catching Rosso when he is having engine trouble, Curtis shoots down Rosso's plane. Undeterred, Rosso takes the remains of his plane to be fixed by Mr. Piccolo in Italy, who proposes that his 17-year-old granddaughter Fio fix Rosso's plane. Rosso is reluctant, but is persuaded by Fio's skill. Fio accompanies Rosso after he leaves, and when a gang of air pirates threatens to destroy Porco's plane and beat him up, Fio deftly compliments the pirates, getting them to agree to leave the plane she built alone, and to let Porco have a rematch with Curtis. She also foolishly bets Curtis: if Rosso wins, Curtis pays his bills, but if Curtis wins, Fio will marry him. Rosso shows up to face Curtis, winning the match and escaping just before the arrival of the Italian Air Force.

Cast:

Role	English	Japanese
Porco Rosso	Michael Keaton	Shūichirou Moriyama
Donald Curtis	Cary Elwes	Akio Ōtsuka
Fio Piccolo	Kimberly Williams-Paisley	Akemi Okamura
Gina	Susan Egan	Tokiko Kato
Grandpa Piccolo	David Ogden Stiers	Sanshi Katsura
Mamma Aiuto Boss	Brad Garrett	Tsunehiko Kamijou
Mamma Aiuto Gang	Bill Fagerbakke	Reizou Nomoto
Mamma Aiuto Gang	Kevin Michael Richardson	Osamu Saka
Mamma Aiuto Gang	Frank Welker	Yuu Shimaka

Music Highlights: "Sakuranbo no Minoru Koro (Le Temps des Cerises)" (Jean-Baptiste Clément/ Antoine Renard) performed by Tokiko Katô. "Le Temps des Cerises (Gina's Song)" by Susan Egan, "Toki ni wa Mukashi no Hanashi Wo" (Katô) performed by Tokiko Katô. Music by Joe Hisaishi.

Film Facts

- The story was based on Hayao Miyazaki's 1989 manga *Hikōtei Jidai* (*The Age of the Flying Boat*).
- The project was begun as a much shorter in-flight film to be shown on Japan Airlines.
- Grandmother Piccolo resembles Sophie (as an old woman) from *Howl's Moving Castle* (2004).

The Prince of Egypt (PG)

Theatrical release date: December 18, 1998
Production Company: DreamWorks Animation
Length: 109 minutes
Directed by: Brenda Chapman, Steve Hickner, Simon Wells
Written by: Philip LaZebnik

Synopsis: When the ancient Egyptian Pharaoh Seti orders that all newborn Hebrew boys be killed, Moses' mother Yocheved sends him down the Nile in a basket, and sees him retrieved at the Pharaoh's palace, where he is raised as a brother to Rameses. While following Tzipporah, a slave who has run away from the palace, Moses finds his brother and sister Aaron and Miriam, who call him brother, to his confusion. He learns the truth from his father, as well as learning about the earlier infanticide. Moses flees into the desert, and helps three girls he finds being harassed by two brigands at an oasis. The girls are the younger sister of Tzipporah and daughters of Jethro, the high priest of Midian, who honors Moses for his kindness. In time, Moses marries Tzipporah, and while working as a shepherd, finds a burning bush and hears the voice of God, telling him that he must lead the Hebrews out of Egypt to freedom. Moses returns to see Rameses, now Pharaoh, and asks that he free the Hebrews, but many challenges lie ahead of him, requiring that he rely on his faith in God.

Cast: Val Kilmer as Moses/God
Ralph Fiennes as Rameses
Michelle Pfeiffer as Tzipporah
Sandra Bullock as Miriam
Jeff Goldblum as Aaron
Danny Glover as Jethro
Patrick Stewart as Seti

Helen Mirren as The Queen
Steve Martin as Hotep
Martin Short as Huy
Bobby Motown as Rameses Son
Eden Riegel as Young Miriam
Ofra Haza as Yocheved

Music Highlights: "Deliver Us" (Schwartz) performed by Ofra Haza and Eden Riegel, "River Lullaby" (Schwartz) performed by Ofra Haza, "River Lullaby (Reprise)" (Schwartz) performed by Brenda Chapman, "All I Ever Wanted" (Schwartz) performed by Amick Byram, "Queen's Reprise" (Schwartz) performed by Linda Dee Shayne, "Through Heaven's Eyes" (Schwartz) performed by Brian Stokes Mitchell, "Playing with the Big Boys" (Schwartz) performed by Steve Martin and Martin Short, "The Plagues" (Schwartz) performed by Ralph Fiennes and Amick Byram, "When You Believe" (Schwartz) performed by Michelle Pfeiffer and Sally Dworsky. End credits: "When You Believe" (Schwartz/Babyface) performed by Whitney Houston and Mariah Carey, "I Will Get There" (Warren) performed by Boyz II Men. Score by Hans Zimmer.

Film Facts

• Stephen Schwartz is known for the stage musicals *Godspell* (1971), *Pippin* (1972), and *Wicked* (2003), and films *Pocahontas* (1995), *The Hunchback of Notre Dame* (1996), and *Enchanted* (2007).
• The opening of the film notes that the story is based on the book of Exodus from the Bible.
• The film was banned in Egypt and a handful of other countries.

The Princess and the Frog (G)

Theatrical release date: December 11, 2009
Production Company: Walt Disney Pictures, Walt Disney Animation Studios
Length: 97 minutes
Directed by: John Musker, Ron Clements
Screenplay by: Ron Clements & John Musker and Rob Edwards, story by Ron Clements & John Musker and Greg Erb & Jason Oremland, story inspired in part by *The Frog Princess* by E.D. Baker

---

Synopsis: After Prince Naveen is turned into a frog through voodoo, he persuades young waitress Tiana to kiss him to break the curse, but she turns into a frog herself. The pair seek help from voodoo expert Mama Odie, but in the end find there is more than one transformation at work.

Cast: Anika Noni Rose as Tiana
Bruno Campos as Prince Naveen
Keith David as Dr. Facilier
Michael-Leon Wooley as Louis
Jennifer Cody as Charlotte
Jim Cummings as Ray
Peter Bartlett as Lawrence
Jenifer Lewis as Mama Odie
Oprah Winfrey as Eudora
Terrence Howard as James
John Goodman as "Big Daddy" La Bouff
Elizabeth Dampier as Young Tiana
Breanna Brooks as Young Charlotte
Ritchie Montgomery as Reggie
Don Hall as Darnell
Paul Briggs as Two Fingers
Jerry Kernion as Mr. Henry Fenner
Corey Burton as Mr. Harvey Fenner
Michael Colyar as Buford
Emeril Lagasse as Marlon the Gator

Music Highlights: "Down in New Orleans" (Newman) performed by Dr. John, "Almost There" (Newman) performed by Anika Noni Rose, "Friends on the Other Side" (Newman) performed by Keith David, "When We're Human" (Newman) performed by Michael-Leon Wooley, Bruno Campos, Anika Noni Rose, and Terence Blanchard, "Gonna Take You There" (Newman) and "Ma Belle Evangeline" (Newman) performed by Jim Cummings, "Dig a Little Deeper" (Newman) performed by Jenifer Lewis, "Never Knew I Needed" (Ne-Yo) performed by Ne-Yo. Score by Randy Newman.

Film Facts

• The 49th of the Disney animated classics, *The Princess and the Frog* was developed and directed by John Musker and Ron Clements, the team behind *The Great Mouse Detective* (1986), *The Little Mermaid* (1989), *Aladdin* (1992), *Hercules* (1997), *Treasure Planet* (2002), and later *Moana* (2016). The story was based on the children's novel *The Frog Princess* by E.D. Baker. Baker's novel was based on the Brothers Grimm fairy tale "The Frog Prince."

• Tiana appeared in the series *Sophia the First,* in the episode "Winter's Gift" (season 2, episode 20), and made a cameo in *Ralph Breaks the Internet* (2018). The live-action series *Once Upon a Time* included Tiana, Prince Naveen, Dr. Facilier, and Eudora in its 7th season.

• Several changes were made: the title *The Frog Princess* was seen as a slur toward the French, the heroine was to be named Maddy (too close to "mammy"), Maddy worked as a chambermaid (a position of servitude), and her love interest was not black, so the title became *The Princess and the Frog,* Maddy became Tiana, Tiana worked as waitress, and her love interest became Prince Naveen.

The Proud Family Movie (TV-G)

Broadcast date: August 19, 2005
Production Company: Walt Disney Television Animation, Hyperion Pictures, Jambalaya Studio
Length: 92 minutes
Directed by: Bruce W. Smith
Screenplay by: Ralph Farquhar, Calvin Brown Jr., John Patrick White, Stiles White

---

Synopsis: The scheming Dr. Carver works to turn a common peanut into a G-Nome warrior, so he can take over the world. While making a presentation at WASTE, Penny Proud's father, Oscar, bumps into Dr. Carver, who sees that Oscar's dipping sauce multiplies peanuts. Meanwhile, Penny is celebrating her 16th birthday, and is thrilled to be chosen for Fifteen Cent's dance group, the Spare Change dancers. When Oscar sees her kissing Fifteen Cent, she is grounded. Scheming to get his formula, Dr. Carver tells Oscar he's won a family vacation to Legoom Island. Penny is grumpy over not being able to join the Spare Change dancers, but the rest of the family enjoys the island. Dr. Carver charms Oscar, seeking the formula, but a peanut in the jungle warns Oscar that the doctor is trying to take over the world. When Oscar doesn't hand over the formula, Dr. Carver begins a series of tortures: the tickle chair, electric eels, and making Oscar watch the children's show "Thingy," finally unleashing clones of the family. Penny escapes the island to head back home, and is joined by the clone family, while the clone of Penny joins the real Proud Family. The family is startled to run across a second Dr. Carver on the island, learning that they've been dealing with the real Dr. Carver's clone. Oscar's recipe is hidden in Penny's necklace, and it's up to her and her friends to stop the clone doctor's evil scheme.

Cast: Kyla Pratt as Penny Proud
Tommy Davidson as Oscar Proud
Paula Jai Parker as Trudy Parker-Proud
Jo Marie Payton as Suga Mama
Orlando Brown as Sticky Webb
Soleil Moon Frye as Zoey
Alisa Reyes as LaCienega Boulevardez

Karen Malina White as Dijonay Jones
Omarion as Fifteen Cent
Arsenio Hall as Dr. Carver/Bobby Proud
Tara Strong as Bebe Proud/Cece Proud/Cashew
Jeremy Suarez as Wally
Carlos Alazraqui as Puff/Board Member
Alvaro Guttierez as Papi Boulevardez

Music Highlights: "Blowin' Up the Spot" (Anderson/John) performed by Omarion, "Right Here" (Fitzpatrick/Corante/Johnson) performed by Jhené Aiko, "Boom Boom Boom" (Petersen/Quinn) performed by Arsenio Hall, "If I Ruled the World" (Anderson) performed by A. Hall, "Looking for the Perfect Beat" (Baker/Robie/Aasim) performed by Afrika Bambaataa & Soulsonic Force, "Together Makes it Better" (Houston) performed by Pratt, Reyes, White, and Frye. Score by Frank Fitzpatrick.

Film Facts

• The film debuted as a Disney Channel Original Movie on August 19, 2005, and served as a finale to *The Proud Family* animated series, broadcast September 15, 2001 - August 19, 2005.
• The DVD offers an extended version with an alternate ending.

Puss in Boots (PG)

Theatrical release date: October 28, 2011
Production Company: DreamWorks Animation
Length: 90 minutes
Directed by: Chris Miller
Screenplay by: Tom Wheeler, story by Brian Lynch, Will Davies and Tom Wheeler

> **Synopsis**: Puss in Boots, the swashbuckling lover, fighter, and outlaw, learns that the notorious Jack and Jill have magic beans, and sets out to steal them, to pay an old debt. He is interrupted by the skilled fighter Kitty Softpaws, and is shocked to find her working with his "brother" from an orphanage, Humpty Alexander Dumpty. Puss and Humpty grew up as thieves, stealing to find the fabled magic beans, but with no success. One day Puss decided to turn away from theft, but Humpty tricked him into participating in a bank robbery, turning him into an outlaw. Puss reluctantly agrees to partner with Humpty once more, to repay the stolen money and regain his honor. They obtain the beans and grow a beanstalk, taking a gosling that lays golden eggs, only to find that a huge creature is chasing them. They escape down the beanstalk, but Puss soon faces a betrayal that dashes his hopes of making amends. Some unexpected help gives Puss a chance to save his town and clear his name.

Cast: Antonio Banderas as Puss in Boots
Salma Hayek as Kitty Softpaws
Zach Galifianakis as Humpty Alexander Dumpty
Billy Bob Thornton as Jack
Amy Sedaris as Jill
Constance Marie as Imelda
Guillermo del Toro as Moustache Man/Comandante

Mike Mitchell as Andy Beanstalk
Rich B. Dietl as Bounty Hunter
Ryan Crego as Luis
Tom Wheeler as Bartender/Mean Boy/
    Wagon Driver/Hotel Owner/Rodrigo
Conrad Vernon as Raoul/Soldier

Music Highlights: "Venimos Cantando" (Felix Vizcaino/Federico Alonso Pernia/Francisco Garcia Tejero) performed by Los Choqueros, "Te Quiero Conocer" (Miguel Angel Ruiz) performed by Las Ondas Marteles, "Hanuman" (Rodrigo Pineda Sanchez/Gabriela Quintero Lopez) performed by Rodrigo y Gabriela, "Diablo Rojo" (Rodrigo Pineda Sanchez/Gabriela Quintero Lopez) performed by Rodrigo y Gabriela, "Americano" (Stefani Germanotta/Brian Lee/Fernando Garibay/DJ White Shadow) performed by Lady Gaga. Music by Henry Jackman, featuring Rodrigo y Gabriela.

Film Facts

• The film was originally to be direct-to-video, titled *Puss in Boots: The Story of an Ogre Killer.*
• The world premiere took place on October 16, 2011, on the Royal Caribbean International cruise ship "Allure of the Seas," when it was docked in Fort Lauderdale, Florida.
• The film was nominated for the "Best Animated Feature" Academy Award and Golden Globe.
• The DVD offers an "Easter Egg": in the Bonus Features menu, press right at "Deleted Scenes."
• Additional appearances: *Shrek 2* (2004), *Shrek the Third* (2007), *Shrek Forever After* (2010), "Scared Shrekless" short (2010), "The Three Diablos" short (2012), "Shrek the Halls" short (2007), *The Adventures of Puss in Boots* TV series (2015–2018).

Quest for Camelot (G)

Theatrical release date: May 15, 1998
Production Company: Warner Bros. Feature Animation
Length: 86 minutes
Directed by: Frederik Du Chau
Screenplay by: Kirk De Micco and William Schifrin and Jacqueline Feather & David Seidler, based on the novel *The King's Damosel* by Vera Chapman

---

Synopsis: Sir Lionel, the bravest of King Arthur's knights, is felled while defending the king from an attack by the power-mad Ruber, who seeks to overthrow the kingdom, leaving Lionel's wife Juliana and daughter Kayley heartbroken. Years later, King Arthur's sword Excalibur is stolen by Ruber's griffin, but the sword is lost in the Forbidden Forest. Kayley races to the forest to retrieve the sword, only to meet Ruber's minions. She is saved by the blind hermit Garrett and his falcon Ayden. They befriend the two-headed dragon Devon/Cornwall, which helps them escape Ruber. Garrett explains that he was a stable boy in Camelot, who was blinded in an accident, after which Kayley's father was training him to be a knight. Relentlessly pursued by Ruber, Kayley and Garrett finally find Excalibur, but Garrett is reluctant to return. Kayley is caught by Ruber, who seizes Excalibur, and forces Juliana to get him into Camelot. When Devon and Cornwall explain what's happened, Garrett returns, and he and Kayley face Ruber together.

Cast: Jessalyn Gilsig as Kayley
Cary Elwes as Garrett
Gary Oldman as Ruber
Eric Idle as Devon
Don Rickles as Cornwall
Jane Seymour as Juliana

Pierce Brosnan as King Arthur
Bronson Pinchot as Griffin
Jaleel White as Bladebeak
Gabriel Byrne as Lionel
Sir John Gielgud as Merlin
Frank Welker as Ayden

Music Highlights: "United We Stand" (Carole Bayer Sager/David Foster) performed by Steve Perry, "On My Father's Wings" (Sager/Foster) performed by Andrea Corr, "Ruber" (Sager/Foster) performed by Gary Oldman, "The Prayer" (Sager/Foster) performed by Céline Dion, "I Stand All Alone" (Sager/Foster) performed by Bryan White, "If I Didn't Have You" (Sager/Foster) performed by Eric Idle and Don Rickles, "Looking Through Your Eyes" (Sager/Foster) performed by Andrea Corr and Bryan White. End credits: "Looking Through Your Eyes" (Sager/Foster) performed by LeAnn Rimes, "I Stand Alone" (Sager/Foster/Perry) performed by Steve Perry, "The Prayer/La Preghiera" (Sager/Foster, trans. Renis/Testa) performed by Andrea Bocelli. Score by Patrick Doyle.

Film Facts

• Singing voices were provided by Andrea Corr as Kayley, Bryan White as Garrett, Céline Dion as Juliana, and Steve Perry as King Arthur.
• "If I Didn't Have You" cameos (39:12): Simba, Godzilla, Red Hot Riding Hood, Sonny & Cher, Elvis.
• Vera Chapman's novel *The King's Damosel* (1976) is the second book of *The Three Damosels* trilogy, in between *The Green Knight* (1975) and *King Arthur's Daughter* (1976).

Rango (PG)

Theatrical release date: March 4, 2011
Production Company: Paramount Pictures, Nickelodeon Movies, Blind Wink Productions
Length: 107 minutes
Directed by: Gore Verbinski
Written by: John Logan, story by John Logan, Gore Verbinski, and James Ward Byrkit

---

Synopsis: The desert lizard Lars, fond of acting with a cast of inanimate objects, is forced to relocate when a car destroys his puddle oasis. The wise armadillo Roadkill sends him to the town of Dirt, where he meets the tough-as-nails lizard lady rancher Beans, prone to episodes of catatonia, who takes him into town. Lars's temptation to act gets the better of him in a local saloon, and he poses as the dangerous desperado Rango. A visit by Bad Bill and his gang soon leads to a showdown between Rango and Bill. The face off is interrupted the arrival of the deadly hawk, which Rango kills by accident, proving his reputation in the eyes of the town. The mayor appoints Rango sheriff, in charge of solving the town's water crisis, as a weekly flow of water from a local spigot has mysteriously ceased. Rango forms a posse to investigate the drought, and as he begins to suspect the mayor is behind things, the mayor sends the dreaded Rattlesnake Jake to the town. When Lars is shown not to be who he said he was, he has to decide who he really wants to be.

Cast: Johnny Depp as Rango/Lars
Isla Fisher as Beans
Abigail Breslin as Priscilla
Ned Beatty as Mayor
Alfred Molina as Roadkill
Bill Nighy as Rattlesnake Jake
Stephen Root as Doc/Merrimack/
      Mr. Snuggles
Harry Dean Stanton as Balthazar

Timothy Olyphant as Spirit of the West
Ray Winstone as Bad Bill
Ian Abercrombie as Ambrose
Gil Birmingham as Wounded Bird
James Ward Byrkit as Waffles/Gordy/
      Papa Joad/Cousin Murt/Curlie/
      Knife Attacker/Rodent Kid
Claudia Black as Angelique
Blake Clark as Buford

Music Highlights: "Rango" (John Thum/David Thum) performed by Mariachi Sol de Mexico de Jose Hernandez and Mariachi Reyna de Los Angeles, "Rango Theme Song" (John Thum/David Thum) performed by Los Lobos. Music by Hans Zimmer.

Film Facts

• The film won the Academy Award for "Best Animated Feature."
• *Rango* was also the name of a short-lived 1967 comedy western starring Tim Conway.
• An owl seems to holds the "Dead Man's Hand" of black aces and black eights (21:38), said to be the hand held by lawman and gunfighter "Wild Bill" Hickok when he was gunned down.
• Director Gore Verbinski and actors Johnny Depp and Bill Nighy also worked together on *Pirates of the Caribbean: Dead Man's Chest* (2006) and *Pirates of the Caribbean: At World's End* (2007).

Ratatouille (G)

Theatrical release date: June 29, 2007
Production Company: Pixar Animation Studios, Walt Disney Pictures
Length: 111 minutes
Directed by: Brad Bird
Written by: Brad Bird, original story by Jan Pinkava, Jim Capobianco, Brad Bird

---

Synopsis: Remy, a common French rat with an uncommon appreciation for fine cuisine, is guided by visions of Gusteau, a great chef whose motto is "Anyone can cook." Remy ends up at a gourmet restaurant and assists the hapless young Linguini, secretly helping him pose as an up-and-coming chef. The surly head chef, Skinner, is suspicious of Linguini, but allows him to cook under the supervision of the tough but proficient chef Colette. Remy and Linguini's ultimate test comes when the impossible-to-please critic Anton Ego arrives, ready to cut Linguini down to size. Everyone's faith is tested as the truth is revealed.

Cast: Patton Oswalt as Remy
Iam Holm as Skinner
Lou Romano as Linguini
Brain Dennehy as Django
Peter Sohn as Emile
Peter O'Toole as Anton Ego
Brad Garrett as Gusteau
Janeane Garofalo as Colette
Will Arnett as Horst

Julius Callahan as Lalo & Francois
James Remar as Larousse
John Ratzenberger as Mustafa
Teddy Newton as Lawyer (Talon Labarthe)
Tony Fucile as Pompidou/Health Inspector
Jake Steinfeld as Git (Lab Rat)
Brad Bird as Ambrister Minion
Stephane Roux as TV Narrator

Music Highlights: "Le Festin" (Michael Giacchino) performed by Camille. Score by Michael Giacchino.

Film Facts

• *Ratatouille* was the 8th Pixar film, and in the eyes of many, the studio's most original title to date. Though the final version of the film was directed by Brad Bird (*The Incredibles*), Ratatouille was originally conceived by Jan Pinkava ("Geri's Game" short), who was expected to direct the film. Bob Peterson was added as a co-director before departing to work on *Up,* and Pinkava was ultimately replaced by Bird, who re-wrote the screenplay.
• A large rat habitat was built at Pixar so the animators could study the appearance and movements of rats, and Debbie Ducommun, an expert on rats, was brought on as a consultant.
• Pizza Planet Truck sighting: In the background on the bridge over the Seine river as chef Skinner pursues Remy on a scooter (1:14:14).
• As Remy is climbing through the walls, the dog Dug, from *Up* (2009), barks at him (16:40).
• Bomb Voyage from *The Incredibles* (2004) is featured as a mime on the Paris streets (1:16:29).
• Disneyland Paris features a ride called "Ratatouille: L'Aventure Totalement Toquée de Rémy," while Walt Disney World Resort's Epcot in Florida offers "Remy's Ratatouille Adventure."
• Additional appearances: "Your Friend the Rat" short (2007), included on the DVD/Blu-ray.

Raya and the Last Dragon (PG)

Theatrical/streaming release date: March 5, 2021
Production Company: Walt Disney Pictures, Walt Disney Animation Studios
Length: 107 minutes
Directed by: Don Hall, Carlos López Estrada, co-directed by Paul Briggs, John Ripa
Screenplay by: Qui Nguyen, Adele Lim, story by Paul Briggs, Don Hall, Adele Lim, Carlos López Estrada, Kiel Murray, Qui Nguyen, John Ripa, Dean Wellins

Synopsis: The land of Kumandra was harmonious 500 years ago, living in peace with benevolent dragons, until a plague called the Druun swept the land, turning people and dragons to stone. Sisu, the last dragon, used a gem with the dragons' concentrated magic to defeat the plague, stopping the Druun, but then disappeared from the physical world. Raya, a girl from the tribe of Heart, has trained in swordplay and martial arts, preparing to guard the gem. Her father, Chief Benja, guards the Dragon Gem, which holds the spirit of Sisu, and Raya proudly becomes a Guardian of the Dragon Gem. Hoping to reunite the people of Kumandra, Chief Benja invites delegations from the tribes of Tail, Talon, Spine, and Fang to share a meal. Raya is friendly with Namaari, the princess of Fang, who betrays her, and tries to steal the gem. The leaders of all the tribes arrive, and in their struggle, the gem is broken, freeing the Druun, which once again begin turning people to stone. The fragments of the gem are seized by tribes, and Chief Benja asks Raya to reconstruct the Dragon Gem, just before he is turned to stone himself. Six years later, Raya and her giant rolling pillbug Tuk Tuk are able to bring Sisu back, and they begin seeking the pieces of the Gem, joined by restauranteur Boun and thief Little Noi. Unfortunately, Namaari is dead set on stopping them. In a world that is broken in many ways, Sisu helps Raya begin learning to trust again.

Cast: Kelly Marie Tran as Raya
Awkwafina as Sisu
Izaac Wang as Boun
Gemma Chan as Namaari
Daniel Dae Kim as Benja
Benedict Wong as Tong

Jona Xiao as Young Namaari
Sandra Oh as Virana
Thalia Tran as Little Noi
Lucille Soong as Dang Hu
Alan Tudyk as Tuk Tuk
Jon Park as Chai

Music Highlights: "Lead the Way" (Aiko) performed by Jhené Aiko. Score by James Newton Howard.

Film Facts

• The 59th of the Disney Animated Classics, *Raya and the Last Dragon* featured the first Southeast Asian Disney Princess. The film's fictional Kumandra was inspired by countries such as Thailand, Laos, Vietnam, and the Philippines.
• The original working title for the film was *Dragon Empire*.
• The Philippines version included Disney's first Filipino song, "Gabay" by KZ Tandingan.
• In theaters the film was shown with the short "Us Again."

The Red Turtle (PG)

Theatrical release date: May 18, 2016 (Cannes), Jun 29, 2016 (France), Sep 17, 2016 (Japan)
Country: France, Japan   **French title**: *La Tortue Rouge*
Production Company: Wild Bunch, Studio Ghibli, Why Not, Prima Linea, CN4, Arte France Cinéma
Length: 80 minutes
Directed by: Michael Dudok de Wit
Screenplay by: Pascale Ferran & Michael Dudok de Wit, story by Michael Dudok de Wit

---

Synopsis: A man wakes up alone on the beach of an island. He seeks out sources of food and water, and while exploring the island, slips into an area enclosed by rock, almost drowning. He watches a group of turtles make their way into the sea, and is kept company by a herd of crabs on the shore. He finally fashions a raft and leaves the island, only to have the raft shake as if it was struck, then come apart in the water, sending him back to the island. A second raft meets the same fate. The man falls ill, and begins hallucinating. He finally makes a third attempt at a raft, this time seeing a large red turtle, which strikes the raft from below, destroying it. Back on the island, the turtle comes up on the beach, and the man attacks it and flips it on its back. Later, regretting his anger, the man tries to return the turtle to the water, but its body is lifeless. Later, the shell cracks, and the body of a woman has replaced the turtle. The man brings her water and shade, and during a rain, while the man goes to get more branches for shelter, the woman begins to stir. When the man returns, the shell is empty. The man later sees the woman in the water, and leaves his shirt for her. The woman sends the empty shell into the ocean, and the man sends off his last raft. The two become a couple, and have a son. When the son is older, a tsunami hits the island and the father is swept out to sea, but with the help of some sea turtles, he is rescued. The son eventually feels lonely for a companion, and leaves with the turtles. The couple age on the island, and the man finally dies. The woman reverts to a red turtle, and returns to the sea.

Cast:

Role	Voice Actor
The father	Emmanuel Garijo
The son as a young adult	Tom Hudson
The son as a child	Baptiste Goy
The son as a baby	Axel Devillers
The mother	Barbara Beretta

Music Highlights: String Quartet No. 2 (Leos Janácek) performed by Jerusalem String Quartet, "Flying with the Turtles" (Laurent Perez Del Mar) performed by F.A.M.E.S. Project, "L'au Revoir" (Laurent Perez Del Mar) performed by F.A.M.E.S. Project. Music by Laurent Perez del Mar.

Film Facts

• The production team made the very unusual choice of including no dialogue in the film.
• Studio Ghibli's Hayao Miyazaki admired Dudok de Wit's 2001 short "Father and Daughter."
• The film was nominated for the "Best Animated Feature" Academy Award.

The Rescuers (G)

Theatrical release date: June 22, 1977
Production Company: Walt Disney Productions
Length: 78 minutes
Directed by: Wolfgang Reitherman, John Lounsbery, Art Stevens. Story: Larry Clemmons, Ken Anderson, Frank Thomas, Vance Gerry, David Michener, Ted Berman, Fred Lucky, Burny Mattinson, Dick Sebast, suggested by *The Rescuers* and *Miss Bianca* by Margery Sharp

Synopsis: The mice of the Rescue Aid Society learn that an orphan named Penny is in trouble, and send Miss Bianca and Bernard to free her from the wicked Madame Medusa. Medusa, assisted by her henchman Mr. Snoops and alligators Brutus and Nero, plans to acquire the world's largest diamond, the Devil's Eye. She needs someone small like Penny who can fit through a hole that leads to a pirate's cave where the diamond is believed to be. Fortunately for Penny, the Rescuers are on the case, aided by Orville the albatross and Evinrude the dragonfly.

Cast: Bob Newhart as Bernard
Eva Gabor as Miss Bianca
Geraldine Page as Madame Medusa
Joe Flynn as Mr. Snoops
Jeanette Nolan as Ellie Mae
Pat Buttram as Luke
Jim Jordan as Orville
John McIntire as Rufus

Michelle Stacy as Penny
Bernard Fox as The Chairman
Larry Clemmons as Gramps
James MacDonald as Evinrude
George Lindsey as Rabbit
Bill McMillan as TV Announcer
Dub Taylor as Digger
John Fiedler as Owl

Music Highlights: "The Journey" (Carol Connors/Ayn Robbins) performed by Shelby Flint, "Rescue Aid Society" (Carol Connors/Ayn Robbins) performed by Eva Gabor, Bob Newhart, and Bernard Fox, "Tomorrow is Another Day" (Carol Connors/Ayn Robbins) performed by Shelby Flint, "Someone's Waiting for You" (Sammy Fain/Ayn Robbins/Carol Connors) performed by Shelby Flint. Score by Artie Butler.

Film Facts

• The 23rd of the Disney animated classics, *The Rescuers* was based on the 1959 children's novel of the same name, and in part on the 1962 sequel *Miss Bianca,* both written by English author Margery Sharp. Work on the film began in 1962, but the project was shelved when Walt Disney became dissatisfied with the story. About 10 years later there were plans to develop Sharp's novel *Miss Bianca in the Antarctic,* with Louis Prima as a captive polar bear, but Prima's illness led to the project's cancelation. A revised story focused on Madame Medusa and the Devil's Eye diamond.
• The original plan for the villain was to feature Cruella de Vil from *101 Dalmatians.*
• The 1992/1999 VHS included an image of a woman's breasts as a joke on a single frame of film, though this was unnoticeable without freezing the frame. The prank resulted in the recall of millions of copies of the 1999 VHS, which was re-released a few weeks later.
• Phil Harris (*The Jungle Book, The Aristocats*) was to play a bullfrog, but got cut from the film.
• Additional appearances: *The Rescuers Down Under* (1990).

The Rescuers Down Under (G)

Theatrical release date: November 16, 1990
Production Company: Walt Disney Pictures, Walt Disney Feature Animation
Length: 77 minutes
Directed by: Hendel Butoy and Mike Gabriel
Screenplay by: Jim Cox, Karey Kirkpatrick, Byron Simpson, Joe Ranft

Synopsis: In the Australian outback, the animal loving boy Cody is kidnapped by the evil poacher McLeach and his giant monitor lizard Joanna, who hope to find the location of the rare golden eagle called Marahuté. The mouse Rescue Aid Organization sends rescue mice Miss Bianca and Bernard to assist, transported by albatross Wilbur and guided by the kangaroo rat Jake. The crafty McLeach releases Cody, and follows him to the nest of Marahuté. When McLeach captures Marahuté and Cody, both are imperiled, needing R-E-S-C-U-E from Bernard and Miss Bianca.

Cast: Bob Newhart as Bernard
Eva Gabor as Miss Bianca
John Candy as Wilbur
Tristan Rogers as Jake
Adam Ryen as Cody
George C. Scott as McLeach
Douglas Seale as Krebbs

Frank Welker as Joanna
Bernard Fox as Chairmouse/Doctor
Peter Firth as Red
Billy Barty as Baitmouse
Ed Gilbert as Francois
Carla Meyer as Faloo/Mother
Russi Taylor as Nurse Mouse

Music Highlights: "Black Slacks" (Joe Bennett/Jimmy Denton) performed by Joe Bennett and The Sparkletones, "Home On the Range (McLeach Version)" (Kelley/Higley+Ranft) performed by Frank Welker, "Waltzing Matilda" (A.B. Paterson/Marie Cowan) performed by Wayne Robson. Music by Bruce Broughton.

Film Facts

• The 29th of the Disney animated classics and the second film of the Disney Renaissance (1989-1999), *The Rescuers Down Under* was the first direct sequel to one of the animated classics, following *The Rescuers* (1977). Work on the new film began in 1986, with Mike Gabriel (later to direct *Pocahontas*) and Hendel Butoy (later to direct a segment of *Fantasia 2000*) recruited by the president of Walt Disney Feature Animation, Peter Schneider, to direct the film.
• The mice were originally helped by the albatross Orville in the first film, and are helped by his brother, Wilbur, in this one, a reference to brothers Orville and Wilbur Wright, pioneers in flight.
• The initial poor performance of this film led to television ads being pulled, and led Disney to release most sequels direct-to-video rather than theatrically.
• John Candy, who provided the voice for the albatross Wilbur, was later slated to voice a turkey in *Pocahontas* (1995), but the character was cut after Candy's death.
• In theaters the film was accompanied by the Mickey Mouse featurette "The Prince and the Pauper" (1990), the second new Mickey Mouse title, after *Mickey's Christmas Carol* (1983), since 1953.
• Additional appearances: Sequel to *The Rescuers* (1977).

Rikki-Tikki-Tavi (NR)

Broadcast date: January 9, 1975
Production Company: Chuck Jones Enterprises
Length: 24 minutes
Directed by: Chuck Jones
Screenplay by: Chuck Jones, based on *The Jungle Book* by Rudyard Kipling

---

Synopsis: In India, the English boy Teddy and his father come across a mongoose that is half-drowned. They revive the animal, name him Rikki-Tikki-Tavi, and he soon becomes a part of the household. Out in the garden, the tailor-bird Darzee and his wife tell Rikki about the big black cobra, Nag, and his wife, Nagaina, and Rikki meets them both, knowing they are his natural enemies. Soon after, Teddy is threatened by Karait, the small dusty brown snakeling, which Rikki uses his speed and strength to kill. During the night Rikki encounters Chuchundra the muskrat, who fearfully lets him know that Nag is sneaking into the house to kill the family, so Rikki will leave. Nag coils himself in the bathroom, planning to strike the father in the morning. Rikki carefully strikes Nag above the hood, struggling with him until Teddy's father shoots the snake. While Darzee is delighted with the death of Nag, Rikki knows he must defeat Nagaina as well. Darzee's wife lures Nagaina out by pretending to have a broken wing, while Rikki begins destroying her eggs. Nagaina threatens to strike the family, and Rikki uses one of her eggs to draw her away, chasing her into her hole, defeating the cobra threat once and for all, keeping the garden free of threats from that time onward.

Cast: Orson Welles as Narrator
June Foray as Nagaina/Teddy's Mother/
    Darzee's Wife
Les Tremayne as Father

Michael LeClair as Teddy
Shepard Menken as Rikki-Tikki-Tavi/
    Nag/Chuchundra
Lennie Weinrib as Darzee the Tailor-bird

Music Highlights: "When I Was a Lad" (Gilbert/Sullivan, from *H.M.S. Pinafore*) performed by Michael LeClair, "Darzee's Song" (Marian Dern/Dean Elliott) performed by Lennie Weinrib. Music by Dean Elliott.

Film Facts

• Rudyard Kipling's collection of stories *The Jungle Book* (1894) was also the source of Disney's *The Jungle Book* (1967).

• The narrator, Orson Welles, was legendary for his work in classic films such as *Citizen Kane* (1941), *The Third Man* (1949), and *Touch of Evil* (1958).

• A live-action Indian film, also titled *Rikki-Tikki-Tavi*, was released in 1979.

• Director Chuck Jones, known for his classic Looney Tunes cartoons, created two other animated shorts from Kipling's *The Jungle Book*: *The White Seal* (1975), and *Mowgli's Brothers* (1976).

• Jones also animated *How the Grinch Stole Christmas!* (1966), *Horton Hears a Who!* (1970), *The Phantom Tollbooth* (1970), *The Cat in the Hat* (1971), *The Cricket in Times Square* (1973), and *The Bugs Bunny/Road-Runner Movie* (1977) among many others.

Rio (G)

Theatrical release date: April 15, 2011
Production Company: Blue Sky Studios, 20th Century Fox Animation
Length: 96 minutes
Directed by: Carlos Saldanha
Screenplay by: Don Rhymer and Joshua Sternin & Jennifer Ventimilia and Sam Harper, story by Carlos Saldanha and Earl Richey Jones & Todd Jones

Synopsis: A blue Spix's macaw is captured by exotic pet sellers, but falls off a truck in Moose Lake, Minnesota. He is rescued, named Blu, and lovingly raised by Linda, who opens a bookstore called The Blue Macaw. One day Tulio, an ornithologist, discovers Blu, saying he is the last male Spix's macaw, inviting Blu and Linda to Rio de Janeiro, where the last known female, Jewel, lives, hoping the two could save the birds from extinction. Blu and Jewel are captured by an animal smuggler, but escape, complicated by Blu's inability to fly and by being chained to each other. As Linda and Tulio search for their macaws, Blu and Jewel try to make their way back to the aviary, aided by the toucan Rafael, the cardinal Pedro, and the canary Nico. The smuggler's vicious cockatoo Nigel captures Jewel, who is placed inside a makeshift Carnaval float on the way to the airport. Linda and Tulio learn of their plan, and join the Carnaval parade, stealing a float to try to stop the plane full of birds, but are too late. Blu and Jewel take matters into their own wings, freeing their companions, but when Jewel's wing is injured and she falls from the plane, Blu must make a leap of faith.

Cast: Anne Hathaway as Jewel (parrot)
Jesse Eisenberg as Blu (parrot)
Will.i.am as Pedro (cardinal)
Jamie Foxx as Nico (canary)
George Lopez as Rafael (toucan)
Tracy Morgan as Luiz (bulldog)
Jemaine Clement as Nigel (cockatoo)
Rodrigo Santoro as Dr. Túlio Monteiro
Leslie Mann as Linda Gunderson
Jake T. Austin as Fernando
Jane Lynch as Alice (goose)
Wanda Sykes as Chloe (goose)

Music Highlights: "Real in Rio" (Mendes/Brown/Mutti/Powell/Garrett) performed by The Rio Singers, "Let Me Take You to Rio" (Dean/Brown/Mutti) performed by Ester Dean and Carlinhos Brown, "Say You, Say Me" (Richie) performed by Lionel Richie, "Pretty Bird" (Clement/Powell/ Brenner/Reiss) performed by Jemaine Clement, "Hot Wings (I Wanna Party)" (Adams) performed by Will.i.am, Jamie Foxx and Anne Hathaway, "Fly Love" (Brown/Garrett) performed by Jamie Foxx, "Real in Rio (New Home)" (Mendes/Brown/Mutti/Powell/Garrett) performed by cast. End Credits: "Telling the World" (Cruz/Kasirye) performed by Taio Cruz, "Take You to Rio" (Dean/Eriksen/ Hermansen) performed by Ester Dean. Music by John Powell.

Film Facts

• The equation Blu writes in the dirt (39:33) gives the gravitational attraction between two bodies.
• Oreo created a special *Rio* Oreo with blue cream, also including stickers from the film.
• The Spix's macaw, a real kind of parrot, is considered extinct in the wild.
• Additional appearances: *Rio 2* (2014).

Rise of the Guardians (PG)

Theatrical release date: November 21, 2012
Production Company: DreamWorks Animation
Length: 97 minutes
Directed by: Peter Ramsey
Screenplay by: David Lindsay-Abaire, based on the book series *Guardians of Childhood* by William Joyce, and "The Man in the Moon," a Reel FX short film directed by William Joyce

Synopsis: When an ancient evil, Pitch Black, returns, North (Santa Claus) gathers the other Guardians who watch over the welfare of the children of the world: Tooth (the Tooth Fairy), Bunny (the Easter Bunny), and Sandy (the Sandman). They learn that the Moon is choosing a new Guardian: Jack Frost. Unfortunately, Jack Frost isn't interested in the responsibilities of being a Guardian. They learn that Pitch is stealing the Tooth Fairy's teeth, which contain memories of childhood, and if enough children stop believing, the Guardians will lose their power. The Guardians, including Jack, agree to pull together to collect teeth for the Fairy. On the way, they are attacked by Pitch, whose nightmare forces overcome Sandy. Jack, with no memory of his life before, learns that his childhood memories reside in his lost teeth, which are held by Pitch. Jack is tempted away from the group, and while the Guardians' forces are divided, Pitch uses his nightmares to sabotage an Easter Egg hunt to weaken belief in the Easter Bunny. Jack departs, and after a confrontation with Pitch, is trapped. He is able to use his teeth to remember how he saved his sister from falling into a frozen lake, only to fall in himself, when the Moon saved him by turning him into Jack Frost. When only one last child, Jamie, believes in the guardians, Jack finally finds his center, inspiring Jamie and his friends, who step forward to protect their protectors.

Cast: Chris Pine as Jack Frost
Alec Baldwin as North
Jude Law as Pitch
Isla Fisher as Tooth
Hugh Jackman as Bunny
Dakota Goyo as Jamie Bennett
Khamani Griffin as Caleb

Kamil McFadden as Claude
Georgie Grieve as Sophie Bennett
Emily Nordwind as Jamie's Mom/Jack's Mother
Jacob Bertrand as Monty
Olivia Mattingly as Pippa/Jack's Sister
Dominique Grund as Cupcake
Ryan Crego as Burgess Dog Walker

Music Highlights: "Kemp's Jig" (Bullard) performed by John Bullard, The Firebird, Suite for Orchestra (Stravinsky), "Still Dream" (Desplat/Lindsay-Abaire) performed by Renée Fleming. Music by Alexandre Desplat.

Film Facts

- Author William Joyce also wrote books that became *Meet the Robinsons* (2007) and *Epic* (2013).
- The events in Joyce's book series take place about 300 years before the story of the film.
- A video game was released for PlayStation 3, Wii/Wii U, Xbox 360, Nintendo DS and 3DS.
- A series of mid-credits scenes appear (1:31:32).

The Road to El Dorado (PG)

Theatrical release date: March 31, 2000
Production Company: DreamWorks Animation
Length: 89 minutes
Directed by: Eric "Bibo" Bergeron, Don Paul
Written by: Ted Elliott & Terry Rossio

Synopsis: In 1519 Spain, conquistador Hernán Cortés is preparing to sail to the New World, seeking glory and gold. Lovable scoundrels Tulio and Miguel steal a map said to show the location of a city of gold, and accidentally end up on Cortés's ship. Escaping with the horse Altivo, they begin to follow their map, and run into a native woman, Chel, who is pursued by an armed group. They are all taken to the golden city of El Dorado, where Tulio and Miguel are believed to be two gods described in a prophecy. High priest Tzekel-Kan asks for proof of their divine power, which a coincidental volcanic eruption appears to show. They develop the elaborate plan to "get the gold, go back to Spain." Chel knows they are no gods, and conspires to escape with them. When a human sacrifice is offered as a tribute to the gods, Tulio and Miguel intervene, and are offered gold instead. Saying they need to return to their own world, they ask Chief Tannabok for a ship, to be built in three days time. Tzekel-Kan again offers a sacrifice, but Miguel proclaims an end to human sacrifices, and dismisses Tzekel-Kan, to the delight of the crowd. Tzekel-Kan notices Miguel has a cut, meaning he is not a god. Tzekel-Kan attacks the "gods" with an animated stone jaguar, but is finally defeated. Miguel decides to stay in El Dorado, while Tulio prepares to set sail for Spain, but everyone must work together when they learn that the conquistador Cortés threatens the city.

Cast: Kevin Kline as Tulio
Kenneth Branagh as Miguel
Rosie Perez as Chel
Armand Assante as Tzekel-Kan
Edward James Olmos as Chief
Jim Cummings as Cortes

Frank Welker as Altivo
Tobin Bell as Zaragoza
Duncan Marjoribanks as Acolyte
Elijah Chiang as Kid #1
Cyrus Shaki-Khan as Kid #2
Elton John as Narrator

Music Highlights: "El Dorado" (Elton John/Tim Rice) performed by Elton John, "The Trail We Blaze" (John/Rice) performed by Elton John, "It's Tough to Be a God" (John/Rice) performed by Kevin Kline/Kenneth Branagh, "Without Question" (John/Rice) performed by Elton John, "Friends Never Say Goodbye" (John/Rice) performed by Elton John, "Someday Out of the Blue (Theme from The Road to El Dorado)" (Elton John/Patrick Leonard/Tim Rice) performed by Elton John, "Without Question (End Title)" (John/Rice) performed by Elton John. Score by Hans Zimmer and John Powell.

Film Facts

• Elton John and Tim Rice had previously collaborated on the soundtrack to *The Lion King* (1994).
• Gonzalo Pizarro was the actual Spanish conquistador who sought El Dorado, not Cortés.
• Sequels were planned, but were canceled after very disappointing box-office returns.

Robin Hood (G)

Theatrical release date: November 8, 1973
Production Company: Walt Disney Productions
Length: 83 minutes
Directed by: Wolfgang Reitherman
Written by: Larry Clemmons, based on character and story conceptions by Ken Anderson

---

Synopsis: Robin Hood lives on the run in Sherwood Forest with Little John, Friar Tuck, and other fighters for freedom, evading the wicked Prince John, the Sheriff of Nottingham, and Sir Hiss. When Robin learns that Prince John is holding an archery tournament, with the prize a kiss from his childhood love Maid Marian, he takes part disguised as a stork. Robin wins the tournament, but is captured by Prince John. With the aid of Little John, Robin Hood escapes, but it isn't long before Prince John raises taxes, begins imprisoning those who don't pay, and lays another trap for Robin Hood. Even when things look hopeless, Robin Hood can be counted on to save the day.

Cast: Roger Miller as The Rooster
Peter Ustinov as Prince John: A Lion
Terry-Thomas as Sir Hiss: A Snake
Brian Bedford as Robin Hood: A Fox
Monica Evans as Maid Marian: A Vixen
Phil Harris as Little John: A Bear

Andy Devine as Friar Tuck: A Badger
Carole Shelley as Lady Kluck: A Chicken
Pat Buttram as Sheriff of Nottingham: A Wolf
George Lindsey as Trigger: A Vulture
Ken Curtis as Nutsy: A Vulture

Music Highlights: "Oo-De-Lally" (Roger Miller) performed by Roger Miller, "Not in Nottingham" (Roger Miller) performed by Roger Miller, "Whistle-Stop" (Roger Miller) performed by Roger Miller, "Love" (Floyd Huddleston/George Bruns) performed by Nancy Adams, "The Phony King of England" (Johnny Mercer) performed by Phil Harris. Music by George Bruns.

Film Facts

• The 21st of the Disney animated classics, *Robin Hood* is an animated update of one of Disney's earliest live-action films, *The Story of Robin Hood and His Merrie Men* (1952). The film was directed by veteran Wolfgang Reitherman.

• An alternate ending, in which Robin Hood is wounded and almost killed, was filmed but not used. It is included on the "Most Wanted Edition" of the DVD.

• The film was criticized for reusing animation, by using the same animation at different times within the film, and by copying movements from other films.

• Phil Harris voiced both Baloo in *The Jungle Book* and Little John in *Robin Hood*, giving the bears similar voices as well as appearances.

• The song "Oo-De-Lally" is on *Classic Disney Vol. 3* CD/*Music of Disney: Legacy in Song* CD box, "Love" is on the *Classic Disney Vol. 3* CD.

• Additional appearances: Robin Hood and other characters appeared on the *House of Mouse* animated TV series (2001-2003).

Robots (PG)

Theatrical release date: March 11, 2005
Production Company: Blue Sky Studios, 20th Century Fox Animation
Length: 91 minutes
Directed by: Chris Wedge, co-directed by Carlos Saldanha
Screenplay by: David Lindsay-Abaire and Lowell Ganz & Babaloo Mandel, story by Ron Mita & Jim McClain and David Lindsay-Abaire

Synopsis: Young inventor Rodney hopes to make his father's life as a dishwasher easier by creating an amazing automated dishwashing device. He sets out to Robot City, where he hopes to work for the television personality Bigweld, who encourages new inventions on his show. He meets the fast-talking Fender Pinwheeler before arriving at the gates of Bigweld Industries. Unfortunately, the company has been taken over by the money-hungry Phineas T. Ratchet, who ejects Rodney from the premises. Ratchet's mother has a plan to do away with the older robots, and turn the company into Ratchet Industries. Supported by Fender and his friends, Rodney begins repairing the robots that can't find spare parts. Rodney crashes the annual Bigweld Ball, hoping to tell Bigweld what's happened to the company. He is seized by Ratchet's henchrobots, but saved by the kind-hearted Cappy. Cappy takes Rodney to meet Bigweld, but they find him in a disillusioned state. On the verge of giving up himself, Rodney returns to face Ratchet, and soon finds he has backup from an unexpected source.

Cast: Ewan McGregor as Rodney Copperbottom
Halle Berry as Cappy
Greg Kinnear as Phineas T. Ratchet
Mel Brooks as Bigweld
Amanda Bynes as Piper Pinwheeler
Drew Carey as Crank Casey
Jim Broadbent as Madame Gasket
Stanley Tucci as Herb Copperbottom
Robin Williams as Fender Pinwheeler
James Earl Jones as Voice Box at Hardware Store
Dianne Wiest as Mrs. Copperbottom
Jennifer Coolidge as Aunt Fanny
Paul Giamatti as Tim the Gate Guard
Dan Hedaya as Mr. Gunk
Jay Leno as Fire Hydrant
Natasha Lyonne as Loretta Geargrinder

Music Highlights: "Silence" performed by Gomez, "Shine" performed by Ricky Fante, "Right Thurr" performed by Chingy, "Walkie Talkie Man" performed by Steriogram, "I Like That" performed by Houston feat. Chingy, Nate Dogg & I-20, "(There's Gotta Be) More to Life" performed by Stacie Orrico, "Tell Me What You Already Did" performed by Fountains of Wayne, "Wonderful Night" performed by Fatboy Slim, "Love's Dance" performed Earth, Wind & Fire, "Low Rider" performed by WAR, "Get Up Offa That Thing" performed by James Brown. Music by John Powell.

Film Facts

• Cameos: Rock 'Em Sock' Em Robots (7:17), *The Wizard of Oz* (14:45), magnet game Wooly Willy (24:57), *Star Wars* (34:52), Oscar from *Sesame Street* (42:15), and the game Operation (43:58).
• The Map of the Stars' Homes that Fender Pinwheeler holds up (14:39) includes the names Jeremy Irons, Orson Wheels, Axle Rose, Britney Gears, Farrah Faucet, and M.C. Hammer.
• The DVD includes the short "Aunt Fanny's Tour of Booty."

The Rugrats Movie (G)

Theatrical release date: November 20, 1998
Production Company: Paramount Pictures, Nickelodeon Movies, Klasky-Csupo
Length: 79 minutes
Directed by: Norton Virgien and Igor Kovalyov
Written by: David N. Weiss & J. David Stem

Synopsis: Tommy is upset by all the disruption in the house when his mother has a new baby named Dil, so the rest of the Rugrats gang, Chuckie, Phil & Lil, decide to help Tommy by taking Dil back to the hospital. Tommy protests, and in their struggle they all roll away in a giant toy Reptar wagon, soon pursued by Tommy's mean older sister Angelica and Spike the dog, and later by Tommy's father Stu and Grandpa. In the forest they run across a derailed Monkey Circus train, and Dil is carried off by the monkeys, as Angelica and Spike flee from a huge wolf in the forest. Tommy gets so frustrated with Dil that he wants to give him to the monkeys, but has a change of heart. Angelica finally catches up with the babies, but they are threatened by the wolf, only to be saved by Spike.

Cast: E.G. Daily as Tommy Pickles
Christine Cavanaugh as Chuckie Finster
Kath Soucie as Philip Deville/Lillian Deville/ Betty Deville
Melanie Chartoff as Didi Pickles/Minka
Phil Proctor as Howard DeVille/Igor
Cree Summer as Susie Carmichael
Michael Bell as Chas Finster/Grandpa Boris/ Drew Pickles
Tress MacNeille as Charlotte Pickles
Jack Riley as Stu Pickles
Joe Alaskey as Grandpa Lou Pickles
Cheryl Chase as Angelica Pickles
Tara Charendoff as Dylan "Dil" Pickles

Music Highlights: "A Baby Is a Gift from a Bob" (Mothersbaugh) performed by Cheryl Chase & Cree Summer, "This World Is Something New to Me" (Mothersbaugh) performed by Dawn Robinson, Lisa Loeb, B Real, Patti Smith, Lou Rawls, Laurie Anderson, Gordon Gano, Fred Schneider, Kate Pierson and Cindy Wilson of The B-52's, Phife, Lenny Kravitz, Beck, Jakob Dylan & Iggy Pop, "Dull-A-Bye" (Mothersbaugh) performed by E.G. Daily, Melanie Chartoff & Jack Riley, "Dil-a-Bye" (Mothersbaugh) performed by E.G. Daily, "On Your Marks, Get Set, Ready, Go!" (Smith) performed by Busta Rhymes, "Yo Ho Ho and a Bottle of Yum!" (Mothersbaugh) performed by E.G. Daily, Christine Cavanaugh & Kath Soucie, "Witch Doctor" (Bagdasarian) performed by Devo (orig. by David Seville), "One Way or Another" (Harry/Harrison + Casemiro) performed by Cheryl Chase (orig. by Blondie). End credits: "Take Me There" (Riley/Savage/Nelson/Betha/Foster) performed by Blackstreet and Mya feat. Ma$e and Blinky Blink, "Take the Train" (Saber/Rakim) performed by Rakim & Danny Saber, "I Throw My Toys Around" (Costello/O'Riordan) performed by No Doubt feat. Elvis Costello. Music by Mark Mothersbaugh.

Film Facts

• A post-credits scene appears (1:19:15).
• Additional appearances: *Rugrats* TV series (1991–2006), *Rugrats in Paris* (2000), *Rugrats Go Wild* (2003), *The Rugrats: All Growed Up* TV film (2001), *All Grown Up!* TV series (2003–2008).

Rugrats Go Wild (PG)

Theatrical release date: June 13, 2003
Production Company: Nickelodeon Movies, Klasky Csupo
Length: 80 minutes
Directed by: John Eng, Norton Virgien
Written by: Kate Boutilier

Synopsis: It's vacation time for the Rugrats gang (Tommy, Chuckie, Phil & Lil, Kimi, and Tommy's mean older sister Angelica, along with their parents), as they set off for a tropical paradise, only to end up marooned on an uninhabited island. As it turns out, the Wild Thornberrys are on the island as well, as Nigel Thornberry tries to track down the clouded leopard. While Thorberry hunts the leopard, the Rugrats are hunting him, knowing "Nigel Strawberry" from TV nature shows. When they finally find each other, a blow to the head leaves Nigel somewhat disoriented. With some teamwork and a little luck, the Rugrats are finally located, just in time to begin a real vacation.

Cast: E.G. Daily as Tommy Pickles
Nancy Cartwright as Chuckie Finster
Kath Soucie as Phil DeVille/Lil DeVille/
    Betty DeVille
Dionne Quan as Kimi Finster
Cheryl Chase as Angelica Pickles
Tim Curry as Nigel Thornberry
Joe Alaskey as Grandpa Lou Pickles

Tress MacNeille as Charlotte Pickles
Michael Bell as Drew Pickles/Chaz Finster
Melanie Chartoff as Didi Pickles
Julia Kato as Kira Finster
Phil Proctor as Howard DeVille
Jack Riley as Stu Pickles
Tara Strong as Dil Pickles
Cree Summer as Susie Carmichael

Music Highlights: "The Rugrats Theme" (Mothersbaugh) by Mark Mothersbaugh, "Changing Faces" (E.G. Daily/Greg De Belles) performed by E.G. Daily, "Holiday" (Curtis Hudson/Lisa Stevens) performed by Cree Summer, "Dresses and Shoes" (orig. "Precious and Few") (Walter Nims) performed by Cheryl Chase, "The Morning After" (Al Kasha/Joel Hirschhorn) performed by Cheryl Chase, "Island Princess" (Mark Mothersbaugh/Eryk Casemiro/Kate Boutilier) performed by Cheryl Chase and Cree Summer, "It's a Jungle Out Here" (Mark Mothersbaugh/Hal Waite) performed by Cree Summer, Nancy Cartwright, E.G. Daily, Tara Strong, Kath Soucie and Dionne Quan, "Big Bad Cat" (Alex Greggs/Bradley Ralph/Daniel O'Donoghue/Eryk Casemiro/Kate Boutilier) performed by Bruce Willis and Chrissie Hynde, "Should I Stay or Should I Go" (Mick Jones/Joe Strummer) performed by The Clash. Music by Mark Mothersbaugh.

Film Facts

• Angelica's song, "The Morning After," was originally from *The Poseidon Adventure* (1972).
• Lil DeVille became the second well-known animated character to go vegetarian, a year after Shaggy Rogers in the TV series *What's New, Scooby-Doo?*
• In theaters, the film offered "Odorama," giving audience members "scratch and sniff" cards.
• Chrissie Hynde, voice of Siri the leopard, is best known as the frontwoman of The Pretenders.

Saludos Amigos (Passed)

Theatrical release date: February 6, 1943
Production Company: Walt Disney Productions
Length: 42 minutes
Directed by: Bill Roberts, Jack Kinney, Ham Luske, Wilfred Jackson
Story by: Homer Brightman, Ralph Wright, Roy Williams, Harry Reeves, Dick Huemer, Joe Grant

Synopsis: A mix of brief live-action clips of the Disney creative staff touring different parts of South America, and animated sequences: "Lake Titicaca" featuring Donald Duck and an uncooperative llama, "Pedro" the mail plane's struggle against the elements in Chile, "El Gaucho Goofy" in Argentina, and "Aquarela do Brasil" featuring Donald Duck and the parrot José Carioca in Rio de Janeiro.

Cast: Fred Shields as Narrator
Clarence Nash as Donald Duck

Pinto Colvig as Goofy
José Oliviera as José Carioca the parrot

Also featuring Walt Disney and several Disney employees: Lee Blair, Mary Blair, Norman Ferguson, Frank Graham, Frank Thomas.

Music Highlights: "Saludos Amigos" (Ned Washington/Charles Wolcott), "Aquarela do Brasil" (Ary Barroso) performed by Aloysio de Oliveira, "Tico-Tico no Fubá" (Zequinha de Abreu). Music by Ed Plumb and Paul Smith.

Film Facts

• *Saludos Amigos,* meaning "Greetings, Friends" in Spanish, was the 6th of the Disney animated classics, and the first of six Disney "package" films in the 1940s that combined shorts or featurettes into feature-length films. It was the shortest of all of Disney's feature films, with a running length of only 42 minutes (just over the 40-minute threshold to count as a feature).
• The word *carioca* is a term for a native of Rio de Janeiro. The José Carioca character is popular in Brazilian comics, where he is known as "Zé Carioca."
• This film inspired Chilean cartoonist René Ríos Boettiger, known as "Pepo," to create the famous character "Condorito," drawn from the condor on the Chilean coat of arms.
• Due to concerns about promoting smoking, Goofy's cigarette (23:00) was edited out of the U.S. home video release of *Saludos Amigos.*
• The closely-related film *The Three Caballeros* would follow in December of 1944.
• The *Saludos Amigos* soundtrack was issued on on three 78 RPM records in 1944 (Decca Records A-369): "Saludos Amigos"/"Inca Suite," "Brazil (Aquarela do Brazil)"/"Argentine Country Dances," "Tico-Tico"/"Pedro from Chile." A *Saludos Amigos* LP (Walt Disney Records WDL 3039) was issued in 1958, including tracks from *Saludos Amigos* and *The Three Caballeros.* The soundtrack has never been released on CD, but tracks have appeared on compilations, including the song "Saludos Amigos" on *The Music of Disney: Legacy in Song* box set.
• Additional appearances: *The Three Caballeros* (1945) was a sequel of sorts, featuring Donald and José Carioca. Donald and Carioca, plus the Aracuan Bird also appeared in the "Blame it on the Samba" segment of *Melody Time* (1948).

Samurai Jack (NR)

Broadcast date: August 10, 2001
Production Company: Cartoon Network Studios
Length: 90 minutes
Directed by: Genndy Tartakovsky
Written by: Paul Rudish and Genndy Tartakovsky

Synopsis: The family and land of a young prince are attacked when the demon Aku escapes from imprisonment. The prince escapes with his mother and trains to do battle. When he is ready, he is presented with a magic katana and samurai robes, and after defeating a number of evil minions, does battle with Aku himself. On the verge of defeat, Aku opens a time portal and sends the samurai far into the future. The samurai is startled to see flying cars, and is attacked by one of them, learning that Aku rules this world. Going by the name Jack, the samurai is hired by dog-like miners to defend them against Aku's minions, making it his mission to vanquish Aku's influence, even as he has hopes of returning to his own time.

Cast: Phil LaMarr as Samurai Jack/Guard/
        Homeslice/Dog #1
Mako as Aku
Jeff Glen Bennett as Alien/McDuffy/
        Dreyfuss/Leader/Dog
Jennifer Hale as Girl/Waitress

Rob Paulsen as Cole Lampkin/Lizor/
        Rothchild
Kevin Michael Richardson as Brobot/
        Bouncer/Vada 2
Sab Shimono as Emperor

Music Highlights: Music by James L. Venable

Film Facts

• The film is comprised of the first three episodes of the *Samurai Jack* animated TV series, all three of which were first broadcast on August 10, 2001. The series initially ran for four seasons, from 2001 to 2004. A fifth season, more adult in tone, appeared in 2017.
• The film was shown in select theaters on October 16, 2017, as *Samurai Jack: The Premiere Movie Event,* to promote the release of the home media box set *Samurai Jack: The Complete Series.*
• A *Samurai Jack* comic was produced by comics publisher IDW from 2013 to 2015. The comics were collected in the 444-page paperback *Samurai Jack: Tales of the Wandering Warrior* (2016).
• Video games based on the series included *Samurai Jack: The Amulet of Time* (2003) for Game Boy Advance, *Samurai Jack: The Shadow of Aku* (2004) for GameCube and PlayStation 2, and *Samurai Jack: Battle Through Time* (2020) for Nintendo Switch, PlayStation 4, Xbox One, Microsoft Windows, and Apple Arcade.
• The strategy board game *Samurai Jack: Back to the Past* was issued by USAopoly in 2018.
• Creator Genndy Tartakovsky directed every episode of the animated series. He had previously worked on Cartoon Network's *The Powerpuff Girls* and *Dexter's Laboratory,* and would go on to direct *Star Wars: Clone Wars* (2003-2005), *Sym-Bionic Titan* (2010–2011), and the *Hotel Transylvania* films.

Scooby-Doo franchise

The Scooby-Doo franchise, created by Joe Ruby and Ken Spears, began in 1969 with the Hanna-Barbera cartoon series *Scooby-Doo, Where Are You!*, and became one of the studio's most popular and enduring shows.

Scooby-Doo, Where Are You! TV series (3 seasons, 41 episodes, 1969 – 1970, 1978)

The New Scooby-Doo Movies TV series (2 seasons, 24 episodes 1972 – 1973)

The Scooby-Doo/Dynomutt Hour/Scooby-Doo/Dynomutt Show TV series (1 season, 16 episodes, Sep 11, 1976 – Dec 18, 1976)

Scooby's All-Star Laff-A-Lympics/Scooby's All-Stars (2 seasons, 24 episodes 1977 – 1978)
Scooby's All-Star Laff-A-Lympics: The Scooby-Doo Show, Laff-A-Lympics, The Blue Falcon & Dynomutt, Captain Caveman and the Teen Angels, and Scooby-Doo, Where Are You! reruns.
Scooby's All-Stars: The Scooby-Doo Show, Laff-A-Lympics, Captain Caveman and the Teen Angels.

Note: Although it was originally broadcast under different titles, *The Scooby-Doo Show* ran for a total of 40 episodes over three seasons (1976-1978), on ABC, including 16 episodes as segments of *The Scooby-Doo/ Dynomutt Hour* (1976), 8 episodes as segments of *Scooby's All-Star Laff-A-Lympics* (1977), 9 episodes as *Scooby-Doo, Where Are You!* (1978), and 7 episodes as segments of *Scooby's All-Stars* (1978). Beginning in 1980 the show was broadcast under the name of *The Scooby-Doo Show.*

Scooby Goes Hollywood ABC television special (Dec 13, 1979)

Scooby-Doo and Scrappy-Doo (1 season, 16 episodes, 1979 – 1980)

The Richie Rich/Scooby-Doo Show/The Scooby & Scrappy-Doo/Puppy Hour (3 seasons, 33 episodes 1980 - 1982)

The New Scooby and Scrappy-Doo Show/The New Scooby-Doo Mysteries (2 seasons, 26 episodes 1983 – 1984)

The 13 Ghosts of Scooby-Doo (1 season on ABC, 13 episodes, 1985)

Scooby-Doo Meets the Boo Brothers TV movie (Oct 18, 1987)
Scooby-Doo and the Ghoul School TV movie (Oct 16, 1988)
Scooby-Doo and the Reluctant Werewolf TV movie (Nov 13, 1988)

A Pup Named Scooby-Doo (4 seasons, 27 episodes, 1988 – 1991)

Scooby-Doo on Zombie Island home media film (1998)
Scooby-Doo! and the Witch's Ghost home media film (1999)
Scooby-Doo and the Alien Invaders home media film (2000)
Scooby-Doo and the Cyber Chase home media film (2001)
Scooby-Doo! and the Legend of the Vampire home media film (2003)
Scooby-Doo! and the Monster of Mexico home media film (2003)

What's New, Scooby-Doo? TV series (3 seasons, 42 episodes, 2003 – 2006)

Scooby-Doo! and the Loch Ness Monster home media film (2004)
Aloha, Scooby-Doo! home media film (2005)
Scooby-Doo! in Where's My Mummy? home media film (2005)
Scooby-Doo! Pirates Ahoy! home media film (2006)

Shaggy & Scooby-Doo Get a Clue! TV series (2 seasons, 26 episodes, 2006 – 2008)

Chill Out, Scooby-Doo! home media film (2007)
Scooby-Doo! and the Goblin King home media film (2008)
Scooby-Doo! and the Samurai Sword home media film (2009)
Scooby-Doo! Camp Scare home media film (2010)
Scooby-Doo! Abracadabra-Doo home media film (2010)

Scooby-Doo! Mystery Incorporated TV series (2 seasons, 52 episodes, 2010 – 2013)

Scooby-Doo! Legend of the Phantosaur home media film (2011)
Big Top Scooby-Doo! home media film (2012)
Scooby-Doo! Music of the Vampire home media film (2012)
Scooby-Doo! Mask of the Blue Falcon home media film (2013)
Scooby-Doo! Stage Fright home media film (2013)
Scooby-Doo! WrestleMania Mystery home media film (2014)
Scooby-Doo! Frankencreepy home media film (2014)
Scooby-Doo! Moon Monster Madness home media film (2015)
Scooby-Doo! and Kiss: Rock and Roll Mystery home media film (2015)

Be Cool, Scooby-Doo! TV series (2 seasons, 52 episodes, 2015 – 2018)

Scooby-Doo! and WWE: Curse of the Speed Demon home media film (2016)
Lego Scooby-Doo! Haunted Hollywood home media film (2016)
Lego Scooby-Doo! Blowout Beach Bash home media film (2017)
Scooby-Doo! Shaggy's Showdown home media film (2017)
Scooby-Doo! and the Gourmet Ghost home media film (2018)
Scooby-Doo! & Batman: The Brave and the Bold home media film (2018)
Scooby-Doo! and the Curse of the 13th Ghost home media film (2019)
Scooby-Doo! Return to Zombie Island home media film (2019)

Scooby-Doo and Guess Who? TV series (2 seasons, 40 episodes, 2019 – 2020)

Scoob! theatrical/streaming film (2020)

Happy Halloween, Scooby-Doo! home media film (2020)

Live action/computer animation: *Scooby-Doo* (2002), *Scooby-Doo 2: Monsters Unleashed* (2004).

Comics

Scooby Doo has also appeared in comics published by several companies, starting with 30 issues of the Gold Key Comics series *Scooby Doo...Where Are You!* (1970-1975), followed by March of Comics (1974), Charlton Comics (1975-1976), Marvel Comics (1977-1979), Harvey Comics (1992-1993), Archie Comics (1995-1997), and DC Comics (1997-2021).

Scooby-Doo on Zombie Island (TV-G)

Home media release date: September 27, 1998
Production Company: Hanna-Barbera Cartoons, Warner Bros. Animation, Cartoon Network Studios
Length: 77 minutes
Directed by: Jim Stenstrum
Screenplay by: Glenn Leopold, story by Glenn Leopold & Davis Doi, based upon characters created by William Hanna and Joseph Barbera

Synopsis: The Mystery Inc. gang has retired from solving mysteries, with Daphne and Fred going on to a television show, Scooby and Shaggy working in security, and Velma finding a position in a library. The gang reunites to film material for Daphne's show, and while in New Orleans, Lena Dupree overhears that they want to find a real haunted house. She tells them about Moonscar Island, said to be haunted by the pirate Morgan Moonscar. After a variety of odd occurrences, the gang is horrified to learn that real zombies are roaming the grounds. They are surprised to find that voodoo dolls are being used to control their movements, and even more shocked to see who is behind the supernatural goings-on.

Cast: Scott Innes as Scooby-Doo
Billy West as Shaggy
Mary Kay Bergman as Daphne
Frank Welker as Fred
B.J. Ward as Velma
Adrienne Barbeau as Simone

Tara Charendoff as Lena
Cam Clarke as Beau
Jim Cummings as Jacques/Morgan Moonscar
Mark Hamill as Snakebite Scruggs
Jennifer Leigh Warren as Chris
Ed Gilbert as Mr. Beeman

Music Highlights: "Scooby-Doo, Where Are You?" (David Mook/Ben Raleigh) performed by Third Eye Blind, "The Ghost Is Here" (Tom Snow/Glenn Leopold) performed by Skycycle, "It's Terror Time Again" (Tom Snow/Glenn Leopold) performed by Skycycle. Music by Steven Bramson.

Film Facts

• The film followed the animated TV series *A Pup Named Scooby-Doo* (1988-1991) and a 1997 guest appearance by the Scooby gang on the *Johnny Bravo* episode "The Sensitive Male/Bravo Dooby Doo" (season 1, episode 3). Interest in a new Scooby-Doo vehicle was prompted by the popularity of reruns of earlier Scooby-Doo episodes on Cartoon Network.
• Casey Kasem, who had voiced the part of Shaggy since 1969 in the series *Scooby-Doo, Where Are You!* was slated to return with this film, but had switched to a vegan diet and was reluctant for his animated counterpart to be shown eating meat. When the producers were not sympathetic to his concern, Shaggy was re-cast. Casem was ultimately successful, and in 2002, on the TV series *What's New, Scooby-Doo?*, Shaggy became the first mainstream cartoon character to go vegetarian.
• The film was based on an unused story that Glenn Leopold had originally written for the animated series *SWAT Kats: The Radical Squadron* (1993-1994).
• A sequel to the film, *Scooby-Doo! Return to Zombie Island,* was released in 2019.
• A brief post-credits scene features Scooby and two cats (1:16:12).

Scooby Doo! and the Witch's Ghost (NR)

Home media release date: October 5, 1999
Production Company: Hanna-Barbera Cartoons
Length: 70 minutes
Directed by: Jim Stenstrum
Written by: Rick Copp & David A. Goodman and Davis Doi & Glenn Leoplod

Synopsis: When Mystery Inc. solves a mystery at a Natural History Museum, horror writer Ben Ravencroft invites them to accompany him to Oakhaven, Massachusetts, where he grew up. They find that the quiet town has been turned into a circus by the mayor, promoting the legend of Ben's ancestor, Sarah Ravencroft, the "ghost of Oakhaven." Ben hopes to find Sarah's journal, to prove she was a kind medicine woman, not a witch. Shaggy and Scooby have a run-in with the flying, fireball-throwing Witch's Ghost, and while investigating, the gang finds the gothic band Hex Girls rehearsing. Odd behavior by the mayor and the Hex Girls make the gang suspicious. They lay a trap for the ghost, finding it's Mr. McKnight, the town pharmacist, assisted by the townspeople. Soon after, the gang helps Ben to find Sarah's journal, only to learn it's actually a spell book, and Ben has tricked them into finding it. Ben frees Sarah's ghost, but instead of serving him, she seeks to wreak destruction on the world. Ben tries to stop Sarah, but she traps him, saying only a virtuous soul can stop her. They ask Thorn, leader of the Hex Girls, who is of Wiccan ancestry, to read the incantation. As Sarah's ghost is trapped in the book, she vows not to go alone, taking her revenge on Ben.

Cast: Scott Innes as Scooby Doo/Shaggy
Mary Kay Bergman as Daphne
Frank Welker as Fred
B.J. Ward as Velma
Tim Curry as Ben Ravencroft
Kimberly Brooks as Luna

Jennifer Hale as Thorn
Jane Wiedlin as Dusk
Bob Joles as Jack
Tress MacNeille as Sarah Ravencroft
Peter Renaday as McKnight
Neil Ross as Mayor

Music Highlights: "Scooby-Doo, Where Are You?" (Mook/Raleigh) performed by Billy Ray Cyrus, "Hex Girl" (Chandler/Leopold) performed by Jennifer Hale, Jane Wiedlin, Kimberly Brooks, "Earth, Wind, Fire, and Air" (Chandler/Leopold) performed by Jennifer Hale, Jane Wiedlin, Kimberly Brooks. End credits: "The Witch's Ghost" (Chandler/Leopold) performed by Terry Wood, Angie Jaree, Gigi Worth. Music by Louis Febre.

Film Facts

• Ben reads a newspaper article (44:33) that refers to the "moat monster" from *Scooby-Doo on Zombie Island* (1998).
• The Hex Girls would be recurring characters, also appearing in *Scooby-Doo! and the Legend of the Vampire* (2003), the TV series *What's New, Scooby-Doo?* (2003-2006), and *Scooby-Doo and Guess Who?* (2019-2020), and the comic *Scooby-Doo! Team-Up*.

Scooby-Doo and the Alien Invaders (NR)

Home media release date: October 3, 2000
Production Company: Hanna-Barbera Cartoons, Mook Animation
Length: 73 minutes
Directed by: Jim Stenstrum
Screenplay by: Davis Doi & Lance Falk, story by Davis Doi & Glenn Leopold

Synopsis: When the Mystery Inc. gang is taking a trip through the New Mexico desert, they accidentally end up on restricted government land, where their van, the Mystery Machine, has engine trouble. Daphne, Fred, and Velma go into town while Shaggy and Scooby stay with the van, where they run into a Jackelope, followed by alien creatures on hovercraft. They meet up with the rest of the gang at a diner, where an eccentric old man named Lester says he was abducted by the aliens. It isn't long before Scooby and Shaggy are abducted themselves, and deposited in the desert, where they meet the hippie nature photographer Crystal and her golden retriever, Amber. Shaggy and Scooby are both smitten, and gratefully accept a ride to the diner, where they rejoin the gang. They meet Max, a friendly worker for the government's Search for Alien Life Forms (SALF) program, and while the rest of the gang get a tour of a SALF facility, Shaggy and Scooby go to hang out with Crystal and Amber, searching for the Jackelope. Crystal confesses that she is an undercover government agent investigating alien abductions. Velma gets suspicious when the office workers have mud on their shoes, and they go to Scorpion Ridge to investigate, finding caves with gold ore. Shaggy and Crystal find the gold too, and are discovered and chased by aliens on hovercraft and two Military Police. The gang is captured, and confront the "aliens." When Shaggy and Scooby are cornered, Crystal and Amber show another side of themselves, and the truth of the "alien invaders" is finally revealed.

Cast: Scott Innes as Scooby Doo/Shaggy
Mary Kay Bergman as Daphne
Frank Welker as Fred
B.J. Ward as Velma
Jeff Glen Bennett as Lester
Jennifer Hale as Dottie

Mark Hamill as Steve
Candi Milo as Crystal
Kevin Michael Richardson as Max
Neil Ross as Sergio/Buck
Audrey Wasilewski as Laura

Music Highlights: "Scooby-Doo, Where Are You?" (Mook/Raleigh) performed by Jennifer Love Hewitt, "How Groovy" (Bodie Chandler/Jim Stenstrum) performed by Scott Innes, "The Aliens Are Here" (Bodie Chandler/Lance Falk) performed by The Hippos. Score by Louis Febre.

Film Facts

• Burger King promoted the film with 8 glow-in-the-dark toys.
• The DVD includes "The Making of the Movie" featurette.
• A post-credits scene appears (1:12:16).

Scooby-Doo and the Cyber Chase (NR)

Home media release date: October 9, 2001
Production Company: Hanna-Barbera Cartoons
Length: 75 minutes
Directed by: Jim Stenstrum
Written by: Mark Turosz

Synopsis: The Mystery, Inc. gang goes to visit Fred's high school friend Eric, who is working on a computer game featuring the mystery-solvers. While at the lab, they learn that Eric, his baseball-loving friend Bill, and Professor Kaufman have developed a way to send physical objects into cyberspace, but their experimental laser also produced a Phantom Virus, a computer virus monster made of electricity, that can destroy all the software in the world. The scientists explain that the phantom virus can be stopped by magnets. While chasing the virus, the gang is zapped by Dr. Kafuman's laser, and pulled into Eric's game, along with the Phantom Virus. They are transported from level to level in the game, featuring the surface of the moon, the Roman Colosseum, a dinosaur-filled jungle, sunken treasure, giant ants, a samurai warrior, an Egyptian tomb, a fire-breathing dragon, and the North Pole. They finally reach the final level, meeting video game copies of themselves. The Phantom Virus is found in a batting cage, followed by the appearance of many villains they had faced in the past. Working together with their video game counterparts, they gather enough clues to know who's really responsible for the Phantom Virus, and how to escape.

Cast: Scott Innes as Scooby-Doo/Shaggy
Joe Alaskey as Wembley
Bob Bergen as Eric
Grey DeLisle as Daphne
Tom Kane as Professor Kaufman

Mikey Kelley as Bill
Gary Sturgis as Phantom Virus
B.J. Ward as Velma
Frank Welker as Fred

Music Highlights: "Scooby-Doo, Where Are You?" (David Mook/Ben Raleigh) performed by Cindy, Kate and Fred of The B-52's, "Hello Cyberdream" (Richard Lawrence Wolf) performed by David Nicoll, additional vocals by Wes Quave, "Double Double Joint" (Richard Lawrence Wolf) performed by Richard Lawrence Wolf. Music by Louis Febre.

Film Facts

• The video game versions of the Mystery, Inc. gang wear their classic clothes from the original *Scooby Doo, Where Are You!* animated TV series (1969-1978), with Shaggy's shirt changed from green to red, and Scooby's collar from blue to red.
• There is a post-credits animation (1:09:14), with the gang talking about what their favorite part of the film was.
• Very appropriately, there was a *Scooby-Doo and the Cyber Chase* video game.
• Warner Bros. insisted on using a staff writer, leading the creative team (including Davis Doi, Lance Falk, Glenn Leopold, and Jim Stenstrum) to depart after this film.

Scoob! (PG)

Theatrical/streaming release date: May 15, 2020
Production Company: Warner Animation Group
Length: 93 minutes
Directed by: Tony Cervone
Screenplay by: Adam Sztykiel and Jack C. Donaldson & Derek Elliott and Matt Lieberman, story by Matt Lieberman and Eyal Podell & Jonathon E. Stewart

---

Synopsis: Scooby, Shaggy, Daphne, Fred, and Velma meet as children, solving a haunted house mystery on Halloween. Years later, while out bowling, Shaggy and Scooby are attacked by the villainous Dick Dastardly's robots, and end up on the Falcon Fury aircraft, where they meet Blue Falcon's son Brian, the robot dog Dynomutt, and the pilot Dee Dee Skyes. They are drawn into Dastardly's plans to obtain three skulls which will allow him to open the underworld where his partner, Muttley, was lost years before. After Scooby and Shaggy have a fight, Scooby is captured by Dastardly, and Shaggy leads the gang as they work to stop Dastardly's plans before it's too late.

Cast: Will Forte as Shaggy Rogers
Mark Wahlberg as Blue Falcon
Jason Isaacs as Dick Dastardly
Gina Rodriguez as Velma Dinkley
Zac Efron as Fred Jones
Amanda Seyfried as Daphne Blake
Kiersey Clemons as Dee Dee Skyes
Ken Jeong as Dynomutt
Tracy Morgan as Captain Caveman
Frank Welker as Scooby-Doo/Pterodactyl
Iain Armitage as Young Shaggy
Mckenna Grace as Young Daphne
Pierce Gagnon as Young Fred
Ariana Greenblatt as Young Velma
Simon Cowell as himself
Christina Hendricks as Officer Jaffe
Henry Winkler as Keith
Harry Perry as himself

Music Highlights: "Scooby-Doo, Where Are You?" (David Mook/Ben Raleigh) performed by Best Coast, "On Me" (Andrew Cedar/Ben Johnson/Jim Lavigne/Jason Derulo) performed by Thomas Rhett and Kane Brown feat. Ava Max, "Summer Feelings" (Watson/Puth/Boland/Izquierdo/Wilcox/Stella/Brown) performed by Lennon Stella featuring Charlie Puth. Music by Tom Holkenborg.

Film Facts

• Some characters are drawn from other Hanna-Barbera cartoons: Dick Dastardly and Muttley from *The Wacky Races,* Blue Falcon and Dynomutt from *The Scooby-Doo/Dynomutt Hour,* Captain Caveman and Dee Dee Skyes from *Captain Caveman and the Teen Angels.*
• Other Hanna-Barbera cameos: Fred and Wilma Flintstone (10:38), Magilla Gorilla's Peeble's Pet Shop (28:14), Squiddly Diddly (33:51), Hong Kong Phooey/Laff-a-Lympics/Space Stars (36:35), The Banana Splits' Adventure Hour/Wacky Races/Penelope Pitstop (36:38), Frankenstein, Jr. (37:26), Yogi Bear's Jellystone National Park (44:59), Yankee Doodle Pigeon (53:19), Jabberjaw (1:24:44), the Grape Grape Ape (1:27:52), and Frankenstein Jr. (1:28:05).
• The montage scene (11:47) recreates the opening sequence of *Scooby Doo, Where Are You!* (1969).
• Takamoto Bowl is named for Iwao Takamoto, the original character designer of Scooby-Doo.

The Secret of Kells (NR)

Theatrical release date: Feb 11, 2009 (France/Belgium), Mar 3, 2009 (Ireland), Jun 22, 2016 (US)
Country: Ireland/France/Belgium
Production Company: Les Armateurs, Vivi Film, Cartoon Saloon, France 2 Cinéma
Length: 75 minutes
Directed by: Tomm Moore, co-director Nora Twomey
Screenplay by: Fabrice Ziolkowski, original story by Tomm Moore

Synopsis: Brendan, the nephew of Abbot Cellach, lives in the abbey of Kells. The scribes in Kells tell Brendan of the master illuminator Brother Aiden on the island of Iona, who created the legendary Book of Iona. The abbot is trying to build a wall to protect the abbey from an attack by the Northmen (Vikings), and Brother Aiden, fleeing from just such an attack, arrives at the abbey with his cat Pangur Ban, and his book. Aiden invites Brendan to help him, asking him to go into the woods to gather gall nuts to make ink. In the woods with Pangur, Brendan is saved from a pack of wolves by the fairy Aisling ("ashling"), who helps Brendan find the gall nuts, on the condition that he does not return to her forest. Aisling shows him the nuts, but afterwards Brendan falls into the cave of Crom Cruach, the dark one, and is again saved by Aisling, who says she will permit him to return to the forest. The abbot is angry Brendan left the abbey, and forbids him to go again. Brother Aiden works to turn the gall nuts into a brilliant green ink. Outside the abbey the Northmen began pillaging the lands. Brother Aiden tells Brendan he must complete the Chi-Rho page, the most important page in the Book of Iona, as Aiden is too old. Brendan does not feel worthy, but Aiden tells him of a crystal, the "eye of Columbkille," which would help him in the work, but was lost. The crystal is also known as the eye of Crom Cruach. As Brendan sets out to try to find the eye, the abbot locks him up. Aisling frees him, and at great risk, they retrieve the eye, but further peril awaits when the Northmen reach the abbey of Kells.

Cast: Evan McGuire as Brendan
Christen Mooney as Aisling
Brendan Gleeson as Abbot Cellach
Mick Lally as Aidan

Liam Hourican as Brother Tang/Leonardo
Paul Tylak as Brother Assoua
Michael McGrath as Adult Brendan
Paul Young as Brother Square

Music Highlights: "Aisling Song" (Tomm Moore/Bruno Coulais) performed by Christen Mooney, "Epicy" (Rossa Ó'Snodaigh) performed by Kila, "Cardinal Knowledge" (Colm Ó'Snodaigh), "Opening Brendan" (Colm Ó'Snodaigh), "The Book of Kells" (Dee Armstrong). Music by Bruno Coulais and Kíla.

Film Facts

- The film was nominated for the "Best Animated Feature" Academy Award.
- The Book of Kells is an actual illuminated manuscript, residing at Trinity College Library, Dublin.
- Moore's "Irish Folklore Trilogy" also includes *Song of the Sea* (2015) and *Wolfwalkers* (2020).

The Secret of NIMH (G)

Theatrical release date: July 16, 1982
Production Company: United Artists, Aurora Productions, Don Bluth Productions
Length: 82 minutes
Directed by: Don Bluth
Story adaptation by: Don Bluth, John Pomeroy, Gary Goldman, Will Finn, based on the novel
Mrs. Frisby and the Rats of NIMH by Robert C. O'Brien

Synopsis: After the death of her husband, Jonathan, the mouse Mrs. Brisby is fearful when one of her children, Timmy, is very ill with pneumonia. She is given medicine by Mr. Ages and advised not to move Timmy for three weeks, On the way home Mrs. Brisby runs into the crow Jeremy, whom she saves from a cat. Mrs. Brisby gives Timmy his medicine, but the family has to move due to the farmer plowing the field. They buy some time by disabling the farmer's tractor, and are sent by the Great Owl to seek out the rats under a rose bush near the farmhouse, led by the mysterious Nicodemus, so they can move her house. Though first chased away by the nasty guard Brutus, Mrs. Brisby is taken by Mr. Ages to meet the kind Captain of the Guard, Justin, the power-mad Jenner, and Nicodemus. She learns that her late husband, Mr. Ages, and the rats were part of experiments at the National Institute of Mental Health (NIMH) which increased their intelligence and extended their lives, and that the rats plan to move their headquarters to Thorn Valley, far from the humans. Nicodemus tells Mrs. Brisby about the experiments at NMH, and gives her an amulet that glows red when worn by one with a courageous heart. The rats agree to move Mrs. Brisby's cinderblock home, but during the move Jenner cuts the ropes to kill Nicodemus. Meanwhile, Mrs. Brisby has agreed to drug the cat Dragon, and is captured by the farmer's son, where she learns that NIMH is coming to capture or kill the rats. She escapes, only to find that Jenner is trying to seize power, while her home sinks in the mud, requiring an act of a truly courageous heart.

Cast: Derek Jacobi as Nicodemus
Elizabeth Hartman as Mrs. Brisby
Arthur Malet as Mr. Ages
Dom DeLuise as Jeremy
Hermione Baddeley as Auntie Shrew
Shannen Doherty as Teresa
Wil Wheaton as Martin
Jodi Hicks as Cynthia
Ian Fried as Timothy
John Carradine as Great Owl
Peter Strauss as Justin
Paul Shenar as Jenner

Music Highlights: "Flying Dreams" lullaby (Goldsmith/Williams) performed by Sally Stevens, "Flying Dreams" (Goldsmith/Williams) performed by Paul Williams. Music by Jerry Goldsmith.

Film Facts

• Wham-O, makers of the Frisbee toy, objected to the name "Mrs. Frisby," so it became Mrs. Brisby.
• The National Institute of Mental Health (NIMH) has indeed engaged in animal experimentation.
• Additional appearances: *The Secret of NIMH 2: Timmy to the Rescue* (1998). Jane Leslie Conly wrote *Racso and the Rats of NIMH* (1986) and *R-T, Margaret, and the Rats of NIMH* (1990).

The Secret World of Arrietty (G)

Theatrical release date: July 17, 2010 (Japan), February 17, 2012 (US)
Country: Japan   Japanese title: *Kari-gurashi no Arietti* (lit. "Arrietty the Borrower")
Production Company: Studio Ghibli
Length: 95 minutes
Directed by: Hiromasa Yonebayashi
Screenplay by: Hayao Miyazaki, Keiko Niwa, based on *The Borrowers* by Mary Norton

Synopsis: A boy named Shawn, who is in poor health, goes to spend a week in the country with his great aunt Jessica and her maid Hara. Shawn's arrival is noticed by the Arrietty, one of the "Borrowers," tiny people who borrow from the "beans" (human beings). That night, Arrietty goes with her father, Pod, on her first borrowing mission to gather food. During the outing, Arrietty is seen by Shawn as he lies in bed. He asks her to stay, but she hurries away. Curious, she breaks the rules and goes to talk briefly with Shawn at his window, but a crow sees her and attacks. Shawn is able to save her, but when Hara comes to get rid of the crow, Arrietty slips away again. It is the Borrowers' way to move when they are discovered by humans, and the tiny family prepares to move. Shawn, trying to be kind, pulls out the Borrowers' kitchen and replaces it with a working kitchen from a dollhouse. Arrietty lets Shawn know that the Borrowers need to leave, and he tells her that he has a serious heart condition. Their conversation is interrupted when Hara discovers Arrietty's mother, Homily, and puts her in a glass jar, calling an exterminator to come capture the other Borrowers. Working together, Shawn and Arrietty free Homily and hide any evidence of the Borrowers, making Hara doubt her sanity. The Borrowers finally depart, going to find Homily's family, but Shawn catches up with them, to say goodbye.

Cast:

Role	English	Japanese
Arrietty	Bridgit Mendler	Mirai Shida
Homily	Amy Poehler	Shinobu Otake
Pod	Will Arnett	Tomokazu Miura
Hara/Haru	Carol Burnett	Kirin Kiki
Shawn/Shō	David Henrie	Ryunosuke Kamiki
Aunt Jessica/Sadako Maki	Gracie Poletti	Keiko Takeshita
Spiller	Moisés Arias	Tatsuya Fujiwara

Music Highlights: "Arrietty's Song" (Corbel) performed by Cécile Corbel, "Summertime" (Mendler) performed by Bridgit Mendler. Score by Cécile Corbel.

Film Facts

- Outside of Japan and the U.S./North America, the film was simply titled *Arrietty*.
- The film won the "Animation of the Year" Japan Academy Prize.
- A UK dub featured Saoirse Ronan, Mark Strong, Olivia Colman, and Tom Holland's debut.

Shaun the Sheep Movie (PG)

Theatrical release date: February 6, 2015 (UK), August 5, 2015 (US)
Production Company: Aardman Animations, iStudioCanal, Lionsgate
Length: 85 minutes
Directed by: Mark Burton, Richard Starzak
Written by: Mark Burton, Richard Starzak

Synopsis: Tired of their boring daily routine at the Mossy Bottom farm, the sheep conspire to put the farmer to sleep, so they can have fun in the farmhouse. The farmer's dog, Bitzer, catches them, but while he is trying to rouse his owner, the trailer the farmer is sleeping in rolls away. The farmer ends up in the big city, suffering from memory loss after his head is bumped. Back at the farm, the sheep miss having their food trough filled, and are locked out of the house by the pigs. It's up to Shaun the Sheep to find the farmer. Unfortunately, all the sheep from the farm follow, requiring some dodgy disguises. Shaun is eventually captured by the overzealous Animal Containment officer A. Trumper, and caged with a scary-looking dog. Meanwhile, the farmer flees the hospital, and while passing an upscale hairstyling salon, recognizes the clippers from sheep-shearing on the farm, seizes a celebrity, and shears his head. The shocked celebrity ends up loving his new hairstyle, and the farmer, dubbed Mr. X from his hospital bracelet, becomes an in-demand hairstylist. Once the sheep rescue Shaun and Bitzer from the pound, they try to take "Mr. X" back to the farm, but he still doesn't remember them. They decide the best way to get him out of the big city is the way that got him there in the first place — sound asleep.

Cast: Justin Fletcher as Shaun/Timmy
John Sparkes as The Farmer/Bitzer
Omid Djalili as Trumper
Richard Webber as Shirley
Kate Harbour as Timmy's Mum/Meryl
Tim Hands as Slip
Andy Nyman as Nuts

Simon Greenall as Twins
Emma Tate as Hazel
Jack Paulson as Celebrity with Hair Trouble
Sean Connolly as Maitre D /Golfer/Stylists/
    Angry Panto Horse/Hospital Characters
Henry Burton as Junior Doctor/Animal
    Containment Visitor

Music Highlights: "Big City" (Ilan Eshkeri/Nick Hodgson) performed by Eliza Doolittle. "Feels Like Summer" (Ilan Eshkeri/Nick Hodgson/Tim Wheeler) performed by Tim Wheeler, "Shaun The Sheep - Life's a Treat" (Mark Thomas) performed by Mark Thomas & Vic Reeves. Music by Ilan Eshkeri.

Film Facts

• The film is based on the UK TV series *Shaun the Sheep* which began in 2007, and its spinoff series, *Timmy Time* (2009). Shaun debuted in the Wallace & Gromit short "A Close Shave" (1995).
• Shaun the Sheep creator Nick Parks makes an animated cameo as a birdwatcher (13:13).
• The name of the French restaurant, "Le Chou Brule," translates to "Cabbage is Burning"
• A dumpster reads "ST-S27M5" (1:06:36), the letters of which stand for **S**haun **T**he **S**heep **M**ovie.
• Additional Appearances: *A Shaun the Sheep Movie: Farmageddon* (2019).

A Shaun the Sheep Movie: Farmageddon (G)

Release dates: UK theatrical Oct 18, 2019, UK home media Feb 10, 2020, Netflix Feb 14, 2020
Production Company: Aardman Animations, Creative Europe MEDIA, Anton Capital Entertainment
Length: 86 minutes
Directed by: Richard Phelan & Will Becher
Written by: Mark Burton and Jon Brown, based on an idea by Richard Starzak

Synopsis: When an alien craft lands near Mossy Bottom, Shaun the Sheep helps the young alien Lu-La escape government agents looking for her, and tries to help her return home. Meanwhile, the Farmer schemes to create Farmageddon, an alien theme park, to cash in on UFO fever. Shaun and Lu-La try to fly her ship, but end up crashing it, and head back to Mossy Bottom to try to call her parents, heading high up to the top of the Farmageddon stage to send a signal. Things get complicated when government agents crash the party.

Cast: Justin Fletcher as Shaun/Timmy
John Sparkes as The Farmer/Bitzer
Amalia Vitale as Lu-La/Me-Ma
Kate Harbour as Agent Red/Timmy's Mum
David Holt as Mugg-1NS
Andy Nyman as Nuts

Richard Webber as Shirley/Ub-Oo
Emma Tate as Hazel
Simon Greenall as Twins
Chris Morrell as Farmer John
Joe Sugg as Pizza Boy

Music Highlights: "Real Life" (Walker/Taylor) performed by Tom Walker, "Blow the Wind Southerly" (Trad.) performed by Mike Smith, "Everything is Better" (Shudall) performed by Kieran Shudall and Heather Shudall, "Lazy" (Hayward-Young/Intonti/Lanham/Cowan/Arnason/Greif-Neill) performed by The Vaccines and Kylie Minogue, "Out of Control (Farmageddon Remix)" (Rowlands/ Simons/Sumner) performed by The Chemical Brothers, "I Can't Be My Old Self Forever" (Smith/ Compass) performed by Jorja Smith, "House of Fun" (Barson/Thompson) performed by Mike Smith (orig. by Madness), "Forever Autumn" (Wayne/Osborne/Vigrass) performed by Justin Hayward, "Shaun the Sheep (Life's a Treat)" (Farmageddon Remix) (Thomas/Bell/Rose) performed by Toddla T feat. Nadia Rose/Vic Reeves, "Renegade Sheep" (Cardy) performed by Rat Boy, "Things Can Only Get Better" (Cunnah/Petrie) performed by Mike Smith (orig. by D:Ream). Music by Tom Howe.

Film Facts

- There are many references to classic sci-fi: *Contact* (1:14), H.G. Wells (1:39), *Close Encounters of the Third Kind* (2:54, 36:52), *Arrival*: pizza box (9:51), *E.T. The Extra-Terrestrial* (11:59, 20:38, 26:21), *Alien* (14:31), *Signs* (19:04), *2001: A Space Odyssey* (19:11, 53:22, 1:09:57), *WALL-E* (22:51), *Hitchhiker's Guide to the Galaxy*: "Milliway's" (31:59), *Star Trek IV: The Voyage Home* (36:20), *Dr. Who* (38:44, 1:02:39, 1:03:09), *Star Trek*: door (40:12), *The X-Files* (45:53), *Logan's Run* (50:22), *Red Dwarf* (53:34), *Space Quest* (53:46), *Futurama* (1:01:34), *Robocop* (1:04:15, 1:07:20), and *Star Wars: Return of the Jedi* (1:13:40), plus a *Blue Peter* badge (53:46).
- Aardman cameos: Wallace and Gromit (1:30), *Chicken Run* (3:40), Morph (1:18:03).
- Post-credits: Brian Cox of D:Ream briefly performs "Things Can Only Get Better" (1:25:58).
- Farmer Ted's Adventure Farm, which has a Shaun the Sheep Adventure, is thanked in the credits.

Shrek (PG)

Theatrical release date: May 18, 2001
Production Company: DreamWorks Animation
Length: 90 minutes
Directed by: Andrew Adamson and Vicky Jenson
Written by: Ted Elliott & Terry Rossio and Joe Stillman and Roger S.H. Schulman, based upon the book by William Steig

Synopsis: Solitary ogre Shrek is incensed when Lord Farquaad exiles all magical creatures to Shrek's formerly tranquil swamp. Accompanied by the chatty Donkey, Shrek confronts Farquaad, ending up on a quest to save the fair Princess Fiona. As they face harrowing exploits — fire breathing dragons, royal betrayal, singing and dancing merry men — Shrek and Fiona both learn that appearances can be deceiving.

Cast: Mike Myers as Shrek
Eddie Murphy as Donkey
Cameron Diaz as Princess Fiona
John Lithgow as Lord Farquaad
Vincent Cassel as Monsieur Hood
Peter Dennis as Ogre Hunter
Clive Pearse as Ogre Hunter
Jim Cummings as Captain of Guards

Bobby Block as Baby Bear
Chris Miller as Geppetto/Magic Mirror
Cody Cameron as Pinocchio/Three Pigs
Kathleen Freeman as Old Woman
Michael Galasso as Peter Pan
Christopher Knights as Blind Mouse
Simon J. Smith as Blind Mouse
Conrad Vernon as Gingerbread Man

Music Highlights: "All Star" (Camp) performed by Smash Mouth, "Escape (The Piña Colada Song)" (Holmes) performed by Rupert Holmes, "Bad Reputation" (Jett/Laguna/Cordell/Kupersmith) performed by Joan Jett & the Blackhearts, "I'm on My Way" (Reid/Reid) performed by The Proclaimers, "Merry Men" (Tepper/Adamson/Vernon) performed by Vincent Cassel, "My Beloved Monster" (E) performed by eels, "You Belong to Me" (King/Stewart/Price) performed by Jason Wade, "Hallelujah" (Cohen) performed by John Cale (orig. by Leonard Cohen), "I'm a Believer" (Diamond) performed by Smash Mouth (orig. by Neil Diamond), "Stay Home" (Matt Mahaffey) performed by Self, "Best Years of Our Lives" (Jaymes/Deane) performed by Baha Men, "Like Wow!" (Harry/St. Victor) performed by Leslie Carter, "It Is You (I Have Loved)" (Gregson-Williams/Powell/ Greenaway/Glover) performed by Dana Glover. Score by Harry Gregson-Williams and John Powell.

Film Facts

- Mike Myers recorded his dialogue with different accents until hitting upon Scottish.
- The descriptions of bachelorette #1, #2, and #3 are based on the 60s/70s show *The Dating Game*.
- Shrek has a star on the Hollywood Walk of Fame.
- The film won the first ever "Best Animated Film" Academy Award in 2001.
- Additional appearances: *Shrek 2* (2004), "Far Far Away Idol" short (2004), *Shrek the Third* (2007), "Shrek the Halls" short (2007), *Shrek Forever After/The Final Chapter* (2010), "Scared Shrekless" short (2010), "Donkey's Christmas Shrektacular" short (2010), "Thriller Night" short (2011), *Shrek's Thrilling Tales* video (2012).

Shrek 2 (PG)

Theatrical release date: May 19, 2004
Production Company: DreamWorks Pictures, PDI, DreamWorks Animation
Length: 93 minutes
Directed by: Andrew Adamson, Kelly Asbury, Conrad Vernon
Screenplay by: Andrew Adamson and Joe Stillman and J. David Stem & David N. Weiss, story by Andrew Adamson, based upon the book by William Steig

---

Synopsis: Shrek and Fiona are enjoying married life, until Fiona's parents, the King and Queen of Far, Far Away, ask to meet Fiona's "Prince Charming." The King and Queen are shocked that Fiona has married an ogre, and Shrek clashes with the royals. The King is angrily confronted by Fiona's Fairy Godmother, who's son, Prince Charming, has been pushed out by Shrek marrying the princess. Fairy Godmother tells the King to get rid of Shrek, and he hires Puss in Boots to do the job. After an initial battle, Puss becomes an ally. They take a "Happily Ever After" potion from the Fairy Godmother, which turns Shrek and Fiona human, and donkey into a horse. The only catch is that to make the change permanent, Shrek and Fiona need to kiss by midnight, but Fairy Godmother is determined to stop them.

Cast: Mike Myers as Shrek
Eddie Murphy as Donkey
Cameron Diaz as Princess Fiona
Julie Andrews as Queen
Antonio Banderas as Puss in Boots
John Cleese as King
Rupert Everett as Prince Charming

Jennifer Saunders as Fairy Godmother
Aron Warner as Wolf
Kelly Asbury as Page/Elf/Nobleman/Son
Cody Cameron as Pinocchio/Three Pigs
Conrad Vernon as Gingerbread Man/Cedric/
    Announcer/Muffin Man/Mongo
Christopher Knights as Blind Mouse

Music Highlights: "Accidentally in Love" (Duritz/Vickrey/Immerglück/Malley/Bryson) performed by Counting Crows, "Le Freak" (Rodgers/Edwards) performed by Chic, "Funkytown" (Greenberg) performed by Lipps Inc., "Fairy Godmother Song" (Adamson/Barton/Dohrn/Gregson-Williams/ Smith/Warner) performed by J. Saunders, "Little Drop of Poison" (Waits/Brennan) performed by Tom Waits, "I Need Some Sleep" (E) performed by eels, "Ever Fallen in Love" (Shelley) performed by Pete Yorn (orig. by Buzzcocks), "Tomorrow" (Charnin/Strouse) performed by Eddie Murphy, "Changes" (Bowie) performed by Butterfly Boucher/David Bowie, "People Ain't No Good" (Cave) performed by Nick Cave, "Holding Out for a Hero" (Pitchford/Steinman) performed by J. Saunders/ Frou Frou (orig. by Bonnie Tyler), "Livin' La Vida Loca" (Child/Rosa) performed by E. Murphy/A. Banderas (orig. by Ricky Martin), "You're So True" (Arthur) performed by Joseph Arthur, "As Lovers Go" (Carrabba) performed by Dashboard Confessional. Music by Harry Gregson-Williams.

Film Facts

- Disney parody cameos include The Little Mermaid (3:30) and Cogsworth and Lumiere (46:46).
- Business parodies include Burger Prince (Burger King) Olde Knavery (Old Navy) Farbucks Coffee (Starbucks), Friar's Fat Boy (Bob's Big Boy), and Saxon Fifth Avenue (Saks Fifth Avenue).
- Mid-credits scene: Donkey sings Eric Carmen's "All By Myself" (1:24:01).

Shrek the Third (PG)

Theatrical release date: May 18, 2007
Production Company: DreamWorks, DreamWorks Animation, Pacific Data Images
Length: 93 minutes
Directed by: Chris Miller, co-directed by Raman Hui
Screenplay by: Jeffrey Price & Peter S. Seaman and Chris Miller & Aron Warner, story by Andrew Adamson, based upon the book by William Steig

Synopsis: When the King of Far Far Away croaks, Shrek and Fiona are set to become the next king and queen. Unfortunately, Shrek is not a good match for the job, and sets out with Donkey and Puss in Boots to locate Arthur, the only other person who can take the job. As they are departing, Fiona tells Shrek she is pregnant, leaving Shrek worried about whether he can raise a child. The party arrives at Worcestershire, and find that Arthur, or "Artie," is a geeky high school student who is happy to leave the bullies behind. On the trip back, Artie has second thoughts and decides he doesn't want to be king, not feeling up to the job after being abandoned by his father at his school. Back in Far Far Away, Fiona's baby shower is interrupted when the kingdom is invaded by the bitter Prince Charming, leading an army of rogues and villains. Charming declares himself king, locking up Fiona and the others. When Shrek learns that Fiona is in trouble, the retired wizard Merlin uses magic to send the heroes back, but Donkey and Puss switch bodies in the process. Shrek is captured, so Fiona leads the princesses in a rescue mission. A confrontation with Charming's armed thugs looms, until Artie helps everyone see a new way, and Shrek is freed to focus on his family.

Cast: Mike Myers as Shrek
Eddie Murphy as Donkey
Cameron Diaz as Princess Fiona
Antonio Banderas as Puss in Boots
Julie Andrews as Queen
John Cleese as King

Rupert Everett as Prince Charming
Eric Idle as Merlin
Justin Timberlake as Artie
Susanne Blakeslee as Evil Queen
Cody Cameron as Pinocchio/Three Pigs
Larry King as Doris

Music Highlights: "Royal Pain" (E) performed by eels, "Live and Let Die" (P. McCartney/L. McCartney) performed by Wings, "Joker & The Thief" (Heskett/Ross/Stockdale) performed by Wolfmother, "9 Crimes" (Rice) performed by Damien Rice & Lisa Hannigan, "Barracuda" (Wilson/Wilson/DeRosier/Fisher) performed by Fergie, "Final Showdown" (Lindsay-Abaire/Dohrn/Tesori) performed by cast, "Losing Streak" (E) performed by eels. End credits: "Thank You (Falettin Me Be Mice Elf Again)" (Stewart) performed by Eddie Murphy & Antonio Banderas, "Best Days" (White) performed by Matt White, "What I Gotta Do" (Hinds/Lopez/Ruzumna/Villaroman/ Speir) performed by Macy Gray, "Other Ways" (Hall) performed by Trevor Hall. Music by Harry Gregson-Williams.

Film Facts

• The film was released May 18, 2007, six years after the first *Shrek* premiered, on May 18, 2001.
• McDonalds sold 10 different *Shrek the Third* promotional Happy Meal figures.
• The Queen sings "My Favorite Things," sung by Julie Andrews in *The Sound of Music* (1:05:25).

Shrek Forever After/The Final Chapter (PG)

Theatrical release date: May 21, 2010
Production Company: DreamWorks Animation
Length: 93 minutes
Directed by: Mike Mitchell
Written by: Josh Klausner and Darren Lemke, based upon the book by William Steig

Synopsis: While Fiona was still a prisoner in a tower, the King and Queen of Far Far Away almost gave Rumpelstiltskin their kingdom to save her, when news came that Shrek had rescued her. In the present day, Shrek feels confined by his domestic life, raising three children with Fiona. Rumpelstiltskin persuades Shrek to trade a day of his life for a day that he could be a free ogre like he used to be. After he signs, Shrek finds the world has changed, and Rumpelstiltskin rules a cruel version of Far Far Away. Rumpelstiltskin explains that the day he took was the day Shrek was born, so Shrek never rescued Fiona, and the King and Queen signed over Far Far Away. Donkey knows the contract has a hidden "exit clause," which they learn is "true love's kiss." Unfortunately, Fiona, who leads the ogre resistance, does not know who Shrek is. Shrek begins a charm offensive, but the kiss does not work, as Fiona does not love him. Shrek learns that Rumpelstiltskin, worried he'll break the curse, has offered a wish to whoever turns Shrek in. Shrek turns himself in, using his wish to free the ogres. His kindness changes Fiona's feelings, setting the stage for true love's kiss.

Cast: Mike Myers as Shrek
Eddie Murphy as Donkey
Cameron Diaz as Princess Fiona
Antonio Banderas as Puss in Boots
Julie Andrews as Queen
John Cleese as King
Walt Dohrn as Rumpelstiltskin

Jon Hamm as Brogan
Jane Lynch as Gretched
Craig Robinson as Cookie
Lake Bell as Patrol Witch/Wagon Witch #2
Kathy Griffin as Dancing Witch/Wagon Witch #1
Mary Kay Place as Guard Witch
Kristen Schaal as Pumpkin Witch/Palace Witch

Music Highlights: "You've Got a Friend" (King), "Isn't It Strange" (Hoffman/Sellards) performed by Scissor Sisters, "Top of the World" (R. Carpenter/Bettis) performed by Carpenters, "Rumpel's Party Palace" (Simpson) instrumental, "Click Click" (Wakeling/Charlery/Morton/Steele/Cox) performed by Light FM feat. Lloyd Hemmings (orig. by The Beat), "Darling I Do" (Pigg/Schwartz) performed by Landon Pigg & Lucy Schwartz. End Credits: "I'm a Believer" (Diamond) performed by Weezer, "For Once in My Life" (Murden/Miller) performed by Stevie Wonder, "Right Back Where We Started From" (Edwards/Tubbs) performed by Maxine Nightingale. Music by Harry Gregson-Williams.

Film Facts

• The film's title was originally going to be *Shrek Goes Fourth,* with *Shrek Forever After* more subtly referring to this being the fourth film.
• McDonalds sold 8 Happy Meal toys and a Shrek watch to promote the film.
• The Shrek series was followed by the spin-off film *Puss in Boots* (2011).

Sinbad: Legend of the Seven Seas (PG)

Theatrical release date: July 2, 2003
Production Company: DreamWorks Animation
Length: 86 minutes
Directed by: Tim Johnson, Patrick Gilmore
Written by: John Logan

Synopsis: Sinbad and his pirate crew seek to steal the mystical Book of Peace, which Sinbad's childhood friend Prince Proteus is taking to his home of Syracuse. As the theft is underway, Eris, the Goddess of Discord, looks forward to creating chaos on Earth, sending her giant sea monster Cetus to attack. Sinbad and Proteus work together to defeat Cetus, but Sinbad is pulled underwater with the monster. He is saved by Eris, who tasks him with stealing the Book of Peace, which he agrees to take to her in Tartarus in return for a fortune. They follow Proteus to Syracuse, where Sinbad meets Proteus' fiancée, Marina. Disguised as Sinbad, Eris steals the Book of Peace, and Sinbad is soon sentenced to death. Proteus takes Sinbad's place, asking Sinbad to travel to Tartarus to return the book. Sinbad plans to escape to Fiji, but soon finds Marina is on his ship, agreeing to change course to Tartarus when she bribes him with gems. All is nearly lost when the male crew falls under the spell of sirens, but Marina is immune to their song, and saves the ship. Eris continues to send obstacles, freezing the ocean, and sending giant birds to attack. Finally reaching the gates of Tartarus, Sinbad and Marina learn the truth about Eris's plan. A final test of Sinbad determines the fate of Proteus and Syracuse, and Marina must also make a life changing decision.

Cast: Brad Pitt as Sinbad
Catherine Zeta-Jones as Marina
Michelle Pfeiffer as Eris
Joseph Fiennes as Proteus
Dennis Haysbert as Kale
Timothy West as Dymas
Adriano Giannini as Rat

Raman Hui as Jin
Chung Chan as Li
Jim Cummings as Luca
Conrad Vernon as Jed
Andrew Birch as Grum/Chum
Chris Miller as Tower Guard
Jim Cummings as Additional Voices

Music Highlights: Music by Harry Gregson-Williams.

Film Facts

• Sinbad originated in the Middle Eastern folktale collection *One Thousand and One Nights* (also called *Arabian Nights*). For the DreamWorks film the setting was relocated to Greece.
• Plans for possible sequels were not developed after the film's disappointing box office returns.
• After this film, DreamWorks switched to computer generated animation.
• Stop-motion animator Ray Harryhausen worked on three live-action Sinbad films: *The 7th Voyage of Sinbad* (1958), *The Golden Voyage of Sinbad* (1973) and *Sinbad and the Eye of the Tiger* (1977).
• Additional appearances: The DVD includes the "Cyclops Island" short in interactive form, while the VHS included a non-interactive version.

Sing (PG)

Theatrical release date: December 21, 2016
Production Company: Illumination Entertainment
Length: 108 minutes
Directed by: Garth Jennings, co-director Christophe Lourdelet
Screenplay by: Garth Jennings

Synopsis: Theater-owning koala Buster Moon has fallen on hard times, having trouble paying his bills. He dreams up a talent contest with a $1,000 prize, that his clumsy assistant Miss Crawly accidentally types as $100,000. Buster chooses several contestants, including pigs Rosita and Gunter, gorilla Johnny, mouse Mike, singing frogs, and punk porcupine Ash, overlooking Ash's partner Lance and the gifted elephant Meena. The show offers a chance for performers to escape their past: Rosita as an overworked mother, Johnny as a getaway driver, Ash's bad relationship, and Meena's passivity. Buster seeks funding from his friend Eddie's wealthy grandmother Nana, but when thugs to whom Mike owes a debt steal the prize money, the theater is destroyed in the process. After a brief stint washing cars, Buster hears Meena's astounding singing, and the show is back on in the theater's ruined remnants.

Cast: Matthew McConaughey as Buster Moon
Reese Witherspoon as Rosita (pig)
Seth MacFarlane as Mike (mouse)
Scarlett Johansson as Ash (porcupine)
John C. Reilly as Eddie (sheep)
Taron Egerton as Johnny (gorilla)
Tori Kelly as Meena (elephant)
Jennifer Saunders as Nana (sheep)
Jennifer Hudson as Young Nana (sheep)
Garth Jennings as Miss Crawly (lizard)
Peter Serafinowicz as Big Daddy (gorilla)
Nick Kroll as Gunter (pig)
Beck Bennett as Lance (porcupine)
Jay Pharoah as Meena's Grandfather (elephant)

Music Highlights: "Golden Slumbers" (Lennon/McCartney) performed by Hudson, "Gimme Some Lovin'" (Winwood/Davis/Winwood) performed by Spencer Davis Group, "The Way I Feel Inside" (Argent) performed by Egerton, "Firework" (Perry/Wilhelm/Dean/Eriksen/Hermansen) performed by Katy Perry/Witherspoon, "I Don't Wanna" (Jennings/Bassett) performed by Johansson/Bennett, "Venus" (Leeuwen) performed by Kroll/Witherspoon, "Bamboleo" (Diaz/Baliardo/Bouchikhi/Reyes) performed by Gipsy Kings, "Hallelujah" (Cohen) performed by Kelly, "Under Pressure" (Queen/Bowie) performed by Queen & David Bowie, "Shake It Off" (Swift/Schuster/Martin) performed by Kroll/Witherspoon, "I'm Still Standing" (John/Taupin) performed by Egerton, "Set It All Free" (Bassett) performed by Johansson, "My Way" (François/Revaux/Anka) performed by MacFarlane, "Don't You Worry 'Bout a Thing" (Wonder) performed by Kelly, "Faith" (Tedder/Wonder/Starlight) performed by Stevie Wonder feat. Ariana Grande. Score by Joby Talbot.

Film Facts

- The gorillas wear Snowball masks (5:09, 51:18) from Illumination's *The Secret Life of Pets* (2016).
- Taron Egerton, who sings Elton John's "I'm Still Standing," played John in *Rocketman* (2019).
- The red pandas sing "Kira Kira Killer" (Nakata) by Japanese singer Kyary Pamyu Pamyu.
- Additional appearances: "Gunter Babysits," "Love at First Sight," "Eddie's Life Coach" shorts.

Sleeping Beauty (G)

Theatrical release date: January 29, 1959
Production Company: Walt Disney Productions
Length: 75 minutes
Supervising director: Clyde Geronimi/Sequence dir. Eric Larson, Wolfgang Reitherman, Les Clark
Story Adaptation: Erdman Penner, from the Charles Perrault version of Sleeping Beauty, additional story: Joe Rinaldi, Winston Hibler, Bill Peet, Ted Sears, Ralph Wright, Milt Banta

---

Synopsis: As a baby, Princess Aurora is given a fatal curse by the evil Maleficent in retribution for not being invited to the celebration of her birth: on Aurora's 16th birthday she would prick her finger on the spindle of a spinning wheel and die. With the help of good fairies Flora, Fauna, and Merryweather, the curse is weakened so that rather than dying she will simply sleep. For her safety Aurora is raised in the woods by the fairies as "Briar Rose," where she meets Prince Phillip. Despite efforts to prevent it, Aurora does prick her finger on a spinning wheel and falls into a deep sleep. Prince Philip combats Maleficent in order to wake the Sleeping Beauty.

Cast: Mary Costa as Princess Aurora
Bill Shirley as Prince Phillip
Eleanor Audley as Maleficent
Verna Felton as Flora/Queen Leah

Barbara Luddy as Merryweather
Barbara Jo Allen as Fauna
Taylor Holmes as King Stefan
Bill Thompson as King Hubert

Music Highlights: "Hail to the Princess Aurora" (Tom Adair/George Bruns) performed by chorus, "The Gifts of Beauty and Song" (Tom Adair/George Bruns) performed by chorus, "Blue Bird - I Wonder" (Winston Hibler/ Ted Sears/George Bruns) performed by Mary Costa, "Once Upon a Dream" (Sammy Fain/Jack Lawrence) performed by Mary Costa and Bill Shirley, "Skumps" (Tom Adair/Erdman Penner/George Bruns) performed by chorus, "Sleeping Beauty" (Tom Adair/George Bruns) performed by chorus. Music by George Bruns, adapted from Tchaikovsky's ballet Sleeping Beauty.

Film Facts

• The 16th of the Disney animated classics, *Sleeping Beauty* was a classic fairy tale, which Disney hoped could replicate the enormous success of *Cinderella* (1950). The story had its origins in a six-volume French romance *Perceforest* from the 1300s, later adapted by other writers and collected by the Brothers Grimm in *Children's and Household Tales,* often known as *Grimms' Fairy Tales*.
• Eleanor Audley, who voiced Maleficent, also voiced Cinderella's stepmother, Lady Tremaine.
• Looney Tunes director Chuck Jones briefly worked on *Sleeping Beauty* during a closure of the "Termite Terrace" studio at Warner Bros., but found work for Walt Disney confining.
• Prince Phillip was the first Disney prince to be named: the royal in *Snow White and the Seven Dwarfs* was simply "the Prince," and *Cinderella* featured "Prince Charming."
• Additional appearances: "Keys to the Kingdom" on *Disney Princess Enchanted Tales: Follow Your Dreams* DVD (2009), cameos in *House of Mouse* (2001-2003) and *Ralph Breaks the Internet* (2018). Maleficent was in the live-action *Maleficent* (2014) and *Maleficent: Mistress of Evil* (2019).

Smallfoot (PG)

Theatrical release date: September 28, 2018
Production Company: Warner Animation Group, Zaftig Films
Length: 96 minutes
Directed by: Karey Kirkpatrick
Screenplay by: Karey Kirkpatrick and Clare Sera, screen story by John Requa & Glenn Ficarra and Karey Kirkpatrick

Synopsis: All is well in the Himalayan yeti village, with strict traditions and guidance provided by the Stonekeeper, who reads the stones that provide the village laws. One day a plane crashes and the young Migo sees a human, known to the yeti as a "smallfoot," who is carried away by his parachute before anyone else can see him. The Stonekeeper says that smallfoots don't exist, and when Migo is unwilling to say he didn't see what he saw, he is cast out from the village. Wandering in the snow, he is found by the yetis Kolka, Gwangi, and Fleem, who take him to a secret meeting of the Smallfoot Evidentiary Society (SES), headed by Meechee, the Stonekeeper's daughter. With the encouragement of the SES, Migo travels below the clouds to the base of the mountain. He runs into another smallfoot, animal documentary personality Percy Patterson, planning to take the terrified filmmaker to the yeti village to prove that smallfoots do exist. They are waylaid by a blizzard, ending up in a cave, where they begin to develop trust in each other. Percy agrees to go along with Migo to the yeti village, prompting a crisis for those who rigidly follow tradition.

Cast: Channing Tatum as Migo
James Corden as Percy
Zendaya as Meechee
Common as Stonekeeper
LeBron James as Gwangi
Danny DeVito as Dorgle
Gina Rodriguez as Kolka

Yara Shahidi as Brenda
Ely Henry as Fleem
Jimmy Tatro as Thorp
Patricia Heaton as Mama Bear
Justin Roiland as Garry
Jack Quaid as Pilot
Sarah Baker as Soozie's Mom

Music Highlights: "Perfection" (W. Kirkpatrick/K. Kirkpatrick) performed by Channing Tatum, "Wonderful Life" (W. Kirkpatrick/K. Kirkpatrick) performed by Zendaya, "Crazy" (Burton/Callaway/Reverberi/Reverberi), "Percy's Pressure" (orig. "Under Pressure" by Bowie/Deacon/May/Mercury/Taylor, additional lyrics by W. Kirkpatrick/K. Kirkpatrick) performed by James Corden, "Blue (Da Ba Dee)" (Randone/Gabutti/Lobina), "Wonderful Questions" (W. Kirkpatrick/K. Kirkpatrick) performed by Channing Tatum and Zendaya, "Let It Lie" (W. Kirkpatrick/K. Kirkpatrick) performed by Common, "Moment of Truth" (W. Kirkpatrick/K. Kirkpatrick) performed by CYN, "Finally Free" (Franzino/Haas/Ryan/Bunetta/Horan) performed by Niall Horan. Music by Heitor Pereira.

Film Facts

• The story was from the unpublished book *Yeti Tracks* by Sergio Pablos (*Despicable Me, Klaus*).
• "Mammoths all the way down" is based on the concept "Turtles all the way down."
• There is a brief mid-credits scene featuring Percy (1:31:05).

The Smurfs and the Magic Flute (TV-G)

Theatrical release date: November 25, 1983 (US), October 7, 1976 (Belgium/West Germany)
Country: Belgium Belgian title: *La Flûte à Six Schtroumpfs*
Production Company: Belvision, Dupuis Audiovisuel
Length: 89 minutes
Directed by: José Dutilliew
Written by: Peyo & Yvan Delporte

Synopsis: In the middle ages, there is a festival at the King's castle. A music merchant loses an unusual 6-holed flute when it falls off of his cart. The King retrieves it, but believing it to be poorly made, tosses it in the fire. Young Peewit rescues it, and finds that it's a magic flute that makes people dance when he plays it. A stranger, Matthew "Oily" McCreep, hears of the flute, and arrives at the Kingdom at the same time that two mysterious tiny blue figures, the Smurfs, fly in on a stork. McCreep steals the flute, using it to rob others, and Peewit and the knight John pursue him, but are stopped by the power of the flute. The magician Homnibus helps them visit the Smurf village, and the Smurfs agree to make a second magic flute to stop McCreep, who meanwhile is raising an army to do battle with the King. With the aid of the Smurfs, Peewit duels McCreep on the flute, finally defeating him. They make the decision to return the flutes to the Smurfs, but Peewit secretly plans to keep one, replacing it with a duplicate. In the end, he mixes them up, giving away the magic flute.

Cast: Role	English (US)	French
Johan/John	Grant Gottschall	William Coryn
The King	Michael Sorich	Georges Pradez
Homnibus	Ted Lehman	Henri Crémieux
Mortaille/Mumford/Earl Flatbroke	Ron Gans	Jacques Dynam
Torchesac/Matthew "Oily" McCreep	Mike Reynolds	Albert Médina
Pirlouit/William/Peewit	Cam Clarke	Michel Modo
Papa Smurf	Bill Capizzi, Michael Sorich	Michel Elias
Smurf #1	Robert Axelrod	Jacques Ruisseau
Smurf #2	Michael Sorich	Roger Crouzet

Music Highlights: Music by Michel Legrand. Songs by Yvan Delporte & Peyo, English lyrics by Roger Guertin.

Film Facts

• In the 1960s T.V.A. Dupuis created a handful of black & white animated Smurfs shorts for Belgian TV, five of which were collected in the theatrical film *The Adventures of the Smurfs* (1965).
• Additional appearances: *The Smurfs* animated TV series (1981–1989), live-action/animated film *The Smurfs* (2011), live-action/animated film *The Smurfs 2* (2013), and animated film *Smurfs: The Lost Village* (2017).

Smurfs: The Lost Village (PG)

Theatrical release date: April 7, 2017
Production Company: Columbia Pictures, Sony Pictures Animation, Kerner Entertainment Company
Length: 90 minutes
Directed by: Kelly Asbury
Written by: Stacey Harman and Pamela Ribon, based on the characters and works of Peyo

Synopsis: When Smurfette ends up near the Forbidden Forest, she sees an unknown Smurf. She is captured by the bird Monty and taken to the evil wizard Gargamel, who uses his magic to learn that there is a another Smurf village near three tall trees. Brainy, Hefty, and Clumsy rescue Smurfette, but even when an angry Papa Smurf grounds them, the four are determined to solve the mystery of the Lost Village. As they approach the village, they run afoul of Gargamel, a swarm of dragonflies, a dark cavern, and a dangerous river. By chance they end up at Smurfy Grove, a village of female Smurfs, and are taken by SmurfLily to meet their leader, SmurfWillow. Papa Smurf follows them, and it isn't long before Gargamel attacks the Grove with freezeballs. As Gargamel uses his evil powers to steal the Smurfs' magic, Smurfette shocks everyone by leading Gargamel to the Smurf Village. They soon come to know that although she was created by Gargamel, she is the truest Smurf of all.

Cast: Demi Lovato as Smurfette
Rainn Wilson as Gargamel
Joe Manganiello as Hefty Smurf
Jack McBrayer as Clumsy Smurf
Danny Pudi as Brainy Smurf
Mandy Patinkin as Papa Smurf
Dee Bradley Baker as Monty
Frank Welker as Azrael
Michelle Rodriguez as SmurfStorm
Ellie Kemper as SmurfBlossom

Julia Roberts as SmurfWillow
Ariel Winter as SmurfLily
Meghan Trainor as SmurfMelody
Bret Marnell as Snappy Bug/Handy Smurf
Brandon Jeffords as Cauldron
Kelly Asbury as Nosey Smurf
Jake Johnson as Grouchy Smurf
Gabriel Iglesias as Jokey Smurf
Tituss Burgess as Vanity Smurf
Jeff Dunham as Farmer Smurf

Music Highlights: "Smurfs Theme (La La Song)" (Barbera/Hanna/Curtin), "Here It Comes Now" (Keefe/O'Donis) performed by Brothers and Sisters, "Heroes (We Could Be)" (Bowie/Eno+Lindblad/Lo) performed by Alesso featuring Tove Lo, "Delirious (Boneless)" (Aoki/Beck/Collins/Lake/Phillips/Vaughan/Vllasaliu) performed by Steve Aoki, Chris Lake & Tujamo feat. Kid Ink, "Blue (Da Ba Dee)" (Lobina/Randone/Gabutti) performed by Eiffel 65, "You Will Always Find Me In Your Heart" (Lennertz /Tunstall) performed by Shaley Scott, "I'm a Lady" (Trainor /René) performed by Meghan Trainor. Music by Christopher Lennertz.

Film Facts

• This release returns the franchise to fully-animated films, after the live-action/animation hybrids *The Smurfs* (2011) and *The Smurfs 2* (2013).
• Gargmel, Azrael, and Monty appear in a mid-credits scene (1:24:57).
• The film is dedicated to Peyo's wife, Janine "Nine" Culliford, who first painted the Smurfs.

Snow White and the Seven Dwarfs (Approved)

Theatrical release date: Feb 4, 1938 (premiere Dec 21, 1937 at Carthay Circle Theatre, Hollywood)
Production Company: Walt Disney Productions
Length: 83 minutes
Supervising Director: David Hand. Sequence Directors: Perce Pearce, William Cottrell, Larry Morey, Wilfred Jackson, Ben Sharpsteen
Story Adaptation: Ted Sears, Richard Creedon, Otto Englander, Dick Rickard, Earl Hurd, Merrill De Maris, Dorothy Ann Blank, Webb Smith, adapted from *Grimms' Fairy Tales*

Synopsis: The kind princess Snow White flees when her vain stepmother, the wicked Queen, seeks to kill her, because Snow White's beauty surpasses her own. Snow White happens upon seven dwarfs in the woods, and takes shelter with them. While disguised as an old woman, the Queen gives Snow White a poisoned apple, causing her to collapse, appearing to die. After the dwarfs lament this tragedy, she is awakened by a prince's kiss.

Cast: Adriana Caselotti as Snow White
Lucille la Verne as the Queen/Witch
Moroni Olsen as the Magic Mirror
Stuart Buchanan as the Huntsman
Harry Stockwell as the Prince
The Dwarfs: Roy Atwell as Doc, Eddie Collins as Dopey, Pinto Colvig as Sleepy/Grumpy, Billy Gilbert as Sneezy, Otis Harlan as Happy, Scotty Mattraw as Bashful

Music Highlights: "I'm Wishing" performed by Adriana Caselotti, "One Song" performed by Harry Stockwell, "Whistle While You Work" performed by Adriana Caselotti, "Heigh-Ho" performed by the Dwarf Chorus, "Bluddle-Uddle-Um-Dum (The Dwarfs' Washing Song)" performed by the Dwarf Chorus, "The Dwarf's Yodel Song (The Silly Song)" performed by the Dwarf Chorus, "Some Day My Prince Will Come" performed by Adriana Caselotti. All songs by Larry Morey/Frank Churchill. Score by Frank Churchill, Leigh Harline, Paul Smith.

Film Facts

• The iconic first feature film of Walt Disney Productions, *Snow White and the Seven Dwarfs* premiered at the Carthay Circle Theatre in Hollywood on December 21, 1937, and was released nationally on February 4, 1938. The story is loosely based on the German fairy tale "Snow White" included in the 1812 first edition of the classic collection *Children's and Household Tales,* also known as *Grimms' Fairy Tales,* telling the story of the kind Snow White, whose jealous step-mother, the Queen, attempts to do away with her, before she is saved by a septet of idiosyncratic dwarfs.
• The film began production in 1934, as the first full-length animated feature ever produced.
• The original focus of the film was to be the wacky antics of the dwarfs, but gradually shifted to the more serious rivalry between the Queen and Snow White.
• *Snow White and the Seven Dwarfs* was the first American film to issue a soundtrack.
• DisneyToon Studios was developing a CGI prequel, *The Seven Dwarfs*. It was canceled in 2006.
• Additional appearances: "The Dinner Dance" on *Princess Stories Vol. 2* DVD (2005), dwarves in *The 7D* animated TV series (2014-2016), cameos in *House of Mouse* (2001-2003), *The Lion King 1 1/2* (2004), and *Ralph Breaks the Internet* (2018). Dwarfs were in the shorts "Standard Parade" (1939), "The Seven Wise Dwarfs" (1941), "All Together" (1942) & "The Winged Scourge" (1943).

Song of the Sea (PG)

Theatrical release date: Sep 6, 2014 (Canada, TIFF), Jul 10, 2015 (Ireland), Nov 20, 2015 (US)
Country: Ireland, Belgium, Denmark, France, Luxembourg   Irish title: *Amhrán na Mara*
Production Company: Cartoon Saloon, Big Farm, Melusine Productions, Backup Media
Length: 93 minutes
Directed by: Tomm Moore
Written by: William Collins, based on an original story by Tomm Moore

Synopsis: Ben's mother is lost the night his sister Saoirse ("seer-sha") is born, making Ben impatient and unkind with Saoirse, who at the age of six, still does not speak. The children's grandmother comes to the house to help their father, Conor, care for them. One night Saoirse plays a tune on her mother's seashell, which creates a trail of glowing dots. The trail takes her to a white coat, which she puts on, and to the sea, where she meets a group of seals in the water. As she enters the water she transforms into a seal, as she is a mythological creature called a "selkie." After she swims with the seals underwater, her grandmother finds her happily washed up on the shore in human form. Fearing for the children's safety, Conor throws the coat in the sea and sends the children to live with their grandmother in the city. Saoirse again plays a tune on the seashell, wrapping herself in her grandmother's coat in an effort to again turn into a seal, but without success. Three mysterious figures appear, seeking the selkie. They take Saoirse to their home, bringing Ben along, explaining that Saoirse is a selkie, and her white coat must be found. Saoirse begins to fall ill, and when they seek shelter at a holy well, she jumps in, with Ben following. He must face many challenges as he seeks to find Saoirse, from facing the owl witch Macha to looking at his own selfish behavior. His bravery unlocks much lost family history.

Cast: David Rawle as Ben
Brendan Gleeson as Conor/Mac Lir
Fionnula Flanagan as Granny/Macha
Lisa Hannigan as Bronach
Lucy O'Connell as Saoirse
Jon Kenny as Ferry Dan/The Great Seanachaí

Pat Shortt as Lug
Colm Ó'Snodaigh as Mossy
Liam Hourican as Spud/Bus Driver
Kevin Swierszcz as Young Ben
William Collins as Additional Voices
Paul Young as Additional Voices

Music Highlights: "The Song" performed by Lisa Hannigan & Lucy O'Connell, "Song of the Sea" performed by Lisa Hannigan, "Song of the Sea (Lullaby)" performed by Nolwenn Leroy. Music by Bruno Coulais and Kíla, performed by Bruno Coulais, Kila band, Lisa Hannigan. Lucy O'Connell, Slim Pezin, Nolwenn Leroy, Liam Hourican, and Karl Odlum.

Film Facts

- Saoirse and Ben pass the famous Dublin statue Molly Malone (30:55).
- Aisling the fairy from Tomm Moore's *The Secret of Kells* (2009) appears on the bus (38:02).
- The Irish band Kila has recorded several albums, including *The Secret of Kells* soundtrack (2009).
- The film was was nominated for the "Best Animated Feature" Academy Award.

Soul (PG)

Streaming/theatrical release date: Dec 25, 2020 (premiere Oct 11, 2020 at London Film Festival)
Production Company: Pixar Animation Studios, Walt Disney Pictures
Length: 100 minutes
Directed by: Pete Docter, co-directed by Kemp Powers
Story and Screenplay by: Pete Docter, Mike Jones & Kemp Powers

Synopsis: Joe Gardner is a middle school music teacher, who gets an opportunity to perform at the Half Note club supporting jazz singer Dorothea Williams. Falling into an open manhole, Joe is transported to a conveyer belt heading into a bright light, the Great Beyond. He runs the opposite direction, and ends up falling into the Great Before, where souls are given personalities before life on Earth. Joe, under the guise of a mentor, is matched with the contrary soul "22," tasked with helping her find the "spark" that will complete her personality. They go to the Hall of Everything to explore activities, but nothing catches 22's interest. They run across Moonwind, who leads a group of mystics that help lost souls reconnect with their bodies. In his rush to reunite with his body, Joe bumps into 22. To their mutual horror, 22 ends up in Joe's body, while Joe is in the body of a therapy cat. They escape from the hospital to find the Earthly form of Moonwind. While they wait for a time they can return, they prepare Joe's body for his jazz gig. As 22 experiences life through Joe's body, she finally gets her "spark." The agent Terry takes Joe and 22 back to the Great Before, where 22 is finally given her pass to Earth. Joe returns to play the jazz gig, but finds it less fulfilling than he thought. He keeps thinking about 22, and Moonwind tells him she's become a lost soul. Joe must rethink what's truly most important to him.

Cast: Jamie Foxx as Joe
Tina Fey as 22
Graham Norton as Moonwind
Rachel House as Terry
Alice Braga as Counselor Jerry

Richard Ayoade as Counselor Jerry
Phylicia Rashad as Libba
Donnell Rawlings as Dez
Ahmir-Khalib Thompson a.k.a. Questlove as Curley
Angela Bassett as Dorothea

Music Highlights: "II B.S." (Mingus) performed by Charles Mingus, "Subterranean Homesick Blues" (Dylan) performed by Bob Dylan, "Body and Soul" (Green/Heyman/Sour/Eyton) performed by Herbie Hancock, "Apple Tree" (Wright/Bradford) performed by Erykah Badu, "We Get Along" (Crispiano/Guy/Jones/Orchard/Roth/Steinweiss) performed by Sharon Jones & the Dap-Kings, "Rappin' CED" (Diggs) performed by Daveed Digs, "Check the Rhime" performed by A Tribe Called Quest, "Parting Ways" (Chesnutt) performed by Cody Chesnutt, "It's All Right" (Mayfield) performed by Jon Batiste and Celeste. Score by Trent Reznor and Atticus Ross. Jazz compositions by Jon Batiste.

Film Facts

- In the US the film was released for streaming on Disney+, and in theaters in other countries.
- A poster shows Portorosso (57:39), the setting of Pixar's next film, *Luca* (2021).
- *Soul* won the "Best Animated Feature Film" Golden Globe.

Spirit: Stallion of the Cimarron (G)

Theatrical release date: May 24, 2002
Production Company: DreamWorks Animation, Dreamworks Pictures
Length: 83 minutes
Directed by: Kelly Asbury, Lorna Cook
Screenplay by: John Fusco

Synopsis: Spirit is a colt born free in the open plains of the Old West. After happening upon sleeping US Army soldiers, he is captured and taken to an Army fort, where an effort is made to break him. Unable to do so, they deprive Spirit of food and water for three days. When a Native American called Little Creek is captured, he and Spirit escape together. Spirit is taken to the Lakota camp, where he meets the painted horse Rain, and she shows him the ways of the Lakota. Spirit is treated with kindness, but still doesn't want to be ridden, and Little Creek finally lets him go. After US soldiers attack the tribe, Spirit jumps into a river to save Rain, and they both fall down a waterfall. While they rest, Spirit is again captured by the Army, and sent to work on a railroad, which he realizes is headed straight toward his homeland. Sprit is able to thwart the project, and is unexpectedly found by Little Creek. After one final fierce pursuit by the Army, Spirit earns his freedom, and reuniting with Rain, the pair return to Spirit's home as free horses.

Cast: Matt Damon as Spirit
James Cromwell as The Colonel
Daniel Studi as Little Creek
Chopper Bernet as Sgt. Adams
Jeff LeBeau as Murphy/Railroad Foreman
John Rubano as Soldier
Richard McGonagle as Bill
Matthew Levin as Joe

Adam Paul as Pete
Robert Cait as Jake
Charles Napier as Roy
Meredith Wells as Little Indian Girl
Zahn McClarnon as Little Creek's Friend
Zahn McClarnon, Michael Horse
      as Little Creek's Friends
Don Fullilove as Train Pull Foreman

Music Highlights: "Here I Am" (Adams/Peters/Zimmer), "This is Where I Belong" (Adams/Lange/Zimmer), "You Can't Take Me" (Adams/Greenaway/Lange), "Get Off My Back" (Adams/Kennedy), "Sound the Bugle" (Greenaway/Horn), "I Will Always Return (Finale)" (Adams/Lange/Zimmer), "Here I Am (End Title)" (Adams/Peters/Zimmer), "Don't Let Go" (Adams/Greenaway/Lange/Peters) with Sarah McLachlan, "Brothers Under the Sun" (Adams/Jablonsky/Peters). All songs performed by Bryan Adams. Music by Hans Zimmer.

Film Facts

- The film earned praise for its accurate depiction of the movements of horses.
- The famous mountain Half-Dome of Yosemite is seen next to Spirit's homeland (1:15:53).
- Bryan Adams sang both the English and the French version of the soundtrack. The Spanish version of the film featured vocals by Raúl Malo of the country band The Mavericks.
- Additional appearances: *Spirit Riding Free* animated TV series (2017-2020), *Spirit Untamed* animated film (2021).

Spirited Away (PG)

Theatrical release date: July 20, 2001 (Japan), September 20, 2002 (US limited)
Country: Japan Japanese title: *Sen to Chihiro no Kamikakushi* (lit. "Sen and Chihiro's Spiriting Away")
Production Company: Studio Ghibli
Length: 125 minutes
Directed by: Hayao Miyazaki
Written by: Hayao Miyazaki

Synopsis: The girl Chihiro is moving to a new house with her parents, and on the way they find a doorway that leads to an empty train station and abandoned theme park. Her parents find an unattended buffet, and begin eating, but Chihiro is uneasy, and instead wanders the grounds. She finds an intense boy, Haku, who tells her she has to leave before it gets dark. Chihiro rushes back to her parents, and as it gets dark shadowy figures begin to appear. Her parents have turned into huge pigs, and water now surrounds the park. Haku guides Chihiro through a strange world of odd creatures, telling her that to save her parents she must get a job at the bathhouse. She meets the six-armed boiler man Kamaji, who agrees to hire her if Yubaba allows it. Yubaba, manager of the bathhouse for the spirits, reluctantly agrees to give her a job, re-naming her Sen. She is assigned to work with Lin, and accidentally invites in No-Name, a black figure with a white mask, which later causes chaos at the bathhouse. Sen is tasked with serving an oozing stink spirit that turns out to be a river spirit, which rewards her kindness. Soon it is Sen's turn to help Haku, and she hopes that she can eventually make it home, if she can negotiate the perils of Yubaba, No-Name, and Yubaba's sister Zeniba.

Cast:

Role	English	Japanese
Chihiro/Sen	Daveigh Chase	Rumi Hiiragi
Yubaba/Zeniba	Suzanne Pleshette	Mari Natsuki
Haku	Jason Marsden	Miyu Irino
Lin	Susan Egan	Yoomi Tamai
Kamaji	David Ogden Stiers	Bunta Sugawara
Chihiro's mother	Lauren Holly	Yasuko Sawaguchi
Chihiro's father	Michael Chiklis	Takashi Naitō
Assistant Manager	John Ratzenberger	Takehiko Ono
Boh (Baby)	Tara Strong	Ryūnosuke Kamiki

Music Highlights: "Itsumo Nando-demo" (Kaku/Kimura) performed by Yumi Kimura, "Paradise" (Castonguay/Terenzi/Bledsoe) performed by Natural and Ben Bledsoe. Music by Joe Hisaishi.

Film Facts

• Often considered Studio Ghibli's best, the film won the "Best Animated Feature" Academy Award, and the "Best Film" Japan Academy Film Prize, becoming the highest grossing film in Japan.
• Screenwriters Cindy Davis Hewitt and Donald H. Hewitt wrote English dialogue to match the animated lip movements of the characters.

Star Wars: The Clone Wars (PG)

Theatrical release date: August 15, 2008
Production Company: Lucasfilm Animation, Lucasfilm Ltd.
Length: 98 minutes
Directed by: Dave Filoni
Written by: Henry Gilroy, Steven Melching, Scott Murphy

Synopsis: Set after *Star Wars: Episode II – Attack of the Clones* (2002), the evil Count Dooku has control of the major hyperspace lanes through his droid army, dividing the Republic from most of its clone army, with more planets joining Dooku's Separatists. The Jedi have been occupied fighting a war, and crime has spread during this time, with Jabba the Hutt's son, Rotta, kidnapped by pirates. Jabba asks the Jedi to come to his rescue, which they agree to, as Jabba controls the Outer Lanes, which the Jedi need to move their troops. As Anakin Skywalker and Obi-Wan Kenobi lead a battle with a droid army on the planet Christophsis, the young Ahsoka Tano is sent by Yoda to retrieve them, explaining that she is to be a Padawan apprentice to a reluctant Anakin. When a droid force field stops the Jedi, Anakin and Ahsoka go on a stealth mission to knock it out, as Obi-Wan stalls the General, and the battle is soon won. Yoda sends Anakin and Ahsoka to the planet Teth to rescue Rotta, as Obi-Wan talks with Jabba. After a battle with droid soldiers, Anakin and Ahsoka retrieve Rotta, but are framed for kidnapping him by Count Dooku and his apprentice, Asajj Ventress. Obi-Wan battles Ventress while Anakin and Ahsoka try to get Rotta back. Ventress lies that Anakin killed Rotta, and Dooku tells Jabba that Anakin is coming to kill him, asking that he be allowed to stop Anakin. Padmé Amidala attempts to persuade Jabba's uncle Ziro to help, but he is in league with Dooku. While Dooku confronts Anakin, Ahsoka is tasked with getting Rotta to Jabba's palace, with the fate of the galaxy in the balance.

Cast: Matt Lanter as Anakin Skywalker
Ashley Eckstein as Ahsoka Tano
James Arnold Taylor as Obi-Wan Kenobi/4-A7
Dee Bradley Baker as Clone Troopers/
    Captain Rex/Cody
Tom Kane as Yoda/Narrator/Admiral Yularen
Nika Futterman as Asajj Ventress/Tee-C-Seventy
Ian Abercrombie as Chancellor Palpatine/
    Darth Sidious
Corey Burton as General Loathsom/
    Ziro the Hutt/Kronos-327
Catherine Taber as Padmé Amidala
Matthew Wood as Battle Droids
Kevin Michael Richardson as Jabba the Hutt
David Acord as Rotta the Huttlet
Samuel L. Jackson as Mace Windu
Anthony Daniels as C-3PO
Christopher Lee as Count Dooku

Music Highlights: Score by Kevin Kiner, original *Star Wars* themes and score by John Williams.

Film Facts

- The film was followed by the *Star Wars: The Clone Wars* animated series (2008–2020).
- Anakin's armor resembles the armor of Darth Vader.
- A post-credits scene featuring Jawas appears (1:37:53).

Stellaluna (G)

Home media release date: July 12, 2004
Production Company: Tundra Productions, Scholastic Productions
Length: 41 minutes
Directed by: William R. Kowalchuk
Screenplay by: Rachel Koretsky and Steve Whitestone, based on the book by Janell Cannon

Synopsis: When the young fruit bat Stellaluna is separated from her mother by an owl, a kind mother bird agrees to raise her alongside her own three children, Pip, Flitter, and Flap, as long as she agrees to follow "the rules of the nest." Stellaluna is glad for the safety of the nest, but feels out of place among the birds, with no feathers, a tendency to hang upside down, no interest in eating bugs, and staying awake at night. When a "superhero jumping spider" named Askari gets too close to the bird nest, he offers to be Stellaluna's bodyguard if she doesn't eat him. One day when playing a game, Stellaluna falls out of the nest, and she, Pip, Flitter, and Flap end up in the owl's nest. They are able to escape into a bush, but can't find their way home. Stellaluna realizes she can see in the dark, and decides to search for their home while the other birds sleep. She gets help from the friendly parrots Kasuku and Horatio, who help her believe in herself. When she sees the owl, she hurries back to lead Pip, Flitter, and Flap into a cave for safety. While there, Stellaluna's mother finds them and is overjoyed, explaining that Stellaluna is a fruit bat and part of the "brave and daring flying foxes." The reunion is cut short when Askari comes to say that the mother bird has been captured by the owl. All of the bats fly together to confront the owl, which flees in fear. Stellaluna and her adoptive siblings finally understand why Stellaluna was such an unusual "bird," and as she leaves with her mother, they agree that they will always be friends.

Cast: Chiara Zanni as Stellaluna/Flitter
Eric Pospisil as Pip
Matthew Prior as Pip
Brittany Moldowan as Flap
Scott McNeil as Horatio
Kathleen Barr as Kasuku/Skeptical Bat

Brenda Crichlow as Nestra/
  Friendly Bat
Lee Tockar as Askari
Blu Mankuma as Great White Owl
Judith Maxie as Estrella

Music Highlights: "Upside Down" (Jody Gray/June Rachelson-Ospa) performed by Chiara Zanni, "Best in You" (Jody Gray/June Rachelson-Ospa) performed by Kathleen Barr and Scott McNeil. Music by Jody Gray.

Film Facts

• An audio recording of the book won the "Best Spoken Word Album for Children" Grammy Award.
• Chiara Zanni (Stellaluna) later voiced Daring Do in *My Little Pony: Friendship Is Magic*.
• The book was on the National Education Association's "Teachers' Top 100 Books for Children" list.

Steven Universe: The Movie (TV-PG)

Broadcast date: September 2, 2019
Production Company: Cartoon Network Studios
Length: 82 minutes
Directed by: Rebecca Sugar, co-directed by Joe Johnston, Kat Morris
Written by: Various

Synopsis: The gem homeworld was ruled by the four Diamonds: White, Yellow, Blue, and the youngest, Pink. Steven Universe, now age 16, is the son of the late Pink Diamond, and declines to join the other Diamonds in ruling their world, preferring to stay on Earth with his friends Pearl, Amethyst, and Garnet. They are soon confronted by the villainous Spinel, who uses an energy scythe to turn Pearl, Amethyst, and Garnet into gems (with garnet splitting into Sapphire and Ruby), and causes Steven's gem to malfunction. Steven turns Spinel into a gem as well, and while the five gems soon return to humanoid form, they have no memory. Peridot, Bismuth and Lapis Lazuli aid Steven as he tries to help his friends recover their memories. One by one they begin to remember, but when Spinel's spacecraft injects a toxic fluid into the Earth, they need her to remember her past. She recalls how she and Pink were happy in their garden, when Pink left for Earth, leaving Spinel alone for 6,000 years, until she learned that Pink had been destroyed. Spinel agrees to stop her injector, but when her insecurities lead her to doubt Steven's sincerity, she resumes her attack. When all seems lost, Steven must remember his own truth.

Cast: Zach Callison as Steven Universe
Michaela Dietz as Amethyst
Estelle Swaray as Garnet
Deedee Magno Hall as Pearl
Sarah Stiles as Spinel
Uzo Aduba as Bismuth

Christine Ebersole as White Diamond
Lisa Hannigan as Blue Diamond
Erica Luttrell as Sapphire
Kate Micucci as Sadie Miller
Ted Leo as Steg (Steven/Greg Fusion)
Patti LuPone as Yellow Diamond

Music Highlights: "The Tale of Steven" (Sugar/Tran/Velema/Ball), "Let Us Adore You" (Sugar/Tran/Velema/Liu), "Happily Ever After" (Sugar/Tran/Velema/Liu), "Other Friends" (Sugar/Tran/Velema/Liu), "system/BOOT.pearl_final(3).Info" (Sugar/Tran/Velema/Liu), "Who We Are" (Sugar/Tran/Velema), "Isn't It Love?" (Sugar/Estelle/Fauntleroy/Tran/Velema), "No Matter What" (Sugar/Tran/Velema/Liu), "Disobedient" (Sugar/Krol), "Independent Together" (Sugar/Leo/Stemage), "Drift Away" (Sugar/Mann/Tran/Velema), "Found" (Sugar/Tran/Velema/Liu), "True Kinda Love" (Sugar/Stewart/Chance the Rapper/Stewart/Tran/Velema/Fauntleroy/Sanchez), "Change" (Sugar/Tran/Velema/Liu), "Finale" (Sugar/Gallant/Tran/Velema). Music by Rebecca Sugar et al.

Film Facts

• Spinel was inspired by some of the more "cartoony" characters from the 1920s and 30s.
• Additional appearances: *Steven Universe* animated TV series (2013-2019), *Steven Universe Future* limited animated TV series (2019-2020).

Strange Magic (PG)

Theatrical release date: January 23, 2015
Production Company: Lucasfilm, Industrial Light & Magic, Touchstone, Walt Disney Pictures
Length: 99 minutes
Directed by: Gary Rydstrom
Screenplay by: David Berenbaum, Irene Mecchi, Gary Rydstrom, story by George Lucas

Synopsis: The fairy Marianne, just before her marriage to the amorous warrior Roland, ventures into the Dark Forest, seeking a primrose flower, a key ingredient in love potions. She flees after a close call with the minions of the Bog King, ruler of the Dark Forest. The Bog King orders all the primroses destroyed, in the hopes of destroying love. Marianne is heartbroken when she sees Roland kissing another fairy, but he still pursues Marianne, who rejects him. Roland sends the elf Sunny to free the Sugar Plum Fairy from the Dark Forest to make him a love potion. With the help of an imp, Sunny gets the potion from the fairy, but the Bog King pursues Sunny to the Elf Festival. During an attack by the Bog King's minions, Marianne's sister Dawn is hit with the love potion. The Bog King demands the potion back by moondown, or he will attack, taking Dawn with him. Dawn, bewitched by the love potion, falls in love with the Bog King, despite his cruelty. The fairies fly to Dawn's rescue, and the ensuing struggles make it clear that love is indeed strange.

Cast: Alan Cumming as Bog King
Evan Rachel Wood as Marianne
Elijah Kelley as Sunny
Meredith Anne Bull as Dawn
Sam Palladio as Roland
Kristin Chenoweth as Sugar Plum Fairy
Alfred Molina as Fairy King
Maya Rudolph as Griselda

Bob Einstein as Stuff
Peter Stormare as Thang
Kevin Michael Richardson as Brutus
Llou Johnson as Pare
Robbie Daymond as Fairy Cronies
Brenda Chapman as Imp
Tony Cox as Plum Elf

Music Highlights: "Can't Help Falling in Love" (Elvis Presley), "Crazy in Love" (Beyoncé ft. Jay Z), "I'll Never Fall in Love Again" (Dionne Warwick), "Three Little Birds" (Bob Marley & the Wailers), "C'mon Marianne" (The Four Seasons)/"Stronger (What Doesn't Kill You)" (Kelly Clarkson), "I Wanna Dance With Somebody (Who Loves Me)" (Whitney Houston), "People Are Strange" instrumental (The Doors), "Trouble" (Elvis Presley), "Love is Strange" (Mickey & Sylvia), "Say Hey" (Michael Franti & Spearhead), "Mistreated" (Deep Purple), "I Can't Help Myself (Sugar Pie Honey Bunch)" (The Four Tops), "Straight On" (Heart), "Strange Magic" (ELO), "Crazy Little Thing Called Love" instrumental (Queen), "Tell Him" (Johnny Thunder)/"Wild Thing" (orig. by The Wild Ones, popularized by The Troggs). Music by Marius de Vries.

Film Facts

• The story's mixed-up passions were inspired by Shakespeare's *A Midsummer Night's Dream*.
• A mid-credits scene with Roland (1:32:40), and a post-credits scene (1:38:42) appear.
• Lucas wanted to make this as a film for his daughters. It was in production off and on for 15 years.

Summer Wars (PG)

Theatrical release date: August 1, 2009
Country: Japan **Japanese title**: *Samā Wōzu*
Production Company: Madhouse
Length: 114 minutes
Directed by: Mamoru Hosoda
Screenplay by: Satoko Okudera, original story by Mamoru Hosoda

Synopsis: Kenji Koiso, a math prodigy and maintenance coder for the online virtual world of OZ, accompanies classmate Natsuki Shinohara to celebrate her great-grandmother Sakae's 90th birthday. Kenji learns that Natsuki has told her family that they are dating, hoping that her grandmother's health would hold out until she met Natsuki's "boyfriend." While there, they meet Natsuki's uncle Wabisuke, who had a falling out with his relatives for selling the family's property. When a mysterious code shows up on Kenji's phone, he solves it, and the next morning learns that the code was used to break through OZ's security, and he is wanted by the authorities. Kenji's friend sends him an avatar so he can enter OZ, where Kenji battles whoever has stolen his avatar. He gets assistance from Sakae's grandson Kazuma, who owns the powerful avatar King Kazma, but Kenji's stolen avatar powers up and prevails. Kenji is arrested, and in the real world chaos develops, with traffic jams, broken water mains, and false alarms, as the powerful AI hacking software Love Machine, responsible for stealing Kenji's avatar, wreaks havoc. Unable to get through the traffic, Kenji is returned to Sakae's home. Wabisuke reveals he developed Love Machine for the US military, and Sakae chases him off. Sakae passes away, her health monitor not functioning due to Love Machine. Kazuma lures Love Machine into a trap, but when it escapes, they learn that it controls a satellite headed toward a nuclear reactor. Soon, with the support of her family, it is Natsuki's turn to battle Love Machine, with everything on the line.

Cast:

Role	English	Japanese
Kenji Koiso	Michael Sinterniklaas	Ryunosuke Kamiki
Natsuki Shinohara	Brina Palencia	Nanami Sakuraba
Sakae Jinnouchi	Pam Dougherty	Sumiko Fuji
Takashi Sakuma	Todd Haberkorn	Takahiro Yokokawa
Wabisuke Jinnouchi	J. Michael Tatum	Ayumu Saito
Kazuma Ikezawa	Maxey Whitehead	Mitsuki Tanimura
Mansuke Jinnouchi	John Swasey	Ichirō Nagai

Music Highlights: "Bokura No Natsu No Yume" (Yamashita) performed by Tatsurô Yamashita. Music by Akihiko Matsumoto.

Film Facts

• Mamoru Hosoda's films include *The Girl Who Leapt Through Time, Wolf Children,* and *Mirai.*
• The film is set in the Japanese city of Ueda.

Surf's Up (PG)

Theatrical release date: June 8, 2007
Production Company: Sony Pictures Animation
Length: 85 minutes
Directed by: Ash Brannon, Chris Buck
Screenplay by: Don Rhymer and Ash Brannon & Chris Buck & Christopher Jenkins, story by Christopher Jenkins and Christian Darren

Synopsis: A documentary tells the story of Cody Maverick, a northern rockhopper penguin who is the best surfer in Antarctica, tracing his family life with his mother and brother Glen. Cody describes his idol, the revered surfing pioneer Big Z. Cody enters the Big Z Memorial surfing competition on Pen Gui Island, where he is quickly smitten with the lifeguard Lani, and finds conflict with the arrogant Tank. They face off surfing, but Cody is impaled by a sea urchin. Lani takes him to see a local surfer called "Geek," who cures his foot. When Cody is discouraged, the Geek insists on making him a board out of koa wood. They happen upon a small beach, where Cody finds a shack with Big Z's original surf boards, and is shocked to find that Geek is Big Z. After initially rejecting Z's guidance, Cody ask for help making his board. Cody finally relaxes, and Z gives him surfing tips. When Z confesses he disappeared because he was not good enough to compete, it's Cody's turn to inspire his idol.

Cast: Shia LaBeouf as Cody Maverick
Jeff Bridges as Zeke "Big Z" Topanga/"Geek"
Zooey Deschanel as Lani Aliikai
Jon Heder as Chicken Joe
James Woods as Reggie Belafonte
Diedrich Bader as Tank "The Shredder" Evans
Mario Cantone as Mikey Abromowitz
Kelly Slater as Kelly
Rob Machado as Rob
Sal Masekela as SPEN Announcer

Music Highlights: "Welcome to Paradise" (Armstrong/Pritchard/Wright) performed by Green Day, "Drive" (Boyd/Einziger/Katunich/Pasillas/Kilmore) performed by Incubus, "Stand Tall" (Bushnell/Watson/Frazier/Fox) performed by Dirty Heads, "Forrowest" (Continentino/Refosco) performed by Forro in the Dark, "Pocket Full of Stars" (Forrest/Jones/Cohen/Galley/Hutchinson) performed by Nine Black Alps, "Into Yesterday" (Frazier/Fox) performed by Sugar Ray, "Big Wave" (Vedder/Ament) performed by Pearl Jam, "Run Home" (Dyball/Heppner/Nudo/Watchorn) performed by Priestess, "What I Like About You" (Palamarchuk/Marinos/Skill) performed by The Romantics, "Hawaiian War Chant (Ta-Hu-Wa-Hu-Wai)" (Leleiohaku/Freed) performed by Bob Wills & His Texas Playboys, "You Get What You Give" (Alexander/Nowels) performed by New Radicals. End credits: "Reggae Got Soul" (Hibbert/Lyn) performed by 311, "Wipe Out" (Surfaris) performed by The Queers, "Lose Myself" (Hill) performed by Lauryn Hill. Music by Mychael Danna.

Film Facts

- The voices of the documentary filmmakers are the actual directors, Ash Brannon and Chris Buck.
- There is a brief post-credits scene with Glen (1:24:59).
- The film was nominated for the "Best Animated Feature" Academy Award and Annie Award.
- Additional Appearances: *Surf's Up 2: WaveMania* (2017), which received unfavorable reviews.

The Sword in the Stone (G)

Theatrical release date: December 25, 1963
Production Company: Walt Disney Productions
Length: 79 minutes
Directed by: Wolfgang Reitherman
Story by: Bill Peet, based on the book by T.H. White

Synopsis: In a story drawn from the mythology of King Arthur, after the death of the King of England, a mysterious anvil holding an immovable sword appears in London, with an inscription saying that whoever removes the enchanted sword from the anvil will become the new King of England. Many years after the appearance of the sword, the wizard Merlin has foreseen that Arthur, a 12-year old orphan nicknamed Wart, will become the King, and takes him on as a student. Merlin puts Wart through a series of lessons preparing him for his role as England's future monarch, including adventures as a fish and as a squirrel, learning to fly with Merlin's owl, Archimedes, and one misadventure with the witch, Madam Mim. Wart is also a squire to his foster brother, Kay, and when he forgets Kay's sword during an important tournament, unwittingly retrieves the "sword in the stone" as a replacement.

Cast: Sebastian Cabot as Sir Ector
Karl Swenson as Merlin
Rickie Sorensen as Wart
Junius Matthews as Archimedes
Ginny Tyler as Little Girl Squirrel

Martha Wentworth as Madam Mim/Squirrel
Norman Alden as Sir Kay
Alan Napier as Sir Pellinore
Richard Reitherman as Wart
Robert Reitherman as Wart

Music Highlights: "The Legend of the Sword in the Stone" performed by Fred Darian, "Higitus Figitus" performed by Karl Swenson, "That's What Makes the World Go Round" performed by Karl Swenson/Rickie Sorensen, "A Most Befuddling Thing" performed by Karl Swenson, "Mad Madame Mim" performed by Martha Wentworth, "Blue Oak Tree" performed by Sebastian Cabot/Alan Napier. All songs by Richard M. Sherman/Robert B. Sherman. Score by George Bruns.

Film Facts

• The 18th Disney animated classic, *The Sword in the Stone* is the first book in T.H. White's tetralogy, *The Once and Future King*. It was the last film released in Walt Disney's lifetime.
• Much of the soundtrack remains unavailable in official digital format, with no CD of the soundtrack issued. The song "Higitus Figitus" is included on *Music of Disney: Legacy in Song* box.
• While director Wolfgang Reitherman's sons Richard and Robert voiced Wart, a third son of Reitherman's, Bruce, would later voice Mowgli in *The Jungle Book* (1967) and Christopher Robin in "Winnie the Pooh and the Honey Tree" (1966).
• The DVD features a deleted song, "The Magic Key."
• The King Arthur Carrousel, inspired by the film, was added to Fantasyland at Disneyland.
• Additional appearances: "That's What Makes the World Go 'Round" and "Higitus Figitus" on *Sing Along Songs: Collection of All Time Favorites: The Magic Years* 1997 VHS.

The Tale of Despereaux (G)

Theatrical release date: December 19, 2008
Production Company: Universal Pictures, Relativity Media, Larger Than Life Prod., Framestore
Length: 93 minutes
Directed by: Sam Fell, Rob Stevenhagen
Screenplay by: Gary Ross, screen story by Will McRobb & Chris Viscardi, based on the book
The Tale of Despereaux by Kate DiCamillo

Synopsis: In the kingdom of Dor, renowned for its delicious soups, Chef Andre prepares his annual creation, secretly aided by his magical assistant Boldo. The ship rat Roscuro is tempted by the aroma of the soup, ending up in the Queen's bowl, who dies of fright. In his grief, the king outlaws both soup and rats, and a long, grey drought begins. In Mouseworld, the strangely brave young mouse Despereaux reads tales of chivalrous knights, and fearlessly talks to the sad but kind Princess Pea. For his unmouselike behavior, the mice banish Despereaux to the dungeon of Dor, where the rats live in darkness. Despereaux is nearly killed by the order of the cruel rat leader Botticelli, but Roscuro saves him. Despereaux tells Roscuro about honor and chivalry, and the two pledge themselves to helping the Princess. Overhearing servant Miggery Sow say she served the Princess, Roscuro goes to see Princess Pea, trying to apologize, but is treated harshly. Embittered, Roscuro persuades Miggery to take the Princess prisoner, then traps Miggery as well. The Princess sends Despereaux for help, and as he tries to raise the alarm, chef Andre decides to begin cooking soup again. As the steam rises to the sky, rain begins to fall. Despereaux persuades Boldo to try to rescue the Princess, but when things look hopeless, a change of heart begins a process of forgiveness that transforms the kingdom for all its inhabitants.

Cast: Matthew Broderick as Despereaux
Dustin Hoffman as Roscuro
Emma Watson as Princess Pea
Tracey Ullman as Miggery Sow
Kevin Kline as Andre
William H. Macy as Lester
Stanley Tucci as Boldo
Ciarán Hinds as Botticelli

Robbie Coltrane as Gregory
Tony Hale as Furlough
Frances Conroy as Antoinette
Frank Langella as Mayor
Richard Jenkins as Principal
Christopher Lloyd as Hovis
Charles Shaughnessy as Pietro
Sigourney Weaver as Narrator

Music Highlights: "Soup" (Ballard/Ross/Stewart) performed by Glen Ballard, Gary Ross and David A. Stewart, "It's Great to Be a Rat" (Ballard/Ross/Stewart) performed by Glen Ballard, Gary Ross and David A. Stewart. Music by William Ross.

Film Facts

• The film was originally to be directed by Sylvain Chomet, but Universal replaced him.
• Roscuro's name comes from the art technique "chiaroscuro" (light/dark), while Botticelli and Boldo are named after the Italian artists Sandro Botticelli and Giuseppe Arcimboldo.

The Tale of the Princess Kaguya (PG)

Theatrical release date: November 23, 2013 (Japan)
Country: Japan   Japanese title: *Kaguyahime no Monogatari*
Production Company: Studio Ghibli
Length: 137 minutes
Directed by: Isao Takahata, English production directed by Jamie Simone
Screenplay by: Isao Takahata & Riko Sakaguchi, story by Isao Takahata, adaptation by Mike Jones

Synopsis: One day a bamboo cutter finds a stalk that blooms to reveal a tiny princess in a robe, who quickly falls asleep. The bamboo cutter gently takes her to his wife, and the princess turns into a baby that they raise. She develops rapidly, and soon inexplicably can walk and talk. The wood cutter finds gold and beautiful fabrics among the bamboo, and makes plans to take the girl to the capital so she can be a proper princess, which he believes will make her happy. The girl, nicknamed "L'il Bamboo," was happy exploring the fields and playing with her friends, especially an older boy named Sutemaru. Lady Sagami comes from the palace to educate the Princess in proper behavior for a noble lady, and forbids the Princess to frolic or make art, and her father scoffs at inviting her friends from the village. Named the Princess Kaguya, she devotes herself to her studies, is accepted by the nobility, and has many suitors, but is deeply unhappy. One day the Princess tells her parents she must return to where she came from, and explains why she came in the first place.

Cast: Role	English	Japanese
The Princess Kaguya	Chloë Grace Moretz/Caitlyn Leone	Aki Asakura
The Bamboo Cutter	James Caan	Takeo Chii
Bamboo Cutter's Wife/Narrator	Mary Steenburgen	Nobuko Miyamoto
Sutemaru	Darren Criss	Kengo Kora
Lady Sagami	Lucy Liu	Atsuko Takahata
Prince Kuramochi	Beau Bridges	Isao Hashizume
Prince Ishitsukuri	James Marsden	Takaya Kamikawa
Lord Minister of the Right Abe	Oliver Platt	Hikaru Ijūin
Me no Warawa	Hynden Walch	Tomoko Tabata
The Mikado	Dean Cain	Nakamura Shichinosuke II
Great Counselor Otomo	Daniel Dae Kim	Ryudo Uzaki
Inbe no Akita	George Segal	Tatekawa Shinosuke

Music Highlights: "Inochi no Kioku (When I Remember This Life)" (Nikaido) performed by Kazumi Nikaido, "Warabe Uta" (Takahata/Sakaguchi), "Tennyo no Uta" (Takahata/Sakaguchi). Music by Joe Hisaishi.

Film Facts

• The story "The Tale of the Bamboo Cutter" dates back to the 9th/10th century.
• A documentary, *Isao Takahata and His Tale of the Princess Kaguya,* shows the making of the film.
• The film was nominated for the "Best Animated Feature" Academy Award.

Tales of the Night (NR)

Theatrical release date: July 20, 2011 (France), September 26, 2012 (US, limited)
Country: France French title: *Les Contes de la Nuit*
Production Company: Nord-Ouest Films, Studio O, StudioCanal
Length: 84 minutes
Written and Directed by: Michel Ocelot

Synopsis: Three members of a theater troupe brainstorm ideas for stories they could enact:

• **Night of the Werewolf**. After he confesses he is a werewolf, the prince Jan is betrayed by his fiancée, who tells everyone that the wolf killed Jan and must be destroyed. The wolf helps his fiancée's sister, who tells the story of how she helped Jan when he was imprisoned, not knowing that the one she told the tale to was Jan himself.

• **Jon Jon and Beauty Not Knowing**. In the Caribbean, the boy Jon Jon (Tijean) enters the Country of the Dead. A man tells him he could marry the king's daughter, and how to defeat three animals that will stand in his way, but Jon Jon chooses to feed them instead. He finally sees the King, and must pass three suitor's tests. The animals he once helped now help him.

• **The Chosen One of the Golden City**. In a golden Aztec city, the prettiest girls are sacrificed to the city's Benefactor. An outsider comes to propose a new way of life.

• **Tom-Tom Boy**. An African boy wishes to drum, but has no instrument. He meets the keeper of a Magic Tom-Tom, which causes people and animals to dance. After practicing, he returns to his village, and plays to cure the dying king, then uses his drum to end an enemy attack. When the drum is destroyed, the true magic is revealed.

• **The Boy Who Never Lied**. In Tibet, a wager is made between royals over whether a boy who never lies can be made to do so.

• **The Young Doe and the Architect's Son**. An evil sorcerer forbids Maud to see her love, Thibault, locking her in a fortress. Thibault scales the fortress, telling Maud to agree to marry the sorcerer, as his father had built the cathedral, and Thibault knows its secrets.

Cast: Marine Griset as Girl/Heroine (Annie)
Julien Béramis as Boy/Hero
Yves Barsacq as Théo/Sorcerer
Michel Ocelot as Melonghi

Olivier Claverie as The Great Shepherd, King of the Dead, King of Tibet
Michel Elias as the Father, Old West Indian, Neighboring Monarch, Guardian

Music Highlights: "Sababou" (Grazaï/Diawara) performed by Fatoumata Diawara, "Tolon" (Grazaï/Diawara) performed by Fatoumata Diawara, "Monneka" (Grazaï). Music by Christian Maire.

Film Facts

• The film is made from five episodes of the animated French TV show *Dragons et Princesses* (2010), plus the new segment "The Young Doe and the Architect's Son."
• Michel Ocelot also directed *Kirikou and the Sorceress* (1998) and *Azur & Asmar* (2006).
• The English cast included John Haslar, Jo Wyatt, Nigel Lambert, Jonathan Keeble, & Emma Tate.

Tangled (PG)

Theatrical release date: November 24, 2010
Production Company: Walt Disney Pictures, Walt Disney Animation Studios
Length: 100 minutes
Directed by: Nathan Greno, Byron Howard
Screenplay by: Dan Fogelman

Synopsis: When a King's pregnant wife is deathly ill, he seeks to heal her with a magic flower which has been jealously guarded for many years by Gothel, an old woman who uses it to stay young. The flower gives their daughter, Rapunzel, long magical hair. "Mother" Gothel steals Rapunzel and hides her in a tower, using her hair to stay young, and frightening her into staying in the tower with tales of the world's cruelty. Rapunzel longs see the world, especially the lights that appear in the sky each year on her birthday, so when cynical thief Flynn Rider steals a crown and hides in Rapunzel's tower to evade the determined horse Maximus, Rapunzel captures him and strikes a deal: if she frees him, he will be her guide in the world, to learn the truth about the floating lights — and about herself.

Cast: Mandy Moore as Rapunzel
Zachary Levi as Flynn Rider
Donna Murphy as Mother Gothel
Ron Perlman as Stabbington Brother
M.C Gainey as Captain of the Guard
Jeffrey Tambor as Big Nose Thug
Brad Garrett as Hook Hand Thug
Paul F. Tompkins as Short Thug (white beard)
Richard Kiel as Vlad (unicorn collector)
Delaney Rose Stein as Young Rapunzel/Little Girl
Nathan Greno as Guard 1/Thug 1
Byron Howard as Guard 2/Thug 2
Tim Mertens as Guard 3
Frank Welker as Maximus (horse)

Music Highlights: "When Will My Life Begin" performed by Mandy Moore, "Incantation Song" performed by Donna Murphy/Mandy Moore, "Mother Knows Best" performed by Donna Murphy, "I've Got a Dream" performed by Garrett, Tambor, Moore, Levi and ensemble, "I See the Light" performed by Moore/Levi, "Something That I Want" (Potter) performed by Grace Potter. Music by Alan Menken/lyrics by Glenn Slater unless otherwise indicated. Score by Alan Menken.

Film Facts

• The 50th of the Disney animated classics, the working title of *Tangled* was *Rapunzel Unbraided*, a story based on the "Rapunzel" fairy tale collected in 1812 by the Brothers Grimm in *Children's and Household Tales* (also known as *Grimms' Fairy Tales*), though the roots of the tale go back to "Petrosinella," a 1634 Italian story by Giambattista Basile.
• Cameos include Pinocchio and a punked-up Pumbaa (40:39), and for the very sharp-eyed, books in the bookshop from *Sleeping Beauty, Beauty and the Beast,* and *The Little Mermaid* (1:03:54).
• The scene as Rapunzel looks at a mosaic of herself (1:02:56) recalls *Ferris Bueller's Day Off* (1986), as Cameron has an art museum epiphany while looking at a pointillistic painting (57:45).
• The King/Queen/second Stabbington Brother don't have voice credits because they don't speak.
• Additional appearances: "Tangled Ever After" short (2012), *Tangled: Before Ever After* Disney Channel Movie (2017), *Tangled: The Series/Rapunzel's Tangled Adventure* TV series (2017-2019).

Tangled: Before Ever After (TV-Y7)

Broadcast date: March 10, 2017
Production Company: Disney Television Animation
Length: 55 minutes
Directed by: Tom Caulfield, Stephen Sandoval
Written by: Jase Ricci

Synopsis: Rapunzel and Eugene are enjoying life in the Kingdom of Corona, on the eve of Rapunzel's coronation day. After an adventurous ride, Rapunzel is guided in royal life by the confident, protective Cassandra. Rapunzel begins to feel the weight of royal responsibilities, and when Eugene unexpectedly proposes, she leaves the castle with Cassandra. Cassandra shows her mysterious black spikes growing out of the ground where the magic flower from *Tangled* was found. When Rapunzel touches one of the spikes, her hair turns blonde and grows to a great length again. New spikes begin sprouting from the ground, following Rapunzel, who flees back to the castle. With her long, blonde hair hidden, Rapunzel's coronation ceremony begins. The outlaw Lady Caine frees a group of criminals, and led by Pocket, they disrupt the ceremony, and begin taking the nobility prisoner. Rapunzel, Eugene, and Cassandra work together to defeat the villains, but after Rapunzel tells her father how she snuck out, he angrily forbids her to leave the castle without his permission. Eugene apologizes to Rapunzel for putting her on the spot with his public proposal, and she asks him to be patient with her, as she plans to investigate the mysterious spikes.

Cast: Zachary Levi as Eugene
Mandy Moore as Rapunzel
Eden Espinosa as Cassandra
Clancy Brown as King Frederic
Julie Bowen as Queen Arianna
Laura Benanti as Lady Caine
Jeffrey Tambor as Big Nose

M.C. Gainey as Captain of the Guard
Sean Hayes as Pete the Guard
Diedrich Bader as Stan the Guard
Jess Harnell as Pocket
Kevin Michael Richardson as Otter
Alan Dale as The Vicar
Dee Bradley Baker as Pascal/Maximus

Music Highlights: "Life After Happily Ever After" (Alan Menken/Glenn Slater) performed by Mandy Moore, Zachary Levi and Clancy Brown, "Wind in My Hair" (Alan Menken/Glenn Slater) performed by Mandy Moore, "Wind in My Hair Reprise" (Alan Menken/Glenn Slater) performed by Mandy Moore. Music by Alan Menken and Glenn Slater.

Film Facts

• The film introduced the series *Tangled: The Series,* later called *Rapunzel's Tangled Adventure* (2017-2020), taking place between *Tangled* (2010) and the short "Tangled Ever After" (2012).
• In contrast to the computer animation of *Tangled, Tangled: Before Ever After* used 2D animation.
• The film debuted as a Disney Channel Original Movie on March 10, 2017, and was issued on DVD on April 11, 2017. The DVD included the first four "Tangled: Short Cuts" shorts (out of 9 total). A DVD titled *Tangled: Queen for a Day* was also issued from the TV series.

Tarzan (G)

Theatrical release date: June 18, 1999
Production Company: Walt Disney Pictures, Walt Disney Feature Animation
Length: 88 minutes
Directed by: Kevin Lima and Chris Buck
Screenplay by: Tab Murphy and Bob Tzudiker & Noni White, based on the story *Tarzan of the Apes* by Edgar Rice Burroughs

Synopsis: Tarzan is discovered as a baby by the kind gorilla Kala, and rescued from the ferocious leopard Sabor. After fighting over the years to be accepted by the apes, and especially his adoptive father, Kerchak, Tarzan is fascinated when humans arrive in the jungle, and torn about where he truly belongs.

Cast: Tony Goldwyn as Tarzan
Glenn Close as Kala
Minnie Driver as Jane
Brian Blessed as Clayton
Nigel Hawthorne as Professor Porter

Rosie O'Donnell as Terk
Wayne Knight as Tantor
Lance Henriksen as Kerchak
Alex D. Linz as Young Tarzan

Music Highlights: "Two Worlds" (Collins) performed by Phil Collins, "You'll Be In My Heart" (Collins) performed by Phil Collins and Glen Close, "Son of Man" (Collins) performed by Phil Collins, "Trashin' the Camp" (Collins) performed by Rosie O'Donnell, "Strangers Like Me" (Collins) performed by Phil Collins. Score by Mark Mancina.

Film Facts

• The 37th of the Disney animated classics, *Tarzan* was based on the 1912 serial/novel *Tarzan of the Apes* by Edgar Rice Burroughs. Tarzan's full name is John Clayton, Earl of Greystoke.
• The filmmakers wanted to include music, but did not want to make the film a musical, finding it hard to picture Tarzan breaking into song, so the decision was made to hire pop singer Phil Collins, both because his music could reach people emotionally, and because he was a percussionist, and they wanted to honor Africa's rich tradition of drumming (versus the emphasis on African vocal music in *The Lion King*). The score was composed by Mark Mancina, and Collins and Mancina would work together again on *Brother Bear* (2003).
• Phil Collins' tender song "You'll Be in My Heart" won both an Academy Award and a Golden Globe, while the soundtrack won a Grammy.
• Like *Beauty and the Beast* and *The Lion King*, *Tarzan* was made into a stage musical, with a book by David Henry Hwang. The production opened on Broadway in 2006, with additional productions in the Netherlands, Sweden, and Germany.
• There are a few cameos in the film: The teapot and cup seen when Terk is "Trashin' the Camp" look suspiciously like Mrs. Potts and Chip from *Beauty and the Beast* (43:10), and a toy of the dog Little Brother from *Mulan* falls out of Professor Porter's pocket (59:53).
• This was the last film of the Disney Renaissance.
• Additional appearances: Followed by *The Legend of Tarzan* TV series (2001-2003), *Tarzan & Jane* (2002), *Tarzan II* (2005).

Tarzan & Jane (G)

Home media release date: July 23, 2002
Production Company: Walt Disney Television Animation, Walt Disney Video Premiere, Toon City Animation, Walt Disney Animation Australia, Wang Film Productions, Hana Animation
Length: 75 minutes
Directors/writers: "Tarzan & Jane" film directed by Steve Loter, written by Bill Motz & Bob Roth
"British Invasion" segment directed by Don Mackinnon, written by Mirith Colao
"Volcanic Diamond Mine" segment directed by Victor Cook, written by John Behnke, Rob Humphrey, Jim Peterson
"Flying Ace" segment directed by Victor Cook, written by Jess Winfield, story by Jess Winfield, David Bullock, Adam Van Wyck

Synopsis: A series of stories featuring Tarzan and Jane, as, on the couple's first wedding anniversary, Jane thinks back on their adventures. Stories include: "The British Invasion," in which Jane's friends come to rescue her, only to find that she decided to stay in the jungle. Jane invites her friends to a picnic, but all must flee when the panthers Sheeta and Nuru crash the party. In "Volcanic Diamond Mine" treasure hunters enlist Tarzan's help to obtain diamonds believed to be inside a volcano, complicated by the fact that the volcano is active. In "Flying Ace" Jane is visited by a pilot she knows, intent on recovering a very special music box.

Cast: Michael T. Weiss as Tarzan
Olivia d'Abo as Jane
Jeff Bennett as Professor Porter
Jim Cummings as Tantor
April Winchell as Terk
Rene Auberjonois as Reynard Dumont
Grey Delisle as Greenly
Alexis Denisof as Nigel Taylor
John O'Hurley as Niels
Phil Proctor as Captain Jerrold
Nicollette Sheridan as Eleanor
Tara Strong as Hazel

Music Highlights: "Two Worlds" (Phil Collins) performed by Phil Collins and Mandy Moore, "The Song of Life" (Don Harper/Mark Mancina) performed by Mandy Moore, "Jane's Theme" (Mark Mancina). Score by Don Harper and Dave Metzger.

Film Facts

• The three segments of the film were episodes of *The Legend of Tarzan* animated TV series that had not yet been aired.
• Both Michael T. Weiss and Olivia d'Abo voice acted in the *Justice League* (2002-2005) series. Olivia d'Abo also portrayed Kevin Arnold's sister Karen on *The Wonder Years*, as well as voice acting on *Batman Beyond, The Animatrix, Ultimate Avengers,* and *Star Wars: The Clone Wars.*
• The three "episodes" that Jane recalls in this movie were produced for a second season of *The Legend of Tarzan*. They were finally broadcast in 2003.
• Additional appearances: Sequel to *Tarzan* (1999) and *The Legend of Tarzan* TV series, followed by the "midquel" *Tarzan II: The Legend Begins* (2005).

Tarzan II: The Legend Begins (G)

Home media release date: June 14, 2005
Production Company: DisneyToon Studios, Toon City Animation, Walt Disney Pictures
Length: 72 minutes
Directed by: Brian Smith
Screenplay by: Jim Kammerud & Brian Smith and Bob Tzuiker & Noni White, based on the "Tarzan" stories created by Edgar Rice Burroughs

> **Synopsis**: Taking place in the midst of the events of the first *Tarzan* film (1999), *Tarzan II* follows Tarzan's exploits as a child, with comic relief by gorillas Kago and Uto. When Tarzan is chased far from his home by Sabor, the leopardess, he encounters the Dark Mountain where a fearsome monster, the Zugor, is believed to dwell. After Tarzan hears the frightening cry of the monster, he flees, encountering an irritable old gorilla. He soon learns that things are often not what they appear to be, when it comes to monsters, enemies, and friends.

Cast: Harrison Chad as Tarzan
George Carlin as Zugor
Brad Garrett as Uto
Ron Perlman as Kago
Estelle Harris as Mama Gunda

Glenn Close as Kala
Lance Henriksen as Kerchack
Brenda Grate as Terk
Harrison Fahn as Tantor

Music Highlights: "Son of Man" (Collins) performed by Phil Collins, "Leaving Home (Find My Way)" (Collins) performed by Phil Collins, "Who Am I?" (Collins) performed by Phil Collins. Score by Mark Mancina.

Film Facts

• *Tarzan II* was produced by DisneyToon Studios, which specialized in "direct-to-video" home media releases, and occasional theatrical features.
• New roles included comedian George Carlin (*Cars*) as Zugor, Brad Garrett (*Finding Nemo, Ratatouille, Tangled*) and Ron Perlman (*Hellboy, Tangled*) as gorilla brothers Uto and Kago, and Estelle Harris (*Seinfeld, Toy Story*) as Mama Gunda, mother of the brothers.
• Phil Collins returned to write and perform the new songs "Leaving Home (Find My Way)" and "Who Am I?", with the score composed by Mark Mancina (*Planes, Moana*), Collins' partner on the soundtrack for the first first *Tarzan* film (1999), and on *Brother Bear* (2003). Collins would continue to develop the music from the Tarzan films for the 2006 Broadway musical *Tarzan*.
• Phil Collins' song "Leaving Home (Find My Way)" later became the song "I Need to Know" in the *Tarzan* Broadway musical.
• As a "midquel," this film takes place in the midst of the events during the song "Son of Man" from *Tarzan* (1999).
• No soundtrack was issued, but "Son of Man" is available on the first *Tarzan* soundtrack (1999).
• Additional appearances: Prequel/midquel to *Tarzan* (1999), *The Legend of Tarzan* TV series, and *Tarzan & Jane* (2005).

Teen Titans Go! To the Movies (PG)

Theatrical release date: July 27, 2018
Production Company: Warner Bros. Animation, DC Entertainment
Length: 84 minutes
Directed by: Peter Rida Michail and Aaron Horvath
Written by: Michael Jelenic & Aaron Horvath

Synopsis: After defeating Balloon Man, The Teen Titans — Robin, Beast Boy, Starfire, Cyborg, and Raven — find that they are not respected by the older superheroes. When they go to see Batman's movie, they conclude that if Robin can acquire an archnemesis, he could get a movie made about him, and he would have the respect he wants. Robin tries to face the supervillain Slade, master of mental manipulation, but when he escapes, Robin is left discouraged. Even worse, famed superhero movie director Jade Wilson tells him the only way she would make a movie about Robin is if there were no other superheroes. Taking up the challenge, Robin convinces the Teen Titans to help him use a time machine to prevent the creation of the other heroes, but when this leads to catastrophe, they reverse their actions. Taking on Slade again, Robin finally acquires an archnemesis, and the Titans are invited by Jade Wilson to a movie set. When Jade decides the Titans are too immature, she offers to make a movie just about Robin, and the Titans are disappointed when he agrees to do it. All is not as it seems, and it isn't long before Slade acquires the Ditronium Crystal, which he plans to use to control the world.

Cast: Greg Cipes as Beast Boy
Scott Menville as Robin
Khary Payton as Cyborg
Tara Strong as Raven
Hynden Walch as Starfire
Will Arnett as Slade
Kristen Bell as Jade Wilson

Eric Bauza as Aquaman/Stan Lee's Assistant
Michael Bolton as Tiger
Nicolas Cage as Superman
Joey Cappabianca as Plastic Man
Greg Davies as Balloon Man
John DiMaggio as Guard/Synth Skate Voice
Halsey as Wonder Woman

Music Highlights: "Go!" (Faber/Michail) performed by cast, "Check This Out" (Faber/Michail) performed by Jared Faber and Joel Virgel, "Upbeat Inspirational Song About Life" (Faber/Jefferies/Jelenic/Michail) performed by cast, "My Superhero Movie" (Faber/Jefferies/Michail) performed by Jacob Jefferies, "Take On Me" (Furuholmen/Harket/Waaktaar) performed by A-Ha, "Crystals" (Gemmill), "Back in Time" (Colla/Lewis/Hayes/Hopper) performed by Huey Lewis & The News, "Shenanigans" (Faber /Michail) performed by Peter Rida Michail. End Credits: "Go!" (Remix) (Faber/Michail/Rahman/Seeff) performed by Lil Yachty, "Upbeat" (Reprise) by Michael Bolton & Scott Menville, "Teen Titans Theme" (Sturmer) performed by Puffy AmiYumi. Music by Jared Faber.

Film Facts

- Voice actors included Nicholas Cage's son Kal-El Cage as Young Bruce Wayne.
- Though they are far more common in Marvel movies, a Stan Lee cameo appears (27:00).
- Additional Appearances: *Teen Titans Go!* animated TV series (2013-2020).

The Three Caballeros (Approved)

Theatrical release date: Dec 21, 1944 (Mexico), Feb 3, 1945 (US premiere), Feb 22, 1945 (US)
Production Company: Walt Disney Productions
Length: 71 minutes
Production Supervision and Direction by: Norman Ferguson, sequence direction by
Clyde Geronimi, Jack Kinney, Bill Roberts
Story: Homer Brightman, Ernest Terrazas, Ted Sears, Bill Peed, Ralph Wright, Elmer Plummer,
Roy Williams, William Cottrell, Del Connell, James Bodrero

Synopsis: Donald Duck opens birthday gifts from Latin American friends: a film projector
with a documentary about *aves raras*, or "rare birds," including a penguin and the Aracuan
Bird; a book from José Carioca describing the Brazilian state of Bahia; and after meeting
Panchito Pistoles of Mexico, a birthday piñata. As with *Saludos Amigos*, the film mixes live-
action and animation.

Cast: Sterling Holloway as Narrator
Clarence Nash as Donald Duck
Joaquin Garay as Panchito Pistoles
José Oliveira as José Carioca
Frank Graham as Narrator
Fred Shields as Narrator
Aurora Miranda of Brazil (singer)
Carmen Molina of Mexico (singer)
Dora Luz of Mexico (singer)
with Almirante, Trio Calaveras, Ascenci del Rio Trio, and Padua Hills Players

Music Highlights: "The Three Caballeros" (Manuel Esperón), "Baîa" (Ary Barroso), "Os Quindins
de Yayá" (Ary Barroso) performed by Aurora Miranda/Charles Wollcott/Nestor Amaral/Bando Da
Lua, "You Belong to My Heart" (Agustín Lara) performed by Dora Luz, "Mexico" (Charles Wolcott)
performed by Carlos Ramírez. Music by Charles Wolcott, Paul J. Smith, and Edward Plumb, lyrics by
Ray Gilbert.

Film Facts

• The 7th of the Disney animated classics, and the second of Disney's six 1940s "package" films,
The Three Caballeros was similar to *Saludos Amigos* (1943), though it was not billed as a sequel.
• The Aracuan bird is also in the "Johnny Appleseed" short in *Melody Time* (1948).
• The film was re-released as a featurette in 1977, accompanying the 1964 live-action Dick Van
Dyke film *Never a Dull Moment*.
• Tracks from *The Three Caballeros* were included on the 1959 *Saludos Amigos* reissue LP (Walt
Disney Records WDL 3039), also on iTunes. "You Belong to My Heart" was included on the
Classic Disney Vol. 5 CD and on *The Music of Disney: Legacy in Song* box set.
• Additional appearances: Preceded by *Saludos Amigos* (1943). Donald and José Carioca also
appeared in the "Blame it on the Samba" segment of *Melody Time* (1948).

Thunder and the House of Magic (NR)

Theatrical release date: December 25, 2013 (Belgium/France), December 25, 2015 (US)
Country: Belgium/France French title: *Le Manoir Magique*
Production Company: nWave Pictures, Anton Capital Entertainment, uMedia
Length: 85 minutes
Directed by: Ben Stassen & Jeremie Degruson
Screenplay by: James Flynn, Domonic Paris, Ben Stassen, story by Ben Stassen

Synopsis: An orange tabby cat is abandoned by his family, and a vicious dog chases him onto the grounds of a spooky mansion. As a storm approaches, the cat climbs a tree and enters the house, meeting the mistrustful Jack the rabbit and Maggie the mouse, who chase him out. Fleeing the rain, the cat ends up in the basement of the house, and finds his way into a room where the elderly magician Mr. Lawrence is working on his mechanical automaton companions. Mr. Lawrence is soon visited by his irritable nephew, Daniel, who wants him to move out of the mansion. Mr. Lawrence finds the cat and names him Thunder, but when the magician has a bicycle accident and is taken to the hospital, Daniel schemes to sell the house. The animals and automatons work together to thwart Daniel's plans until their beloved magician can return.

Cast: Murray Blue as Thunder/Dylan
Doug Stone as Lawrence
George Babbit as Carlo/Jack/Zoltar
Shanelle Gray as Maggie
Grant George as Daniel
Joey Camen as Chihuahua
Sage Sommer as Izzy
Cinda Adams as Nurse Baxter
Kathleen Browers as Carla

Joseph W. Terry as Reggie Willis
Nina Grillo as Audrey
Joey Lotsko as Mr. Eames
Millie Mup as Mrs. Eames
Kendra Leif as Lasondra
Goldie Jonsie as Old Lady
Will Parks as Mike Mathews
Kyle Hebert as Mark Mathews
Michael Sorich as Crane Operator

Music Highlights: "The Lovecats" (Robert Smith) performed by The Cure, "Maybe It's Magic" (Rosas/Healy/Bard) performed by Blake Healy, "House of Fun" (Mike Barson/Lee Thompson) performed by Madness, "This Ole House" (Stuart Hamblen) performed by Shakin' Stevens, "Am I Wrong" (William Wiik Larsen/Nico Sereba/Vincent Dery) performed by Nico & Vinz, "Hit the Lights" (Leah Haywood, Daniel James, Tony Nilsson) performed by Selena Gomez. Music composed by Ramin Djawadi.

Film Facts

• The voice actress for Thunder, "Murray Blue," is a stage name of Brianne "Bree" Siddall, also known as Brianne Brozey, Ian Hawk, Jetta E. Bumpy, and Jetta Bird.
• In 2017 TeamTO and Nexus Factory announced the new TV series *Presto! School of Magic*.
• Co-director Ben Stassen also directed *A Turtle's Tale: Sammy's Adventures* (2010), *The Son of Bigfoot* (2017), and *The Queen's Corgi* (2019).

Tinker Bell (G)

Theatrical release date: Sep 11, 2008 (Argentina), El Capitan Theatre in L.A. Sep 19 - Oct 2, 2008
Home media release date: October 28, 2008
Production Company: Walt Disney Pictures, DisneyToon Studios, Prana Studios
Length: 78 minutes
Directed by: Bradley Raymond
Screenplay by: Jeffrey M. Howard, original story by Jeffrey M. Howard, Bradley Raymond

Synopsis: Tinker Bell is born from a baby's laugh (as all fairies are), and upon arriving in Pixie Hollow, discovers her talent as a tinker fairy. She dearly wants to cross the sea to the mainland to help spring arrive, but learns that only nature-talent fairies are allowed to do so. She asks her friends to teach her their talents, including water fairy Silvermist, light fairy Iridessa, and animal fairy Fawn, but all her efforts end in disaster. The scheming fast-flying fairy Vidia tricks Tinker Bell into trying to catch the wild "sprinting thistles," but they end up stampeding through Pixie Hollow, destroying months of preparations for spring. Tinker Bell finally accepts her tinkering talent, and creates a series of new inventions that allow the fairies to usher spring in on time. As a reward, Tinker Bell is allowed to go to the mainland to return a musical figurine of a dancer she fixed to a familiar little girl named Wendy…

Cast: Mae Whitman as Tinker Bell
Kristin Chenoweth as Rosetta (garden fairy)
Raven-Symoné as Iridessa (light fairy)
Lucy Liu as Silvermist (water fairy)
America Ferrera as Fawn (animal fairy)
Jane Horrocks as Fairy Mary (tinker fairy)

Jesse McCartney as Terence (dust-keeper fairy)
Jeff Bennett as Clank (tinker fairy)
Rob Paulsen as Bobble (tinker fairy)
Pamela Adlon as Vidia (fast-flying fairy)
Anjelica Huston as Queen Clarion
Loreena McKennitt as Narrator

Music Highlights: "To the Fairies They Draw Near" (McKennitt) performed by Loreena McKennitt, "Fly to Your Heart" (Tumes) performed by Selena Gomez. Score by Joel McNeely.

Film Facts

• The role of Tinker Bell was originally going to be voiced by Brittany Murphy (*Clueless, Girl Interrupted, Just Married*) before going to Mae Whitman.
• The film had a limited run at El Capitan Theatre in Los Angeles, September 19 to October 2, 2008.
• The final release was preceded by many script revisions and personnel changes.
• Canadian singer/songwriter Loreena McKennitt wrote "To the Fairies They Draw Near" in the studio after meeting with the creative team at Disney.
• The book *In the Realm of the Never Fairies: The Secret World of Pixie Hollow* (2006) by Monique Peterson inspired the filmmakers' development of Pixie Hollow and its residents.
• Additional appearances: Tinker Bell appeared in *Peter Pan* (1953) and *Return to Never Land* (2002), followed by *Tinker Bell and the Lost Treasure* (2009), *Tinker Bell and the Great Fairy Rescue* (2010), "Pixie Hollow Games" short (2011), *Secret of the Wings* (2012), "Pixie Hollow Bake Off" short (2013), *The Pirate Fairy* (2014), & *Tinker Bell and the Legend of the Neverbeast* (2014).

Tinker Bell and the Lost Treasure (G)

Home media release date: Oct 27, 2009 (premiere Oct 25, 2009 at UN Headquarters, New York)
Production Company: DisneyToon Studios, Prana Studios, Walt Disney Pictures
Length: 81 minutes
Directed by: Klay Hall
Screenplay by: Evan Spiliotopoulos, original story by Klay Hall, Evan Spiliotopoulos

Synopsis: It is a special year in Pixie Hollow, as the Great Autumn Revelry celebration coincides with a blue harvest moon. Tinker Bell is chosen to create a new scepter to mark the occasion, topped by the rare, fragile moonstone, which will create blue pixie dust to rejuvenate the pixie dust tree. Tinker Bell's friend Terence tries to help her, but ends up annoying her to the point that she accidentally shatters the moonstone, leading her to blame Terence. Tinker Bell sets out to find the lost enchanted Mirror of Incanta, which can grant a wish. With the help of a friendly firefly named Blaze she finds the mirror, but after her wish goes amiss, Tinker Bell and Terence both recognize the importance of forgiveness. Working together, they realize how the fall scepter can be restored.

Cast: Mae Whitman as Tinker Bell
Jesse McCartney as Terence
Jane Horrocks as Fairy Mary
Lucy Liu as Silvermist
Raven-Symoné as Iridessa
Kristin Chenoweth as Rosetta
Angela Bartys as Fawn
Rob Paulsen as Bobble/Tall Troll/Owl

Jeff Bennett as Clank/Small Troll/Fairy Gary
Grey DeLisle as Lyria/Viola/Narrator
John DiMaggio as Minister of Autumn
Eliza Pollack Zebert as Blaze
Bob Bergen as Bugs and Creatures/Cheese
Roger Craig Smith as Bolt/Stone
Allison Roth as French Fairy
Anjelica Houston as Queen Clarion

Music Highlights: "If You Believe" (Brendan Milburn/Valerie Vigoda) performed by Lisa Kelly, "Fairy Tale Theatre" (Joel McNeely/Seth Friedman) performed by Grey DeLisle and Jule Garnye, "Gift of a Friend" (Adam Watts/Andy Dodd/Demi Lovato) performed by Demi Lovato, "Where the Sunbeams Play" (Joel McNeely/Brendan Milburn/Valerie Vigoda) performed by Méav Ní Mhaolchatha. Music by Joel McNeely.

Film Facts

• The story was inspired by the book *Tink, North of Neverland* (2007) by Kiki Thorpe.
• Lisa Kelly, singer of "If You Believe," is a member of the Irish singing ensemble Celtic Woman.
• The soundtrack CD includes songs not in the film: "Take to the Sky," "Road to Paradise," "I'll Try," "Magic Mirror," "The Magic of a Friend," "Fly Away Home," and "Pixie Dust."
• Tinker Bell emulates Indiana Jones when weighing out pixie dust (35:00).
• A regular *Tinker Bell and the Lost Treasure* soundtrack CD was released by Walt Disney Records in 2009, followed by a score soundtrack CD by Intrada in 2014.
• The film premiered at the UN Headquarters in New York, where the Under-Secretary-General for Communications and Public Information, Kiyotaka Akasaka, named Tinker Bell an "honorary Ambassador of Green" in order to increase environmental awareness among children.

Tinker Bell and the Great Fairy Rescue (G)

Home media release date: September 21, 2010 (premiere Aug 8, 2010 at May Fair Hotel, London)
Production Company: DisneyToon Studios, Walt Disney Pictures
Length: 76 minutes
Directed by: Bradley Raymond
Screenplay by: Bob Hilgenberg & Rob Muir and Joe Ansolabehere & Paul Germain, story by Bradley Raymond and Jeffrey M. Howard

Synopsis: Tinker Bell's curiosity gets the best of her during a trip to fairy camp on the mainland, and while she explores near a human house (despite Vidia's protests), she is captured by the girl who lives there, Lizzie Griffiths. Lizzie thinks better of showing the fairy to her scientist father, Dr. Griffiths, after she notes the butterflies he has pinned to a display, instead talking with Tinker Bell herself. Though she's terrified at first, Tinker Bell realizes Lizzie is kind, and teaches her about the fairy world, which Lizzie takes down in a journal. When Dr. Griffiths dismisses Lizzie's journal as nonsense, Tink angrily reveals herself, to the doctor's amazement. He tries to capture her, but ends up capturing Vidia instead, planning to share this discovery with the scientific community. Lizzie and the fairies must try to persuade him that keeping the fairy world secret is the right thing to do.

Cast: Mae Whitman as Tinker Bell
Lauren Mote as Lizzy Griffiths
Michael Sheen as Dr. Griffiths
Pamela Adlon as Vidia
Lucy Liu as Silvermist
Raven-Symoné as Iridessa
Kristin Chenoweth as Rosetta

Angela Bartys as Fawn
Rob Paulsen as Bobble
Jeff Bennett as Clank/Driver
Jesse McCartney as Terence
Cara Dillon as Narrator
Faith Prince as Mrs. Perkins
Bob Bergen as Cheese/Additional Voices

Music Highlights: "Summer's Just Begun" (Brendan Milburn/Valerie Vigoda) performed by Cara Dillon, "How to Believe" (Adam Iscove) performed by Holly Brook, "Come Flying With Me" (Joel McNeely/Brendan Milburn/Valerie Vigoda) performed by Cara Dillon. End credits: "How to Believe" (Adam Iscove) performed by Bridgit Mendler. Score by Joel McNeely.

Film Facts

• Cara Dillon's contributions to the soundtrack, the opening song "Summer's Just Begun" and "Come Flying With Me," reflect a strong Celtic influence. Holly Brook (AKA Skylar Grey) contributed "How to Believe," and Bridgit Mendler performed another version of the song for the end credits. In 2015 a soundtrack was issued by the Intrada Records/Disney partnership.
• While making the boat, Bobble says to Clank, "This one goes there. That one goes there. Right?" (20:30), an exact quote of Han Solo in *Star Wars: The Empire Strikes Back* (29:43). Another Han Solo quote is heard in *Tinker Bell and the Legend of the NeverBeast* (2014).
• The film had the working title *Tinker Bell: A Midsummer Storm*.
• A number of differences can be seen between the preview of the film included on the home media release of *Tinker Bell and the Lost Treasure*, and the final version of the film.

Tinker Bell/Disney Fairies: *Pixie Hollow Games* (NR)

Broadcast date: November 19, 2011 (Disney Channel), DVD release date: August 20, 2013
Production Company: DisneyToon Studios, Prana Studios, Walt Disney Pictures
Length: 21 minutes
Directed by: Bradley Raymond
Screenplay by: Jeffrey M. Howard

Synopsis: Chloe, the enthusiastic rookie member of the Garden Fairies team in the Pixie Hollow Games, hopes to break the team's losing streak, despite her partner Rosetta's pessimism. Inspired by Chloe's spirit, and emboldened by the taunts of their obnoxious Storm Fairy competitor Rumble, Rosetta finds a new resolve to compete against the other teams: the Fast-Flying Fairies, the Dust-Keeper Fairies, and the Storm Fairies. Challenging her aversion to dirt, Rosetta helps Chloe take the lead, but their car is destroyed by a lightning bolt from Rumble. Though they have no hope of winning, Rosetta and Chloe cross the finish line together, only to find that Rumble's team mate, Glimmer, chose not to cross the finish line, allowing the Garden Fairies their rightful win.

Cast: Megan Hilty as Rosetta
Brenda Song as Chloe
Jason Dolley as Rumble
Tiffany Thornton as Glimmer
Zendaya as Fern
Mae Whitman as Tinker Bell
Lucy Liu as Silvermist
Raven-Symoné as Iridessa
Angela Bartys as Fawn

Pamela Adlon as Vidia
Jeff Bennett as Clank/Fairy Gary
Rob Paulsen as Bobble/Buck
Jane Horrocks as Fairy Mary
Kari Wahlgren as Ivy
Jessica DiCicco as Lilac/Lumina
Jesse McCartney as Terence
Daniel Curtis Lee as Starter Sparrowman
Anjelica Huston as Queen Clarion

Music Highlights: Title theme: "Dig Down Deeper" (Milburn/Vigoda) performed by Zendaya. Score by Joel Neely.

Film Facts

• The film centered on the rivalry between the Garden Fairies (Rosetta and Chloe) and the Storm Fairies (Glimmer and Rumble). Other teams included the Dust-Keepers (Terence and Fairy Gary), Fast-Flying Fairies (Vidia and Zephyr), Light Fairies (Iridessa and Lumina), Animal Fairies (Fawn and Buck), Tinkers (Tinker Bell and Fairy Mary), and Water Fairies (Silvermist and Marina).
• The story was originally to be titled *Tinker Bell: Race through the Seasons*, in which Clank and Bobble represent the Tinker Fairies in a race through the four seasons, complicated by Bobble's hopes to impress a Lightning Fairy, threatening Clank and Bobble's friendship.
• Megan Hilty replaced Kristin Chenoweth as Rosetta from this title forward.
• Zendaya, star of the Disney Channel series *Shake It Up* (2010-2013) and *K.C. Undercover* (2015-2018), voiced the minor character Fern, also singing the inspirational "Dig Down Deeper."
• The composers of "Dig Down Deeper," Valerie Vigoda and Brendan Milburn, are members of the New York band GrooveLily.

Tinker Bell/Disney Fairies: *Secret of the Wings* (G)

Limited theatrical release date: August 31, 2012 (premiere August 16, 2012, Ukraine)
Home media release date: October 23, 2012
Production Company: DisneyToon Studios, Prana Studios, Walt Disney Pictures
Length: 75 minutes
Directed by: Peggy Holmes, co-directed by Bobs Gannaway
Screenplay by: Bobs Gannaway & Peggy Holmes and Ray Rowe and Tom Rogers

Synopsis: While helping Fawn usher some animals into Winter, Tinker Bell sneaks from Spring into Winter, finding that her wings sparkle mysteriously. She learns that the Keeper, in the Winter realm, can tell her what it means. Braving the cold of Winter, Tinker Bell finds Dewey, the Keeper, as well as Periwinkle, a white-haired Frost Fairy. Tinker Bell and Periwinkle's wings glow and sparkle when they are together, and they learn that they are twins. Though warm fairies are forbidden in Winter due to the risk of illness, Tinker Bell and Periwinkle spend time getting to know each other. Tinker Bell tinkers a snow machine to allow Periwinkle to visit Pixie Hollow, but during the visit Periwinkle falls ill, leading Winter Lord Milori to cast Tinker Bell's snow-making machine into the river. The machine begins generating snow in Spring, throwing the seasons out of balance and putting the Pixie Dust Tree in jeopardy. A team of Winter fairies place a protective frost on the Pixie Dust Tree to save it, but Tinker Bell's wing is broken by the cold. To the surprise of all, when Tinker Bell and Periwinkle put their wings together, it heals the broken wing, and it is learned that Winter fairies can frost the wings of Spring fairies to allow them to visit Winter.

Cast: Mae Whitman as Tinker Bell
Lucy Hale as Periwinkle
Timothy Dalton as Lord Milori
Jeff Bennett as Dewey/Clank
Lucy Liu as Silvermist
Raven-Symoné as Iridessa
Megan Hilty as Rosetta

Pamela Adlon as Vidia
Angela Bartys as Fawn
Matt Lanter as Sled
Debby Ryan as Spike
Grey DeLisle as Gliss
Rob Paulsen as Bobble
Jane Horrocks as Fairy Mary

Music Highlights: Title theme: "The Great Divide" (Milburn/Vigoda) performed by the McClain Sisters, "We'll Be There" (Milburn/Vigoda) performed by Sydney Sierota. Score by Joel McNeely.

Film Facts

• The Blu-ray includes "Pixie Hollow Games" and "Fright Light" bonus shorts.
• In researching the film director Holmes consulted with an expert on what happens when separated twins are reunited.
• The McClain Sisters' music video for "The Great Divide" is included on the DVD/Blu-ray.
• Despite the strict separation of Winter fairies from Pixie Hollow in the film, Winter fairies are present in *Tinker Bell* (2008) when Tinker Bell is born (3:36 and 5:02).
• The CD *Disney Fairies: Faith, Trust And Pixie Dust* (2012) includes "The Great Divide" and "We'll Be There" by Thia Megia (replacing the film version sung by Sydney Sierota of Echosmith).

Tinker Bell/Disney Fairies: *The Pirate Fairy* (G)

Limited theatrical release: Feb 13, 2014 (Denmark), Apr 1, 2014 (US), Home media: Apr 1, 2014
Production Company: DisneyToon Studios, Prana Studios
Length: 78 minutes
Directed by: Peggy Holmes
Screenplay by: Jeffrey M. Howard and Kate Kondell, story by John Lasseter, Peggy Holmes, Bobs Gannaway, Jeffrey M. Howard, Lorna Cook, & Craig Gerber

Synopsis: After DustKeeper fairy Zarina breaks the rules and experiments with pixie dust, she loses her post. Leaving Pixie Hollow, Zarina becomes a Pirate Fairy. She returns and spreads pink fairy dust, putting all the fairies to sleep except for Tinker Bell, her friends, and the Tinker fairy Clank, then steals Pixie Hollow's precious supply of blue pixie dust. Tinker Bell and her friends follow Zarina to a pirate ship, where they learn Zarina has made a deal with the pirates to be their captain, with the plan of using pixie dust to create a flying pirate ship. Once the pirates have the pixie dust, Zarina is betrayed and Tinker Bell and the fairies are trapped. With the help of a tiny crocodile the fairies are freed and save Zarina, working as a team to stop the pirates and retrieve the precious blue pixie dust.

Cast: Mae Whitman as Tinker Bell
Christina Hendricks as Zarina
Tom Hiddleston as James
Lucy Liu as Silvermist
Raven-Symoné as Iridessa
Megan Hilty as Rosetta
Pamela Adlon as Vidia

Angela Bartys as Fawn
Jim Cummings as Oppenheimer/Port
Carlos Ponce as Bonito
Mick Wingert as Starboard
Kevin Michael Richardson as Yang
Jeff Bennett as Smee/Clank/Fairy Gary
Rob Paulsen as Bobble

Music Highlights: Title theme: "Who I Am" (Adam Watts/Andy Dodd) performed by Natasha Beddingfeld, "The Frigate That Flies" (Gaby Alter/Itamar Moses) performed by pirate cast, "Weightless (Less is More Version)" (Natasha Bedingfield/Stephen Kipner/Wayne Wilkins/Andre Merritt) performed by Natasha Bedingfield. Score by Joel McNeely.

Film Facts

• The story for *The Pirate Fairy,* the sixth Disney Fairies film, was a team effort, with input from Peggy Holmes, John Lasseter, Bobs Gannaway, Jeffrey M. Howard, Lorna Cook, and Craig Gerber, with a screenplay by Jeffrey M. Howard and Kate Kondell. Peggy Holmes, co-director of *Secret of the Wings* (2012), returned as the director for the film. Noted fashion designer Christian Siriano of *Project Runway* was brought on to design the pirate costumes.
• The film's working titles were *Quest for the Queen* and *Tinker Bell and the Mythical Island.*
• The DVD includes a "Croc-u-menatary" and the Disney Fairies shorts "Aaarrgh!" (1:09) and "Treasure Chest" (1:31). The Blu-ray adds "Second Star to the Right: The Legacy of Never Land."
• This was the first Disney Fairies film to introduce clear elements of *Peter Pan* (1953). The identity of James, leader of the pirates, is kept as a surprise for the audience until late in the film, but once revealed, places the Disney Fairies adventures several years before the events depicted in *Peter Pan.*

Tinker Bell and the Legend of the NeverBeast (G)

Theatrical release date: December 12, 2014 (UK/Ireland), DVD release date: March 3, 2015
Production Company: DisneyToon Studios, Prana Studios
Length: 76 minutes
Directed by: Steve Loter
Screenplay by: Tom Rogers and Robert Schooley & Mark McCorkle, and Kate Kondell, story by Steve Loter and Tom Rogers

---

Synopsis: Devoted animal fairy Fawn, after being chastised by Queen Clarion for caring for a dangerous baby hawk, hears a roar in the woods and discovers a huge, strange creature in a cave. Despite the creature's resistance, Fawn succeeds in removing a thorn from its paw, and is convinced that it is friendly despite its gruff manner (which leads her to name him Gruff). Fawn introduces Gruff to her friends, and they are puzzled by his strange behavior as he gathers large piles of rocks. Meanwhile, aggressive scout fairy Nyx, who heard the same roar as Fawn, researches a legend about a creature called the NeverBeast, and from the fragmentary information she has, believes the creature will cause a storm that will destroy Pixie Hollow. When Gruff grows wings and horns and a storm approaches, as predicted by Nyx, even Fawn fears what Gruff might do. The fairies must decide whether Gruff is friend or foe, with the safety of Pixie Hollow hanging in the balance.

Cast: Ginnifer Goodwin as Fawn
Mae Whitman as Tinker Bell
Rosario Dawson as Nyx
Lucy Liu as Silvermist
Raven-Symoné as Iridessa
Megan Hilty as Rosetta

Pamela Adlon as Vidia
Danai Gurira as Fury
Chloe Bennet as Chase
Thomas Lennon as Scribble
Jeff Corwin as Buck
Olivia Holt as Morgan

Music Highlights: Title theme: "1,000 Years" (Bleu) performed by Bleu & KT Tunstall, "Float" (Bleu) performed by KT Tunstall, "Strange Sight" (Rob Cantor) performed by KT Tunstall. Score by Joel McNeely.

Film Facts

• Ginnifer Goodwin (Judy Hopps in *Zootopia*, Mary Margaret in *Once Upon a Time*) replaces Angela Bartys as Fawn for this film.
• The DVD includes "5 Essential Ingredients to Getting Gruff" and the Disney Fairies short "Tink'n About Animals." The Blu-ray adds "My Dad's Movies: The True Story of the NeverBeast."
• Fawn tells Tinkerbell to "fly casual" (5:18), a phrase Han Solo used in *Star Wars: Return of the Jedi* (55:19). Another Han Solo quote is heard in *Tinker Bell and the Great Fairy Rescue* (2010).
• Fawn mentions the Latin names of two animals (19:35): "Didelphis marsupialis" means opossum, and "Bison occidentalis" is an extinct species of bison.
• Director Steve Loter had been listening to the work of producer/musician Bleu, and approached him to provide music for the film.
• Songs include KT Tunstall's "Float," "Strange Sight," and the Bleu/Tunstall duet "1,000 Years."

Titan A.E. (PG)

Theatrical release date: June 16, 2000
Production Company: Fox Animation Studios, David Kirschner Productions
Length: 94 minutes
Directed by: Don Bluth & Gary Goldman
Screenplay by: Ben Edlund and John August and Joss Whedon, story by Hans Bauer and Randall McCormick

---

Synopsis: At the dawn of the 31st century, the Titan project provokes an attack by the alien Drej. The young Cale is sent on a shuttle with the friendly alien Tek, while his father leaves in the Titan, just before Earth is destroyed by the Drej. Fifteen years later, Cale is working at a salvage station, where he meets Korso, captain of the Valkyrie, who invites Cale to go on a mission with him and the pilot Akima. Cale learns that a ring his father gave him is a map to the Titan. When Drej warriors come to kill Cale, he flees on the Valkyrie, where he meets the crew: first mate Preed, navigator Gune, and the irritable weapons expert Stith. They head to the planet Sesharrim, learning the Titan is in the Andali Nebula. Cale is captured by the Drej, who copy his map, but he soon escapes, stealing a Drej ship and rejoining the Valkyrie. When faced with a betrayal on the ship, Cale and Akima escape, and a race is on to see who can find the Titan first. When Cale finally reaches the Titan, a message from his father tells him what the ship is really for — if he can just survive long enough to use it.

Cast: Matt Damon as Cale
Bill Pullman as Korso
John Leguizamo as Gune
Nathan Lane as Preed
Janeane Garofalo as Stith
Drew Barrymore as Akima
Ron Perlman as Professor Sam Tucker
Alex D. Linz as Young Cale

Tone Lōc as Tek
Jim Breuer as The Cook
Christopher Scarabosio as Queen Drej
Jim Cummings as Chowquin
Charles Rocket as Firrikash/Slave Trader Guard
Ken Campbell as Po
Tsai Chin as Old Woman
Crystal Scales as Drifter Girl

Music Highlights: "Cosmic Castaway" (Nisbet) performed by Electrasy, "Down to Earth" (Cunniff) performed by Luscious Jackson. "It's My Turn to Fly" (Ewing/Grable/Jost/Magness/Pessoni) performed by The Urge, "Over My Head" (Popoff) performed by Lit. End Credits: "Not Quite Paradise"(Ballard/Goff) performed by Bliss, "Like Lovers (Holding On)" (Ballard/McElhone/Spiteri) performed by Texas. Score by Graeme Revell.

Film Facts

• The initials "A.E." stand for "After Earth."
• The story was originally planned to be a live-action film.
• *Star Wars* homages: the Death Star appears in the Drifter Colony (52:15), and Akima says "Should I get out and push?" (1:00:49) when a ship won't start, paraphrasing Princess Leia in *The Empire Strikes Back* (1981), "Would it help if I got out and pushed?"

A Town Called Panic (TV-PG)

Theatrical release date: June 17, 2009
Country: Belgium French title: *Panique au Village*
Production Company: La Parti Production, Mélusine Productions, Made in, Les Films du Grognon
Length: 75 minutes
Directed by: Stéphane Aubier and Vincent Patar
Screenplay by: Vincent Patar, Guillaume Malandrin, Stéphane Aubier, Vincent Tavier

Synopsis: Cowboy and Indian learn that it is Horse's birthday on June 21st, and decide to build a barbecue for him. They send Horse off to pick up their neighbor Steven's animals from music school while they order bricks for the barbecue, accidentally ordering 50 million bricks. Horse is quite taken with the animals' music teacher, Mrs. Longray (also a horse), and signs up for music lessons with her. Horse returns for a lovely party, but unfortunately, Cowboy and Indian put the extra bricks from the 50 million on their roof, which ends up crushing their house. Horse directs rebuilding of the house using the bricks. During the night the new house is stolen, and their neighbor Steven is wrongly accused of the theft. Horse, Cowboy, and Indian track one of the real thieves to their lair, but fall into a deep hole that leads them to a snowy wasteland. They follow the footprints of the thief, and are scooped up by a team of mad scientists in a penguin-shaped snowball machine, which they are forced to clean. While the scientists are distracted, they try to escape in a snowball, but the thief changes the settings so the snowball lands in the ocean, near his home. Our heroes are chased by barracuda, but finally escape, leading to a huge battle at their home. NOTE: While many aspects of the film will appeal to younger viewers, it contains some profanity, use of alcohol, and a fair amount of comedic violence.

Cast: Stéphane Aubier as Cowboy/
        Max Briquenet/Mr. Ernotte
Jeanne Balibar as Madame Longrée
Nicolas Buysse as Mouton/Jean-Paul
François De Brigode as Journaliste Sportif
Véronique Dumont as Janine
Bruce Ellison as Indian (Indien)
Christine Grulois as Cow (Vache)/Étudiante
Frédéric Jannin as Policeman (Gendarme)/
        Gérard/Livreur de briques
Bouli Lanners as Facteur/Simon/Vache

Christelle Mahy as Poule
Eric Muller as Rocky Gaufres/Étudiant chorale 1
François Neyken as Cochon
Vincent Patar as Horse (Cheval)/Maman Atlante
Pipou as Rire de Michel
Franco Piscopo as Bear (Ours)
Benoît Poelvoorde as Steven
David Ricci as Ane/Michel
Ben Tesseur as Scientifique 1
Alexandre von Sivers as Scientifique 2

Music Highlights: Music by Dionysos, French Cowboy.

Film Facts

• The film is based on the Belgian TV series *Panique au village* (2002-2003).
• GKIDS released a 2017 English Blu-ray of the TV series, *A Town Called Panic: The Collection*.

Toy Story (G)

Theatrical release date: November 22, 1995
Production Company: Pixar Animation Studios, Walt Disney Pictures
Length: 81 minutes
Directed by: John Lasseter
Screenplay by: Joss Whedon, Andrew Stanton, Joel Cohen and Alec Sokolow, original story by John Lasseter, Pete Docter, Andrew Stanton, Joe Ranft

Synopsis: Woody the cowboy, longtime "favorite toy" of the boy Andy, suddenly gets competition from the exciting new space ranger toy Buzz Lightyear, and their rivalry puts them both at risk, landing them at the home of Andy's next door neighbor Sid, known for destroying his toys. Finally working together, Woody and Buzz escape, but their road home is complicated when the other toys mistakenly think Woody is trying to harm Buzz. Classic supporting toys include the dinosaur Rex, Mr. Potato Head, Slinky Dog, piggy bank Hamm, army man Sergeant, and doll Bo Peep.

Cast: Tom Hanks as Woody
Tim Allen as Buzz Lightyear
Don Rickles as Mr. Potato Head
Jim Varney as Slinky Dog
Wallace Shawn as Rex
John Ratzenberger as Hamm

Annie Potts as Bo Peep
John Morris as Andy
Erik von Detten as Sid
Laurie Metcalf as Mrs. Davis
R. Lee Ermey as Sergeant
Penn Jillette as TV Announcer

Music Highlights: "You've Got a Friend in Me," "Strange Things," "I Will Go Sailing No More." All songs written and performed by Randy Newman. Score by Randy Newman.

Film Facts

• *Toy Story* was the first Pixar feature film. The original story was conceived by Pixar creative team members John Lasseter, Pete Docter, and Andrew Stanton. The protagonists, initially from an unproduced holiday special to be called *A Tin Toy Christmas,* were "Tinny" (from the Pixar short "Tin Toy") and a ventriloquists dummy, while Woody was to be a villain. The story was re-developed by Lasseter, Docter, Stanton, and Joe Ranft, with a screenplay by Stanton with Joss Whedon (*Buffy the Vampire Slayer, The Avengers*), Joel Cohen (*Fargo*) & Alec Sokolow (*Garfield*).
• Billy Crystal was offered the role of Buzz Lightyear, but to his later chagrin, turned it down. He was later given the role of Mike Wazowski in *Monsters, Inc.* (2001) as a consolation.
• *Toy Story* is the first appearance of the Pizza Planet truck, which makes cameos in Pixar films.
• Some book titles are the names of early Pixar short films (4:57): "Knick Knack" (1989), "Tin Toy" (1988), and "Red's Dream" (1987).
• "Hakuna Matata" from *The Lion King* plays in the car on the drive to Andy's new house (1:12:06).
• John Lasseter received a "Special Achievement" Academy Award for the film, among other Oscar nominations, and the film also won an Annie Award for "Best Animated Feature."
• Additional appearances: Followed by *Toy Story Treats* TV mini-shorts (1996), *Toy Story 2* (1999), *Buzz Lightyear of Star Command: The Adventure Begins* (2000), *Buzz Lightyear of Star Command* TV series (2000-2001), *Toy Story 3* (2010), *Toy Story Toons* short series (2011-2012), *Toy Story of Terror!* TV special (2013), *Toy Story That Time Forgot* TV special (2015), *Toy Story 4* (2019).

Toy Story 2 (G)

Theatrical release date: Nov 24, 1999 (premiere Nov 13, 1999 at El Capitan Theatre, Hollywood)
Production Company: Pixar Animation Studios, Walt Disney Pictures
Length: 92 minutes
Directed by: John Lasseter, co-directed by Lee Unkrich and Ash Brannon
Screenplay by: Andrew Stanton, Rita Hsiao, Doug Chamberlin & Chris Webb, original story by John Lasseter, Pete Docter, Ash Brannon, Andrew Stanton

---

Synopsis: Woody is kidnapped by toy collector Al McWhiggin to complete his collection of "Roundup Gang" toys, along with cowgirl Jessie, horse Bullseye, and the Prospector. The toy collector soon has plans to sell the set of toys to a museum in Japan. While Woody wants to return home, the other toys will be put in storage if he does not go, and Jessie suffers from claustrophobia. Jessie and the Prospector convince Woody to go to the museum, until Buzz reminds him that a toy's purpose is to be played with. Woody invites the rest of the Roundup Gang to come to Andy's home with him, but complications arise when not everyone agrees to go, and when Buzz's enemy, the Evil Emperor Zurg, shows up.

Cast: Tom Hanks as Woody
Tim Allen as Buzz Lightyear
Joan Cusack as Jessie
Kelsey Grammer as Prospector
Don Rickles as Mr. Potato Head
Jim Varney as Slinky Dog
Wallace Shawn as Rex
John Ratzenberger as Hamm
Annie Potts as Bo Peep

Wayne Knight as Al McWhiggin
John Morris as Andy
Laurie Metcalf as Andy's Mom
Estelle Harris as Mrs. Potato Head
R. Lee Ermey as Sarge
Jodi Benson as Barbie
Jonathan Harris as The Cleaner
Joe Ranft as Wheezy
Andrew Stanton as Emperor Zurg

Music Highlights: "Woody's Roundup" (Randy Newman) performed by Riders in the Sky, "When She Loved Me" (Randy Newman) performed by Sarah McLachlan, "You've Got a Friend in Me (Wheezy's Version)" (Randy Newman) performed by Robert Goulet. Music by Randy Newman.

Film Facts

• *Toy Story 2*, the 3rd Pixar film, achieved a rare feat: it was a sequel which was as enjoyable as the first film. Director John Lasseter was joined by co-directors Lee Unkrich (*Monsters, Inc., Finding Nemo*) and Ash Brannon (*The Little Mermaid, Surf's Up*).
• Soon after *Toy Story* became a hit with audiences, plans began for a sequel. Disney originally considered releasing the film as a "direct to video" home media release, and debated whether it would be computer animated by Pixar or traditionally animated by Walt Disney Feature Animation.
• Toymaker Mattel gave permission for Barbie to appear after the first *Toy Story* was a blockbuster.
• The character "The Cleaner" (first appearing at 38:50) is from the Pixar short "Geri's Game" (1997) about a chess game. Chess pieces can be seen in his drawer (39:19).
• Jessie's line upon meeting Woody, "Sweet mother of Abraham Lincoln!" (21:26) refers to Lincoln's mother, Nancy Hanks, an actual distant relative of Woody's voice actor Tom Hanks.

Toy Story: *Buzz Lightyear of Star Command:*
The Adventure Begins (NR)

Home media release date: August 8, 2000
Production Company: Walt Disney Television Animation, Pixar Animation Studios
Length: 70 minutes
Directed by: Tad Stones
Written by: Mark McCorkle & Bob Schooley and Bill Motz & Bob Roth

Synopsis: Buzz Lightyear, a Space Ranger working for Star Command, keeps law and order in the universe. Buzz and his partner, Warp Darkmatter, search for three missing Little Green Men (LGM), finding them in the lab of the evil Emperor Zurg. As they rescue the LGM, Warp is caught in an explosion, leaving Buzz grief stricken. Over his objections, Buzz is assigned to work with Princess Mira Nova, a Tangean who possesses ghosting powers. Zurg, working with his minion Agent Z, seeks to control the LGM'S Uni-Mind, which connects the minds of the LGM. The LGM respond by building the robot XR. Zurg turns the Uni-Mind into a Mega-Ray, used for mind control. Desperate to stop Zurg, Mira steals a ship, unknowingly carrying the alien janitor Booster and XR as stowaways. When Zurg uses the Mega-Ray on Star Command, it's up to Buzz, Mira, Booster, and XR to stop him, and in the process they learn the shocking identity of Agent Z. Conquering his fear of working with others, Buzz forms "Team Lightyear" with Mira, Booster, and XR.

Cast: Tim Allen as Buzz Lightyear
Nicole Sullivan as Mira Nova
Larry Miller as XR
Stephen Furst as Booster

Wayne Knight as Emperor Zurg
Adam Carolla as Commander Nebula
Diedrich Bader as Warp Darkmatter/Agent Z
Patrick Warburton as LGM

Music Highlights: Music by Adam Berry.

Film Facts

• This film launched the animated TV series *Buzz Lightyear of Star Command* (2000-2001). The first season of the series was broadcast as a daily cartoon on UPN, with a second season shown during Disney's One Saturday Morning programming block on ABC. The series was also shown on the Disney Channel.
• The film begins with a short scene of the *Toy Story* gang gathering to watch the movie on TV.
• Patrick Warburton originally voiced the role of Buzz in the film, but his lines were replaced by Tim Allen for the home media release. Warburton voiced Buzz for the subsequent TV series.
• The film was divided into three parts when broadcast as part of the TV series, and Patrick Warburton's original voice recordings were used for the TV broadcast.
• The houses of the Space Rangers are inspired by the 1957-1967 Disneyland attraction Monsanto House of the Future, and Star Command resembles the Disneyland ride Space Mountain.
• A video was created by Activision for PlayStation, Game Boy Color, Sega Dreamcast, and PC.

Toy Story 3 (G)

Theatrical release date: June 18, 2010 (premiere June 12, 2010 at Taormina Film Fest, Italy)
Production Company: Pixar Animation Studios, Walt Disney Pictures
Length: 103 minutes
Directed by: Lee Unkrich
Screenplay by: Michael Arndt, story by John Lasseter, Andrew Stanton, and Lee Unkrich

Synopsis: When Andy leaves for college, Woody, Buzz, and the toys end up at Sunnyside Daycare. They are warmly welcomed by Lots-O'-Huggin' Bear, and delighted to have lots of children who want to play with them, including the kind girl Bonnie, but soon learn that the toy paradise they have found is not quite what it seems.

Cast: Tom Hanks as Woody
Tim Allen as Buzz Lightyear
Joan Cusack as Jessie
Ned Beatty as Lotso
Don Rickles as Mr. Potato Head
Michael Keaton as Ken
Wallace Shawn as Rex
John Ratzenberger as Hamm
Estelle Harris as Mrs. Potato Head
John Morris as Andy
Jodi Benson as Barbie
Emily Hahn as Bonnie

Laurie Metcalf as Andy's Mom
Blake Clark as Slinky Dog
Teddy Newton as Chatter Telephone
Bud Luckey as Chuckles
Beatrice Miller as Molly
Javier Fernandez-Peña as Spanish Buzz
Timothy Dalton as Mr. Pricklepants
Lori Alan as Bonnie's Mom
Charlie Bright as Young Andy
Kristen Schaal as Trixie
Jeff Garlin as Buttercup
Bonnie Hunt as Dolly

Music Highlights: "You've Got a Friend in Me" (Newman) performed by Randy Newman, "You've Got a Friend in Me (Para Buzz Español)" (Newman) performed by Gipsy Kings, "Dream Weaver" (Wright) performed by Gary Wright, "Le Freak" (Edwards/Rodgers) performed by Chic. End credits: "We Belong Together" (Newman) performed by Randy Newman. Music by Randy Newman.

Film Facts

• *Toy Story 3*, the 11th Pixar film, almost wasn't made by Pixar. According to the original deal struck between Disney and Pixar, Disney would distribute the first seven Pixar films, and had the right to make sequels to any of them, but had to offer Pixar the first opportunity to make the sequel (the "right of first refusal"). Disney's Circle 7 Animation, modeled after Pixar (but dubbed "Pixaren't" by skeptics), began developing a third Toy Story film, in which Buzz Lightyear malfunctioned and was shipped to Taiwan, supposedly to get fixed. The toys learned that all the Buzz Lightyear action figures had actually been recalled, and embarked on a rescue mission to Taiwan.
• Barbie's clotheshorse counterpart Ken is the 1988 "Animal Lovin' Ken" model.
• Totoro from Hayao Miyazaki's 1990 film *My Neighbor Totoro* makes cameos (35:45, 1:36:09).
• Cameos include references to *Cars, WALL-E, Monsters, Inc., A Bug's Life, The Incredibles, Up, Finding Nemo,* and early Pixar shorts *Tin Toy,* and *The Adventures of Andre and Wally B.*
• Angus MacLean wrote and directed a series of promotional mini-shorts called *Ken's Dating Tips* ("#24: Know Yourself, Be Yourself," "#31: Play Hard to Get," "#48: Communication is Key").

Toy Story of Terror! (TV-G)

Broadcast date: October 16, 2013, Home media release date: August 19, 2014
Production Company: Pixar Animation Studios, Walt Disney Television Animation,
Walt Disney Pictures
Length: 22 minutes
Written and Directed by: Angus MacLane

> **Synopsis**: On a trip with their child Bonnie, the toys watch a horror movie in the trunk of the car, before a flat tire forces a stop at the creepy Sleep Well motel. Before long toys begin disappearing, and it's up to Jessie to save the day by facing her fear of enclosed spaces, aided by the one-handed lost toy Combat Carl.

Cast: Tom Hanks as Woody
Tim Allen as Buzz Lightyear
Joan Cusack as Jessie
Carl Weathers as Combat Carl/
      Combat Carl Jr.
Stephen Tobolowsky as Ron the Manager
Timothy Dalton as Mr. Pricklepants
Wallace Shawn as Rex
Don Rickles as Mr. Potato Head
Kristen Schaal as Trixie
Kate McKinnon as PEZ Cat
Lori Alan as Bonnie's Mom

Peter Sohn as Transitron
Emily Hahn as Bonnie
Dawnn Lewis as Delivery Lady
Jason 'Jtop' Topolski as Vampire/
      Tow Truck Guy
Ken Marino as Pocketeer
Christian Roman as Old Timer
Laraine Newman as Betsy
Tara Strong as Computer
Angus MacLane as Officer Wilson
Josh Cooley as Officer Phillips
Dee Bradley Baker as Mr. Jones

Music Highlights: Music by Michael Giacchino.

Film Facts

• The short was written and directed by Angus MacLane, an animator on many Pixar films and shorts. MacLane directed the *WALL-E* short "BURN-E" (2008), three "Ken's Dating Tips" shorts to promote *Toy Story 3* (2010), the *Toy Story Toons* short "Small Fry" (2011), and co-directed *Finding Dory* (2016).
• Combat Carl is based on a role Carl Weathers played in the sci-fi/action movie *Predator* (1987).
• Easter eggs: One tombstone reads "R.I.P. Simon J. Paladino, a public servant with a unique vision" (0:15). Paladino is the secret identity of Gazerbeam from *The Incredibles* (2004). Toy-collecting Al from *Toy Story 2* wins the bidding for Woody, with Al McWhiggin/Al's Toy Barn on the label (12:50). The Luxo Ball appears as a drawing under the sink (8:47). The Pizza Planet truck is on a flyer next to the calendar in Ron's office (10:36). The Buy and Large "BnL" logo from *WALL-E* (2008) is on the motel door (16:56). Bonnie wears a shirt with DJ Blue Jay from the *Toy Story Toons* short "Small Fry" (19:17).
• This is the first Pixar production not to include a vocal performance by John Ratzenberger.
• The music titles from the soundtrack are hilarious (e.g., "The Suspension is Killing Me," "Motel Me a Scary Story," "Nobody Puts Jessie in the Box") — look them up on iTunes.

Toy Story That Time Forgot (TV-G)

Broadcast date: December 2, 2014, Home media release date: November 3, 2015
Production Company: Pixar Animation Studios, Walt Disney Television Animation,
Walt Disney Pictures
Length: 22 minutes
Written and Directed by: Steve Purcell

Synopsis: Just after Christmas, the toys enjoy a creative in-home play session with their girl Bonnie, with her triceratops, Trixie, cast as a reindeer. They expect even more fun when Bonnie packs a backpack of her toys for a playdate at her friend Mason's house, only to find that Mason is obsessed with his new Optimum X video game console. Even worse, Bonnie tosses her backpack of toys into Mason's play room and joins Mason. The toys find a tribe of dinosaur warriors, the Battlesaurs, led by head warrior Reptillus Maximus and the cruel Cleric. Delight turns to horror as the Battlesaurs conduct vicious arena fights, and it becomes clear that the Battlesaurs have never been played with. It's up to Trixie to show Reptillus Maximus that "surrender" to a child is very unlike surrender on a battlefield. The story closes with wisdom from the Angel Kitty.

Cast: Tom Hanks as Woody
Tim Allen as Buzz Lightyear
Kristen Schaal as Trixie
Kevin McKidd as Reptillus Maximus
Emily Hahn as Bonnie
Wallace Shawn as Rex
Steve Purcell as The Cleric
Jonathan Kydd as Ray-Gon

R.C. Cope as Mason
Don Rickles as Mr. Potato Head
Timothy Dalton as Mr. Pricklepants
Lori Alan as Bonnie's Mom
Joan Cusack as Jessie
Emma Hudak as Angel Kitty
Ron Bottitta as Mason's Dad

Music Highlights: Score by Michael Giacchino.

Film Facts

• The title is based on the Edgar Rice Burroughs novel *The Land That Time Forgot* (1924).
• Easter eggs: The snow globe from the "Knick Knack" short appears in the bottom left corner of the screen (0:08), and a LEGO Pizza Planet truck is on the table in Mason's playroom (2:13). From *Toy Story of Terror!* (2013), a poster of Transitron is in Mason's room (4:17), and the iguana Mr. Jones is in a glass case (19:08).
• The Cleric bears a strong resemblance to the Skeksis from *The Dark Crystal* (1982), and his statement "I find their lack of armor disturbing" is a paraphrase of Darth Vader's "I find your lack of faith disturbing" from *Star Wars: A New Hope* (1977).
• Kristen Schaal (Trixie) also voiced Mabel in *Gravity Falls* (2012-2016).
• Kevin McKidd was chosen to voice Reptillus Maximus due to his role in *Rome* (2005-2007).
• Additional appearances: Follows *Toy Story* (1995), *Toy Story 2* (1999), *Buzz Lightyear of Star Command: The Adventure Begins* (2000), *Buzz Lightyear of Star Command* animated TV series (2000-2001), *Toy Story 3* (2010), *Toy Story Toons* short series (2011-2012), and *Toy Story of Terror!* TV special (2013), followed by *Toy Story 4* (2019).

Toy Story 4 (G)

Theatrical release date: June 21, 2019 (premiere June 11, 2019 at El Capitan Theatre, Hollywood)
Production Company: Pixar Animation Studios, Walt Disney Pictures
Length: 100 minutes
Directed by: Josh Cooley
Screenplay by: Andrew Stanton & Stephany Folsom, story by John Lasseter, Andrew Stanton, Josh Cooley, Valerie LaPointe, Rashida Jones, Will McCormack, Martin Hynes, Stephany Folsom

Synopsis: Woody notices that Bonnie plays with him less and less, preferring other toys. On her first day of kindergarten, Bonnie makes a new toy, "Forky," out of a discarded spork. Forky meets the other toys, but thinks of himself as trash, repeatedly trying to throw himself away. When Bonnie's family goes on vacation in an RV, Forky jumps out the window, with Woody following so he can return Forky to Bonnie. On the way back, in an antique store window, Woody sees the lamp of Bo Peep, who lived with the toys in Andy's house years before. Woody and Forky enter the store, encountering a vintage Gabby Gabby doll and her creepy ventriloquist dummy henchmen. They soon learn that Gabby's voice box is defective, and she wants to take Woody's. Woody escapes, but Forky is held captive. A reunion with an ownerless and empowered Bo Peep gives Woody a new perspective. After an elaborate rescue of Forky, and selfless efforts to aid Gabby, Woody makes a life-changing decision.

Cast: Tom Hanks as Woody
Tim Allen as Buzz Lightyear
Annie Potts as Bo Peep
Tony Hale as Forky
Keegan-Michael Key as Ducky
Madeleine McGraw as Bonnie
Christina Hendricks as Gabby Gabby
Jordan Peele as Bunny
Keanu Reeves as Duke Caboom
Ally Maki as Giggle McDimples
Jay Hernandez as Bonnie's Dad
Lori Alan as Bonnie's Mom
Joan Cusack as Jessie
Bonnie Hunt as Dolly
Kristen Schaal as Trixie
Emily Davis as Billy/Goat/Gruff
Wallace Shawn as Rex
John Ratzenberger as Hamm
Blake Clark as Slinky Dog
June Squibb as Margaret the Store Owner
Carl Weathers as Combat Carl
Lila Sage Bromley as Harmony
Don Rickles as Mr. Potato Head
Jeff Garlin as Buttercup

Music Highlights: "You've Got a Friend in Me" (Newman) performed by Randy Newman, "I Can't Let You Throw Yourself Away" (Newman) performed by Randy Newman, "The Ballad of the Lonesome Cowboy" (Newman) performed by Chris Stapleton. Score by Randy Newman.

Film Facts

• When Woody pretends to be a phone he strikes the same pose as the classic Mickey Mouse phone.
• One of the items Bo's sheep bring her is the grape soda cap from *Up* (2009).
• Buzz's prerecorded phrase, "Open the pod bay doors!" is from *2001: A Space Odyssey* (1968).
• The film earned the "Best Animated Feature" Academy Award and a Golden Globe nomination.
• A 10-episode educational short series, *Forky Asks a Question* (2019) premiered on Disney+, and a new Toy Story short, "Lamp Life," followed in 2020.

Treasure Planet (PG)

Theatrical release date: November 27, 2002
Production Company: Walt Disney Pictures, Walt Disney Feature Animation
Length: 95 minutes
Directed by: John Musker and Ron Clements
Screenplay by: Ron Clements & John Musker and Rob Edwards, adapted from the novel
Treasure Island by Robert Louis Stevenson

Synopsis: Young Jim Hawkins obtains a mysterious sphere from wounded pilot Billy Bones shortly before he dies, and must flee from the inn where he lives when pirates attack. Assisted by Dr. Doppler, Jim learns that the sphere is a map, and hires the crew of the R.L.S. Legacy, under the command of Captain Amelia, to voyage to the legendary Treasure Planet.

Cast: Roscoe Lee Browne as Mr. Arrow
Corey Burton as Onus
Dane A. Davis as Morph
Joseph Gordon-Levitt as Jim Hawkins
Tony Jay as Narrator
Austin Majors as Young Jim
Patrick McGoohan as Billy Bones
Michael McShane as Hands
Laurie Metcalf as Sarah
Brian Murray as John Silver
David Hyde Pierce as Doctor Doppler
Martin Short as B.E.N.
Emma Thompson as Captain Amelia
Michael Wincott as Scroop

Music Highlights: "I'm Still Here (Jim's Theme)" (John Rzeznik) performed by John Rzeznik, "Always Know Where You Are" (John Rzeznik) performed by John Rzeznik. Score by James Netwton Howard.

Film Facts

• The 43rd of the Disney animated classics, *Treasure Planet* is based on Robert Louis Stevenson's classic novel *Treasure Island* (1883). Co-directors Ron Clements and John Musker met during work on *The Fox and the Hound* (1981), and collaborated as part of a team on *The Great Mouse Detective* (1986). During a 1985 pitch meeting at Disney, Clements proposed ideas for *The Little Mermaid* and "Treasure Island in Space." *The Little Mermaid* was developed into a script with Musker, resulting in the 1989 hit film that kicked off the Disney Renaissance. Clements and Musker later proposed a revised *Treasure Planet* concept, but were again denied, instead accepting work on *Aladdin* (1992). A third effort to get *Treasure Planet* approved failed, and the duo agreed to direct *Hercules* (1997), with the understanding that they would get to produce *Treasure Planet* afterwards.
• Songwriter John Rzeznik is best known as the singer/guitarist from the rock band Goo Goo Dolls.
• The initials in the ship's name, R.L.S. Legacy, are a reference to the author of *Treasure Island,* Robert Louis Stevenson.
• Billy Bones is voiced by Patrick McGoohan, famous for his role as "Number 6" in the short-lived cult British spy series *The Prisoner* (1967-1968).
• An earlier live-action Italian/German mini-series, *L'isola del Tesoro* or *Il Pianetta Del Tesoro* (1987) had already depicted *Treasure Island* in a futuristic setting.
• Stitch, of *Lilo & Stitch,* is seen on Jim's shelf at the beginning of the film (1:43).
• A planned sequel would have pitted Jim Hawkins against Ironbeard (to be voiced by Willem Defoe), a villain set on staging a jailbreak on the Botany Bay Prison Asteroid.

Trolls (PG)

Theatrical release date: November 4, 2016
Production Company: DreamWorks Animation
Length: 92 minutes
Directed by: Mike Mitchell, co-director Walt Dohrn
Screenplay by: Jonathan Aibel & Glenn Berger, story by Erica Rivinoja, based on the Good Luck Trolls created by Thomas Dam

Synopsis: The happiest creatures in the world, the Trolls, were discovered by the Bergens, miserable creatures who were only happy when they ate trolls, and who created an annual holiday called Trollstice. As the Bergen prince Gristle Jr. is about to eat his first troll, King Peppy and his baby daughter, Poppy, escape, leading King Gristle to banish his chef. Twenty years later, Poppy celebrates their escape, but the commotion of their party reveals their location to Chef, who kidnaps several trolls, including Poppy's love Creek. It's up to Poppy and Branch to venture into Bergen Town to try to rescue their friends, and avoid the treachery of King Gristle (junior) and Chef.

Cast: Anna Kendrick as Poppy
Justin Timberlake as Branch
Zooey Deschanel as Bridget
Christopher Mintz-Plasse as King Gristle
Christine Baranski as Chef
Russell Brand as Creek
Gwen Stefani as DJ Suki

John Cleese as King Gristle Sr.
James Corden as Biggie
Jeffrey Tambor as King Peppy
Ron Funches as Cooper
Aino Jawo as Satin
Caroline Hjelt as Chenille
Kunal Nayyar as Guy Diamond

Music Highlights: "Hair Up" (Timberlake/Martin/Shellback/Kotecha/Holter) performed by Justin Timberlake, Gwen Stefani and Ron Funches, "Can't Stop the Feeling!" (Timberlake/Martin/Shellback) performed by Justin Timberlake and cast, "Move Your Feet" (Mortensen)/"D.A.N.C.E." (Augé/Chaton/de Rosnay)/"It's a Sunshine Day" (McCarthy) performed by cast, "Get Back Up Again" (Pasek/Paul) performed by Anna Kendrick, "The Sound of Silence" (Simon) performed by Anna Kendrick, "Hello" (Richie) performed by Zooey Deschanel, "I'm Coming Out" (Rodgers/Edwards)/"Mo Money Mo Problems" (Combs/Wallace/Betha/Jordan/Rodgers/Edwards) performed by cast, "They Don't Know" (Timberlake/Kotecha/Ilya) performed by Ariana Grande, "True Colors" (Kelly/Steinberg) performed by Anna Kendrick and Justin Timberlake, "September" (White/McKay/Willis), "What U Workin' With" (Timberlake/Martin/Kotecha/Svensson/Ilya) performed by Gwen Stefani feat. Justin Timberlake, "September" (White/McKay/Willis) performed by Justin Timberlake and Anna Kendrick, featuring Earth, Wind & Fire. Music by Christophe Beck.

Film Facts

• The song "Can't Stop the Feeling!" was nominated for the "Best Original Song" Academy Award.
• Hasbro produced Troll-themed games, such as Twister, Operation, and Trouble.
• Additional Appearances: *Trolls Holiday* TV special (2017), *Trolls: The Beat Goes On!* animated TV series (2018-2019), *Trolls World Tour* film (2020), *Trolls: TrollsTopia* TV series (2020-2021).

Trolls: World Tour (PG)

Theatrical/streaming release date: April 10, 2020
Production Company: DreamWorks Animation
Length: 90 minutes
Directed by: Walt Dohrn, co-director David P. Smith
Screenplay by: Jonathan Aibel & Glenn Berger, Maya Forbes & Wally Wolodarsky, Elizabeth Tippet, story by Jonathan Aibel & Glenn Berger

Synopsis: The trolls come from six musical tribes, Pop, Rock, Techno, Funk, Classical, and Country, and each tribe has a magic string with their music's energy. The leader of the Rock tribe, Queen Barb, gathers the tribes, planning to steal the strings and rule over all of them. Meanwhile Cooper, raised in the Pop tribe, discovers he is a lost prince of the Funk tribe, and while in the classical city Symphonyville, learns of Barb's efforts. Poppy begins to rally the trolls against Barb's coup, but it will not be an easy task to stop her, especially once she is able to obtain all six strings.

Cast: Anna Kendrick as Poppy
Justin Timberlake as Branch
Rachel Bloom as Barb
James Corden as Biggie
Ron Funches as Cooper
Kelly Clarkson as Delta Dawn
Anderson .Paak as Prince D
Sam Rockwell as Hickory
George Clinton as King Quincy
Mary J. Blige as Queen Essence
Kenan Thompson as Tiny Diamond
Kunal Nayyar as Guy Diamond
Caroline Hjelt as Chenille
Aino Jawo as Satin
J Balvin as Tresillo
Flula Borg as Dickory

Music Highlights: "The Other Side" (Timberlake/Göransson/Martin/Aarons/Rowe) performed by SZA & Timberlake, "Trolls Wanna Have Good Times," "Don't Slack" (Anderson/Göransson/Timberlake) performed by Paak & Timberlake, "It's All Love (History of Funk)" (Fauntleroy/Göransson/Shirley) performed by Timberlake, Paak, Blige, Clinton, "Just Sing" (Timberlake/Göransson/Martin/Aarons), "One More Time" (Bangalter/Homem-Christo/Moore) performed by Anthony Ramos, "Atomic Dog" (Clinton/Shider/Spradley) performed by Clinton, Paak, Blige, "Rainbows, Unicorns, Everything Nice" (Jensen) performed by Dohrn & Shirley, "Rock N Roll Rules" (Göransson/A. Haim/D. Haim/E. Haim) performed by HAIM & Ludwig Göransson, "Leaving Lonesome Flats" (Timberlake/Stapleton) performed by Dierks Bentley, "Born to Die" (Timberlake/Stapleton) performed by Clarkson, "Trolls 2 Many Hits Mashup," "Barracuda" (DeRosier/Fisher/Wilson/Wilson) performed by Bloom, "Yodel Beat" (Göransson) performed by Ludwig Göransson, "Crazy Train" (Osborne/Rhoads/Daisley) performed by Bloom, "I Fall to Pieces" (Cochran/Howard) performed by Rockwell, "Perfect for Me" (Timberlake/Göransson/Dixon), "Rock You Like a Hurricane" (Schenker/Meine/Rarebell) performed by Bloom. Music by Theodore Shapiro.

Film Facts

• *Trolls: World Tour* was released simultaneously in theaters and by streaming.
• The DVD and Blu-ray include the short "Tiny Diamond Goes Back to School."
• The film was followed by the animated TV series *Trolls: TrollsTopia* (2020-2021).

Turbo (PG)

Theatrical release date: July 17, 2013
Production Company: DreamWorks Animation
Length: 96 minutes
Directed by: David Soren
Screenplay by: David Soren and Darren Lemke and Robert Siegel, story by David Soren

Synopsis: The little Los Angeles garden snail Theo has big ambitions, and dreams of being a racer, leaving him out of step with the sluggish snails around him. After making a wish to be speedy, Theo is sucked into a Chevrolet Camaro, where nitrous oxide creates a miraculous mutation, making him the fastest snail on earth. His enthusiasm causes an accident, getting both Theo and his brother Chet fired. Chet is abducted by a crow, and Theo catches up with him at the Starlight Plaza strip mall, where they are caught by taco truck driver Tito Lopez, who enters them in a snail race. Theo earns the nickname "Turbo" from his amazing speed. Tito has hopes that Turbo's powers will help Starlight Plaza recover its former glory, but his brother, Angelo, is skeptical. The snails scheme to waylay a tour bus, bringing much needed business to Starlight Plaza, after which Tito agrees to enter Turbo in the Indianapolis 500. Turbo is not allowed to enter the competition, but an encounter with his hero, race car driver Guy Gagné, gives the snail a chance to show what he can do, leading the public to demand he be allowed to race. Turbo has a rough time before the race, arguing with Chet and getting discouraged by Gagné, and his low morale brings his performance down. His team inspires him during a pitstop, and he begins making up lost ground, only to struggle with Gagné breaking the rules, damaging both Turbo's shell and his will. It takes a team effort to stand up to Gagné and mount a comeback, bringing glory to Starlight Plaza.

Cast: Ryan Reynolds as Turbo
Paul Giamatti as Chet
Michael Peña as Tito
Samuel L. Jackson as Whiplash
Luis Guzmán as Angelo

Bill Hader as Guy Gagné
Snoop Dogg as Smoove Move
Maya Rudolph as Burn
Ben Schwartz as Skidmark
Richard Jenkins as Bobby

Music Highlights: "It's Tricky" (McDaniels/Jay/Rubin/Simmons) performed by Run-D.M.C., "Krazy" (Spanish Version) (Perez/Smith/Franchi) performed by Pitbull featuring Lil Jon, "Goin' Back to Indiana" (Gordy/Richards/Perren/Mizell) performed by Jackson 5, "The Snail is Fast " (Theodore/Yaeger/Cabral/Jackson/Da Fonseca) performed by V12 and Nomadik, "Eye of the Tiger" (Sher Gunn Remix) (Peterik/Sullivan) performed by Survivor. Music by Henry Jackman.

Film Facts

• Director David Soren proposed the film when DreamWorks invited all employees to pitch a story.
• A short mid-credits scene appears (1:28:15).
• An animated TV series based on the film, *Turbo Fast* (2013-2016), debuted on Netflix.

Twice Upon a Time (PG)

Theatrical release date: August 5, 1983
Production Company: Korty Films, Lucasfilm, The Ladd Company
Length: 74 minutes
Directed by: John Korty and Charles Swenson
Screenplay by: John Korty, Charles Swenson, Suella Kennedy, Bill Couturié, based on a story by John Korty, Bill Couturié, Suella Kennedy

Synopsis: The people called the Rushers of Din are given sweet dreams from Frivoli, and nightmares from the Murkworks. Synonamess Botch in the Murkworks wants the Rushers to only have nightmares, and seeks control of the Cosmic Clock. Botch's vultures kidnap the Frivolian worker Greensleeves and his Figmen of Imagination. Wanting to save Greensleeves, aspiring heroes Mumford and Ralph, the All-Purpose Animal, are tricked by Botch into taking the main spring from the Cosmic Clock. Flora Fauna is taken to the Murkworks, and some help from a Fairy Godmother does little to remedy matters, so Mumford and Ralph are soon returned to Frivoli and dismissed. Rod Rescueman is able to bring Flora back from the Murkworks, and with assistance from Scuzzbopper, a disgruntled former nightmare screenwriter in the Murkworks, Mumford, Ralph, Flora, and Rod make their way to save Greensleeves. Through bravery, strength, and a bit of trickery, the heroes work to stop the evil plans of Botch, and free the frozen Rushers of Din.

Cast: Lorenzo Music as Ralph, the
       All-Purpose Animal
Judith Kahan Kampmann as The Fairy Godmother
Marshall Efron as Synonamess Botch
James Cranna as Rod Rescueman/Scuzzbopper
Julie Payne as Flora Fauna
Hamilton Camp as Greensleeves
Paul Frees as Narrator/Chef of State/
       Judges/Bailiff
Mum as Himself

Music Highlights: "Heartbreak Town" (Bruce Hornsby/John Hornsby) performed by Bruce Hornsby, "Life Is But a Dream" (Maureen McDonald/Tom Ferguson/Michael McDonald) performed by Maureen McDonald, "Twice Upon A Time" (Maureen McDonald/Tom Ferguson/Michael McDonald) performed by Maureen McDonald. "Out On My Own" (Maureen McDonald/Tom Ferguson/David Moordigian) performed by Maureen McDonald, "Champagne Time" (George Cates) performed by Lawrence Welk and His Orchestra. Music by Dawn Atkinson and Ken Melville.

Film Facts

• The version of the film envisioned by director John Korty was family-friendly, but in an effort to appeal to college students and other older viewers, the studio made a version with more profanity. Korty did not learn of this change until the film was being released.
• John Korty also directed the *Star Wars* special *Caravan of Courage: An Ewok Adventure* (1984).
• Henry Selick worked as a sequence director on the film, going on to direct *The Nightmare Before Christmas* (1993), *James and the Giant Peach* (1996), and *Coraline* (2009).
• A children's book of *Twice Upon a Time* was written by Avery Hall and John Korty.

Up (PG)

Theatrical release date: May 29, 2009
Production Company: Pixar Animation Studios, Walt Disney Pictures
Length: 96 minutes
Directed by: Pete Docter, co-directed by Bob Peterson
Screenplay by: Bob Peterson, Pete Docter, story by Pete Docter, Bob Peterson, Tom McCarthy

Synopsis: Inspired by thrilling newsreels of adventurer Charles Muntz, childhood friends Carl and Ellie make a pact to move their clubhouse to the exotic Paradise Falls. The pair grow up, get married, and find that their fund to go to Paradise Falls is repeatedly depleted for more mundane needs. Finally on the verge of departing, the elderly couple is waylaid by a sudden illness which claims Ellie's life. Lost, lonely, and faced with the prospect of life in a retirement home, Carl unfurls an immense expanse of helium balloons to fly his entire house to Paradise Falls. He soon discovers a stowaway, the eager scout Russell, and when they arrive at Paradise Falls, Russell bonds with "Kevin," a rare flightless bird which is pursued by Dug, one of a team of dogs in search of the bird. On the verge of being attacked by the pack of dogs, Carl and Russell are rescued by none other than Charles Muntz - but they soon learn that the man is very unlike the myth.

Cast: Ed Asner as Carl Fredricksen
Christopher Plummer as Charles Muntz
Jordan Nagai as Russell
Bob Peterson as Dug/Alpha
Delroy Lindo as Beta
Jerome Ranft as Gamma
John Ratzenberger as Construction Foreman Tom
David Kaye as Newsreel Announcer

Elie Docter as Young Ellie
Jeremy Leary as Young Carl
Mickie T. McGowan as Police Officer Edith
Danny Mann as Construction Worker Steve
Don Fullilove as Nurse George
Jess Harnell as Nurse AJ
Josh Cooley as Omega
Pete Docter as Campmaster Strauch

Music: Score by Michael Giacchino.

Film Facts

• Carl Fredricksen is voiced by Ed Asner, most famous for portraying Lou Grant on the *Mary Tyler Moore Show* (1970-1977), while Charles Muntz is voiced by Christopher Plummer, best known as Captain von Trapp from the musical *The Sound of Music* (1965).
• Cameos: The theater from the "Presto" (2008) short (1:54), Buy n Large logos (20:29) from *WALL-E* (2008), Lotso (22:02) from *Toy Story 3* (2010), the Pixar ball (22:02), and the *Toy Story* Pizza Planet Truck (22:10).
• In one scene the dogs mimic Cassius Marcellus Collidge's famous "dogs playing poker" paintings (1:15:39).
• The name of Charles Muntz is quite similar to that of Charles Mintz of Universal Pictures, who acquired (some have said stole) the rights to Walt Disney's "Oswald the Lucky Rabbit" cartoons.
• Additional appearances: "Dug's Special Mission" short (2009). Disney also created three promotional shorts, or "UPisodes": "Animal Calls," "First Aid," and "Snipe Trap."

Wallace & Gromit: The Curse of the Were-Rabbit (G)

Theatrical release date: October 7, 2005
Production Company: Aardman Animations, DreamWorks Animation
Length: 85 minutes
Directed by: Nick Park & Steve Box
Written by: Steve Box & Nick Park, Mark Burton and Bob Baker

Synopsis: When Wallace and Gromit's Anti-Pesto humane pest control company is called to help Lady Campanula Tottington with a rabbit infestation, Wallace tries to brainwash the rabbits into no longer wanting vegetables. The process goes awry, and the rabbit Hutch has to be forced off of Wallace's head. Soon there is a "night of vegetable carnage," caused by a mysterious creature called a Were-Rabbit, a crisis for the community of growers looking forward to an upcoming giant vegetable competition. The hunter Victor Quartermaine wishes to slay the beast, but kind Lady Tottington gives Wallace and Gromit another chance to subdue the creature. They believe the monster is the rabbit Hutch, but Gromit finds a set of muddy footprints, which turn from rabbit's feet to human feet, and lead to Wallace's room, where the stolen vegetables are found. It turns out that while Wallace has taken on qualities of a rabbit, Hutch has taken on some of Wallace's personality as well, including an affinity for cheese and the power of speech. The Were-Rabbit is unable to stay away from the vegetable competition, and Victor, who knows the creature is really Wallace, is determined to shoot the Were-Rabbit, requiring Gromit to come to the rescue.

Cast: Peter Sallis as Wallace/Hutch
Ralph Fiennes as Victor Quartermaine
Helena Bonham Carter as Lady
      Campanula Tottington
Peter Kay as PC Mackintosh
Nicholas Smith as Reverend Clement Hedges
Liz Smith as Mrs. Mulch
John Thomson as Mr. Windfall

Mark Gatiss as Miss Blight
Vincent Ebrahim as Mr. Caliche
Geraldine McEwan as Miss Thripp
Edward Kelsey as Mr. Growbag
Dicken Ashworth as Mr. Mulch
Robert Horvath as Mr. Dibber
Pete Atkin as Mr. Crock
Noni Lewis as Mrs. Girdling

Music Highlights: The Planets: Venus (Holst), "The Stripper" (David Rose) performed by Joe Loss & His Orchestra, "We Plow the Fields and Scatter" (Claudius/Schültz) performed by Nicholas Smith, "Bright Eyes" (Mike Batt) performed by Art Garfunkel, Symphony No. 1: 1st Movement (Elgar). Music by Julian Nott.

Film Facts

• The original title of the film was *Wallace & Gromit: The Great Vegetable Plot*.
• There were tensions between Aardman Studios and DreamWorks during development of the film, as DreamWorks asked for many changes, hoping to make the film more appealing to US audiences.
• The film won the "Best Animated Feature" Academy Award.

Wallace & Gromit: The Complete Collection (NR)

Home media Release date: September 22, 2009 (shorts released 1989, 1993, 1995, and 2010)
Production Company: Aardman Animations
Directed by: Nick Park
Written by: "A Grand Day Out" by Nick Park, "The Wrong Trousers" by Nick Park & Bob Baker, "A Close Shave" by Bob Baker & Nick Park, "A Matter of Loaf and Death" by Nick Park & Bob Baker

---

Synopsis: **"A Grand Day Out"** short (1989, 23 min.): Seeking a place to spend their holiday, Wallace & Gromit build a spaceship and take a trip to the moon. Their picnic on moon cheese is interrupted by a robot that objects to the cheese harvesting. They flee back to their ship, leaving behind metal skis for the robot. **"The Wrong Trousers"** short (1993, 30 min.). Wallace gives Gromit a pair of mechanized "techno trousers" that can take him for a walk. Soon after, due to their limited finances, Wallace advertises a room for rent, and a penguin moves into Gromit's room, with Gromit relegated to a doghouse. The penguin begins to act suspiciously, modifying the techno trousers to control Wallace. Gromit watches the penguin, learning he is planning a robbery of the diamond exhibition at the City Museum — using a sleeping Wallace to commit the crime. Once the diamond is stolen it's up to Wallace and Gromit to work together to bring the notorious Feathers McGraw to justice. **"A Close Shave"** short (1995, 30 min.): In the midst of a sheep rustling and wool shortage crisis, a sheep breaks out of a truck and sneaks into the home of Wallace & Gromit, who work as window washers. While Gromit cleans the windows, Wallace stops by the wool shop to pick up yarn for Gromit's knitting, where he meets Wendolene Ramsbottom, and her grim dog Preston. Returning home, Wallace and Gromit find the sheep has made of mess of their household. Wallace uses a washing machine to clean the sheep, but when the machine malfunctions, the sheep's wool is sheared for Wallace's Knit-O-Matic machine, which knits a sweater. They name the sheep Shaun, and let him wear the sweater, as Preston steals the plans for the Knit-O-Matic. Gromit begins to uncover Preston's scheme, but is framed as a criminal and arrested. Wallace and the sheep break him out of prison, uncovering the truth about the sheep rustling operation. **"A Matter of Loaf and Death"** short (2010, 30 min.): Bakers are being murdered, putting Wallace and Gromit, owners of the Top Bun bakery, at risk. Piella Bakewell and her poodle charm Wallace, but Gromit fears skullduggery.

Cast: Peter Sallis as Wallace
Anne Reid as Wendolene ("A Close Shave")

Sally Lindsay as Piella Bakewell ("A Matter of Loaf and Death")

Music Highlights: Music by Julian Nott.

Film Facts

- Popular Aardman Animations character Shaun the Sheep debuted in "A Close Shave."
- "The Wrong Trousers" & "A Close Shave" won the "Best Animated Short Film" Academy Award.
- Peter Sallis, who voiced Wallace, retired in 2010, after "A Matter of Loaf and Death."

WALL-E (G)

Theatrical release date: June 27, 2008
Production Company: Pixar Animation Studios, Walt Disney Pictures
Length: 98 minutes
Directed by: Andrew Stanton
Screenplay by: Andrew Stanton, Jim Reardon, original story by Andrew Stanton, Pete Docter

Synopsis: After Earth was overtaken by pollution, humanity boarded a giant space cruiser, leaving Earth in the care of robots designed to clean and organize. One of these robots, WALL-E, diligently cleans and collects artifacts in the desolate wasteland, its only company a hardy cockroach and a videotape of *Hello, Dolly!* After many years, a hair-trigger EVE robot arrives to search for the growth of vegetation. When a small plant is found, WALL-E and EVE get caught up in the return flight to alert humanity that Earth has healed, as well as the struggle against those who would thwart the return to Earth.

Cast: Ben Burtt as Wall-E
Elissa Knight as EVE
Jeff Garlin as Captain
Fred Willard as Shelby Forthright, BnL CEO
MacInTalk as AUTO

Ben Burtt as M-O
John Ratzenberger as John
Kathy Najimy as Mary
Sigourney Weaver as Ship's Computer

Music Highlights: "Put On Your Sunday Clothes" (Jerry Herman) and "It Only Takes a Moment" (Jerry Herman) from *Hello, Dolly!* (1969), "La Vie en Rose" (Marcel Louiguy/Edith Piaf/Mack David) performed by Louis Armstrong, "Down to Earth" (Peter Gabriel/Thomas Newman) performed by Peter Gabriel. Score by Thomas Newman.

Film Facts

• WALL-E, the 9th Pixar film, was directed by Andrew Stanton (*A Bug's Life, Monsters, Inc., Finding Nemo*), from a story Stanton developed with Pete Docter (*Monsters, Inc., Up, Inside Out*), and a screenplay by Stanton and Jim Reardon (*Wreck-It Ralph, Zootopia*). The earliest seeds of the idea came in 1994 at a Pixar staff lunch, attended by Stanton with John Lasseter, Pete Docter, and Joe Ranft, during which they also discussed ideas for *A Bug's Life, Toy Story 2, Monsters, Inc.* and *Finding Nemo*. The original story, titled *Trash Planet*, featured WALL-E inspiring a robot revolution against the "Gels," the cruel, atrophied descendants of humanity.
• WALL-E stands for Waste Allocation Load Lifter - Earth-class. EVE stands for Extraterrestrial Vegetation Evaluator.
• WALL-E is also named after Walter Elias Disney, commonly known as Walt Disney.
• Part of EVE's design came from Jonathan Ive, who designed Apple's iPod.
• Among WALL-E's artifacts: a Rubik's Cube, Atari 2600, lightbulbs, CDs, a Twinkie, and some Pixar cameos: *Toy Story*'s Rex (6:16) and Hamm (24:44), and Mike from *Monsters, Inc.* (9:27).
• The film won the "best animated film" Golden Globe and Academy Award, as well as receiving five other Oscar nominations.
• A video game was made for Mac, Windows, Nintendo DS, PS2/PS3/PS Portable, Wii, Xbox 360.
• Director/animator Angus MacLean created a related short, "BURN-E" a DVD/Blu-ray bonus.

When Marnie Was There (PG)

Theatrical release date: July 19, 2014 (Japan), August 7, 2015 (US)
Country: Japan **Japanese title**: *Omoide no Mānī* (lit. "Marnie of My Memories")
Production Company: Studio Ghibli
Length: 103 minutes
Directed by: Hiromasa Yonebayashi, English production directed by James Simone
Screenplay by: Keiko Niwa, Masashi Ando, Hiromasa Yonebayashi, based on the novel *When Marnie Was There* by Joan G. Robinson

> **Synopsis**: After an asthma attack at school, Anna Sasaki, an introverted 12-year-old orphan who loves to draw, is sent by her foster parents to stay with an aunt and uncle in a quiet seaside town. After sending a postcard, she finds an old mansion, the Marsh House, that somehow feels familiar to her. Anna has a recurring dream of a blonde girl in the house, and after feeling out of place at the town's *Tanabata* festival, she rows to the Marsh House, where she meets the blonde girl Marnie, who says she knows her. They agree to have a secret friendship, and begin to learn about each others' lives. Marnie explains her parents are often away on business, but soon invites Anna to a party at the mansion, where Anna meets Marnie's parents. The next day Anna goes to the Marsh House, finding it dilapidated and seemingly unoccupied. A new family moves in, and the girl in the family, Sayaka, shows Anna an old diary of Marnie's she has found, which gives some clues to who Marnie really is, and how she knows Anna.

Cast:

Role	English	Japanese
Anna Sasaki	Hailee Steinfeld	Sara Takatsuki
Marnie	Kiernan Shipka	Kasumi Arimura
Setsu Oiwa	Grey Griffin	Toshie Negishi
Kiyomasa Oiwa	John C. Reilly	Susumu Terajima[
Hisako	Vanessa Williams	Hitomi Kuroki
Yoriko Sasaki	Geena Davis	Nanako Matsushima
Sayaka	Ava Acres	Hana Sugisaki
Nobuko Kadoya	Raini Rodriguez	Akiko Yoritsune
Nan	Ellen Burstyn	Kazuko Yoshiyuki
Older Woman	Catherine O'Hara	Ryoko Moriyama
Tōichi	Fred Tatasciore	Ken Yasuda

Music Highlights: "Fine on the Outside" (Ahn) performed by Priscilla Ahn, "Atashi-tachi mo Odorimashou!" (Muramatsu) performed by Kasumi Arimura. Music by Takatsugu Muramatsu.

Film Facts

- *Until the End of The Creation of When Marnie Was There* is a documentary about making the film.
- Studio Ghibli head Hayao Miyazaki retired shortly before this film was released.
- After this film, Yonebayashi joined Studio Ponoc, directing *Mary and the Witch's Flower* (2017).
- Studio Ghibli went on hiatus after this film, returning with *The Red Turtle* (2016) co-production.

A Whisker Away (TV-PG)

Streaming release date: June 18, 2020
Country: Japan Japanese title: *Nakitai Watashi wa Neko wo Kaburu*
Production Company: BS Fuji, Dentsu Meitetsu Communications, Fuji Creative
Length: 104 minutes
Directed by: Jun'ichi Satô, Tomotaka Shibayama
Written by: Mari Okada

Synopsis: The middle schooler Miyo "Muge" Sasaki has two main problems: she doesn't get along with her father's new partner, and she is hopelessly smitten with Kento Hinode, a boy who seems to have no interest in her. She also has a secret: using a cat mask she received from a giant cat, she transforms into Tarō, a cute white kitten that, unlike her human form, Kento adores. Kento, for his part, is troubled that his grandfather is retiring and closing the pottery studio he loves. Muge finally decides to write a letter to Kento confessing her love for him, but it's intercepted by a bully who reads it in front of the class, leading a humiliated Kento to say he hates Muge. Even worse, she learns that her father is marrying his partner. Muge's human face, looking like a mask, comes off when she decides she'd prefer to be a cat, and the cat mask seller takes it away, telling her she will soon become a cat forever if she doesn't put it back on. She begins to have second thoughts when everyone, including Kento, is worried about her disappearance. The cat Kinako puts on Muge's human face, and takes her place as Muge. Soon Muge, Kinako, and Kento all learn that what they thought they wanted isn't everything they thought it would be.

Cast:

Role	English	Japanese
Miyo "Muge" Sasaki/Tarō	Cherami Leigh	Mirai Shida
Kento Hinode	Johnny Yong Bosch	Natsuki Hanae
Mask Seller	Keith Silverstein	Kōichi Yamadera
Mizoguchi	Kira Buckland	Rie Hikisaka
Kusunoki	Robert Buchholz	Hiroaki Ogi
Shōta Bannai	Bryce Papenbrook	Wataru Komada
Yumi Hinode	Cristina Vee	Rina Kitagawa
Kinako	Cristina Vee	Eri Kitamura
Yoriko Fukase	Erika Harlacher	Minako Kotobuki
Masamichi Isami	Griffin Burns	Kensho Ono

Music Highlights: End credits: "Usotsuki" (N-buna) performed by Yorushika. Music by Mina Kubota.

Film Facts

- The human masks resemble masks from Noh, a traditional Japanese dance-drama.
- Originally intended for theaters in Japan, due to Coronavirus the film debuted on Netflix.
- The film's Japanese title loosely translates to "I Don't Want to Wear a Cat."

Whisper of the Heart (G)

Theatrical release date: December 13, 1996
Country: Japan Japanese title: *Mimi wo Sumaseba*
Production Company: Studio Ghibli
Length: 111 minutes
Directed by: Yoshifumi Kondô
Screenplay by: Hayao Miyazaki, based on the manga by Aoi Hiiragi, English screenplay by Cindy Davis Hewitt and Donald H. Hewitt

Synopsis: Shizuku Tsukishima, a book-loving junior high student, notices that someone named Seiji Amasawa has checked out many of the same library books that she has. By chance she meets Seiji, who teases her. Later, she finds a cat on a train, following it through the city, ending up at an antique shop. She finds a small statue of a cat, which the shop owner says is called Baron Humbert von Gikkingen. Coming out of the shop, she again runs into Seiji, who has the cat she followed on the back of his bike, and again he teases her. It turns out that Seiji is the grandson of the antique store owner, and he shows her the Baron statue, saying his grandfather would never sell it, as he's looking for its partner, Louise. Seiji is learning to make violins, and gets an opportunity to be an apprentice in Italy. Though she is sad to see him go, Shizuku is inspired to begin writing, starting a fantasy story called "Whisper of the Heart," featuring the Baron. Shizuku's studies begin to suffer greatly as she becomes intensely focused on writing, wanting to complete her story by the time Seiji returns. Once Seiji is back, the two of them begin to plan their future lives.

Cast:

Role	English	Japanese
Shizuku Tsukishima	Brittany Snow	Yōko Honna
Seiji Amasawa	David Gallagher	Issei Takahashi
Asako Tsukishima	Jean Smart	Shigeru Muroi
Seiya Tsukishima	James Sikking	Takashi Tachibana
Baron Humbert von Gikkingen	Cary Elwes	Shigeru Tsuyuguchi
Shirō Nishi	Harold Gould	Keiju Kobayashi
Yūko Harada	Ashley Tisdale	Maiko Kayama
Ms. Kōsaka	Vicki Davis	Minami Takayama
Kinuyo	Mika Boorem	Mayumi Iizuka
Nao	Abigail Mavity	Mai Chiba

Music Highlights: "Take Me Home, Country Roads" (Bill Danoff/Taffy Nivert/John Denver) performed by Olivia Newton-John (orig. by John Denver). Music by Yuji Nomi.

Film Facts

• The film was based on the manga *Mimi o Sumaseba* (1989) created by Aoi Hiiragi, and its sequel *Mimi o Sumaseba: Shiawase na Jikan* (1995), both published in *Ribon* magazine.
• The grandfather clock face reads "Porco Rosso" (25:32), the name of a 1992 Studio Ghibli film.
• Studio Ghibli produced a sequel of sorts, *The Cat Returns,* in 2002.

The Wild (G)

Theatrical release date: April 14, 2006
Production Company: Walt Disney Pictures, Hoytyboy Pictures, Sir Zip Prod., Contrafilm, C.O.R.E.
Length: 82 minutes
Directed by: Steve "Spaz" Williams
Screenplay by: Ed Decter & John J. Strauss and Mark Gibson & Philip Halprin, story by Mark Gibson & Philip Halprin

Synopsis: In the New York Zoo, lion cub Ryan lives in the shadow of his father, the fearsome Samson, who tells tales of his glory days in the wild. Samson is on a turtle-curling team with his friends, the squirrel Benny, Benny's love interest Bridget the giraffe, the snake Larry, and the zoo's mascot, the koala Nigel. After accidentally causing a stampede, Ryan ends up in a cargo container which will be shipped overseas. Samson, accompanied by Benny, Bridget, Nigel, and Larry, set off to rescue Ryan, making their way through New York and to an island where animals are being rescued from a volcano thats about to erupt. Samson admits that despite his tall tales of adventure, he has never actually lived in the wild, as Nigel is captured by a herd of wildebeests. The wildebeest leader Kazar explains to Nigel his plan for the prey to become the predators, beginning with a lion. It isn't long before all the animals end up with the wildebeests, and a battle with Kazar gives Samson a chance to confront his fears from the past.

Cast: Kiefer Sutherland as Samson (lion)
Jim Belushi as Benny (squirrel)
Eddie Izzard as Nigel (koala)
Janeane Garofalo as Bridget (giraffe)
William Shatner as Kazar (wildebeest)
Richard Kind as Larry (snake)
Greg Cipes as Ryan (lion)
Colin Hay as Fergus Flamingo

Miles Marsico as Duke (red kangaroo)
Jack De Sena as Eze (hippopotamus)
Don Cherry as Penguin MC
Christian Argueta as Hamir (pigeon)
David Cowgill as Hamir (still a pigeon)
Lenny Venito as Stan (alligator)
Joseph Siravo as Carmine (alligator)
Patrick Warburton as Blag (wildebeest)

Music Highlights: "Big Time Boppin' (Go Man Go)" (Morris) performed by Big Bad Voodoo Daddy, "Lovin' You" (Riperton/Rudolph) performed by Minnie Riperton, "Clocks" (Berryman/ Buckland/ Champion/Martin) performed by Coldplay, "Really Nice Day" (Idle/Du Prez) performed by Eric Idle and John Du Prez, "Really Nice Day (Finale)" (Idle/Du Prez) performed by Eric Idle and John Du Prez. End Credits: "Real Wild Child" (Greenan/O'Keefe/Owens) performed by Everlife (orig. by Johnny O'Keefe), "Good Enough" (Lifehouse) performed by Lifehouse. Music by Alan Silvestri.

Film Facts

• A number of parallels were noted between this film and DreamWorks' *Madagascar* (2005).
• To promote the film, Hollywood's El Capitan Theatre partnered with the Los Angeles Zoo and Botanical Gardens to present a show of exotic birds, from April 14 through May 11, 2006.
• Nigel appears in a brief post-credits scene (1:21:17).

Winnie the Pooh franchise
Theatrical/Television/Home Media Releases

Winnie the Pooh and the Honey Tree theatrical short (1966)

Winnie the Pooh and the Blustery Day theatrical short (1968)

Winnie the Pooh and Tigger Too theatrical short (1974)

The Many Adventures of Winnie the Pooh theatrical film (1977)

Winnie the Pooh Discovers the Seasons educational short (1981)

Winnie the Pooh and a Day for Eeyore theatrical short (1983)

Welcome to Pooh Corner live-action TV series (1983-1986)

Winnie the Pooh and Friends home media release VHS (1984) with "Winnie the Pooh and a Day for Eeyore," "Hooked Bear," "In the Bag, "Hold That Pose" shorts

The New Adventures of Winnie the Pooh TV series (1988-1991)

Winnie the Pooh & Christmas Too! TV special (1991)

Pooh's Grand Adventure home media release VHS/DVD (1997)

A Winnie the Pooh Thanksgiving TV special (1998, on 1999 *Seasons of Giving* VHS/DVD)

Winnie the Pooh: A Valentine for You TV special (1999)

The Tigger Movie theatrical film (2000)

The Book of Pooh TV series (2001-2003)

A Very Merry Pooh Year home media release VHS/DVD (2002)

Piglet's Big Movie theatrical film (2003)

Winnie the Pooh: Springtime with Roo home media release VHS/DVD (2004)

Pooh's Heffalump Movie theatrical film (2005)

Pooh's Heffalump Halloween Movie home media release VHS/DVD (2005)

My Friends Tigger & Pooh TV series (2007–2010)

    Super Sleuth Christmas Movie home media release DVD (2007)

    Tigger & Pooh and a Musical Too home media release DVD (2009)

    Super Duper Super Sleuths home media release DVD (2010)

Winnie the Pooh theatrical film (2011)

The Mini-Adventures of Winnie the Pooh short series (2011-2014)

Christopher Robin live-action theatrical film (2018)

Winnie the Pooh Home Media: Specials and Series

Storybook Classics/Mini-Classics series:
Winnie the Pooh and the Honey Tree VHS (1991, orig. short 1966)
Winnie the Pooh and the Blustery Day VHS (1991, orig. short 1968)
Winnie the Pooh and Tigger Too VHS (1991, orig. short 1974)
Winnie the Pooh and a Day for Eeyore VHS (1991, orig. short 1983)

The New Adventures of Winnie the Pooh series:
Vol. 1: *The Great Honey Pot Robbery* VHS (1991), Vol. 2: *The Wishing Bear* VHS (1991)
Vol. 3: *Newfound Friends* VHS (1991), Vol. 4: *There's No Camp Like Home* VHS (1991)
Vol. 5: *Wind Some, Lose Some* VHS (1991), Vol. 6: *All's Well That Ends Well* VHS (1991)
Vol. 7: *King of the Beasties* VHS (1992), Vol. 8: *The Sky's the Limit* VHS (1992)
Vol. 9: *Everything's Coming Up Roses* VHS (1992), Vol. 10: *Pooh to the Rescue* VHS (1992)

Winnie the Pooh - Learning series: *Helping Others* VHS (1994), *Making Friends* VHS (1994),
Sharing and Caring VHS (1994), *Growing Up* VHS (1995), *Working Together* VHS (1996)

Winnie the Pooh - Playtime series: *Cowboy Pooh* VHS (1994), *Pooh Party* VHS (1994)
Detective Tigger VHS (1994), *Fun 'n Games* VHS (1995), *Happy Pooh Day* VHS (1996)

Winnie the Pooh - Friendship series: *Clever Little Piglet* VHS (1997), *Pooh Wishes* VHS (1997),
Tigger-iffic Tales VHS (1997), *Imagine That, Christopher Robin!* VHS (1998),
Three Cheers for Eeyore and Rabbit VHS (1998)

Sing Along Songs: *Sing a Song with Pooh Bear* VHS (1999)
Sing a Song with Tigger VHS (2000)
Sing a Song with Pooh Bear & Piglet Too VHS/DVD (2003)

The Book of Pooh series: *The Book of Pooh: Stories from the Heart* VHS/DVD (2001), *Fun With
Friends* VHS (2001), *Just Say Boo!* VHS (2002), *A Valentine for Eeyore* VHS (2002), *Fun With
Make Believe* VHS (2002), *Fun With Manners* VHS (2003), *Fun With Words* VHS (2003)

Growing Up with Winnie the Pooh DVD series: *Friends Forever* (2005), *All for One, One For All:
Adventures in Sharing and Caring* (2005), *A Great Day of Discovery* (2005), *It's Playtime with
Pooh* (2006), *Love & Friendship* (2006)

Winnie the Pooh specials: *Winnie the Pooh and Christmas Too* TV special VHS (1994, orig. 1991),
Un-Valentine's Day VHS (1995), *Frankenpooh* VHS (1995/2001), *Spookable Pooh* VHS (1996),
Boo to You Too! VHS (1997), *Seasons of Giving* VHS (1999/2000), DVD (2003/2009): *A Winnie the
Pooh Thanksgiving* + 2 episodes, *A Valentine For You* VHS (2000, orig. 1999), DVD (2010),
Frankenpooh/Spookable Pooh DVD (2002), *Un-Valentines Day/A Valentine for You* DVD (2004)

My Friends Tigger & Pooh TV series: *Super Sleuth Christmas Movie* DVD (2007),
Tigger & Pooh and a Musical Too DVD (2009), *Super Duper Super Sleuths* DVD (2010)

Winnie the Pooh featurettes
1966, 1968, 1974, 1983 theatrical featurettes + 1981 educational short

---

Synopsis: In "Winnie the Pooh and the Honey Tree" (1966), Pooh runs out of honey, and goes on a mission to find more. After disguising himself as a "little black raincloud" in order to infiltrate a beehive, Pooh invites himself over to Rabbit's house and consumes all of his honey. Pooh is so full that he gets stuck in Rabbit's door, leading to a lengthy team effort to extract him. In "Winnie the Pooh and the Blustery Day" (1968), Pooh goes to visit his thoughtful spot on a windy day, receiving a warning from Gopher to seek shelter because it is "Winds-day." Pooh, getting the warning wrong, sets out to wish his friends a happy Winds-day, with chaotic results. "Winnie the Pooh and Tigger Too" (1974) offers a series of adventures focused on Tigger, including Rabbit's plan to cure Tigger of his excessive bouncing, ice skating with Roo, and efforts to get Tigger out of a tree. "Winnie the Pooh and a Day for Eeyore" introduces the sticks-dropped-in-water game "poohsticks," followed by a birthday celebration for the gloomy donkey Eeyore.

Walt Disney always had his eyes open for good source material, and The Winnie the Pooh featurettes came about because Disney's daughter, Diane, was enjoying A.A. Milne's books. Disney first began seeking the rights for the stories in the late 1930s, obtaining them in 1961. Adjustments and additions were made to the original stories, including the creation of the character of Gopher (at one point Gopher says, "I'm not in the book, but I'm at your service!"). Wolfgang Reitherman was chosen to direct the first two featurettes, with John Lounsbery directing the third. All of the screenplays were adapted by Disney's writing staff.

The voice cast for the initial featurettes included Sterling Holloway as Winnie-the-Pooh, John Fiedler as Piglet, Junius Matthews as Rabbit, Paul Winchell as Tigger, Hal Smith as Owl, Barbara Luddy as Kanga, Clint Howard and Dori Whitaker as Roo, Ralph Wright as Eeyore, Howard Morris as Gopher, and Bruce Reitherman, Jon Walmsley, and Timothy Turner as Christopher Robin, with narration by Sebastian Cabot.

The songs were provided by Richard M. Sherman and Robert B. Sherman, including some of their best-known work: "Winnie the Pooh," "Up, Down, Touch the Ground," "Rumbly in My Tumbly," "(I'm Just a) Little Black Raincloud," "The Wonderful Thing About Tiggers," and "Heffalumps and Woozles."

"Winnie the Pooh and the Honey Tree" received mixed reviews, but was popular enough to merit a second film. After "Winnie the Pooh and the Blustery Day" won the Academy Award for "Best Animated Short Film," Pooh's place in the Disney pantheon was established, setting the stage for numerous sequels over many years.

Winnie the Pooh featurettes

Production Company: Walt Disney Productions

Cast: Winnie-the-Pooh: Sterling Holloway (1-3), Hal Smith (4-5)
Piglet: John Fiedler (2-5)
Christopher Robin: Bruce Reitherman (1), Jon Walmsley (2), Timothy Turner (3), Kim Christianson (4-5)
Rabbit: Junius Matthews (1-3), Ray Erlenborn (4), Will Ryan (5)
Tigger: Paul Winchell (2, 3, 5)

Owl: Hal Smith (1-2, 4-5)
Kanga: Barbara Luddy (1-3), Julie McWhirter Dees (5)
Roo: Clint Howard (1-2), Dori Whitaker (3), Dick Billingsley (5)
Eeyore: Ralph Wright (1, 2, 5), Ron Feinberg
Gopher: Howard Morris (1-2)
Narrator: Sebastian Cabot (1-3), Laurie Main (4-5)

1. *Winnie the Pooh and the Honey Tree* 26 minute featurette (Feb 4, 1966), dir. Wolfgang Reitherman, screened with the 1966 film *The Ugly Dachshund*. When Pooh runs out of honey, he sets about to get more, dressing as a little black rain cloud to fool bees in a neighboring tree. Later, he invites himself to lunch at Rabbit's, and gets stuck in Rabbit's front door. Songs: "Winnie the Pooh," "Up, Down, Touch the Ground," "Rumbly in My Tumbly," "Little Black Raincloud."

2. *Winnie the Pooh and the Blustery Day* 25 minute featurette (Dec 20, 1968), dir. Wolfgang Reitherman, Screened with the 1968 film *The Horse in the Gray Flannel Suit*. After Gopher warns Pooh about the coming wind, Pooh sets off to wish everyone a happy "Winds-day," with tumultuous results. The tiger-like Tigger visits Pooh, warning him about "Heffalumps and Woozles" that steal honey, leading a series of nightmares for Pooh. A flood in the area washes Piglet away, leading all his friends to help. Songs: "The Wonderful Thing About Tiggers," "Heffalumps and Woozles."

3. *Winnie the Pooh and Tigger Too* 25 minute featurette (Dec 20, 1974), dir. John Lounsbery, screened with the 1974 film *The Island at the Top of the World*. Annoyed with Tigger's bouncing, Rabbit schemes to temporarily lose Tigger in the forest. The plan backfires, with Rabbit, Pooh, and Piglet lost instead. Later Tigger babysits Roo, but after some chaotic ice skating ends up stuck in a tree, requiring the narrator's assistance. Songs: "The Honey Tree," "Birthday, Birthday."

4. "**Winnie the Pooh Discovers the Seasons**" 8 minute short (Sep 6, 1981), dir. Rick Reinert. Not released theatrically. Pooh, Piglet, Owl, Rabbit, and Eeyore learn about the seasons.

5. *Winnie the Pooh and a Day for Eeyore* 25 minute featurette (Mar 11, 1983), dir. Rick Reinert. Screened with the 1983 re-release of *The Sword in the Stone*. During a game Pooh's called Poohsticks (racing objects dropped in the river) Eeyore is spotted floating in the river, after having been bounced by Tigger. Pooh learns it's Eeyore's birthday, and a party is organized.

Releases: *Winnie the Pooh and the Honey Tree* VHS (1991/2000), *Winnie the Pooh and the Blustery Day* VHS (1991/2000), *Winnie the Pooh and Tigger Too* VHS (1991/2000), *Winnie the Pooh and a Day for Eeyore* VHS (1991/2000), *The Many Adventures of Winnie the Pooh* Blu-ray (2013).

Film Facts

- Gopher's character was created by Disney, not appearing in the stories by A.A. Milne.
- Walt Disney learned of Winnie the Pooh when his daughter, Diane, was reading the books.
- *Winnie the Pooh and the Blustery Day* won the "Best Animated Short Film" Academy Award.

The Many Adventures of Winnie the Pooh (G)

Theatrical release date: March 11, 1977
Production Company: Walt Disney Productions
Length: 74 minutes
Directed by: Wolfgang Reitherman, John Lounsbery
Story: Larry Clemmons, Ralph Wright, Vance Gerry, Xavier Atencio, Ken Anderson, Julius Svendsen, Ted Berman, Eric Cleworth, based on the books written by A.A. Milne

> **Synopsis**: Combines three previously made featurettes based on A.A. Milne's classic children's stories, "Winnie the Pooh and the Honey Tree" (1966), "Winnie the Pooh and the Blustery Day" (1968), and "Winnie the Pooh and Tigger Too" (1974).

Cast: Sterling Holloway as Winnie the Pooh
Paul Winchell as Tigger
Sebastian Cabot as the Narrator
Junius Matthews as Rabbit
Barbara Luddy as Kanga
Howard Morris as Gopher
John Fiedler as Piglet
Ralph Wright as Eeyore
Hal Smith as Owl
Clint Howard as Roo
Bruce Reitherman as Christopher Robin
Jon Walmsley as Christopher Robin
Timothy Turner as Christopher Robin
Dori Whitaker as Roo

Music Highlights: "Winnie the Pooh" performed by Disney Chorus/Thurl Ravenscroft, "Up, Down, Touch the Ground" performed by S. Holloway, "Rumbly in My Tumbly" performed by S. Holloway, "(I'm Just a) Little Black Raincloud" performed by S. Holloway and Bruce Reitherman, "Mind Over Matter" performed by Holloway, Reitherman, Matthews, Wright, Howard, Luddy, Fiedler, & Smith, "Like a Rather Blustery Day" performed by S. Holloway, "The Wonderful Thing About Tiggers" performed by Paul Winchell, "Heffalumps and Woozles" performed by Disney Chorus, "The Rain, Rain, Rain, Came Down, Down, Down" performed by Disney Chorus, "Hip-Hip Pooh-Ray!" performed by cast. All songs by Richard M. Sherman/Robert B. Sherman. Score by Buddy Baker.

Film Facts

- The 22nd of the Disney animated classics, *The Many Adventures of Winnie the Pooh* combined the three Winnie the Pooh theatrical featurettes into one film, using a storybook frame to unite them.
- Winnie and other characters were named after toys of Christopher Robin, A.A. Milne's son.
- A stuffed toy sold by Harrods department store as "Edward Bear" was renamed by the real Christopher Robin as Winnie the Pooh, after Winnie, a bear at the London Zoo, and Pooh, a swan.
- Disney had originally wanted to complete a feature film, but decided to release a series of featurettes to familiarize audiences in the United States with the Winnie the Pooh characters, which were better-known in the UK.
- The film was first released on a double bill with the live-action *The Littlest Horse Thieves* (1977).
- *The Many Adventures of Winnie the Pooh* and *Dumbo* were the first two animated Disney features released on VHS and Betamax tapes, on June 28, 1981 (shorts and live-action films began in 1978).
- Additional appearances: See Winnie the Pooh franchise overview.

Winnie the Pooh and Christmas Too! (TV-G)

Broadcast date: December 14, 1991
Production Company: Walt Disney Television Animation, Walt Disney Animation France, Sunwoo Animation
Length: 26 minutes
Directed by: Jamie Mitchell
Written by: Karl Geurs, Mark Zaslove

Synopsis: This holiday special served as the finale for *The New Adventures of Winnie the Pooh* animated TV series, which was broadcast from January 17, 1988 to October 26, 1991. In a letter to Santa, Christopher Robin takes down the Christmas wishes of the inhabitants of the Hundred Acre Wood. The letter is thrown to the wind to be carried to the North Pole, but Piglet realizes Pooh didn't include his wish. They retrieve the letter, Rabbit provides a pencil to add Pooh's wish, and the letter is thrown back to the wind. When the letter is blown back and there's no time for it to get to Santa, Pooh and Piglet fear that everyone's Christmas will be ruined. Determined not to let this happen, they dress Pooh as Santa and Piglet as a reindeer and cobble together gifts for their friends. The kind ruse is revealed, and Rabbit figures out that the letter was incorrectly sent on the south wind (Pooh figuring "S" stood for Santa). Pooh finally sets out to hand-deliver the letter, but it escapes his grasp. Christopher Robin arrives on a new sled, with gifts for all, including a new honeypot for Pooh.

Cast: Jim Cummings as Winnie the Pooh
Peter Cullen as Eeyore
John Fiedler as Piglet
Michael Gough as Gopher

Edan Gross as Christopher Robin
Ken Sansom as Rabbit
Paul Winchell as Tigger

Music Highlights: Music by Steve Nelson.

Film Facts

• The special was made by the creative team from Disney's animated TV series *The New Adventures of Winnie the Pooh* (1988-1991).
• The special was released on VHS in 1994, adding the episode "The Magic Earmuffs," directed by Karl Geurs, story by Terrie Collins & Mark Zaslove, teleplay by Carter Crocker.
• Rabbit's fur attracted attention in this special for its odd greenish color.
• A version of *Winnie the Pooh and Christmas Too!* was included on the *Winnie The Pooh: A Very Merry Pooh Year* DVD (2002), which has Christopher Robin's lines re-recorded by William Green (Christopher Robin's voice actor for *A Very Merry Pooh Year*), and adjusted the color of Rabbit's fur.
• Composer Steve Nelson also worked on *Winnie the Pooh: Seasons of Giving* and *The New Adventures of Winnie the Pooh* TV series, as well as *Sesame Street*, *Webster*, and *Good Grief*.
• The special was nominated for an "Outstanding Children's Program" primetime Emmy Award in 1992.

Boo to You Too! Winnie the Pooh (TV-G)

Broadcast date: October 25, 1996
Production Company: Walt Disney Television Animation, Toon City Animation, Thai Wang Film Productions
Length: 21 minutes
Directed by: Rob LaDuca
Written by: Carter Crocker

> **Synopsis**: When Piglet is afraid of the spooky aspects of Halloween, he tries to face his fears, but between a frightening thunderstorm and Tigger's scary stories, he ends up hiding at home. Pooh, Tigger, and Eeyore decide to help by throwing a "Hallo-wasn't" party at his home that isn't scary. Trying to be in the Halloween spirit, they dress up in costumes, which scares Piglet all over again. He runs away, looking for Pooh, Tigger and Eeyore, as they look for him. Piglet fears his friends have been captured by "Spookables," and when he happens upon Tigger and Eeyore, still in costume, trying to get Pooh unstuck from a tree branch, he thinks Pooh is under attack by Spookables. When his friend needs him, Piglet finds the courage to come to the rescue. Having overcoming his fears of Halloween, Piglet is free to join his friends for trick-or-treating.

Cast: Peter Cullen as Eeyore
Jim Cummings as Winnie the Pooh/Tigger
John Fiedler as Piglet

Michael Gough as Gopher
John Rhys-Davies as Narrator
Ken Sansom as Rabbit

Music Highlights: "I Wanna Scare Myself" (Michael Silversher/Patty Silversher) performed by Jim Cummings, "I Am Not Afraid" (Michael Silversher/Patty Silversher) performed by John Fiedler. Music by Mark Watters.

Film Facts

• Like *Winnie the Pooh and Christmas Too!,* the special was made by the creative team that produced the animated TV series *The New Adventures of Winnie the Pooh* (1988-1991).
• This is the second of the Winnie the Pooh specials.
• Animator Phil Spencer won the "Outstanding Individual Achievement in Animation" Primetime Emmy Award in 1997 for his work.
• This special was incorporated into the home media film *Pooh's Heffalump Halloween Movie* (2005) as a flashback.
• Following the model of the Peanuts specials, the first three Winnie the Pooh TV specials were Christmas, Halloween, and Thanksgiving-themed (despite the fact that Thanksgiving is not celebrated in England).
• Other Halloween home media releases were issued, including *Spookable Pooh* (1996) and *Frankenpooh* (1999), both drawn from episodes from Disney's animated TV series *The New Adventures of Winnie the Pooh* (1988-1991), as well as *Pooh's Heffalump Halloween Movie* (2005).

Pooh's Grand Adventure: The Search for Christopher Robin (G)

Home media release date: August 5, 1997
Production Company: Walt Disney Television Animation, DisneyToon Studios,
Walt Disney Video Premiere, Walt Disney Animation Japan
Length: 76 minutes
Directed by: Karl Geurs
Screenplay by: Karl Geurs and Carter Crocker, inspired by the stories of A. A. Milne

Synopsis: When Christopher Robin disappears and leaves a note for Winnie the Pooh, Owl misinterprets it, leaving the residents of the Hundred Acre Wood fearful that Christopher Robin has gone to a distant cave called Skull, where the frightening Skullasaurus dwells. Pooh, Piglet, Tigger, and Rabbit set out with a map provided by Owl to rescue their friend, making their way through "the Great Unknown." Each member of the search party faces a setback, leaving them feeling defeated, afraid, and lost. Despite these challenges, they are able to rally, finding inspiration in each other and an understanding that others can provide strength even when they are far away.

Cast: Jim Cummings as Winnie the Pooh/
     Skullasaurus growls
John Fiedler as Piglet
Ken Sansom as Rabbit
Andre Stojka as Owl

Peter Cullen as Eeyore
Brady Bluhm as Christopher Robin
David Warner as The Narrator
Paul Winchell as Tigger
Frankie J. Galasso as Christopher Robin (singing)

Music Highlights: "Forever and Ever" (Abbott/Weeks) performed by Jim Cummings & Frankie J. Galasso, "Adventure Is a Wonderful Thing" (Abbott/Weeks) performed by Andre Stojka, "If It Says So" (Abbott/Weeks), performed by Jim Cummings and Ken Sansom, "Wherever You Are" (Abbott/Weeks) performed by Jim Cummings, "Everything Is Right" (Abbott/Weeks) performed by Jim Cummings, Frankie J. Galasso, Ken Sansom, Steven Schatzberg, Andre Stojka, and Dylan Watson. End credits: "Wherever You Are" (Abbott/Weeks) performed by Barry Coffing and Vonda Shepard. Music by Carl Johnson.

Film Facts

• The UK title of the film was *Pooh's Most Grand Adventure: The Search for Christopher Robin*.
• The film was a series finale for the TV show *The New Adventures of Winnie the Pooh* (1988-1991).
• As with the previous two specials, this film is primarily based on an original story, rather than drawn from A.A. Milne's work.
• Paul Winchell, voice of Tigger since the original 1960s shorts, was having voice difficulties, leading Jim Cummings to perform Tigger's singing parts. Winchell retired from voicing Tigger after *Winnie the Pooh: A Valentine for You* (1999).
• Hundred Acre Wood residents Kanga, Roo, and Gopher are not included in the film.
• The *Pooh's Grand Adventure: The Search for Christopher Robin* soundtrack CD/cassette (Walt Disney Records, 1997) featured songs from the film with additional songs by Kathie Lee Gifford.

A Winnie the Pooh Thanksgiving (G)

Broadcast date: November 22, 1998, Home media release date: Nov 9, 1999 (on *Seasons of Giving*)
Production Company: Walt Disney Television Animation, Walt Disney Pictures
Length: 22 minutes
Directed by: Jun Falkenstein
Written by: Carter Crocker

Synopsis: The residents of the Hundred Acre Wood gather to celebrate Thanksgiving with a potluck of honey, "haycorns" (acorns), biscuits, thistles, lemonade, and ice cream, until Rabbit, a stickler for protocol, insists that this is not a traditional Thanksgiving dinner. Taking charge of the situation, Rabbit asks Tigger and Eeyore to find cranberries, Gopher to bake a pumpkin pie, and Owl to clean and polish the dinnerware, appointing himself to see to the decorations, and sending Winnie the Pooh and Piglet in search of a turkey. A traditional Thanksgiving meal appears to be developing, until the "turkey" Pooh and Piglet captured turns out to be Tigger and Eeyore. By chance the food and decorations end up spoiled, and Rabbit believes that Thanksgiving is ruined, telling everyone there's nothing to be thankful for. After everyone heads home feeling discouraged, Pooh realizes he can share the little honey he has with his friends. He gathers everyone again and the original meal is re-assembled. Rabbit realizes that being with loved ones is what Thanksgiving is truly about.

Cast: Jim Cummings as Winnie the Pooh,
      Tigger's singing voice
John Fiedler as Piglet
Steven Schatzberg as Piglet's singing voice
Paul Winchell as Tigger
Peter Cullen as Eeyore

Ken Sansom as Rabbit
Andre Stojka as Owl
Michael Gough as Gopher
Brady Bluhm as Christopher Robin
David Warner as Narrator

Music Highlights: "Hooray, Hooray!" performed by Jim Cummings, "The Turkey Song" performed by Jim Cummings Steve Schatzberg, "Berrily We Roll Along" performed by Jim Cummings, "Our Thanksgiving Day" performed by cast. All songs by Michael & Patty Silversher. Score by Carl Johnson.

Film Facts

• The special was broadcast on Thanksgiving Day in 1998, and was nominated for the "Outstanding Children's Program" Primetime Emmy.
• Director Jun Falkenstein went on to direct *Mickey's Once Upon a Christmas* (1999), *The Tigger Movie* (2000), and the live-action version of *The Jungle Book* (2014).
• *A Winnie the Pooh Thanksgiving* is included on the *Seasons of Giving* VHS (1999/2000), *Seasons of Giving* DVD (2003), *Seasons of Giving* 10th Anniversary Edition DVD (2009).
• The narration in *A Winnie the Pooh Thanksgiving* is altered on the *Seasons of Giving* VHS/DVD.
• This was one of Paul Winchell's final appearances as Tigger, followed by *Winnie the Pooh: A Valentine for You* (1999).
• Some viewers found it odd that an American holiday was celebrated in the Hundred Acre Wood.

Winnie the Pooh: A Valentine for You (NR)

Broadcast date: February 13, 1999
Production Company: Walt Disney Television Animation
Length: 22 minutes
Directed by: Keith Ingham
Written by: Carter Crocker

Synopsis: Valentine's Day is coming to the Hundred Acre Wood, and Winnie the Pooh is worried that Christopher Robin hasn't been coming by lately. When Christopher Robin writes a card to "Winifred," Owl explains that Christopher Robin has been bitten by a Smitten love bug, and is suffering from a "love sickness." Tigger and Rabbit reason that if he's bitten by a second Smitten, it should cancel out the first bite. A firefly is mistaken for a Smitten, and they follow it into the heart of the Hundred Acre Wood, getting lost in the process. Pooh finally catches the bug, but decides to let it go, and the light of the bug leads the friends back together. Upon meeting Christopher Robin again, Pooh doesn't have the heart to sic the bug on him, but, to his relief, learns that Christopher will always love him.

Cast: Jim Cummings as Winnie the Pooh/Tigger (singing)
Paul Winchell as Tigger
John Fiedler as Piglet
Steve Schatzberg as Piglet (singing)
Peter Cullen as Eeyore
Ken Sansom as Rabbit
Andre Stojka as Owl
Michael Gough as Gopher
Brady Bluhm as Christopher Robin
Frankie J. Galasso as Christopher Robin
 (singing)
David Warner as Narrator

Music Highlights: "Winnie the Pooh" instrumental (Sherman/Sherman), "Girls Are Like Boys" (Michael Silversher/Patty Silversher) performed by Andre Stojka (Owl), "When The Love Bug Bites" (Michael Silversher/Patty Silversher), performed by Jim Cummings (Tigger/Pooh), Ken Sansom (Rabbit) and Steven Schatzberg (Piglet), "Places in the Heart" (Michael Silversher/Patty Silversher) performed by Jim Cummings (Pooh/Tigger), Frankie J. Galasso (Christopher Robbin) and Ken Sansom (Rabbit). Songs arranged by Carl Johnson. Score by Carl Johnson.

Film Facts

• After its initial February 13, 1999 broadcast on ABC, home media releases included the *Winnie the Pooh: A Valentine for You* VHS (2000), the *Un-Valentine's Day* and *A Valentine for You* Double Feature DVD (2004), and the *Winnie the Pooh: A Valentine for You* Special Edition DVD (2010).
• This was Paul Winchell's final appearance as Tigger. He would be succeeded by Jim Cummings in *The Tigger Movie* (2000).
• Michael Silversher (music) and Patty Silversher (lyrics) composed the songs, also writing songs for *DuckTales* (1987-1990), *Chip 'n Dale Rescue Rangers* (1989-1990), *TaleSpin* (1990-1991), *The Little Mermaid* animated TV series (1992-1994), *The Return of Jafar* (1994), *Boo to You Too! Winnie the Pooh* (1996), *Winnie the Pooh: A Valentine for You* (1999), *The Little Mermaid II: Return to the Sea* (2000), and *A Very Merry Pooh Year* (2002).

Winnie the Pooh: *The Tigger Movie* (G)

Theatrical release date: February 11, 2000 (premiere February 6, 2000 at El Capitan Theatre, L.A.)
Production Company: Walt Disney Pictures, Walt Disney Television Animation,
Disney MovieToons, Walt Disney Animation Japan
Length: 77 minutes
Directed by: Jun Falkenstein
Screenplay by: Jun Falkenstein, story by Eddie Guzelian

Synopsis: The residents of the Hundred Acre Wood have difficulty keeping up with Tigger's energetic bouncing, so, at the suggestion of Roo, Tigger seeks his family, sending off a letter to them. When he has no luck, his friends write a letter back, posing as his family, and Tigger mistakenly thinks his relatives are coming to visit. To avoid disappointing Tigger, his friends dress as Tiggers. Tigger sees through the ruse, and angrily leaves into a storm. A search party is formed and Tigger finally realizes he's been with his family the whole time.

Cast: Jim Cummings as Tigger/Winnie the Pooh
Nikita Hopkins as Roo
Ken Sansom as Rabbit
John Fiedler as Piglet
Peter Cullen as Eeyore

Andre Stojka as Owl
Kath Soucie as Kanga
Tom Attenborough as Christopher Robin
John Hurt as Narrator
Frank Welker as additional voices

Music Highlights: "Your Heart Will Lead You Home" (Sherman/Sherman/Loggins) performed by Kenny Loggins with chorus, "The Wonderful Thing about Tiggers" (Sherman/Sherman) performed by cast/chorus, "Someone Like Me" (Sherman/Sherman) performed by cast, "The Whoop-de-Dooper-Bounce" (Sherman/Sherman) performed by cast/chorus, "Pooh's Lullabee" (Sherman/Sherman) performed by cast/chorus, "Round My Family Tree" (Sherman/Sherman) performed by cast/chorus, "How to Be a Tigger" (Sherman/Sherman) performed by cast. Score by Harry Gregson-Williams.

Film Facts

• After *The Many Adventures of Winnie the Pooh* debuted in theaters in 1977, Disney had produced several Winnie the Pooh projects, but *The Tigger Movie* was the first theatrical follow-up.
• The original title of the film was *Winnie the Pooh and the Family Tree*.
• One of the most momentous events in the development of the film was the return of the Sherman Brothers (*Mary Poppins*, *The Jungle Book*, *The Aristocats*) to Disney.
• The original voice of Tigger, Paul Winchell, passed the role to Jim Cummings from this film on.
• The DVD (2012) includes five 3-4 minute shorts from *The Mini-Adventures of Winnie the Pooh*: "The Most Wonderful Thing About Tiggers," "Eeyore's House," "Someone Like Tigger," "Lullabee," and "The Super Bounce." The Blu-ray adds five more: "Pooh and Tigger," "What Tiggers Do Best," "Tigger Goes Ice Skating," "The Jagular," and "Unbouncing Tigger."
• The film was originally planned as a home media release, but was upgraded to a theatrical film when an early version was screened at Disney.
• Soundtracks included *The Tigger Movie…& More!* Canadian CD (Walt Disney Records, 1999) and *The Tigger Movie: Songs & Story* (Walt Disney Records, 2000).

Winnie the Pooh: *A Very Merry Pooh Year* (G)

Home media release date: November 11, 2002
Production Company: Walt Disney Video Premiere, Walt Disney Television Animation, DisneyToon Studios, Walt Disney Pictures, Walt Disney Animation France, Wang Film, Sunwoo Animation
Length: 65 minutes
Directors/Writers: "Happy Pooh Year" directed by Gary Katona, Ed Wexler, written by Brian Hohfeld, "A Very Merry Pooh Year" (interstitials) written by Ted Henning/Karl Geurs, "Winnie the Pooh and Christmas Too," directed by Jamie Mitchell, written by Karl Geurs/Mark Zaslove

Synopsis: The film begins with new interstitials of Pooh's friends arriving on Christmas Eve to help trim his Christmas tree, before segueing into the 1991 TV special "Winnie the Pooh and Christmas Too" (running from 6:38 to 30:38) as Rabbit tells Roo the story of when a letter to Santa from the residents of the Hundred Acre Woods got waylaid. In the "Happy Pooh Year" segment (beginning at 35:22), Pooh learns of New Years Resolutions from Christopher Robin. After Rabbit becomes irritated with his friends' quirks, Pooh resolves not to eat honey, Piglet not to be afraid, Eeyore to be cheerful, and Tigger not to bounce. Before long Pooh acts like Eeyore, Piglet like Tigger, Eeyore like Pooh, and Tigger like Piglet, but they end up irritating Rabbit even more. They fear that their friend will leave the Hundred Acre Wood, but Rabbit finally realizes that their quirks are part of who his friends are.

Cast: Jim Cummings as Winnie the Pooh/Tigger
Peter Cullen as Eeyore
John Fiedler as Piglet
Michael Gough as Gopher
William Green as Christopher Robin

Nikita Hopkins as Roo
Ken Sansom as Rabbit
Kath Soucie as Kanga
Michael York as Narrator

Music Highlights: "Winnie the Pooh" (Sherman/Sherman) performed by Carly Simon with Jim Cummings, "Auld Lang Syne" (Burns, additional lyrics by Carly Simon) performed by Carly Simon and cast, "Jingle Bells" (Pierpont) performed by cast, "Snow Snows" (Michael Silversher/Patty Silversher) performed by Jim Cummings, "Happy Pooh Year" (M. Silversher/P. Silversher) performed by Jim Cummings, "Hunny, No Not For Me" (M. Silversher/P. Silversher) performed by Jim Cummings. Score by Mark Watters.

Film Facts

• Carly Simon began a series of collaborations on Winnie the Pooh films with this title.
• Christopher Robin's voice in the "Winnie the Pooh and Christmas Too" portion of the special, originally voiced by Edan Gross, was re-recorded by William Green for this release.
• Michael and Patty Silversher wrote music for several Disney titles, including *The Little Mermaid* TV series (1993), *The Return of Jafar* (1994), *Boo to You Too! Winnie the Pooh* (1996), *Winnie the Pooh: A Valentine for You* (1999), and *The Little Mermaid II: Return to the Sea* (2000).
• Releases included *A Very Merry Pooh Year* VHS (2002), *A Very Merry Pooh Year* DVD (2003/2013), and *A Very Merry Pooh Year* (Gift of Friendship Edition) Blu-ray/DVD/Digital Copy (2013).

Winnie the Pooh: *Piglet's Big Movie* (G)

Theatrical release date: March 21, 2003
Production Company: Walt Disney Pictures, DisneyToon Studios, Walt Disney Animation Japan, Toon City Animation (Philippines)
Length: 75 minutes
Directed by: Francis Glebas
Screenplay by: Brian Hohlfeld, adapted from and inspired by the works of A.A. Milne

> **Synopsis**: Piglet is feeling unappreciated, as Pooh, Tigger, Rabbit, and Eeyore plan to get some honey while avoiding the bees, but exclude Piglet due to his small size. He is unnoticed even after he outsmarts the bees when things go wrong, and sadly departs. Once Piglet's absence is noticed, a scrapbook journal he complied of their adventures together is used to guide the search, which reveals what a big difference Piglet has made in everyone's life. A scuffle over the journal leads to its loss in a river, and while trying to retrieve it, Pooh ends up hanging at the edge of a waterfall. Piglet is able to save Pooh, and everyone realizes that small stature does not mean small importance.

Cast: John Fiedler as Piglet
Jim Cummings as Winnie the Pooh/Tigger
Andre Stojka as Owl
Kath Soucie as Kanga

Nikita Hopkins as Roo
Peter Cullen as Eeyore
Ken Sansom as Rabbit
Tom Wheatley as Christopher Robin

Music Highlights: "Winnie the Pooh" (Sherman/Sherman) performed by Carly Simon with Ben Taylor, "If I Wasn't So Small (The Piglet Song)" (Simon) performed by Carly Simon, "Mother's Intuition" (Simon) performed by Carly Simon, "Sing Ho for the Life of a Bear" (Simon) performed by Carly Simon and cast, "The More It Snows (Tiddely-Pom)" (Simon/lyrics adapted from A.A. Milne) performed by John Fiedler and Jim Cummings, "With a Few Good Friends" (Simon/Hohlfeld) performed by Carly Simon with Ben Taylor and Sally Taylor, "With a Few Good Friends (Reprise)" (Simon/Hohlfeld) performed by cast, "The More I Look Inside" (Simon) performed by Carly Simon, "Comforting to Know" (Simon) performed by Carly Simon with Ben Taylor, guest vocal performance by Renée Fleming. Score by Carl Johnson.

Film Facts

- The film draws from A.A. Milne's books *Winnie-the-Pooh* (chapters 5, 7, and 8) and *The House at Pooh Corner* (chapters 1 and 3).
- *Piglet's Big Game* was released for Nintendo GameCube/Game Boy Advance, Sony PS2, and PC.
- Christopher Robin's drum (33:03) looks the same as the drum in *The Many Adventures of Winnie the Pooh* (7:48, 24:02).
- Carly Simon wrote several original songs for the film, and is joined by her children, Ben and Sally, on some tracks. "Winnie the Pooh (Theme Song)" and "With a Few Good Friends" are on the 2005 CD *The Best of Pooh & Heffalumps Too*.
- This was the 3rd theatrical Pooh film, after *The Many Adventures of Winnie the Pooh* (1977) and *The Tigger Movie* (2000), followed by *Pooh's Heffalump Movie* (2005), and *Winnie the Pooh* (2011).

Winnie the Pooh: Springtime with Roo (G)

Home media release date: March 9, 2004
Production Company: Walt Disney Pictures, DisneyToon Studios, Toon City Animation (Philippines)
Length: 65 minutes
Directed by: Elliot M. Bour & Saul Andrew Blinkoff
Screenplay by: Tom Rogers

Synopsis: On Easter morning, Pooh, Piglet, Tigger, Eeyore and Roo head over to Rabbit's for an Easter egg hunt, only to be drafted by Rabbit to help with Spring cleaning. In the process they discover Rabbit's Easter decorations and put them out, angering Rabbit to the point that he throws everyone out of the house. Tigger returns, and with the help of the Narrator, remind Rabbit that he used to enjoy Easter. Rabbit is shown a past Easter, when his fussiness interfered with everyone's enjoyment of the holiday, then a future Easter, when Rabbit's irritable ways have driven everyone away. When he returns to the present, Rabbit has a chance to mend his ways by sharing the joy of Easter with all.

Cast: Jim Cummings as Winnie The Pooh/Tigger
Ken Sansom as Rabbit
Jimmy Bennett as Roo
David Ogden Stiers as Narrator

Kath Soucie as Kanga
John Fiedler as Piglet
Jeff Bennett as Piglet (singing)
Peter Cullen as Eeyore

Music Highlights: "Winnie the Pooh" (Sherman/Sherman), "The Wonderful Thing About Tiggers" (Sherman/Sherman), "We're Huntin' Eggs Today" (John Kavanaugh) performed by Jim Cummings, Peter Cullen, John Fiedler, Jimmy Bennett, "Sniffly Sniff" (Rogers/Kavanaugh) performed by Jim Cummings, "Easter Day With You" (Kavanaugh) performed by Jim Cummings, Peter Cullen, Jeff Bennett, Jimmy Bennett, "The Way It Must Be Done" (Rogel/Geissman) performed by Ken Sansom, Jim Cummings, Peter Cullen, John Fiedler, Jimmy Bennett, "Easter Day With You (Reprise)" (Kavanaugh) performed by Jimmy Bennett, "The Grandest Easter of All (Rabbit's Reprise)" (Rogel/Geissman), "Easter Day With You" (Finale), performed by cast. Score by Mark Watters.

Film Facts

• The story is patterned after the Ghost of Christmas Past and the Ghost of Christmas Yet to Come from Charles Dickens' *The Christmas Carol*.
• Narrator David Ogden Stiers has an extensive voice acting resume, including Cogsworth in *Beauty and the Beast* (1991), Governor Ratcliffe in *Pocahontas* (1995), the Archdeacon in *The Hunchback of Notre Dame* (1996), Jumba in *Lilo & Stitch* (2002), and Mr. Harcourt in *Atlantis: The Lost Empire* (2001).
• Writer Tom Rogers also worked on *Lady and the Tramp 2* (2001), *The Jungle Book 2* (2003), *The Lion King 1 1/2* (2004), *The Little Mermaid: Ariel's Beginning* (2008), *Secret of the Wings* (2012), *Tinker Bell & the Legend of the NeverBeast* (2014), and the *Elena of Avalor* TV series.
• The film was released on DVD in 2004, and as the *Winnie the Pooh: Springtime with Roo* Hippity Hoppity Roo Edition Blu-ray/Digital HD in 2014.

Winnie the Pooh: *Pooh's Heffalump Movie* (G)

Theatrical release date: February 11, 2005
Production Company: Walt Disney Pictures, DisneyToon Studios, Walt Disney Animation Japan
Length: 68 minutes
Directed by: Frank Nissen
Screenplay by: Brian Hohlfeld and Evan Spiliotopoulos

Synopsis: After strange trumpeting sounds are heard, Tigger's house is damaged, and large, mysterious animal tracks are found, it is believed that there is a dreaded Heffalump on the loose in the Hundred Acre Woods (Tigger had warned Pooh about Heffalumps in the 1968 short *Winnie the Pooh and the Blustery Day*). Rabbit organizes a Heffalump expedition to capture the creature, excluding Roo due to his youth. While the others are anxiously searching, Roo strikes out on his own and encounters the young Heffalump, a friendly, elephant-like creature named Lumpy (short for Heffridge Trumpler Brompet Heffalump IV). Lumpy tries to call out to his mother, but is not able to make the right sound so she can hear him. When the others return, they mistakenly think Lumpy is a threat to Roo, and frighten Lumpy with the traps they've set, though Roo's mother, Kanga, learns the truth. After Roo is accidentally stuck on some logs, Lumpy is finally able to call his mother to come help.

Cast: Jim Cummings as Winnie the Pooh/Tigger
John Fiedler as Piglet
Nikita Hopkins as Roo
Kath Soucie as Kanga

Ken Sansom as Rabbit
Peter Cullen as Eeyore
Brenda Blethyn as Mama Heffalump
Kyle Stanger as Lumpy

Music Highlights: "The Horribly Hazardous Heffalumps!" (Carly Simon/Brian Hohlfeld) performed by Carly Simon, Jim Cummings, Ken Sansom, Peter Cullen, John Fiedler, Nikita Hopkins, "Little Mr. Roo" (Simon) performed by Carly Simon and Kath Soucie, "The Name Game" (Simon/Hohlfeld) performed by Kyle Stanger and Nikita Hopkins, "Shoulder to Shoulder" (Simon) performed by Carly Simon with The Heffalump Chorus, "In the Name of the Hundred Acre Wood/What Do You Do?" (Simon) performed by Carly Simon with The Heffalump Chorus. Score by Joel McNeely.

Film Facts

• Carly Simon contributed the name Heffridge Trumpler Brompet Heffalump IV. Simon also wrote and performed songs for *Piglet's Big Movie* (2003).

• Kanga is caught in a trap made from a life preserver from the HMS Ashdown (50:07). The Hundred Ace Wood is inspired by Ashdown Forest, south of London.

• Roo lassos a barrel with a rope (at 10:15), but a few seconds later the rope has mysteriously vanished.

• *The Best of Pooh & Heffalumps Too* CD (Walt Disney Records, 2005) includes several songs from the film, plus new recordings and two songs from *Piglet's Big Movie* (2003): "Winnie the Pooh (Theme Song)" and "With a Few Good Friends," sung with Simon's children Ben Taylor and Sally Taylor.

Winnie the Pooh: *Pooh's Heffalump Halloween Movie* (G)

Home media release date: September 12, 2005
Production Company: DisneyToon Studios, Toon City Animation (Philippines)
Length: 67 minutes
Directed by: Elliot M. Bour & Saul Andrew Blinkoff
Written by: Brian Hohlfeld & Evan Spiliotopoulos

Synopsis: It is Halloween in the Hundred Acre Wood, and Tigger tells a tale of the "Gobloon," a monster that turns its victims into "jaggedy lanterns," but will grant a wish if it is captured. When Pooh eats all of Rabbit's Halloween candy, Roo and Lumpy the Heffalump set out to catch the Gobloon to wish for more candy. Lumpy's courage wavers, so Roo tells him the story of when Piglet overcame his fear of trick-or-treating (from the 1997 special *Boo to You Too! Winnie the Pooh*). They believe the Gobloon is coming, and Lumpy accidentally falls into the trap he and Roo had set, and when Roo sees a jack-o'-lantern that looks like Lumpy, he thinks the Gobloon has transformed his friend. Roo rallies Pooh, Piglet, Tigger, Rabbit and Eeyore to rescue Lumpy, and when they arrive at the trap, they believe Lumpy is the Gobloon. It is later revealed that Roo and Lumpy mistook Kanga for the Gobloon, and it was she that dropped a jack-o'-lantern that looked like Lumpy.

Cast: Jimmy Bennett as Roo
Peter Cullen as Eeyore
Jim Cummings as Winnie-the-Pooh/Tigger
John Fiedler/Travis Oates as Piglet

Ken Sansom as Rabbit
Kath Soucie as Kanga
Kyle Stanger as Lumpy
David Ogden Stiers as Narrator

Music Highlights: "Winnie the Pooh" (Sherman/Sherman), "As Long As I'm Here With You" (Mark Watters/Lorraine Feather) performed by Joey Lawrence, "Trick R' Treating With Our Friends" (Michael Silversher/Patty Silversher) performed by Jim Cummings, Ken Sansom, Peter Cullen, John Fiedler and Jimmy Bennett, "Brave Together" (Silversher/Silversher) performed by Jimmy Bennett and Kyle Stanger, "Trick R' Treating With Our Friends (Finale)" (Michael Silversher and Patty Silversher) performed by Jim Cummings, Ken Sansom, Peter Cullen, John Fiedler, Jimmy Bennett and Kyle Stanger, "I Wanna Scare Myself!" (Silversher/Silversher) performed by Jim Cummings, "I Am Not Afraid" (Silversher/Silversher) performed by John Fiedler. Score by Mark Watters.

Film Facts

• This was John Fiedler's last performance as Piglet. Travis Oates completed Piglet's remaining lines after Fiedler passed away in June, 2005.
• Like *Pooh's Heffalump Movie* (2005), *Pooh's Heffalump Halloween Movie* was written by Brian Hohlfeld and Evan Spiliotopoulos.
• Previous Pooh Halloween titles included *Spookable Pooh* (1996), a home media release of two episodes of *The New Adventures of Winnie the Pooh* (1988-1991), "A Knight to Remember" and "Rock-a-Bye Pooh Bear," and *Boo to You Too! Winnie the Pooh* (1997).

Winnie the Pooh (G)

Theatrical release date: July 15, 2011
Production Company: Walt Disney Pictures, Walt Disney Animation Studios
Length: 63 minutes
Directed by: Stephen Anderson, Don Hall
Story by: Stephen Anderson, Clio Chiang, Don Dougherty, Don Hall, Kendelle Hoyer, Brian Kesinger, Nicole Mitchell, Jeremy Spears, based on the *Winnie the Pooh* works by A.A. Milne and E.H. Shepard

Synopsis: As with *The Many Adventures of Winnie the Pooh* (1977), this film features three stories largely based on chapters from A.A. Milne's books: "In Which Eeyore Loses a Tail and Pooh Finds One" and "In Which Piglet Meets a Heffalump" from *Winnie-the-Pooh* (1926) and "In Which Rabbit Has a Busy Day and We Learn What Christopher Robin Does in the Mornings" from *The House at Pooh Corner* (1928).

Cast: John Cleese as Narrator
Jim Cummings as Winnie the Pooh
Bud Luckey as Eeyore
Craig Ferguson as Owl
Jack Boulter as Christopher Robin
Travis Oates as Piglet
Kristen Anderson-Lopez as Kanga
Wyatt Dean Hall as Roo
Tom Kenny as Rabbit
Jim Cummings as Tigger
Huell Howser as Backson

Music Highlights: "The Tummy Song" performed by Jim Cummings and Robert Lopez, "A Very Important Thing to Do" performed by Zooey Deschanel, "The Winner Song" performed by cast, "The Backson Song" performed by Craig Ferguson and cast, "It's Gonna Be Great" performed by Jim Cummings and Bud Luckey, "Everything is Honey" and "Finale" performed by Jim Cummings, Zooey Deschanel, Robert Lopez, and cast, "Winnie the Pooh" (Richard M. Sherman/Robert B. Sherman) performed by Zooey Deschanel and M. Ward, "So Long" (Zooey Deschanel) performed by Zooey Deschanel and M. Ward. All songs by Kristen Anderson-Lopez and Robert Lopez unless otherwise indicated. Score by Henry Jackman.

Film Facts

• The 51st of the Disney animated classics, *Winnie the Pooh* was inspired by stories from the same A.A. Milne books as Disney's original 1960s featurettes. The film was co-directed by Stephen Anderson (*Meet the Robinsons*) and Don Hall (*Big Hero 6, Moana*), featuring a story developed by Anderson and Hall with a team of story artists.
• The character of gopher was not in the original books by A.A. Milne, and is not included in *Winnie the Pooh* (2011).
• Five songwriting teams were invited to submit songs for the film. Kristen Anderson-Lopez and Robert Lopez (soon to write songs for *Frozen*) were the winning favorites.
• Zooey Deschanel and M. Ward also perform as the duo She and Him.
• The Backson appears in a brief post-credits scene (1:01:48) that many viewers missed.
• The next Winnie the Pooh film to be developed by Disney would be the live-action *Christopher Robin* (2018), starring Ewan McGregor.

Wolf Children (PG)

Theatrical release date: July 21, 2012
Country: Japan Japanese title: *Ôkami Kodomo no Ame to Yuki* (lit. *Wolf Children: Ame and Yuki*)
Production Company: Studio Chizu
Length: 117 minutes
Directed by: Mamoru Hosoda
Screenplay by: Mamoru Hosoda & Satoko Okudera, story by Mamoru Hosoda

Synopsis: College student Hana is intrigued with a mysterious man who shows up in her class one day. They begin to have feelings for each other, and Hana learns that the man is a wolf-man, a descendent of the Honshu wolf, with both wolf and human blood. The couple have a daughter, Yuki, then a son, Ame, but one day their father is killed while in wolf form. Hana quits school to care for her two children, and faces several problems: the children turn into wolves and tear up the apartment, Ame cries, the children howl, and child services asks so see the children. Hana gives the children the choice of living as children or wolves, and they move to the country. They begin to grow vegetables, getting help from their neighbors, starting with the grouchy Grandpa Nirasaki. Yuki asks to go school when she is 6, making friends there, and Hana begins working at a nature center, where a captive wolf is kept. One day a new boy, Soehi, joins Yuki's class, and they grow close. Ame, meanwhile, finds a fox who teaches him about the wild, and Hana does her best to help each child in their world.

Cast: Role	English	Japanese
Hana	Colleen Clinkenbeard	Aoi Miyazaki
Father	David Matranga	Takao Osawa
Yuki	Jad Saxton, Lara Woodhull (child)	Haru Kuroki, Momoka Ono (child)
Ame	Micah Solusod, Alison Viktorin (child)	Yukito Nishii, Amon Kabe (child)
Sōhei	Jason Liebrecht	Takuma Hiraoka
Sōhei's mother	Lydia Mackay	Megumi Hayashibara
Hosokawa	R. Bruce Elliott	Tadashi Nakamura
Yamaoka	Bill Flynn	Tamio Ōki
Mrs. Nirasaki	Wendy Powell	Tomie Kataoka
Mr. Nirasaki	Kenny Green	Takashi Kobayashi
Mr. Tanabe	Sonny Strait	Shota Sometani
Nirasaki	Jerry Russell	Bunta Sugawara

Music Highlights: "Okaa-san no Uta" (Masakatsu Takagi/Mamoru Hosoda) performed by Ann Sally. Music by Masakatsu Takagi.

Film Facts

• Mamoru Hosoda previously directed *The Girl Who Leapt Through Time* (2006) and *Summer Wars* (2009), going on to direct *The Boy and the Beast* (2015), *Mirai* (2018), and *Belle* (2021).
• Ame means "rain" in Japanese, and Yuki means "snow." Both are associated with their element.
• The film won the "Animation of the Year" Japan Academy Film Prize.

Wolfwalkers (PG)

Theatrical release date: October 30, 2020 (UK), November 13, 2020 (US)
Country: Ireland/Luxembourg
Production Company: Cartoon Saloon, Mélusine
Length: 104 minutes
Directed by: Tomm Moore and Ross Stewart
Screenplay by: Will Collins

Synopsis: In Killkenny, Ireland, in the 1500s, the English girl Robyn Goodfellowe craves excitement, wishing she could go outside the walls of the town and hunt the dreaded wolves in the forest, like her father, Bill, but the Lord Protector insists that children stay inside. Robyn sneaks out with her crossbow and her falcon, Merlyn. When wolves begin attacking a shepherd, Robyn tries to shoot the wolf, but accidentally shoots Merlyn. The wounded bird is taken by a feral girl with red hair. Woodcutter Seán Óg tells Robyn that the red-haired girl is a Wolfwalker, who can talk with wolves and who has healing powers. Robyn sneaks out again and finds Merlyn, who has made friends with a wolf, protecting it from Robyn. She follows them, getting visions of the red-haired girl as she looks at the wolf. She enters a cave where the wolf turns to spirit form and enters the body of the sleeping girl, who wakes. The spirited girl, Mebh Óg MacTíre, heals Robyn, but taunts her and has the wolves chase her. As they head back to the town, they become friends, and Mebh says her mother is looking for a new place for them to live. In the town, Robyn is called by a caged wolf in the Lord Protector's quarters. That night, she finds that, like Mebh, when she sleeps her spirit becomes a wolf. She flees to find Mebh, who shows her life as a wolf. Once she returns to the town, she is seen and attacked, but catches the scent of the wolf in the cage, learning it is Mebh's mother. Robyn tells Mebh her mother wants her to take the wolves out of the forest, but Mebh returns to free her mother. As the Lord Protector seeks to destroy them, the wolves defend their home, and Bill Goodfellowe struggles with where his loyalty lies.

Cast: Honor Kneafsey as Robyn Goodfellowe
Eva Whittaker as Mebh Óg MacTíre
Sean Bean as Robyn's Father, Bill Goodfellowe
Simon McBurney as Lord Protector
Tommy Tiernan as Seán Óg
Maria Doyle Kennedy as Mebh's Mother, Moll MacTíre
Jon Kenny as Stringy Woodcutter, Ned
John Morton as Stumpy Woodcutter
Nora Twomey as Head Housekeeper, Bridget

Music Highlights: "Wolfwalkers Theme" (Coulais) performed by Sofia Coulais and Camille Joutard, "Running with the Wolves" (Aksnes/Rebscher/Leonard) performed by Aurora, "Moll's Song" (Stewart/Moore/Kila) performed by Maria Doyle Kennedy. Music by Bruno Coulais, Kíla.

Film Facts

• The film was nominated for the "Best Animated Feature" Academy Award and Golden Globe.
• In Tomm Moore's "Irish Folklore Trilogy," after *The Secret of Kells* (2009), *Song of the Sea* (2014).
• The name "Robin Goodfellow" (or Puck) is from Shakespeare's *A Midsummer Night's Dream*.

Wreck-It Ralph (PG)

Theatrical release date: November 2, 2012
Production Company: Walt Disney Pictures, Walt Disney Animation Studios
Length: 108 minutes
Directed by: Rich Moore
Screenplay by: Phil Johnston, Jennifer Lee, story by Rich Moore, Phil Johnston, Jim Reardon

---

Synopsis: Frustrated with his villain role in the "Fix-It Felix Jr." video game and the ostracism that goes with it, Ralph tries to fit in, only to face the challenge of earning a medal to prove he's a good guy. Ralph infiltrates the "Hero's Duty" game to get a medal, leading Fix-It Felix Jr. to shut down in the absence of its villain. While getting his medal, Ralph tangles with a cy-bug and ends up crash landing with it in the "Sugar Rush" go-kart race game. He loses his medal to Vanellope von Schweetz, a sassy misfit known as "the glitch," who is snubbed as much as Ralph. Ralph and Vanellope form a pact to help each other, as Felix and Hero's Duty commander Calhoun seek to stop the rapidly-multiplying cy-bugs from destroying Sugar Rush, exposing the secrets of King Candy and Sugar Rush along the way.

Cast: John C. Reilly as Ralph
Sarah Silverman as Vanellope
Jack McBrayer as Felix
Jane Lynch as Calhoun
Alan Tudyk as King Candy
Mindy Kaling as Taffyta Muttonfudge
Joe Lo Truglio as Markowski
Ed O'Neill as Mr. Litwak

Dennis Haysbert as General Hologram
Edie McClurg as Mary
Raymond S. Persi as Gene and Zombie
Jess Harnell as Don
Rachael Harris as Deanna
Skylar Astin as Roy
Adam Carolla as Wynnchel
Horatio Sanz as Duncan

Music Highlights: "When Can I See You Again?" (Adam Young/Matthew Thiessen/Brian Lee) performed by Owl City, "Wreck-It, Wreck-It Ralph" (Jamie Houston) performed by Buckner & Garcia, "Shut Up and Drive" (Gillian Gilbert/Peter Hook/Stephen Morris/Evan Rogers/Carl Sturken/Bernard Sumner) performed by Rihanna, "Sugar Rush" (Yasushi Akimoto) performed by Jamie Houston, "Bug Hunt" (Skrillex) performed by Skrillex. Score by Henry Jackman.

Film Facts

• The 52nd of the Disney animated classics, *Wreck-It Ralph* was a huge hit for Disney in the Fall of 2012, making heroes out of two outcasts. Rich Moore (*The Simpsons, Futurama, Zootopia*) was asked to direct the film. Moore developed the story with Phil Johnston (*Zootopia*) and Jim Reardon (*WALL-E, Zootopia*). Johnston and Jennifer Lee (*Frozen, Zootopia*) wrote the screenplay.
• Musicians Buckner & Garcia, who performed "Pac-Man Fever" in 1982, were tapped to record "Wreck It, Wreck It Ralph."
• Video game characters in the movie included Q*Bert, Pac-Man, Sonic the Hedgehog, and Frogger.
• The Bad-Anon members include *Pac-Man* ghost Clyde, Bowser from *Super Mario Bros.*, Dr. Eggman from *Sonic*, Zangief from *Street Fighter II*, and Neff from *Altered Beast*.
• Sugar Rush racer "Minty Zaki" was named after esteemed Japanese director Hayao Miyazaki.
• The film was nominated for the "Best Animated Feature" Academy Award and Golden Globe.

Wreck-It Ralph: *Ralph Breaks the Internet* (PG)

Theatrical release date: November 5, 2018
Production Company: Walt Disney Pictures, Walt Disney Animation Studios
Length: 112 minutes
Directed by: Rich Moore, Phil Johnston
Screenplay by: Phil Johnston, Pamela Ribon, story by Rich Moore, Phil Johnston and Jim Reardon, Pamela Ribon, Josie Trinidad

Synopsis: Six years after the events in *Wreck-It Ralph,* video game villain Ralph is delighted to spend time with Sugar Rush racer Vanellope after work, but Vanellope has begun to feel restless with the routine. Ralph tries to fix this by altering her game, but the change ends up damaging the console's steering wheel. When replacement of the old part is too expensive, Sugar Rush is shut down, leading Ralph and Vanellope to enter the dizzying world of the internet in search of a new steering wheel. The good news is that they buy one on eBay, the bad news is that it costs $27,001, and they only have 24 hours to pay for it. With the help of J.P. Spamley, they set out to earn their fortune, which leads them to the cutthroat racing game Slaughter Race, which is everything Vanellope's been looking for. BuzzzTube's Yesss helps Ralph earn money by creating a series of viral videos, but as Vanellope is drawn toward a life in Slaughter Race, money may not be the solution to all of his problems.

Cast: John C. Reilly as Ralph
Sarah Silverman as Vanellope
Gal Gadot as Shank
Taraji P. Henson as Yesss
Jack McBrayer as Felix

Jane Lynch as Calhoun
Alan Tudyk as KnowsMore
Alfred Molina as Double Dan
Ed O'Neill as Mr. Litwak
Sean Giambrone as The Eboy

Music Highlights: "Zero" (Imagine Dragons) performed by Imagine Dragons, "A Place Called Slaughter Race" (Alan Menken/Phil Johnston/Tom MacDougall) performed by Sarah Silverman and Gal Gadot, "In This Place" (Tom MacDougall/Phil Johnston/Alan Menken) performed by Julia Michaels. Score by Henry Jackman.

Film Facts

• The 57th of the Disney animated classics, *Ralph Breaks the Internet* expanded Ralph and Vanellope's story from the confines of Litwak's arcade to the world wide web.
• The film was originally to be titled *Ralph Breaks the Internet: Wreck-It Ralph 2*.
• The majority of the Disney Princesses were voiced by their original voice actresses, with the exceptions of Snow White, Cinderella, and Sleeping Beauty.
• Cameos when Vanellope arrives at Oh My Disney (52:00) include Kermit the Frog, Star Wars vehicles, Dumbo, Buzz Lightyear, Baymax, Disney Princesses, Eeyore, Clarabelle Cow, Groot, Stormtroopers, Gamora, R2-D2, Iron Man, Nick Wilde, Grumpy, Peter Pan/Tinker Bell, & Hei Hei.
• A rather cruel mid-credits scene appears (1:41:58), followed by an even crueler post-credits scene (1:51:33).
• Additional appearances: Sequel to *Wreck-It Ralph* (2012).

Yellow Submarine (G)

Theatrical release date: November 13, 1968
Production Company: Apple Films, King Features Syndicate, TVC London
Length: 89 minutes (US theatrical release 85 minutes)
Directed by: George Dunning, musical director George Martin
Screenplay by: Lee Minoff and Al Brodax, Jack Mendelsohn and Erich Segal, original story by Lee Minoff, based upon a song by John Lennon and Paul McCartney

Synopsis: In the earthly paradise of Pepperland, 80,000 leagues under the sea, all is well until the Blue Meanies attack. Fred is appointed Lord Admiral and sent in the Yellow Submarine to get help. One by one, Fred picks up Ringo, John, George, and Paul, passing through the Sea of Time, the Sea of Science, the Sea of Monsters, and the Sea of Nothing. They meet the pseudo-intellectual academic/artist Jeremy Hillary Boob, Ph.D., who accidentally strands the Beatles in the Foothills of the Headlands. In the Sea of Holes Jeremy disappears, and the Beatles finally arrive in Pepperland, where they battle the Blue Meanies with music. The Blue Meanies put up a fight, deploying the Glove and their four-headed dog, but the Beatles prevail. An offer of friendship leads to a change of heart in the Blue Meanies, and the live-action Beatles close the film with "All Together Now."

Cast: John Clive as John Lennon
Geoff Hughes as Paul McCartney
Peter Batten as George Harrison
Paul Angelis as Ringo Starr/Chief Blue Meanie/
    Narrator/George Harrison
Dick Emery as Max/Lord Mayor/Jeremy Hillary Boob

Lance Percival as Fred
John Lennon
Paul McCartney
George Harrison
Ringo Starr

Music Highlights: "Yellow Submarine" (Lennon/McCartney), "Eleanor Rigby" (Lennon/McCartney), "Love You To" (Harrison) fragment, "A Day in the Life" (Lennon/McCartney) fragment, "All Together Now" (Lennon/McCartney), "When I'm Sixty-Four" (Lennon/McCartney), "Only a Northern Song" (Harrison), "Nowhere Man" (Lennon/McCartney), "Lucy In The Sky With Diamonds" (Lennon/McCartney), "Think For Yourself" (Harrison) fragment, "Sgt. Pepper's Lonely Hearts Club Band" (Lennon/McCartney), "With A Little Help From My Friends" (Lennon/McCartney) fragment, "All You Need Is Love" (Lennon/McCartney), "Baby You're A Rich Man" (Lennon/McCartney) fragment, "Hey Bulldog" (Lennon/McCartney), "It's All Too Much" (Harrison), "All Together Now" (Lennon/McCartney). All songs performed by The Beatles. Instrumental music by George Martin.

Film Facts

• Lance Percival voiced Paul and Ringo in the ABC animated TV series *The Beatles* (1965-1967).
• The film/soundtrack included the new songs "All Together Now," "It's All Too Much," "Only a Northern Song," and "Hey Bulldog." "Yellow Submarine" is from the album *Revolver* (1966).
• The Beatles owed United Artists a third film, after *A Hard Day's Night* (1964) and *Help!* (1965), and satisfied their contractual obligation with a live-action appearance at the end of this film.

Zootopia (PG)

Theatrical release date: Mar 4, 2016 (premiere Feb 13, 2016 at Brussels Animation Film Festival)
Production Company: Walt Disney Pictures, Walt Disney Animation Studios
Length: 108 minutes
Directed by: Byron Howard and Rich Moore
Screenplay by: Jared Bush and Phil Johnston, story by: Byron Howard, Rich Moore, Jared Bush, Jim Reardon, Josie Trinidad, Phil Johnston, Jennifer Lee

Synopsis: Rookie police officer Judy Hopps, a petite but determined rabbit, comes to the city of Zootopia ready to fight for justice, but is discouraged by the lackluster assignments she receives. While pursuing petty criminal Nick Wilde, a cynical yet cheerful fox, Hopps begins to uncover clues as to why a string of citizens of Zootopia are suddenly turning feral, threatening the peaceful coexistence of predators and prey. When she impulsively agrees to find the missing Emmitt Otter, Hopps is briefly fired by the irritable Chief Bogo, but is reinstated when assistant mayor Dawn Bellwether praises her, with the understanding that she will resign if she cannot solve the missing otter case in 48 hours.

Cast: Ginnifer Goodwin as Officer Judy Hopps
Jason Bateman as Nick Wilde
Idris Elba as Chief Bogo
Jenny Slate as Dawn Bellwether
Nate Torrence as Officer Benjamin Clawhauser
Bonnie Hunt as Bonnie Hopps
Don Lake as Stu Hopps
Tommy Chong as Yax

J.K. Simmons as Leodore Lionheart
Octavia Spencer as Mrs. Otterton
Alan Tudyk as Duke Weaselton
Shakira as Gazelle
Raymond S. Persi as Flash/Officer Higgins
Maurice LaMarche as Mr. Big
Phil Johnston as Gideon Grey
Kristen Bell as Priscilla

Music Highlights: "Try Everything" (Sia Furler/Tor Erik Hermansen/Mikkel S. Eriksen) performed by Shakira. Score by Michael Giacchino.

Film Facts

• The 55th of the Disney animated classics, the story for *Zootopia* was a combination of concepts drawn from six film ideas pitched to Disney by Byron Howard (*Bolt, Tangled*).
• Alan Tudyk voices Duke Weaselton, inspired by the Duke of Weselton from *Frozen* (2013).
• The film was called *Zoomania* in Germany, as the title was similar to the kids' book *Zootopolis*.
• Priscilla, the co-worker of Flash at the DMV, is voiced by Kristen Bell (*Frozen, Veronica Mars*).
• The pirated DVDs for sale by Weaselton are parodies of a variety of movies: "Pig Hero 6," "Wrangled," "Wreck-It Rhino," "Meowana," "Floatzen 2," and "Giraffic" (1:22:14). "Giraffic" refers to *Gigantic*, a Jack and the Beanstalk film that Disney was developing, but canceled.
• Judy's music player (10:05) shows the artists The Beagles (The Beatles), Black Sable (Black Sabbath), Catty Perry (Katy Perry), Destiny's Cub (Destiny's Child), Ewe 2 (U2), Fleetwood Yak (Fleetwood Mac), Fur Fighters (Foo Fighters), Guns N' Rodents (Guns N' Roses), Hyena Gomez (Selena Gomez), and Mick Jaguar (Mick Jagger).
• The film won the "Best Animated Feature" Academy Award and Golden Globe.

Appendices

Noteworthy Directors

Brad Bird
The Iron Giant (1999, PG)
The Incredibles (2004, PG)
Ratatouille (2007, G)
Incredibles 2 (2018, PG)

Chris Buck
Tarzan (1999, G) with Kevin Lima
Surf's Up (2007, PG) with Ash Brannon
Frozen (2013, PG) with Jennifer Lee
Frozen II (2019, PG) with Jennifer Lee

Brenda Chapman
The Prince of Egypt (1998, PG) with Steve Hickner, Simon Wells
Brave (2012, PG) with Mark Andrews, Steve Purcell

Dean DeBlois
Lilo & Stitch (2002, PG) with Chris Sanders
How to Train Your Dragon (2010, PG) with Chris Sanders
How to Train Your Dragon 2 (2014, PG)
How to Train Your Dragon: The Hidden World (2019, PG)

Peggy Holmes
Mickey's Twice Upon a Christmas segment "Belles on Ice" (2004, G)
The Little Mermaid: Ariel's Beginning (2008, G)
Disney Fairies: *Secret of the Wings* (2012, G) with Bobs Gannaway
Disney Fairies: *The Pirate Fairy* (2014, G)

Mamoru Hosoda
Digimon: The Movie (2000, PG)
The Girl Who Leapt Through Time (2006, TV-PG)
Summer Wars (2009, PG)
Wolf Children (2012, PG)
The Boy and the Beast (2015, PG-13)
Mirai (2018, PG)
Belle (2021)

Chuck Jones
How the Grinch Stole Christmas! (1966, NR) with Ben Washam
Horton Hears a Who! (1970, NR) with Ben Washam
The Phantom Tollbooth (1970, G) with Abe Levitow
The Cricket in Times Square (1973, NR)
A Very Merry Cricket (1973, NR)
Rikki Tikki Tavi (1975, NR)
Yankee Doodle Cricket (1975, NR)
The White Seal (1975, NR)
Mowgli's Brothers (1976, NR)
The Bugs Bunny/Road-Runner Movie (1977, G)

Jennifer Lee
Frozen (2013, PG) with Chris Buck
"Frozen Fever" short (2015, G) with Chris Buck
Frozen II (2019, PG) with Chris Buck

Hayao Miyazaki
Nausicaä of the Valley of the Wind (1984, PG)
Castle in the Sky (1986, PG)
My Neighbor Totoro (1988, PG)
Kiki's Delivery Service (1989, G)
Porco Rosso (1992, PG)
Princess Mononoke (1997, PG-13)
Spirited Away (2001, PG)
Howl's Moving Castle (2004, PG)
Ponyo (2008, G)
The Wind Rises (2013, PG-13)

John Musker and Ron Clements
The Great Mouse Detective (1986, G) with Burny Mattinson and Dave Michener
The Little Mermaid (1989, G)
Aladdin (1992, G)
Hercules (1997, G)
Treasure Planet (2002, PG)
The Princess and the Frog (2009, G)
Moana (2016, PG) with Don Hall and Chris Williams

Jennifer Yuh Nelson
Kung Fu Panda 2 (2011, PG)
Kung Fu Panda 3 (2016, PG) with Alessandro Carloni

Carlos Saldanha
Ice Age (2002, PG) with Chris Wedge
Robots (2005, PG) with Chris Wedge
Ice Age: The Meltdown (2006, PG)
Ice Age: Dawn of the Dinosaurs (2009, PG) with Mike Thurmeier
Rio (2011, G)
Rio 2 (2014, G)
Ferdinand (2017, PG)

Chris Sanders
Lilo & Stitch (2002, PG) with Dean DeBlois
How to Train Your Dragon (2010, PG) with Dean DeBlois
The Croods (2013, PG) with Kirk DeMicco
+ live-action *The Call of the Wild* (2020, PG)

Chris Wedge
Ice Age (2002, PG) with Carlos Saldanha
Robots (2005, PG) with Carlos Saldanha
Epic (2013, PG)

Best Movies for Families with Older Kids

Some films may be appreciated more by older viewers, either because of more mature themes that younger viewers might not understand, or because of higher levels of action, violence, or other more mature content. Many of the films on this list may be fine for younger viewers as well, but tweens and teens might get more out of them.

- *April and the Extraordinary World* (2015, PG, StudioCanal)
- *Batman: Mask of the Phantasm* (1993, PG, Warner Bros. Animation)
- *The Boxtrolls* (2014, PG, Focus Features/Laika Entertainment)
- *Castle in the Sky* (1986, PG, Studio Ghibli)
- *Coraline* (2009, PG, Focus Features/Laika Entertainment)
- *Corpse Bride* (2005, PG, Tim Burton Productions/Laika Ent.)
- *Fantastic Mr. Fox* (2009, PG, American Empirical Pictures/Indian Paintbrush)
- *The Girl Who Leapt Through Time* (2006, TV-PG, Madhouse)
- *The Illusionist* (2010, PG, Pathé/Django Films/Ciné B)
- *The Iron Giant* (1999, PG, Warner Bros. Feature Animation)
- *Kahlil Gibran's The Prophet* (2014, PG, Ventanarosa/Doha Film Institute)
- *Kubo and the Two Strings* (2016, PG, Laika Entertainment/Focus Features)
- *Legend of the Guardians: The Owls of Ga'Hoole* (2010, PG, Village Roadshow)
- *Long Way North* (2015, PG, Sacrebleu Productions/Maybe Movies)
- *Mirai* (2018, PG, Studio Chizu)
- *A Monster in Paris* (2011, PG, EuropaCorp)
- *My Beautiful Girl, Mari* (2002, TV-G, Daewoo Entertainment)
- *Nausicaä of the Valley of the Wind* (1984, PG, Studio Ghibli)
- *The Painting* (2011, TV-PG, Blue Spirit Animation/Be-Films)
- *ParaNorman* (2012, PG, Laika)
- *The Prince of Egypt* (1998, PG, DreamWorks)
- *Rango* (2011, PG, Paramount Pictures/Nickelodeon Movies)
- *The Red Turtle/La Tortue Rouge* (2016, PG, Wild Bunch/Studio Ghibli)
- *Samurai Jack* (2001, NR, Cartoon Network Studios)
- *The Secret of Kells* (2009, NR, Les Armateurs/Vivi Film/Cartoon Saloon)
- *Song of the Sea* (2015, PG, Backup Media/Big Farm)
- *Soul* (2020, PG, Pixar/Disney)
- *Spirited Away* (2001, PG, Studio Ghibli)
- *Summer Wars* (2009, PG, Madhouse)
- *The Tale of The Princess Kaguya* (2013, PG, Studio Ghibli)
- *A Town Called Panic* (2009, TV-PG, La Parti Production)
- *Up* (2009, PG, Pixar/Disney)
- *When Marnie Was There* (2014, PG, Studio Ghibli)
- *Whisper of the Heart* (1995, G, Studio Ghibli)
- *Wolf Children* (2012, PG, Studio Chizu)

Best Movies for Younger & Older Viewers Watching Together

It can be a challenge to balance the tastes of different ages, but there are several films that have managed to walk this line quite well. If you want a movie that has something for everyone, these titles are worth considering:

- *The Adventures of Tintin* (2011, PG, Amblin/Paramount/Nickelodeon)
- *Bee Movie* (2007, PG, DreamWorks)
- *Big Hero 6* (2014, PG, Disney)
- *Brave* (2012, PG, Pixar)
- *Chicken Run* (2000, G, DreamWorks)
- *The Croods* (2013, PG, DreamWorks)/*The Croods: A New Age* (2020, PG, DreamWorks)
- *Despicable Me* (2010, PG, Universal Pictures/Illumination Entertainment)
- *How to Train Your Dragon* (2010, PG, DreamWorks)
- *Howl's Moving Castle* (2004, PG, Studio Ghibli)
- *Ice Age* (2002, PG, Blue Sky Studios/20th Century Fox Animation)
- *The Incredibles* (2004, PG, Pixar/Disney)/*Incredibles 2* (2018, PG, Pixar/Disney)
- *Klaus* (2019, PG, The SPA Studios/Atresmedia Cine)
- *Kung Fu Panda* series
- *Meet the Robinsons* (2007, G, Disney)
- *Megamind* (2010, PG, DreamWorks)
- *Missing Link* (2019, PG, Laika)
- *Moana* (2016, PG, Disney)
- *Monsters, Inc.* (2001, G, Pixar/Disney)/*Monsters University* (2013, G, Pixar/Disney)
- *My Little Pony: Equestria Girls* (2013, TV-Y, DHX/Hasbro)
- *My Neighbor Totoro* (1988, PG, Studio Ghibli)
- *Onward* (2020, PG, Pixar/Disney)
- *Phineas and Ferb the Movie: Across the 2nd Dimension* (2011, TV-G, Disney)
- *Phineas and Ferb the Movie: Candace Against the Universe* (2020, TV-G, Disney)
- *The Pirates! Band of Misfits* (2012, PG, Sony Pictures Animation/Aardman Animation)
- *Ponyo* (2008, G, Studio Ghibli)
- *Shrek* (2001, PG, DreamWorks)
- *Sinbad: Legend of the Seven Seas* (2003, PG, DreamWorks)
- *Sing* (2016, PG, Illumination)
- *Smallfoot* (2018, PG, Warner Animation Group/Zaftig Films)
- *Surf's Up* (2007, PG, Sony Pictures Animation)
- *Tangled* (2010, PG, Disney)
- *WALL-E* (2008, G, Pixar/Disney)
- *Wallace & Gromit: The Curse of the Were-Rabbit* (2005, G, Aardman/DreamWorks)
- *Wolfwalkers* (2020, PG, Cartoon Saloon)
- *Wreck-It Ralph* (2012, PG, Disney)
- Wreck-It Ralph: *Ralph Breaks the Internet* (2018, PG, Disney)
- *Zootopia* (2016, PG, Disney)

Representation

African American/Black
Home (2015, PG)
Kirikou and the Sorceress (1998, NR)
Madagascar (2005, PG), *Madagascar: Escape 2 Africa* (2008, PG)
Madagascar 3: Europe's Most Wanted (2012, PG)
The Painting (2011, TV-PG)
The Princess and the Frog (2009, G)
The Proud Family Movie (2005, TV-G)
Soul (2020, PG)
Spider Man: Into the Spiderverse (2018, PG)
Adventures in Zambezia (2012, PG)

Asian
Abominable (2019, PG, US/China)
Big Hero 6 (2014, PG)
The Girl Who Leapt Through Time (2006, TV-PG, Japan)
Kubo and the Two Strings (2016, PG)
Lilo & Stitch (2002, PG)
Mirai (2018, PG, Japan)
Moana (2016, PG)
My Beautiful Girl, Mari (2002, TV-G, Korea)
My Neighbor Totoro (1988, PG, Japan)
Spirited Away (2001, PG, Japan)

Latinx/Hispanic
Anina (2013, NR, Uruguay)
The Book of Life (2014, PG, US, Mexico, Canada)
Boy and the World (2013, PG, Brazil)
Coco (2017, PG)
Ferdinand (2017, PG)
Puss in Boots (2011, PG)
El Ratón Pérez live-action/animation (2006, TV-Y7, Argentina)
The Road to El Dorado (2000, PG)
Una Película de Huevos (2006, TV-PG, Mexico)
Underdogs/Metegol (2013, PG, Argentina)

Middle East/Persian
Aladdin (1992, G)
Aladdin: *The Return of Jafar* (1994, G)
Aladdin and the King of Thieves (1996, NR)
Azur & Asmar: The Princes' Quest (2006, PG)
The Breadwinner (2017, PG-13)
Kahlil Gibran's The Prophet (2014, PG)
Persepolis (2007, PG-13)
The Prince of Egypt (1998, PG)
Sahara (2017, TV-Y7)

Native American

Brother Bear (2003, G)
Brother Bear 2 (2006, G)
The Emperor's New Groove (2000, G)
The Legend of Sarila (2013, TV-G)
Pachamama (2018, PG)
Pocahontas (1995, G)
The Road to El Dorado (2000, PG)
Spirit: Stallion of the Cimarron (2002, G)

LGBTQ

Coraline (2009, PG)
The Dragon Prince TV series (2018-2021, TV-Y7)
How to Train Your Dragon 2 (2014, PG)
The Legend of Korra TV series (2012–2014, TV-Y7-FV)
The Mitchells vs. the Machines (2021, PG)
The Owl House TV series (2020, TV-Y7-FV)
ParaNorman (2012, PG)
Revolutionary Girl Utena TV series (1997, TV-14), *Revolutionary Girl Utena: The Movie* (1999, NR)
Sailor Moon TV series (1992-1997, TV-PG)
She-Ra and the Princesses of Power TV series (2018-2020, TV-Y7-FV)
Steven Universe TV series (2013-2020, TV-PG), *Steven Universe: The Movie* (2019, TV-PG)

Strong Female Leads

April and the Extraordinary World (2015, PG)
Brave (2012, PG)
The Croods (2013, PG)
Frozen (2013, PG)
The Girl Who Leapt Through Time (2006, TV-PG)
Howl's Moving Castle (2004, PG)
Lilo & Stitch (2002, PG)
Moana (2016, PG)
My Little Pony: Equestria Girls (2013, TV-Y)
My Neighbor Totoro (1988, G)
Nausicaä of the Valley of the Wind (1984, PG)
Ponyo (2008, G)
The Secret of Kells (2009, NR)
The Secret World of Arrietty (2010, G)
Sing (2016, PG)
Spirited Away (2001, PG)
Strange Magic (2015, PG)
The Tale of The Princess Kaguya (2013, PG)
Tangled (2010, PG)
Tinker Bell (2008, G)
Whisper of the Heart (1995, G)
Wolf Children (2012, PG)
Wolfwalkers (2020, PG)
Zootopia (2016, PG)

Best Animated Feature awards

Academy Award

<u>2001 (74th)</u>
Shrek (winner)
Jimmy Neutron: Boy Genius
Monsters, Inc.

<u>2002 (75th)</u>
Spirited Away (winner)
Ice Age
Lilo & Stitch
Spirit: Stallion of the Cimarron
Treasure Planet

<u>2003 (76th)</u>
Finding Nemo (winner)
Brother Bear
The Triplets of Belleville (PG-13)

<u>2004 (77th)</u>
The Incredibles (winner)
Shark Tale
Shrek 2

<u>2005 (78th)</u>
*Wallace & Gromit: The Curse of the
          Were-Rabbit* (winner)
Corpse Bride
Howl's Moving Castle

Golden Globe

<u>2006 (79th)</u>
Happy Feet (winner)
Cars
Monster House

<u>2006 (64th)</u>
Cars (winner)
Happy Feet
Monster House

<u>2007 (80th)</u>
Ratatouille (winner)
Persepolis (PG-13)
Surf's Up

<u>2007 (65th)</u>
Ratatouille (winner)
Bee Movie
The Simpsons Movie

<u>2008 (81st)</u>
WALL-E (winner)
Bolt
Kung Fu Panda

<u>2008 (66th)</u>
WALL-E (winner)
Bolt
Kung Fu Panda

Academy Award

2009 (82nd)
Up (winner)
Coraline
Fantastic Mr. Fox
The Princess and the Frog
The Secret of Kells

2010 (83rd)
Toy Story 3 (winner)
How to Train Your Dragon
The Illusionist

2011 (84th)
Rango (winner)
A Cat in Paris
Chico & Rita (NR/17+)
Kung Fu Panda 2
Puss in Boots

2012 (85th)
Brave (winner)
Frankenweenie
Wreck-It Ralph
ParaNorman
The Pirates! In an Adventure with Scientists!/
The Pirates Band of Misfits

2013 (86th)
Frozen (winner)
The Croods
Despicable Me 2
Ernest & Celestine
The Wind Rises

2014 (87th)
Big Hero 6 (winner)
How to Train Your Dragon 2
The Boxtrolls
Song of the Sea
The Tale of the Princess Kaguya

Golden Globe

2009 (67th)
Up (winner)
Coraline
Fantastic Mr. Fox
The Princess and the Frog
Cloudy with a Chance of Meatballs

2010 (68th)
Toy Story 3 (winner)
How to Train Your Dragon
Despicable Me
Tangled

2011 (69th)
The Adventures of Tintin (winner)
Rango
Arthur Christmas
Cars 2
Puss in Boots

2012 (70th)
Brave (winner)
Frankenweenie
Wreck-It Ralph
Hotel Transylvania
Rise of the Guardians

2013 (71st)
Frozen (winner)
The Croods
Despicable Me 2

2014 (72nd)
How to Train Your Dragon 2 (winner)
Big Hero 6
The Boxtrolls
The Book of Life
The Lego Movie

Academy Award

2015 (88th)
Inside Out (winner)
Shaun the Sheep Movie
Anomalisa (R)
Boy and the World
When Marnie Was There

2016 (89th)
Zootopia (winner)
Kubo and the Two Strings
Moana
My Life as a Zucchini (PG-13)
The Red Turtle

2017 (90th)
Coco (winner)
The Boss Baby
The Breadwinner (PG-13)
Ferdinand
Loving Vincent (PG-13)

2018 (91st)
Spider-Man: Into the Spider-Verse (winner)
Incredibles 2
Isle of Dogs (PG-13)
Mirai
Ralph Breaks the Internet

2019 (92nd)
Toy Story 4 (winner)
Missing Link
How to Train Your Dragon: The Hidden World
I Lost My Body (TV-MA)
Klaus

2020 (93rd)
Soul (winner)
Onward
Over the Moon
Wolfwalkers
A Shaun the Sheep Movie: Farmageddon

Golden Globe

2015 (73rd)
Inside Out (winner)
Shaun the Sheep Movie
Anomalisa (R)
The Good Dinosaur
The Peanuts Movie

2016 (74th)
Zootopia (winner)
Kubo and the Two Strings
Moana
My Life as a Zucchini (PG-13)
Sing

2017 (75th)
Coco (winner)
The Boss Baby
The Breadwinner (PG-13)
Ferdinand
Loving Vincent (PG-13)

2018 (76th)
Spider-Man: Into the Spider-Verse (winner)
Incredibles 2
Isle of Dogs (PG-13)
Mirai
Ralph Breaks the Internet

2019 (77th)
Missing Link (winner)
Toy Story 4
How to Train Your Dragon: The Hidden World
Frozen II
The Lion King

2020 (78th)
Soul (winner)
Onward
Over the Moon
Wolfwalkers
The Croods: A New Age

Made in the USA
Middletown, DE
30 September 2021